ANSELM STUDIES

Anselm Studies
An Occasional Journal

II

PROCEEDINGS
OF
THE FIFTH INTERNATIONAL SAINT ANSELM CONFERENCE:
ST. ANSELM AND ST. AUGUSTINE—EPISCOPI AD SAECULA

edited by

Joseph C. Schnaubelt, OSA
Thomas A. Losoncy
Frederick Van Fleteren
Jill A. Frederick

KRAUS INTERNATIONAL PUBLICATIONS
White Plains, New York
A Division of Kraus-Thomson Organization Limited
1988

The paper used in this publication meets the minimum
requirements of American National Standard for
Information Science — Permanence of Papers for
Printed Library Materials, ANSI Z39.48-1984.

Contents

Preface

Thomas A. Losoncy

With its general theme of *St. Anselm and St. Augustine: Episcopi ad Saecula*, the Fifth International St. Anselm Conference met at Villanova University from the 16th to the 21st of September, 1985. This St. Anselm Conference was held in conjunction with the Tenth International Patristic, Medieval, and Renaissance Conference, sponsored and hosted by the Augustinian Historical Institute at Villanova University. This Anselmian conference explored and updated points of convergence between the two thinkers: previous international conferences of St. Anselm scholars had highlighted areas of influence and juncture, but this conference presented the first opportunity for extended scrutiny, bringing to bear the latest information and insights about the fifth-century Doctor of Grace and the eleventh-century Abbot of Bec.

The present Abbot of Bec, Dom Paul Grammont, OSB, opened the Conference with remarks on the significance of St. Anselm as monk. The papers which followed Dom Grammont's presentation, examined in detail St. Anselm's life and work: these papers treat Anselm's own understanding of the monk's place in society and in the Church, the influences of previous ecclesiastical figures on his view of the monastic life, and the connections of his vision of such a life with the views of St. Augustine.

St. Augustine's argument for the existence of God in the *De libero arbitrio* provides a background for St. Anselm's *Proslogion* argument. The historical foundations of Anselm's argument, especially its nascence in the thought of St. Augustine, and its subsequent influence on philosophical and theological writings, provided the focus for the next group of papers.

Another convergence between the thought of St. Anselm and St. Augustine concerns their respective views on "truth," metaphysical and moral. The third group of papers expands on the various facets of this topic, for example, theories of will, evil, and linguistic matters.

Another group of papers examines general influences of St. Augustine on St. Anselm, among them the philosophical and monastic character of Anselm's theology and the relationship between faith and reason that this theology employed. Other papers address the role of Scripture and the fathers in Anselm's theological enterprise.

A final area of exploration discusses St. Anselm's spirituality and the world-outlook it has fostered. This collection examines various works and appraises their place in the culture of Anselm's day, while studying their impact upon subsequent centuries as well.

The aims of the conference were ambitious and directed towards an area of Anselmian studies much in need of exposition. We thank all those who were able to contribute to making Anselm's thought and influence better known to the academic community at large. In a special way, we wish to thank Villanova University and its president, Rev. John M. Driscoll, OSA, for sponsoring this endeavor and for providing a warm and gracious setting for the labors of those who attended.

Foreword

Fides quaerens intellectum

Fides quaerit; intellectus invenit.

Frederick Van Fleteren

An important part of the testament bequeathed by Augustine to the Western world, especially the Christian West, resides in his speculations on faith and reason. Though Augustine was not the first Christian to approach this problem -- Justin martyr was -- his deliberations about faith and reason have had an extraordinary influence on the West because of his special place in Western thought. Augustine's influence on Anselm in this matter of faith and reason has been well-documented, so it is fitting, then, that in a volume on the relationship between Augustine and Anselm, the relationship between faith and reason takes such an important place.

In Augustine's own life, tension between faith and reason existed from childhood. What he may have learned about the Christian faith on his mother's knee must remain a matter of speculation, but we know that, though not baptized, he was raised a "Catholic Christian." His first encounter with "reason" took place at the age of nineteen when he read Cicero's *Hortensius*, a protreptic to philosophy in the style of Aristotle. This work placed within him a desire for wisdom and led him by a strange twist of fate to the Manichaeans, a gnostic sect of the late Roman Empire. Its deterministic theory of evil aside, Augustine was attracted to that sect by its rationalism, that is by its promise of complete understanding by reason alone without any appeal to faith. Through nine long years as an "auditor," and through two more with some proximity to the sect, the young Augustine sought the understanding it promised. When he realized that this promise could not be fulfilled, even in the person of its leader, Faustus, Augustine left the Manichaeans. The young rhetor had begun to reason that faith had a place even in mundane matters. Augustine's later speculations concerning faith and reason form a counterpoint to these Manichaean teachings.

In the evolution of Augustine's thought on faith and reason, the importance of Ambrose, the Bishop of Milan, remains undisputed. Through Ambrose's preaching and "spiritual exegesis," the imperial rhetor of Milan began to see that the Scriptures did not contradict reason and that a way of salvation existed for mankind through them. Prepared by

Ambrose's use of the "Platonists" in his preaching, Augustine gleaned certain philosophical doctrines from the *libri Platonicorum*, that is, "reason," which helped him to understand the Christian mysteries. This conversion of intellect, accompanied by his conversion of will (to the celibate life), formed the basis from which he approached his intellectual speculations for the remainder of his life.

The young convert, of course, was much more optimistic than the more mature bishop about the possibility of the convergence of Platonism and Christianity as well as the human possibility of knowing the divine. The convert's fundamental insight, however, remains the same: Christianity is the "true philosophy"; reason's task is to understand, insofar as possible, the truths of faith; reason has an ontological priority in the sense that rational understanding (limited as it is for man) of matters of faith is the purpose of the theological enterprise; faith has a temporal priority because it offers the matter to be studied, that is, the truths of faith (to study anything else would be idle curiosity), and shows us the moral precepts providing the indispensable pre-condition of intellectual insight. Augustine's conviction remains from first to last, the ultimate harmony between faith and reason, the unity of truth. Truth, wherever it is, remains the property of God.

As the idealism of youth gave way to the realism of maturity, Augustine's expectations from his speculations diminished. Whether looking for images of the divine in man or understanding the mystery of God's grace together with human freedom, the elder bishop was not as sanguine as the young convert about man's ability to comprehend. And yet, his enterprise remained fundamentally the same: to understand the truths of faith by means of reason, although the complete fulfillment of this task will come only in the direct vision of God, when there will be but "one Christ, loving himself."

It is but a short step from the *fides quaerit; intellectus invenit* of Augustine to the *fides quaerens intellectum* of Anselm, although the world had obviously changed a great deal during the nearly six hundred years which separated these giants. Anselm as monk, prior, and abbot of the monastery at Bec, and later as the twice-exiled Archbishop of Canterbury, provided one of the links between Augustine and the High Middle Ages. He endeavored to provide the "necessary reasons" for the mysteries of faith. Whether his speculations concerned an argument for the existence of God, the necessity of the incarnation, or the ultimate harmony between divine foreknowledge and human freedom, Anselm conceived his task as providing understanding for the mysteries of faith. His expectations of success in this enterprise may be compared to the similar expectations of the young Augustine, and his underlying presuppositions are Augustinian: rational understanding remains the goal; faith provides the matter and the moral purification necessary; the unity of truth is preserved. That history's judgement of the success of Anselm's enterprise is mixed provides as much a tribute to the loftiness of his aspirations as it does to the finitude of the human intellect.

These two giants laid the foundations on which Western Christian thought has been built. Consequently, it is indeed fitting that, on the occasion of the Fifth International Congress of Anselmian Studies and the sixteenth centenary of the conversion and baptism of Augustine of Hippo, so many scholars of international repute have studied the relationship between them so thoroughly. The editors hope that this volume will illuminate the two essential principles which guided the thought of both Anselm and Augustine, the unity of truth in God himself and the harmony between faith and reason, and that these honorable principles will continue to guide speculation in our own time.

Abbreviations

AA:	*Analecta Anselmiana*
BA	*Bibliothèque Augustinienne*
CC:	*Corpus Christianorum*
CSEL:	*Corpus scriptorum ecclesiasticorum latinorum*
DTC:	*Dictionnaire de théologie catholique*
Historia novorum:	Eadmer, *Historia novorum in Anglia*, ed. M. Rule. Rolls Series, No. 51. 1834; rpt. London: Kraus, 1965.
LTK:	*Lexikon für Theologie und Kirche*
MGH:	*Monumenta Germaniae historica*
NCE:	*New Catholic Encyclopedia*
PG:	J. P. Migne, *Patrologiae Graecae cursus completus*
PL:	J. P. Migne, *Patrologiae Latinae cursus completus*
SB I:	*Spicilegium Beccense.* Vol. I. Paris: J. Vrin, 1959.
SB II:	*Spicilegium Beccense.* Vol. II. Paris: Éditions du Centre national de la recherche scientifique, 1984.
Schmitt:	F. S. Schmitt, OSB, *Sancti Anselmi Cantuariensis archiepiscopi opera omnia.* Vols. I–VI. Edinburgh, Thomas Nelson, 1938–61.
Vita Anselmi:	Eadmer, *The Life of Saint Anselm, Archbishop of Canterbury*, ed. R. W. Southern. London: Nelson, 1962.

§

Introduction

Anselm

[Scripturam meam] saepe retractans nihil
potui invenire me in ea dixisse, quod non catho-
licorum patrum et maxime beati AUGUSTINI scrip-
tis cohaereat. Quapropter si cui videbitur,
quod in eodem opusculo aliquid protulerim, quod
aut nimis novum sit aut a veritate dissentiat:
rogo, ne statim me aut praesumptorem novitatum
aut falsitatis assertorem exclamet, sed prius
libros praefati doctoris AUGUSTINI *De trinitate*
diligenter perspiciat, deinde secundum eos
opusculum meum diiudicet.

(*Monologion*, prologus)

Note: Anselm as Abbot of Bec

Joseph C. Schnaubelt, OSA

In 1060 Anselm entered the newly formed Abbey of Bec in Normandy. Three years later Anselm was elected to succeed Lanfranc of Pavia as prior of the abbey. And when Herluin, founding abbot of Bec, died in 1078, Anselm was unanimously elected to succeed him. Initially reluctant to accept this office, Anselm proved an excellent administrator, especially in developing the abbey into a center of philosophical and theological studies. During this period, Anselm wrote a series of theological works, which he published at the insistence of his community.

Recognized as comparable, in some measure, to the writings of Augustine of Hippo for insight and originality, these works are commonly divided into three categories: systematic treatises, prayers and meditations, and letters. The systematic works include the *Monologion*, which deals with the existence of God and His attributes; the *Proslogion*, which presents Anselm's famous "ontological argument"; four dialogues between teacher and students: the *De grammatico*, which debates whether grammar should be considered as a substance or as a quality; the *De veritate* and the *De libertate arbitrii*, which give Anselm's definitions of truth and free will; and the *De casu diaboli*, which investigates angelology; the *Epistola de incarnatione verbi*, which defends the doctrine of the Holy Trinity; a dialogue on the Incarnation, the *Cur deus homo*, which is considered Anselm's main work; the *De conceptu virginali et de originali peccato*, which considers how Christ, in spite of descent from Adam, remained sinless; the *De processione spiritus sancti*, which advanced the doctrine of the Trinity; and the *De concordia praescientiae et praedestinationis et gratiae dei cum libero arbitrio*, which reconciled the attributes of God with human free will. The prayers and meditations include nineteen prayers and three meditations. Among the latter, the *Meditatio redemptionis humanae* is outstanding as a summary of the *Cur deus homo*. The letters, a collection of four hundred seventy-five items from and to Anselm, furnish insights into his personality and life, especially as a bishop.

All of these writings can be perceived as the fruit of Anselm's ardent spirituality, which blossomed in the religious milieu of the Abbey of Bec. In his introductory remarks at the Fifth International St. Anselm Conference, Dom Paul Grammont, the present Abbot of Bec, emphasized this aspect of Anselm's persona.

Saint Anselme, le Moine

Paul Grammont, OSB

Il est difficile de donner quelques traits de la physionomie d'un moine. Car ce que l'on voit, ce que l'on peut relever dans sa vie, pour essayer d'en faire un portrait, n'est que reflet d'un mystère d'une vie cachée en Dieu, et surtout d'une vie qui tend sans cesse à une plus parfaite unité -- unité du regard, tourné vers Dieu, l'Invisible, l'Innommable -- unité du coeur, orienté par l'amour de Dieu, de son Verbe incarné -- unité de l'esprit, préoccupé par l'Absolu, l'Indépassable. D'où il résulte une unité dans la vie même, traversée par de multiples épreuves, et obligée de faire face à des évènements, des rencontres qui suscitent des comportements variés, adaptés au moment, et qui révèlent une personnalité complexe.

Au creux, à la racine de toute la vie du moine, il y a la quête de Dieu, la conscience de sa présence, l'expérience peut-on dire de cette présence perçue, connue comme un don, une grâce requise en pure gratuité, et une proximité qui est intérieure et extérieure à soi -- cette présence vivante et agissante, cette vie intérieure et en même temps reconnue dans de multiples méditations, au dehors de soi, dans les autres rencontres, les évènements, les choses, et surtout dans la Bible lue, entendue, méditée, la Parole de Dieu goûtée.

Mais il faut le dire ici, cette présence se donne, surtout pour le moine, dans un profond silence tout d'écoute, calme, paisible habituellement, dont l'Evangile nous présente un exemple dans l'épisode de Marthe et Marie (Lk 10:38-42).

Deux mots peuvent résumer ce qui caractérise le milieu, l'ambiance monastique: *unité* et *paix*.

C'est-à-dire *l'unité* dans le sens d'unification de la vie du moine. Il ne peut être dans la vérité de sa vocation sans être *un*, sans partage, tout saisi par la consécration qui le met à part et le pénètre. C'est toute une existence, sous toutes ses formes et ses expressions, qui est investie et pénétrée par la louange, la bénédiction adressée à Dieu -- unité d'un coeur simple, sans repli, par l'exercice constant de l'humilité qui garde la mémoire de Dieu sans cesse recherché.

D'une manière semblable, on reçoit *la paix* aux sens de pacification de l'être tout entier, réconcilié avec soi, habitant tranquillement avec soi. Et cette paix, qui ne va pas sans combat, résulte d'une victoire sur les passions qui

peuvent traverser le coeur de l'homme -- une paix faite de
don et de pardon, pardon reçu et donné, dans une charité
informée par la foi en un Dieu qui donne et se donne, qui
pardonne et accueille. Le moine cherche Dieu, ce faisant il
cherche la paix, puisque Dieu est un Dieu de paix, et que
Jésus Christ donne et laisse la paix, non pas celle que
donne le monde, mais *la sienne*, toute d'amour créateur et
re-créateur.

Toutes ces considérations sont tirées de la Règle de
Saint Benoît, fondées sur l'Ecriture, et forment le cadre
dans lequel se situent toutes les figures de moines. En
Saint Anselme, nous les retrouvons jusque dans les traits de
son caractère, ferme et doux à la fois, très contemplatif et
porté à la méditation; ses traités, ses prières en gardent
bien la marque.

Mais chez lui, tout se ramène à un principe fondamental,
une expérience en toute sa vie, l'intuition de la grandeur
de Dieu et de sa relation à l'homme. Aussi bien dans ses
réflexions les plus spéculatives, *Monologion*, *Proslogion*, et
ainsi de suite, que dans sa piété, Anselme se réfère toujours à la grandeur de Dieu qui surpasse toute pensée qu'on
puisse avoir de lui. Et c'est cela qui fait l'unité de sa
vie.

Comme cette grandeur de Dieu est amour, et qu'il ne la
considère pas seulement dans la création, mais aussi en
lui-même, elle modèle son comportement de fermeté, de
fidélité et de douceur à la fois. C'est peut-être à cause
de cela qu'Anselme, fidèle à la Règle de Saint Benoît, vou-
lait que le moine évite toute négligence, et pratiquant les
vertus parvienne à la grande pureté d'intention qui n'estime
rien de petit au service de Dieu. Cette attitude se traduit
par la *rectitude*, mot bien cher à Anselme. Pénétré de la
présence de Dieu à qui rien n'est caché, qui voit dans le
secret des coeurs, le moine est invité à une grande
délicatesse de conscience.

Anselme attire l'attention sur la droiture du coeur et
la pureté de l'intention. Il écrit: "Ne considérez pas
seulement ce que vous faites, mais ce que vous voulez;
examinez moins quelles sont vos oeuvres que la nature de
votre intention, car toute action droite tire sa rectitude
de la juste volonté qui la dirige" (*Epistola 414*).[1] Ce
souci de la pureté d'intention, de la rectitude, vient du
respect devant Dieu, dont la grandeur en tout, vérité,
bonté, justice, amour, appelle de la part de l'homme une
conformité entre le coeur et l'action, la parole et les
actes.

En cela, Anselme traduit directement la Règle de Saint Benoît et sa pédagogie: le sens de l'omniprésence de Dieu engendre la gravité de la vie et fait fuir la légèreté d'esprit; l'intention doit informer les actions, les qualifier et leur donner valeur. La rectitude d'esprit qu'Anselme recommande est l'expression de l'unité de l'être recherchée dans la vie du moine; elle est le fruit de sa quête de Dieu et de l'hommage qui lui est rendu.

Volontiers on rapprocherait du terme de *rectitude* celui de *gravité* employé plusieurs fois dans la Règle des Moines. Il s'agit en effet du sérieux dans l'attention à faire correctement, droitement, ce qui procède d'une intention bien orientée et pleine de la "mémoire" de Dieu.

En pleine consonance avec cette rectitude, il est nécessaire de reconnaître en Saint Anselme un souci très grand d'intériorité. Son tempérament spéculatif l'y portait sans doute, mais aussi sa vocation monastique, car l'existence du moine est toute tendue vers une vie intérieure, emplie de la pensée de Dieu, où la prière continuelle exerce une attirance devenue naturelle.

Ses lettres, ses méditations trahissent l'écartèlement dont il souffrait, tiraillé pendant son épiscopat par les soucis multiples de sa charge. Déjà lorsqu'il fut appelé par l'Abbé Herluin à succéder à Lanfranc comme prieur, il supplia d'être enlevé de cette fonction. Il n'en fut rien. Et à la mort d'Herluin, il fut élu pour lui succéder comme Abbé du Bec. Il fit tout pour s'y soustraire, mais il dut céder. Et malgré ses nouvelles occupations, il ne cessa pas de s'adonner autant qu'il le pouvait à la contemplation, nous dit son biographe Eadmer.

Lorsqu'il écrit sa *Méditation sur la Rédemption de l'Homme*, Anselme nous livre quelque chose de sa démarche contemplative: "Considère, ô mon âme, concentre *tout ce qu'il y a de plus intime en toi, et vois* jusqu'où la totale substance de mon être se doit au Christ." Et il poursuit aussitôt, reprenant la grande intuition qui domine sa vie: "Assurément, Seigneur, parce que *tu m'as créé*, je me *dois tout entier* à ton amour parce que tu es ma rédemption, je me dois tout entier . . ." C'est bien sur cette dépendance fondamentale de l'homme par rapport à son Créateur et Sauveur, qu'il appuie sa contemplation, sa prière: "Bien plus, je dois à ton amour infiniment plus que moi-même, et de ceci autant que tu es plus grand que moi, moi pour qui tu t'es livré toi-même et à qui tu t'es promis." Et il conclut: "Mon être tout entier t'appartient par sa condition, accorde lui d'être tien tout entier par l'amour."[2]

N'y a-t-il pas là la physionomie monastique d'Anselme?
Saisi par le mystère d'intériorité de l'âme où se *vérifie*
l'expérience de Dieu créateur, par la reconnaissance de sa
trace, Anselme est emporté dans la contemplation de ce grand
Dieu indépassable même par la pensée, et qui se révèle amour
libérant. Il montre en même temps l'étonnante vocation de
l'homme à se dépasser pour entrer dans la joie du Dieu
amour, créateur et sauveur. C'est au creux de son expérience d'intériorité qu'il découvre aussi cette prodigieuse
présence. C'est pourquoi Anselme ose ce précepte: "Entre
dans la cellule de ton âme."³ Et c'est là que se situe la
reconnaissance de la présence à soi, et à l'Autre, et à
l'Universel. C'est aussi le lieu du jaillissement de la
louange et de l'adoration, de la source même de la bénédiction qui met l'âme en état de prière continuelle.

Aussi Anselme a-t-il su reconnaître, comme l'a écrit
Aimé Forest, "l'achèvement de la philosophie réflexive dans
la philosophie spirituelle."⁴ En même temps, Anselme sait
que Dieu en nous reste lui-même, il est amour, et l'amour
nous établit dans l'intériorité, comme il est aussi principe
d'unité et de liaison; par l'amour, l'âme retrouve du dedans
d'elle-même la liberté la plus haute, la paix la plus
grande.

Aussi l'humanité d'Anselme se révèle accueillante et
discrète, et très fidèle. Ses lettres nous le montrent
d'une tendresse étonnante dans ses amitiés, et en même temps
très respectueux des personnes et de leur liberté. Pour
l'Eglise dont le zèle l'habitait, il avait la passion de sa
liberté, et l'a montré dans sa résistance aux volontés dom-
inatrices et indiscrètes du roi Guillaume le Roux.

Par contre, il gardait le souci et le sens de la conciliation, de la pacification des conflits, mettant tout en
oeuvre pour favoriser des rencontres et des entretiens entre
des théologiens dont le langage n'était pas accordé, par
exemple au Concile de Bari entre Orientaux et Occidentaux au
sujet de la procession du Saint Esprit. C'est ainsi que cet
homme de paix trouvait dans sa vie intérieure la force
nécessaire pour promouvoir à tous les niveaux l'unité et la
liberté.

Toujours habité par le sens de l'infini, Anselme accomplit le rôle prophétique du moine dans l'Eglise et le monde,
qui est témoigner de l'Au-delà de tout. Cet Au-delà qui ne
peut se comparer à aucune grandeur, tant il est toujours
plus grand, et qui pour cela se manifeste aussi bien "le
plus grand" dans l'humilité de la Croix que dans l'acte
créateur, révèle par là qu'en Lui-même c'est toute liberté
d'amour pour accueillir dans la communion trinitaire ce

qu'il a créé: pardonnant son péché, il fait de l'homme un fils dans le Fils par le souffle de l'Esprit.

La contemplation de l'acte rédempteur jusqu'à l'exténuation du plus grand que tout dans la mort, rejoint l'acte créateur dans la Résurrection et l'espérance qu'elle projette sur toute la création.

Notes

[1] *Epistola 414*, Ad Robertum eiusque moniales: Schmitt III,360,17-19.

[2] Cf. *Meditatio redemptionis humanae*: Schmitt III, 91,191-200.

[3] Cf. *Proslogion* I: Schmitt I,96,7.

[4] Cf. A. Forest, "L'Argument de Saint Anselme dans la philosphie réflexive," *SB* I, 273-94, cf. 283.

Joseph C. Schnaubelt, OSA

As already indicated, Anselm entered religious life in 1060.   Three years later, Lanfranc, the Prior of Bec, was elevated to the Archbishopric of Canterbury, the primatial see of the English Church.   The community at Bec then elected Anselm to succeed Lanfranc as prior.   Thirty years later, Anselm, Abbot of Bec since 1078, was again chosen to succeed Lanfranc, this time as Primate of England.   Lanfranc had died in 1089, but the king, William Rufus, left this see and others vacant, so that he could appropriate the revenues of the Church.   Only serious illness moved William Rufus to appoint a new archbishop.   Realizing he could not cooperate with such a king, Anselm resisted the appointment, until he was persuaded to accept for the good of the Church.   Accordingly, Anselm was ordained bishop on December 4, 1093.

As a proponent of Church reform, Anselm had associated himself with the policies of Gregory VII (1073-1085).   Gregory's pontificate had been marked by drastic efforts to abolish lay investiture by kings and princes, who awarded ecclesiastical offices through the presentation of ring and crozier.   Anselm was therefore immediately at loggerheads with William Rufus, who opposed any kind of reform.   Moreover, the king refused Anselm permission to visit Rome to receive the *pallium* from Pope Urban II (1088-1099), inasmuch as Urban had not been recognized in England as the rightful pope.   But because he himself had already recognized Urban, Anselm had recourse to a council of the English bishops and nobles to determine if his obedience to the Holy See could be reconciled with his loyalty to the king.   At the Council of Rockingham, the bishops, out of fear of the king, sided against Anselm, but the secular princes prevented his removal.   Consequently, the king requested the *pallium* himself in order to confer it on another, but Walter, the cardinal-legate who had brought the *pallium*, refused to surrender it.   At this point, October 15, 1097, Anselm realized he must leave the country.   In Rome, Anselm was graciously received by Pope Urban, who refused his resignation. While in Italy, Anselm took part in the Council of Bari, where he was able to delay the excommunication of William Rufus.   He also attended the Easter Synod of 1098 at the Lateran, which did pronounce excommunication against kings and princes who participated in lay investiture.

Two years later at Lyons, Anselm received the news that King William Rufus had died on August 2, 1100.   Henry I,

William Rufus' successor, immediately recalled Anselm, but
the new king was soon in conflict with the archbishop, when
Anselm refused to take an oath of allegiance to Henry
because of the decrees of the Council of Bari. The king's
subsequent request for the archbishop to go to Rome meant
another three years in exile for Anselm. Finally, in 1106,
a compromise was reached: the king renounced the right of
investiture, and the archbishop agreed not to refuse episcopal consecration to anyone who had sworn allegiance to the
king.

The comparative tranquility of Anselm's last years was
disturbed by the claim of the See of York to the primacy
which had always resided in the See of Canterbury. The end
of all earthly strife came for Anselm when he died on
Wednesday of Holy Week, April 21, 1109. He was canonized in
1163 and declared a Doctor of the Church in 1720.

By a comparison of two contemporaries, Ivo of Chartres
and Anselm of Canterbury, Lynn K. Barker draws a picture of
the reform bishop struggling against lay investiture.

Ivo of Chartres and Anselm of Canterbury

Lynn K. Barker

In March 1093, from what he took to be his deathbed, William Rufus nominated Anselm, Abbot of Bec, to fill the long vacancy at Canterbury, a post to which the abbot was consecrated on 4 December, after the king had recovered and begun to repent of his choice. Three years earlier, in November 1090,[1] Ivo, Prior of the regular canons of St. Quentin, Beauvais, had been elevated -- likewise under troubled circumstances -- to one of the important royal sees of France. Tenure of the See of Chartres had been disrupted ever since the time of Gregory VII, under whom Ivo's predecessor had been charged with a variety of crimes including simony. Only in 1090 and with the evident cooperation of Philip I and Urban II was Geoffrey at last ousted -- he took refuge in a priory of Chartres in Normandy -- and Ivo elected. Ivo was invested with his bishopric by King Philip; then, because Richer of Sens, his metropolitan, was a friend of Geoffrey of Chartres and refused to consecrate the usurper from Beauvais, he was consecrated bishop by Urban II.[2]

Ivo's early years as bishop were troubled ones. His predecessor did not retire gracefully, and then in 1092 Philip I eloped with the (possibly fourth) wife of the count of Anjou.[3] Ivo's opposition to the marriage led to attacks against the lands belonging to Chartres and to the bishop's imprisonment for at least several months.[4] In many letters of this period Ivo lamented his circumstances and his own ineffectiveness. He felt called by God to the unwelcome task of bishop and responsible to Urban, who had placed him at Chartres. Nevertheless he was at least tempted to resign his office and to return to the *otium* of the canons' cloister at Beauvais.[5]

It was in these turbulent early years of his own pontificate, then, that Ivo in 1094 drafted a letter to the newly consecrated Anselm of Canterbury -- the only letter between the two that survives. Despite basic differences, the two men had much in common. They were both prelates and religious, reformers and reluctant participants in the Investiture Controversy, fellow alumni of Lanfranc's school at Bec, and respected intellectual figures, although engaged in very disparate endeavors. The paths of Archbishop Anselm and Bishop Ivo would have occasion to cross many times in the coming years.

Scholars' assumptions about the relations between the two have spanned a wide spectrum. At one end, by casting doubt on whether Ivo ever studied at Bec, Margaret Gibson would undermine what scholars had long assumed was the basis of any friendship between the two.[6] At the other end we find the view that Ivo and Anselm were so close that the bishop of Chartres personally intervened to end the English Investiture Controversy.[7] What I would like to do is to examine the old evidence afresh and to suggest some new avenues of inquiry into the ties between the two prelates. The resulting view falls somewhere between these extremes. It shows more points of contact, even coincidence, than fundamental similarities of outlook. What we can discover about Ivo's other ties to the Anglo-Norman episcopate and his stance in the Canterbury/York dispute mitigates any impression that he was uncritically loyal to Anselm. Yet there is one area of long-term importance to the English church on which they may have cooperated, namely the introduction of regular canons into England.

Ivo's Letter to Anselm

Epistola XXXIX in Ivo's correspondence is addressed "to Anselm, the reverend Archbishop of Canterbury, from Ivo, humble servant of the church of Chartres."[8] In it Ivo seeks Archbishop Anselm's support in prayer and offers his own. In this respect, it resembles several of Ivo's long-distance letters, especially those to England and Normandy.

Ivo begins with a reference to Anselm's having been invited "up higher," his favorite biblical allusion to episcopal selection. He refers to old affection between the two, expressing hope that despite his promotion Anselm has not forgotten those whom he loved and whose loyalty he formerly enjoyed.[9] Ivo promises Anselm his own unstinting help. As an example he points out that just this year he supported the monks of Bec in their case against Molesmes, at least as far as "reason and authority" would allow. This he says he did because of his strong friendship for Anselm (*pro multa in te benivolentia*). He would have seen to it that the monks were rendered full justice in their case regarding Poissy had they not preferred to seek the king's favor (*benivolentiam*).[10]

Finally, the letter served as a letter of reference. Ivo commends to Anselm's care the bearer, Brother Rothard, who was being sent to England (*ad partes istas*) on business for his community (*per obedientiam confratrum*).

Ivo at Bec

The way in which Ivo invoked an earlier friendship with
Anselm in *Epistola XXXIX* seems to recall time spent together
in the past, and it is natural for us to wonder if Ivo could
here be referring to experiences shared at Bec. The tradition that Ivo was a student of Lanfranc's at Bec is a long-
standing one, but it has received criticism. The twelfth-
century chronicler Robert of Torigni wrote that "When he was
young [Ivo] heard Master Lanfranc, the Prior of Bec, teach
on secular and divine letters in that celebrated school
which he held at Bec."[12]

Margaret Gibson mentions a "real and continuing doubt"
about whether Ivo was Lanfranc's student and discredits Robert's *Chronicle* as too late a source to be deemed reliable.
Nevertheless she appreciates the many connections between
Ivo and Bec and concludes that he was possibly part of a
"miscellaneous group of Beauvais men who had an interest in
Bec."[13]

In defense of the traditional view, we must remember
that Robert himself was a monk at Bec from 1128 -- and prior
from 1149 -- until he was elected Abbot of Mont-Saint-Michel
in 1154. He shows us that he had detailed knowledge of
scholarly life at Bec in Lanfranc's day. He describes, for
instance, Lanfranc's textual emendations and observes that
the master had his students collate and correct texts.[14]
It is true that by around 1150, when Robert wrote, Lanfranc's school and Ivo's student days were nearly a century
in the past. Yet what Robert records has the ring of the
sort of corporate memory characteristic of a medieval monastic community. There is no positive evidence to discredit
Robert's statement; the relatively late date calls for caution, but we may conclude that the account is probably
true.[15]

Lanfranc had arrived at Bec around 1042 and was soon
encouraged by the founder Herluin to open an extern school,
which he conducted presumably until he was called to Caen as
abbot in 1063 at the behest of Duke William. Later chroniclers gave Lanfranc credit for renewing learning in northern Europe, and many of Bec's alumni went on to positions of
authority in the church. Other alumni of the school of Bec
in the time of Lanfranc include[16] Pope Alexander II,[17]
William Bona Anima, Archbishop of Rouen, Guitmund of Aversa,
Gundulf and Ernulf, Bishops of Rochester, Fulk, Bishop of
Beauvais, among others. Many of these were Ivo's correspon-
dents; others we know were his friends or perhaps disciples.

In his study of "sacred and divine letters," Ivo might
have picked up some of his interest in canon law under Lan-

franc's influence.[18]   One peculiarity of Ivo's *Decretum* is
its inclusion of materials relating to the Eucharistic controversy with Berengar, including excerpts from Lanfranc's
De corpore et sanguine Domini.[19] On the whole, however,
little has been done to explore connections between Lanfranc's work and Ivo's.[20]

Ivo and the English Investiture Controversy

While Norman F. Cantor's *Church, Kingship and Lay Investiture in England 1089-1135* has been criticized on many
points,[21] the work made a lasting contribution by exposing
what Cantor terms the "Ivo of Chartres thesis" about the end
of the English Investiture Controversy.[22] Apparently first
suggested by Ernst Bernheim and further developed by Felix
Liebermann, this view held that Ivo's ideas and intervention
brought about the compromise settlement with Henry I in 1107
and even paved the way for the Concordat of Worms in 1122.[23]
Cantor's refutation counters Liebermann's two chief
points. On the subject of Ivo's personal involvement, Cantor shows that Ivo is not mentioned in connection with the
compromise of 1107. What this absence from contemporary
sources amounts to is that Eadmer does not mention Ivo in
his account of these events.
According to Eadmer's *Historia novorum,* Anselm was at
Chartres three times during his exile from 1103 to 1106. The
first was at Pentecost 1103, when he arrived at Chartres
from Bec on his way to see the pope. Eadmer tells us that
Bishop Ivo of Chartres and others persuaded Anselm to avoid
the extreme heat of Italy by postponing his trip until the
end of summer. Anselm returned to Bec, passing through
Chartres a second time in August, when he set out again for
the papal court.[24]
In 1105 Anselm returned from Lyon, where he had spent
most of the exile in the company of the papal legate, Archbishop Hugh. His purpose in returning was to excommunicate
Henry I, who was then occupied with the conquest of Normandy. Hearing that Countess Adela was ill at Blois, he
agreed to visit her there, and then, as she recovered and
showed concern for her brother's impending excommunication,
Anselm was persuaded to accompany her to Chartres. Eadmer
does not say what happened at Chartres, only that shortly
afterwards Adela escorted Anselm into Normandy, where the
two met with Henry I. These negotiations led to the agreement of 1107 whereby the English king gave up investitures
but retained a claim to homage by his churchmen.   The   pre-

sumption then is that Adela was instrumental in bringing about the negotiations if not the actual settlement. Eadmer does not mention Ivo in this context or in connection with Anselm's 1105 visit to Chartres.[25]

Cantor places great weight on Eadmer's omission. Neither Eadmer nor Anselm, who endorsed the *History*, "had . . . cause to deny to the great canonist, a friend of the Archbishop of Canterbury, recognition for his role in ending the English Investiture Controversy."[26] Yet, as we will see, Ivo enjoyed friendly ties with several of Anselm's opponents, and he failed to offer unequivocal support for Canterbury's primacy over the English church. We are left to wonder if Eadmer had as little reason for slighting Ivo as Cantor believed.

Far more convincing than Eadmer's silence is Cantor's simple demonstration that the views embodied in the compromise of 1107 do not reflect those of the Bishop of Chartres. Briefly stated: in the agreement of 1107, the English king gave up the right to invest bishops. This implies that the parties to the settlement recognized that investiture conveyed something spiritual which the king had no right to confer. By the time of Anselm's dispute with Henry, however, Ivo was on record as saying that investiture by laymen did not convey anything spiritual regardless of the ceremonial involved.

Even if Ivo did take part in the discussions of 1105; even if he discussed the issues with Anselm in 1103; and even if Eadmer had his own reasons for leaving Ivo out of the picture, there are still no grounds for holding Ivo responsible for the resulting settlement. For most of a century scholars assumed that Ivo's role in the English Investiture Controversy was the chief manifestation of his friendship for Anselm. While we can qualify Cantor's account, his refutation of the view that Ivo settled the English Investiture Controversy stands, and we must look elsewhere to find the friendship yielding results.

Ivo's Contacts with Other Bec Alumni and Anglo-Normans

Ivo's letter to Anselm was only one of several letters of prayer confraternity and spiritual friendship addressed to churchmen in the Anglo-Norman realm. In tone it was not as warm as some others. Unlike these others, it displays a deferential, almost detached, quality and deals largely with business. Throughout his correspondence we catch sight of Ivo's extensive network of Anglo-Norman connections.

Examining these can deepen our appreciation for Ivo's ties
with the Anglo-Norman realm and with the Archbishop of
Canterbury.

A famous letter is addressed to William, Abbot of
Fécamp, who had consulted Ivo as to whether an altar that
had been moved needed to be reconsecrated. In the letter
Ivo quoted extensively from a letter he had sent earlier to
Gerard, Abbot of St. Wandrille.[29] Interestingly, in his
search for an answer, William had posed the same question to
Anselm.[30]

Guitmund of Aversa was a monk of St.-Croix-le-Leufroy at
Evreux and a student of Lanfranc's; he wrote a work on the
Eucharist against Berengar, and in 1088 Urban made him
bishop of Aversa. Ivo mentions him in a letter in which he
refers to several churchmen whom he may have known personally.[31] Historians of the Gregorian Reform are familiar
with a passage ascribed to Gregory VII in which the pope
argued that Christ said, "I am the truth," not, "I am custom." What is less well known is that the passage was preserved only through Ivo's three canon law collections and
that the letter from which it was taken was addressed by
Gregory to Guitmund of Aversa.[32] It is tempting to conclude
from these two bits of information that Ivo was acquainted
with Guitmund (they were also both episcopal creations of
Urban), and, since Guitmund was a student of Lanfranc's, it
is tempting to see Bec as the common denominator.

In the same letter in which he mentioned Guitmund, Ivo
referred also to Ernulf, monk of St. Symphorien, Beauvais,
who left the monastery to become prior at Canterbury. Ivo
was trying to show that for good cause, in this case the
church's need for worthy leaders, a monk might transfer from
his monastery. It is interesting that two of the contemporary examples he adduced, Guitmund and Ernulf, were alumni
of Bec with whom he seems to have been acquainted.[33]

Among the many glimpses we have of Ivo's Anglo-Norman
connections, what best lends perspective to our view of his
relations with Anselm is a group of letters to certain
Anglo-Norman bishops. These include Walkelin of Winchester,
Samson of Worcester and his son Robert of Bayeux, and Robert
Bloet of Lincoln -- all curialist bishops, all opponents of
Anselm.[34] Ivo's letters to these men show a remarkable
homogeneity, including several traits that set them apart
from most of his other correspondence. Like the letter to
Anselm, they offer and request prayer support. In them Ivo
sometimes acknowledges receipt of a gift: liturgical slip-
pers from Samson, a chrism vessel requested from Walkelin.[35]
Frequently they achieve a friendly tone of episcopal colle-

giality.   They   are   letters of friendship of the sort more
common in the later twelfth century.

These men were royal appointees, curialists, members of
the   old school.   Ivo's relations with them were at least as
friendly as those he enjoyed with Anselm.   Two other features strike us in these letters.   The first is that several
of Ivo's Anglo-Norman friends belonged to a remarkable
ecclesiastical dynasty that included Samson of Worcester
-- his brother was Thomas I of York, a student of Lanfranc's
-- and his two sons, Thomas II of York and Robert of Bayeux.
That the feelings Ivo expressed may have been more than formal sentiments is suggested by his intercession with papal
legate Cono of Palestrina on behalf of his dear friend --
amicissimo -- Robert, Bishop of Bayeux, who was suffering
under Cono's excommunication of all Norman bishops for their
failure to attend the legate's councils.[36]   The second
striking feature is that Ivo's ties to this family seem to
have made him a friend of the See of York.

Two of Ivo's letters are addressed to Samson of Worcester.[37] Chaplain and nominee of William Rufus, consecrated by
Anselm on 8 June, 1096, Samson was the brother of Thomas I
of York.[38]   Modern studies have tried to show that he had a
chief role in compiling the Domesday survey. Married and
only a subdeacon at the time of his appointment, Samson was
the son of a priest and had close family ties to the chapter
of Bayeux, where he himself served as treasurer and dean.
Samson   enjoyed   the   patronage of Bishop Odo and the
Conqueror, who, according to Orderic Vitalis, had tried to
make him bishop of Le Mans (Samson begged off, Orderic tells
us, because of the weight of his sins). William of Malmesbury's prejudiced account of Samson the glutton was probably
influenced by the monastic historian's perception of Samson
as an enemy of monks -- an episcopal quality that would not
necessarily have troubled Ivo. Anselm consulted Samson concerning the rights of Canterbury. Samson replied that it
ill befitted a bishop to become so heated over the issue.[39]

Ivo's friendship with the family extended to Samson's
sons, since he wrote warmly on behalf of Robert of Bayeux
and addressed a friendly letter of support to Thomas on his
election to York.[40]

His Anglo-Norman correspondence confirms the likelihood
that Ivo was linked to Anselm as a Bec alumnus.   On the
other hand, it points out the complexities of his relations
with the Anglo-Norman church.[41]   Many and close ties to
Anglo-Norman churchmen would not automatically make Ivo a
supporter of Anselm in the archbishop's struggle against the
English king over investitures.   It is clear that Ivo's

ties with York must also be weighed in any effort to assess
his relations with the archbishop of Canterbury.

Canterbury and York[42]

The dispute between Canterbury and York concerned Canterbury's claim to primacy of the English church and dated
(in its Anglo-Norman manifestation) to the time of Lanfranc.
Thomas I,[43] Samson's brother, had refused for two years to
make the profession of obedience that Lanfranc had required
of him in 1070. While Thomas finally yielded to the combined pressure of king and fellow archbishop, the conflict
between York and Canterbury was renewed with nearly every
election of a new archbishop for the next fifty years.

Ivo's ties to Canterbury, through Lanfranc, Anselm,
Ernulf, and perhaps others, did not keep him from supporting
York against Canterbury's claims. He was a friend of Thomas
II, the nephew of Thomas I, and he urged the pope to let
Thurstan be consecrated despite his refusal to profess
obedience to Canterbury.[44]

Frank Barlow feels that Anselm was not particularly keen
to defend Canterbury's status.[45]   Southern, on the other
hand, sees the setbacks of Anselm's pontificate as the
result of circumstances and not due to any lack of dedication on Anselm's part.[46]   Recent work by Sally Vaughn,
however, argues that the Canterbury primacy was one of
Anselm's chief concerns and stresses his success at achieving his goals.[47]

In 1102 Paschal II granted the primacy to Anselm personally "as to his predecessors"[48] and later in that year
ordered Gerard of York to make profession.[49] The next year
marked the high point of Canterbury's success, when, in
exile at the papal court, Anselm secured papal confirmation
of the Canterbury primacy (described vaguely as that which
his predecessors had enjoyed) to his successors.[50]

In the last year of his life Anselm was much preoccupied
with exerting his primacy over the newly elected Thomas II,
even threatening to go into a third exile if he could not
get papal support for his position.[51] The last letter in
his correspondence suspended Thomas from the priesthood
until he should submit to Canterbury.[52]

Ivo outlived Anselm by six years, long enough to see the
opening salvos of Thurstan's campaign.   One of *his* last
letters was a plea for Paschal II to permit Thurstan to be
consecrated despite his refusal to obey Canterbury. Thurstan, who succeeded Thomas in 1114, was unwilling to compromise and went into exile for his refusal to recognize Can-

terbury. He was at last consecrated by Pope Calixtus II before the Council of Reims in 1119 and, reconciled to Henry after the wreck of the White Ship, he was enthroned (1122-23), still refusing to make profession.[53]

Despite these several factors, I suspect the fundamental answer has less to do with the personalities involved or with English ecclesiastical organization than with what primacy meant to Ivo. It is true that in the later years of the dispute, towards the end of Ivo's life, it was York rather than Canterbury that enjoyed papal support. Thurstan was consecrated by the pope; the Canterbury forgeries were derided at the papal court.[56] But these episodes need not have affected Ivo's attitude toward the primacies in 1108 or in 1114. On the contrary, one suspects that Ivo's attitude toward the issues was formed by events of an earlier day. Ivo, like Geoffrey of Rouen, was acquainted with the primacy as a centralizing tool of the Gregorian papacy.

Ivo's *Epistola LX* is addressed to Hugh of Die, who was Archbishop of Lyon, papal legate, and Primate of Gaul. The primacy of Lyon had been set up by Gregory VII to enhance papal control over Sens, Reims, Tours, and Rouen.[57] Ivo was writing to defend his newly elected metropolitan, Daimbert of Sens, from Hugh's refusal to let Daimbert be consecrated until he had recognized the primacy of Lyon.

The letter is one of Ivo's two chief contributions to the polemical literature of the Investiture Controversy, and while investiture is discussed -- Daimbert was alleged to have received investiture from the king -- the real subject of dispute was that Daimbert refused to make profession recognizing the primacy of Lyon over Sens. It is only one of several indications of the tension between Ivo and the papal legate Hugh, whose reforming zeal even Gregory VII himself had been forced to temper and who had been deposed on Gregory's death, before having his commission renewed by Urban II. As we know from a later letter, Ivo's defense of Daimbert incurred the pope's displeasure.[58] It was the sort of episode that would have impressed Ivo with the primacy as a tool of "Gregorian" centralization and with the foolish consistency of his opponents in the matter of investitures. Was it enough to make him see in Canterbury's claims the same forces and the same unreasonableness?

We know from ideas at Rouen that contemporaries engaged in the continental struggles over primacy might well draw a parallel to the Canterbury/York dispute. The See of Rouen was both an opponent of Lyon and a supporter of York. Mary Cheney has suggested a connection between the two positions.[59] She feels that Archbishop Geoffrey of Rouen (1111-28) made use of a York privilege "not because of any

direct interest in Thurstan's position, but because the text
might be useful in his own similar struggle against the primatial claims of the archbishops of Lyon."[60] The Norman
Anonymous likewise defended Rouen and York against the primatial arrangements of the Gregorian papacy.[61] That Ivo
directed the opposition of Sens against Lyon places him in
company with the views expressed at Rouen; like Geoffrey or
the Norman Anonymous, he may have had similar motives for
his attitude toward York.

It does not surprise us then to learn that Ivo was
remembered with respect and that his writings were preserved
and studied at York. It is perhaps no accident that it was
a York writer, Hugh the Chantor, and not Eadmer, who
recorded the one -- favorable -- twelfth-century English
assessment of Ivo's views on investitures.[62]

Regular Canons in England: Chartres and Beauvais

We have seen, then, that traditional views of Ivo's and
Anselm's relations must be considerably revised. Not only,
as Cantor had shown, was Ivo not responsible for ending the
English Investiture Controversy. His relations with the
Anglo-Normans were more varied, his possible motives more
complex, than has previously been appreciated. These contacts and motives make him more than a simple friend to Canterbury. What is left of Ivo's and Anselm's friendship? One
further area suggests friendly cooperation between the two
prelates in reforming the life of the clergy, namely, the
introduction of regular canons into England.

The man who led the introduction of regular canons into
England was a priest named Norman from St. Botolph's,
Colchester. A history of one of St. Botolph's priories
tells us that Norman had studied in France with "Anselm."
When he wished to embrace the full common life in keeping
with the Rule of St. Augustine, he and his brother, Bernard,
set out for the continent with a letter of introduction from
Anselm to the house of Mt.-Saint-Eloi. But as J. C. Dickinson tells us, the letter was not used because "for some
unexplained reason" the brothers studied instead at Chartres
and then at Beauvais. It is Dickinson's belief that
Anselm's meetings with Ivo are responsible for the switch.[63]

Ivo was the Prior of St. Quentin, Beauvais, from its
foundation in the 1070s until his election to Chartres in
1090. In 1099 he turned St.-Jean-en-Vallée, Chartres, into
a house of regular canons, probably after unsuccessful
efforts to introduce the common life at the cathedral.[64]
Among Anselm's acquaintances, Ivo was the leading proponent

of the full common life for clergy. Anselm sent Norman and Bernard on their way; Ivo's houses received them. It is not at all unlikely that Anselm referred them to Ivo. Moreover, Ivo was on friendly terms with Henry I and his queen, Matilda, who was herself one of the greatest patrons of the regular life in the generation after its introduction into England.[65] Although the details are hidden from us, we can have no doubt that Ivo and Anselm shared responsibility for the introduction of regular canons into England. One point that calls for further investigation is the number of English Ivonian MSS whose provenance can be traced to these early houses of regular canons.

Conclusion

Ivo cannot accurately be described as a Gregorian. His real contribution to the Investiture Controversy was a theory of dispensation that allowed the reformers to avoid intransigence on the issue of investiture -- an approach often adopted by both Urban II and Paschal II, with whom Ivo was generally on very cordial terms. Nor was he a friend to "Gregorian" methods of centralizing church power. For Ivo the office of reform belonged properly to the bishop. And that reform, far from being political, was chiefly the reform of the religious life. Inasmuch as Ivo and Anselm cooperated as prelate-reformers, then, this was done not on the subject of investitures (or of church-state relations in general) nor in matters touching Canterbury's primacy, but in bringing the regular canons to England.

Notes

[1] On Ivo in general see R. Sprandel, *Ivo von Chartres und seine Stellung in der Kirchengeschichte*, Pariser Historische Studien, No. 1 (Stuttgart: Hiersemann, 1962); Leclercq, below, n. 2; E. Amann and L. Guizard, *DTC*, XV, 3625-40; on Ivo and the Investiture Controversy, see note 23, below.

[2] *Epistolae I-II*:   PL CLXII,11-13; CLI,325-27; also in Yves de Chartres, *Correspondance*, ed. and trans. J. Leclercq, Les classiques de l'histoire de France au moyen âge, No. 22 (Paris: Société d'Edition "Les Belles Lettres," 1949) (hereinafter cited as Leclercq), I, 2-11; Leclercq, p. ix, says Ivo was consecrated by Urban at Capua shortly before 24 November, almost certainly in 1090.

[3] According to M. Chibnall, Count Fulk Nerra of Anjou had been married at least three times when he married Bertrada; at least two of her predecessors had been repudiated by Fulk; Ordericus Vitalis, *The Ecclesiastical History of Ordericus Vitalis*, ed. and trans. M. Chibnall (Oxford: Clarendon Press, 1969-80) (hereinafter cited as Ordericus), IV, 186-87 and n. 3.

[4] Ivo was imprisoned by Hugh of Le Puiset at Philip's command; Suger, *Vie de Louis VI le Gros*, ed. and trans. H. Waquet, Les classiques de l'histoire de France au moyen âge, No. 11 (Paris: Société d'Edition "Les Belles Lettres," 1929) (hereinafter cited as Suger), pp. 134 and 135; but cf. Leclercq, p. 82; Sprandel, *Ivo*, p. 103; A. Fliche, *Le règne de Philippe 1er, roi de France* (Paris: Société française d'imprimerie et de librairie, 1912), pp. 46-77.

[5] *Epistolae III, XII, XVII: PL* CLXII,13-14, 24-25, 29-31; on Ivo's relations with St.-Quentin, Beauvais, see above, p. 13.

[6] M. Gibson, *Lanfranc of Bec* (Oxford: Clarendon Press, 1976), pp. 36-37.

[7] This view prevailed until the publication of N. F. Cantor, *Church, Kingship, and Lay Investiture in England 1089-1135*, Princeton Studies in History, No. 10 (Princeton: Princeton Univ. Press, 1958); above, p. 4.

[8] *Epistola XXXIX: PL* CLXII,50-51; Leclerq, pp. 162-64; *Epistola 181*: Schmitt IV,65-66; the date of the letter seems to be soon after Anselm's consecration, so probably 1094; Sprandel, *Ivo*, p. 186.

[9] . . . quos aliquando in Christo dilexerat, vel a quibus pro Christo aliquod obsequium fraternitatis acceperat, *Epistola XXXIX: PL* CLXII,51.

[10] . . . de Pixiacensi monasterio plenam per nos consecuti fuissent justitiam nisi quod prius affectabant regis captare benivolentiam, *Epistola XXXIX: PL* CLXII,51; Poissy-sur-Seine was a priory of Bec in the diocese of Chartres and the subject of a dispute between Bec and Molesmes; *Epistola IX: PL* CLXII,21, to Philip I, also concerns the case; here Ivo insisted that the settlement he had effected had done no harm to Bec. See also Leclercq, pp. 38-39; A. A. Porée, *Histoire de l'abbaye du Bec* (Evreux: Hérissey, 1901), I, 241.

¹¹Rothard is unidentified; Ivo's use of *confrater* frequently refers to a regular canon; on Ivo's language regarding regular canons, see L. K. Barker, "Clerical Reform and the Typological Exegesis of Ivo of Chartres," *Proceedings of the PMR Conference* 9 (1984), 51-58.

¹²Hic dum esset juvenis audivit magistrum Lanfrancum, priorem Becci, de secularibus et divinis litteris tractantem in illa famosa scola quam Becci tenuit, *Chronique de Robert de Torigni, abbé du Mont-Saint-Michel,* ed. L. Delisle (Rouen: le Brumen, 1872) (hereinafter cited as Robert of Torigni), I, 153; trans. Gibson, *Lanfranc,* p. 36.

¹³Gibson, *Lanfranc,* p. 36; on the schools at Bec in general, Porée, *Histoire de l'abbaye du Bec;* R. Foreville, "L'école du Bec et le 'studium' de Canterbury aux XIe et XIIe siècles," *Bulletin philologique et historique (jusqu'à 1715)* 1955-1956, 357-74; T. Maze, "L'abbaye du Bec au XIe siècle," in *La Normandie bénédictine au temps de Guillaume le Conquérant (XIe siècle)* (Lille: Facultés Catholiques de Lille, 1967), pp. 229-47, at 233-34; and now Vaughn, "Lanfranc," n. 46, below.

¹⁴Robert of Torigni, I, 74: . . . quia scripturae scriptorum vitio erant nimium corruptae, mones tam veteris quam novi Testamenti libros, necnon etiam scripta sanctorum patrum, secundum orthodoxam fidem studuit corrigere, et etiam multa de his quibus utimur die ac nocte in servitio ecclesiae, ad unguem emendavit, et hoc non tantum per se, sed etiam per discipulos suos fecit; reference to a surviving manuscript in G. Nortier, *Les bibliothèques médiévales des abbayes bénédictines de Normandie,* 2nd ed., Bibliothèque d'histoire et d'archéologie chrétiennes, No. 9 (Paris: Lethielleux, 1971), p. 35.

¹⁵See also Sprandel, *Ivo,* p. 7; D. Knowles, *The Monastic Order in England: A History of Its Development from the Times of St. Dunstan to the Fourth Lateran Council, 940-1216,* 2nd ed. (Cambridge: Univ. Press, 1963), pp. 88-92. When this paper was presented, Sally Vaughn very kindly brought her recent work on Lanfranc to my attention; her discussion of Ivo's association with the school of Bec agrees with the above in substance and detail: "Lanfranc of Bec: A Reconsideration," *Albion* 17 (1985), 135-48, esp. 136-37.

¹⁶Hugh the Chantor, *The History of the Church of York 1066-1127,* ed. and trans. C. Johnson, Medieval Texts (Lon-

don: Nelson, 1961), p. 2, observes that Lanfranc had taught
almost everyone who had any reputation for learning   at   the
time (sub cuius magisterio de Gallie, Germanie, Italie fini-
bus omnes fere didicerant, inter   quos   et   prefatus   Thomas
[Thomas I of York], ubicunque tunc temporis scientia litterarum aliquantum nomen habebat); for lists of Lanfranc's students, Porée, *Histoire . . . du Bec*, I, 102; S. N. Vaughn,
The Abbey of Bec and the Anglo-Norman State 1034-1136 (Wood-
bridge, Suffolk: Boydell, 1981), pp. 148-49, n. 27.

[17]Alexander,   the   former Anselm of Baggio, continued to
honor Lanfranc even after he was   pope,   e.g.,   during Lanfranc's 1071   visit   to   Rome;   T.   Schmidt, *Alexander II
(1061-1073) und die Römische Reformgruppe seiner Zeit*,
Päpste und Papsttum, No. 11 (Stuttgart: Hiersemann, 1977),
pp. 10-25, reexamines the question of   Alexander's   association with the school of Bec.

[18]Z.   N.   Brooke, *The English Church and the Papacy from
the Conquest to the Reign of King   John* (Cambridge: Univ.
Press,   1931),   pp.   57-83 on Lanfranc's canon law study and
manuscripts; Foreville, "L'école," p.   359,   observes   that
Lanfranc   as   a   teacher   of   liberal arts would have taught
"*sans doute, ce que la   rhétorique   préservait de connais-
sances   et   d'art   juridique*"; cf. Gibson, *Lanfranc*, p. 37:
"At most Lanfranc's instruction in the   arts   gave   Ivo   the
tools   with which to organize and clarify the study of canon
law."   For the question of whether Lanfranc practiced law in
his   native   Pavia,   Gibson,   pp. 6-11, and older literature
cited in Foreville, "L'école," p. 360, n. 1.

[19]*Decretum* II,9:   *PL* CLXI,152-60   (from   Lanfranc's   *De
corpore et sanguine Domini*); *Decretum* II,10:   *PL* CLXI,160-62
(Berengar's profession of faith); J. de Ghellinck, *Le mouvement   théologique du XIIe siècle*, 2nd ed. (Bruges: Editions
"De Tempel," 1948), p.   447,   believes Ivo was   the   first   to
include   these two works in canon law collections.   Guitmund
and Ascelin were Bec alumni who participated in the literary
exchange;   on the controversy between Lanfranc and Berengar,
Gibson, *Lanfranc*, pp. 63-97; J.   de   Montclos,   *Lanfranc et
Bérenger: La controverse eucharistique du XIe siècle*, Spicilegium sacrum Lovaniense,   No.   37 (Louvain: Spicilegium
sacrum   Lovaniense,   1971); R.   W.   Southern, "Lanfranc of Bec
and Berengar of Tours," in *Studies in Medieval History Presented   to Frederick Maurice Powicke*, eds. R. W. Hunt, W. A.
Pantin,   and   R.   W.   Southern,   (Oxford: Clarendon   Press,
1948),   pp.   27-48; A. J. MacDonald, *Berengar and the Reform
of Sacramental Doctrine* (London: Longmans, Green, 1930).

[20] Sprandel, *Ivo*, pp. 34, 64; Gibson, *Lanfranc*, p. 36 and n. 4, compared an unpublished fragment of an Exodus commentary attributed to Ivo, MS Oxford Bodl. Laud Misc. 216, fol. 2v, and found no similarity to Lanfranc's thought.

[21] Reviews of Cantor include: C. R. Cheney, *Speculum* 34 (1959), 653-56; R. van Caenegem, *Revue belge de philologie et d'histoire* 38 (1960), 885-88; M. J. Wilks, *Medium aevum* 30 (1961), 134-36; W. Holtzmann, *Deutsches Archiv* 75 (1959), 295-96; C. N. L. Brooke, *English Historical Review* 75 (1960), 116-20; most reviews were critical of several aspects of the work, but accepted the refutation regarding Ivo; cf. the review by T. Schieffer, *Historische Zeitschrift* 192 (1961), 690-95, whose reluctance to abandon the "Chartrain theory" extended to rejecting the conclusions of Hoffmann, "Ivo von Chartres und die Lösung," below, note 23.

[22] Cantor, *Church, Kingship*, pp. 202-16.

[23] E. Bernheim, *Zur Geschichte des Wormser Concordates* (Göttingen: Peppemüller, 1878), p. 12; F. Liebermann, "Anselm von Canterbury und Hugo von Lyon," in *Historische Aufsätze dem Andenken Georg Waitz gewidmet* (Hanover: Hahn, 1886), pp. 194-96; cited in Cantor, *Church, Kingship*, p. 203; repeated e.g. by A. L. Poole, *From Domesday Book to Magna Carta 1087-1216*, 2nd ed. (Oxford: Clarendon Press, 1955), pp. 179-80; R. W. Southern, *Saint Anselm*, p. 177, n. 1, endorses Cantor's refutation, "with whose judgment on this point I am in complete agreement"; on Ivo and the Investiture Controversy, see especially H. Hoffmann, "Ivo von Chartres und die Lösung des Investiturproblems," *Deutsches Archiv* 15 (1959), 393-440 and the literature cited there, pp. 405-06, no. 6.

[24] *Historia novorum*, p. 151.

[25] Ibid., pp. 164-66.

[26] Cantor, *Church, Kingship*, p. 205.

[27] It is interesting to note that, unlike other twelfth-century accounts, Eadmer's one reference to Ivo fails to pay tribute to the bishop's great reputation for learning, although Eadmer does link Ivo with "others . . . whose counsel was not to be slighted," *Historia novorum*, p. 151: accepti ab Ivone civitatis episcopo et a multis non spernendi consilii viris; with other writers such praise is somewhat formulaic: Robert of Torigni, I, 153: "Vir reli-

giosus et magnae litteraturae"; Suger,, p. 84: "venerabili et sapientissimo viro Ivone, Carnotensi episcopo," and p. 134: "Carnotensi venerabili Ivone"; Orderic, 4.262: "Eruditissimus quoque Iuo Carnotensi preerat aeclesiae, cui perhibet euidens testimonium laus bonae vitae et rectae doctrinae," and 6.42: "Tunc uenerabilis Iuo Carnotenae urbis episcopus inter precipuos Franciae doctores eruditione litterarum tam diuinarum quam secularium floruit"; Hugh the Chantor, *The History of the Church of York*, p. 14: "venerabilem Ivonem Carnotensem episcopum, quo nec alter in Gallis tempore suo melius in divinis eruditus et exercitatus, nec fide et doctrina magis catholicus extitit."

[28] *Epistola LX* to Hugh of Lyon, 1097: *PL* CLXII,73, Leclercq, p. 246: "Quae concessio sive fiat manu, sive nutu, sive lingua, sive virga, quid refert? cum reges nihil spirituale se dare intendant . . ."; the letter circulated independently of Ivo's main collection as part of the polemical literature on investitures; in *Libelli de lite*: ed. E. Sackur, *MGH* II,640-47; the letter brought Ivo into conflict with Urban II; *Epistola LXVII*: *PL* CLXII,85: "Audivi dulcedinem vestram in me amaricatam . . .," and later statements were more diplomatic; Ivo's attitude toward the Gregorian legislation is discussed in a study I am preparing on his historical thought.

[29] Cf. *Epistola LXXII* to Gerard, Abbot of St. Wandrille: *PL* CLXII,92; *Epistola LXXII* is quoted extensively in *Epistola LXXX* to William of Fécamp: *PL* CLXII,101-03; it is one of his most popular letters and circulated apart from the main letter collection.

[30] R. W. Southern, *Saint Anselm and His Biographer* (Cambridge: Univ. Press, 1963), p. 126, Ivo and Anselm gave similar answers: no reconsecration, but reconciliation.

[31] *Epistola LXXVIII*: *PL* CLXII,100, in which he also mentions Ernulf of Rochester; s.v. Guitmund, *LTK* IV, 1272, and *NCE*, VI, 858-59, with bibliography.

[32] *Decretum* IV,213: *PL* CLXI,311; *Panormia* IV,166: *PL* CLXI,1121; *Tripartita*, MS Paris B.N. lat. 3858B, fol. 148v; see G. Ladner, "Two Gregorian Letters on the Sources and Nature of Gregory VII's Reform Ideology," *Studi Gregoriani* 5 (1956), 221-42; H. E. J. Cowdrey, ed. and trans., *The Epistolae Vacantes of Gregory VII* (Oxford: Clarendon Press, 1972), p. 151, no. 67; J. Gilchrist, "The Reception of Gregory VII into the Canon Law (1072-1141) [Part 1]," *Zeit-*

schrift der Savigny-Stiftung für Rechtsgeschichte. Kanonistische Abteilung 90 (1973), 61-64.

[33] On Ernulf, monk at Beauvais, Prior of Canterbury, Abbot of Peterborough from 1107, and finally Bishop of Rochester 1115-24, see *LTK*, I, 889, s.v. Arnulf von Beauvais; and Southern, *Saint Anselm*, pp. 269-79, who mentions that Ernulf may have been a disciple of Ivo's.

[34] *Epistola XXXVIII*: PL CLXII,50 (Walkelin of Winchester); *Epistolae CLXV and CCVII*: PL CLXII,168-69, 212-13 (Samson of Worcester); *Epistola CCLXXVIII*: PL CLXII,279-80 (Robert of Lincoln); *Epistola CCXV* : PL CLXII,219-21 (Thomas II of York); W. Fröhlich, "Die bischöflichen Kollegen des heiligen Erzbischofs Anselm von Canterbury," Diss., Univ. of Munich, 1971, a shorter version of which appeared earlier under the same title in *AA* 1 (1969), 223-67 and 2 (1970), 117-68 (subsequent references are to the dissertation); E. U. Crosby, "The Organization of the English Episcopate under Henry I," *Studies in Medieval and Renaissance History* 4 (1967), 1-88.

[35] *Epistola CCVII*: PL CLXII,13, and *Epistola XXXVIII*: PL CLXII,50; cf. *Epistola VI* to Gerard, possibly canon of Ham, on receipt of a liturgical comb; on this letter, Leclercq, *Correspondance*, pp. 18-23 and his "Pour l'histoire du canif et de la lime," *Scriptorium* 26 (1972), 294-300, esp. 298.

[36] *Epistola CCLXXIII*: PL CLXII,275-76; the suspensions and excommunications occurred at Châlons-sur-Marne in July 1115; on Cono's legation, T. Schieffer, *Die päpstlichen Legaten in Frankreich, vom Vertrage von Meersen (870) bis zum Schisma von 1130*, Historische Studien, No. 263 (Berlin: Ebering, 1935; rpt. Vaduz: Kraus, 1965), pp. 198-212, esp. 202.

[37] *Epistolae CLXV and CCVII*: PL CLXII,168-69, 212-13; V. H. Galbraith, "Notes on the Career of Samson, Bishop of Worcester (1096-1112)," *English Historical Review* 82 (1967), 86-101; qualifications by F. Barlow, *English Church*, p. 71, n. 91.

[38] Fröhlich, *Bischöflichen Kollegen*, pp. 108-18; Crosby, "Organization," pp. 19-20.

[39] Southern, *Saint Anselm*, p. 140: Samson, he says, was of the "old school" and "everything that the Hildebrandine

Church abhorred" but a friend of Marbod of Rennes' and
Ivo's.

⁴⁰*Epistola CCLXXIII*:   *PL* CLXII,275-76; *Epistola CCXV*:
PL CLXII,219-20.

⁴¹Ivo's other Anglo-Norman contacts include: Ouen of
Evreux; William of Rouen; Gerard of St. Wandrille, O. of
Jumièges; Ernulf of Canterbury and Rochester; Ralph of
Rochester; Turgis of Avranches; William Rufus; Henry I;
Queen Matilda; Robert of Meulan; Robert of Bellême; Eudo,
the steward (*dapifer*); I am at present preparing a study on
Ivo's relations with the Anglo-Norman realm.

⁴²On the issue of Canterbury's primacy during this
period, Southern, *Saint Anselm*, pp. 127-42; Barlow, *English
Church*, esp. pp. 39-45; M. Brett, *The English Church under
Henry I* (Oxford: Univ. Press, 1975), esp. pp. 12-15, 38-42,
45-48; M. Richter, "Archbishop Lanfranc and the Canterbury
Primacy: Some Suggestions," *Downside Review* 90 (1972),
110-18; D. Bethell, "William of Corbeil and the Canterbury
York Dispute," *Journal of Ecclesiastical History* 19 (1968),
145-59; M. Düball, *Der Suprematstreit zwischen den
Erzdiözesen Canterbury und York 1070-1126: Ein Beitrag zur
Geschichte der englischen Kirche im Zeitalter des Gregorian-
ismus*, Historische Studien, No. 184 (Berlin: Ebering, 1929;
rpt. Vaduz: Kraus, 1965).

⁴³" . . . the protégé of Lanfranc's rival, Odo of
Bayeux," Barlow, *English Church*, p. 40; D. R. Bates, "The
Character and Career of Odo, Bishop of Bayeux
(1049/50-97)," *Speculum* 50 (1975), 1-20, esp. 13; Fröhlich,
Bischöflichen Kollegen, pp. 50-52.

⁴⁴*Epistola CCLXXVI* to Paschal on behalf of Thurstan: *PL*
CLXII,278-79; *Epistola CCXV*:   *PL* CLXII,219-20, is evidently
addressed to Thomas II, although in some MSS the address is
to Thurstan; the letter's location in the correspondence
suggests that it is to Thomas; D. Nicholl, *Thurstan Archbishop of York (1114-1140)* (York: Stonegate, 1964), p. 41,
says the letter is to Thurstan without mentioning the other
possibility.

⁴⁵Barlow, *English Church*, p. 43.

⁴⁶Southern, *Saint Anselm*, pp. 135-36.

47 S. N. Vaughn, "St. Anselm: Reluctant Archbishop?" *Albion* 6 (1974), 24-50; "St. Anselm of Canterbury: The Philosopher-Saint as Politician," *Journal of Medieval History* 1 (1975), 279-306; "Robert of Meulan and Raison d'Etat in the Anglo-Norman State, 1093-1118," *Albion* 10 (1978), 352-73; "St. Anselm and the English Investiture Controversy Reconsidered," *Journal of Medieval History* 6 (1980), 61-86; *The Abbey of Bec and the Anglo-Norman State*, pp. 23-41; I have not yet seen "Anselm in Exile, 1103-6: The Creation of Public Images and the Uses of Propaganda in the Anglo-Norman State," *Annales canossani*, forth-coming.

48 *Epistola 222*: Schmitt IV,124-25; J. L. 5908.

49 *Epistola 283*: Schmitt IV,200; J. L. 5930.

50 *Epistola 303*: Schmitt IV,224-24; J. L. 5955.

51 *Epistola 451*: Schmitt V,398-99.

52 *Epistola 472*: Schmitt V,420.

53 *Epistola CCLXXVI*: PL CLXII,278-79; Thurstan announced his appeal to Rome at a meeting at Salisbury, 20 March 1116. Messengers from York to Rome soon returned with a letter in which Paschal forbade Thurstan's profession to Ralph of Canterbury (*The History of the Church of York*, p. 44; a similar letter had been received earlier, *The History of the Church of York*, p. 40; perhaps this first letter was in part a response to Ivo's intervention.

54 One example was his intervention for Ralph of Rochester, Anselm's successor at Canterbury, *Epistola CCL*: PL CLXII, 255-57.

55 This rivalry was a factor in the dispute; Barlow, *English Church*, p. 41.

56 The famous Canterbury forgeries were apparently produced around 1120 in the time of Archbishop William of Corbeil, although some scholars have tried to date them around 1070; see the summary of scholarship given by Barlow, *English Church*, p. 41, n. 60; Barlow accepts the views of M. Gibson that the documents were begun soon after 1070. Thomas II, who was the nephew of Thomas I and had been raised at York, was contesting Canterbury's claims when Anselm died, 21 April, 1109. A settlement was reached in 1125, and because Thurstan still would not make profession to William,

the pope sought to satisfy Canterbury with a papal vicarate and legateship.

[57] *Epistola LX:*   *PL* CLXII,70-75; Leclercq, pp. 238-54; but cf. *Epistola L:* *PL* CLXII,61-62, perhaps more sympathetic to Lyon's primacy because Hugh was then exerting his claims against Archbishop Richer; Leclercq, pp. 200-07; on Gregorian use of primacy, see A. Fliche, "La primatie des Gaules depuis l'époque Carolingienne jusqu'à la fin de la querrelle des investitures (876-1121)," *Revue historique* 173 (1934), 329-42; for the primacy in general, H. Fuhrmann, "Studien zur Geschichte mittelalterlicher Patriarchate," *Zeitschrift der Savigny-Stiftung für Rechtsgeschichte. Kanonistische Abteilung* 39 (1953), 112-76; 40 (1954), 1-84; 41 (1955), 95-183.

[58] Above, note 28.

[59] M. Cheney, "Some Observations on a Papal Privilege of 1120 for the Archbishops of York," *Journal of Ecclesiastical History* 31 (1980), 429-39.

[60] Ibid., p. 435.

[61] K. Pellens, *Die Texte des Normannischen Anonymus* (Wiesbaden: Steiner, 1966), tract J2, pp. 7-19: "*De equalitate ecclesiarum provinciarum et de unitate ordinis episcopalis . . . ,*" deals with the defense of Rouen against Lyon.

[62] *The History of the Church of York,* p. 14: Credo equidem de investituris sane sensisse venerabilem Ivonem Carnotensem episcopum, quo nec alter in Gallis tempore suo melius in divinis eruditus et exercitatus, nec fide et doctrina magis catholicus extitit. Dicebat parum interesse qualiter investiture fierent, sive virga, sive anulo, sive manu, sive mica, seu quocunque modo, dum canonica eleccio et libera consecracio ecclesiis servarentur, nec quicquam Symoniace contagionis inesse, cum neque dans neque accipiens intelligat sacramentum vel rem sacramenti dare vel accipere, set villas, predia, reditus que de munificencia regum et principum ecclesiis collata sunt; this passage shows close dependence upon Ivo's *Epistola LX:* *PL* CLXII,73.

[63] J. C. Dickinson, *The Origins of the Austin Canons and their Introduction into England* (London: SPCK, 1950), pp. 98-103; and his "Saint Anselm and the First Regular Canons in England," *SB* I, pp. 541-46.

[64] Sprandel, *Ivo*, pp. 130-37; C. Dereine, "Les coutumiers de Saint-Quentin de Beauvais et de Springiersbach," *Revue d'histoire ecclésiastique* 43 (1948), 411-42; L. Fischer, "Ivo von Chartres, der Erneuerer der Vita canonica in Frankreich," in *Festgabe Alois Knöpfler zur Vollendung des 70. Lebensjahres*, ed. J. Geitl and G. Pfeilschifter (Freiburg: Herder, 1917), pp. 67-88; L. Milis, "Le coutumier de Saint-Quentin de Beauvais," *Sacris erudiri* 21 (1972-73), 435-81; *PL* CLXII,293-95 (foundation charter for St.-Jean-en-Vallée).

[65] Dickinson, *Austin Canons*, pp. 108-31.

I

Anselm's Monasticism

Anselm

. . . et ei quem divina pietas vobis prae-
esse voluit, humilem in omnibus oboedientiam
exhibeatis, memores illius praecepti, quo nos
idem apostolus admonet dicens: "Oboedite prae-
postis vestris et subicite vos eis."
(*Epistola 165*)

Augustine

Praeposito tamquam patri oboediatur, honore
servato, ne in illo offendatur deus . . .
(*Praeceptum* VII,1)

Über das Monastische in der Theologie
des Heiligen Anselm

Helmut Kohlenberger

Unbestritten ist, dass in der Theologie des Heiligen Anselm ein Höhepunkt in der Geschichte monastischer intellektueller Kultur erreicht wurde. Wir haben uns daran gewöhnt, nach dem Zusammenhang von Lebens- und Denkformen zu fragen. Aufs engste ist die Geschichte des Denkens mit den wechselnden Formen des Lebens verbunden. Gewiss gibt es eine Eigendynamik des Denkens, die für eine Weile von den Lebensformen absehen lässt. Nur so ist zu verstehen, dass Anselms Argumentum nicht nur Theologen und Kirchenhistoriker interessiert. Aber diese Eigendynamik ist selbst keineswegs zu lösen von den Gemeinsamkeiten unserer westlichen rationalen Kultur. Es gibt einen Duktus zur Universalisierung, zur Legitamation in argumentativen Verfahren, der heute allerdings nicht selten als "In-der-Welt-Sein," als Gefangenschaft im System erfahren wird. Bei Anselm können wir die Eingangsbedingungen dieses Universalisierungsduktus kennenlernen. Sie sind auch dann noch wirksam, wenn ihre Umstände vergessen oder verdrägt worden sind.

Zu den Eingangsbedingungen der westlichen Rationalität gehört das Mönchtum insbesondere in seiner benediktinischen Gestalt. Anselm als Theologe des Mönchtums gehört somit entscheidend in die Geschichte unserer rationalen Kultur. Es geht also um den Reflex des Mönchtums in Anselms Theologie und dessen Konsequenzen für das westliche Denken. In diesem Beitrag müssen wir uns auf drei Gesichtspunkte beschränken:

(1) Was verstehen wir unter Mönchtum im Blick auf Anselm?

(2) Wie reflektiert sich das Mönchtum in Anselms Theologie?

(3) Welches sind die Konsequenzen und Grenzen dieses Denkens in der Geschichte des Denkens?

Der letzte Gesichtspunkt kann nur exemplarisch mit Hinweisen auf Descartes' *Meditationen* und den *Tractatus* von Wittgenstein angedeutet werden.

1. Über das Mönchtum im Blick auf Anselm

Die benediktinischen Mönchsgemeinschaften können als kulturelle Kontinuität zwischen dem abreissenden römischen Reich und der entstehenden westlichen Christenheit angesehen werden. Im Zusammenbruch des römischen Familienprinzips entsteht eine autoritär geführt Lebensform von Menschen des gleichen Geschlechts, in deren Zentrum die Liturgie und die geistliche Lesung steht. Aus der evangelischen Predigt vom Ende der Welt entsteht eine Gegenwelt, in der nicht die Herkunft, die Genealogie, sondern die Zukunft, das ausstehende Reich Gottes bestimmt. In dieser Gegenwelt wird Augustins Vision der *civitas dei* ernst genommen. Christus allein soll herrschen, dessen Wort in der Schrift darum im Mittelpunkt steht. Im Kloster wurde die eschatologische Dimension des Evangeliums auf Dauer gestellt. Das Gericht am Ende aller Tage war der entscheidende Gesichtspunkt der Lebensführung. Vom Gericht ging ein alle erfassender Universalisierungsduktus aus. So unterschiedlich die Position eines jeden auf Erden sein mochte, so war doch jeder angesichts der Verantwortung vor dem Gericht jedem anderen gleich.

Das hatte viele Konsequenzen. Eine Konsequenz war, dass angesichts des sicheren Endes aller Zeit Zeit überhaupt als endlich erfahren wurde und darum der Zeitablauf organisiert werden musste. Eine erste Form dieser Organisation der Zeit war das Stundengebet. Die gleiche Stellung aller vor dem letzten Gericht war das Zentrum der kulturellen Identifikation. Das "Buch des Lebens," das im letzten Gericht zur Grundlage der Verhandlung dient, verband Lebende und Tote.[1] Im liturgischen Gedenken, in der Lesung aus dem "Buch des Lebens," im Kloster wurde somit die Kontinuitätsgarantie schlechthin gesehen. Den Klöstern kamen darum Stiftungen zugute und sie wurden zu Zentren geistlicher Bruderschaften, die auch Nichtklosterangehörige umfassten. Inmitten einer anarchischen politischen Szenerie wurden vom kultischen Totengedenken her Inseln rechtlicher Ordnung freigelegt. Im Chaos der Natur wurde gerodet. Die Unabhängigkeit der Klöster und ihrer Rechtsordnung war nicht ein für alle Mal verbürgt. Die Gegenwelt des Klosters war der Welt der Stammeshäuptlinge und des Adels strikt entgegengesetzt. Wollte sie bestehen, so musste sie straff organisiert sein. Der Prior, Abt und Erzbischof Anselm stand mitten in diesem Gegensatz und musste darum auf *disciplina* dringen.

Anselm stellt darum den Gedanken einer geradezu militärischen Disziplinierung des Mönches in den Mittelpunk der wenigen Anspielungen auf Mönchtum, die sich bei ihm explizit finden. Er apostrophiert den Heiligen Benedikt als Führer (*dux*), der Mönch ist dessen Gefolgsmann (*miles*).[2] Bei

Eadmer findet sich ein schönes Zeugnis. In seiner Ansprache an die Mönche in Canterbury spricht er mit Verweis auf 2 Tm 2:4 und den Prolog der Benediktsregel von den *Deo milita-turi*. In Entsprechung zum Dienst bei Hofe und seinen Glie-derungen gibt es einen Gottes Dienst, den die Engel im Him-mel, auf Erden die Söldner und die ganz Gott geweihten Mönche versehen.

> Habet quoquo nonnullos qui die noctuque suae voluntati inhaerentes ad regnum caelorum quod in patris sui Adae culpa perdiderunt, haereditario jure pervenire contendunt. Sed nobis ad beatorum spirituum societatem magis est suspirandum, quam de eorum procinctu quo Deo perenniter astant in praesenti disputan-dum. Ad solidarios Dei milites verba ver-tamus.[3]

Darum steht auch der Gehorsam im Zentrum von Anselms Auffas-sung des Mönchtums. Wiederholt schärft er in Briefen diesen Gehorsam ein.

> Regula docet ut monachus omni oboedientia se subdat maiori et ut ad exemplum domini oboedientiam servemus "usque ad mortem."[4]

Dem Gehorsam ist der Eigenwille entgegengesetzt:

> Cum enim professus sum monachum, abnegavi meipsum mihi, ut deinceps meus non essem, id est non viverem secundum propriam volunta-tem, sed secundum oboedientiam.[5]

Der Ungehorsam vertrieb den Menschen aus dem Paradies, eine Rückkehr gibt es nur im Gehorsam.[6] Der Gehorsam ist aber nicht Kadavergehorsam.

> Non enim debet monachus exspectare oris imperium, si novit voluntatem abbatis sui aut consilium.[7]

Das Kloster ist Ort des Gehorsams, insofern es auch Ort geistlicher Schulung ist. Der Heilige Benedikt ist ebenso *magister* wie *dux*.[8]

> O tu, mi bone dux, o suavis magister, o dul-cis pater benedicte BENEDICTE, oro, obsecro per misericordiam quam erga alios habuisti,

et per illam quam erga te deus habuit, com-
patere miseriae meae, qui congratulor feli-
citati tuae.[9]

2. Das Mönchtum in Anselms Theologie.

In der schulmässigen Disziplinierung des Klosters wird
die *rectitudo* zur Lebensform. Mit diesem Grundwort Anselmischen Denkens ist die allen Trennungen vorausliegende Einheit von Gottes Ordnung, Einstellung und Einsicht des Menschen bezeichnet. Sie ist die Einheit von Gottes Ordnung
und Freiheit. Christus ist die Wirklichkeit dieser Einheit.
Anselms Lehre von der Erlösung -- *sola ratione* -- ist eine
Christologie im Ausgang von der *rectitudo* als dem monastischen Lebensprinzip. Nur durch Gehorsam konnte das Leben,
das durch Ungehorsam verwirkt worden war, zurückkommen.[10]
Gehorsam schuldet der Mensch Gott jedenfalls:

In oboedientia vero quid das deo quod non
debes, cui iubenti totum quod es et quod
habes et quod potes debes?[11]

Dieser Gehorsam ist nicht erzwungen, er wird freiwillig
geleistet.

Iam tunc est simplex vera oboedientia, cum
rationalis natura non necessitate, sed
sponte servat voluntatem a deo acceptam.[12]

Der geschuldete Gehorsam aus freien Stücken ist die Voraussetzung der Anselmischen Erlösungslehre. Die Erlösung fordert ja, dass der Mensch mehr als den Gehorsam leistet, den
er ohnedies Gott schuldet. Christus tritt für die Bedingtheit des Menschen ein, für das Unentwirrbare seiner Situation. Er bringt dem Menschen die *rectitudo* zurück.
    Nur im ausgegrenzten Bereich des Klosters wird die mit
der rectitudo gesetzte Eindeutigkeit der Lebensform zum Vor-
Schein einer künftigen allumfassenden Wirklichkeit. In der
Welt ist die *rectitudo* beständig gefährdet.

O rationalis natura, an est hoc rationabile
consilium ut, quia ubique est periculum, ibi
eligas manere, ubi maius est periculum?[13]

In der Gegenwelt des Klosters ist schon jetzt das Paradies
auf Erden. In einem Brief an einen Bischof, der in Bec ein-
trat, heisst es:

> In viam paradisi vos direxit divina clemen-
> tia, immo in quendam paradisum huius vitae
> vos introduxit, cum vos in claustralem con-
> versationem monachi propositi introduxit.[14]

Trotz der Ambivalenz der Welt, in der sich schon einem
Augustinus so vieles verdüsterte, gibt es den Weg der
rationalen Natur in die Vollendung, der oft -- so scheint es
-- die Bedingtheiten des Erdenlebens vergessen lässt.

Das zeigt sich nicht zuletzt auch im entscheidenden
Lebenselement des monastischen Lebens, in der Schriftlesung.
In der Lesung wird die Unabgeschlossenheit der Welt stets
neu bewusst. Nicht um das sich absichernde Zitat, einen
Beweis, der auf *auctoritas* gestützt ist, sondern um Einsicht
geht es. In *De concordia* heisst es:

> . . . ita corda humana sine doctrina, sine
> studio sponte quasi germinant cogitationes
> et voluntates nihil utiles saluti aut etiam
> noxias, illas vero, sine quibus ad salutem
> animae non proficimus, nequaquam sine sui
> generis semine et laboriosa cultura conci-
> piunt aut germinant. Unde illos homines,
> quibus talis cultura impenditur, "agricultu-
> ram dei" vocat apostolus. Et autem semen
> huius culturae verbum dei, immo non verbum,
> sed sensus qui percipitur per verbum. Vox
> namque sine sensu nihil constituit in corde.
> Nec solum sensus verbi, sed omnis sensus vel
> intellectus rectitudinis, quem mens humana
> sive per auditum, sive per lectionem, sive
> per rationem, sive quolibet alio modo conci-
> pit, semen est recte volendi. Nullus namque
> velle potest, quod prius corde non conci-
> pit.[15]

Nicht um Reproduktion von Wortwörtlichkeit geht es, sondern
um das lebendige Wort, das im Schriftwort empfangen wird.

Anselms Auffassung vom Wort zeigt einen deutlichen
Hiatus zur Tradition, der es um die Wörtlichkeit selbst
ging. Die Transformation der Schriftlesung in Richtung auf
Empfängnis des Sinnes der Schrift kann nicht eindrucksvoller
gezeigt werden als mit den Begleitumständen der Abfassung
des *Proslogion*. Die Tafeln, auf die Anselm sein Argument
niederschrieb, liessen sich trotz sorgsamer Verwahrung nicht
finden. Nach wiederholter Niederschrift fanden sich die
Tafeln zerbrochen am Boden.[16] Die sich aus der Bindung ans
geschriebene Wort befreiende Haltung widersetzte sich der

Schriftlichkeit.   So verwundert es nicht, dass Anselm
zunächst glaubte, einer Versuchung zu erliegen, zumal die
Aufmerksamkeit, die das Argument für sich beanspruchte, ihn
von der geistlichen Lesung abzuhalten schien.   Erst die
Erleuchtung inter *nocturnas vigilias* überzeugte Anselm von
der geistlichen Bedeutung seiner Konzeption.[17]   In dieser
Erleuchtung während der Lesung ist die Voraussetzung von
Anselms Denken zu sehen.   Das Argument ist die rationale
Fassung dieser Erleuchtung.   In diesem Sinne ruht es in sich
selbst, entsprechen Form und Vollzug des Denkens einander.
So ist das Argument eine Aktualisierung des in jedem Wort --
wenn auch noch so abgeschwächt -- sich durchhaltenden Wortes
der Schöpfung.

Diese Denkform wird schon im Monologion deutlich.
Anselm nennt es ein *exemplum meditandi*.   Es ist geschrieben
*sub persona secum sola cogitatione disputantis et investi-
gantis ea, quae prius non animadvertisset.*[18]   Nichts wird im
Rückgriff aufs Schriftwort gesagt, obschon nichts gesagt
wird, was nicht mit der Tradition der Kirche zusammen-
hängt.[19]   Es wird gewagt, im Rahmen der Schriftlesung das
Wort der Schrift zu denken.   Anselm denkt es im Akt der
Schöpfung.   Grammatik, Logik und Schöpfung fordern sich
gegenseitig.   In jeder Aussage, die etwas gut oder gerecht
nennt, hält sich durch, was es ermöglicht, dieses gut bzw.
gerecht zu nennen.   Im 1. Kapitel heisst es:

> Ergo cum certum sit quod omnia bona, si ad
> invicem conferantur, aut aequaliter aut
> inaequaliter sint bona, necesse est, ut
> omnia sint per aliquid bona, quod intelligi-
> tur idem in diversis bonis, licet aliquando
> videantur bona dici alia per aliud.[20]

Sprechen und Schöpfungsakt sind einunddasselbe.   Beide
setzen nur sich selbst voraus.   Nur das ist zu zeigen:
dass diese Voraussetzungslosigkeit der Durchbruch der Wirklichkeit ist.   Es gibt keine Vermittlung mit der uns bekannten Welt der Dinge.   Alle Vergleiche reichen nicht hin.   Der
Vergleich mit dem Handwerker bzw. Künstler hinkt, denn er
setzt voraus, dass es neben dem Schöpfer noch Materie gibt,
die zu etwas gestaltet wird.   Das Sprechen bzw. Schaffen
sieht von jeder Materie ab und transformiert das Urbild.
Dem Bild muss Sprache gegeben werden.   Es wird zurück-
gelassen.   Anselm spricht von *exemplum, forma, similitudo,
regula.*[21]   Das sind Worte für die Stelle des Bildes im
Schöpfungswort.   Damit ist ein Doppeltes gesagt:

(1) Die Unabhängigkeit des Schöpfungswortes wird ausgesprochen.

(2) Es wird zugleich festgestellt, dass das Sprechen nicht ins Leere geht.

Zusammenfassend heisst es bei Anselm:

> Mentis autem sive rationis locutionem hic intelligo, non cum voces rerum significativae cogitantur, sed cum res ipsae vel futurae vel iam existentes acie cogitationis in mente conspiciuntur.[22]

Schöpfung, Sprechen ist nicht Verursachen. Anselm weist darum alle ihm geläufigen Vorstellungen von Verursachung zur Erläuterung des Schöfungsaktes im Wort zurück. Solche Vorstellungen sind Verursachung *per aliquid efficiens aut ex aliqua materia* oder andere Ursachen.[23] Nichts macht den Schöpfungsakt so deutlich wie das Leuchten des Lichts.

> Quemadmodum enim sese habent ad invicem lux et lucere et lucens, sic sunt ad se invicem essentia et esse et ens, hoc est existens sive subsistens.[24]

Sprechen und Schau sind einunddasselbe. In der Erleuchtung, im Blitz der Erkenntnis ist ganz gegenwärtig, was ist. Anselm spricht vom *maxime proprium et principale rei verbum*. Dieses Wort ist naturgegeben, es liegt aller Trennung voraus. Vergleichbar ist es der Ursprünglichkeit eines Vokals. Anselm bleibt bei dieser Feststellung nicht stehen. Er deutet das aller Trennung vorausliegende Wort im Sinne technisch-philosophischer Bestimmungen z.B. *animal rationale mortale*.[25] Damit hat er den Grund für Terminologisierung und Eigendynamik des philosophischen Diskurses akzeptiert. Die Bedingungen der Terminologisierung werden nicht mitbedacht. Ein Universum argumentativer Verfahren, das von allen einschränkenden Bedingungen der Sinne frei und doch in sich geschlossen ist, entsteht. Denn die höchste Wesenheit trägt, überragt, umschliesst und durchdringt alles.[26] Selbstredend weist Anselm daraufhin, dass das göttliche Sprechen und das aus der Erleuchtung im Wort entstehende Sprechen des Menschen einander zwar ähnlich, in grösserem Masse aber unähnlich ist. Doch bleibt der Grad der Unähnlichkeit unbestimmt. Sie ermöglicht es, dass sowohl von einer graduellen Differenzierung überhaupt gesprochen wird (cf. *maius* im Argumentum) als auch die absolute

Negation endlicher Erkenntnisbedingungen gedacht werden
kann. Die Universalität des Wortes hat einen absoluten
ausschliessenden Charakter. Das Heil ist angeboten, aber
keineswegs selbstverständlich.

Im *Proslogion* finden wir den reifsten Ausdruck des
Erkennens aus der Erleuchtung. Bekannt sind die Worte, mit
denen zur Kontemplation aufgefordert wird:

> Eia nunc, homuncio, fuge paululum occupa-
> tiones tuas, absconde te modicum a tumul-
> tuosis cogitationibus tuis . . .

Gott wohnt in "unzugänglichem Licht."

> Et ubi est lux inaccessiblis? Aut quomodo
> accedam ad lucem inaccessibliem? Aut quis
> me ducet et inducet in illam, ut videam te
> in illa?

Wir sind im Exil, im Konflikt widerstreitender Gedanken,
fern der beseligenden Schau.[27] Die Aporie zwischen der Welt
der Dinge, die sich im Vollkommenheitsgrad unterscheiden,
und dem allumfassenden Schöpfungswort wird zum *unum argumen-*
tum. Die Schriftlesung führt zum Problem, Anselm nimmt das
"*non est Deus*" des *insipiens* auf.[28] Aber das Denken allein
spricht die Aporie in der Kategorie der Grösse und im absoluten Wider-Spruch zur Welt des Exils aus. Das Argument ist
der Ausdruck vollkommenster Freiheit in einer der erfahr-
baren Welt entgegengesetzten Gegen-Welt. Das Denken kann
nicht anders als sich an sich selbst halten, es lässt alle
Brücken hinter sich. Die Bilder haben keine Bedeutung, es
sei denn, sie sind Modelle, die zur Realisierung drängen.
Mit dem Wegfall der Welt der Bilder bleibt nur die Kategorie
der Grösse. Anselm verliert sich nicht in dieser Kategorie
wie der *insipiens*. Für Anselm ist die Grösse immer gebunden
an den absoluten Wider-Spruch zur Welt der Dinge.

> Ergo, Domine, non solum es quo maius cogi-
> tari nequit, sed es quiddam maius quam cogi-
> tari possit.[29]

So sehr Gottes Sprechen alles umschliesst, so wenig reicht
das Denken hin, ihn und die Welt zu umschliessen. Es bleibt
das Bewusstsein des offenen Horizontes. Aus dem Argument,
das mit der Kategorie der Grösse im Widerspruch zur Welt der
Bilder das Sprechen in der Erleuchtung auf die Ebene des
technisch-philosophischen Diskurses bringt, lässt sich
nicht eine geschlossene Welt als Welt schlechthin kon-

struieren. Das Kloster, die selige Insel des Gaunilo, die Utopie der Neuzeit sind nicht die Welt als solche. Es bleibt die Spannung zum Exil, so sehr auch Anselm das Kloster als Vorwegnahme des Künftigen ansehen mag. Gaunilo erinnert zurecht an die Bedingtheit der seligen Insel -- er rennt offene Türen ein.[30] So ist das *Proslogion*-Argument Ausdruck der Spannung zwischen Schöpfungswort und Exil, gebunden an die Bedingungen des Wortes in der Erleuchtung der Schriftlesung.

Das Argument formuliert die Spannung des Klosters zur Welt, der zukünftigen Gottesschau zur Welt der Bilder und der Sinne. Nichts ist weniger selbstverständlich als die Geltung argumentativer Verfahren, rationaler Argumentation. Es bedurfte der Disziplinierung im Sinne der *militia Christi*, der Freiheit von allen genealogischen Bedingtheiten, um die Eigenständigkeit des Denkens zu formulieren. Alles Bildhafte, zuletzt noch alles Zeichenhafte, der Buchstabe der Schrift wird zurückgedrängt, um dem *sensus rectitudinis* Platz zu schaffen. Jedes Sprechen steht im Gehorsam gegenüber dem Wort der Schrift, im Wider-Spruch zur Welt der Bilder. Die Teilnahme am Schöpfungswort weist nicht zurück auf einen Anfang, sondern voraus auf das himmlische Jerusalem, das im Kloster schon konkrete Form angenommen hat. Anselms Denken ist die Aktualisierung dieser Teilnahme am Schöpfungswort im Gehorsam gegenüber der disponierten *rectitudo*, die Aktualisierung der Einheit von Grammatik und Eschatologie.[31]

Mit dem Gehorsam gegenüber der *rectitudo*, in dem sich Christi und unser aller Freiheit erfüllt, steht Anselm im Widerspruch zur Welt der Bilder, überschreitet er die Reihe der endlichen Wesen und transformiert so die Negation des *insipiens* zur Freisetzung der Grösse ohne Angabe einer bestimmten Masseinheit. Anselms Denken ist offen, es ist an kein gegebenes Mass gebunden. Es ist aber an Messung, an das Denken selbst gebunden. Erst in der kartesianischen Version des *Argumentums* wird der Charakter der Autonomie, der Selbsterzeugung dieses Denkens klar. Es setzt die Welt der Grösse frei. Betrachten wir in der Folge einige Konsequenzen der sich im Zeichen der Mathematisierung des Denkens etablierenden Gegenwelt.

3. Die Gegenwelt der "Neuzeit": Voraussetzungen und Grenzen.

Descartes versuchte, aus der Spannung zwischen Kloster und Welt, Gottesschau und Sinnlichkeit herauszukommen und setzte auf Eindeutigkeit. Diese Eindeutigkeit sollte sich

im Durchgang durch den alles in Zweifel setzenden Wider-
spruch zur Welt der Bilder und damit der Sinne einstellen.
Was sich dem Widerspruch gegenüber hielt, das war das
schlechthinige Fundament der Wahrheit.

Descartes ist darüber betroffen, dass wir in Bildern
gefangen sind. Es sind die Bilder unserer Träume. Wir
können nicht einmal sicher zwischen Traum und Wachen unterscheiden.[32] Zuerst müssen wir sogar einsehen lernen, dass
es Träume sind, denen wir ausgesetzt sind;

> iam autem certo scio me esse, simulque fieri
> posse ut omnes istae imagines, et generali-
> ter quaecumque ad corporis naturam referun-
> tur, nihil sint praeter insomnia.[33]

Erst am Ende formuliert Descartes ein Unterscheidungskrite-
rium zwischen Traum und Wachen -- die Kontinuität einer Ein-
zelwahrnehmung mit dem gesamten Lebenszusammenhang.[34] An
die Stelle der Wahrnehmung ist ein abstraktes Konzept -- die
Kontinuität einer Totalität getreten.

Der Preis ist die Ausschaltung des Körpers. Es ist
zweifelhaft, ob der Körper überhaupt begriffen werden kann.
Viel deutlicher als die Vorstellung vom Körper ist der
Geist.[35] Das Vorstellen des Körpers scheint über die Grenzen des Wahrscheinlichen nicht hinauszukommen. Wenn man
aber den Körper sich nicht einbildet, sondern denkt, wird
alles ganz klar. Jetzt ist die Mathematik am Zug.[36] Darum
ist es am besten, den Körper als Uhr aufzufassen. Das Stundengebet, die Organisation der Zeit wird zum Erkenntnisprin-
zip schlechthin und bestimmt auch noch das Materiale der
Erkenntnis, den Körper. Das Universum des Geistes, das sich
der Ausschaltung der Wahrnehmung verdankt, ist die Organisation, das Schema der Zeit.

Nur der Wille hält sich nicht an diese Organisation der
Erkenntnis. Auch in Belangen, in denen ich über keine
Erkenntnis verfüge, muss ich wollen.[37] Es ist, als ob sich
das Erkennen von der alles umfassenden *rectitudo* emanzipiert
habe. Nur in der Voraussetzung der Wahrhaftigkeit Gottes
ist die Anselmische Einheit der Ordnung Gottes noch da. Und
diese Voraussetzung ist ein Rekurs auf den nicht zu dome-
stizierenden Willen, der in der Folgezeit das *movens* des
Philosophierens abgibt -- in der Unabhängigkeit der prakti-
schen Vernunft, schliesslich im "Willen zur Macht." Vom
Willen kann ich schlechterdings nicht absehen, er ist ja
noch das *movens* des Zweifelns. So kann und soll man Gott
nicht den freien Willen vorwerfen, sagt Descartes.[38] Er ist
allerdings eine Versuchung. Diese Versuchung ist nicht nur
ein biographisches Korollar, sondern gehört in den Gang der

Argumentation selbst. In der Gestalt des *genius malignus* wird die Intensität dieser Versuchung erfahren. Der Wille, dieser Bastard des Glaubens, ist der einzige Widerstand gegen das geschlossene Universum der Mathematik. Im Widerspruch zur Welt des Körpers stellt sich das mathematische Universum ein. Descartes' Vorbild ist Archimedes, der nichts als einen festen Punkt verlangte, um die Welt bewegen zu können.[39] Denn auch im radikalsten Zweifel kann nicht bestritten werden:

> dass ich nichts bin, solange ich mir bewusst
> bin, etwas zu wissen, oder dass es zu irgend-
> einer Zeit wahr wird, dass ich nie existiert
> habe, wo es doch jetzt wahr ist, dass ich
> existiere oder etwa, dass 2 + 3 mehr oder
> weniger seien als 5 und dergleichen, worin
> ich nämlich einen offenen Widerspruch
> erkenne.[40]

Das zweifelsfreie Denken konstitiert sich in den Konzepten Substanz, Dauer und Zahl.[41] Damit ist das konstituierte Universum als Bereich der organisierten Zeit, der Kausalität festgelegt.

> Iam vero lumine naturali manifestum est tan-
> tumdem ad minimum esse debere in causa effi-
> ciente et totali, quantum in eiusdem causae
> effectu, nam quaeso undenam posset assumere
> realitatem suam effectus, nisi a causa?[42]

Jede Erkenntnis geht von der Grösse und von grundlegenden Bestimmungen wie Figur, Zahl und Bewegung aus.[43] Über den Status mathematischer Bestimmungen ist sich Descartes natürlich im Klaren -- sie haben eine unveränderliche und vom aktuellen Denken unabhängige Natur.[44] Sie wird mit den traditionellen Bestimmungen -- Idee, Archetypus, aber auch Akt-Potenz -- Unterscheidung usw. -- benannt. So wird die Kontinuität der Weltauffassung demonstriert. Das gilt zeitlich: Kein Bruch mit der Tradition ist beabsichtigt, Descartes widmet die *Meditationes* der Theologischen Fakultät der Universität Paris. Das gilt der Sache nach: Im Konzept der Kausalität wird die Schöpfungslehre domestiziert. Descartes profitiert von der Unterbestimmtheit des Unendlichen.[45] Das Unendliche ist nicht einfach Negation im Sinne der Polarität von Licht und Dunkel, Berg und Tal, sondern enthält mehr Sachgehalt (*plus realitatis*), so dass "der Begriff des Unendlichen dem des Endlichen, d.i. der Gottes dem meiner selbst gewissermassen vorhergeht."[46] Bezeichnen-

derweise erläutert Descartes das *plus realitatis* mit dem
Akt-Potenz-Schema:

> Deum autem ita judicio esse actu infinitum,
> ut nihil eius perfectioni addi potest. Ac
> denique percipio esse objectivum ideae non a
> solo esse potentiali, quod proprie loquendo
> nihil est, sed tantummodo ab actuali, sive
> formali posse produci.[47]

Wie so oft ist es die Funktion eines traditionellen Vokabu-
lars, die Verschiebung von Problemlagen zu tabuisieren.

Im kartesianischen Universum der Mathematik lebt die
monastische Lebensform in transformierter Weise fort. Die
Ausschaltung des Körpers im Status des aus allen genealogischen Bindungen emanzipierten disziplinierten Mönches in
einem antizipierten Paradies hat zu einer Welt geführt, in
der die organisierte Zeit rundum das Geschehen bestimmt und
in der allenfalls der Wille zur Bedrohung werden kann. Die
Welt der Bilder weicht dem Gesetz der Kausalität, in dem der
Schöpfungsakt aktualisiert gedacht wird. Bilder, Körper und
Macht werden allenfalls im Rahmen einer Sekundärerfahrung
zugänglich. In dieser geschlossenen Welt fühlen wir uns
zunehmend gefangen. Die Selbstverständlichkeit dieser Welt
hat bedeutend abgenommen. Auswege zeigen sich nicht.
Wittgenstein hat auf diese Welt gewissermassen zurück-
geschaut und Grenzerfahrungen zum Ausdruck gebracht. Wie
ein später Reflex der Schöpfungslehre mutet Satz 5.123 des
Tractatus an:

> Wenn ein Gott eine Welt erschafft, worin
> gewisse Sätze wahr sind, so schafft er damit
> auch schon eine Welt, in welcher alle ihre
> Folgesätze stimmen. Und ähnlich könnte er
> keine Welt schaffen, worin der Satz "p" wahr
> ist, ohne seine sämtlichen Gegenstände zu
> schaffen.

Die Gegenständlichkeit der Welt wird nicht einfach unter-
schlagen, verschwindet nicht in den Konstruktionsprinzipien
von Grammatik und Logik. Die Gegenstände erhalten ihre
Würde zurück. Es heisst an anderer Stelle:[48] "Der Gegenstand ist einfach." Grundsätzlich ist jeder Gegenstand mit
anderen in Verbindung.[49] Es verbietet sich die Reduktion
auf ein Unteilbares, worin Descartes das den Geist (als
Reduktionsprinzip) Auszeichnende sah. Die Unendlichkeit
begehrt auf gegen alle Versuche der Domestikation. Darum
gibt es kein philosophisches System, dem eine ausgezeichnete

Zahl zugrundeliegt (z.B. *Monismus, Dualismus*).[50] Logik ist
nicht mehr eine Art Metatheorie, sondern der Aufweis der
sich in Bildern, Modellen der Welt zei-genden Formen der
Abbildung.[51] Aufgewiesen wird eine "innere Ähnlichkeit,"
ein Gesetz der Projektion, eine Übersetzungsregel.[52]
Die Bilder und Körper kehren zurück. Die Negation verliert
ihren himmelstürmenden *Gestus* als absolute Negation endlicher Erkenntnisbedingungen, als *Movens* des erkenntnislei-
tenden Zweifels. Sie "bezieht sich schon auf den logischen
Ort, den der verneinte Satz bestimmt."[53] "Nimmt man die
Sätze der Logik für sich und fragt, was sie sagen -- so
sieht man, sie sagen dasselbe. Nämlich Nichts."[54] Mit der
Einsicht in den regulativen Charakter der Logik wird auch
dem Kausalitätsprinzip sein für neuzeitliches Denken konstitutiver Charakter genommen. Es ist nicht ein Gesetz, sondern die Form eines Gesetzes.[55] Wittgenstein versucht angesichts der Einseitigkeit des monastisch-mathematischen Universums der Neuzeit einen Balance-akt. Im Zuge logischer
Erörterungen kehrt alles Verdrängte wieder, fordert sein
Recht ein. Nicht alles was aufbricht ist schon zur Sprache
gereift. "Das Gefühl der Welt als begrenztes Ganzes ist das
mystische."[56] An anderer Stelle heisst es vom Mystischen,
dass es unaussprechlich sei, dass es sich zeige.[57] Logik
und Mystik ist eines gemeinsam; beide sind verwiesen auf
etwas, das sich zeigt.

In Wittgensteins Denken bahnt sich die Wirklichkeit
gegen die Konstruktion einen Weg. Die Möglichkeit der Balance des geschlossenen Universums der Mathematik mit der
Offenheit der Wirklichkeit wird geahnt. Es wird akzeptiert,
dass sich etwas zeigt, das ich nicht ableiten kann. Anselms
Denkanstoss aus der Erleuchtung kehrt nach dem Gang durch
das Gefängnis des geschlossenen Universums wieder. Gewiss
hat Anselms Denken das monastisch-mathematische Universum
entscheidend disponiert, insofern der terminologisierte Dis-
kurs direkt aus dem erleuchteten Denken zu folgen schien.
Noch Descartes konnte sich aufs *lumen naturale* berufen.
Aber nie hat das Konstitutionsgesetz des mathematischen Universums das Denken aus der Erleuchtung bei Anselm aufge-
sogen. Anselms Denken ist nicht an eine Masseinheit gebunden. Gott ist immer noch grösser als er je gedacht werden
kann, so sehr er auch gedacht werden kann. Inmitten des
monastisch-mathematischen Universums bricht nun unvermittelt
das Mystische auf. In einer Zeit, in der das Mystische die
rationale Universalisierung in den verschiedensten Formen
der Regression (z.B. Bedeutung der Träume, Riten, Körper-
therapien, Feminismus, Ökologie) zu unterlaufen scheint, ist
es heilsam, sich eines Denkens zu erinnern, das im Mystischen zugleich den Weg zur Logik fand.

Anmerkungen

[1] Cf. mein Art. "Buch des Lebens," in *Historisches Wörterbuch der Philosophie* (Basel-Stuttgart: B. Schwabe, 1971), I, 956f.

[2] *Oratio 15*: Schmitt III,61-64.

[3] *Vita Anselmi*, p. 95 (ch. II,21).

[4] *Epistola 123* 14-16: Schmitt III,264.

[5] *Epistola 156* 91-93: Schmitt IV,20.

[6] *Epistola 231* 30-32: Schmitt IV,137.

[7] *Epistola 137* 53f.: Schmitt III,283.

[8] *Oratio 15*,51-54: Schmitt III,63.

[9] Ibid.

[10] *Cur Deus homo* I,3: Schmitt II,51,5-7.

[11] Ibid. I,20: Schmitt II,87,22-24.

[12] Ibid. I,10: Schmitt II,65,17-19.

[13] *Epistola 121* 26-28: Schmitt III,261.

[14] *Epistola 418* 13-15: Schmitt IV,364.

[15] *De concordia* III,6: Schmitt II,270,18-28.

[16] *Vita Anselmi*, p. 30f. (ch. I,19).

[17] Ibid.

[18] *Monologion*, Prologus: Schmitt I,8,18f.

[19] Ibid.: Schmitt I,8,8f.

[20] Ibid.: Schmitt I,14,15-18.

[21] Ibid. IX: Schmitt I,24,13f.

[22] Ibid. X: Schmitt I,7ff.

[23] Ibid. VI: Schmitt I,18-20.

[24] Ibid.: Schmitt I,20,15f.

[25] Ibid. X: Schmitt I,7ff.

[26] Ibid. XIV: Schmitt I,27,23f.

[27] *Proslogion* I: Schmitt I,97,4f.; 98,4-6; cf. *Vita Anselmi*, p. 30f.

[28] *Proslogion* II: Schmitt I,101,6f.

[29] Ibid. XV: Schmitt I,112,14f. Über den Gesichtspunkt der Grösse im Argument, cf. Coloman Viola, "La dialectique de la grandeur: Une interprétation du *Proslogion*," *Recherches de Théologie ancienne et médiévale* 37 (1970), 23-55. J. Vuillemin hat die Grenzen betont, die das Konzept der Grösse für Anselms Gottesbegriff mit sich bringt. Er macht aus dem Gottesbegriff einen Komplementärbegriff zur Erfahrung schlechthin (cf. *Le Dieu d'Anselme et les apparences de la raison* [Paris: Aubier, Editions Montaigne, 1971], 80ff.). Dazu gehört nach Vuillemin auch die Formulierung des *Proslogion* XV (cf. 20f.). Genau hier setzt die Zäsur ein zwischen der Akzeptanz einer mystischen Eigendynamik und der konsequent wissenschafts-immanenten Auffassung, für die Vuillemin eintritt.

[30] Im Zusammenhang der argumentativen Defizienz der Formulierung *maius omnibus* erörtert Anselm den Einwand Gaunilos, der das Beispiel der glückseligen Insel einführt, cf. Schmitt I,135f.

[31] Jean Leclercq sah in Grammatik und Eschatologie die entscheidenden Stichworte monastischer Bildung; cf. *Wissenschaft und Gottverlangen: Zur Mönchstheologie des Mittelalters* (Düsseldorf: Patmos, 1963), bes. 9ff.

[32] Descartes, *Meditationes de prima philosophia* I,6.

[33] Ibid. II,7.

[34] Ibid. VI,24.

[35] Ibid. IV,1.

[36] Ibid. VI,10.

[37] Ibid. IV,9.

[38] Ibid. IV,14.

[39] Ibid. II,1.

[40] Ibid. III,4; deutsche Fassung in der A. Buchenau folgenden Ausgabe von L. Gäbe, (Hamburg: F. Meiner Verlag, 1959), pp. 63-65.

[41] Ibid. III,21.

[42] Ibid. III,14.

[43] Ibid. V,3ff.

[44] Ibid. V,5.

[45] Diese Unterbestimmtheit lässt den Spiegelungscharakter zu -- Gott ist ein ins Unendliche gehender Spiegel des Ichs, aber auch die zur Welterhaltung aktualisierte Schöpfunglehre im Sinne einer ontologischen Priorität Gottes; cf. *Meditationes* III,31f.

[46] Ibid. III,24 (nach der oben genannten Übersetzung, p. 83).

[47] Ibid. III,27.

[48] L. Wittgenstein, *Tractatus logico-philosophicus* 2.02.

[49] Ibid. 2.0121.

[50] Ibid. 4.128.

[51] Ibid. 2.17, 4.12, 4.121.

[52] Ibid. 4.0141.

[53] Ibid. 4.0641; cf. auch 4.0621, 5.5151.

[54] Ibid. 5.43; cf. auch 5.142.

[55] Ibid. 6.32.

[56] Ibid. 6.45.

The Monastic Sources of Anselm's Political Beliefs: St. Augustine, St. Benedict, and St. Gregory the Great

Sally N. Vaughn

Looking back on his enthronement as archbishop of Canterbury in 1093, Anselm wrote to the bishops of Ireland:

> Proinde insulatus sedule quid Christo, quid eius ecclesiae pro loco, pro officio deberem cogitare coepi, et pastorali regimine vitia resecare, praesumptores coercere, et quaeque inordinata, ut me intererat, ad ordinem debitum volui revocare.[1]

How did Anselm conceive of his "duty", to what pastoral "rule" and to what "ordinances" (or "laws") did he refer? And what did he mean by "due order"? It is the thesis of this paper that Anselm's conception of "due order" was in fact his political philosophy: that the "ordinances" and "rules" to which he refers reflect the outlines of this political philosophy; and that he saw as his duty the enforcement of this political philosophy -- "due order" -- in a particular way. His "coercing" of presumers, "cutting off" of evil deeds, and "recalling the inordinate back to due order" was done by the guidance of a particular conception of "pastoral rule." In each case he is relying on particular patristic sources, all of which are monastic. A partial list of these sources would include the writings of St. Augustine of Hippo, St. Benedict, and St. Gregory the Great.

Anselm seldom quoted his sources. Modern students of Anselm's theology have concluded that St. Augustine of Hippo was Anselm's major theological source, although Augustine is only directly cited six times in Anselm's theological works. As Jasper Hopkins states, "Even where Anselm does not cite him directly, he appropriates examples, poses problems in exactly the same way, and borrows arguments without acknowledgment."[2] Thus it seems reasonable to approach Anselm's sources for his political philosophy expecting Anselm to refer to his sources in precisely the same way -- by inference and allusion rather than direct quotation. We may look at Anselm's own letters for these references, but perhaps we might also look with profit at the writings of Anselm's student and companion Eadmer, who in many cases provides us with eyewitness accounts and quotations of Anselm's words. We might also investigate with profit the historical writings emanating from the school of Bec, where Anselm spent

thirty-three years as monk, prior, abbot and teacher,
expecting in these to find a clear imprint of Anselm's
thought.

But we already know that a clear imprint of Augustine's
thought appears in Anselm's theology, and it is logical to
begin the search for his sources for political ideas there.
Let us begin with Anselm's clear statement that he conceived
of the existence of "due order." Looking to Augustine's
major political work, *The City of God*, we find that he does
speak of order in a particularly illuminating way, in the
context of a discussion of "peace" and the "highest good":

> We may say of peace what we have said of
> eternal life -- that it is our highest good;
> . . . Peace between mortal man and his maker
> consists in ordered obedience, guided by
> faith, under God's eternal law; peace
> between man and man consists in regulated
> fellowship. . . . Peace, in its final sense,
> is the calm that comes of order. Order is
> an arrangement of like and unlike things
> whereby each of them is disposed in its
> proper place.[3]

Thus Augustine equates "peace" to the "highest good," to
"eternal life," to "ordered obedience . . . under God's
eternal law, " and to "regulated fellowship," and finally to
"order." Anselm's words "due order" seem to echo this discussion. His letter to the Irish bishops contains many of
the elements Augustine discusses in this passage -- order,
law, and, by inference, obedience and regulated fellowship.
To Anselm, steeped in the "order" envisioned in the *Benedictine Rule*, this passage may have had particular meaning.
And it may not be coincidental that at about the time to
which Anselm refers in the letter -- his installation in
1093 -- he wrote to the monks of Bec referring to "the invi-
olate order of the monastery" -- *monasterii ordo inviolata*
-- of Bec, [4] suggesting that order was important to him at
Bec as well as Canterbury. Bec's "order" may well have been
determined by the *Benedictine Rule*.[5]

And many other intellectuals of Anselm's day were thinking in terms of "right order" -- Peter Damiani, Humbert, and
Pope Gregory VII, to name a few.[6] As is well known, they
began with a search of the writings of the Church Fathers,
and sought to find here guidance for the restructuring of
society along more authoritative lines. But Damiani and
Humbert interpreted these sources quite differently -- and
Gregory VII applied them in quite a revolutionary way with

the writing of *Dictatus Papae* and his vigorous efforts to
impose a new vision of order on the kings and clergy of
Europe. As an intellectual, a philosopher, and an ecclesiastical ruler -- first at Bec, then at Canterbury --
Anselm would have been vitally interested in these developments. It may well be significant that just at the time
that the research and thinking on these matters was gearing
up -- 1049 to 1059 -- Anselm's teacher Lanfranc spent nearly
a full year at the papal court, and thenceforth became
active in the reform of the Norman church.[7] It was during
that latter part of this decade that Lanfranc selected
Anselm as his foremost student, and it is nearly inconceiv-
able that the two intellectuals would not have discussed
these issues, even though neither wrote formal tracts on the
subject. Whether or not they discussed these issues, it
would not surprise us that Anselm -- the foremost intellect
of his day -- might also give the matter some thought.

Anselm did indeed express a particular conception of
"due order," as reported by his student and companion
Eadmer:

> Aratrum ecclesiam perpendite . . . Hoc ara-
> trum in Anglia duo boves caeteris praecel-
> lentes regendo trahunt et trahendo regunt,
> rex videlicet et archiepiscopus Cantuarien-
> sis iste saeculari justitia et imperio, ille
> divina doctrina et magisterio.[8]

This metaphor, I propose, is the main outline of Anselm's
political philosophy; it makes king and archbishop co-equals
in the rule of the church and the land -- for each is an
oxen in a team "foremost above the rest," pulling the plow
of the church through the land of England. Curiously, this
seems to suggest that the king is a co-priest while the
archbishop is a co-regent. The church, as the plow, appears
as the major mechanism for ruling the land. To the king is
attributed "justice" and the rather Gelasian *potestas*, while
to the archbishop the power of rule comes from divine doctrine and, curiously, teaching. Once more, there seems to be
a faint echo of Augustine's words on order -- and on God's
eternal law, which might have been phrased here as divine
doctrine. We shall return to the subject of archiepiscopal
teaching.

It is important to note the context in which Anselm
expressed his idea of "due order." Anselm was resisting the
attempts of the English bishops to forcibly consecrate him
as Archbishop of Canterbury, and protested to them that they
were trying to yoke an old sheep to an untamed bull -- him-

self as a scholar and teacher now in his sixties, and the
ruthless oppressor of the church King William Rufus. But
rather than negating the ideal vision of "due order" which
follows this statement, Anselm's words serve to heighten the
co-equal emphasis of king and archbishop in his metaphor --
for he is comparing an actual state of affairs with an ideal
one in a very clear way.

This ideal image is clarified by further statements
attributed by Eadmer to Anselm, in a progressive set of
revelations elaborating and enlarging this philosophy to
King William Rufus. The second time this subject was presented to Rufus begins with Anselm's request of the king to
restore all Canterbury lands as they had been held by
Anselm's archiepiscopal predecessor Lanfranc. Then Anselm
continues:

> Ad haec, volo ut in iis quae ad Deum et
> Christianitatem pertinent te meo prae cae-
> teris consilio credas, ac, sicut ego te volo
> terrenum habere dominum et defensorem, ita
> et tu me spiritualem habeas patrem et animae
> tuae provisorem.[9]

Now the relationship between king and archbishop gains
greater clarity -- for us, as for Rufus. The king is a feudal lord and guardian, and the archbishop is a kind of parallel protector of the king's soul. While the echo of Gela-
sius is obvious, a distinctly feudal image is injected.
Anselm seems to be reinterpreting the Gelasian theory in
terms of his own eleventh-century feudal environment, equating "king" with "lord and protector," and seeing himself as
archbishop in the context of the feudal court -- the *magister* is also the king's first counsellor. Anselm ends with a
plea that Rufus acknowledge Urban, as yet unrecognized in
England, as pope.

Eadmer makes it appear that it is this last point over
which Rufus and Anselm disagreed, and he may well have been
reporting accurately. Nevertheless, discussion on this
point did not begin immediately, and in the spring of 1094,
while Rufus was awaiting favorable winds to cross the chan-
nel and invade Normandy, Anselm presented Rufus with a third
expression of his philosophy on due order, invoking an even
clearer Gelasian image, with a few added details. Anselm
begs the king to restore Christianity "to its rightful
place" -- *suum statum* -- by holding councils *ex antiquo usu*:

> Sed conemur una, queso, tu regia potestate
> et ego pontificali auctoritate, quatenus

> tale quid inde statuatur, quod cum per totum
> fuerit regnum divulgatum solo etiam auditu
> quicunque illius fautor est paveat et depri-
> matur.[10]

Not only does Anselm seem to refer to the same "due order"
here that he has been invoking all along, in his concept
that the church has a "rightful state," but also to an image
of due order "from ancient usage." The specific "ancient
usage" to which he refers is the holding of councils to correct the evils in England, and these, he implies, are to be
done jointly, with the king using his power and the archbishop his authority in a united effort to restore what is
"legislated" -- *statuatur*. But the holding of councils was
not the only "ancient usage" that Anselm was concerned with.

Another "ancient usage" was the relative independence of
the Archbishop of Canterbury from papal control, along with
the complete dependence not only of every prelate in England
but also of every prelate in Scotland, Ireland, and the
Orkneys -- all Britain -- to Canterbury. These last two
elements of Anselm's political philosophy become clear
through Anselm's correspondence, Eadmer's accounts, and
Anselm's charters. Eadmer repeatedly insists that every
bishop in Britain owed submission and obedience to Anselm as
Archbishop of Canterbury -- and this he most often refers to
as "the customary profession" to Canterbury.[11] He refers
repeatedly to Canterbury as "the mother of the whole of
England, Scotland, and Ireland, and of the adjacent
isles."[12] Anselm clearly corroborates this view in his own
letters and charters. The term "Primate of all Britain"
occurs in every written profession rendered to Anselm during
his archiepiscopate.[13] And although Anselm continued to
assert his personal unworthiness to be archbishop, he also
stressed the grandeur of his primatial office. He styled
himself "Archbishop of Canterbury and Primate of all
England, Scotland, Ireland and the adjacent Isle,"[14] and
called the Church of Canterbury "the first of all the
churches in all England." He called himself *Cantuariensis
archiepiscopus et majoris Britannie atque Hybernie primas*,
and referred to Canterbury as the see *que omnium ecclesiarum
totius Anglie prima est*[15] in a charter to Norwich Cathedral
issued under extremely telling circumstances.

Just at the time this charter was issued, 1095, a papal
legate, Cardinal Walter of Albano, was staying in England,
having been summoned by King William Rufus to grant Anselm
his pallium, the symbol of his office. Rufus had hoped, by
recognizing Urban as pope, to reinforce his royal power over
Anselm by handing the pallium to the archbishop himself.

Walter would not permit this, and Anselm won the right to
take the pallium from the altar of Canterbury Cathedral "as
if from the hand of St. Peter."[16] But Walter did not return
to Rome immediately, remaining in England in hopes of
reforming the English church. In two carefully worded letters to Walter, Anselm told him that the church of England
could not be reformed without the king's assent: "We two
can effect nothing unless it would be suggested to the king,
so that with his assent and aid what we dispose may be led
to effect."[17] To a second admonition by Walter, this time
more strongly worded and stating that he wanted to act in
his person "as if the holy apostle Peter through his vicar
Urban were present," Anselm replied that the correction of
the Church of England could not be done without the aid and
consent of the king, nobles, bishops, and "others *to whom it
pertains*" -- a testy hint that Walter's efforts were indeed
unwelcome. Anselm firmly concluded the letter with a statement that he did not expect to see Walter again before the
legate left the kingdom.[18]

This letter is confirmed by a subsequent letter from
Anselm to Urban's successor Paschal:

> When I was at Rome I plainly showed [Urban]
> concerning legations from Rome to the realm
> of England how the men of that kingdom
> asserted [the legateship] to have been held
> from ancient times up to our own by the
> Church of Canterbury; how necessary it must
> therefore be to have it so, and that it
> could not be otherwise except to the injury
> of both Roman and English churches. The
> Lord Pope did not take away from me that
> legation which up to our time the church had
> retained. . . . What a great difficulty, nay
> even total impossibility it would be those
> comprehend who have had the experience of
> the long and perilous extent of seas and
> kingdoms between England and [Rome].[19]

Thus Anselm, in addition to viewing the Archbishop of Canterbury as co-ruler with the king, viewed himself as
uniquely independent of the pope -- a papal legate for
England, a vicar of the vicar of Christ -- or perhaps, as
Pope Alexander II is reported to have colorfully expressed
the idea to Anselm's predecessor Lanfranc, the Archbishop of
Canterbury was "Pope of another world."[20] And Pope Paschal
II later granted something like this position to Anselm in a
letter of 1103:

> The primacy we do indeed confirm to you
> . . . in as full and undiminished measure as
> it is known to have been held by your prede-
> cessors, and to you personally we grant this
> additional privilege: that . . . you are to
> be subject only to our judgment and not at
> any time to that of any legate.[21]

Thus Anselm eventually gained a quasi-independence from Pope
Paschal, which we must assume was part of his political philosophy.

Let us now turn to a closer look at Anselm's view of
kingship. Anselm had a very positive -- almost priestly
-- view of the role of the king in England, despite his long
and arduous struggles with Kings William Rufus and Henry I
of England. He wrote four letters expressing his view of
kingship, which is epitomized by his words to Baldwin, king
of Jerusalem: God chooses kings, and therefore kings should
devote themselves to "the will of God and his service," gov-
erning themselves and their people "according to the law and
will of God," and setting a good example for other kings.[22]
But other letters make it clear that kings were to set a
good example for their people, too, by the righteousness of
their lives and the justice of their rule. To Alexander,
King of Scotland, Anselm writes:

> Kings rule well when they live according to
> God's will and serve him with reverence; and
> when they keep rule over themselves nor
> yield to vicious ways, but with steadfast
> strength conquer those importunate tempta-
> tions. For constancy in virtue and royal
> fortitude are not inconsistent in a king
> . . . [nor] with royal power. Some kings,
> as David, both lived holily and ruled the
> people committed to their charge with strict
> justice and gentle kindness, according as
> need required. So behave yourself that the
> bad shall fear you and the good love you,
> and that your life may always please God.[23]

Kings were also chosen to bring order and peace to God's
church and people. As Anselm writes to King Murchertach of
Ireland: "Upon this foundation of peace, it is easy to
build the other things which are required by the religion of
the Church." The king is to examine and correct anything at
fault in his kingdom, no matter how trifling, and to always
progress from good to better, with the good intention that

God will approve.[24] In short, Anselm regarded the ideal
king as God's appointed viceroy to maintain peace, law and
order with "strict justice and gentle kindness," and to protect and nurture God's church, which was "committed to his
care." Christianity and Christian living in the kingdom
were to be fostered by his own good example. Thus Anselm's
view of kings was not at all negative. Rather, it envisions
the king's role as a constructive one in Christendom. It
clearly follows St. Paul's injunction to pray for kings and
all others in authority so that men can live in peace and
quietness (1 Tm 2:2), and his long discussion of how God has
put government in place, so that those who refuse to obey
the laws of the land are refusing to obey God (Rm 13:1-2,
cf. 5-7). This view is immediately preceded by a discussion
of how each person should use the particular talents God has
given him to the utmost of his ability, for this is God's
intention (Rm 12:6-8).

This view is crystallized in Anselm's letter to King
Henry I congratulating Henry on his victory at Tinchebrai in
1106, by which the king conquered Normandy:

> I rejoice and I give thanks to God with as
> much affection as I can . . . for your pro-
> sperity and your successes . . . because
> with earthly prosperity His grace so illumi-
> nates your heart that you attribute nothing
> in God's gift and in your own advancement to
> yourself or to human strength, but totally
> to God's mercy. And I rejoice and give
> thanks that you have promised the peace and
> liberty of God's church with all your heart.
> . . . I counsel . . . that you persevere in
> this . . .[25]

Clearly, Anselm considered Henry a good king at this point,
and approved of his conquest of Normandy to bring peace and
order to the land, as Henry himself had claimed was the purpose of his conquest of Normandy.[26]

Significantly, Anselm's view of kingship exactly coincides with his view of the role of the ideal bishop. Anselm
himself clearly stated that he conceived his role as archbishop to "set a good example" to the people of his kingdom:

> For the weak brethren in God's church are
> much injured by the opinion of any wicked-
> ness in any man . . . and most of all if it
> be of wickedness in him who is so placed in

the Catholic Church as that by word and
example he should and can be of use to
others.

He goes on to state that he is Archbishop of Canterbury
because the will of God has chosen him for this office, and
not from his own will and desire.[27] In other words, the
archbishop is chosen by God to rule much as the king is chosen to rule, as God's vicar, and like the king, is to serve
as a model of morals and behavior for the people committed
to his care, lay or ecclesiastical. We have already seen
that the archbishop, like the king, is to rule the land, but
with divine doctrine and teaching. And while the archbishop's authority extended somewhat wider than that of the
king -- throughout the British Isles, including Ireland,
Scotland, and the Orkneys -- his requirement of a written
oath of obedience from every prelate in this realm was not
unlike the oath of fealty required by the king from every
important man in England.[28]

Likewise, apparently, neither king nor archbishop were
to be under the direct control of the pope. Nevertheless,
while we have seen that Anselm did not want the pope
directly interfering in England, Anselm considered the pope
to be one of the sources of the divine doctrine or law by
which both king and archbishop were to rule. In a series of
letters to Pope Paschal, Anselm entreated him to exempt
England from the papal decrees against investiture and
homage:

> [The king and nobles] asserted forcibly that
> if I would join my entreaties to those of
> the bishops, your highness would be pleased
> to lessen the severity of [the decrees
> against investiture and homage] . . . I pray
> that so far as your authority under God
> allows, you would yield to this petition.[29]

This letter makes clear that both Anselm and King Henry I
were at once resisting the imposition of papal pronouncements that they were unwilling to accept for England, but
that both were willing to go somewhat further than their
predecessors King William and Archbishop Lanfranc in recognition of the authority of the pope to make laws.[30]

We have now been able to piece together Anselm's political philosophy -- his concept of "due order", as an echo of
St. Augustine's concern with "order" being the same as
"peace", "eternal life", and "the highest good", all con-

sisting in "regulated fellowship" in obedience to "God's
eternal laws." We have not yet looked at Anselm's sources
for the concrete structure of the philosophy itself -- the
"two oxen" theory, the regal role of the archbishop, the
priestly role of the king, the quasi-independence of England
from papal control, and the interesting conception of the
archbishop as "teacher."

How did Anselm arrive at these ideas? We have already
seen echoes of Augustine's high regard for "peace" and
"order" as "the highest good." Other passages from Augustine also seem to be echoed in Anselm's political philosophy. Anselm's insistence on his own and the king's
obedience to the will of God also echoes Augustine's view
that obedience is "the mother and guardian of all virtues of
a rational creature" who ought to yield to its Creator's
will.[31] Here, Augustine is speaking of obedience as the
supreme virtue, especially obedience to God, as Anselm
repeatedly emphasized. Augustine also speaks of hierarchies
in relation to the Highest Good and the Highest Virtue:

> It is good for some to be in an inferior
> position, and . . . it is for the good of
> all . . . to be subject to God . . . . What
> fragment of justice can there be in a man
> who is not subject to God, if . . . such a
> man cannot rightfully exercise dominion?[32]

As a variation on the earlier-quoted Pauline passage from
Romans on obedience to rulers, Anselm would have clearly
understood Augustine's meaning. Anselm's view of kings also
echoes Augustine's statements that

> on this earth . . . rule by good men is a
> blessing bestowed not so much on themselves
> as on mankind. . . . Hence, if the true God
> is adored, and if He is given the service of
> the true sacrifice and of an upright life,
> then it is beneficial for good men to extend
> their empire far and wide and to rule for a
> long time.[33]

This kind of thinking may well explain Anselm's effusively
congratulatory letter to King Henry I on his conquest of
Normandy in 1106, praising him for imputing his victory to
God rather than himself and for promising to protect the
church.

These passages from Augustine, clearly based on Pauline Scripture, as Anselm would have seen, may explain also why Anselm himself took such an active role in promoting the primacy of Canterbury, gaining for his church, as Sir Richard Southern has shown, greater dominion over the churches of the British Isles than either his predecessors or successors enjoyed. Southern calls these achievements the "high water mark" of the Canterbury primacy.[34] Likewise, Anselm's exalted view of the Church of Canterbury as the Mother of the English Church and of himself as its Primate gain some illumination in a theoretical sense.

We have also seen Anselm taking somewhat of an active role in the securing of papal approval for the primacy of Canterbury, by actively asserting to Popes Urban and Paschal Canterbury's right to serve as papal legate in England, and to assure that the papal legate Walter did not reform the English Church by right of his papal appointment, in opposition to Anselm's theories that it pertained to himself, the king, and the barons and clergy of England. Anselm's endeavors find strong support in these further Augustinian statements:

> Take the three modes of life: the contemplative, the active, the contemplative-active. A man can live the life of faith in any of these three and get to heaven . . . No man must be so committed to contemplation as . . . to give no thought to his neighbor's needs, nor so absorbed in action as to dispense with the contemplation of God . . . Nor should the man of action love worldly position or power . . . but only what can be properly and usefully accomplished by means of such position and power . . . contributing to the eternal salvation of those committed to one's care. Thus, as St. Paul wrote, "If anyone is eager for the office of bishop, he desires a good work" (1 Tm 3:1). He wanted to make clear that the office of bishop implies work rather than a dignity.[35]

This passage is clearly echoed in *Vita Herluini*, written during Anselm's episcopate by Anselm's close friend Gilbert Crispin. Gilbert speaks of Herluin and Lanfranc as almost twin rulers embodying the active-contemplative principle. Gilbert explicitly states, in discussing the role of Abbot

Herluin and Prior Lanfranc over Bec, that "each was a model
for the flock, one of the active life, the other of the contemplative."[36]   Anselm,   as   a   son   of   Bec, may well have
shared this concept. Clearly the above Augustinian passage
had been noticed and emphasized at Bec.

In the same passage, Crispin speaks of Herluin's "prudence" -- practical common wisdom.   This   trait   was   also
attributed to Anselm.   Eadmer   states that King William I
respected both Lanfranc and Anselm for their "prudence," and
for this reason listened to them before all others.[37]   St.
Augustine regarded prudence as one of the four cardinal virtues, along with courage, justice, and temperance: "Prudence shall provide . . ."[38]

Anselm speaks often in his letters too of "usefulness,"
specifically of *utilitas ecclesiae*, and often in the context
of a practical necessity of the church, as in *Epistola 214*,
quoted above, in which Anselm suggests that the long
expanses of land and sea between Rome and England make it
more "useful" both to the Church of Rome and the Church of
England for the Archbishop of Canterbury to exercise the
role of papal legate in England.[39] And Anselm's concern with
practical utility predated his archiepiscopate, for he spoke
of *utilitas ecclesiae* of Bec in a letter advising his successor Abbot William to follow his example in caring for
it.[40]   We shall return to this letter later. Anselm's
prudence -- practical common sense -- and his concern for
practical utility must have aided Anselm greatly in his
strenuous struggle to bring "due order" to England during
the investiture contest. And St. Augustine makes clear that
a bishop is supposed to be an effective ruler:

> . . . a bishop is supposed to superintend
> those over whom he is set in the sense that
> he is to oversee or look out for those under
> him . . . thus no man can be a good bishop
> if he loves the title but not the task . . .
> the position of dignity [of bishop] . . . is
> necessary for government . . . of course the
> dignity itself and its use are not wrong in
> themselves . . . [only the ambition for the
> title is wrong] . . . Once the burden is on
> the back, it should be carried, since *cari-
> tas* so demands.[41]

Anselm's apparent belief that the role of king almost
exactly parallels the role of bishop would make these ideas
applicable to the king as well as to the archbishop -- and

nowhere is this more plainly shown than in Anselm's enthu-
siastic letter of congratulation to King Henry I on his victory at Tinchebrai, quoted above. Henry is doing and has
done his proper duty as king.

But before the joyous victory at Tinchebrai, Anselm had
been engaged in a monumental struggle with Henry over the
issues of lay investiture and homage, stretching from 1100
to 1106. I have discussed this struggle elsewhere in
detail,[42] noting that the investiture contest was in fact a
three way struggle, between king, pope, and archbishop, and
that Anselm's major goals were to promote the primacy of
Canterbury above all else. In the context of the discussion
of Anselm's "due order" above, some further words of St.
Augustine on the subject of peace -- and indirectly order
-- may well have held particular meaning for Anselm.

> Any man who has examined history and human
> nature will agree with me that there is no
> such thing as a human heart that does not
> crave for joy and peace. One only has to
> think of men who are bent on war. What they
> want is to win . . . their battles are but
> bridges to glory and to peace. The whole
> point of victory is to bring opponents to
> their knees -- this done, peace ensues.
> Peace, then, is the purpose of waging war;
> and this is true even of men who have a pas-
> sion for the exercise of military prowess as
> rulers and commanders. What, then, men want
> in war is that it should end in peace. Even
> while waging war every man wants peace. And
> even when men are plotting to disturb the
> peace, it is merely to fashion a new peace
> nearer to the heart's desire . . . It is not
> that they love peace less, but that they
> love their kind of peace more.[43]

Anselm himself was no stranger to military matters, having
prepared the defenses of Kent for King William Rufus during
the rebellion of 1095. Indeed, he was designated commander
of those defenses, in expectation of a rebel attack (which
never occurred).[44] Again, in 1101, Anselm camped with the
Canterbury knights in the field as King Henry awaited the
invasion from Normandy by his brother Duke Robert Curthose.[45] And in the investiture contest, Anselm was clearly
trying to impose his kind of peace on England -- "due
order."

    Thus Anselm's political philosophy and some of his
political goals seem to echo passages in St. Augustine of
Hippo. But other patristic sources also echoed these ideas,
expanded them, and would have served to reinforce Anselm's
views. Most prominent of these are the writings of St. Gregory the Great and St. Benedict, and perhaps also the writings of John Cassian, although echoes of his work do not
reverberate as clearly as those of Benedict and Gregory.
Anselm's own teacher and predecessor at Canterbury, Lanfranc, explicitly cited Bede's *Ecclesiastical History*,
containing many letters of St. Gregory, to Pope Alexander II
as a source for precedents defining the Canterbury traditions. He wrote to Alexander that:

          passages were read out which proved to
          everyone's satisfaction that from the time
          of St. Augustine, the first Archbishop of
          Canterbury, until the last years of Bede
          himself . . . my predecessors exercised pri-
          macy over the Church of York and the whole
          island which men call Britain and over Ire-
          land as well; they extended pastoral care to
          all; they ordained bishops and held councils
          where they thought fit . . .[46]

Lanfranc seems to have been using Bede as a handbook for
Canterbury traditions (taken along with other texts and the
testimony of witnesses), and it is not unreasonable to suggest that Anselm did the same.
    For Anselm too was vitally concerned with the use of
precedents -- both ancient usages and the actions of his
predecessor -- and he was concerned lest his own actions
would set precedents for the future. Once he wrote from
exile that he was afraid to return to England at that time
for fear that he would establish "evil customs" for himself
and his successors.[47] And his letters abound with similar
references to his own actions as precedents.[48] Thus the
"ancient usages" to which he referred may well have involved
those of his own predecessors, and he was himself concerned
not to introduce usages disadvantageous to his own successors.
    When we turn to Bede for sources of Anselm's political
theory, we find a striking letter from St. Gregory to Ethel-
bert, England's first Christian king, reflecting both St.
Augustine of Hippo's political statements, and foreshadowing
Anselm's ideas:

> The reason why Almighty God raises good men
> to govern nations is that through them he
> may bestow the gifts of his mercy on all
> whom they rule. . . . Zealously foster the
> grace that God has given you and press on
> with the task of extending the Christian
> faith among the people committed to your
> charge . . . Make their conversion your
> first concern . . . raise the moral stan-
> dards of your subjects by your own innocence
> of life, encouraging, warning, persuading,
> correcting, and showing them an example by
> your good deeds . . . So it was that the
> devout Emperor Constantine in his day turned
> the Roman state from its ignorant worship of
> idols by his own submission to our Lord . .
> . Our most reverend brother Augustine has
> been trained under monastic rule, has a com-
> plete knowledge of Holy Scripture, and . . .
> is a man of holy life. Therefore I beg you
> to listen to his advice ungrudgingly, follow
> it exactly, and store it carefully in your
> memory; for he speaks in God's name. . . .
> Work sincerely with him in fervent faith,
> and support his efforts with all the
> strength God has given you . . .[49]

This letter exactly mirrors Anselm's political philosophy
outlined above, including both "due order" and his view of
kingship: the divinely chosen king who acts as a steward of
God to the "people committed to [his] care" much as the
priest or bishop receives the stewardship of his church or
see. Like the bishop, the king is to set a good example
through his own life, and to teach and correct the people.
And he is to be advised and taught in turn by his archbishop
of Canterbury, following his advice exactly, "for he speaks
in God's name." Finally, king and archbishop are to work
together.

Anselm's use of this letter as a pattern for "due order"
is confirmed by Eadmer's use of exactly the same pattern in
his summaries of the joint rule of King Edgar and Archbishop
Dunstan. Eadmer begins the text of *Historia novorum* with
these words:

> While . . . King Edgar was reigning in
> England, and diligently governing the whole

> realm with sacred laws, Dunstan, priest of
> Canterbury, a man of unblemished goodness,
> disposed all Britain by administering Chris-
> tian law. Under his influence and counsel,
> King Edgar showed himself a devoted servant
> of God.[50]

A clear summation of Anselm's "two oxen" statement as well
as Gregory's plan for England emerges from this passage, and
both seem to agree with the statements of St. Augustine of
Hippo. According to Eadmer, King William and Archbishop Lanfranc likewise followed the pattern:

> Lanfranc had the ear of King William . . .
> as his principal advisor . . . He always
> took great pains both to make the king a
> faithful servant of God and to renew reli-
> gion and right living among all classes
> throughout the whole kingdom.[51]

Eadmer goes on to state that Lanfranc's "example will be a
lesson to his successors."[52]

   That Anselm strove to follow this example and eventually
did bring "due order" to England is shown by a letter from
Anselm to the abbot of St. Ouen, a former monk of Bec, written in 1106, shortly after Henry won Normandy at the Battle
of Tinchebrai: "What you have heard is true; that my lord
the king committed to me his kingdom and all his possessions
so that my will shall be done in all things that are his."[53]
This statement is substantiated in several places. Writing
from Normandy in March, 1109, Henry told Anselm that the
management of affairs in England in his absence was "to be
governed by your will and settled by your advice. Indeed, I
have made this known to our justiciars."[54] And in 1107,
after Henry returned in triumph to England from Normandy, he
and Anselm jointly held a great council in London. Together
they announced to England their new peace and concord,
passed many measures for the reform of the church, and
jointly appointed new pastors to England's widowed churches
and abbeys, and to some in Normandy as well.[55] As Anselm
wrote to Pope Paschal in reporting the council, "now the
king, in choosing persons for preferment, does not consult
his own wishes at all but relies entirely on the advice of
men of religion,"[56] the chief and master of whom in England
was the Archbishop of Canterbury, Anselm. We have already
seen that Anselm persuaded Pope Paschal to confirm the Canterbury primacy to him, along with the legateship in
England, in a letter quoted above.

How did Anselm bring this "due order" into being? His initial words on the subject of "due order" give us some clues. He seems to have set out to "teach" it to the king and to the people of England. We know something of how Anselm was accustomed to teach because his student Eadmer, once a student at Bec,[57] had observed Anselm's teaching firsthand both at Bec and at Canterbury. Thus Eadmer gives us eyewitness accounts: in one instance, he reports that Anselm led a young monk Osbern to a holy life by loving him and caring for him, offering him many privileges and bland-ishments as concessions to his youth and to win his love, but later lovingly withdrew them when Osbern had reached a more mature state of spiritual development, and then later advocated applying blows when Osbern was strong enough for them to be effective.[58] Eadmer elaborates this methodology in at least four other places in *Vita Anselmi*. Anselm, he says, preferred to teach young men who, being of an age like soft wax, could be molded and shaped and could easily take the impress of a seal, Anselm's model of an ideal person.[59] Elsewhere Anselm advises another abbot not to beat and mal-treat young boys, because they will then grow up to be brutes. Rather, he should gently bend and train them up, carefully and lovingly guiding them like saplings into strong and straight trees. And finally, Eadmer reports Anselm to have said that young boys[60] should be gently shaped, bent, and molded much as a goldsmith gently shapes, bends and presses the precious gold or silver into a beauti-ful work of art, not with blows, but with gentle tapping.[61]

These methods -- which are most detailed in the case of Osbern -- Eadmer says Anselm used on all the monks of Bec when they rebelled at his "election" as prior on 1063. Ead-mer calls these methods "holy guile" -- *sancta calliditas* -- and says that the rebellious monks (who surely had not therefore "elected" Anselm) were won over "by Anselm's guile", *quo dolo Anselmi*.[62] If Eadmer is correct in his descriptions, this holy guile involved gentle love and prom-ises and concessions, later to be withdrawn gradually as the student progressed to maturity. Anselm's letters seem to confirm this style of teaching. While yet a simple monk, Anselm wrote:

> But since anger is shown only against an adversary, if the guilty one associates him-self with the one offended, by agreement with his opinion, the impulse of the offended one must subside, since he can find no enemy to strike at.[63]

And to Prior Henry of Canterbury, his former student at Bec, Anselm wrote:

> . . . There is never so great need of kind-
> ness as in the early incomplete conversion
> from a bad to a good life, lest the immature
> virtues which may be nourished and brought
> to full growth by the consolation of kind-
> ness should be checked or quite crushed by
> austere hardness. Therefore I beg of you
> . . . since wisdom in government becomes you
> . . . [to overlook] his past perversity and
> nourish the infancy of his good intentions
> with the milk of perceptible kindness lest
> he fall back into wickedness not from weak-
> ness but from malice.[64]

A careful reading of the *Benedictine Rule* reveals that these principles are embedded therein, and quite reasonably so, as they seem to be derived clearly from several of the Pauline epistles. Paul speaks often of immature Christians being nourished with milk until they are ready for more sub-stantial spiritual food (1 Th 2:7, 11; 2 Tm 4:2; 1 Co 2:4, 6; 3:1-12), and of course the preceding statement echoes Christ's dictum to turn the other cheek. But Benedict had studied these words long before Anselm, and had interpreted them in a way that Anselm, knowing them, would have espe-cially understood. Benedict spends an entire chapter on the abbot as teacher. He begins by advocating a two-fold teach-ing method; by words and example. "To such as are under-standing," the teacher may use words. "To the hard-hearted and simple-minded, he must manifest the Divine precepts in his life." "As occasions require, he ought to mingle encouragement with reproofs." "To the more unctious and apprehensive, he may for the first or second time use words of warning." One may be led by gentle words, another by sharp reprehension, another by persuasion, and thus shall he so shape and adapt himself to the character and intelligence of each . . . to rejoice in the good growth [of his flock]."[65] Thus Benedict well understood the tone of the Pauline letters addressed with deep knowledge of Jewish cul-ture and special concerns to Christian Jews (such as the Epistle to the Hebrews) and Paul's equally well-informed discussions of the major concerns of Gentile Christians (such as Corinthians). In 2 Timothy, he urges the new pas-tor to correct and rebuke his people when they need it, encouraging them to do right, while all the time patiently feeding them with God's word (2 Tm 4:2).

We have already seen how Anselm was determined always "by word and example" to be "of use" to others. This too is largely taken from the Pauline Epistles, where the importance of setting a good example is repeatedly stressed (see, for example, Rm 14; 1 Th 1:7; 2 Th 3:7; 1 Tm 1:16). But Benedict elaborates this method further on in the *Rule*. In subsequent chapters, he pictures a ladder of climbing deeds leading to perfection like Jacob saw in his dream.[66] In two different places he states that every age and state of intelligence ought to be governed in the way suitable to it. Thus the faults of those who are children or youths are to be overlooked, and the weakness of children is always to be taken into account by the granting of indulgences.[67] Some sins may be kept secret, and disclosed only to the abbot, for the house of God ought to be ruled by wise men.[68] Finally, the abbot must be learned in divine law. And

> even in his corrections he should act with
> prudence -- lest by scouring off the rust
> the vessel might be broken. The abbot must
> be prudent, discreet, and moderate, and use
> principles of discretion, the mother of vir-
> tues.[69]

Thus Anselm's teaching methods directly mirror the precepts of St. Benedict, which in turn reflect the Pauline epistles. Why, then, does Eadmer call Anselm's use of them "holy guile"? Here too our answer is to be found both in Scripture and in the patristic writings. Jesus said to his disciples, "Behold, I send you out as sheep among wolves; be therefore wise [sometimes translated as "guileful"] as serpents and as innocent as doves (Mt 10:16).

St. Gregory the Great seems to have been well aware of this dictum, interpreting it in conjunction with the Pauline sources cited above and expanding upon St. Benedict's use of them, in both another "book of rules," St. Gregory the Great's *Pastoral Care*, and in his letters preserved in Bede, to which Anselm would have had access.

In Gregory's *Pastoral Care* these same Pauline and Benedictine principles are stated with even greater clarity but in a different context. The *Pastoral Care* is written as a handbook to guide the bishop in the rule of his see. Significantly, Gregory regards the bishop's role primarily as that of teacher. He believes teaching to be "the craft of all crafts." He describes the process of learning "as on a ladder, step by step, nearer and nearer, until it stands fast in the upper room of the mind."[70] And while Gregory devotes the greater part of his work to the spiritual quali-

ties of the teacher-bishop and to the spiritual subject
matter to be taught, nevertheless he also devotes a small
portion of *Pastoral Care* to teaching methods. And these are
elaborations of Benedict's principles, but now set in a secular framework rather than a monastic context. The implication is that the bishop is to teach laymen, not the young
boys which St. Benedict envisioned in the monastery. And it
is clear that Anselm too made a similar transition from
abbot to bishop, and therefore must adapt his teaching methods in the same way as Gregory adapted the precepts of St.
Paul and the *Rule*.

By inference, then, Gregory speaks to the education of
laymen, and primarily to adults.

> The speech of teachers ought to be fashioned
> according to the condition of the hearers,
> that it may . . . be suited to each for his
> own needs . . . Whence also every teacher,
> to the end that he may edify all in the one
> virtue of *caritas*, ought to touch the hearts
> out of one system of teaching, but not with
> one and the same address . . . sometimes the
> faults of subjects are discreetly to be
> winked at but to be shown that they are
> winked at; sometimes even when they are
> openly acknowledged they are in their season
> to be borne; . . . sometimes they are to be
> gently reproved, at others sharply rebuked
> . . .[71]

Gregory continues to elaborate elsewhere in the same vein:

> Different admonitions are to be addressed to
> the wise in this world and to the dull . . .
> The one, for the most part, are converted by
> arguments of reasoning, the other better by
> examples . . . [the teacher] must understand
> that he is not to draw the mind of his
> hearer beyond his strength lest . . . the
> string of the soul, being stretched beyond
> what it can endure, be broken; for all deep
> things ought to be covered over when there
> are many hearers, and scarcely opened to a
> few.[72]

Gregory's letters in Bede show how this originally
monastic program for teaching was turned to the teaching of

laymen and to political purposes in England. Gregory wrote
to St. Augustine of Canterbury, England's first archbishop,
not to destroy the pagan temples but to cleanse them and
turn them into Christian churches, installing relics in
place of pagan images, because the people were accustomed to
worshipping there. Likewise, he advised Augustine not to
abolish pagan sacrifices and feasts, but to turn them into
feasts of thanksgiving to God.

> For it is certainly impossible to eradicate
> all errors from obstinate minds at one
> stroke, and whoever wishes to climb to a
> mountaintop climbs gradually step by step,
> and not in one leap. It was in this way
> that the Lord revealed himself to the Israe-
> lite people in Egypt, permitting the sacri-
> fices formerly offered to the devil to be
> offered thenceforward to himself instead
> . . . Once they had become enlightened,
> they might abandon one element of sacrifice
> and retain another.[73]

That Anselm was following this teaching is shown by a
letter he wrote to Pope Paschal II not only exactly mirror-
ing one of Gregory's letters in Bede, but also almost par-
aphrasing the thrust of Gregory's thought. Gregory's letter
consists of his quotation of a series of questions that St.
Augustine of Canterbury had posed to him regarding the
reform of the English Church, following each question with
an answer to it. In one of his replies, Gregory makes the
following statement:

> For in these days the Church corrects some
> things strictly, and allows others out of
> lenience. Others again she deliberately
> glosses over and tolerates and by so doing
> often succeeds in checking an evil of which
> she disapproves. . . . For in spiritual
> matters we may often with advantage follow
> the customs of the world, so that we may
> arrange things carefully and wisely.[74]

The implication is that "due order" must sometimes be
arranged in non-spiritual, practical ways, and that prudence, practical commonsense, must often be used.

One letter in Anselm's correspondence almost exactly
mirrors Gregory's letter in Bede. It is a letter from Pope
Paschal II to Anselm, quoting Anselm's questions about the

governance of the English Church and answering each   one   in
turn.   In Anselm's sixth question, he seems to mirror the
above statement of St. Gregory:

> Often it is necessary to relax something
> from the apostolic and canonical laws so as
> to compromise, and especially in a kingdom
> in which nearly all things are corrupt and
> perverse, so that scarcely anything is able
> to be done following ecclesiastical law; I
> ask that through your license I may be able
> to temper certain things, in proportion as
> God will give me discretion. Which I sought
> from the lord Pope Urban, and he placed it
> in my deliberation.[75]

Nowhere in Anselm's correspondence is his reliance on Pope
Gregory the Great's records in Bede more clearly shown. But
this evidence seems to make clear that just as Anselm
referred often in his theological works indirectly to the
works of St. Augustine, so also in the conduct of practical
affairs -- in the teaching methods that seem to have become
his political methods -- Anselm relied on the works of St.
Gregory that were available to him. Thus echoes of the
Benedictine Rule and *Pastoral Care* reverberate in a subdued
way in Anselm's correspondence. But they appear very
clearly in Eadmer's works, particularly *Vita Anselmi*.   For
example, Eadmer states that Anselm

> adapted his words to every class of men, so
> that his hearers declared that nothing could
> have been spoken more appropriate to their
> station. He spoke to monks, to clerks, and
> to laymen, ordering his words to the way of
> life of each.[76]

So it seems that just as the theoretical and philosophical
writings of St. Augustine of Hippo patterned Anselm's political philosophy when combined with the "ancient usages" of
England now placed in the feudal context, so the practical
and useful writings of St. Benedict and St. Gregory the
Great -- and certainly as extensions of Pauline dictums on
teaching -- seem to have inspired at least some of Anselm's
political behavior.
    But the test of this theory is to look at some of
Anselm's political behavior in detail, to see if he is
applying any of these Gregorian and Benedictine principles
of teaching. It is impossible to go through every political

action of Anselm's archiepiscopate here; indeed, I have done so elsewhere.[77] Eadmer's accounts indeed so obscure what Anselm actually did in trying to present Anselm as the model archbishop that an entire volume was needed to untangle the web. Anselm's political methods are further obscured by his own efforts to portray himself "by word and example" as a perfect model archbishop by collecting and editing his own letters, as Walter Fröhlich has shown. Fröhlich believes that Anselm was creating a "public image,"[78] and this may well stem from Anselm's efforts to set a good example for his successors. As well, St. Gregory had enjoined that "some deep things are to be hidden, and revealed only to a few." Anselm seems to have been following this doctrine in editing his letters. As he explicitly stated, regarding a certain important letter from King Henry to Pope Paschal, he "did not think it useful that it be preserved."[79] And we must also think of this editing of the letter collection in terms of the deep concern Anselm showed for the danger of setting "evil customs" or precedents for his successors at Canterbury. For custom was law in the Anglo-Norman state.

Because Anselm collected his archiepiscopal letters in an apparent effort to create a public image, it is possible to compare the "unofficial" accounts of Anselm's pontificate to these letters to see what Anselm perhaps did not want to be known, for understandable reasons of his own. These unofficial accounts include Eadmer's *Vita Anselmi* and *Historia novorum*, and the letters preserved at Bec not included in the Canterbury collection. And because Eadmer writes differently about the reigns of King William Rufus and King Henry I in *Historia novorum* -- the former being more or less a prose account and the latter being primarily quotations of Anselm's letters -- Anselm's political methods appear more clearly in the accounts of Rufus's reign than in the accounts of Henry's. Let us then look at one particular set of events that particularly reveal the somewhat typical political methods Anselm was using.

Anselm was consecrated as archbishop on December 4, 1093. Only one week later, King William Rufus summoned all his vassals (including Anselm) to his Christmas court. As he was planning to invade Normandy the following spring to win it from his brother, Duke Robert Curthose, the king requested "voluntary gifts" from his court. But Anselm was concerned that a large gift from him would appear to be a simoniacal payment so soon after his installation. Nevertheless, so Eadmer states, Anselm offered five hundred pounds, a considerable sum. Rufus at first agreed to accept it, but his advisors were outraged and told the king to demand twice or four times as much. Significantly, four

times as much would equal about a year's income from Canterbury estates,[80] the typical simoniacal payment.

Eadmer remarks at this point that the king was "in the
habit of treating in this way all those over whom he rules,"
thereby gaining his demands. But on the king's refusal to
accept the five hundred pound gift, Anselm promptly gave the
money to the poor, considering the matter closed. When the
king, seeing later that Anselm would never give more, later
agreed to the original five hundred pound gift, Anselm
replied that the money was gone, given to the poor.[81]
Later, Anselm wrote to his friend Hugh, archbishop of Lyon,
explaining the incident in a letter preserved at Bec, but
not at Canterbury:

> Before [the king] had asked me for anything,
> by advice of my friends I promised him no
> small sum; God knows with what intention.
> He rejected it as too little, that I might
> give more; but I would not. Thanks be to
> God, who, pitying the simplicity of my
> heart, caused it to happen thus, lest, if I
> had promised little or nothing, there might
> have seemed a just cause for anger; or, if
> he had accepted it, it might have turned
> into an accusation of nefarious purchase.[82]

Anselm had carefully and completely analyzed the situation.
He seems to have surmised precisely the right amount to
offer the king to ensure rejection, being fully aware, as
Eadmer implies, of the king's habitual behavior, and the
inclinations of the king's counselors. Characteristically,
Anselm attributes the outcome to the will of God, the cause
of all events. But if the great theologian thought consistently about his own political theories as outlined above,
he would also have had the view that God had chosen him for
Canterbury for a specific purpose, and that he was to carry
out God's will. He clearly believed that God had ordained
him for Canterbury. At one point in his letters, he speaks
of his own *ingenium*, cleverness, and although he goes on to
say that God's *ingenium* was greater than his own, nevertheless the implication is that he felt himself possessed of
intelligence and cleverness.[83] Doubtless he had read the
Pauline Epistle, two of which go on at great length on the
virtue of using effectively any God-given talents (Rm
13:6-8; 1 Co 12:4-11).

Eadmer states that Anselm

> was able by God's help to see into and
> unravel many most obscure and previously
> insoluble questions[84]

and that

> he so understood the characters of people of
> whatever sex or age that you might have seen
> him opening to each one the secrets of his
> heart and bringing them into the light of
> day. . . . He uncovered the origins . . .
> the very seeds and roots and process of
> growth of all virtues and vices . . .[85]

The outcome of Anselm's encounter with Rufus in December 1093 may have been ordained by God, but surely Anselm's talents also contributed. The result was that Anselm appeared neither ungenerous nor simoniacal. Rufus was simply left outmaneuvered and empty-handed. "Yesterday," he said, "I hated him with great hatred; today with still greater hatred; and he can be sure that tomorrow I shall hate him with ever fiercer and more bitter hatred."[86]

Anselm's attempt to teach the king with his methods of compromise, loving concessions to an immature spirit, and initial agreement with his opinions did not work in this case -- and really never worked on Rufus' hardened soul. Nevertheless, here we can see Anselm undergoing a transition in which he began to apply his teaching methods to the world of high politics.

Anselm characteristically responded to Rufus' hatred with his theories of teaching by love. Anselm was with Rufus as the king awaited favorable winds to cross to Normandy for the invasion of 1094 shortly after the incident reported above. Anselm had been slowly and progressively revealing to Rufus the elements of his "two oxen" theory, as noted above. In the third such revelation, Anselm entreated the king to work together with him -- to use royal power and archiepiscopal authority jointly -- to correct specific evils in England, including holding councils to correct immoral behavior such as illicit sexual practices of all kinds, and specifically the homosexuality of which the king is now suspected.[87] Rufus belligerently refused and departed England unblessed by Anselm.

A careful reading of *Historia novorum* reveals that Anselm was gradually unfolding his political vision to the king bit by bit, presumably adjusting his revelations to the king's growing ability to accept them.[88] But the king was very resistant, and eventually he and his court accused

Anselm   repeatedly   of   "trying to rob the king . . . of his
crown and the jewel of his sovereignty."[89]   The   "two oxen"
theory did not sit well with the king. Rufus' statement to
his bishops that "you can be sure that, while I live, I will
brook   no   rival in my kingdom"[90] seems to show clearly that
Rufus was   well   aware   of   its   consequences and that he
resisted it with all his might.

      But   Henry   I, Rufus' successor, was a different sort of
man, more cooperative and more reasonable. Anselm did succeed   with   Henry as he had failed with Rufus to educate the
king and convince him to recognize "due order" in England,
as we have seen above in both Anselm's congratulatory letter
to Henry after the Battle of Tinchebrai, and in Henry's
grants   to   Anselm of a kind of co-rule. The correspondence
between Anselm and Henry from 1103 to 1107 was a delicate
ballet   of   mutual   expressions   of   love and affection and
blandishments from both sides, each masking a hard position.
Despite the   fact   that   Henry had informed Anselm that the
archbishop would not be permitted to return to England so
long as he supported the papal bans on clerical homage and
lay investiture, Anselm addressed Henry consistently as "his
honored   lord"   and   assured   the king of "his faithful service."[91] Henry, for his part, replied that "I wish to have
no   mortal   man   with me in my kingdom more willingly than
you."[92] But in the end Henry yielded to Anselm's teaching.

      We have one striking letter in which Anselm expresses
how   his   teaching   methods   were transformed into political
methods in his own words.   In 1093 Anselm wrote   to   William
of Beaumont, his successor as Abbot of Bec:

> Remember   . . . for what reason I was always
> careful to acquire friends for the church of
> Bec,   and   by this example you should hasten
> to acquire friends from every side, striving
> after   the good work of hospitality, extend-
> ing kindness to all, and when this is not
> feasible,   reaching   out   to please with
> affable words. Nor believe yourself ever to
> have enough friends, but gather all to you
> in friendship whether rich or poor; so that
> this can both bring profit for the utility
> of your church and can increase the safety
> of those you love.[93]

Here, Anselm clearly refers to his teaching method of
extending love, friendship, kindness, good words, and even
blandishments, implying in the process that faults are to be
overlooked, at least for a time.   The   implication here is

that when it is not possible to extend kindness, at least let your words (possibly even of rebuke) be loving and affable.

Characteristically Anselm's teaching methods are methods of love. And they seem clearly derived from the Pauline letters, the *Benedictine Rule*, and *Pastoral Care*. Anselm may well also have connected these educational methods with St. Augustine of Hippo's *Confessiones*, containing a clearly stated belief that Augustine himself was educated by God through his experiences as he was maturing. Thus, one's experiences teach one lessons. The next logical step, which Anselm seems to have taken, is to teach by experience. In the case of William Rufus and the five hundred pounds, Anselm expertly maneuvered the king into the consequences of his greed and disregard for God's law against simony. And he did this in his official capacity of archbishop, vicar of God in England, for the *utilitas ecclesiae*, as he had once made friends for the utility of Bec.

Another point needs stressing. Benedict and Gregory both advocated overlooking the faults of the young and the immature in spirit, glossing over lesser misdeeds for the sake of correcting greater. As we have seen, Gregory goes on at some length on this point in a number of different places. These statements imply a theory of lesser goods and greater goods that Anselm himself seems to have endorsed in his questions to Paschal quoted above, suggesting that some of the laws for the Church of England be "relaxed" according to the archbishop's discretion. And we have noted that Anselm seems to echo Augustine's passage equating peace with eternal life and with order, all as manifestations of the Highest Good. We have noted also that the students of Bec -- probably including Anselm -- were so deeply impressed with Augustine's discussion of the three modes of life -- the active, the contemplative, and the active-contemplative -- that they portrayed their rulers as jointly exhibiting the best mode: the contemplative-active. Augustine makes another statement that seems to put Anselm's political career particularly in the context of this line of thinking:

> Socrates was . . . so highly distinguished both in life and death that he left behind him numerous disciples. They rivaled one another in zealous discussions of those ethical problems where there is a question of the supreme good, and hence of happiness. . . . Now the truth is that the supreme good is that which, attained, makes all men happy. . . . [Moral philosophy] deals with

> the supreme good, by reference to which all
> our actions are directed. It is the good we
> seek for itself and not because of something
> else and, once it is attained, we seek noth-
> ing further to make us happy. This, in
> fact, is why we call it our end, because
> other things are desired on account of this
> *summum bonum*. . . . Hence those who are said
> to have added to the list of goods their
> "extrinsic" goods -- such as honor, glory,
> wealth, and so on -- did not mean this as
> though it were a supreme good to be sought
> for its own sake, but merely as a relative
> good and one that was good for good men but
> bad for the wicked.[94]

Anselm devoted all his energy in the later years of his life
to the active life, to bringing "due order" to England. And
in the course of this active struggle, he mentioned at least
once that he saw his vow of obedience to the will of God as
superseding all other vows, when he wrote to the monks of
Bec explaining why he had accepted the archbishopric, thus
breaking his previous vow never to leave Bec and its monks
and to always be their abbot.[95] In a later incident at the
court of William Rufus in 1097, Anselm repeated this concept
and this reasoning in a particularly striking way. Rufus
had just returned from two successful military campaigns,
one to "subdue and settle Normandy, " which he had just
received in pledge from his brother Robert Curthose; and the
second to subdue the Welsh. "So he obtained peace from all
his enemies." On his return, he complained that the sol-
diers Anselm had sent for his campaign were "neither suitably trained nor fit for war," and summoned the archbishop
to appear before his court to be judged at law. Eadmer then
clearly states that Rufus had been practicing delaying tac-
tics against the archbishop's requests for king and archbishop to reform the Church of England: "the king, when
asked . . . would often reply that he could not attend to
the matter because of the enemies that encompassed him on
all sides." Now, with peace on all sides, Rufus had turned
on Anselm with a false accusation, "willfully fabricated to
preclude Anselm from having any opportunity of approaching
the king *to speak for God*." Anselm then deliberated and
concluded that it was "unseemly" for the archbishop as spo-
kesman for God to "sue as a litigant . . . or to submit the
question of his truth to the judgment of the court -- a
judgment not based on any law, equity, or reason."[96] At

length, Anselm determined to go to Rome for advice in the matter, asked the king's permission, and was refused three times. At this, Anselm replied, "If he refuses to give it, then I shall take it upon myself; for it is written 'It is right to obey God rather than men.'"[97]

Anselm then appealed to the bishops to rally to his side and support him, but "they chose one and all to follow the will of an earthly man, saying: 'We owe allegiance to the king and from that allegiance we will not depart.'"[98] And together with all the barons of England, they reminded Anselm of a vow he had made at the Council of Rockingham two years earlier in 1095:

> You then promised the king that you would thenceforth in every respect and at all times maintain his usages and laws and against all men would loyally defend them. The king, led to trust these promises, had then hopes that for the future he would have peace. But from that promise, that plighted word, already you are clearly departing when you threaten to go to Rome without waiting for the king's permission. It is a thing unheard of in his realm and utterly contrary to the usages that anyone of his princes should arrogate to himself any such right as that and most of all that you should do so.[99]

Eadmer shows here that Anselm clearly intended to break his former vow to the king.

Anselm's own words, as reported by Eadmer, echo the monastic teaching methods outlined above:

> You say that I promised you to uphold your usages and customs and with you against all men loyally to defend them. That I admit I should recognize as a true statement, if you qualify it by the stipulation which I quite clearly remember was made at the time the promise of which you speak was given. I know that I did indeed promise that your customs, that is those which you hold in your kingdom rightly and according to the will of God, I would according to the will of God maintain and would by all just means against all men defend them to the utmost of my power.

When Anselm had taken the oath, it was of course routine to
make it "under God." What Anselm had kept secret at the
time were the full implications of this phrase, which
amounted to a loop-hole which he now invoked when the king
was behaving badly, according to the archbishop's judgment
-- and Anselm, as we have seen, believed that his role was
to "speak for God" in England.

Thus Anselm clearly had a concept of "greater goods" and
"lesser goods," and the *summum bonum* is here revealed as
"God's will," which was the "due order" that Anselm conceived for Canterbury. And he seems to have been using
important aspects of the monastic teaching methods outlined
by Benedict and Gregory in his dealings with Rufus.   Anselm
had tolerated the king's sins (for a council to correct the
evils in England -- including homosexuality -- had never
been held at that point), nevertheless rebuking them gently,
trying to correct what evils he could in England. He tried
to educate Rufus by example and by words, revealing to Rufus
what the king could understand in his vow of fidelity and
service, and only later revealing the deeper meaning of the
vow, which he had kept secret for immature souls.

Anselm himself, in his correspondence, corroborates that
he was using these teaching methods on the king, but this
time it was Rufus' brother and successor, Henry I.   He had
written to his close friend and advisor -- and fellow primate -- Hugh Archbishop of Lyon. It is in Hugh's reply to
Anselm that we see his thoughts, for Hugh quoted Anselm's
words, apparently exactly. Anselm had written to Hugh seeking advice because he had reached a compromise with Henry at
the castle of Laigle in Normandy over the issues of homage
and investiture. Anselm's letter to Hugh asked for advice,
for "the king, although he grants that he is vanquished by
the apostolic decrees concerning the investiture of
churches, nevertheless does not yet wish, he says, to set
aside the homage of prelates."[100] Henry appears to have
made this compromise as a result of Anselm's threat to
excommunicate him if he did not obey the papal decrees.[101]
Hugh repeats Anselm's words to him verbatim: "According to
the report of Dom Baldwin . . . because you have labored so
hard to attain this end and not only your own goods but even
your very self have you offered up, by the grace of God, at
length already have you to a great degree attained it.   So
that you can be animated to hope for that which remains."[102]
Hugh then warned Anselm that he might be thought to have
taken apostolic authority upon himself by making the compromise, but he will, as Anselm had requested, send his own
advice to the pope to ratify the agreement.

And Pope Paschal's reply clearly echoes Anselm's words
in Hugh's letter:

> That God Almighty has inclined the heart of
> the King of England to obey the Apostolic
> See, for this we give thanks to that same
> Lord of mercies in whose hand the hearts of
> kings are held.   We feel no doubt at all
> that it is due to your gracious love and to
> your persistent prayers that this has been
> brought about. . . . Since the Lord almighty
> has granted us to progress this far in the
> kingdom of England, do you, my brother, now
> bring to bear upon the king and the princes
> such gentleness, tact, wisdom and foresight
> that those things which have not yet been
> set right as they should be may with the
> help of our Lord God through your devoted
> care be fully amended. You can be sure that
> in this task you . . . have our full sup-
> port, so that what you loose we loose and
> what you bind we bind too.[103]

And Paschal also clearly echoes Anselm's teaching methods,
which had by now become political methods to win "right
order" for the Church -- in this case, the church of Rome.
But notice that Anselm was at the same time winning "due
order" for England, for Paschal's letter clearly confirms in
a most striking way Anselm's legatine authority to "loose
and bind," and he does not limit it to England necessarily.
As well, the Laigle compromise at length permitted Anselm to
return to England having won Canterbury's rights from the
king, as we have seen above.

Anselm reveals his devotion to this highest good through
his singlemindedness of purpose even to the point of death.
For he suffered two painful exiles under Rufus and Henry,
and struggled up to the end of his life for the realization
of the complete political philosophy he had conceived for
England. The last two years of his life were spend working
in harmony with King Henry, but were marred by the refusal
of the archbishop of York to render "due obedience" to
Canterbury.

Two of the last letters Anselm wrote were intended to
put this last element in Anselm's great design in place.
First he wrote to Pope Paschal gently but clearly stating
that he would once again go into exile if Paschal consecrated Thomas Archbishop of York before Thomas had professed

obedience to Canterbury. Paschal, embroiled in his own
political problems with Germany, as Anselm knew, could not
afford to permit a man of Anselm's holiness to enter into
such a public display against the papacy, and relented.[104]
Finally, on his deathbed, Anselm wrote to all the bishops of
England that if anyone consecrated or accepted Thomas as
Archbishop of York before he had made his due profession to
Canterbury, by Anselm's decree he would be placed under
anathema and excommunication.[105]   Thomas was forced to
render the obedience.[106]

As Anselm tried to recall everything irregular back to
due order in England, he may well have been inspired, as the
burden of the task grew more and more onerous, by these
words of Pope Gregory the Great to the small group of monks
about to convert England to Roman Catholicism at the very
beginning of the Canterbury history:

> My very dear sons, it is better never to
> undertake any high enterprise than to aban-
> don it when once begun. So, with the help
> of God you must carry out this holy task
> which you have begun. Do not be deterred by
> the troubles of the journey or by what men
> say.   Be constant and zealous in carrying
> out this enterprise, which, under God's
> guidance, you have undertaken; and be
> assured that the greater the labor, the
> greater will be the glory of your eternal
> reward.[107]

Was Anselm's enterprise any less high, or the troubles of
the journey any less vexing, or the criticism of his contemporaries any less biting? Anselm's remarkable achievement
was to bring "due order" to England, according to the concepts in his political philosophy, a set of ideas gleaned
from conventional sources but remarkable for its differences
from contemporary political ideas derived from similar
sources. And he achieved this by methods gleaned from these
same traditional sources, seeing his behavior, teaching, and
example as applicable to political situations with the same
clear vision that he wrote his better known and more famous
theological tracts.

Notes

[1] The *Epistolae* of St. Anselm are found in Schmitt III–V.

[2] J. Hopkins, *A Companion to the Study of St. Anselm* (Minneapolis: Univ. of Minnesota Press, 1972), p. 16.

[3] *De civitate dei* XIX,13:   *CSEL* XL,395–97.

[4] *Epistola 165*:   Schmitt IV,38.

[5] Gilbert Crispin, *Vita Herluini*, in J. A. Robinson, *Gilbert Crispin, Abbot of Westminster* (Cambridge: Univ. Press, 1911), p. 93, suggests that Herluin was using at least some documents including the Benedictine Rule: ". . . [Herluin] ruled most strictly, but in the manner of the earlier Fathers . . ." The later *Vita Lanfranci*:   *PL* CL,33, explicitly refers to a certain "order" which at one point Lanfranc felt the monks were transgressing -- it must certainly have been the *Rule*. Lanfranc himself, Anselm's teacher at Bec, often referred to the decrees of the seventh century councils of Toledo in his letters as if they were definitive rules for the primacy of Canterbury. Note the frequent mention of "canon law" in *The Letters of Lanfranc*, ed. H. Clover and M. Gibsdon (Oxford: Clarendon Press, 1979), passim, esp. p. 11. For a full discussion of the unique sense of the "order" of Bec, see S. N. Vaughn, *Anselm of Bec and Robert of Meulan: The Innocence of the Dove and the Wisdom of the Serpent* (Berkeley: Univ. of California Press, 1987), ch. 2, pp. 19–77, especially pp. 70–77.

[6] Cf. G. Tellenbach, *Church, State, and Christian Society at the Time of the Investiture Contest*, trans. R. F. Bennett (Oxford: Blackwell, 1970), for a discussion of papal attempts to bring about "right order"; and G. Barraclough, *The Medieval Papacy* (Norwich: Jarrold, 1968), pp. 94–101 for a discussion of Urban II and his efforts to collect canon law.

[7] S. N. Vaughn, "Lanfranc at Bec: A Reinterpretation," *Albion* 17 (1985), 135–48.

[8] *Historia novorum*, p. 36.

[9] Ibid., pp. 39–40.

[10] Ibid., pp. 48–49.

[11] Ibid., pp. 47, 63, 73-74, 194-206, esp. 197-98 and 206, 189, 210, 216.

[12] Ibid., pp. 26, 63, 42-43; cf. 12-13, 14, 189.

[13] *Canterbury Professions*, ed. M. Richter (Torquay: Devonshire Press, 1973), nos. 50a-61; cf. p. lix, n. 2.

[14] *Historia novorum*, pp. 189, 26.

[15] *The Charters of Norwich Cathedral Priory, Part One*, ed. B. Dodwell, Pipe Roll Society (London: Ruddoch, 1974), no. 260.

[16] *Historia novorum*, pp. 70-73; *Vita Anselmi*, p. 87.

[17] *Epistola 191*: Schmitt IV,77-78.

[18] *Epistola 192*: Schmitt IV,78-81.

[19] *Epistola 214*: Schmitt IV,111-14.

[20] *Historia novorum*, p. 11; *Vita Anselmi*, p. 105. Cf. M. Brett, *The English Church Under Henry I* (Oxford: Univ. Press, 1975), pp. 12-14; William of Malmesbury, *Gesta Pontificum*, ed. N. E. S. A. Hamilton, Rolls Series (1870; rpt. London: Kraus, 1965), p. 100.

[21] *Epistola 222*: Schmitt IV,124-25.

[22] *Epistola 324*: Schmitt V,255; cf. *Epistola 248*: Schmitt IV,158-59; and *Epistola 249*: Schmitt IV,158-60.

[23] *Epistola 413*: Schmitt V,358-59.

[24] *Epistola 427*: Schmitt V,373-74; *Epistola 435*: Schmitt V,382-83.

[25] *Epistola 402*: Schmitt V,346.

[26] Orderic Vitalis, *The Ecclesiastical History of Orderic Vitalis*, ed. M. Chibnall (Oxford: Clarendon Press, 1980), VI, 87-88; cf. pp. 57, 61, 65. Henry's own justification for his conquest of Normandy in fact mirrors Anselm's philosophical views.

[27] *Epistola 160*: Schmitt IV,29-31; cf. *Epistola 355*: Schmitt V,295-97; *Epistola 176*: Schmitt IV,57-60; *Epistola*

201: Schmitt IV,92-93; *Epistola 210*: Schmitt IV,105-07; *Epistola 251*: Schmitt IV,162-63; *Epistola 264*: Schmitt IV,179; *Epistola 293*: Schmitt IV,213-14; *Epistola 311*: Schmitt V,235-38; *Epistola 318*: Schmitt V,246; and *Epistola 319*: Schmitt V,247-48, for Anselm's stress of "good examples," and *Epistola 148*: Schmitt IV,3-6; *Epistola 151*: Schmitt IV,12-13; *Epistola 156*: Schmitt IV,17-23; *Epistola 159*: Schmitt IV,26-29; and *Epistola 160*: Schmitt IV,29-31, for Anselm's belief that the will of God drove him to the archbishopric.

[28] See D. Douglas, *William the Conqueror* (Berkeley: Univ. of California Press, 1964), pp. 355-56.

[29] *Epistola 217*: Schmitt IV,118-19; *Epistola 218*: Schmitt IV,120; *Epistola 219*: Schmitt IV,121; and *Epistola 220*: Schmitt IV,122-23.

[30] Lanfranc, too, recognized the pope only as a distant authority, for when Pope Gregory VII demanded that King William I do homage to him, Lanfranc not only sided with the king's refusal to do so, but refused to visit Rome at the Pope's request: *The Letters of Lanfranc*, pp. 38 and 39.

[31] *De civitate dei* XIV,12: *CSEL* XL,30.

[32] Ibid. XIX,21: *CSEL* XL,408-10.

[33] Ibid. IV,4: *CSEL* XL,166-67,.

[34] R. W. Southern, *St. Anselm and His Biographer* (Cambridge: Univ. Press, 1966), p. 137; cf. pp. 132-39.

[35] *De civitate dei* XIX,19: *CSEL* XL,405-07.

[36] *Vita Herluini*, p. 96.

[37] *Historia novorum*, p. 23: King William respected Lanfranc and Anselm above all other men for their "prudence." Cf. *De libertate Beccensis monasterii*, in *Annales ordinis sancti Benedicti*, ed. J. Mabillon (Lucca: Enturini, 1745), V, 601: Count Robert of Meulan was astonished at Anselm's "prudence."

[38] *De civitate dei* V,20: *CSEL* XL,254-55.

[39] *Epistola 214*: Schmitt IV,111-14; *Epistola 165*: Schmitt IV,38-40; *Epistola 340*: Schmitt V,278.

[40] *Epistola 165*:   Schmitt IV,38-40.

[41] *De civitate dei* XIX,19:   *CSEL* XL,405-07; cf.   Anselm's letters in 1093 denying that he sought the office of archbishop because of cupidity, but stating that rather the "will of God" was driving him to office: *Epistola 148*: Schmitt IV,3-6; *Epistola 151*:   Schmitt IV,12-13; *Epistola 156*:   Schmitt IV,17-23; *Epistola 159*: Schmitt IV,26-29; *Epistola 160*:   Schmitt IV,29-31.

[42] Cf. S. N. Vaughn, "St. Anselm and the English Investiture Controversy Reconsidered, " *Journal of Medieval History* 6 (1980), 61-86.

[43] *De civitate dei* XIX,12:   *CSEL* XL,390-94.

[44] *Epistola 191*:   Schmitt   IV,77-78;   *Epistola 192*: Schmitt IV,77-81.

[45] *Historia novorum*, p. 127.

[46] *The Letters of Lanfranc*, p. 4; cf. *Epistola 65*: Schmitt III,183,60-61, for Anselm's only reference to Gregory's letter, according to Schmitt.

[47] *Epistola 311*:   Schmitt IV,235-38.

[48] *Epistola 176*:   Schmitt   IV,57-60; *Epistola 210*: Schmitt IV,105-06; *Epistola 251*:   Schmitt   IV,162-63; *Epistola 264*:   Schmitt IV,179; *Epistola 293*:   Schmitt I,217-18; *Epistola 311*:   Schmitt V,235-38; *Epistola 319*:   Schmitt V,247-48.

[49] Bede, *Historia ecclesiastica* I,32; cf. *Epistola 149*, Schmitt IV,6-10, from Osbern, monk of Canterbury, outlining the Canterbury tradition and calling St. Gregory the founder of Canterbury tradition. He also mentions St. Dunstan, whom Eadmer also considers a model; see below and note 50.

[50] *Historia novorum*, p. 3.

[51] Ibid., p. 12.

[52] Ibid., pp. 21-23.

[53] *Epistola 407*:   Schmitt V,352,3; cf. *Historia novorum*, p. 197.

[54] *Epistola 461*:   Schmitt V,410-11.

[55] *Historia novorum*, p. 186.

[56] *Epistola 430*:   Schmitt V,376.

[57] *Epistola 209*:   Schmitt IV,104-05:   domnus Edmeris,
. . . monachus Becci . . . ut filius eius; and J. H. Round,
Calendar of Documents Preserved in France (London: Eyre and
Spottiswoode, 1899), no. 209, witnessed by Eadmer   as   "chaplain of   the   above named church," which appears to be Bec
when taken in conjunction with Anselm's statement   in   *Epistola 209*.

[58] *Vita Anselmi*, pp. 16-17.

[59] Ibid., pp. 20-21.

[60] Ibid., pp. 37-39,

[61] Ibid., p. 38.

[62] Ibid., p. 16.

[63] *Epistola 9*:   Schmitt III,111-12.

[64] *Epistola 67*:   Schmitt III,187-88.

[65] *Regula* II: *PL* LXVI,263-66; cf. *Epistola 37*:   Schmitt
III,144-48; *Epistola 88*:   Schmitt III,213-14; *Epistola   105*:
Schmitt III,238;   *Epistola 176*:   Schmitt IV,57-60; *Epistola
199*:   Schmitt IV, 90-91; *Epistola 231*:   Schmitt   IV,136-38;
Epistola 232:   Schmitt   IV,138-39;   *Epistola 251*:   Schmitt
IV,162-63; *Epistola 286*:   Schmitt IV,205-06;   *Epistola   293*:
Schmitt IV,213-14;   *Epistola 313*:   Schmitt V,240; *Epistola
337*:   Schmitt V,274-75; *Epistola 410*:   Schmitt V,355;   *Epis-
tola 421*:   Schmitt V,366-67; *Epistola 434*: Schmitt V,380-81;
Epistola 436:   Schmitt   V,384-85;   for references   to   the
Regula.   Anselm also cites John Cassian, *Collatio*, once, in
Epistola 425:   Schmitt V,370-72.

[66] *Regula* III: *PL* LXVI,287-88.

[67] Ibid. XXX: *PL* LXVI,533-34; XXXVII: *PL* LXVI,599-600.

[68] Ibid. XLVI: *PL* LXVI, 693-94; LIII: *PL* LXVII, 749-52.

[69] Ibid. LXIV: *PL* LXVI,879-82.

[70] *Liber regulae pastoralis* I, prologus: *PL* LXXVII,13.
Cf. *Epistola 1*:   Schmitt III,97-98; *Epistola 23*: Schmitt
III,130-31; *Epistola 25*:   Schmitt III,132-33; *Epistola 222*:
Schmitt IV,124-25 for Anselm's and Paschal's references to
the *Life* of Gregory, the *Moralia in Job*, and the *Dialogues*.
The *Liber regulae pastoralis* is not cited by Schmitt, nor is
Bede.

[71] *Liber regulae pastoralis* III, prologus: *PL* LXXVII,49;
II,9-10: *PL* LXXVII,41-48; III,19:   *PL* LXXVII,81-83.

[72] Ibid. III,6 and 39:   *PL* LXXVII,56-57 and 124.

[73] Bede, *Historia ecclesiastica* I,30:   *PL* XCV,70-71.

[74] Ibid. I,27:   *PL* XCV,57-68.

[75] *Epistola 223*:   Schmitt IV,126-29.

[76] *Vita Anselmi*, p. 55.

[77] S. N. Vaughn, *Anselm of Bec and Robert of Meulan*,
pp. 149-366.

[78] W. Fröhlich, "The Letters Omitted from Anselm's Col-
lection of Letters," *Anglo-Norman Studies* 6 (1984), 58-71;
"The Genesis of Anselm's Letters," *American Benedictine
Review* 35 (1984), 249-60.

[79] *Epistola 379*:   Schmitt V,323-4.

[80] F. R. H. DuBoulay, *The Lordship of Canterbury* (New
York: Barnes and Noble, 1966), pp. 42-59, 195-204, and esp.
205, which states that in the mid-twelfth century, gross
annual receipts averaged £1560 per year.

[81] *Historia novorum*, pp. 44-45.

[82] *Epistola 176*:   Schmitt IV,57-60.

[83] *Epistola 156*:   Schmitt IV,22,132-34: "I presumed to
defend myself by my own fortitude and *ingenium*" -- but God's
ingenium, he goes on to state, was greater.   Nevertheless,
Anselm thought of himself as possessing *ingenium*, or cleverness.

[84] *Vita Anselmi*, p. 12.

85 Ibid., p. 13.

86 *Historia novorum*, p. 52.

87 Ibid., pp. 48-49; see above, p. 8.

88 Ibid., pp. 36, 40, 48-49, 53-62.

89 Ibid., pp. 53, 54, 58-61; cf. 62.

90 Ibid., p. 62.

91 *Epistola 308*:   Schmitt   IV,230-31; cf. *Epistola 319*: Schmitt V,247-48; *Epistola 321*:   Schmitt V,250-51;   *Epistola 329*:   Schmitt   V,261-62;   *Epistola 346*:   Schmitt V,284-85; *Epistola 347*:   Schmitt   V,285-86;   *Epistola 368*:   Schmitt V,311-12.

92 *Epistola   318*:   Schmitt   V,246;   cf.   *Epistola   317*: Schmitt V,244-46; *Epistola 319*:   Schmitt V,247-48;   *Epistola 367*: Schmitt V,311; *Epistola 371*:   Schmitt V,314.

93 *Epistola 165*:   Schmitt III,38-40

94 *De civitate dei* VIII,4:   *CSEL* XL,358-60.

95 *Epistola   156*:   Schmitt   III,17-23;   cf.   *Historia novorum*, p. 8.

96 *Historia novorum*, pp. 77-78.

97 Ibid., p. 81.

98 Ibid., pp. 82-83.

99 Ibid., p. 84.

100 *Epistola 389*:   Schmitt V,333-34

101 *Historia novorum*,   pp.   165-67;   cf.   p.   170,   where Anselm mentions in a letter to King Henry the agreement made at Laigle. *Epistola 389* and *Epistola 390*, written just after the   meeting   at   Laigle   and accompanying Anselm's letter to Pope Paschal explaining the results of   that   meeting,   also substantiate that the agreement was made at Laigle.

102 *Epistola 390*:   Schmitt V,334-35.

[103] *Epistola 398*:   Schmitt V,343.

[104] *Epistola 451*:   Schmitt   V,398-99; *Historia novorum*, p. 207.

[105] *Epistola 472*:   Schmitt V,420.

[106] *Historia novorum*,   p.   210;   cf.   Hugh   the   Chantor, *History of the Church of York*, ed. C. Johnson (London: Nelson, 1961), pp. 29-30.

[107] Bede, *Historia ecclesiastica* I,23:   *PL* XCV,52-54.

ST. ANSELM AND HOMOSEXUALITY[1]

Glenn W. Olsen

In his widely discussed, award winning, *Christianity,
Social Tolerance, and Homosexuality: Gay People in Western
Europe from the Beginning of the Christian Era to the Fourteenth Century*,[2] John Boswell argues two closely related
propositions: (1) that St. Anselm was gay, and (2) that
when, against a background of earlier tolerance, the Council
at Westminster (the Council of London) of 1102 took measures
to be sure that sodomy be understood by all as sinful and a
matter for confession, Anselm, probably out of both self-
interest and sympathy for the Gregorian moderation in dealing with homosexuality among the clergy, saw that this legislation never was promulgated.[3] Both these claims deserve
scrutiny, but for this background and definition of terms
are necessary.

The question of St. Anselm's possible gayness can not
profitably be pursued unless there is some agreement on
terms, and here the problems are formidable indeed. Boswell, as others before him, notes that the term "homosexuality," and more importantly the abstract classification
that it stands for, is modern.[4] The ancients and medievals
had words for specific homosexual acts, but, especially
before the thirteenth century, no abstract nouns corresponding to the modern terms for "sexuality" and "homosexuality,"
and virtually no terminology at all to express a distinction
between homosexual acts and a homosexual inclination.[5] This
latter is of special importance for the case of Anselm,
because Boswell does not claim that he engaged in homosexual
acts, only that he had an erotic inclination towards or
preference for members of his own sex, that is, that he was
what Boswell calls "gay." Although, both in the title and
text of his book, Boswell uses the term "homosexuality," his
preferred word for the description of what he believes is an
ancient and medieval reality is the term "gay." "Homosexual" is the broader term for him, comprising "all sexual
phenomena between persons of the same gender," while "gay"
describes "persons who are conscious of erotic preference
for their own gender."[6] Note should be made, because of its
relevance to the question of Anselm's gayness, that for Boswell's definition to be satisfied a person must not only in
fact prefer his or her own gender, but be conscious of this
preference. Also important for the study of Anselm is Boswell's assertion that "any distinction between "friendship"
and "love" must be extremely arbitrary."[7] This assertion

has been discussed in my review of Boswell's book, and we will return to this below, but here we must understand that Boswell's analysis proceeds on the assumption that what earlier scholars have treated as "friendship" may, sometimes as much as evidence for "love," be taken as manifesting a gay orientation.[8]

Boswell's terminology has already occasioned widespread discussion and dissent. More than one reviewer has pointed out how difficult of application it is, and many have questioned Boswell's conclusions in the matter of the classification of the sexual orientation of this or that writer.[9] This discussion merges with a more primordial question, and that is the nature of homosexuality itself. The range of opinion on the nature of homosexuality is wide indeed.[10] Many look upon a homosexual orientation as genetic, or at least congenital, some look upon it as learned, and of course some see it as lying somewhere between these alternatives, or as an undifferentiated term covering a variety of phenomena.[11] Gore Vidal has recently announced in the pages of *The New York Review of Books* "that there is no such thing as a homosexual or a heterosexual person. There are only homo- or heterosexual acts. Most people are a mixture of impulses if not practices. . . ."[12] It is a part of Boswell's *parti pris* that, in spite of the fact that the jury is still out on this central question, he speaks of gay people having a "permanent sexual preference."[13] Logic suggests this can only be so if being gay is congenital. Nevertheless, although Boswell's notion of "gayness" in fact assumes congenitality, it could be saved by refashioning the idea of "permanent sexual preference" into a learned or habitual sexual preference: in the concrete case of examining the life and writings of an individual like Anselm, analysis can proceed as long as there is evidence of some kind of a relatively stable and conscious orientation. This, as we shall see, is the real question.

The problem of terminology, of which Boswell himself is acutely aware, has recently been revealed in all its historical complexity in the study of *Sex and the Penitentials*, by Pierre J. Payer. This work bears extended summary, for it makes vivid the fact that, beyond Anselm's day, the really operative terms, as nouns, were either the catch-all *fornicatio* = sexual offence, or terms like *sodomita* = sodomist.[14] That is, into the twelfth century, to judge by the penitentials, medieval thinkers wavered between the very general (*fornicatio*) and the description, often in great detail, of specific sexual offences. What was real were the acts, and not some "sexual preference" of which they were the expression. A *sodomita* was most commonly someone who engaged in

anal intercourse, not someone who preferred his own sex.[15]
Indeed, if we were faithful to the medieval terminology, we
would have to say that no one before Anselm's day, using
whatever kind of terminology, posed the question of what his
or her attitude should be toward "gayness" or "homosexuality":[16] if this were our only concern, the present paper
would have better been titled "St. Anselm and Sodomy," meaning, "What did Anselm think of acts of sodomy?"

Payer's analysis is very precise, and throws much of
Boswell's understanding of the history of homosexuality in
the period down to Anselm into doubt. Boswell had claimed
that the New Testament had no position on homosexuality, and
that only after Anselm's time and through social influences
exterior to itself, did Christianity become intolerant of
homosexuality. This argument has already been attacked by
the reviewers at a number of points: we need not, for the
purpose of understanding Anselm, pause over this debate as
it touches on the biblical and patristic periods.[17] But the
situation of the early middle ages is different. In the
long period from the decline of Roman might to the urban
recovery advancing in Anselm's day, the materials for understanding any aspect of the history of human sexuality are
not very plentiful.[18] The kind of literary materials that
Boswell was forced to rely on for a picture of these long
centuries do not, any more than the ancient materials, permit us to answer many questions we would like to ask. For
the most part, one has to be content with the history of
attitudes and ideas, primarily of the clergy and nobility,
and with the early medieval writers' impressions of how rare
or common this or that practice was. This being so, Payer
now argues, Boswell seriously underestimated the importance
of the penitentials for understanding this obscure period.

Boswell does devote four pages to the evidence for attitudes toward homosexuality in the early medieval penitentials.[19] He concludes, however, that the penitentials are
not "an index of medieval morality," and that they reveal "a
relatively indulgent attitude adopted by prominent churchmen
of the early Middle Ages toward homosexual behavior."[20]
Payer has now argued in considerable detail that both these
judgments are incorrect. Payer's position is that, because
"the penitentials . . . were mediators between the general,
theoretical ideas they sought to apply and the level of
actual practice that was their sphere of immediate concern,"
they are a specially privileged source for the knowledge of
early medieval sexual attitudes and practice.[21] This is
undoubtedly true as far as it goes, but we have learned from
the *annalistes* of the frequently immense gulf between
learned and popular culture, and it might be fairer to say

that the penitentials articulate attitudes toward sexual
practices that the Church hoped the laity would adopt, and
also incidentally give some evidence of what people were
doing. In this sense they neither are nor are not "an index
of medieval morality." They give us the best idea we have
of what, in an effective pastoral situation -- which must
frequently have been absent -- was communicated from priest
to penitent. They are, and fortunately for a study of
Anselm this is what we need, an index of the morality clerics were supposed to communicate.

Beginning in the sixth century in Ireland, these manuals
for confessors spread first to Anglo-Saxon England and then
to the Continent, where, for five hundred years, that is to
Anselm's day, they were the chief written instrument for the
formation of Western European ideas about sexual ethics.[22]
We do not know with certitude how they were used in practice, but Payer makes the reasonable speculation that "they
served as reference works and guides, informing the priest
of . . . aggravating and mitigating circumstances, and providing suggestions for appropriate penances," and suggests
that most of them are short enough so that after a period of
use a priest would have tended to know them by memory.[23]
Presumably the penitentials "reflect what people were doing
sexually," and Payer attacks a residual "Victorian" modesty
still found among many scholars, who refuse to believe that
the detailed description of a wide variety of condemned
practices reveals anything more than a morbid monkish imagination, or refuse to believe the penitentials when they
state that sodomy is a common sin.[24] He makes the obvious
point that these penitentials had a very long and widespread influence, and that from time to time they were
reformed and reformulated for new social conditions, or at
least new perceptions of what the Christian life should be:
this is not likely unless they were regularly being used.[25]

Payer assumes that the penances given for specific sins
by the penitentials "are at least rough indicators of the
perceived gravity of the various offences".[26] His examination of fourteen penitentials composed before 813, that is
of the penitential literature which was at the core of all
the succeeding literature, shows that every penitential has
at least one canon on homosexuality.[27] In these certain
distinctions, also found where relevant in the discussion of
heterosexual practices, regularly appear. Intercourse "*in
tergo*," meaning anal intercourse, is regularly used in homosexual contexts, and in a number of sources seems to be
taken as analogous to bestiality.[28] Therefore, homo- or
heterosexual, it receives heavy penances.[29] Oral sex is
frequently mentioned, and Payer argues against some earlier

scholars that these references in the earliest penitentials are uniformly to homosexual practices, with only the later *Tripartite of St. Gall* making the sole clear condemnation of heterosexual oral relations.[30] Femoral intercourse and mutual masturbation are usually distinguished from sodomy, and receive somewhat lighter penances.[31] A possible conclusion which can be drawn from the early evidence Payer presents is that homosexuality was more disapproved than fornication among the unmarried laity.[32] Although the *Canons of Theodore* assigns a penance of seven years to *molles*, apparently meaning a man who takes the passive role in a homosexual relation, later writers reduced this penance to one year and apparently did not understand the term as Theodore had.[33] In assigning penances for homosexual acts, the gravity of the penance regularly depends on factors like the age and rank of the offenders: homosexual practices among boys often receive lighter penances.[34] Before 813 there is very little appeal to biblical or conciliar sources as authorities for the judgments made against homosexual acts, and furthermore no articulated rationale explaining their sinfulness: these were seen as unnecessary and beside the point in brief works intended for practical confessional application.[35]

Some of the Carolingian reformers, with their passion for a return to the sources, thought otherwise, and turned against the penitentials of the previous two-and-a-half centuries because they adduced few or no authorities for their prescriptions.[36] But new forms of pastoral literature by no means drove out the old, and, old, new, or mixed, the pastoral, penitential, and legal literature of the next three centuries maintained the teaching on homosexuality of the original penitentials. From the beginning of the tenth century, the old penitential sources entered on a large scale into canonical collections like the *Decretum* of Burchard of Worms.[37] In a sense this gave the penitential materials a status they had not previously possessed, because they were now mixed in the legal collections with a variety of authoritative sources and by this fact obtained "a quasi-juridical status."[38] The penitential materials were by no means unaffected in this process, and particularly the penances prescribed for specific sins were often modified (but with no clear pattern, as far as sodomy was concerned).[39] As we enter the period of the Gregorian Reform, some collections dropped the penitential materials dealing with sexual questions altogether, and this has sometimes been taken as manifesting hostility to these materials. However, Payer argues that there was no general Gregorian hostility to the penitentials: rather, the purposes of some of the Gregorian

collections did not include pastoral care. Others of these
collections, like those of Anselm of Lucca and Ivo of
Chartres, did continue to treat penance, and in these collections, albeit in a more limited way than in the still
popular *Decretum* of Burchard, a restricted amount of penitential material was still found.[40] While the question of
St. Anselm's knowledge of these collections is still being
debated, taken together they are representative of what was
being taught across Europe in his day, and manifest a uni-
form serious opposition to "homosexuality."[41] Things clearly
were changing in Anselm's time, and Payer has noted "the
waning influence of the penitentials" in Ivo of Chartres,
the *Polycarpus*, and, somewhat later, in Gratian.[42] Nevertheless, rather than expressing any general hostility to the
teaching of the penitentials, this seems to have been the
inevitable effect of the legal and theological developments
of the day, with their quest for a more consistent and
rationalized treatment of penance than the traditional penitential materials could supply: the outcome of this was to
be the appearance of the *summae confessorum*, but as far as
Anselm himself is concerned, in the degree that penitential
materials on homosexuality were present in his time, they
continued traditional teaching and attitudes.

Payer draws a number of general conclusions about sexuality in the period from 550 to 1100 which, in the specific
case of describing and explaining the history of homosexuality, seem much more helpful than the perspectives advanced
by Boswell. It may be a statement of the obvious to insist
that, "Sexual behaviour in early medieval society was governed by a fundamental principle which had been elaborated
much earlier: sexual intercourse was permitted only between
a man and a woman who were legitimately married to one
another, and then only if done for the sake of procre-
ation,"[43] but a number of reviewers have noted that Boswell's book is out of focus because it overlooks the obvious. That is, Boswell never systematically places his history of homosexuality within the larger framework of the
history of the biblical and Christian attitude toward marriage.[44] If he had, he would have had to stress that,
granted the purposes and nature of marriage beginning with
the Genesis account, "the logical implication was quite
clear -- all other forms of sexual contact must be considered to be forbidden."[45] Even in the pre-Carolingian
period, but more generally during all the centuries before
Anselm, when there was little explanation of why the various
homosexual practices are wrong, the nevertheless instinctive
sense that sodomy is "unnatural" and somehow analogous to
bestiality, is perfectly comprehensible when the larger

Christian understanding of marriage is considered. But if
this is so, then Boswell's argument that it was social factors exterior to Christianity which eventually led to the
Christian attack on homosexuality in the later Middle Ages
is wrongheaded, or rather, very incomplete. It could be
more plausibly argued that the religion itself, in varying
degrees but at all periods according to the level of reflection present, of its nature carried the seeds of a condemnation of sodomy, and then homosexuality. This is not to deny
that exterior factors of the type Boswell delineates could
force the issue, but it is to affirm that, as often in the
history of ideas, there was an intrinsic logic following
from long-standing Christian understanding of the purposes
of marriage that made hostility to sodomy virtually inevitable. It should not be forgotten that in the period under
discussion Christianity was a missionary religion, and the
blunt prescriptions of the penitentials on sex should be
seen as an attempt to educate newly converted peoples --
whose ideas about sexual matters, we may gather from the
penitentials, were often at great variance with Christianity[46] -- in the fundamentals of Christian moral conduct.
One must conclude that Christianity itself was a great motor
force in spreading antipathy to all the "sins against
nature," and that later writers like Aquinas merely worked
out the logic of long-standing positions.

The present study can not survey all the non-penitential
materials that might indicate attitudes toward or the practice of homosexuality in Anselm's day. Boswell clearly has
established that in Anselm's time there was appearing a literature celebrating, or at least favorable to, specific
homosexual activities, with an occasional text showing conscious erotic same-sex gender preference. One could also
build up a list of materials condemning specific "homosexual" activities.[47] The purposes of this study only require
that we be able to place Anselm within this context, to show
where he stood on this issue of the day, and, if possible,
what his personal inclination was. The foregoing survey
suggests that, however widely homosexual acts occurred in
Anselm's day, at least the better-educated among the clergy
commonly could have no doubt that the Church as revealed in
its pastoral manuals and law was deeply opposed to a long
list of homosexual activities. Anselm's own behavior and
statements both before and in regard to the Council at Westminster in 1102 leave no doubt that he understood sodomy to
be sinful and condemned.[48] Our question now is, rather, was
Anselm himself gay?

Boswell's presentation of Anselm is curiously indirect.
The discussion has little point unless the claim is that

Anselm was gay, and this is implied in more than one comment, but never in complete clarity. Boswell first discusses Anselm's role in prohibiting the publication of the
decree of the Council at Westminster of 1102, which had
insisted that sodomy be confessed as a sin. Here he suggests that Anselm "may . . . have had personal reasons for
suppressing the council's decree," and then notes R. W.
Southern's comment that "love and friendship are the dominant feature of his early and middle years."[49] We may take
it, in the light of Boswell's discussion two pages later,
that this is meant to suggest that because of his own sexual
orientation Anselm may have suppressed the Council's decree.
This is what Boswell writes of the years from 1050 to
1150:[50]

> The same period witnessed the first efforts
> to formulate a theology which could incorpo-
> rate expressions of gay feelings into the
> most revered Christian life-style, monasti-
> cism. Saint Anselm . . . was probably the
> most imposing intellectual figure of his
> day. It was he who brought the tradition of
> passionate friendship among monks into the
> limelight of medieval society (as he also
> prevented the promulgation of the first
> anti-gay legislation in England).

We shall see soon enough that Boswell misunderstands
Anselm's role at the Council at Westminster, but this quotation manifests the problems in trying to figure out exactly
what Boswell is claiming. "The tradition of passionate
friendship among monks" introduced by Anselm into medieval
society is apparently -- the transition from the first to
the second sentences quoted is rather abrupt -- to be
equated with "expressions of gay feelings." Presumably the
conclusion follows that Anselm himself was gay.

In Boswell's subsequent discussion, he notes that Anselm
was both committed to the ideal of celibacy and "had
extraordinary emotional relationships, first with Lanfranc
and then with a succession of his own pupils."[51] Anselm's
frequent use of expressions like "*dilecto dilectori*,"
"beloved lover," in addressing males is noted, but it is
specifically denied that erotic interest was "the primary
component of most of Anselm's relationships. . . ."[52] Yet,
Boswell claims, "some of his epistolary output appears
erotic by any standards."[53] In support of this claim,
Boswell cites a letter from Anselm to Gislebert, "brother,
friend, beloved lover":[54]

> sweet to me, sweetest friend, are the gifts
> of your sweetness, but they cannot begin to
> console my desolate heart for its want of
> your love.

Having used the classical commonplace, not specifically
identified by Boswell, that being separated from one's
friend is like being separated from one's other half, Anselm
continues:

> The anguish of my heart just thinking
> about this bears witness, as do the tears
> dimming my eyes and wetting my face and
> the fingers writing this.
> You recognized, as I do now, my love
> for you, but I did not. Our separation
> from each other has shown me how much I
> loved you . . . Not having experienced
> your absence, I did not realize how sweet
> it was to be with you and how bitter to be
> without you.
> But you have gained from our very sep-
> aration the company of someone else, whom
> you love no less -- or even more -- than
> me; while I have lost you, and there is no
> one to take your place. You are thus
> enjoying your consolation, while nothing
> is left to me but heartbreak.

Boswell proceeds to argue that because of Anselm's personal
prestige, it was this form of monastic love or friendship
which was, more than "the erotic friendships which had previously appeared in small literary circles," to influence
subsequent generations.[55] Anselm had achieved a kind of
synthesis of male affection with spirituality, and this was
to continue with many of the great twelfth century monastic
and clerical writers.[56]
    A number of reviewers have taken exception to this ana-
lysis. Peter Linehan, in criticizing Boswell for his handling of a variety of late eleventh and early twelfth century
figures, observes that, whereas in his chapter on "Definitions," Boswell holds that "there is no conceivable way of
quantifying the homosexual versus heterosexual experience of
most historical personages" . . . "as he approaches the
twelfth century, . . . he casts aside all discretion and
utters judgments which appear sexually innumerate."[57]
Further, while holding that it is possible for the historian
to distinguish homosexual attachments from simple friend-

ship, Boswell "neglects the possibility, earlier suggested,
that 'effusive romantic expressions between persons of the
same gender . . . may be hyperbolic manifestations of distinctly nonerotic friendships or even of simple charity.'"[58]
In short, Boswell's treatment of many of the great twelfth
century figures is a real muddle, in which he does not with
consistency or method explain how the various "effusive
romantic expressions" are classified. Linehan's strictures
are directed particularly against Boswell's treatment of
Ailred of Rielvaux, and his virtual non-treatment of Bernard
of Clairvaux, but they apply equally to his discussion of
Anselm.

Coming to Anselm, Linehan declares, "Boswell's account
of St. Anselm of Canterbury is as much tendentious as misin-
formed." Linehan disagrees with virtually everything Boswell
says about Anselm: "Inference breeds implication, and what
is implied here is unwarranted, and not only as to 'the Lanfranc set.'" Boswell's reading of Anselm's letters is
called "very literal and insensitive . . . the leaden interpretation of the obsessive inquisitor rather than of the
dispassionate inquirer." Especially important is the observation, originally made by R. W. Southern and seconded by
Keith Thomas, that Anselm "not uncommonly used physical
imagery in writing to people he did not know."[59] Moreover,
"physical imagery remains *imagery*. . . ." Linehan's points
are well taken.

J. Robert Wright, in also objecting to Boswell's tendency "at least by suggestive inference, to insinuate evidence of 'gay' where previous scholars have not found it,"
as in the case of Anselm, makes a point very damaging to
Boswell's book: "Boswell's medieval 'gays' do not in fact
say they are conscious of an erotic preference for their own
gender, much less that they consciously prefer this to a
heterosexual inclination."[60] This criticism, completely
sound as far as Anselm and most writers considered by Boswell are concerned, is nevertheless somewhat overstated.
Some of the poetry beginning with contemporaries of Anselm
analyzed by Boswell, or now available in the translation of
Thomas Stehling, does seem to satisfy Boswell's definition
of "gay," and returns us to a world something like that of
Plato's *Symposium* 191E-192D, a world in which some people
"have no great fancy" for people of the other sex, and are
"inclined" to their own.[61] Indeed, although it goes beyond
the goals of the present study, both topical and chronological, to show this in detail, if one were to eliminate from
Boswell's book all the materials which do not satisfy his
definition of "gay," one might arguably be left with the

truly novel and important observation that, as far as the Middle Ages are concerned, it was about 1100 in certain poems of Marbod of Rennes, and then later in the century in writers like Bernard of Cluny and Walter of Chatillon, and above all in the late twelfth century "A Debate Between Ganymede and Helen," that we see the appearance of a clear erotic preference for one's own sex that, by still being called "sodomy," began the expansion of that term into the modern "homosexuality."[62]

But to continue with the reviewers' critiques, Thomas, having wondered whether many medievalists will accept Boswell's reading of Anselm, returns to Southern's biography, which comments about Anselm's passionate letters: "'Anselm's response was excited by their monastic vocation and not by their personalities, of which he knew nothing.' His letters were 'a product of philosophy rather than feeling.'"[63] Although Thomas does not note that Southern is speaking in the first quotation of Anselm's letters to relatives, it is true that the sharp distinction which Anselm drew between the monastic and all lesser ways of life led him virtually to identify his "friends" as those who had taken, or could be persuaded to take, up monasticism. In this sense Southern and Thomas are precisely right: although Anselm could address an occasional layman with the language of friendship, what excited him and led most commonly to his language of love was not males, but monastic vocations.

Such has been some of the most important critical response. What may we conclude about the question of Anselm's gayness? The best study, though not without flaws, of Anselm's sexuality remains that of Brian McGuire. Indeed, an examination of G. R. Evans' recently published *A Concordance of the Works of St. Anselm*[64] reveals no telltale pattern, implicit or explicit, that would take us beyond what McGuire has already said about Anselm's sexuality. We all know of Anselm's frequent use of words for affection and love, both through his own writings and Eadmer's biography, but when we look for a specifically homosexual vocabulary we find none. The word *sodomitico* occurs only once, and that in the well-known *Epistola 257*, already mentioned. Absent is any other word for sodomy or other homosexual acts, and any pattern of usage of words for love which would suggest a gay preference. The state of the question thus is as McGuire left it.[65]

With his beloved mother dead, Anselm had left Aosta forever at age twenty-three, deeply alienated from his father, whom he hated, and who in turn showed only contempt for his

son.[66] At Bec, three years later, he has found a new
"father," Lanfranc, and in turn becomes a "father" to
others:[67]

> The fatherless, homeless young man estab-
> lishes himself as a centre of paternal
> affection and builds around him a group of
> followers that stimulates him both emotion-
> ally and intellectually. . . . It is no won-
> der that almost every time Anselm had a
> chance, he wrote letters to friends, rela-
> tives, and totally unknown people urging
> them passionately to enter a monastery.

The initial devotion to Lanfranc was total, and the admiration unbounded, but then Lanfranc left in 1063 to become
abbot of Caen, and Anselm was made prior at Bec in his
place.[68] If Southern is right in thinking that *Meditatio 2:
Deploratio virginitatis male amissae*, is the earliest of
Anselm's works, and therefore is to be dated to this period,
Anselm seems to have been going through "a great emotional
crisis."[69]   *Meditatio 2*, with its strong language of
self-accusation, is especially difficult to   interpret.
Anselm writes, for instance:[70]

> It is a bitter grief which burns me, to have
> lost virginity; but it is anguish and heavy
> sorrow, and fear of heavier yet, to have
> committed fornication. . . . O my soul,
> . . . it is of your own free will that you
> are miserably cast down from highest virgi-
> nity into the lowest pit of fornication.

One can not rule out the possibility that Anselm here was
confessing some form of homosexual activity. But positively
so to conclude would be incautious: better to say with
McGuire that the Meditation is concerned with some kind of
sexual sin "probably from his own experience. . . . the meditation indicates that the temptations are far from over.
. . ."[71]

Although even here we can not specify what Anselm is
writing about, he never again would indulge in such personal
revelation. McGuire concludes that whatever had occasioned
this outburst, "the temptation or cause or habit, whatever
it was, was overcome. . . ."[72] Overt sexual activity, if it
had ever existed, was driven out of Anselm's life, but in
its place, according to McGuire, came "a completely non-

physical love affair with a young monk named Osbern during the late 1060's or beginning of the 1070's."[73] Through Anselm's love, Osbern was transformed from a recalcitrant to an exemplary monk. Here we have a problem. McGuire designates this a "love affair," while pointing out that Eadmer (probably wishing to deflect any suggestion of impropriety) is careful to insist that Anselm was "inspired by the holy fire of charity."[74] The chapter in Eadmer's life which is almost our sole source for this story is too long to quote here, but it is hard to see that anything in it demands the use of the term "love affair," with its inevitable sexual connotations. Anselm clearly deeply loved Osbern, and Eadmer explicitly tells us that when Osbern, still young, died, Anselm never again centered his affections on a single person.[75] While it is difficult to speak with authority to the question of the sexual component in any form of love, the favoritism shown by Anselm toward Osbern, the affection and delight, do not seem clearly to differ from that shown by a parent to a child who is at once difficult but loveable (Eadmer describes Osbern as *aetate adolescentulus, puer*, and *in juvene*). Certainly this is how Eadmer, who describes Anselm as Osbern's "good father (*bonum patrem*)" and "friend (*amicum*)," saw the relationship.[76]

The most intimate of Anselm's letters were written in the years before he became Abbot of Bec in 1078, and McGuire argues that they tend to reflect an abstract idea of friendship, rather than the warmth and individualized passion that had been shown toward Osbern.[77] Perhaps this is because, as McGuire speculates, Anselm had now "a deep fear of new intimate relationships," but we are on firmer ground if we stress Anselm's commitment, after Osbern's death, to be all things to all men, that is, to avoid preferential loves.[78] Having analyzed Anselm's chief epistolary relationships in this period, McGuire draws a conclusion that compels assent:[79]

> Anselm's idea and practice of friendship with men thus becomes clear. He wanted to share his mind and heart with people who would be affectionate toward him but who would not come to expect too much of him. He was always on his guard for the moment when a friend started claiming exclusiveness. Such a friend, if he continued in his demands, would eventually be dropped. Anselm wanted to love, but gently and from a distance. For him the individual was only a

stepping stone, and a fragile and dubious
one, to the much more dependable world of
unchanging ideas and truths.

The analysis thus far must have raised in the reader's
mind the question of whether, especially before becoming
archbishop of Canterbury, the nature of Anselm's expression
of love had not been dictated by the fact that, in spite of
the role he took on himself of spiritual director to a number of women, he lived in an almost wholly masculine world,
and McGuire next takes up the question of Anselm's contact
with women. Not surprisingly, he concludes, "Anselm sought
friendship and love only from men."[80] This for McGuire
raises the further question of whether Anselm was a latent
homosexual, a question he correctly says "cannot be answered
in any final sense."[81] He notes that Anselm could comment
on the physical beauty of a young man, although in the particular letter under discussion (*Epistola 117*) the point is
that an exceptionally favored young man had been able to
give up all to become a monk at Bec.[82] Eadmer tells us that
Anselm gave more attention to young men than to others, but
this for the obvious reason that this was their formative
time.[83] On one occasion when one of his monks came to him
to complain of pain in his genitals, Anselm dealt with the
problem in a straight-forward manner which leads McGuire to
conclude "Anselm shows here a frankness and directness in
dealing with a sexual problem that hardly is the sign of
someone obsessed with male sexuality."[84] The same conclusion, for McGuire, is to be drawn from Anselm's decision
temporarily not to enforce the decree of excommunication of
the Council at Westminster in regard to sodomy.[85] Moreover,
McGuire makes the speculative point, which works in the
opposite direction of Boswell's handling of Anselm's letters, that:[86]

> If Anselm had been afraid of his sexual
> inclinations, then he would have tried to
> eliminate from the declarations of affection
> so common in his letters any sexual inter-
> pretation. He would have had to protest the
> innocence of his desires . . . But Anselm
> did not have to plead his innocence and
> purity, for the possibility of impurity in
> his desires never came to the surface of his
> mind. Anselm's very naivety about kissing
> and being together with his beloved monks
> indicates that homosexual contact with men
> was not on his mind.

While speculative, such a conclusion has common sense in its favor. Anselm's letters were intended for public reading, and this makes it most unlikely that they would have included anything which could be understood in the way Boswell has read the letter to Gislebert. Clearly, if we remain faithful to Boswell's criterion that to be gay one must consciously prefer one's own sex, there is no evidence at all that Anselm was gay. But perhaps McGuire somewhat muddies the water by continuing, "we are dealing with a man who was homoerotic but not homosexual," meaning that while all Anselm's "desires for love were centred on men, . . . this did not lead to any need for physical expression of this love." While the factual situation is thus, so far as we know, correctly described, the use of the label "homoerotic" to describe this is perhaps not very useful. Anselm not only lived in an overwhelmingly masculine world; as monk, abbot, and archbishop, many public expectations were placed on him. In this world, if he were to love anyone with the vivid language of his letters, it would by definition be a relative or a man. Expectations were that he would maintain a formal distance from women. If "homoerotic" describes the mere fact that Anselm loved only his mother and males, the term is not useful. Since McGuire himself rules out the possibility that "homoerotic" designates a conscious preference for males, it cannot mean "gay" in Boswell's sense. Thus the term can only suggest a "latent homosexuality," a possibility that can not be ruled out for any person, but that can not be clearly shown from the evidence, each piece of which, as briefly has been shown, can be read without recourse to such a theory.

The more important point is that McGuire's generally helpful reading of Anselm provides us with the materials for seeing the dangers of anachronism in Boswell's approach to the eleventh and twelfth centuries. If at least those learned men in these centuries who have left written evidence thought most commonly in terms of specific acts, like "sodomy," and only haltingly could extend this term to cover acts other than anal intercourse under the organizing principle of a gender preference, generally rather grouping such acts under a classification such as "acts against nature" or "fornication," in which "marriage" rather than gender preference was the defining norm, we must be very cautious in our use of the term "gay." If the main contrast for this period was between licit marital intercourse, celibacy, and a not very differentiated "everything else," that is, "acts against nature," this made it difficult, though not impossible, to see oneself as erotically preferring one sex to the other. Obviously Boswell has performed a great service in tracing the origins of a range of attitudes and practices relevant to what a later period called homosexuality. But he has not conveyed a sense of how concrete and realistic medieval thinking about sex still was in Anselm's day, concentrating as it did on the description, praise, or disapproval of this or that act, but not on any clearly generalized categories of sexual preference. Perhaps, as in the condemnation of the "crime of sodomy" at the Council at Westminster of 1102, to which we now turn, there was attached an understood reference to other sexual acts than anal intercourse, that is, perhaps, as may have occurred sometimes earlier, a concrete term like *sodomitico* was already attracting to itself a class of acts that would eventually be labelled homosexual, but we can not say this for sure.[87] In sum, the evidence does not suggest Anselm was gay; it does suggest that while some people were conscious of "liking sodomy" or some other practice, and thus could understand themselves as "sodomites," people in his day, with few exceptions, did not clearly perceive themselves as gay.

We come then to the Council at Westminster of 1102, of which Boswell's reading can be stated very briefly. Boswell understands the Gregorian papacy from the 1050's to have been quite tolerant of the practice of homosexuality -- criticism of this idea would involve another study.[88] Against this background, in an England in which there had previously been no statutes against homosexuality, the Council at Westminster condemned sodomy and stated that henceforth it was to be confessed. From Anselm's statement that "this sin has hitherto been so public that hardly anyone is embarrassed by it, and many have therefore fallen into it because they were unaware of its seriousness," Boswell concludes "that the average Englishman was not already aware" that sodomy was wrong and to be confessed.[89] Anselm had reservations about publishing the conciliar decision, and these probably were due to his having realized that it violated Leo IX's decree "forbidding extreme measures of this sort in dealing with homosexuality among the clergy," and to the personal reasons we already know Boswell believes Anselm had for treating homosexuality lightly.[90] Nevertheless -- and this is not in dispute -- "the stated reasons for the suppression of the decree were that it had been drafted hastily and needed revision. . . . In fact the edict was apparently never published."[91]

This description of the Council at Westminster raises as many problems as Boswell's treatment of Anselm's personality. Here it is more economical, rather than summarizing separately the criticism of the reviewers, to present an alternative reading of the Council which, it will be seen, disagrees with Boswell on most important points. Unfortunately it would lead us too far afield to examine the question of whether, in the period up to 1102, it was widely known in England that sodomy was a serious sin. Payer's research would suggest that this was so, but one can legitimately wonder how widely lay society grasped the penitential teaching of the Church, in what degree this was enforced, and how strong the old penitential tradition, which as we have seen was rapidly changing about 1100, still was: without a complete survey of the Anglo-Saxon period and the Conquest, discussion is premature.[92] What we will shortly see, however, is that Anselm's words about the public visibility of sodomy and the general lack of awareness of its seriousness around 1100 can be subject to a different reading than that given by Boswell.

The background for the Council at Westminster of 1102 is the following. The view, common now for a century, that William Rufus was homosexual and fostered around himself a court in which homosexuals were prominent, rests, according to Boswell, on untrustworthy evidence, chiefly the witness some years later of Orderic Vitalis, who also insinuated that Rufus' brother, Robert, Duke of Normandy, was guilty of the same sin.[93] Boswell rejects Orderic's testimony as it touches on this alleged homosexual activity, noting that of the "monkish chroniclers" who unanimously charge William Rufus with a variety of sins of the flesh, "only Ordericus Vitalis mentions homosexual relations specifically, and he does so only in passing."[94] Perhaps, for the sake of precision, as the discussion of Orderic which follows is intended to bring out, it should immediately be pointed out that while Orderic indeed does mention sodomy, he never unequivocally says that either William Rufus or Robert practiced it. What he says is that sodomy was rife during Robert's reign, and at William's court. A more important preliminary point is that Boswell seems to be wrong in saying that Orderic is the only monastic writer to mention homosexual relations specifically: this leaves out the account of Eadmer in the *Historia novorum*, with what will be taken below to be its blunt exchange between Anselm and Rufus on the matter of sodomy.[95]

A review of what Orderic and Eadmer have to say is in order. We can not dismiss Orderic as untrustworthy, because he does not seem in fact to stand alone in his witness. In describing Robert's government of Normandy as "weak and ineffectual," Orderic tells us, "in such times as these sodomy walked abroad unpunished, flaunting its tender allurements and foully corrupting the effeminate, dragging them

down to Hell."[96]   While Robert's reign is associated with
sodomy, no accusation is made here against him, and indeed
Orderic's point is that the appearance of sodomy was one of
the signs of the absence of good government. Orderic's
famous description of the foppishness found at King Rufus'
court occurs some pages later. "Frivolous men in search of
novelties," had adopted shoes with long, pointed toes,
and:[97]

> At that time effeminates set the fashion in
> many parts of the world: foul catamites,
> doomed to eternal fire, unrestrainedly pur-
> sued their revels and shamelessly gave them-
> selves up to the filth of sodomy. They
> rejected the traditions of honest men, ridi-
> culed the counsel of priests, and persisted
> in their barbarous way of life and style of
> dress. They parted their hair from the
> crown of the head to the forehead, grew long
> and luxurious locks like women, and loved to
> deck themselves in long, over-tight shirts
> and tunics.

Orderic goes on to describe the frivolity of the courtiers,
their feasting, drinking, and gambling, and then generalizes
to the whole population:[98]

> . . . after the death of Pope Gregory and
> William the Bastard and other pious leaders,
> the healthy customs of our fathers almost
> wholly disappeared in the regions of the
> west. . . . Our wanton youth is sunk in
> effeminacy . . . almost all our fellow coun-
> trymen are crazy and wear little beards,
> openly proclaiming by such a token that they
> revel in filthy lusts like stinking goats.

In sum -- we postpone to below a consideration of the possibly heterosexual implications of the references to "beards"
and "goats" -- Orderic presents sodomy as a practice that
has recently become a public scandal epitomized by the life
at William Rufus' court. We may reasonably see him as the
representative of a disciplined mode of life, both clerical
and monastic, appalled by the undisciplined life of the
court, which obeys neither the "counsel of priests" nor follows a proper lay marital code. He closes this account by
telling us of earlier satirists and moralists, beginning in
the Old Testament and continuing until the recent past, who

had condemned their times. "Following their example,"
Orderic says he condemns the practices of his times: "I
would far rather write of holiness . . . But I have no power
to force [our princes and bishops] . . . to live holy lives;
and so . . . I write a factual account of what they really
do."[99] Orderic wants us to believe that, though his lament
on the times stands in a venerable genre, he is nevertheless
speaking the truth.

It is to be emphasized that in this last passage Orderic
does not attack "homosexuality": if our argument above has
been correct, such a label was not available to him. In
condemning a whole range of vices, some heterosexual, he
here condemns "effeminates," "catamites," that is, those who
play the passive role in sodomy, and "sodomy," all of which
seem closely associated in his mind. This is a point which
needs further exploration. In 1 Co 11:14, St. Paul had
asked "whether nature itself does not tell you that long
hair on a man is nothing to be admired," and throughout this
letter and elsewhere had urged distinctions in dress and
decorum between men and women: this had fed a distaste for
effeminacy and sexual passivity already found in the ancient
world and still very much alive in Orderic's day.[100] Thus,
as Boswell's book itself bears witness, in the ancient and
earlier medieval world, if one looks for attitudes toward
"homosexuality," what one finds beyond the polar attitudes
of advocacy of same-sex love or condemnation of sodomy, is
some degree of distaste or scorn for effeminacy and playing
the passive role in sexual relations: this latter is often
the subject of taunts. What seems generally of greatest
concern to writers like Orderic is the (probably often subconscious) assertion of gender expectation, of the superiority of the masculine and the active, rather than the condemnation of a generalized class of homosexual activities. In
a society with as clearly differentiated masculine and feminine expectations as that of Orderic, the superiority,
power, control, and virility of the masculine could be
threatened in a thousand ways. If "little things" like the
charms and potions women add to food could be perceived as a
threat to or attempt to manipulate virility,[101] how much
more to be feared was a world in which men were losing their
grip on what defined them, were slipping into their opposite, were becoming like women. Our texts tell us a great
deal about this fear, but rather less about what we call
"homosexuality." We must not expect our materials, which
generally are more concerned that men live up to male gender
expectations than anything else, to give clear evidence
about homosexuality. If we approach these materials looking

for Boswell's "gayness," we will be disappointed, for at a non-theological level the concern of the literary evidence seems centered rather on the condemnation of effeminateness, of which sodomy is most commonly but a sign. In addition, in the passage just considered and in a number yet to be described, we seem to have a fear, not unlike that much earlier articulated by John Chrysostom, that letting children's or young men's hair grow long would make them appear effeminate and thus attractive for sodomy.[102]

Eadmer, without making any specific reference to sodomy, gives us a very similar picture of life at William Rufus' court. Speaking of the period shortly after Anselm's consecration as archbishop in 1093, Eadmer comments that "nearly all the young men of the Court . . . grow their hair long like girls" and "glancing about them and winking in ungodly fashion, they would daily walk abroad with delicate steps and mincing gait."[103] In response to this, Eadmer continues, Anselm made this court life one subject of his Ash Wednesday sermon at the beginning of Lent in 1094. Many were led to repentance, cut their hair, "and adopted again such bearing as becomes a man." Anselm refused the penitential ashes and absolution to those who would not. Again, what was condemned here was overt effeminacy, and we can only guess that by implication sodomy was included. At the least, from the beginning of his archbishopric Anselm had declared himself against the life of the court.

Orderic's comment on William Rufus himself might, but does not have to, be taken as an accusation of sodomy. Having criticized William for having favored certain underlings who had flattered him, Orderic remarks: "He never had a lawful wife, but gave himself up insatiably to obscene fornications (*obscenis fornicationibus*) and repeated adulteries."[104] We already know that the accusation of fornication can cover anything, and whatever else is intended, it is only the accusation of heterosexual offences that is clear. A similar description of Duke Robert as "sunk . . . in indolence and voluptuousness (*socordia . . . mollicieque*)," need not even bear a sexual reference, though again the Latin has associations of softness, passivity, and thus effeminacy.[105]

In the last passage of Orderic relevant to our theme, Robert is again accused of laxness in government and a whole range of sins including harlotry. The sins mentioned are all either "heterosexual" or simply express dissoluteness, and seem signs for Orderic that Robert was not "acting the man" as Duke. The setting is 1105. William Rufus is dead, and in a sermon preached before Henry I in Normandy his gathered courtiers are criticized for "all" wearing their hair long, and 1 Co 11:14-15 is cited in condemnation of this. Long hair is appropriate for penitents, of which it is said:[106]

> Long beards give them the look of he-goats, whose filthy viciousness is shamefully imitated by the degradations of fornicators and sodomites, and they are rightly abominated by decent men for the foulness of their vile lusts. By growing their hair long they make themselves seem like imitators of women, and by womanly softness they lose their manly strength and are led to sin . . .

These last are words attributed to Serlo, Bishop of Séez, preached, according to Orderic, before Henry I. The passage describes penitents, and not directly the courtiers, but Serlo obviously transfers his remarks to the courtiers. For, although no one is specifically accused of sodomy, the reaction reported by Orderic is dramatic: "the bishop, ready for action, immediately drew scissors from his cloak-bag and proceeded to cut the hair, first of the king, and then of the count [of Meulan] and most of the magnates with his own hands. The king's whole household and all who flocked to follow their example were close-shorn. . . ."[107] Paris may be worth a mass but apparently Normandy could be had for a haircut.

What are we to make of all this? The emphasis in this passage again lies in the effeminacy expressed by long hair on men, but the comparison of the bearded to he-goats, reminiscent of *Historia ecclesiastica* VIII,10, considered above, who in turn are apparently associated with an overactive indiscriminate hetero- and homosexuality (if thus we may understand "fornicators and sodomites" -- mistresses are mentioned some lines before), gives us an entrance into Orderic's thinking. Here and in a number of passages already presented he seems to be condemning at once men who are not manly enough, that is, are effeminate, and yet are "too manly," that is, practice sexual license. The present passage is particularly interesting because both accusations are brought against the same men, and are associated with sodomy. Orderic seems to use an understood acceptable male sexuality as actively expressed only in marriage and in moderation as a norm by which he condemns the defect of effeminacy and the excess of fornication, both included in the he-goat image of an untamed sexuality which one way or another evades the discipline necessary to "be a man" and a

leader of men.[108]   Orderic continues   by   saying   that   "the
Roman   pontiffs and other bishops have prohibited" the wearing of long hair, which Chibnall reasonably takes   to   be   a
reference   to the canons of the Council of Rouen of 1096 and
of Westminster of 1102, to be described below. Again,   long
hair   is   seen   as pleasing to mistresses, so the context is
not simply condemnation of effeminacy and   sodomy.   Orderic
is,   then,   as   he   says, the moralist, and just as with the
earlier penitential writers, the assumed   standard   of   male
sexuality is intercourse within marriage.

We   can not trace the history of tonsorial practice further in Orderic's pages, but as Chibnall   indicates   in   her
notes,   there is a larger context for this seemingly trivial
moralizing that bears directly on the   Council   at   Westminster.   The   evidence   that thus far has been presented only
shows that Anselm, as distinguished from Orderic and Eadmer,
condemned   long   hair   as a sign of effeminacy, and does not
absolutely prove that Anselm understood his attack   on   long
hair in his Lenten preaching of 1094 to be an attack on sodomy.   But there can be no doubt that Anselm did condemn sodomy,   for   in   the   very   next   paragraph following Eadmer's
account   of   Anselm's   Lenten   preaching of 1094,   Eadmer
describes   the following extraordinary exchange between William Rufus and Anselm, in response to Anselm's request   that
a   general   council   of   the English bishops be held. Unac-
countably,   Boswell does not   discuss   this   text   either   in
regard   to his argument that Anselm was gay, or in regard to
his assertion that Rufus was not.   The King asked,[109]

> mockingly, "But you, what   would   you   speak
> about   in   such   a Council?"   To this Anselm
> replied: "That most shameful crime of   sod-
> omy,   not   to   speak   of   illicit   marriages
> between persons of kindred blood . . .   that
> crime,   I   say, of sodomy, but lately spread
> abroad in this land, has already borne fruit
> all too abundantly and has with its abomina-
> tion defiled many.   If it   be   not   speedily
> met   with   sentence of stern judgment coming
> from you and by rigorous discipline   on   the
> part   of   the Church, the whole land will, I
> declare,   become   little   better   than   Sodom
> itself."

Anselm   requested   that the two of them work together -- and
here we are at the source of the impetus behind the legislation against sodomy of the later Council at Westminster:

"to establish some decree against it such
that, when it is published up and down the
land, even the hearing of it will make
everyone that is addicted to such practices
tremble and be dismayed." These things
found no home in the heart of the King and
he made but brief answer saying, "What good
would that do for you?" "If not for me,"
said Anselm, "it should, I trust, do so for
God and for you." "Enough," said the King,
"say no more about it."

To repeat, this exchange, which seems to bear with it the
suggestion of a personal accusation of sodomy against Rufus
-- "if not for me . . . for you" -- follows immediately upon
Eadmer's description of Rufus' courtiers, and of Anselm's
sermon on long hair. That this is an accusation can not be
absolutely proved, but the likelihood is that Eadmer saw,
and by the sequence of his narrative was trying to convey,
both a condemnation of Rufus by Anselm, and a connection
between the condemned long hair in the previous paragraph
and the sodomy attacked here. Perhaps Anselm, in addition
to condemning the effeminacy of long hair and sodomy separately, also saw this latter connection: here the larger
context becomes relevant.

Two years later, Orderic tells us, a council held in
Rouen decreed "that no man shall grow his hair long."[110] We
are not told the reason for this decree, although the punishment specified, exclusion from church and prohibition
that any priest perform any divine office or burial for the
long-haired, is quite severe. But immediately we suspect a
connection between the court life described by Orderic in
VIII,10, and XI,17, and Eadmer in the *Historia novorum* 48,
and this decree from Rouen. The question, then, so far as
understanding Anselm's context, is not so much whether William Rufus and Duke Robert in fact practiced sodomy,
although the evidence that Rufus did is circumstantially
strong and has led his most recent biographer to say without
qualification that Rufus was a homosexual.[111] The question
is rather whether, by the 1090's, an association had been
made between wearing long hair and a life of dissipation,
including both homo- and heterosexual offences. Put this
way, we see that Eadmer's and Orderic's pages looking back
to this time are clear witness to a court life that displeased reform-minded churchmen, and that was symbolized by,
among other things, wearing hair in the manner of a woman,
and expressed in the "womanish" practice of sodomy.

That the Council of Rouen itself made this association
between hair length and a life of dissipation is by itself
only a speculation, although, placed within the other evidence already presented, and with note taken that the decree
at Rouen was directed against laymen, a reasonable speculation. Here we can uncover the probable background for the
decision at Rouen. A whole symbolism in which the head and
the hair expressed the dignity of the human person, and
especially the highest faculty of the mind, had developed
beginning in the ancient Church. Without laying all of this
bare here, we may simply note that the Carolingian liturg-
ist, Amalarius, had expressed the heart of this teaching in
the ninth century, and that this had been taken over in the
1060's by John of Avranches (John of Bayeux), who was to be
archbishop of Rouen from 1067-79, in his *De officiis ecclesiasticis.*[112] Near the beginning of his work, John took up
the question of the *corona* or tonsure that the clergy were
to wear, and stated that it was to be short. His argument
was that the upper part of the head was to be shaved as a
sign that all superfluous and temporal concerns had been cut
off from the mind, which is symbolized (*exprimitur*) by the
head. The crown of hair which is left is not to cover the
ears or eyes, that they not be impeded from seeking out good
works. The beard, which manifests the strength (*virtus*) of
the body, is shaved to show that fierceness (*feritatem*) of
mind has been driven off.[113] Although we have no evidence
that this work had a wide influence, it was used by John's
predecessor at Rouen, and was known in twelfth century
England. Its obvious importance is that, existing at Rouen
in the 1090's, it was likely known to those at the Council
of Rouen in 1096.[114] While written for the clergy, its
presentation of the symbolism of hair could as easily be
applied to laymen, and we can only guess that this is what
was done at the Council of Rouen in 1096. Further, we may
have here one influence on Orderic's comment about the
bearded expressing the wildness or virility of the he-goat.
Just as the beard expresses man's strength, so the shaved
beard expresses a controlled or disciplined strength, a
proper masculinity. We can only suggest that such ideas lay
behind what the Council at Westminster and Anselm himself
were to say about the hair styles of both clergy and laity.
Once again, ideas developed initially in a clerical context
seem to have expanded to form expectations concerning proper
lay decorum.

In addition to its condemnation of sodomy, the Council
at Westminster of 1102, like that of Rouen, condemned the
wearing of long hair: "That men wearing hair are to have it
cut so as to leave part of their ears visible and their eyes

not covered."[115]   No specific association is made between
long hair and any form of "effeminacy."[116]   But in his
Epistola 257 on interpreting this Council, Anselm proceeded
immediately from his discussion of how the canon on sodomy
was to be applied to an explanation of the canon on hair
which seems to look back to the kind of punishment laid down
at Rouen -- Westminster specified no punishment for long
hair.[117]   Anselm does not, as Rouen had, exclude the long-
haired from church. Rather, they were to be allowed to
attend mass, but they were to be warned that, in Chibnall's
interpretation, "they did so at the peril of their
souls."[118]   Although the canon on hair had preceded that on
sodomy by five canons in the decisions of Westminster, and
here Anselm discussed it immediately following his discussion of sodomy, this is not conclusive evidence that either
Westminster or Anselm associated the two issues. But, in
conclusion, the likelihood is that all these documents are
to be read together, and that Eadmer's and Orderic's
descriptions of the Anglo-Norman courtiers, taken together
with John of Avranche's explanation of the significance of
hair-length, are a key to understanding what was afoot at
Rouen, at Westminster, and in Anselm's mind. The matter of
sodomy had to be taken up at Westminster because the recent
dissoluteness of the royal court, still fresh in memory and
symbolized in its still-prevalent sartorial and tonsorial
practices, had become a public scandal leading some to think
that sodomy was a sin of little account.

The immediate background of Westminster, then, is that
Henry I, who, whatever his heterosexual excess, had driven
out the courtiers of the type fostered by Rufus (although to
judge by Orderic's account of Serlo's sermon of 1105, the
long hair remained), was sympathetic toward his bishops taking up Anselm's program of moral reform which had languished
under William Rufus.[119]   Anselm was given his chance to
press legislation on the issue of sodomy, which had concerned him for at least the better part of a decade. Various versions of the decisions at Westminster survive, and
are catalogued by Whitelock, Brett, and Brooke. In Eadmer's
version the decision of the Council concerning sodomy
reads:[120]

> Those committing the crime of sodomy and
> those voluntarily abetting them were in this
> Council condemned and subjected to a heavy
> curse until by penitence and confession they
> proved themselves fit to receive absolution.
> Anyone found notoriously guilty of this
> crime, . . . if he be one of the religious

order, is not to be preferred to any further
step in the hierarchy; and, if he already
holds any such preferment, is to be deposed
from it. If a layman, he is throughout the
whole of England to be deprived of the status which by law belongs to his rank; and no
one except a bishop is henceforth to presume
to give absolution from this crime to any
who have not vowed to live under rule. It
was also decreed that throughout the whole
of England such excommunication should be
renewed in all Churches every Sunday.

The Council was unusually short, lasting only two days, and
its decisions composed in some haste: afterwards Anselm
decided that a further meeting would be necessary to prepare
a proper text for publication.[121]   However, his departure
for Rome in 1103 and following exile, which took him from
England for three years, prevented the calling of a second
council, and there is no record that a corrected version was
ever prepared or circulated. All we know is that Anselm
apparently believed the concluding sentence of the canon on
sodomy too severe, and dispensed "for the time being" from
the requirement that the excommunication of sodomists be
renewed each Sunday.[122] In addition he wrote to the arch-
deacon of Canterbury, William, probably in 1103:[123]

. . . Concerning those who have committed
the sin of Sodom either before or after the
excommunication, not knowing that it had
been promulgated, the sentence in both cases
will be equal and similar if they confess
and seek to do penance. You will assign
penances at your discretion, taking into
consideration the age of the offenders, the
duration of the sin, and whether or not they
have wives; and also how you see them performing their penance, and what promise they
show of true amendment thereafter. It must
be remembered that this sin has been pub-
licly committed to such an extent that it
scarcely makes anyone blush, and that many
have fallen into it in ignorance of its gravity. As for those who defile themselves
with this sin after learning of the excommunication, they ought to be dealt with more
severely by way of penance. But we leave

> this to your discretion on the lines
> suggested.

It is quite possible that Anselm's statement here that many had fallen into sodomy in ignorance of its seriousness is to be taken at face value, as Boswell does, but also still in Anselm's mind was the recent scandalous life of the courtiers, with the bad example it had set for all. In any case, Anselm's first concern seems to be a good pastor of souls, not to suppress distasteful legislation. Especially difficult to reconcile with Boswell's interpretation of Anselm is Anselm's statement here that those who know of this decree and then commit sodomy should be given more severe penance: these are not the words of a man set on suppressing the Council's decisions.

Although we presumably will never know all that transpired in these months, the sequence of events just indicated is sufficient to explain what Boswell takes to be Anselm's "suppression" of the Council's decisions on sodomy.[124] *Councils and Synods* has collected what evidence has survived, and this shows that while the circulation of various unofficial forms of the canons from Westminster was limited, this "did not . . . prevent their being enforced. The decrees against married clergy and sodomy were pursued for a while with some zeal. . . ."[125] Further, Anselm, by an initiative that was not then considered necessary, and was not usual, obtained papal confirmation of the conciliar decisions.[126] That later councils, such as that of 1108 at London, did not again take up the question of sodomy cannot therefore be taken as evidence that Anselm, who now also was in ill health, had through some unspoken personal motive successfully suppressed the question of sodomy.

We know from Eadmer that at least the problem of effeminacy and long hair remained after Anselm's death:[127]

> . . . the men with long hair were, as we
> very well know, excommunicated by Father
> Anselm and banished from the doors of holy
> Church; yet they now so abound and so boast-
> ingly pride themselves on the shameful girl-
> ish length of their locks that anyone who is
> not long-haired is branded with some oppro-
> brious name, called "country bumpkin" or
> "priest." The rest of such doings, no less
> hatefully shameful, I shall pass over in
> silence.

Perhaps this refers to nothing more than a persistent fashion which continued to irritate old-fashioned monks and
ecclesiastics, but as McGuire suggests, the things Eadmer
"passes over in silence" may be continuing homosexual behavior.[128] We do not know for sure, and it is useless to
speculate on why the Council of 1108 at London, meeting in
the year before Anselm's death, did not take up this question again. Yet Eadmer's last word on the subject presents
an interesting conflation of ideas. So far as we know,
Anselm and the councils with which he was connected had
never given the punishment of excommunication for wearing
long hair, only for sodomy. But so closely are the two connected in Eadmer's mind that the sodomists that Westminster
had excommunicated become "the men with long hair." Almost
certainly, then, the things "passed over in silence" are
sodomous practices. More importantly, writing not long
after Anselm's death, it never occurred to Eadmer to look
upon the decisions of Westminster as having been suppressed.
Ineffective in the long run they may have been, but Eadmer
still sees the canon against sodomy as having been the personal work of Anselm.[129]

Notes

[1] I wish to thank the College of Humanities of the University of Utah for a grant supporting the research and
writing of this article.

[2] J. Boswell, *Christianity, Social Tolerance, and Homosexuality: Gay People in Western Europe from the Beginning
of the Christian Era to the Fourteenth Century* (Chicago:
Univ. of Chicago Press, 1980), received the 1980 Melcher
Book Award of the Unitarian Universalist Association, and
the 1981 American Book Award in History. G. W. Olsen, "The
Gay Middle Ages: A Response to Professor Boswell," *Communio*
8 (1981), 119-38, lists some of the earlier reviews. Further and later bibliography is listed in J. R. Wright's sub-
stantial "Boswell on Homosexuality: A Case Undemonstrated,"
Anglican Theological Review 66 (1984), 79-94.

[3] Boswell, *Christianity*, pp. 215-16, 218-20, 235. I
conclude that Boswell means to ascribe "self-interest" to
Anselm from the discussion following the comment, p. 216,
that Anselm "may also have had personal reasons for suppressing the council's decree." See below n. 49. Boswell,
with the older literature, refers to "the Council of London
of 1102." The current referent, however, is the "Council at

Westminster":   M.   Brett,   *The English Church under Henry I* (Oxford: Univ. Press, 1975), index under   "Councils,   Westminster   (1102)," and   D. Whitelock, M. Brett, and C. N. L. Brooke, eds., *Councils and Synods, with Other Documents Relating to the English Church*, I, Part II: *1066-1204* (Oxford: Clarendon Press, 1981), pp. 668-88.

⁴ Boswell, *Christianity*, esp. ch. 2.   Unfortunately (see below nn. 16, 60-62, 81, 87), Boswell does not seem fully to appreciate the importance of this fact.

⁵ P. J. Payer, *Sex and the Penitentials: The Development of a Sexual Code, 550-1150* (Toronto: Univ. of Toronto Press, 1984), as at pp.   14-15,   40,   82,   135-38,   140-44. Payer considers lesbianism, but the present paper will not. Cf. for St. Paul, Olsen, "Gay Middle Ages," p. 132.

⁶ Boswell, *Christianity*, pp. 43-44.

⁷ Ibid., pp. 46-47 at 46.

⁸ Olsen, "Gay Middle Ages," p. 127.

⁹ See as examples K. Thomas,   "Rescuing Homosexual History,"   *The New York Review of Books* 27, No. 19 (December 1980),   26-29, at 26 and 29 (the latter   disputing   Boswell's reading of   Anselm);   J.   duQ. Adams in *Speculum* 56 (1981), 350-55 at 352-54; P. Linehan, "Growing Hostile to Gays," *New York Times*, 23 Jan. 1981, Times Literary Supplement, p. 73; M. M. Sheehan, "Christianity and Homosexuality," *Journal of Ecclesiastical History* 33 (1982), 438-46 at 443, and see 444 for Sheehan's understanding of   Anselm;   and   Wright,   "Boswell," 90-91.

¹⁰ P.   Coleman,   *Christian Attitudes to Homosexuality* (London: SPCK, 1980), esp. Part A; V. L. Bullough, *Homosexuality: A History* (New York: New American Library, 1979), esp. ch. 1; A. P. Bell and M. S. Weinberg,   *Homosexualities: A Study of Diversity among Men and Women* (New York: Simon and Schuster, 1978); R. Bayer,   *Homosexuality and American Psychiatry: The Politics of Diagnosis* (New York: Basic Books, 1981); K. Plummer, *The Making of the Modern Homosexual* (Totowa, NJ: Barnes and Noble, 1981); M. Pollack, "Male Homosexuality -- or Happiness in   the   Ghetto,"   in   *Western Sexuality: Practice and Precept in Past and Present Times*, ed. P. Ariès and A. Béjin, trans. A. Forster (Oxford: Blackwell,   1985), pp. 40-61.   On both biological and theological questions, see *Sex and Gender: A Theological and Scientific*

Inquiry,   ed. M. Schwartz, A. Moraczewski, and J. Monteleone
(St. Louis: Pope John Center, 1984), with the review by J.
R. Connery in *Theological Studies* 46 (1985), 373-74.

[11] For the poles of opinion, compare n. 13 below with L.
McCandlish, "Concerning Sexual Orientation," *Fidelity* 4, No.
6 (May 1985), 18-22 at 18. As I write this, a controversy
has broken out in New York City about the opening of the
country's first gay high school. As reported in the *Deseret
News*, 7 June 1985, one party to the controversy sees the
opening as "an act of compassion," while the executive
director of the United Federation of Teachers holds that
"it's unclear whether teens should be regarded as confirmed
homosexuals."

[12] G. Vidal, "Immortal Bird," *The New York Review of
Books* 32, No. 10 (June 1985), 5-10 at 6. Such a view,
although it could not have been expressed in these terms, is
arguably close to ancient (this much Boswell, *Christianity*,
p. 59, allows) and medieval attitudes, as we will see, and
also to the views of Michel Foucault (see below n. 16).
When finally in the late Middle Ages we find records like
the register of Jacques Fournier, Bishop of Pamiers, which
give detailed descriptions of the sexual practices of people
at many levels of society, we typically find those engaged
in sodomy also engaged in heterosexual relations, with
little or no conscious expression of gender preference. See
the very interesting partial translation in the Appendix to
M. Goodich, *The Unmentionable Vice: Homosexuality in the
Later Medieval Period* (Santa Barbara: ABC-Clio, Inc.,
1979), and E. L. Ladurie, *Montaillou: The Promised Land of
Error*, trans. B. Bray (New York: George Braziller, 1978),
pp. 144-49.   While using, inappropriately, the term "homosexuality," Ladurie says of the person for whom we have the
most evidence (pp. 148-49): "Arnaud seems not to have
regarded his own homosexuality as a form of real love, consciously expressed and organized. . . . Arnaud might have
experienced . . . feelings [of love] towards some of his
friends. But he never dreamed of mentioning them in words .
. . [to the Inquisitor]. It is more likely that on such
feelings Arnaud maintained a silence which amounted to a
cultural 'expression gap.' Pamiers was not pagan Greece,
and to talk of love in connection with sodomy, even if such
love had been 'objectively' real, would have been meaning-
less.
     So Arnaud's evidence presents homosexuality not as an
expression of real feeling, but as a cure for lust.   After
between a week and a fortnight of chastity, Arnaud claimed

he could not help throwing himself into some man's arms; except, of course, in the unusual case when a woman was available."

[13] Boswell, *Christianity*, p. 109.

[14] See above n. 5, esp. Payer, *Sex*, pp. 13-14, 40, 82, 135-36, 141-53, and below n. 46. For patristic understanding of fornication, see M. Foucault, "The Battle for Chastity," in *Western Sexuality*, ed. Ariès and Béjin, pp. 14-25 (with some material on homosexuality), and V. L. Bullough and J. Brundage, *Sexual Practices and the Medieval Church* (Buffalo, NY: Prometheus Books, 1982). esp. chs. 1-2 and index under "Fornication" and "Sodom and sodomy," with ch. 6.

[15] Payer, *Sex*, pp. 40-41. I write "most commonly" because Boswell, *Christianity*, pp. 202-04, notes some evidence of "sodomy" covering more than anal intercourse (not all the texts cited on these pages seem to me correctly interpreted). See also below n. 31. One must keep in mind the general perspective suggested by M. Foucault, *An Introduction*, Vol. I of *The History of Sexuality*, trans. R. Hurley (New York: Pantheon Books, 1978), pp. 18-19, who saw the "nakedness of the questions formulated by the confession manuals of the Middle Ages" as "little by little . . . veiled" in the modern period (see all of ch. 1 on how this perspective is to be related to the other long-term impressions Foucault had of the history of sexuality).

[16] More generally, "Strictly speaking, the medievals did not speak about sex as such": Payer, *Sex*, p. 14. Foucault, *Sexuality*, I, 43, sees the nineteenth century as the origin of basic categories unknown to the Middle Ages: "As defined by the ancient civil or canonical codes, sodomy was a category of forbidden acts; their perpetrator was nothing more than the juridical subject of them. The nineteenth-century homosexual became a personage . . . in addition to being a type of life . . . Homosexuality appeared as one of the forms of sexuality when it was transposed from the practice of sodomy onto a kind of interior androgyny, a hermaphrodism of the soul. The sodomite had been a temporary aberration; the homosexual was now a species." As has been noted above nn. 4 and 15, and will be noted below, nn. 60-62, 87, Boswell's book is basically flawed by the anachronistic claim to have found a "permanent gay orientation" in many writers and centuries for whom such categories of self-understanding were unavailable. As should become clear in the following

pages (see below n. 44), if we are looking for general classifications in the early middle ages, the basic one we find is the contrast between legitimate marital intercourse and "sins against nature," that is, everything else.

[17] Two of the best statements of the deficiencies, both methodological and substantial, of Boswell's book here are Wright, "Boswell," pp. 81-91, and J. F. Harvey, review in *Linacre Quarterly* (August 1981), 265-75, at 267-71, 274.

[18] See for instance G. R. Taylor, *Sex in History* (New York: Thames and Hudson, 1954), pp. 19-71. J. T. Noonan, Jr.'s *Contraception: A History of its Treatment by the Catholic Theologians and Canonists* (New York: The New American Library, 1965), receives some criticism for our period from Payer, *Sex*, p. 29, n. 60, and p. 34. Of the other histories of homosexuality (see above nn. 10 and 14), D. S. Bailey, *Homosexuality and the Western Christian Tradition* (London: Longmans, Green, 1955), was a pioneering study, and Goodich, *Unmentionable Vice*, only briefly mentions Anselm: see Sheehan, "Christianity," pp. 439-40.

[19] Boswell, *Christianity*, pp. 180-83. Compare Goodich, *Unmentionable Vice*, pp. 25-32.

[20] Boswell, *Christianity*, pp. 182-83, quoted by Payer, *Sex*, pp. 135-39, at 135, in his important "Appendix D: Homosexuality and the Penitentials."

[21] Payer, *Sex*, pp. 3-5, 52, 119. It should be pointed out that, because we have little idea of how strictly the penances prescribed by the penitentials were enforced, they are a better indication of what was held to be normative behavior, and of what was thought to be the frequency of specific sins, than they are of the actual frequency of sexual practices, or of tendencies for pastoral or other reasons to mitigate the severity of their enforcement. On commutation of penances, see Payer, pp. 13-14, 132. Foucault, *Sexuality*, I, 101, writing with a frustrating lack of chronological precision about a period apparently later that ours, gives some indirect evidence that a sin like sodomy could simultaneously be heavily punished when punished, but also commonly tolerated, at least within certain social groups, if not officially. In the middle of the eleventh century, of course, Peter Damian, *Liber Gomorrhianus* VII: *PL* CVL,167, had made a famous protest against the laxness of confession when sodomists confessed to sodomists: see Bailey, *Homosexuality*, pp. 111-15.

[22] Payer, *Sex*, pp. 5, 139. A new edition of these works by R. Kottje has been announced for *CC* CLVI.

[23] Payer, *Sex*, p. 8, and see also pp. 12 ff.

[24] Ibid., pp. 12-13; 41-42.

[25] Ibid., pp. 5, 10.

[26] Ibid., pp. 13-14, 129-34, at 13.

[27] Ibid., pp. 40-46, 125-26.

[28] Ibid., pp. 29, 41, 45-46, 57, 136, 143.

[29] Ibid., pp. 30-31, 41-42.

[30] Ibid., pp. 29-30, 41.

[31] Ibid., p. 41.

[32] Ibid., pp. 37-38, 43-44. Bullough, *Homosexuality*, p. 26, in showing that for Augustine "only in marriage with children as a hoped-for end . . . could sex be justified," (see below nn. 43-45) points out the logic that seems still to have underlaid the penitentials: "All other kinds of intercourse were evil. Some acts were less evil than others. Simple fornication was a sin, but since children might well result, it was much less a sin than sodomy or lesbianism."

[33] Payer, *Sex*, pp. 40-41, 108, is uncertain of the later meaning of the term. Compare Boswell, *Christianity*, pp. 76, 180, n. 38, and P. Ariès, "St. Paul and the Flesh," in *Western Sexuality*, ed. Ariès and Béjin, pp. 36-39.

[34] See n. 26 above, and Payer, *Sex*, pp. 41, 44, 135-39.

[35] Ibid., pp. 44, 46, 53.

[36] On this and the following, see ibid., pp. 53, 55-71.

[37] On this and the following, see ibid., pp. 71-114. On Burchard see my "Reference to the 'Ecclesia Primitiva' in the *Decretum* of Burchard of Worms," in *Proceedings of the Sixth International Congress of Medieval Canon Law*, ed. S. Kuttner and K. Pennington, Subsidia, Vol. VII of Monumenta iuris canonici, Series C (Città del Vaticano: Biblioteca Apostolica Vaticana, 1985), pp. 289-307.

[38] Payer, *Sex*, p. 73. A. Gauthier, "La sodomie dans le droit canonique médiéval," in *L'érotisme au moyen âge*, ed. B. Roy (Montréal: Aurore, 1977), pp. 111-22, is superficial.

[39] In addition to Payer, *Sex*, p. 73, see pp. 130, 136-37.

[40] Ibid., pp. 73, 75-77, 81-87.

[41] I have considered the question of St. Anselm's canonical knowledge briefly in "The Image of the First Community of Christians at Jerusalem in the Time of Lanfranc and Anselm," in *Les Mutations socio-culturelles au tournant des XIe-XIIe siècles*, SB II, pp. 341-53, at 344-45. For England in his day see F. Barlow, *The English Church 1066-1154* (London: Longman, 1979), pp. 82, 145-47, 152-53, 257, 293, 299. Ivo of Chartres, in addition to including canons against sodomy in his works, made protest against the consecration of a notorious sodomist as bishop of Orléans: Goodich, *Unmentionable Vice*, pp. 31-32, and Boswell, *Christianity*, pp. 213-15.

[42] On this and the following, see Payer, *Sex*, pp. 86-87, 120-22, at 86. Relevant here also is Barlow's observation, *English Church 1066-1154*, p. 146: "the law concerning penance as stated in the collections was entirely unsuited to the eleventh-century church, where all men were considered to be Christian and discipline had been relaxed in order to hold the weakest brother within the community." Although Payer has collected too much evidence to say that the penitential law was "entirely unsuited," Barlow draws attention to an important fact. To the extent that we have knowledge of this (see above n. 21), we note that there had long been a tendency to commute the harsh penances originating in the penitential literature. This affected all sins. One can not therefore speak of any particular sin, as sodomy, being more tolerated, but one can say that while the old guides were still used in defining sin, in a degree we can no longer precisely measure, their assignment of penance was commonly modified.

[43] Payer, *Sex*, pp. 3-4, 115, at 115. There is a wealth of information on the patristic period in *Etica sessuale e matrimonio nel cristianesimo delle origini*, ed. R. Cantalamessa (Milan: Vita e pensiero, 1976).

[44] Wright, "Boswell," p. 89, with reference to Coleman, *Christian Attitudes*. See also Sheehan, "Christianity," pp.

440, 443. Boswell, *Christianity*, does of course make scattered comments, as at p. 202.

[45] Payer, *Sex*, p. 115. This is not to say that the understanding of "sins against nature" of theological writers (on the development of which see Brundage, "Sin against Nature," in Bullough and Brundage, *Medieval Church*) was commonly found among the faithful: J.-L. Flandrin, *Le Sexe et l'Occident: Evolutions des attitudes et des comportements* (Paris: Editions du Seuil, 1981), pp. 112ff. Cf. Foucault, *Sexuality*, I, 37-39. Foucault, p. 121, in writing of a much later period says of the working classes that "it is unlikely that the Christian technology of the flesh ever had any importance for them." Though this is undoubtedly an exaggeration, what Foucault shows for the modern period, that techniques for channelling sex first affected the upper classes, is undoubtedly true of the early Middle Ages also. In the West the working out of the logical implications of Christianity in regard to its view of marriage was done by an overwhelmingly clerical-monastic elite, who gradually insinuated their views into the life of the laity. This indeed is a useful perspective for viewing Anselm's work in attacking sodomy through the legislation of the Council at Westminster. What is written here and in the following sentences of the text is meant to take account of the variety of interpretation of sexual matters within the various Christian traditions. Obviously a writer like Augustine left his particular impress on the West: Bullough and Brundage, *Medieval Church*, pp. XI, 1.

[46] The evidence Payer, *Sex*, pp. 44-46, 125-26, 132-33, presents on bestiality suggests that it was quite common, and that there was considerable variation within the penitentials themselves about the severity of the penances to be imposed. See pp. 115, 121, on the missionary enterprise, and Bullough and Brundage, *Medieval Church*, pp. 20-21, on the sexual practices of the Germanic peoples and 72-85, for Scandinavia. R. Manselli, "Vie familiale et éthique sexuelle dans les pénitentiels," in *Famille et parenté dans l'occident médiéval*, ed. G. Duby and J. Le Goff, Collection de l'école française de Rome, No. 30 (Rome: Ecole française de Rome, 1977), pp. 362-78, at 368, 377-78, notes ways in which Christianity introduced new sexual ideas to the convert peoples, and on the larger point writes: "Dans l'optique des pénitentiels, le problème dominant de l'éthique sexuelle devient donc surtout la *fornicatio*, c'est-à-dire le problème de l'illégitimité de tout acte sexuel accompli en dehors du mariage, et, à plus forte raison,

de toutes déviations des manières naturelles de la sexu-
alité." Ladurie, *Montaillou*, as at pp. 150-78, gives much
evidence of country dwellers (including priests) still in
the thirteenth and fourteenth centuries neither accepting
nor practicing a full Christian sexual code.

⁴⁷See below n. 92. In regard to Boswell's comment on
the legislation enacted under Edgar against "homosexuality,"
Christianity, p. 215, n. 24, the complicated question of the
transmission of the canons of the Council of Ancyra (see
Boswell, pp. 178-79, 183, etc.), is further clarified by
Payer, *Sex*, index under "councils."

⁴⁸See below nn. 107, 116 ff. The central document here
is *Epistola 257*: Schmitt IV,169-70. As is the convention,
I will cite this work by the volume numbers of the original
edition. Boswell does not use this standard edition in discussing Anselm. The letter has also been edited from Lambeth
Palace, MS. 59, in *Councils and Synods*, ed. Whitelock,
Brett, and Brooke, I, Part II, pp. 687-88. On Anselm's letters see W. Fröhlich, "The Genesis of the Collections of St.
Anselm's Letters," *The American Benedictine Review* 35
(1984), 249-66. In general on the penitential system in
England in Anselm's day, see Barlow, *English Church
1066-1154*, pp. 132-40, 146ff.

⁴⁹Boswell, *Christianity*, pp. 215-16, at 216 (and see
above n. 3). Boswell misquotes R. W. Southern, *Medieval
Humanism* (New York: Harper and Row, 1970), p. 13.

⁵⁰Boswell, *Christianity*, p. 218.

⁵¹Ibid.

⁵²Ibid., giving references.

⁵³Ibid., p. 219.

⁵⁴*Epistola 84*: Schmitt III,208-09; trans. Boswell,
Christianity, p. 219, who, because he does not use the
critical edition of Schmitt, gives the addressee as "Gilbert" and numbers the letters following Migne.

⁵⁵Boswell, *Christianity*, pp. 219-20. Cf. now *Medieval
Latin Poems of Male Love and Friendship*, trans. T. Stehling
(New York: Garland Publishers, 1984).

⁵⁶Boswell, *Christianity*, pp. 219ff.

[57] Ibid., p. 42. Boswell's point is that one can not conclude from the sexual *actions* of a given person as to his or her sexual *orientation*. Boswell seems to me to remain consistent in this point of view in the sense that he does not attempt to quantify sexual activity in order to deduce sexual orientation, or to consider only people known to be sexually active: his goal is to discover the sexual orientation of his subjects. Perhaps Linehan, "Growing hostile to gays," p. 73 (all further references to Linehan are to this page), does not quite understand this. Yet, if we, while recognizing that Linehan here may be writing at cross-purposes, take him to mean Boswell's "method" involves a kind of highly subjective enumeration, not of evidence of sexual activity but of claimed sexual orientation, in which on the basis of sufficient, or sufficiently intense, documentation, the homo- is separated from the heterosexual, Linehan has a point. Initially clearer is the review by Harvey, *Linacre Quarterly* (August, 1981), 266, but there is a confusion similar to Linehan's in the discussion of Paulinus of Nola, p. 269, and on p. 271.

[58] Boswell, *Christianity*, p. 47, slightly misquoted by Linehan.

[59] R. W. Southern, *St. Anselm and his Biographer* (Cambridge: Cambridge Univ. Press, 1963), p. 74; Thomas, "Rescuing Homosexual History," p. 29. At one point Linehan seems again (see above n. 57) to misunderstand Boswell's analysis, for he criticizes him for not citing B. P. McGuire's conclusion in "Love, Friendship and Sex in the Eleventh Century: The Experience of Anselm," *Studia Theologica* 28 (1974), 111-52, that, in Linehan's words, "there is no evidence of Anselm's ever having given physical expression to his affections." As noted above in the text before n. 6, Boswell does not claim that Anselm engaged in homosexual activity.

[60] Wright, "Boswell," p. 91.

[61] The translation of the *Symposium* from which the phrases quoted are taken is that of W. R. Lamb (London: William Heinemann, 1932), on which see V. L. Bullough, *Sexual Variance in Society and History* (New York: John Wiley and Sons, 1976), pp. 15-16. Plato's perhaps facetious treatment of sexual preference in this passage is not typical of the ancient world: see above n. 12, and, for the Greeks, K. Dover, *Greek Homosexuality* (Cambridge, MA: Harvard Univ. Press, 1978), at pp. 11-13, 153-68, on Plato.

The twelfth century poem which begins "A perverse custom   it
is   to   prefer   boys   to   girls" (Boswell, *Christianity*, pp.
389-92) nicely illustrates the difficulties in finding
gender preference even in likely places. What follows this
promising line is (condemnation of) preference for one male
submitting to another. This seems to reflect more preference for a specific sexual act, than for one's own gender.
On the other hand the poem of Marbod of Rennes which Boswell, pp. 248-49, 370, titles "An Argument against Romance"
seems to me to express a "gay" sensibility that satisfies
his definition. The "Argument" of this poem is not clear in
either Boswell's discussion of it, or in his partial translation: see, however, the same poem in Stehling, *Medieval
Latin Poems*, no. 47, pp. 32-35. A girl desires Marbod. The
boy who sets Marbod on fire loves this girl. She spurns the
boy, and is rejected by Marbod. As a younger man Marbod
would have been aroused by the girl. But as long as his
"madness grows (presumably his desire for the boy)," he must
reject the girl. "The kindling of this new vice kills the
other's power." We seem to have a man formerly heterosexu-
ally indulgent who from desire for a boy has lost his desire
for girls. All this, however, is the thought world of one
poem, and in another poem (Boswell, p. 248, n. 19), Marbod
says that now the embraces of both sexes have become unap-
pealing, and repents of what we would call active bisexu-
ality. Nevertheless, if we find a "gay" sensibility in
Anselm's day at all, it would be in the former poem.

[62] See above n. 61. The very interesting, but difficult
to interpret, lines from Bernard of Cluny cited as no. 75 in
Stehling, *Medieval Latin Poems*, both suggest conscious gay
preference (see also nos. 80, 88, 114), and that sodomites
are a kind of hermaphrodite (see also no. 79, and above n.
16).   In no. 119 it is anachronistic to translate *corrigere
sodomita* as "curb your homosexuality." We will not analyze
further the materials after Anselm's day gathered by Boswell
and Stehling.

[63] Thomas, "Rescuing Homosexual History," p. 29, citing,
with some alteration, Southern, *Anselm*, pp. 73-74. The
comments in the following sentences were suggested by the
address "St. Anselm's *Weltbild* as Conveyed in his Letters,"
by W. Fröhlich, delivered at the Fifth International St.
Anselm Conference, Villanova University, Sept. 16-21, 1985.
For friendship with laymen, see J. F. A. Mason, "Saint
Anselm's Relations with Laymen: Selected Letters," *SB* I,
pp. 547-60, esp. 559-60. J. Leclercq, *Monks and Love in
Twelfth-Century France* (Oxford: Clarendon Press, 1979), pp.

8-26, associates "old monasticism" or the Black monks with oblate recruitment and "new monasticism" with adult recruitment. Bec and Anselm practiced both (see below nn. 73-76), and do not easily fit into this schema, but Leclercq, p. 104, noting that Anselm uses few metaphors drawn from sexual relations (adultery, marriage, etc.), holds that this is because his audience had been brought up in the cloister instead of the world. M. Chibnall, *The World of Orderic Vitalis* (Oxford: Clarendon Press, 1984), p. 73, suggests a mixed audience of *nutriti* and *conversi*.

[64] G. R. Evans, *A Concordance of the Works of St. Anselm*, 4 vols. (Millwood, NY: Kraus International Publications, 1984). In addition to having gone over Anselm's entire corpus for earlier studies, I have gone through Evans' *Concordance* looking for medieval words for homosexual activities, as suggested by the studies in the present article, and by works like J. N. Adams, *The Latin Sexual Vocabulary* (London: Duckworth, 1982).

[65] McGuire, "Love, friendship and sex," p. 112, gives up any claim to be "remotely scientific."

[66] McGuire, ibid., pp. 113-15, says at p. 113, "However trite it may sound, the Oedipus complex lies just below the surface of Eadmer's narration."

[67] Ibid., pp. 115-16, at 116.

[68] Ibid., pp. 115-17.

[69] Southern, *Anselm*, p. 46; McGuire, "Love, friendship and sex," p. 117. See *Meditatio 2*: Schmitt III, 80-83; see also *The Prayers and Meditations of Saint Anselm*, trans. B. Ward (Harmondsworth: Penguin Books, 1973), pp. 225-29.

[70] Ward, trans., *The Prayers*, pp. 225-26. Leclercq, *Monks and Love*, pp. 45-47, stresses that this Meditation uses the language of adultery, the soul having been seduced away from God. This makes it unlikely that it refers to some "homosexual" experience in Anselm's life.

[71] McGuire, "Love, friendship and sex," p. 119. If there had been some indiscretion, this could explain Anselm's later zeal (see n. 103ff. below) in attacking effeminacy and sodomy: others were not to make the mistake he had.

[72] Ibid., p. 119.

[73] Ibid., p. 121; see also pp. 121-27. McGuire uses the expressions "one great love of his life," and "son-disciple-lover."

[74] Ibid., pp. 121, 123, 127; *Vita Anselmi* I,10: Southern, p. 17. Eadmer was generally concerned to enhance Anselm's reputation, and his acount is "loving and partisan . . . designed to defend him against criticism": Barlow, *English Church 1066-1154*, p. 23.

[75] *Vita Anselmi* I,10: Southern, pp. 16-20.

[76] Ibid.: Southern, p. 17.

[77] McGuire, "Love, friendship and sex," pp. 127ff.

[78] Ibid., at p. 131. McGuire does not point out that the *Rule of St. Benedict*, 2,16-22, taught "the abbot should avoid all favoritism in the monastery. He is not to love one more than another unless he finds someone better in good actions and obedience. . . . the abbot is to show equal love to everyone and apply the same discipline to all according to their merits." See *The Rule of St. Benedict*, ed. and trans. T. Fry (Collegeville, MN: The Liturgical Press, 1981), pp. 174-75. Anselm, even before becoming an abbot, had perhaps begun to see some wisdom in this. The subject of "peculiar friendships" is of course widely discussed in subsequent twelfth century monastic literature.

[79] McGuire, "Love, friendship and sex," p. 143.

[80] Ibid., p. 145. On the "dearest mothers" (dependent religious) living under the protection of Bec, see Chibnall, *World of Orderic Vitalis*, p. 80.

[81] McGuire, "Love, friendship and sex," p. 145.

[82] Ibid., p. 146.

[83] *Vita Anselmi* I,11: Southern, p. 20; not quite correctly described by McGuire, "Love, friendship and sex," p. 147, as saying that "Anselm preferred to be with young men."

[84] *Vita Anselmi* I,14: Southern, pp. 23-24; McGuire, "Love, friendship and sex," p. 147.

[85] McGuire, "Love, friendship and sex," pp. 147-49.

[86] Ibid., p. 149.

[87] Thus Bailey, *Homosexuality*, p. 124, unaware of the issues discussed in the present study, takes the Council at Westminster of 1102 to be referring to "homosexual offences." McGuire, "Love, friendship and sex," p. 147, does the same. Boswell, *Christianity*, p. 215, says the Council designates "homosexual behavior as sinful." Brundage, "Sin against Nature," in Bullough and Brundage, *Medieval Church*, pp. 62-63, notes that because the Council did not define sodomy, it is not clear that the average Englishman would have understood what this term entailed. It is premature to judge whether "sodomy" around 1100 long had been or only just was becoming "that utterly confused category" (Foucault, *Sexuality*, I, 101) which it was to remain in the modern period. We have noted above, n. 15, that there is at least limited early medieval evidence of "sodomy" covering more than anal intercourse, although the penitentials almost always distinguish the various acts. There also had been ambiguity in patristic reference to sodomy. Perhaps around 1100 the specificity of the early medieval penitentials, which had likely always been more precise than other kinds of evidence, was being diluted by the process in which the concrete act of "sodomy" would, over many centuries, become a catch-all term for the various forms of homosexual act, and, finally, one synonym for "homosexuality." The point cannot be established without much more philological study, and is almost hopelessly complicated by the absence of many examples of non-learned or non-clerical usage from the early Middle Ages. Perhaps for the non-learned, the concept of "sodomy" had been either foreign or confused across the centuries. Indeed the confusion Foucault finds in the modern period may be one result of the availability of increasing amounts of non-clerical evidence, but Brundage has shown that there is much ambiguity and confusion among the legal and theological writers themselves from the twelfth century, and among the late medieval penitential writers, as to how sodomy was to be defined: Bullough and Brundage, *Medieval Church*, pp. 61-71 (one could argue that when writers like Albert the Great and Jean Gerson defined sodomy as *masculi cum masculo, vel foeminae cum foemina*, the word was on its way to becoming the modern "homosexuality"). See also p. 208, and below n. 92.

[88] Boswell, *Christianity*, pp. 211-16, 365-66. In response to my review of Boswell, I received a letter of August 20, 1981, from the Rev. Donald Hendricks, taking

exception to Boswell's handling and interpretation of Latin
texts at a number of points. In regard to Leo IX's *Ad splendidum nitentis*, Fr. Hendricks writes: "As Boswell points
out   in   his footnotes, this   matter   has   been previously
treated by Mann, Bailey, and McNeil. When I had read them,
it was plain that the first two had read the document in the
Latin, but that McNeil only knew it from Mann.   If you check
Mann, you will see that he has the old habit of leaving tags
of Latin (from the document translated) in parentheses in
the   translation.   This led McNeil to suppose that the words
Nos humanius agentes were the title of the document.   On
page 365 of Boswell, the same mistake occurs.   The correct
citation is *Ad splendidum nitentis* (at the end of the first
sentence   in B.'s translation: *Nos humanius agentes* appears
on the fifteenth line on page 366.) . . ."   Although not
directly related to this paper, perhaps it would be useful
to record here Fr. Hendricks' further correction: ". . .
on page 236, he describes God as simply laughing at homosexuality and in the footnote points out that the phrase seems
original to the author. . . . the phrase is a quote from the
Vulgate of the 2nd Psalm. . . ."

[89] *Epistola 257*:   Schmitt IV,170; Boswell, *Christianity*,
p. 215.

[90] Boswell, *Christianity*, p. 215, and above n. 3.   When
Boswell speaks of "homosexuality" instead of "sodomy," I
repeat his terminology in describing his position.

[91] Ibid., p. 215, n. 27, and p. 216.

[92] There   are   surveys of early medieval legislation, and
of some of the literary sources, in Boswell, *Christianity*,
pp. 169ff., and Goodich, *Unmentionable Vice*, pp. 71-75.   The
circle of glossators around Anselm of Laon described sodomy
as a sacrilege for which the death penalty was appropriate:
Goodich, pp. 7, 35-39.   Further afield, Ulrich of Imola (ca.
1060) argued for the gravity of sodomy: Goodich, pp. 23-24;
see above n. 21.   Writing in 1115 very antagonistically
against dualist heretics, Guibert of Nogent, *De vita sua*
III,17:   ed. E. R. Labande (Paris: Belles Lettres, 1981),
p. 428; trans. in J. F. Benton, *Self and Society in Medieval
France: The Memoirs of Abbot Guibert of Nogent* (New York:
Harper, 1970), p. 212, says that "men are known to lie with
men and women with women . . ." See above n. 87.   Several
of the poems of the late eleventh and early twelfth centuries in Stehling, *Medieval Latin Poems* (see nos. 48-49, 65),
condemn sodomy.   The late medieval evidence (largely

Cathar), gathered by Ladurie (above n. 46), suggests not simply a chasm between official teaching and actual practice, but an ignorance of Church teaching. There had been an instance under Lanfranc when the allegation of widespread sodomy among his own monks at Canterbury had been made: Barlow, *English Church 1066-1154*, p. 191; see also p. 259, n. 235.

⁹³Orderic Vitalis, *Historia ecclesiastica* VIII,4 and 10; X,2 and 17; XI,17: ed. M. Chibnall, *The Ecclesiastical History of Orderic Vitalis* (Oxford: Clarendon Press, 1969-80), IV, 146, 188-92; V, 202, 300; VI, 62-66, discussed by Bailey, *Homosexuality*, pp. 122ff., and Boswell, *Christianity*, pp. 229-30, 281, n. 40, with references to other later medieval historians who make similar charges. See also William of Malmesbury, *De gestis pontificum Anglorum*: ed. N. E. S. A. Hamilton (London: Rolls Series, 1870), p. 79. Boswell's reference to the two volume work of E. A. Freeman, *The Reign of William Rufus*, (Oxford, 1882; rp. New York: AMS Press, 1970), presumably also should refer to I, 158-59. It is not clear whether Boswell has made an independent survey of the evidence (see *Christianity*, p. 229, n. 70, and p. 230, nn. 72, 75), but Appendix G of Freeman's study, on which he relies, does not contain the passage from Eadmer discussed below in n. 109.

⁹⁴Boswell, *Christianity*, p. 229. For all questions on the composition and character of Orderic's work, see Chibnall, *World of Orderic Vitalis*, as at pp. 36-40, 169-220. It is common to note the wide network on which Orderic depended for his information: H. Wolker, *Orderic Vitalis: Ein Beitrag zur kluniazenischen Geschichtschreibung* (Wiesbaden: Franz Steiner Verlag, 1955), esp. Part IV. Wolker too singlemindedly makes Orderic into a Cluniac historian.

⁹⁵Boswell does not consider the central evidence in Eadmer's account either in his discussion of Anselm or of the Council at Westminster of 1102, and thus his reference, *Christianity*, p. 230, n. 75, is misleading. For Eadmer, see below nn. 103, 109, 115, 120, 122, 127.

⁹⁶*Historia ecclesiastica* VIII,4: Chibnall IV,146-47: "Inter haec impune procedebat petulans illecebra molles flammisque cremandos turpiter fedabat uenus sodomestica. . . ." Note that the difficult to interpret word *molles* (see above n. 33 and below n. 97) is here clearly used in the context of sodomy; as usual, Orderic stresses the "effeminate" aspect of sodomy. The passage goes on to speak of a

parallel open practice of adultery in these difficult times.
Boswell, *Christianity*, p. 230, n. 71 does not seem to understand the Latin of this passage and what follows in his comment: ". . . in 8.4 he [Orderic] refers to 'the Venus of
Sodom' but seems to clarify it by explaining further that
'maritalem thorum publice polluebant adulteria.' It would
be difficult to demonstrate that 'adulterium' here refers to
homosexuality." Indeed, "adulterium" in what follows refers
to adultery, but as reference to Chibnall's edition and
translation would have made clear for Boswell (who again
does not use the best edition of the author under study), as
another activity parallel to sodomy that showed the lawless-
ness of the times. For the political background, and the
desire at Saint-Evroult, Orderic's monastery, for peace, see
Chibnall, *World of Orderic*, as at pp. 27-28, 31-33, 117-19,
132-45.

     [97] *Historia ecclesiastica* VIII,10:   Chibnall IV,186-89.
The Latin emphasizes the association of effeminacy with sodomy: "Tunc effeminati passim in orbe dominabantur indisci-
plinate debachabantur sodomiticisque spurciciis foedi catamitae flammis urendi turpiter abutebantur." Boswell, *Christianity*, pp. 229-30, n. 71, states that the use of "the
feminine gender of catamite is provocative: it is invari-
ably masculine in Latin." This is not so; see the three
lines of poem 36 (eleventh century) given by Stehling,
Medieval Latin Poems, p. 22: "Propagatur quae latebat
discincta luxuria;/ molles sibi subjugavit Venus sodomestica;/ pro abusu catamitae mulier fit vacua." Although Boswell, p. 230, is correct in stating in regard to these
monastic writers' objections to the beards popular at the
court that beards "could hardly be considered 'effeminate,'"
see the somewhat different approach offered below in nn.
106ff.

     [98] *Historia ecclesiastica* VIII,10:   Chibnall IV,188-89:
"Femineam mollitiem petulans iuuentus amplectitur," again
may have overtones of the "softness" of playing the passive
role in sodomy (see above n. 96), but only explicitly refers
to the decadence of court life (and passes immediately to an
accusation of heterosexual lewdness). A further reference
in the same passage to shaving the front part of the head,
but letting the back grow very long "like harlots," may also
emphasize the effeminacy of the youth, but may rather emphasize their lust. This passage seems at once to criticize
effeminacy and heterosexual lust, long hair and beards, in
the manner more clearly present below in n. 106.

[99]*Historia ecclesiastica* VIII,10:   Chibnall IV,190–93.

[100]Trans. *Jerusalem Bible* (Garden City, NY: Doubleday, 1966).   The   Pauline   text is cited in the passage discussed below n. 106.   See for this and the following the very useful   introduction on beards in the Middle Ages by G. Constable to Burchard, *Apologia de barbis*:   ed. R. H. C.   Huygens, *Apologiae   Duae*,   *CC* LXII,45–130, at 78–79, 85–88, 103, 111, 114.   It is clear from the texts gathered by Constable that, whatever   the   specific historical circumstances of Orderic, Anselm, and Eadmer, the prejudices   they   expressed   against long   hair   and   beards were widespread.   See also Stehling, *Medieval Latin Poems*, p. xxii, and   Bullough,   *Sexual Variance*, pp. 178–79, with p. 64, n. 57, on the antiquity of the distaste for passivity, and more generally pp. 74–89, on the Jewish   contribution   to   Western sexual attitudes (although the discussion of homosexuality is   unfortunately   based   on Bailey), and p. 179, for the interpretation of the condemnation of the "effeminate" in 1 Co 6:9 (see above   n.   33   and Boswell,   *Christianity*,   pp. 103–14, 106–07, 337–41, 346–49, 353).

[101]For both the specific point and the   larger   context, see C. Walker Bynum, "Fast, Feast, and Flesh: The Religious Significance of Food to Medieval Women," *Representations* 11 (Summer, 1985), 1–25, here at 10, with reference to G. Duby, *The Knight, the Lady and the Priest: The Making   of   Modern Marriage   in   Medieval   France*,   trans.   B.   Bray (New York: Pantheon Books, 1983), pp. 72, 106.   See   also   V.   L.   Bullough,   *The   Subordinate Sex: A History of Attitudes Toward Women* (Urbana, IL: Univ. of Illinois Press,   1973),   as   at pp.   77–96, for the ancient background, and Bullough, *Sexual Variance*, pp. 168–69.   Bynum, as at pp. 11–16, reminds us of other ways in which women were commonly viewed, above all as sexual beings, and as more physical than spiritual, and such associations seem in the passage under discussion and others following to be part of the disgust felt   with   the   effeminate,   whose   sexuality and physicality are constantly stressed.   Nevertheless, these associations do not   seem   as important as those in which the effeminate symbolize the bad order of the times, the loss of manly political control.

[102]John Chrysostom, *Homiliae in Matthaeum* LXXIII,3:   PG LVIII,676–77,   with   Bullough and Brundage, *Medieval Church*, p. 18.   Bullough's   description   of   "Transvestism   in   the Middle   Ages" in the same volume develops the parallel argument (pp. 43–44), that "Western attitudes towards transvestism   have   been   strongly influenced by status concepts about

the role of the sexes." The hostility to the dress of the
effeminates in the text under discussion (above n. 97) might
be taken as a form of hostility to transvestism: the effeminates were slipping toward transvestism, and thus endan-
gering their masculinity.

[103]*Historia novorum*, p. 48; trans. G. Bosanquet,
Eadmer's History of Recent Events in England (London: The
Cresset Press, 1964), p. 49. William of Malmesbury, *Gesta
regum anglorum* IV, 314: ed. W. Stubbs (London: Rolls
Series, 1889), II, pp. 369-70, gives a similar account, saying that young men at William's court were to imitate female
softness of body, and walked around in the nude with a special gait.

[104]*Historia ecclesiastica* X,2: Chibnall V,202-03.

[105]Ibid., X,17: Chibnall V,300-01. See above nn. 33,
96, 98.

[106]*Historia ecclesiastica* XI,17: Chibnall VI,60-67, at
64-67. This is one of the passages discussed by Constable,
Apologiae Duae, p. 59, n. 57, and pp. 67, 96. At p. 51,
Constable remarks of Alan of Lille's attitude toward hair:
"It was beautiful but needed to be controlled. The beard
was manly. . . but it had to be 'corrected' at times by the
razor." Although the symbolism of hair varied from author
to author, this was a common idea. At p. 59, n. 57, Constable observes: "Orderic and Serlo of Séez . . . clearly
associated beards with lust." Thus long beards "uncor-
rected" by the razor for them synbolized lust unbridled. At
p. 65, Constable finds quite a different symbolism in the
Bayeux Tapestry portrayal of Edward the Confessor with a
long beard , construing it ". . . doubtless as a mark of
his wisdom and dignity as well as of his age," and, at p.
95, he states that by the second half of the eleventh century "many if not most" men in France and England shaved.
See also pp. 99-102, and below n. 113. Needless to say (but
see above n. 97), there need be no formal logic to the signs
chosen for sexual license, weakness, and effeminacy. A man
(whether or not there is substance to the accusation) may be
accused at once of harlotry, that is, of heterosexual
offence, and of effeminacy and/or sodomy. I am not claiming
that the main category being offended against is an always
consciously defended "masculinity," but rather that in the
conscious attack on a whole range of evils, writers like
Orderic defend the goods they believe in, such as good government, in ways which reveal a strong distaste for both

lust and "effeminateness" in men, hyper- and deficient masculinity.

[107]*Historia ecclesiastica* XI,17: Chibnall VI,66-67.
Orderic liked to craft the speeches he relates, so we should
not believe we have here the actual words spoken. See Chibnall, *World of Orderic*, pp. 196-201.

[108]Throughout his *Monks on Marriage: A Twelfth-Century
View* (New York: The Seabury Press, 1982), J. Leclercq notes
medieval stress on moderation and discipline in love and
loving. On p. 97 he says that for Bernard of Clairvaux "Mary
Magdalen is a . . . model of conversion from savage, uncontrolled love to faithful bridal love."

[109]*Historia novorum*, pp. 48-49; trans. Bosanquet, pp.
49-50.

[110]*Historia ecclesiastica* IX,3: Chibnall V,22-23 , with
VI,66, n. 1. Constable, *Apologiae Duae*, pp. 96-97, gives
some additional twelfth century evidence of the personal
condemnation of long hair.

[111]F. Barlow, *William Rufus* (Berkeley: Univ. of
California Press, 1983), index under "homosexuality," and
English Church 1066-1154, pp. 66-67, 70, 128-29, 287-88,
297. Examination of these books will show that Boswell's
discussion of Rufus examines only a fraction of the evidence. In *English Church 1066-1154*, p. 297, Barlow suggests, with reference to Anselm's *Epistola 210*, that
Anselm's exile of 1098 was caused in part by Rufus'
"encouragement of sodomy." In *Epistola 210*: Schmitt
IV,105-07, there is no specific mention of sodomy.

[112]See *Le De officiis ecclesiasticis de Jean
d'Avranches, Archevêque de Rouen (1067-1079)*, ed. R. Delamare (Paris: A. Picard, 1923), pp. xxxviii-xxxix and 4, on
John's general dependence on Amalarius, and also his specific dependence in this passage, and the unpaginated introduction for dating. Amalarius' *De officiis* was present in a
number of Norman monasteries, and was still being read and
modified into the twelfth century: Chibnall, *World of
Orderic Vitalis*, pp. 87-89.

[113]*De officiis ecclesiasticis*: Delamare, p. 4. Gregory
the Great had stated in the *Moralia* II,52, that "To shave
the head is . . . to cut superfluous thoughts from the

mind," and Bruno of Segni (d.1123) held that a beard was a sign of idleness and vanity; cf. Constable, *Apologiae Duae*, 69-79, discussing Isidore of Seville, Amalarius, and others (but not John of Avranches). See above n. 106.

[114] *De officiis ecclesiasticis*:   Delamare, unpaginated Introduction and p. xxxi (listing of *De officiis* in Rouen chapter library catalogue from 1111-28), and p. xlvff.

[115] Canon 24, *Councils and Synods* I, Part II: Whitelock, Brett, and Brooke, pp. 677-78; recorded by Eadmer, *Historia novorum*, p. 143; trans. Bosanquet, p. 151, from which this translation is taken. Canon 13 deals with the *corona* of clerics, but Canon 24 occurs in a series dealing with laymen.

[116] *Councils and Synods*, I, Part II: Whitelock, Brett, and Brooke, p. 678, n. 1.

[117] *Epistola 257*:   Schmitt IV,170:   De iis qui tonderi nolunt, dictum est, ut ecclesiam non ingrederentur; non tamen praeceptum est, ut, si ingrederentur, cessarent sacerdotes, sed tantum annuntiarent illis quia contra deum et ad damnationem suam ingrediuntur.

[118] *Historia ecclesiastica*:   Chibnall VI,66, n. 1.

[119] Barlow, *English Church 1066-1154*, p. 76.

[120] *Historia novorum*, pp. 143-44; trans. Bosanquet, p. 152.

[121] For background and another translation of the decisions on sodomy, see Bailey, *Homosexuality*, pp. 124-25. More recent accounts are found in McGuire, "Love, friendship and sex," pp. 147-49; M. Brett, The *English Church under Henry I* (Oxford: Univ. Press, 1975), pp. 76-79; Barlow, *English Church 1066-1154*, pp. 122, 128-29; and, along with the texts, in *Councils and Synods*, I, Part II: Whitelock, Brett, and Brooke, pp. 668-89. Anselm's *Epistola 257*: Schmitt IV,169, opens with a description of the problems with the publishing of the conciliar acts.

[122] *Historia novorum*, p. 144; trans. Bosanquet, p. 152. Some manuscripts of William of Malmesbury's *De gestis pontificum Anglorum*: Hamilton, p. 121, n. 1, follow the presentation of the decrees from Westminster with the statement:

"Illud sane praeceptum de Sodomitis omni Dominico die excommunicandis, Anselmus ipse postea, quibusdam rationabilibus exigentibus causis, immutavit."

[123] *Epistola 257*: Schmitt IV,169-70: De illis qui ante excommunicationem, vel post excommunicationem nescientes eam factam, sodomitico peccato peccaverunt. . . . The translation is from Bailey, *Homosexuality*, p. 125.

[124] Cf. *Councils and Synods*, I, Part II: Whitelock, Brett, and Brooke, p. 670, with Boswell, *Christianity*, pp. 215-16.

[125] *Councils and Synods*, I, Part II: Whitelock, Brett, and Brooke, p. 670. Cf. Barlow, *English Church 1066-1154*, p. 129.

[126] C. R. Cheney, "Legislation of the Medieval English Church, Part I," *English Historical Review* 50 (1935), 203, n. 1, cites David Wilkins, *Concilia* (1737), i. 382 (= C. R. Cheney, *The English Church and its Laws 12th-14th Centuries* [London: Variorum Reprints, 1982], No. I). Presumably this means that Anselm had taken a copy of the conciliar decisions with him to Rome, and then perhaps into exile. Pages 208 and 210 of this article discuss the drafting and circulation of the acts of the Council at Westminster of 1102. Cheney, p. 208, n. 2, suggests that the "purpose of the council which Anselm announced to the archbishop of York for Christmas 1103" may have been to prepare the new recension of the Acts of Westminster of 1102, but, if so, this was aborted by Anselm's departure from England after Easter 1103.

[127] *Historia novorum*, p. 214; trans. Bosanquet, p. 229.

[128] McGuire, "Love, friendship and sex," p. 149.

[129] For the dating of the *Historia novorum*, see the Foreword by R. W. Southern to trans. Bosanquet, p. xi.

Ernulf of Rochester and the Problem of Remembrance

P. J. Cramer

The circle of men who came into contact with Anselm at one time or another made up a diverse group: Gilbert Crispin, whose theological response to gentile and Jew shows more sensitivity than much of the later work on the same theme; the monk Rodulfus, whose identity remains an enigma, and who made it his task to interpret some of the salient thoughts of his master in a more practical light; and then Eadmer, the historian and biographer, and Elmer, and others who were connected with the recording of Anselm's thoughts in the *Dicta*, the *De moribus* and so forth.[1] It is the purpose of this paper to consider the figure of Ernulf of Rochester, who was at both Bec and Canterbury with St. Anselm, and to trace some aspects of the history of juridical and ethical ideas as they emerge from the period.[2]

The context is not an easy one to make clear. The history of ideas in and about law operates not only on the level of explicit philosophical thought, but has to be sought out from various approaches and activities oblique to it; the evolution of moral awareness is still less refractible. Perhaps it is enough for the time being to try and sketch as much as can be seen on the surface, and to notice that over this period of the eleventh and twelfth centuries, there begins to develop in certain areas of discourse a lucid notion of man as a moral and juridical agent, a notion quite distinct from the earlier ethic of submission and obedience prevailing in monastic culture. In his admittedly modest letters, one on some problems raised in the new theology of the eucharist, the other on a case in the canon law of marriage, Ernulf nonetheless provides an insight into this novelty of perception.

Ernulf's canonical letter is a reply to bishop Walkelin of Winchester, who has asked whether a woman who has committed adultery with her stepson, should be separated from her husband by ecclesiastical judgement.[3] The argument which follows from Ernulf is interesting for a number of reasons: for the language of rhetoric it uses, for the method of dialectic, and for the type of source material, legal and patristic and biblical, which it rests on. In all these characteristics, it has moved beyond the legal procedure of the earlier period, in which the predominant method was not discussion, or opposition and juxtaposition of texts, but invocation and direct application of them to circumstance. Where once God had intervened in person, he was

now represented, as it were, in the course of the argument.
This is the difference between the law-codes of the Anglo-
Saxons and the Franks, in which the law is regarded as the
static deposit of God's vice-gerent, and the court of a
Henry II Plantagenet, where it is subject to the fluid process of argument. Again, and more strikingly still, it is
the difference between the *False Decretals* of pseudo-
Isidore, where the arrangement is chronological, and the
analytical collections of canons of the eleventh century and
after -- the *Decretum* of Burchard of Worms, the *Decretum* of
Ivo of Chartres, eventually, about 1140, the *Decretum* of
Gratian -- where canons are grouped according to subject-
matter: baptism, the eucharist, marriage, the law pertaining to the laity, and so on.[4]

The apparently surprising thing about Ernulf is that he
is using one or several of this second species of canonical
collection, the systematic variety. In the 1930's, Z. N.
Brooke showed that a manuscript of Trinity College, Cambridge, was Lanfranc's personal copy of an abridged version
of pseudo-lsidore. His *marginalia* are identifiable. It is
clear from Brooke's study that Lanfranc's abridgement of
pseudo-Isidore, and copies made from it, remained the basis
of church law in England until about the middle of the
twelfth century. The anomaly of Ernulf's canonical letter
is that already in the last decade of the eleventh century,
it makes careful, knowing use of a systematic collection or
collections.[5] From the councils cited by Ernulf, several of
which do not figure in pseudo-Isidore or its abridgements,
it can be shown that he was referring to one of the more
recent compilations, possibly a text dependent on Burchard's
Decretum.[6] In what he writes to Walkelin, in 1098 or
shortly before, the effect of such *ordinatio* of the text on
the nature of legal argument is made very evident. The same
effect is visible in the preface which Ivo of Chartres gave
to his own work of gathering canons, and is appended to manuscripts of both his *Decretum* and *Panormia*. It is unlikely
that Ernulf was using either of these collections, since
they do not seem to have entered England until the twelfth
century. Yet he was familiar with the principles enunciated
in the Preface, and from external evidence it is almost certain that the two men -- Ivo and Ernulf -- knew one another,
first at Bec, then later in Beauvais.

The argument in Ernulf's letter sets out from the recognition that the corpus of legislation received from the past
is not an undifferentiated mass which can be brought to bear
in each judgement; it is rather the raw material from which
particular judgements can be drawn by a process of argument.
The authority of the judgement is in this dialectic, and

therefore in the relation between the judge and the *traditio* from which he takes his judgement. It is true that this principle of relationship is partially weakened by the basis of all judicial authority in absolute and unquestionable precepts found in the New Testament, but on the other hand the main purpose of legal thinking in Ivo, Ernulf, and then even more fully in Gratian, is to find out through intellectual dialogue how these precepts are relevant. The notion of law as an inquiry of this kind is quite alien to what had gone before it, and to the legislation associated with chronological collections such as pseudo-Isidore.[7] In his letter on the incestuous wife and her stepson, to take an example, Ernulf establishes the relative quality of the law from the outset: he carefully cites the authorities for both points of view, first those that forbid, or appear to forbid, the separation of man and wife, then those which demand it. The first group includes the appropriate excerpts from Matthew, Mark, Luke and Paul (Romans and 1 Corinthians), the second a number of Frankish councils. Superficially, the weight seems to lie with the first judgement, that the two should be reconciled; but Ernulf has already anticipated his case, which is that the absolute injunctions of the Gospel writers make an exception in the event of fornication by one of the partners: "*excepta causa fornicationis*". It is not enough however to have shown this: the argument can only be closed when the apparent conflict within *traditio*, and between the different grades of authority -- gospel, Pauline epistles, the Fathers, decretals and councils -- is seen to be part of a harmonious whole. The particularity of the various sources make them participants in the single *veritas;*[8] from the differing forms which the *veritas* takes, in the words of an evangelist, in the specific judgement of a council or a pope, in the exhortations of Paul to the peoples, emerges a precept.[9] To all this Ivo, who is dealing generally with jurisprudence in his preface, adds another variable, the immediate consideration of the health of the soul.[10] Ernulf himself uses the medicinal metaphor, but only to dismiss it, pointing out with Augustine that, if a clear precept exists, it cannot fade before mere human weakness.[11] There is a difficulty here in the attempt to lay a groundwork for rational judgement, from which Ernulf shrinks. It is the question of what happens when two precepts are in conflict. A satisfactory discussion of this would only come with Abelard.[12]

The working assumption behind Ivo and Ernulf and the other canonists of this period is fairly clear: judgement is a critical faculty, which operates by discerning the interaction between abiding principle and changing circum-

stance.   The   tools   of   this   discernment,   and no doubt the
origins of the entire idea of this way of doing justice, are
the   supremely   rational   tools   of   dialectic,   grammar,   exegesis, and systematic compilation.[13]   Ernulf, who is referred
to in one of Anselm's letters as a teacher of grammar,[14]
turns to an analysis from grammar in order to show the equivalence of *vir* and *homo* in the remarks of Matthew and Mark
on marriage and separation;[15] exegesis he uses to demonstrate that what Paul says on the matter leaves room for
interpretation according to circumstance, since his text
allows   both for the possibility of separation and reconciliation:

> I order, or rather not I but the Lord, that
> the woman should not leave her husband; if
> she has left him, she should remain unmar-
> ried or otherwise be reconciled to her hus-
> band (1 Co 7:10-11).[16]

Thus Ernulf is able to conclude, against the view that   the
marriage must be maintained, that

> Reconciliari vero non est Domini iussum, sed
> Apostoli permissum, sive consilium.

Indeed, working from a broad definition of *fornicatio*,
inspired by Augustine,[17] his verdict is that the couple must
be parted.

   This foundation of a legal approach in the different new
disciplines of *ratio* or critical intellect places it immediately in a wide context.   The connection with the philosophical method of Anselm, although not exact, is quite apparent, and in the same vein it has been indicated by Sir
Richard Southern and Helmut Kohlenberger how the disposition
of the monk Rodulfus hinges on the use of reason.[18]   Beyond
the   circle   of Anselm, the affiliations which can be traced
are diverse: there is the assault of Berengar of Tours on
reality in the sacraments of baptism and the eucharist;[19] in
the historical writing of Orderic Vitalis, William of Malmesbury, Florence of Worcester, an instinct is developed to
compare sources and to reshape material with reference to a
theme;[20]   at the same time, the artist is moving from an
iconic and predominantly formal depiction to a narrative and
more naturalistic one,[21] and so on.   The habit which is
common to all these activities is that of distancing the
mind from the material it is considering, and then drawing
it back into the mind by continuous interpretation.   The
consequences of this are far-reaching: an alternative is

being offered to the old universe dictated by ritual and
sacrament, in the form of a new one which is primarily ethical and anthropological. Now, the understanding of what is
right and wrong, instead of relying on external forms and
the associations between them, which together make up the
presence of God in nature and man, depends on the ability to
distinguish and discern, to perceive the relation between
principle and circumstance.[22] It would obviously be an
exaggeration to suppose that Ernulf himself was deliberately
fashioning such a new ethic, although the thoroughness and
theoretical content of his letter on marriage suggest some
awareness of the need to advance and defend a position.
This attitude is clearer still in Ivo. Even more radically
than Ernulf, Ivo is inspired in his idea of what is just by
the disagreement between many of the canons he has brought
together in the *Decretum*. There is no cause for alarm in
this confusion, he explains, because the whole body of
ecclesiastical law is subjected to one criterion, that of
charitas.[23] The whole apparatus of *admonitio, praeceptio
mobilis* and *immobilis, prohibitio mobilis* and *immobilis*, and
dispensatio,[24] in other words the gamut of laws both
relative and absolute, are reduced to a consideration of
what is most likely to lead to salvation. The case of a man
who has taken a vow to remain celibate or to fast, cannot
therefore be treated in the same way as that of a man who
has taken no such vow.[25] Law, says Ivo, must be supple: it
is to be the slave neither of convenience nor of necessity,
but it must remain the embodiment of charity.[26] As in
Ernulf (and as in so much of what is said and done at this
time), there is here a strong sense of drawing back to analyse, a sense that more and more emphasis is being given to
critical intention, the intention of the judge, and that of
the individual judged.

It is this critical distance which is on the whole lacking in the forms taken by ritual, and in the kind of ethical
values deriving from the rite. It would be too easy and too
bold simply to claim that the initiative of Ernulf and Ivo
and others of this period was no more than a breaking away
from the embrace of a ritual society and a release into one
based in rational ethics. Yet there are many indications
that this evolution, one which is developed by the anthro-
pologist Hocart in his work on primitive kingship and the
beginnings of government,[27] holds good for the Middle Ages,
and might perhaps serve as a further approach to the so-
called twelfth-century renaissance. Conveniently, the
hypothesis can be tested against the experience of Ernulf,
for the second of his letters is a treatment of some problems raised by the eucharistic controversy.

The letter, written sometime before 1095, is addressed
to Lambert of Saint Bertin, who was himself a teacher of
grammar, philosophy, theology and music.[28] Lambert had,
some two years earlier, asked Ernulf four questions about
the liturgy and theology of the eucharist, and then another
about a verse from the minor prophet Joel.[29] The eucharistic questions are all prompted by the atmosphere of scepticism and perplexity raised by Berengar of Tours, and it is
significant that Ernulf, in answering them, reveals impa-
tience when the friction between reason and faith becomes
too brutal.[30] Here he finds himself on treacherous ground,
and he reacts warily, retreating behind the certainties of
mysterium: his main concern is now that of defining the
limits of reason.

The questions are as follows: why should the bread be
dipped into the wine and given to the faithful in this form,
when it is known that Christ handed round bread and wine
separately? This refers to the practice known as *intinctio*,
which has distant origins, possibly in the Jewish custom of
mixing bread and wine, as at the Last Supper.[31] Secondly,
why is the host divided by the priest into four parts? Both
these queries have much to do with custom, and so Ernulf can
at least begin with the defense of changing custom which is
a part of his legal training. The next two questions call
for more ingenuity: Is the body of Christ taken wholly or
in part, and is it taken wholly from the bread, wholly in
the wine, or partly in each? And, finally, if Christ is
taken as a whole, is his body nevertheless taken without his
soul?[32] All four questions, which sound rather like questions asked of Lambert by his own pupils, have a common
direction: They arise from a literal interpretation of ritual equivalences; they suggest in fact a wilful confrontation between faith and reason. When Berengar had argued in
the 1060's that the physical presence of Christ in the
sacrament was implausible on logical grounds, he had not
fully explored the implications this view would have on the
liturgical mind in general. But the destructiveness of the
view was impossible to escape, and in this questioning is
the recognition of it. Many of the thoughts lying beneath
Lambert's words are ignored by Ernulf, probably quite consciously: if the body and blood of Christ are received
materially, as Lanfranc had maintained so vehemently against
Berengar,[33] and as Berengar had conceded in his recantation,
then how was it acceptable to break up the bread into parts?
And if the bread represents the body, and the wine the soul,
then is it sufficient to take the bread alone? Ernulf's
position is equally consistent. It is based in the argument
that resemblance or *similitudo* is in itself not the source

of power in the rite, but that this power is rather in *fides* or *mysterium*. This position is without doubt a radical one.

The ritual mentality perceives the world as a series of resemblances, which at their most intense become more than mere likeness, and turn into sameness. In the christian rite, this process of identification is most palpable in the eucharist: the bread and the wine become the body and blood of Christ, and in some way which can never be expressed in the discourse of theology proper, the body and blood are absorbed by the communicant. This heightened resemblance, in which the events of the Last Supper are made to happen again, as well as those of death and resurrection, is only possible through a number of lesser resemblances. Ritual, in this sense, is the ultimate theater: instead of a performance representing past event, it uses representation in order to build up an identity with past event. Thus for Rupert of Deutz, as for Godescalc in the ninth century, the eucharist is an incarnation.[34] To say, as Ernulf does, against this background, that resemblance or *similitudo* is not an integral part of the rite, requires an entirely different understanding of why and how a sacrament works.

Lambert's first question suggests that since Christ handed bread and wine to the apostles separately, it would be more appropriate in the celebration to do the same: Ernulf replies almost brusquely: "He said: 'Do this in memory of me,' not, Do it in this way. Likewise, he said: 'Go, baptise all the peoples in the name of the Father, the Son and the Holy Ghost.' He did not say, Baptise in this way, or, immerse once, or immerse three times. He did not say, Perform the scrutiny, or bless the chrism. In this way he seems to have implied that those precepts which must be observed can be done in one way or another, depending on the demands of necessity, or suitability (*honestas*)."[35] In other words, the practicality of custom prevails over any idea of resemblance. If you ask why the bread and wine are not taken singly, he goes on, you might as well ask why they are not taken in the same place, or at the same table.[36] Again, to argue that the host dipped in the wine is somehow made impure by its recollection of the similar host which Jesus gave to Judas, is false, because the two occasions are not the same, nor are the intentions of the recipients:

> Non enim ea operatio congruam habet simili-
> tudinem, quae causae habet dissimilitudi-
> nem.[37]

Ernulf also attaches considerable weight to the apparently banal objection that the wine taken on its own is all too

likely to spill, especially if given to a man wearing a
beard.[38] His self-assurance goes against the grain of most
contemporary practice: Urban II did not approve of intinction, unless demanded by prudence or necessity. It occurs
however in the customs of Cluny, and for the same reasons as
Ernulf gives, although stated more vaguely; it was not
advisable to give the blood separately to *rudes*, who would
almost certainly mishandle it in some way. For the most part
though, communion under one kind was accepted, but not
intinction.[39]

Ernulf continues to put the knife of *ratio* to liturgical
accretions: the host is divided into three parts at the
fractio -- he brushes aside Lambert's enquiry about the four
parts -- in the first place for a historical reason. In the
past, the offering was made by bishop or priest, together
with other ministers, usually a deacon and a subdeacon. The
three parts, one in the chalice, two on the paten, were thus
distributed to each of the three clerics.[40] This kind of
reconstruction of the origins of a custom anticipates a similar instinct in John Beleth, whose *Summa de ecclesiasticis
officiis*, an extended commentary on the liturgy, abounds in
just such researches, though in a more developed form.[41]

With all this, it should be said that Ernulf is not
utterly ruthless. He allows a limited area of resemblance
to remain: the three part host "is not empty of mystery," he
admits. It signifies the three orders of the church as
described by Gregory the Great, the monks (*praepositi*), the
unmarried, and the married; it signifies the Trinity, and in
a more exact manner, the three states of God as man, his
body, his entombed body, and the immortal body of the resurrection.[42] Here he derives his remarks from the tradition
of the *corpus mysticum*. The overall impression of his
thought though is the reduction of resemblance to its bare
minimum. The effect of it is to isolate the matter of the
host from its meaning. The theatrical and ritual supports
have all but gone, and the believer looks onto an open space
between the little "coin" of bread (*panis in forma numi*) --
portiuncula, bucella[43] -- and the overpowering image of the
flesh of the God-man. Ernulf's own horror at the possibility
of the wine dribbling down through a beard already begins to
show the lavish attention given the elements after the declarations of Lanfranc had laid such stress on the real presence. But what comes across more convincingly than this
theological tenet in Ernulf's letter is the tension between
physical element and metaphysical idea. The proliferation
of eucharistic miracles which followed the theological discussion of the sacrament in the early twelfth century was
surely a subconscious ruse to allay this strain by bringing

the two poles together in a single, unequivocal vision.[44]
In this way such miracles were perhaps more a reaction
against the new theology, a manner of setting up a new and
cruder identity, than a simpleton's way of consenting to
it.[45] Certainly among theologians an effort was made to
alleviate this strain on the intellectual imagination by
restoring the sense that the sacrament was no more than an
extension of the working of God in nature. In the scheme of
Ambrose and Augustine, there was no need felt to explain the
mechanism in sacrament because it was simply a more explicit
form than usual of the operation of divine *mirum* which had
begun with creation. In this sacrament was not unlike
miracle. Now Lanfranc, and then Guitmund and others, tried
to make sacrament generally, and the eucharist especially,
conform to a different idea of nature, which had become dis-
satisfied with consigning everything to the unmediated power
of God. They borrowed from Aristotle by way of Boethius a
language of *qualitas* as against *essentia*; or a little later,
of *accidentia* and *substantia*.[46] Guitmund, anticipating
Aquinas on baptism, proposed a progression from nature to
sacrament: in nature as in the Bible, he says, there are
four kinds of substantive change: one in which all things
are created from nothing, one in which all return to nothing, a third by which one substance changes into another (as
an acorn grows into an oak), and a fourth in which something
which is becomes something which already is, as in the
eucharist and the incarnation.[47]

None of this, however, does anything but place the process further beyond the pale of reason, by making more definite the limits of perception.[48] Ernulf, following Lanfranc
in the main, will go only so far in this attempt to re-
assimilate the metamorphosis of bread and wine. Since body
refers to all corporeal substance, he explains, blood is
body and so can be taken separately from the body without
any loss. But as to how the one is taken in the other,
there is no knowing.[49] And the last of Lambert's questions,
whether the body is taken with or without the soul, elicits
the opposition of reason to faith in all its harshness and
abstraction: Such speculations are idle, mere panderings to
the crowd and its applause:

> non est utile animae christianae insolitis
> disputationibus discutere mysteria rede-
> mptionis nostrae;
>
> veritas mentiri non potest.

> This kind of mystery is called a mystery of
> faith [he affirms], because its secret can
> only be grasped by faith, and cannot be fol-
> lowed by reason.[50]

And as to the recently devised doctrine of *substantia* and
qualitas -- these are the terms Ernulf prefers -- he presents it only as a further precision to the confrontation
between sensual evidence and *integritas fidei*.[51]

The tension in Ernulf was a commonplace of the times.
It comes of the need to defend the sacramental order without
the supporting edifice of ritual resemblance. Yet there
were ways of avoiding it. Pére Gy has recently suggested
that the celebration of the eucharist from Carolingian times
turns away from the prayer "*per Christum ad Deum*" and its
accompanying memorial of death and resurrection, and towards
the more personal prayer "*ad Christum*" with its associations
of crucifixion and passion.[52] Both these approaches to the
eucharist avoid crisis by their concentration on prayer
rather than sacrificial species. Again, Pére de Lubac has
shown the endurance, against the odds of scholastic thought,
of the ecclesiological theme of *corpus mysticum*, in which
the equivalence or identity is between the body of Christ
and an idea of the body of the church.[53] And although this
may make use of the material symbolism of the host -- Ernulf
and many besides connect it with the tripartite host -- its
abiding attraction is in the linking of two image-ideas.
Likewise, Rupert of Deutz reveals a tendency to lift the
level of liturgy from a material to an intellectual order of
resemblance.[54]

Enough has been said, I hope, to give some idea of the
character of Ernulf's mind. The brittleness of his opposition of reason and faith, the relief with which he turns
from theology to simple belief, make him in his way, with
his mere two letters, a more illustrative figure than even
Lanfranc, whose treatment of the eucharistic problem is
lengthier but more fluid. Perhaps though, to end, a word
might be said about the relation of Ernulf's writings to the
thought of Anselm. There are both similarities and differences in style: both men were occupied with differentiat-
ing, with drawing a harmonious truth from what seemed a
tangle of inconsistencies; yet Anselm's mind, besides being
so much more penetrating, is not afraid to take this work of
resolution onto another level of perception. If Anselm's
thinking is seen against the contemporary debate over ritual
meanings, this becomes clear: He talks very little about
sacrament itself, and yet his prayers and meditations take
on the rhythm of the liturgy. Rather than comment outright

on the liturgy, as does Rupert of Deutz or John Beleth or Durandus of Mende, he seems to have absorbed it, and lifted it to the level of idea. Like Rupert, although with a more spectacular sleight of hand, he has thus done away with the problem of physical sacrifice. Unlike Rupert's, however, his idea is Janus-faced: rather than turning the liturgy inward so that it becomes self-reflection, Anselm renders it at once a contemplation and a source of moral judgement. His account of redemption derives from incarnation, which is the origin in his thought not only of an explanation of salvation through moral and metaphysical satisfaction, but of an analysis of moral psychology. Where the liturgy develops identities which lie outside man, Anselm proposes one between the idea of incarnation and the intellect and will within man. The presence of God, the playing-out of incarnation, instead of being a performance of liturgical theater, is a performance of moral consciousness.[55] With this anthropological ethics of Anselm, we have returned, although on an almost entirely theoretical level, to Ernulf in his juridical guise: In the discerning lawyer of Ernulf or Ivo or Gratian is a practical and active reflection of Anselm's moral man.

Notes

[1] Gilbert Crispin, *Disputatio judaei et christiani et anonymi auctoris*, ed. B. Blumenkranz (Utrecht: Spectrum, 1956); *Disputatio christiani cum gentili de fide Christi*, ed. C. C. J. Webb, *Medieval and Renaissance Studies* 3 (1954), 58-77; also see J. Armitage Robinson, *Gilbert Crispin, Abbot of Westminster: A Study of the Abbey under Norman Rule*, Notes and Documents relating to Westminster Abbey, No. 3 (Cambridge: Univ. Press, 1911); R. W. Southern, "St. Anselm and Gilbert Crispin, Abbot of Westminster," *Medieval and Renaissance Studies* 3 (1954), 99-115; and J. Leclercq, "La Lettre de Gilbert Crispin sur la vie monastique", *Studia Anselmiana* 31 (1953), 118-23. For Rodulfus, see his *De octo a monachis observandis*, *Studia monastica*, No. 11 (1969), 26-29; and see R. W. Southern, "St. Anselm and his English Pupils," *Medieval and Renaissance Studies* 1 (1941), 3-34, at 24-29, where this author is identified -- conjecturally -- with Ralph d'Escures, Archbishop of Canterbury (1114-1122); but see R. W. Southern and F. S. Schmitt, *Memorials of St. Anselm*, Auctores Britannici Medii Aevi, No. 1 (London: Published for the British Academy by Oxford Univ. Press, 1969), pp. 320-21, where he is referred to tentatively as Ralph of Battle; Eadmer, *Historia novorum in Anglia*, Rolls Series,

No. 81 (London: Longman, 1884); Eadmer, *Vita Anselmi*, in *St. Anselm and his Biographer*, ed. R. W. Southern (Cambridge: Univ. Press, 1962). For Elmer, see J. Leclercq, "Ecrits spirituels d'Elmer de Cantorbéry," *Studia Anselmiana* 31 (1953), 45-117. For works attributed to Anselm, but in fact either recordings of his remarks or recensions of his unfinished material, see Southern and Schmitt, *Memorials*.

[2] I have collected the matter bearing on Ernulf's life, and have discussed in more detail the text and context of his letter on canon law, *De incestis coniugiis*, in an earlier article which will appear in Vol. 40 of the *Journal of Ecclesiastical History* (1989). The *De incestis coniugiis*: PL CLXIII,1457-74, is also in L. D'Achery, *Spicilegium: sive Collectio aliquot scriptorum qui in Galliae bibliothecis delituerant . . .* (Paris: Montalant, 1723), III, 464-70; the letter on the eucharist to Lambert of St.-Bertin, ibid., pp. 470-74. A third letter, which says something about the measured, pragmatic personality of Ernulf, is *Epistola 310*: Schmitt V,233-35, where he writes as prior of Christ Church to the exiled Anselm, taking him to task for his insistence on principle against the king; see *Epistola 311*: Schmitt V,235-38, Anselm's defensive reply.

[3] *De incestis coniugiis*: D'Achery, p. 464: An uxor a filio coniugis non suo adulterium passa, a thoro coniugis merito suo sit pontificali iudicio removenda.

[4] On the the implications of this change for the origins of scholasticism, J. De Ghellinck, *Le Mouvement théologique au xiie siécle* (Bruges: Editions "De Tempel," 1948). The relation of systematic canonical compilations to the early twelfth-century outbreak of encyclopaedism remains obscure: see Honorius Augustodunensis, *Elucidarium sive dialogus de summa totius christianae theologiae*: PL CLXXII,1109-76; see Y. LeFèvre, *L'Elucidarium et les Lucidaires*, Bibliothèque des écoles françaises d'Athènes et de Rome, fasc. 180 (Paris: E. de Boccard, 1954).

[5] On the progressive *ordinatio* of texts, and the growing desire, or need, to make texts more accessible in their parts and under subject-headings, see R. and M. Rouse, *Preachers, Florilegia and Sermons: Studies on the Manipulus Florum of Thomas of Ireland*, Studies and Texts -- Pontifical Institute of Mediaeval Studies, No. 41 (Toronto: Pontifical Institute of Mediaeval Studies, 1979). On the entry of pseudo-Isidore into England after the Conquest, see Z. N.

Brooke, *The English Church and the Papacy, from the Conquest to the Reign of John* (Cambridge: Univ. Press, 1931).

[6] This case, and Ernulf's relation to Ivo, is argued in the unpublished article cited above, note 2, where I have also given the relevant bibliographical indications.

[7] For the background to this, see P. Fournier and G. Le Bras, *Histoire des collections canoniques en occident*, 2 vols. (Paris: Recueil Sirey, 1931–32); G. Fransen, *Les collections canoniques* fasc. 10 of Typologie des sources du moyen âge occidental, (Turnhout: Brepols, 1973); H. Fuhrmann, *Einfluss und Verbreitung der pseudoisidorischen Fälschungen*, 3 vols.: Schriften der *MGH*, No. 24 a, b, c (Stuttgart: Hiersemann, 1972).

[8] *De incestis coniugiis*: D'Achery, p. 466: Aut quomodo ecclesiam Dei rexerunt, verbo et exemplo illustrarunt, si contra Deum, contra Dei apostolum, contra denique totius ferme christianae salutem a veritate missi falsitatis praecones exstiterunt? . . . Liquido igitur constat praecepta corrigendae praesumptionis illicitae, castigandae turpitudinis nefariae talibus scelestis imposita, salubriter esse inventa, divinitus data, pro veritate non contra veritatem loquentia. Praeterea si ab universa ecclesia non fuerunt instituta, non idcirco sunt reprobanda? Numquid decreta et canones universi christianae fidei confessores aut defensores uno spiritu, eodemque sensu decrevere? Pleraque enim ab uno, nonnulla a pluribus definita; quae tamen ab omnibus gratanter sunt accepta, a nemine contempta.

[9] Ibid., p. 468: Quibus rebus dubium non est, morem ecclesiasticum, sive concilia patrum, non modo evangelicae sive apostolicae institutioni non opponi, verum quasi quodam venerabili obsequio famulari. Further, ibid., p. 470: Quod praeceptum est, non fieri non licet, quod permissum est, non fieri licet.

[10] Ivo of Chartres, Preface to the *Decretum*: PL CLXI,48: Sicut enim ratio corporalis medicinae vel depellere morbos, vel curare vulnera salutem servare, vel augere intendit; nec medicus contrarius sibi videtur esse, cum pro qualitate vel quantitate aegritudinis, vel aegrotantis, nunc mordentia, nunc mollientia aegrotanti medicamina apponit; et nunc ferro secat, cui fomento subvenire non poterat, et e converso ei nunc subvenit fomento, quem ferro secare non audebat; ita spirituales medici, doctores videlicet sanctae ecclesiae,

nec a se, nec inter se dissentiunt, cum illicita prohibent,
necessaria iubent, summa suadent, venialia indulgent: cum
secundum   duritiam   cordis   delinquentium   pro   correctione
eorum, vel cautela caeterorum severas poenitentiae leges
imponent; vel cum secundum devotionem dolentium et resurgere
volentium, considerata fragilitate vasis quod portant indul-
gentiae malagma superponunt. Nam, qui indulgent, maioribus
morbis amovendis provident; et qui illicita prohibent, a
morte   deterrent: qui vero necessaria iubent, salutem
cupiunt conservare; qui autem suadent, salutem student
augere.

    [11] *De incestis coniugiis*:   D'Achery. p. 467: Nonnulli
humanam fragilitatem attendentes, aiunt lapsos in coniugio
nullo pacto esse separandos, ne unde procuratur eis medi-
cina, amplior casus deteriorque contingat ruina.   Quia cum
putantur rigore huius disciplinae posse sanari, sua aestu-
ante incontinentia paratur eis laqueus et vorago fornicationis.

    [12]Abelard, *Sic et non: A Critical Edition*, ed. B. B.
Boyer and R. McKeon, 2 vols. (Chicago: Univ. of Chicago
Press, 1976); Abelard, *Ethics: An Edition with Introduction, English Translation and Notes*, ed., introd., trans. D.
E. Luscombe, Oxford Medieval Texts (Oxford: Clarendon
Press, 1971). The instinct of the early and mid-twelfth
century to fragment the vying sources of *traditio*, and then
to reassemble the parts by dependence on the powers of reason and ethical *intentio*, is perhaps a more compelling
characteristic of the period, and certainly more flexible as
a historical category, than that of the twelfth-century
"individual": on this, see C. Morris, *The Discovery of the
Individual, 1050-1200* (London: Harper & Row, 1972); and a
critical response, C. Bynum, "Did the twelfth century really
discover the individual?" in *Journal of Ecclesiastical History* 31 (1980), 1-17

    [13]On dialectic, M.-D. Chenu, "Les *Magistri*: La 'science
théologique,'" in *La Théologie au douzième siècle*, Etudes de
philosophie médiévale, No. 45 (Paris: J. Vrin, 1957).   On
grammar, C. Thurot, *Notices et extraits de divers manuscrits
latins pour servir à l'histoire des doctrines grammaticales
au moyen âge*, Notices et extraits 22.2 (Paris, 1868; rpt.
Frankfurt, 1964); R. W. Hunt, *The History of Grammar in the
Middle Ages: Collected Papers*, ed. and introd. G. L. Bur-
sall-Hall (Amsterdam: Benjamins, 1980), esp.   "Studies in
Priscian" (Art. I). On exegesis, B. Smalley, *The Study of
the Bible in the Middle Ages*, 2nd ed. (Oxford: Blackwell,

1952); H. de Lubac, *L'Exégèse mediévale: Les Quatre sens de l'écriture*, 3 vols. (Paris: Aubier, 1959-61).

[14] Anselm, *Epistola 64*: Schmitt III,180-1.

[15] *De incestis coniugiis*: D'Achery, p. 467.

[16] Ibid., p. 468: Apostolus memorans legem a domino latam: "Praecipio," inquit, "non ego, sed dominus, mulierem a viro non discedere; quod si discesserit, manere innuptam; aut viro suo reconciliari." Hoc quidem aut illud necesse est fieri. Sed non hoc tantum, aut illud tantum fieri necesse est.

[17] Ibid.: . . . quam fornicationem beatus Augustinus in eo libro quem de sermone domini in monte declarato composuit, dicit generalem esse, asseverans videlicet fornicationem esse omnem illam praevaricationem, quae animam male utentem corpore suo, alienam facit a creatore suo. Cf. Augustine, *De sermone domini in monte* XII,36: *PL* 34,1247.

[18] Rodulfus, *Libellus de peccatore qui desperat et de ratione que peccatorum ne desperet confortat*, Bodl. MS. Laud. misc. 363, ff. 1r-55v, of which see extracts printed in R. W. Southern, "St. Anselm and his English Pupils," *Medieval and Renaissance Studies* 1 (1941), 24-29; H. Kohlenberger, "Ratio bei Rodulfus Monachus: Ein Versuch aus der Sicht der historischen Anthropologie," *Anselm Studies* 1 (1983), 201-05.

[19] Berengar of Tours, *De sacra coena adversus Lanfrancum*, ed. A. F. and F. Th. Vischer (Berlin, 1834; rpt. Hildesheim/New York: G. Olms, 1975).

[20] Orderic Vitalis, *Historia ecclesiastica: The Ecclesiastical History of Orderic Vitalis*, ed. and trans. M. Chibnall, 6 vols. (Oxford: Clarendon Press, 1969-80); William of Malmesbury, *De gestis pontificum anglorum*, ed. N. E. S. A. Hamilton, Rolls Series 52 (London: Longman, 1870); idem, *De gestis regum anglorum*, ed. W. Stubbs, 2 vols., Rolls Series, No. 90 (London: Longman, 1887, 1889); Florence of Worcester, *Chronicon ex chronicis*, ed. B. Thorpe, 2 vols., (London: English Historical Society, 1848-49).

[21] Cf. O. Pächt, *The Rise of Pictorial Narrative in Twelfth-Century England* (Oxford: Clarendon Press, 1962); G. B. Ladner, *Ad imaginem Dei: The Image of Man in Mediaeval Art* (Latrobe, Pa.: Archabbey Press, 1965).

[22]On this concern for distinction-making, see M. Foucault, *Les mots et les choses: Une Archéologie des sciences humaines* (Paris: Gallimard, 1966), where, in its Enlightenment form, it is characterised as an *epistémé* inclined to taxonomy.

[23]Ivo, *Preface*: *PL* CLXI,47: Huius aedificationis magistra est charitas, quae saluti proximorum consulens, id praecipit aliis fieri quod sibi quisque vult ab aliis impendi.

[24]Ibid., 49-51.

[25]Ibid., 49D.

[26]Ibid., 57A: Ex necessitate enim fit mutatio legis. But 58B: nec est pro lege habendum quod aut utilitas suasit, aut necessitas imperavit.

[27]A. M. Hocart, *Kings and Councillors: An Essay in the Comparative Anatomy of Human Society*, ed. and introd. R. Needham, foreword E. E. Evans-Pritchard, 2nd ed. (Chicago: Univ. of Chicago Press, 1970)

[28]Lambert is not addressed as abbot: he became abbot of St.-Bertin in 1095 (H. De Laplane, *Les abbés de Saint-Bertin d'après les anciens monuments de ce monastère* [St. Omer: Chanvin fils, 1854-55], p. 175); for his accomplishments as recluse and abbot, ibid., p. 174.

[29]*D'Achery*, p.474.

[30]On the controversy surrounding the real presence, see J. de Montclos, *Lanfranc et Bérenger: La Controverse eucharistique du xie siècle*, Spicilegium sacrum lovaniense: Etudes et documents, fasc. 37 (Louvain: Spicilegium sacrum Lovaniense, 1971); G. Macy, *Theologies of the Eucharist in the Early Scholastic Period: A Study of the Salvific Function of the Sacrament according to the Theologians, c. 1080-1220* (Oxford: Clarendon Press, 1984): the author emphasizes the importance of seeing a wide variety of problems and views pertaining to the eucharist from the creative period of Ambrose and Augustine to the critical period of ninth to twelfth centuries. The account given is thus far more plausible than that which regards the eleventh-twelfth century crisis as simply a theological duel between real presence and symbolism. Also, see R. W. Southern, "Lanfranc of Bec and Berengar of Tours", *Studies in Medieval History*

Presented to Frederick Maurice Powicke, eds. R. W. Hunt, W.
A. Pantin, R. W. Southern (Oxford: Clarendon Press, 1948);
O. Capitani, "'L'affaire bérengarienne' ovvero dell'utilità
delle monografie," *Studi medievali*, 3rd ser., 16, No. 1,
(1975), 353-78.

[31] Cf. Jn 13:26: 'Ille est, qui ego intinctum panem
porrexero.' Et cum intinxisset panem, dedit Iudae Simonis
Iscariotae.

[32] D'Achery, pp. 471-73, passim.

[33] Lanfranc, *De corpore et sanguine domini*, ed. J. A.
Giles, in Vol. II of *Lanfranci opera quae supersunt omnia*,
Patres ecclesiae anglicanae, No. 30 (Oxford: Parker, 1844);
as main source of this materialist view, Paschasius Radber-
tus, *De corpore et sanguine domini*: ed. B. Paulus, *CCCM*
XVI.

[34] The sense in which Rupert considered the eucharist to
be incarnational is characteristically abstruse and allusive: *De divinis officiis* II,9: ed. H. Haacke, *CCCM*
VII,41: Nam cum diceret idem magnus pontifex panem et vinum
tenens: "Hoc est corpus meum, hic est sanguis meus," vox
erat Verbi incarnati, vox aeterni principii, verbum antiqui
consilii. Verbum, quod humanam accepit naturam, idem in
carne manens, panis et vini accipiebat substantiam; vita
media panem cum sua carne, vinum cum suo iungebat sanguine.
Quemadmodum in corporis sensibus menti et corpulento aeri
media lingua intervenit et utrumque coniungens unum sermonem
efficit, quo in aures dimisso id, quod audibile est, cito
absumitur et transit, sensus autem sermonis et in dicente et
in eo, qui audit, integer permanet et inconsumptus, sic Verbum Patris carni et sanguini, quem de utero Virginis assump-
serat, et pani et uino, quod de altari assumit, medium
interueniens unum sacrificium efficit, quod cum in ora fide-
lium sacerdos distribuit, panis et uini species absumitur et
transit, partus autem Virginis cum unito sibi Verbo Patris
et in caelo et in hominibus integer permanet et inconsumptus. And Godescalc, *De corpore et sanguine domini*, ed. D.
C. Lambot, *Oeuvres théologiques et grammaticales de Godescalc d'Orbais*, *Etudes et documents*, No. 20 (Louvain: Spicilegium sacrum lovaniense, 1945), p. 335: Ergo iam modo
pateat placeat libeat rogo quod deus homo "uerbum caro" dat
ecclesiae suae sponsae suae carni scilicet suae manducandum
carnem suam de semetipso dei agno semper tamen manente uiuo
semper integro. For a recent and uninhibited evocation of
this theme of ritual identification, see P. Levi, "Funeral

Oration for David Jones," *The Flutes of Autumn* (London: Harvill Press, 1983). See also G. Dix, *The Shape of the Liturgy* (Westminster [London]: Dacre Press, 1945), esp. pp. 255ff.

[35] D'Achery, p. 471: Redemptor noster veniens in mundum, quia propter hominum salutem inter homines apparuit, quaeque reparationi infirmitatis humanae commoda seu necessaria fore praevidit, sicut oportere vidit in sapientia sua, ita ab hominibus fieri et esse voluit in ecclesia sua. Haec eis, cum quibus conversari dignatus est, verbo vel exemplo insinuavit, quae facienda erant docens, certum quo facienda erant modum praefigere omittens. Hinc esse videtur quod ait: "Hoc facite in meam commemorationem." Non ait, hoc modo facite. Et: "Ite baptizate omnes gentes in nomine Patris, et filii, et spiritus sancti." Non ait, hoc modo baptizate, non ait, semel mergite, aut tertio mergite. Non ait, scrutinium facite, chrisma sacrate. Qua in re insinuasse videtur quae praecepta sunt non fieri non licere; pro ratione vero necessitatis, vel honestatis, alio et alio modo fieri licere.

[36] Ibid.: Qui ergo quaerit, cur non accipiantur exemplo dominico singulatim, quae de altari sumuntur nova consuetudine simul mixta; simili ratione quaerere potest, cur non sumantur in simili loco, aut de simili mensa, vel in simili forma, aut cur etiam aliud sumatur, videlicet aqua, quae a domino non legitur in coena esse porrecta.

[37] Ibid., p. 472; and on p. 471: Arguitur iste mos ex eo quod bucellae intinctae a domino traditori suo porrectae similitudinem videtur habere . . . Si enim exteriora pensentur, nemo dicet justum hominem edere non debere panem intinctum in sua coena, quia id proditor manducavit Judas in dominica coena. Aut nemo ideo non dabit osculum pacis, quia Judas osculo dedit signum proditionis? . . . Si autem interiora cogitemus, propter aliud ille, propter aliud nos. Ille in suae signum nequitiae, in signum doli et proditionis, quam mente gerebat, de manu domini buccellam intinctam intinctus fraude suscepit. Nos carnem domini intinguimus in sanguine domini, non ut designemus malitiam esse in cordibus nostris . . . and Guibert de Nogent, *De bucella Judae data et de veritate dominici corporis*: PL CLVI,527–538 (at 530): At si de bucella agitur, quae ei intincta porrigitur, signum fuit, et non signum: signum plane proditoris, sed non signum sacramenti . . .

[38] D'Achery, p. 471: Evenit enim frequenter, ut barbati, et prolixos habentes granos, dum poculum inter epulas sumunt prius liquore pilos inficiant, quam ori liquorem infundant. See Amalarius of Metz, *Epistola ad Guntradem*: *PL* CV,1338C-D: a reply to a young priest who had shown outrage at Amalarius' spitting after reception of the host.

[39] Council of Clermont (1095), c. 28: Hefelé-Leclercq, *Histoire des conciles*, p. 403; *Consuetudines Cluniacenses* II: *PL* CXLIX,721 (and note 6).

[40] D'Achery, p. 472.

[41] Ed. H. Douteil: *CCCM* XLI, XLIA, written c. the third quarter of the twelfth century.

[42] D'Achery, p. 472.

[43] Ibid. And see Guibert, *De bucella*: *PL* CLVI,534: Quid enim ibi quantitas, in cuius etiam atomo constat salutis universitas? And see below, note 46.

[44] P. Browe, *Die eucharistischen Wunder des Mittelalters*, Breslauer Studien zur historische Theologie, N.F., Bd. 4 (Breslau: Verlag Müller & Seiffert, 1938).

[45] But see Benedicta Ward, *Miracles and the Medieval Mind* (London: Scolar Press, 1982).

[46] On the development of this terminology, see J. de Montclos, *Lanfranc et Bérenger*, p. 580. A little later than the time of Ernulf's letter, Alger of Liège, identifying the eucharistic body with the spiritual body of resurrection, as against the flesh born of the Virgin, uses the term *supersubstantialis*: *De sacramento corporis et sanguinis domini*: *PL* CLXXX,780D; also, Guibert de Nogent, *De pignoribus sanctorum* II,9: *PL* CLVI,641B; Odo of Cambrai, *Expositio in canonem missae*: *PL* CLX,1064C: here the usual philosophical language is avoided in favor of expressive oppositions, founded in the relationship of Old and New Testament. The *carnalis* of the old law becomes the *spiritualis* of the new. Thus: Haec hostia caro est, non carnalis, sed incontaminata lux, et ideo pura. . .

[47] Guitmund, *De corporis et sanguinis Christi veritate in eucharistia*: *PL* CXLIX,1443-44. In this interpretation of nature as transformation, there lies perhaps something of the natural-spiritual procession envisioned by John Scot

Eriugena, (see *Periphyseon*, ed. I. P. Sheldon-Williams, *Scriptores latini Hiberniae*, No. 7 [Dublin: Dublin Institute for Advanced Studies, 1968]).

[48] This tendency of mind may be compared with the more systematic thinking of Anselm, and his definition of God as that which it is not possible not to conceive: in the ontological proof, God is that which the mind can conceive but not encompass; see J. Vuillemin, *Le Dieu d'Anselme et les apparences de la raison* (Paris: Aubier Montaigne, 1971).

[49] D'Achery, p. 473: Quia enim omnem corpoream substantiam constat corpus esse, sanguinem domini corpus esse manifestum est remota omni ambiguitate. Sed cum dominus passionis suae sacramenta commendaret, dicens: "Hoc est corpus meum." Et item: "Hic est calix sanguinis mei." Corpus a sanguine distinxit corpus proprie intelligens quod solidum erat, quod cruci affigendum erat, per sanguinem assignans quod erat liquidum, quod erat effudendum, in utroque passionis suae qualitatem praefigurans. Et nos quoties de corpore et sanguine domini loquimur, in eadam significatione nomina ipsa memoramus. Domini ergo corpus quamquam in sacramentorum velamine sumatur ex toto . . . separatim tamen et sanguis sine corpore, et corpus percipitur sine sanguine. . . . Nec repugnare videtur, si totus sanguis separatim sumatur sine corpore, quem totum credimus sumi cum corpore, cum et totum ab uno, totum a multis corpus dominicum percipi certissime teneatis. In his language, Ernulf is running close to that of Berengar, the difference being that while Berengar places the efficacy of signification in the perceiving mind, Ernulf (along with Lanfranc and the later orthodox writers) makes of it an exterior operation.

[50] Ibid.: Id sane mysterii genus idcirco mysterium fidei vocatur, quia eius secreta sola capit fides, quae ratio assequi non potest.

[51] Ibid. p. 474: Cum ergo manentibus panis qualitatibus, non miremur panis abesse substantiam, sed integritate fidei in substantiam carnis credamus eam adesse, non mutatis eius qualitatibus, permutatam . . .

[52] P. M. Gy, "Evolution historique et spirituelle de l'Eu-charistie au moyen âge," *Segni e Riti nella Chiesa Altomedievale Occidentale*, Settimane di studio del Centro italiano di studi sull'alto Medioevo, No. 33 (Spoleto: Presso la sede del Centro, 1987).

[53] H. de Lubac, *Corpus mysticum: L'Eucharistie et l'église au Moyen Age* (Paris: Aubier, 1944)

[54] Rupert of Deutz, *De divinis officiis*, prologus: *CCCM* VII,5: Altissimarum namque signa sunt rerum et maxima quaeque continent caelestium sacramenta secretorum, quorum ad maiestatem contemplandam non nisi eruditus et religiosus quispiam aspirare idoneus est.

[55] Thus Anselm can show by "necessary reasons," perceptible to the intellect, the impossibility of satisfaction for Adam's sin other than by the incarnation of a god-man; and these reasons derive from a moral understanding of Adam's sin as an offense to God, which, in an equally moral sense (involving *honor* and *iustitia*) has to be made up by the God who is man: *Cur deus homo*, ed. and trans. R. Roques, Sources chrétiennes, No. 91 (Paris: Editions du Cerf, 1963). All moral action then is seen against the paradigm of incarnation: the implications of this, left obscure by Anselm himself, are explored in works associated with his name, especially *De humanis moribus*: Southern and Schmitt, *Memorials*, pp. 36-104.

Relections on Anselm's Friendship and *Conversatio*

Mary-Rose Barral

Studying Anselm is like contemplating a multifaceted diamond. Each face of the gem gives forth a different light. So the various aspects of Anselm's personality regale his admirers with a different hue of virtue. However, there is one reflection coming from Anselm which renders all other virtues brighter and more attractive: his genius for friendship. No matter what he does or what are the circumstances or the events which shape his life, he is sure to approach every person involved with that particular brand of friendship which conquers hearts.

However, can one say that friendship is a virtue in the strict sense of the word? Of course, there are friendships and friendships: not everyone who cultivates a friendship is necessarily a virtuous person thereby. In fact, there may be relations, rightly or wrongly called friendships, which are the occasions for evil, and which, far from bettering the persons involved, contribute further to the depravity of the participants. Can one call "partners in crime" friends? Their relations exhibit some characteristics of friendship, such as concern for each others welfare, may be genuine affection. But, because the aims which bind them or the activities in which they are engaged are not good, it can hardly be the case that they "live" a friendship or a virtue.

Following the classification of Aristotle, friendship arising from common interest is good in its own kind, but not good without qualification; it entails a degree of communication, qualified concern and help, but it is not lasting beyond the common interest and can hardly be held as virtue.

There is also a friendship arising from pleasure, the enjoyment of beauty or of other physical attractions which are short-lived; generally, the enjoyment of each other's company. Such friendships are genuine in their kind and to the limited degree of depth which they may attain, but are likely to exhaust themselves quickly because of their limited purpose and lack of commitment. Virtue here may be limited to some expression of kindness and mutual help. Then, the only kind of friendship worthy of the name is that which Aristotle describes as motivated by the good and obtaining only between and among good persons. This kind of friendship would undoubtedly be virtuous because concerned with the good without qualifications.

What, then, are the characteristics of a virtuous
friendship? Besides being based on goodness, a true friendship seeks the good of the friend unselfishly. A friendship
involves an openness of the spirit and mutual affection.
The deeper the understanding, the truer the friendship.
Friends will, and actually seek the spiritual betterment of
each other, but are concerned with the physical welfare as
well. It is a sign of true friendship not only to grieve
with others in misfortune, but also, and particularly, to
rejoice in their success and good fortune, to aid in the
attainment of each other's goals, and to promote each
other's good in every respect. In a word, friends care for
each other, in the true sense of caring, that is, guiding
and supporting each other in the attainment of full being.

Is there virtue in all these activities of friendship?
No doubt. First of all none of the above mentioned characteristics of friendship would be possible without love.
Love is, in fact, the essence of friendship. It is possible
to love without being a friend, but friendship without love
is not possible. Parents may love their children and be
loved in return in the sense that there is a genuine concern
for one another, and yet not be friends at all -- particularly for what concerns open communication and understanding. One may sincerely love a neighbor, be ready to help
when there is need, yet not offer, or expect, friendship.
One may have a genuine, compassionate love for the poor, but
neither invite, nor expect intimate interchange of communication with them.

However, friendship is not only love, but a special kind
of love, which goes from the intimate self of one to the
personal inner being of the other in the most open exchange
possible between autonomous selves. Actually, this kind of
love already implies, or presupposes, the characteristics
that constitute friendship.

Friendship also requires a profound sense of justice as
foundation to goodness; it necessitates a generous heart and
generous action; readiness to sacrifice; sincerity to reveal
one's true self to the friend so that openness of spirit may
be possible. Can there be any doubt that true friendship
not only is a virtue, but requires a whole array of virtues?
Does it mean then that true friendship is rare? Perhaps;
not only because it requires time for friendships to grow,
but also because, Aristotle said, there are not that many
good persons.[1]

One thing can be taken for granted: Anselm was one of
those "good men." What is to be considered then is whether
Anselm was a friend to many; what motives inspired his
friendships; what kind of friendship he cultivated; what

virtues were evident in his friendships and what effects his virtue had on his friends.

Anselm had strong ties of friendship with Lanfranc with whom he shared a great love of learning and a keen desire to work for the glory of God and the sanctification of the Church. They were one in their friendship, a "glowing attachment of pupil and hero-worshipper."[2] Anselm's biographers are unanimous in celebrating the universal appeal of his friendliness: toward his own as well as towards strangers. Many were so impressed by him that they made use of his inspiring talks to invite others to virtue; in all simplicity perhaps, used his wisdom to enhance their writings; and treasured and preserved his words for the edification of future disciples. His letters and his formal and informal talks contain an abundance of wisdom coupled with a very personal style and originality. He was well versed in the old, basic traditional monastic spirituality, yet was very original in his understanding of the new, "in the penetrating analysis, the striking definitions, and the unfamiliar illustrations."[3]

His "conversation" occurred often at mealtime when he made use of an option to substitute live talk to reading; it also took place on the occasion of daily situations or problems which arose in the community and required his intervention. On these occasions he was always ready with original allegories and parables suited to the occasion and always directed to the strengthening of the spiritual life in the community. To those live talks, he brought the products of a keen, logical mind and a loving heart, the first attaining conviction, the second conquering the affections of his hearers. An episode, quoted by several of his biographers, illustrates both the acuity of his logical mind and his understanding and love for human beings -- especially one dedicated to the Lord. St. Elphege, an English saint, was held to be a martyr by some, but refused the title by Norman detractors: the question was put to Anselm, for the saint in question had not died for the faith, but to spare his people the burden of paying his ransom to his captors. His reply was: "He who is willing to die for the lesser will the more readily die for the greater . . . Elphege preferred death to the impoverishment of his people . . . offering good over evil for the sake of his neighbors."[4] And there was a new martyr.

His live talks contributed greatly to gain him the esteem and the veneration which became friendship of his monks and of those who came in contact with him. Although we do not have a complete body of his live talks, the contributions of Eadmer, Alexander and the anonymous writer of the

Note!

Liber de similitudinis give us an insight into the varied aspects of his spoken word. Eadmer gives us the beauty and originality of Anselm's words; Alexander preserves for us the logical aspects of the discourses, the doctrines therein presented; the anonymous writer preserves Anselm's wise and original sayings, greatly sought after during his time and by posterity. In a discourse on charity, Anselm reasoned that it is better to give than to receive since, "we who give love do not lose it" and the giver has the permanent gift of charity, the receiver only a transient gift. And he concludes, "To love others is, therefore, a greater cause for joy than being loved by them."[5] One of his most celebrated talks was that of the joys of heaven (which will be discussed later); the incident of the hare taking refuge under his horse gave him the occasion to create a parable of life; the incident of an overburdened monk also gave him the occasion to present a vivid image of life and its tasks.

However, it is in his letters that we discover more of Anselm's personality and his charm, which brought him so many friends. As literary works, they are very carefully written; for Southern, in fact, "often too elaborately contrived -- showing the same wealth of rhyme , assonance and antithesis . . . noticed in the early prayers and meditations."[6] The fact that many of his letters were put together for posterity by Anselm himself, because of their content -- to him worthy of preservation for teaching purposes -- explains his care in the matter. Nevertheless, from the point of view of the sentiments expressed therein, this may raise some questions: Is there true spontaneity as can be expected in a friendly correspondence? Still, the desire to fix and preserve beautiful moments in his relationships with his friends may have been the real motive for the preservation of his letters -- in which case spontaneity would be preserved.

At any rate, his letters were a great contribution to literary production of a letter-writing age[7] as letters of friendship and spiritual guidance. His letter writing began in 1070, when some of his monks were transferred from Le Bec to Canterbury where Lanfranc was. Anselm wrote to these men his earlier letters and continued to correspond with them, so much so that they received, according to Southern, nearly half of his total correspondence before 1093. In his letters be dealt only with matters of importance (as he did also in his practical life). He concerned himself with matters falling within the range of his duties, and did not intrude where his intervention was not requested. The spiritual life, the religious discipline, relationships with his monks, with his friends, were his chief concerns, and these were the topics about which he wrote. <u>The most important thing was to communicate, not so much news or information of any kind, but to reveal himself to his friends.</u> This Anselm did with <u>an extraordinary display of affection.</u>

The wording and the emphasis on certain expressions come as a great surprise to twentieth century readers, unused to such free and open display of sentiment from a person in his state of life. There are the letters to his long-term friends, such as Gundulf, a monk who left Le Bec to follow Lanfranc to Canterbury. Anselm writes:

> Everything I feel about you is sweet and pleasant to my heart; whatever I desire for you is the best that my mind can conceive. For such as I have seen you to be, I have loved, as you well know; and such as I now hear you to be, I desire, as God well knows. And so, wherever you go, my love follows you; and wherever I stay, my desire embraces you. Why then do you entreat me through your messengers, exhort me in your letters, and constrain me by your gifts, to remember you? "If I do not remember thee, let my tongue cleave to the roof of my mouth," if I prefer not Gundulf among my chief friends. For how should I forget you? How could he be removed from my memory who is impressed on my heart like a seal of wax?[8]

It is difficult to understand how such very warm feelings could be expressed towards one who had been absent for a good number of years (they had not met in the meantime); also Gundulf was by at least ten years Anselm's senior; this could perhaps be explained as hero worship, as in the case of Lanfranc; still, the whole tenor of the letter seems extravagant, especially when, towards the end, there is a clear implication that this ardent message is not meant for Gundulf alone. His friendship for Gundulf lasted his whole life, and it was precisely in the later years that the two met to rekindle their love for God by holy conversation, as they used to do the first happy years at Le Bec.

Another example of great ardor is found in this letter to William, whom he hoped would leave the world and dedicate his life to God:

> To his loved, his loving and his longed-for William, Brother Anselm, styled Abbot of Le Bec. May he not love the world, nor the

things that are in the world, but enjoy the
love of God, and give Him his love.

I begin by styling him my loved and my
loving one in reply to the request he
makes of my love. A soul dear to my soul
has asked, through the medium of a letter
all fragrant, and all fragrant with affection, asked me, as token of my affection,
for a letter of solace. What is sweeter
and more agreeable to affection or what
greater solace has it than affection.
How, then, can I better solace you in your
love for me than by writing to tell you
that my soul's love for you is such that
my heart will know no consolation and my
longing for you be all unappeased, unless
I have you for my own. Truth to say, when
you ask me for my affection with such fervor, you do more than incline me to love
you; you oblige me to long for you. Your
affection for me makes you crave my hand-
writing for your comfort; mine for you
makes me desire your presence for my joy.
So, then, if you do not wish to do violence to my heart, satisfy the longing you
have taken such pains to kindle.

O dear soul, how can you tell me that
you love me, and yet suffer my heart to
break from love of you? If the same flame
burns in you as burns in me, then your
soul and mine must needs be melting with
one and the same desire. But how can you
wish for my affection without returning me
your own? Be not cruel, therefore, to
your soul and mine; but come and console
your soul and mine.

Then Anselm advises William to take the decisive step
with courage: to leave the world, dedicate himself to God,
and learn the ways of religious life in holy friendship.

And when you leave your city, be like
Lot. Look not back. Look ahead and learn
the way forward; look not behind, but forget the way back. So, with the Apostle,
shall you forget the things that are
behind and reach forward to those that are
before.

Now I tell you what I mean and I tell you frankly. Come, and let our lives be spent together, if you really wish us to be a consolation to each other. I might, my dearest friend, adduce to you numberless places of Holy Writ which exhort you to despise the world and its concupiscence, if you were not already familiar with them. But do not forget that, if we are passing through the false, it is only that we may reach the true. Love not the false if you would have the true . . .

May Almighty God prevent all your wishes and all your actions with his counsel, and further them with his help, friend of mine, dearest to my heart."[9]

This letter is a combination of the affection of a loving friend and the apostolic fervor of the spiritual father who is concerned with the spiritual welfare of the disciple. The change in the tone of the letter is striking. A question that must be asked in this regard is: What is the real meaning of the exuberant affectivity towards a person who "might" be received into the community? Anselm was used to deal in this fashion towards persons who desired to embrace the religious life. There are other examples, even more striking than this one, written to persons as yet unknown:

. . . My eyes eagerly long to see your face most beloved: my arms stretch out to your embrace. My lips long for your kisses; whatever remains of my life desires your company, so that my soul's joy may be full in time to come.[10]

One is hard put to figure out the real sense of these expressions of affection so unusual and extravagant, even if, as Southern says, the expressions of the letter were directed to some relatives (probably not even known personally). The expressions of ardent love in both letters can be misleading: what kind of relation would involve such intense feelings? One could also interpret them as well-intentioned exaggeration in an attempt to show open-hearted *rhetoric* welcome to the candidates, as opposed to formalism in the application of religious statutes. The literal interpretation is also out of the question, unless one considers love purely in a spiritual sense. Southern maintains that such expressions cannot be interpreted in a purely symbolic way , and finds them "only distantly reminiscent of The Song of Songs, which provides the best authority for the expression of spiritual love in terms of physical union."[11] Southern is right in saying that such expressions are undoubtedly an outburst of a personal desire or emotions but it must be admitted that it is not easy to determine whether the passion is actually addressed to the person in question or to the more general love of the religious life, or even to zeal for the glory of God.

Anselm speaks in terms of friendship: But the meaning he assigns to such a term is certainly not that which prevails now. His terms of endearment cannot be interpreted as we would today in a similar friendly situation. True, he is concerned with a spiritual friendship, based, not only on the fellowship of the good, but also of those whose spirit is one with his. But how to explain the expressions of sensible love if the friendship is a communion of souls? Perhaps the only answer is found in the medieval notion of love as a purely spiritual concept; and therefore whatever terms were used to express such love had a spiritual meaning and intent.

Thus it is important, in assessing the real meaning of Anselm's expressions in his correspondence, to understand his psychological use of words: "mind" means the spiritual and rational soul. His employment of this term, so frequent in his letters (my mind, your mind), is signifying the whole personality of the writer or of the recipient of the letter in the sense in which we can say "spirit" and indicate ourselves in our very intimacy. When he uses the term "sense," he understands first of all the manner of experiencing sensations, but then it extends this to all kinds of knowledge, including the personal knowledge which involves feeling about something or someone and even opinion. The "sense" of the will of God is for him the knowledge of God's will. "It is only in the mind that one can savor the sweetness of a sentiment"[12] and "notwithstanding his distance, the spirit of the Archbishop of Canterbury maintained present the affections of his friends . . . "[13]

When he speaks of conscience he does not simply mean the value of the moral judgement, but the interior reality, the attitude of the soul, the intimate and affective essence of the personality. He even speaks of opening the conscience of his heart.[14] This sheds a little more light on the meaning of certain phrases such as, "as unremittingly as my heart burns with love for you, so ardently does it thirst for your true happiness . . . "[15] and "Those whose minds have been fused together by the fire of love not unnaturally find it grievous when distance separates their bodies";[16] or

again, (to the Englishman Osborn, after only a short
acquaintance) "We cannot now be separated without tearing
apart our joint souls and severing our hearts."[17]

Yet, these intimate expressions do not claim exclusi-
vity: (in a letter to Gundulf)

> "Since all who are dear to me are dear to
> you, place in a group together with me in
> the chamber of your memory, where I always
> keep my place, those friends of mine of whom
> I have told you as wishing to be bound by
> the same kind of friendship with us; set
> them in a circle with me; but, oh! dear
> friend, place Osborn's shade in my bosom;
> place him, I beg you, in my bosom, nowhere
> else."[18]

Osborn had been the recipient of Anselm's special care,
first, when the former resented Anselm's elevation to Prior;
then, after the monk had become a devoted disciple, their
friendship became very close, which did not prevent Anselm
from sternly guiding him in the spiritual life, and endured
until beyond the death of the latter (as the above letter
shows). Anselm's friendship for Osborn expressed itself in
more than tender care for all the physical needs of the latter, particularly in his illness, up to his death. Of this,
Rule says:

> The spectacle of that love subdued all
> hearts, and there was not a man at Le Bec
> who did not take shame to himself as he con-
> trasted it with Osborn's happiness and joy,
> a happiness and joy which the heavenly-
> minded Prior had insured him by his attach-
> ment in life and his succor after death; not
> one who did not commit himself and his dear-
> est interests to Anselm in the hope of
> inheriting Osborn's privilege. And he, says
> Eadmer, became all things to all men, that
> he might save all.[19]

His care for his monks extended to all their needs, spiritual as well as physical. His concern extended as well to
other monasteries whose endowment was insufficient to their
needs. This care is "friendship" in the true sense of the
word.[20] Clayton observes:

> Anselm's love for his fellowmen was not ab-
> stract, but personal, rooted in good will --
> part and parcel of love of God; he spread
> peace, had influence on the violent and pas-
> sionate . . .[21]

In a way, his solicitude for his friends was a result of
his innate compassion -- which seems to have extended to
every living thing. "The largess of his heart, with its
sense of kingship with the whole animal creation . . .
astonished the hunting men of the Red King's reign"[22] (On
one occasion he forbade them to harm a hare which had taken
refuge under his horse). Should we say that Anselm had a
friendship with all creation?

His notion of friendship was very special. In one of
the talks he gave (probably on his second visit to Cluny) on
the bliss of heaven, after listing the bliss of the body,
beauty, ability, force, liberty, impassibility, he singled
out pleasure which in heaven will be perpetual and spiritual, so that souls will be inundated with delight. However, high above all that, the blessings of the soul will be
knowledge, concord and friendship. The latter, in particular, is of interest: in heaven, as a consequence of universal knowledge, a collective friendship will unite in perfect
contentment all the elect, members of one body, the Body of
Christ, their head; it is in him that we will love and will
be loved, in him, who will love us personally more than we
love ourselves and the others; likewise, each will love him
with ineffable love more than himself and his brothers. This
friendship will bring joy, which the assurance of an eternal
duration will intensify so as to make of it an ocean of happiness in which the soul will be immersed.[23]
This talk helps us understand better Anselm's notion of
friendship here on earth. He says very emphatically that
pleasure here on earth is imperfect and may bring disillu-
sions because of its transitory character and of animal sensations which accompany it. Now, the language used in
Anselm's letters of friendship wants to approach the characteristics of the heavenly friendship, in which case no
expression of love would be excessive: and its meaning
could not but be spiritual.
At the same time, this notion of friendship raises a
fundamental question: Is the friendship of Saint Anselm a
truly personal relation, or is it a collective kind of relation wherein friends are not really felt to be individual
and unique, as the notion of friendship must intend? This
then would change the understanding of Anselm's friendships
not only as revealed in his letters, but also in his lived

experience. Maybe the term friendship, as understood in the
twentieth century or even as described by Aristotle does not
apply in Anselm's theory and practice of friendship.

Of particular importance is Southern's analysis of
Anselm's friendship:

> He bends his mind to the contemplation of an
> ideal image, he attaches it to himself with
> passionate intensity, he defines its nature,
> and gives it a name. Here the name is that
> of a friend. In his prayers and medita-
> tions, formed under the influence of a simi-
> lar impulse, the name is that of God or of a
> saint. But in the latter, the reality of
> the ideal object was guaranteed in advance;
> in his letters of friendship it was a subtle
> blend of fact and imagination.[24]

This then supports the contention that these friendships
were not really personal relations, but rather a general
attitude towards his fellow religious, new candidates and
others among the laity who fell in some way within the scope
of his religious or pastoral care. His conversations were
not only geared to monastic life and discipline, but also,
and very often, to the hope of the world to come. Friendship was one way, best perhaps? of reaching the hoped-for
blessedness. Friendship, begun in this world, continued
unchanged in heaven; it was of its nature everlasting:
friends would be friends forever. All good qualities and
capacities of human beings are enhanced and transformed in
heaven: friendship alone remains the same.

Again according to Southern, Anselm maintained that
identity of profession was the essence of friendship. But
then, how could Anselm address laymen as friends, as he does
in his letters to Haimo, the Sheriff (of Kent) and to Earl
Robert (of Shrewbury), Earl Arnulf, and others,[25] specifically dealing with material interests; he was certainly not
concerned directly with the religious aspect of life, and
the persons thus addressed were not of his profession --
unless, of course, one wants to accept as "same profession"
the Christian faith. But this seems hardly to be the intention of the definition of that friendship which, begun on
earth, will have its perpetuity in heaven.

Anselm's correspondence was voluminous; but how many of
those who received his ardent letters really felt him to be
their "special friend," how many really understood the love
expressions which had all the markings of "soul-mate" or
"favorite, chosen friend?" Was it the holiness which marked

his life from the beginning that gained him friends, regardless of the words he addressed to them? After all, Anselm
was a philosopher, and, chances are, not all of his friends
were able to follow his intellectual speculation and spiritual insights, the mysterious sense of his ardent expressions of intimacy, or the exhortations to a holy life.
Clayton reports:

> Your conversation is in heaven, holy father
> . . . You are a man of religion and holi-
> ness. But we are bound to this world by the
> friends and relatives we have to think of
> . . . we simply cannot afford to walk on
> the heights where you walk, or go with you
> in your contempt of the world.[26]

Like these words of his suffragans, similar expressions may
have reached Anselm in reply to his exhortations to those
whom he called friends, but who were in the service of the
world rather than of God. Nevertheless, by whatever kind of
friendship they may have felt to be united to Anselm, many
claimed him their friend and he so called them.

Anselm regarded some among the monks of Le Bec his intimate friends, toward whom he expressed his love in ardent
yet spiritual accents. Rule states:

> Thank God, there were round about him a
> sacred inner circle of tried and trusted
> friends, in whose society he could, from
> time to time, enjoy an hour's oblivion of
> sorrow as he expatiated with them now on the
> infinite love of God, now on the mysteries
> in which that love had found its divinest
> exhibition. There was the faithful Gundulf
> who . . . in the cloister of Le Bec had wept
> tears of consolation at the thrilling words
> of the young Aostan, and who was one soul
> with him to the end.[27]

There were others, such as Baldwin of Tournay, whose knowledge, experience, and fertility of resources were placed at
the service of the revered master; Eadmer, truly beloved by
Anselm, for his loyalty, affection, and dedication; there
was Boso with whom Anselm had much in common for he was the
true Benedictine, like Anselm, philosopher, theologian, and
ascetic. With these men Anselm's friendship endured and
they were eager to visit with him whenever possible. Perhaps these were some of Anselm's relations which more

closely realized a friendship which, although always bathed in the love of the supernatural, was also earthy, personal, human and concrete. It is likely that these men, of all others, felt most the friendship to be something special, unique to them, their common purpose being one: to grow in the love of the Lord and to prepare for the place where friendship would be everlasting.

Anselm's friendship was founded on trust and it was only "when tutored by long and sad experience that he could bring himself to believe that his own dependents and friends were capable of playing him false."[28] There was a particular trait in Anselm which was conducive to good relations with others: he was both thoughtful and compassionate; he rejected that rigorism in religious life that took no notice of, nor made allowance for those who had not yet attained the desired level of perfection or, by their past condition, found virtue difficult.

Taking account of all that has been said, it must have happened, at times, that some of Anselm's friends may have been disillusioned at finding that they were not the special friend which his ardent letter implied. Anselm felt very strongly the unity of all men in God; therefore, to him, friendship was prompted by this sense of unity with all men; it extended to all, because all are God's, regardless of their merits. Southern affirms,

> For himself [Anselm] this unity was a pre-
> sent, painful and -- if we are to trust some
> of his expressions -- a shattering experi-
> ence . . . at the command of the most tran-
> sient applicant . . .

Then he relates the story of the fugitive monk, Moses, returning to the monastery, on whose behalf Anselm inter-vened -- a very strange kind of friendship:

> If therefore at any time I have offended any
> of you, scourge the skin of Moses for my
> fault and in him deprive my mouth of food.
> For I have commended my skin to my brother
> Moses for him to keep it carefully as his
> own. Do not spare it on this account; but
> if you beat my skin for his fault, I shall
> require satisfaction from him; and if you
> spare him I shall be thankful.[29]

This is the concretization of Anselm's philosophico-theological theory not only of the unity of mankind on a cosmic level, but also of the homogeneity of human beings, hence of the possibility of one man substituting for another, for whatever reason, particularly for the atonement of sins. Anselm, however, did not seem aware of the utter individuality of human beings, each of whom is uniquely a self, incommunicable as a being in his/her selfhood, and yet made to be with, that is, basically related to every other human being in the cosmos. He did not seem to have realized that it is precisely the intimate relatedness of one being to another which makes for friendship, for atonement, for cooperation (alas, also for discord, conflict, enmity). However, relatedness is not synonymous with identity, and atonement is affected not by substitution, but by compassion and love.

Anselm's friendships, which, as results clearly from his letters, *conversatio* and examples in his lived dedication to his fellowmen, was basically a "love in the Lord," it demanded of him, along with love, firmness and, at times, severity to help the erring return to the right road, or to aid the wavering resolve their doubts and enter the service of the Lord. He did not hesitate to use the strongest language and at times even to foretell God's likely punishments for non-compliance. In his letters, the great concern was always the good of the person in question, and with his monks of Le Bec in particular, the observance of the monastic life was paramount. He held that stability does not concern only the observance of the law of the monastery; it involves, above all, the will to live as monk and concrete fidelity to one's own community and the manner of life therein, customs and usages as well.[30] In any case, he said, the religious profession is without repentance; its duties are valid forever: to evade them is apostasy.[31] How could Anselm, so mild-mannered and so understanding of the weaknesses of human beings, particularly of his brothers in religion, use such a strong word as "apostasy?" It is all in the name of friendship.

For the same reason, he uses extremely strong language in a letter to a nun who is about to leave the monastery, because her expected elevation to abbess did not occur. After calling her the sweetest "beloved friend of mine," "cherished friend and chosen spouse of Christ," he does not hesitate to say that, if she were to choose a mortal man in lieu of Christ, not only would she and he be damned to eternal death, but would cause a tremendous and detestable scandal in the Church; if so much evil were to come from her conduct, it would have been better if she had never been born.[32] It is not clear who the nun was, but the commentator points to a probable woman of royal family; it seems

that there were two letters of Anselm, the first fatherly
and much milder. However, much mystery remains about this
situation. If the person in question was a certain Gunhilde
of Wulstan, then her reputation had not been tainted, except
for what Anselm's letter may have done. This event also
shows that Anselm was not deterred from seeking the good of
his "friends," as he saw it, and the glory of God by any
respect for the great of this world.

Generally, Anselm's letters of exhortation were successful -- and they often contained the prevision of dire
consequences if the will of God were not to be followed. On
some occasions, his pleas went unanswered, as was the case
with a certain Henry, whom he was trying to win over from
the love of the world, and who did not heed either Anselm's
friendly inducements or his forebodings.

Regardless of the results of his exhortations, either by
letters or personally, the influence of Anselm was great.
His biographers affirm that none who met him, even for a
brief moment, failed to be impressed by his holiness, no
less than by his knowledge; and those who hoped to be his
friends were conquered by his charm and cherished his
friendship. During his stay at different monasteries,
visiting abbots and friends, (during the times of his
exiles)

> the peasants knew for a saint the kindly old
> priest who had come to live among them . . .
> among the people of that countryside there
> grew up an immense and wonderful love for
> Anselm; they spoke of his great goodness far
> and wide.[33]

Is Anselm's friendship all virtue? A consistent effort
to be "all things to all men," which was, ultimately, what
Anselm strove to be during his whole life, requires a high
degree of virtue, which Anselm certainly possessed. But virtue is not always sweet and pleasant; friendship is not a
state of endless bliss. So it is not surprising if even for
Anselm, as for his friends, as was mentioned, there were
disappointments, particularly when his counsels were not
followed, or his words of affection not understood or not
reciprocated. Basically, Anselm understood friendship as a
union of soul and will, both subject to the designs of God
upon each one. That is why Anselm did not shrink from causing his community great grief when he understood that the
will of God for him was to be Archbishop of Canterbury. His
friends did not accept this will readily, and there was
great resistance to his leaving: after all, Anselm's elec-

tion to abbot of Le Bec was for life, like a marriage. His
monks felt betrayed; they may well have doubted, at that
point, the sincerity of his friendship.

Anselm accepted the higher will -- God's -- and his
relationship to his friends was thereby changed. Had he
really been a true friend? we may ask. Should a change in
one's way of life extinguish the source of love for one's
friends? It seems not, if it is true friendship. Perhaps
Southern is right, after all, when he says that for Anselm
"the friend is more of an idea than a person."[34] So, when
Anselm left the sheltered atmosphere of the monastery, where
life was peaceful and recollection easy, and relations of
friendship came naturally and delightfully, the burdensome
cares of the archbishopric changed his life: his loving
fervor towards his former monks vanished, although he protested that his friendship remained.

In conclusion, friendship in Anselm was less than it
appeared to be. It did not really express a personal feeling towards a friend, but rather, general benevolence for
his companions in the religious life and for those who came
within the scope of his apostolate. His concrete care for
some particular friends, like Osborn, was an outgrowth of
his love for God. It seems safe to say that feeling and
loving sentiments which usually accompany friendship (which
he, however, expressed so freely) were not the moving force
of his intellect and will: rather a will-to-good was the
source of his friendships.

Is a friendship not a friendship if one loves for the
love of God? No. Love is not of the intellect, but of the
heart; even if God is the moving force, friends love each
other with their total being, sentiments and feelings
included. Anselm, however, did not yet know this: he lived
in medieval times.

Notes

[1] The *Nichomachean Ethics* of Aristotle generally deals
with the subject of friendship.

[2] Joseph Clayton, *Saint Anselm* (Milwaukee: Bruce, 1933),
p. 28.

[3] R. W. Southern, *Saint Anselm and His Biographer*
(Cambridge: Univ. Press, 1966), p. 69.

[4] Clayton, *Saint Anselm*, p. 14.

[5] Ibid., p. 42.

[6] Southern, *Saint Anselm*, p. 68.

[7] Southern, ibid., points out two such great letter-writing periods: from the latter part of the tenth century to the beginning of the thirteenth (Gerbert to Peter of Blois); from the middle of the fourteenth to early sixteenth century (Petrarch to Erasmus).

[8] *Epistola 4*: Schmitt III,103-05, as cited in Southern, *Saint Anselm*, p. 69.

[9] Martin Rule, *The Life and Times of St. Anselm* (London: Kegan Paul, Trench, 1883), I, 258-59.

[10] *Epistola 120*: Schmitt III,258-60, as quoted in Southern, *Saint Anselm*, p. 72.

[11] Ibid.

[12] *Epistola 59*: Schmitt III,173-74, as quoted in Pierre Michaud-Quantin, "Notes sur le vocabulaire psychologique de Saint Anselme," *SB* I, p. 27 (translation mine).

[13] *Epistola 288*: Schmitt IV,207,1; Michaud-Quantin, "Notes," p. 27.

[14] Ibid., p. 29.

[15] Rule, *The Life*, p. 48 (letter to his uncle).

[16] *Epistola 5*, ad Henricum monachum [Prior of Canterbury]: Schmitt III,106,5. Henry did not seem very close to Anselm.

[17] *Epistola 39*: Schmitt III,150,31.

[18] Rule, *The Life*, pp. 158-59.

[19] Ibid.

[20] Cf. Marjorie Chibnall, "The Relations of St. Anselm with the English Dependencies of the Abbey of Bec, 1079-1093," *SB* I, pp. 521-30.

[21] Clayton, *Saint Anselm*, p. 76.

[22] Ibid., p. 45.

[23] Patrice Cousin, OSB, "Les relations de Saint Anselme avec Cluny," *SB* I, p. 444.

[24] Southern, *Saint Anselm*, p. 73.

[25] J. F. A. Mason, "Saint Anselm's Relations with Laymen," *SB* I, passim.

[26] Clayton, *Saint Anselm*, p. 80.

[27] Rule, *The Life*, pp. 117-18.

[28] Ibid., pp. 120-21.

[29] *Epistola 140*: Schmitt III,285-87; Southern, *Saint Anselm*, p. 75.

[30] *Epistola 37*: Schmitt III,144-48, as quoted in P. Salmon, OSB, "L'Ascèse monastique dans les lettres de Saint Anselme de Cantorbery," *SB* I, p. 513.

[31] *Epistola 123*: Schmitt III,263-64; Salmon, "L'Ascèse," p. 513.

[32] A. Wilmart, "Une lettre inédite de S. Anselme à une moniale inconstante", *Revue Benedictine* 40 (1928), 323.

[33] Clayton, *Saint Anselm*, pp. 86, 93.

[34] Southern, *Saint Anselm*, p. 76.

The *Proslogion* Argument

Anselm

Ergo, domine, qui das fidei intellectum, da
mihi, ut quantum scis expedire intelligam, quia
es sicut credimus, et hoc es quod credimus. Et
quidem credimus te esse aliquid quo nihil maius
cogitari possit.

(*Proslogion*, Sumptum ex eodem libello)

Augustine

Ita cogitatur ut aliquid quo nihil melius
sit atque sublimius illa cogitatio conetur
attingere.

(*De doctrina christiana* I,vii,7)

Les preuves cartésiennes et la preuve du *Proslogion*

Jules Vuillemin

Je me propose ici de répondre, de façon indirecte, à la question suivante: quelle est la présupposition métaphysique de la preuve anselmienne du *Proslogion*?

On admet généralement que les preuves du *Monologion* "reposent sur la théorie platonico-augustinienne des idées."[1] En revanche, c'est une question disputée de savoir si la preuve ontologique, sous la forme qu'Anselme lui donne dans le *Proslogion* dépend, pour sa validité, du réalisme des idées.[2]

C'est à l'examen des preuves cartésiennes qu'on demandera de donner une réponse indirecte à cette question. Les critiques de la preuve du *Proslogion* se sont, en effet, jusqu'ici interrogés uniquement sur la question de savoir si l'existence peut être légitimement tenue pour une propriété et, plus rarement, sur la non-contradiction du concept de Dieu dans le *Proslogion*. C'est une troisième sorte d'objection que les *Méditations* de Descartes paraissent formuler par implication[3] et cette objection, qu'on n'a point encore examinée du point de vue anselmien, fait précisément porter l'examen sur la présupposition métaphysique du *Proslogion*.

Je comparerai d'abord la structure des deux argumentations et j'en ferai ressortir les analogies et les affinités.

Celles-ci mises en lumière, il sera plus aisé de comprendre le sens de la critique implicite d'Anselme par Descartes et, en conséquence, les dépendances métaphysiques des deux sortes de preuves.

I

Du *Proslogion*, ne retenons que les textes constitutifs de la preuve ontologique au sens que Descartes, après d'autres, donne au mot: à savoir que l'être souverainement parfait existe nécessairement. C'est au chapitre V du *Proslogion* que nous atteignons cette vérité, à partir de laquelle commence l'enquête proprement théologique sur ses conséquences. Que si, à présent, nous prêtons attention non aux démonstrations elles-mêmes mais aux vérités démontrées, nous observons que les chapitres II, III, et V démontrent respectivement que Dieu existe, qu'il existe nécessairement et qu'étant seul par soi il est créateur de tout ce qui n'est pas lui. Les chapitres I et IV ont un rôle accessoire par

rapport aux démonstrations. L'un, par la grâce de la prière, révèle le vrai sens du mot *Dieu*; l'autre, de l'impossibilité que Dieu ne soit pas, déduit l'impossibilité de
l'athéisme.

Le chapitre I du *Proslogion* est absorbé dans la
troisième *Méditation*, car, selon Descartes, la lumière
naturelle ne peut nous faire défaut au point de nous faire
concevoir l'idée de parfait à la façon des idolâtres. La
quatrième *Méditation* du vrai et du faux, joue, de son côté,
un rôle analogue au chapitre IV du *Proslogion*, puisqu'il
faut expliquer comment moi qui suis fait à l'image de Dieu
et qui possède l'idée du parfait, je puis me tromper,
l'athéisme étant la plus grossière des erreurs possibles.
Restent alors pour les vérités démontrées les correspon-
dances évidentes. Au chapitre II du *Proslogion* répond la
première partie de la troisième *Méditation* ou première
preuve par les effets: Dieu existe. La cinquième
Méditation, comme le chapitre III du *Proslogion*, démontre
que Dieu existe nécessairement. L'objet du chapitre V du
Proslogion, l'existence par soi de Dieu, est enfin repris et
modifié dans la seconde partie de la troisième *Méditation*
(seconde preuve par les effets), où il est démontré que le
Dieu qui me crée ne tient sa cause que de lui-même.

Mais la comparaison aboutit à des analogies de nature
plus intrinsèques, dès qu'on la fait porter sur la preuve
qu'Anselme et Descartes tiennent pour principale en ce
qu'elle est la première et que les deux autres en dépendent.
Cinq traits rapprochent, en effet, le chapitre II du *Proslogion* et la première preuve par les effets de la troisième
Méditation.

Premièrement ces deux preuves ont pour objet l'existence
divine à titre assertorique et non pas apodictique, puisqu'elles établissent cette existence et non pas la nécessité
de cette existence, et elles considèrent cette existence en
tant que telle (*quod*) sans faire intervenir proprement l'essence divine (*quid*) puisqu'elles ne retiennent de cette essence que ce qui est juste nécessaire pour la démonstration
d'existence (le nom de Dieu tel qu'il nous est révélé selon
Anselme,[5] l'idée en nous du parfait selon Descartes). Lorsqu'on compare, dans les deux cas, la première preuve avec la
dernière (qui donc, chez Anselme, établit Dieu comme créateur tandis que, chez Descartes, elle l'établit comme nécessairement existant) on voit que ce passage opère la même
transformation fondamentale de l'enquête. Cette dernière,
dans les premières preuves, conserve un statut épistémologique et relatif à ma science pour atteindre, dans les
dernières, un statut ontologique et relatif à la chose.[6]

Deuxièmement, les deux premières preuves sont fondées sur la considération d'un contenu représentatif (*esse in intellectu* chez Anselme, réalité objective de l'idée chez Descartes) dont on démontrera qu'il n'est tel que parce qu'il lui correspond, au dehors, une existence (*esse in re* chez Anselme, réalité formelle de l'idée chez Descartes). Cette seconde analogie mérite d'être remarquée, sitôt qu'on note le soin que prend Descartes, inspectant le contenu de son esprit, dans la troisième *Méditation*, à écarter d'une part les pensées non représentatives (telles que les actes de la volonté), d'autre part et surtout les jugements, pour retenir uniquement les contenus représentatifs.[7] C'est exactement ainsi, en faisant d'ailleurs l'économie de tout ce grand appareil, que procède Anselme lorsqu'il postule comme objet de foi (*Et quidem credimus te esse*) une description définie prise isolément (*aliquid quo nihil maius cogitari possit*), c'est-à-dire hors de tout jugement et dont on montrera qu'elle ne saurait être que contradictoire avec la même description définie dont l'objet serait requis n'exister que dans l'intelligence. Descartes, comme Anselme, applique le mot *intelligo* à l'action par laquelle nous saisissons cet *esse in intellectu* en quoi consiste, pour nous, un contenu représentatif.[8]

On ne s'étonnera donc pas, troisièmement, si ces deux premières preuves sont dominées par le paradigme de l'image ou du tableau, paradigme caractéristique pour les contenus représentatifs. Le peintre, dit Anselme, lorsqu'il la médite encore (*praecogitat*), n'a la scène représentée que dans son intelligence. La peinture achevée, "*et habet in intellectu et intelligit esse quod iam fecit.*"[9] "La lumière naturelle, dit Descartes, me fait connaître évidemment que les idées sont en moi comme des tableaux ou des images."[10]

Une digression est ici nécessaire, à propos de ce témoignage de la lumière naturelle, dont dépend la validité de la première preuve par les effets. Cette preuve est due au jeu entrecroisé de deux principes. Le principe de causalité affirme qu'il y a au moins autant de réalité dans la cause que dans l'effet. Si l'effet est l'idée en moi du parfait, je ne serai donc fondé à poser nécessairement comme cause qu'une réalité (formelle ou éminente) au plus égale à la réalité de l'effet. Or c'est ici que se pose un dilemme apparemment fatal pour la preuve. Car, pour déterminer la quantité de réalité contenue dans l'effet, nous devons faire appel au second principe qui est celui de la correspondance entre l'idée et l'idéat qui est son modèle ou patron, c'est-à-dire entre réalité objective et réalité formelle. Mais de deux choses l'une. Ou bien il y a égalité complète

entre copie et modèle, ce qui est nécessaire pour la validité de la preuve, mais veut dire aussi que la copie contient toutes les perfections du modèle, y compris l'existence, en conséquence de quoi la preuve est circulaire et,
de plus, l'idée de Dieu en moi vient se confondre avec son
existence. Ou bien on respecte l'expérience, on admet que
l'idée de Dieu en moi représente son modèle sous une forme
nécessairement déchue, puisque le tableau est au moins privé
de l'existence propre au modèle, mais alors la preuve cesse
d'être concluante, puisque d'un effet tel que le fournit le
principe de correspondance et qui est l'idée du parfait
moins l'existence, on est autorisé seulement, en vertu du
principe de causalité, à conclure nécessairement à une cause
parfaite formelle ou éminente, mais dont la perfection
peut-être ne contient pas l'existence.

Cet argument, subtil et puissant, est dû au grand histo-
rien de la philosophie que fut Martial Gueroult.[11] Je ne
vois qu'une parade possible. L'incontestable déchéance du
tableau par rapport au modèle empêche de regarder le principe de correspondance comme postulant une égalité entière
dans la *similitude* ou la *conformitas* entre réalité objective
et réalité formelle.[12] Cependant ce n'est pas parce qu'en
moi le contenu représentatif de la chose n'en contient évidemment pas l'existence qu'il ne contient aucune représentation de cette existence. Soient, en effet, les trois
contenus représentatifs suivants: l'idée d'angle intercepté
par le plus grand côté d'un triangle, l'idée de chèvre,
l'idée de Dieu. Le premier contenu représentatif exclut
l'existence extramentale de la chose; le second ne l'exclut
ni ne l'inclut; le troisième l'inclut, faute de quoi l'idée
du parfait excluerait une perfection et ne serait pas l'idée
du parfait. Donc l'idée du parfait, sans contenir elle-même
l'existence, contient la représentation de l'existence en
tant que perfection. Mais la cause doit avoir autant de
réalité que l'effet. Cet effet, comme réalité objective,
c'est: la toute puissance, la science complète, etc., plus
la représentation de l'existence, représentation unique
parmi toutes les réalités objectives et repésentation d'une
existence, qui ne fait défaut qu'en raison de la déchéance
propre à ce genre de réalité. La cause devra donc contenir
la toute puissance, la science complète, etc., mais aussi
l'existence qui est représentée dans le seul cas de la
réalité objective de Dieu appartenir à cet objet indépendamment de l'impuissance existentielle propre à toute réalité objective. Si donc, dans ce cas, la cause ne contenait
pas l'existence comme perfection, elle violerait la conformité et la similitude représentatives de l'idée du parfait

en ignorant l'une des perfections non pas certes possédées, mais à coup sûr représentées par cette idée.[13]

Revenons, à présent, à la quatrième analogie entre Descartes et Anselme. D'une part la preuve anselmienne est étrangère à la forme positive de la preuve ontologique -- telle que la concevra Descartes dans la cinquième *Méditation* -- elle est à partir des effets exclus et se rapproche par là d'une preuve par les effets telle qu'est la première preuve cartésienne. D'autre part, lorsque Descartes rencontre l'argument essentiel de l'athée, savoir que mes propres perfections en tant que je les imagine s'étendant indéfiniment et que je les fais en puissance plus grandes que ce qu'elles sont en acte, sont peut-être suffisantes pour m'attribuer à moi-même l'idée du parfait,[14] c'est en des termes quasi anselmiens qu'il réfute cet argument. En quoi consiste, en effet, ce Moi infini en puissance sinon en quelque chose qui est tel que je puis toujours penser quelque chose de plus grand que lui? Or cette gradation indéfinie qui est en mon pouvoir et que l'athée identifie à la cause de l'idée du parfait,

> n'est-ce pas [demande Descartes] un argument infaillible et très certain d'imperfection en ma connaissance, de ce qu'elle s'accroît peu à peu, et qu'elle s'augmente par degrés? Davantage, encore que ma connaissance s'augmentât de plus en plus, néanmoins je ne laisse pas de concevoir qu'elle ne saurait être actuellement infinie, parce qu'elle n'arrivera jamais à un aussi haut point de perfection, qu'elle ne soit encore capable d'acquérir quelque plus grand accroissement. Mais je conçois Dieu actuellement infini en un si haut degré, qu'il ne se peut rien ajouter à la souveraine perfection qu'il possède.[15]

Pour Descartes, ces miennes perfections qui sont en puissance ne sont pas en puissance au sens qu'un Aristotélicien donnerait au mot, en leur prêtant une sorte de réalité fantomatique faisant pression pour accéder à l'existence. La puissance, ici, c'est le seul pouvoir de la pensée imaginative qui la produit: *potest cogitari*. Et l'unique différence entre les deux premières preuves, quand on ne regarde que leur objet et qu'on ne le regarde que matériellement, c'est qu'Anselme raisonne sur toute la création, tandis que Descartes borne son argument à la connaissance humaine.

Le cinquième trait qui rapproche enfin Descartes d'Anselme est le recours à la comparaison des perfections ou
quantités d'être attachées chez l'un aux "réalités objectives" ou, chez l'autre, par implication, à l'ensemble des
choses créées.   La perfection servira donc de *tertium com-
parationis* à toutes les idées ou essences des choses.[16]
Voilà pour les analogies et les affinités.

II

Voici maintenant pour les différences.   J'examinerai
d'abord celles qui résultent des deux sortes d'ordre dans
les trois preuves.   Elles conduiront ensuite à la critique
implicite d'Anselme par Descartes et enfin à l'élucidation
métaphysique de cette critique et, par là, des deux sortes
de preuves.

L'ordre anselmien est une progression qui d'une prémisse
identique: la considération épistémologique des effets exclus (*id quo nihil maius cogitari potest*) tire une conclusion de plus en plus forte: l'existence, la nécessité épistémologique (*quod non possit cogitari non esse*), l'essence
positive (*quid es nisi id . . . summum omnium . . .*).   L'ordre cartésien des raisons, en revanche, modifie, pour chaque
preuve, la prémisse et non seulement la conclusion.   Descartes conclut de l'idée du parfait en moi à l'existence du
parfait, puis de Moi qui existe et ai l'idée du parfait à
l'existence créatrice, puis de l'essence du parfait à son
existence nécessaire.   La dernière preuve cartésienne ou
preuve ontologique part de l'essence à laquelle aboutit la
dernière preuve anselmienne.

Dans les deux cas, l'ordre des preuves va à pénétrer de
plus en plus profondément dans l'intelligence de Dieu.   Que
d'ailleurs l'approfondissement de l'intelligence ne puisse
déboucher sur la compréhension de Dieu, c'est ce que garantit chez Anselme la constance de la prémisse par les effets
et chez Descartes soit dans les deux premières preuves la
liaison de la prémisse aux effets, soit la subordination de
la dernière preuve à la première.   En même temps, la progression de la preuve anselmienne laisse entièrement intacte
la constance de la prémisse, tandis que l'ordre cartésien
sépare par le tout de la quatrième *Méditation* la dernière
preuve des deux premières et prend soin d'opposer ces effets
que sont l'idée de Dieu en moi ou moi-même en tant que j'ai
l'idée de Dieu d'une part, l'essence de Dieu d'autre part.
Du point de vue cartésien, le *Proslogion*, si l'on en considère seulement les cinq premiers chapitres ne contient
donc pas de preuve ontologique.

En conséquence, la comparaison des ordres respectifs des preuves oblige à se poser la question suivante: puisque, selon Descartes, la prémisse de la preuve ontologique proprement dite doit être rationnellement fondée, quel est ce fondement? Et si ce fondement fait défaut chez Anselme, par quoi se trouve-t-il remplacé?

Le titre de la cinquième *Méditation* a quelque chose de remarquable. Descartes y traite, en effet, "de l'essence des choses matérielles; et, derechef, de Dieu, qu'il existe."[17] Comme l'a bien montré Martial Gueroult, la validité intrinsèque de la preuve ontologique est égale à la validité intrinsèque d'une vérité mathématique, c'est-à-dire d'une vérité qui porte sur l'essence des choses matérielles. Elle s'impose à l'assentiment de tout esprit attentif en vertu de sa clarté et de sa distinction. Cependant, elle n'échappe pas au doute métaphysique, en d'autres termes à l'hypothèse d'un malin génie, d'un Diable assez puissant pour faire que les idées claires et distinctes ne soient pas vraies. La preuve ontologique ne saurait donc se suffire à elle-même; car l'essence de Dieu, qu'elle suppose, doit d'abord être démontrée véridique en ce sens que, idée claire et distincte, elle possède en tant que telle une valeur objective. Or nous ne pouvons nous assurer d'une telle valeur objective qu'une fois levée l'hypothèse du malin génie et nous ne pouvons lever cette hypothèse qu'en démontrant l'existence d'un Dieu vérace. Ainsi la preuve ontologique n'est valable qu'autant qu'on est en droit d'attribuer une valeur objective aux idées claires et distinctes illustrées tant par les idées mathématiques que par l'idée de Dieu. Tout ce qu'elle montre, c'est que la nature de mon esprit est telle que je ne puis pas plus concevoir l'essence de Dieu séparée de son existence qu'une montagne séparée de sa vallée.[18]

En revanche, la preuve par les effets qui va de l'idée de Dieu en moi à l'existence de Dieu se suffit à elle-même et possède une valeur démonstrative même dans l'hypothèse du malin génie, puisque la prémisse n'est ici que l'idée *en moi* du parfait, autrement dit la présence phénoménologique d'un contenu représentatif, d'une "réalité objective" à laquelle je ne prête nullement de valeur objective et qui, par conséquent, échappe par nature aux prises du doute métaphysique. On peut donc formuler dans les termes suivants la critique implicite du *Proslogion* par Descartes:

> lorsque vous prononcez et entendez les mots: *id quo nihil maius cogitari potest*, je ne conteste pas leur cohérence c'est-à-dire que je ne doute pas qu'il leur corresponde dans

mon entendement une idée aussi claire et
distincte que celle du plus grand côté
intercepté par le plus grand angle d'un
triangle. Je ne mets pas en cause, non
plus, que l'existence compte au nombre des
maiora. Mais je puis imaginer un Grand
Trompeur qui me déçoive dans mes certitudes
les plus constantes et qui ne laisse pas de
me surprendre et de me tromper dès que mes
évidences dépassent la forme de mon Moi.

Qu'on relise à présent les chapitres I et IV du *Proslogion*.   On sera peut-être tenté de croire qu'Anselme répond
par avance à Descartes. Ce qui garantit la validité objective du contenu représentatif, dira-t-on, c'est, en effet,
la foi, qui, une fois l'idolâtrie écartée, nous impose de
Dieu un concept qui serait contradictoire s'il ne contenait
pas l'existence. Cependant, prêtons attention à la fin du
chapitre IV:

> Gratias tibi, bone Domine, quia quod prius
> credidi te donante, jam sic intelligo te
> illuminante, ut si te esse nolim credere,
> non possim non intelligere.[19]

Du point de vue de l'athée, la foi ne fait qu'attirer son
attention sur la véritable idée de Dieu, s'il est toutefois
légitime d'utiliser ici cette désignation positive. Ceci
fait, une fois qu'il a compris de quoi il s'agit, l'athée ne
peut pas ne pas comprendre que Dieu existe, même voudrait-il
ne pas le croire. Mais qui ne voit qu'un tel athée qui prononce dans son coeur les mots par lesquels la foi désigne
Dieu en attachant à ces mots une signification et en leur
attachant une signification qui ne leur soit pas étrangère[20]
peut encore utiliser l'argument cartésien? Car qui a prouvé
que, pour parler le langage de Jean et d'Anselme[21], le
Diable, qui n'est pas demeuré dans la vérité n'est précisément pas en train de nous tromper en suggérant à notre
esprit les mots par lesquels la fois désigne Dieu?
Il reste donc à examiner le sens métaphysique de
l'objection cartésienne et d'examiner par conséquent quel
est le postulat métaphysique dont le *Proslogion* suppose la
validité pour être inconditionnellement démonstratif.
L'opposition qui s'institue, dans les *Méditations* cartésiennes entre la vérité de ma science et la vérité de la
chose, une fois le Dieu vérace démontré par les effets, a
pour conséquence de changer le statut de l'idée. L'idée en
Moi du parfait ne contient pas analytiquement l'existence

que la première preuve par les effets doit lui ajouter, tandis que l'idée de Dieu, dans la preuve ontologique, contient analytiquement cette même existence. La première idée, c'est l'idée-tableau, la seconde c'est l'idée-essence. Ce n'est pas leur perfection ou quantité de réalité qui fait la différence entre ces idées, sinon la possibilité même d'une preuve et d'une connaissance s'effondrerait. Ce qui les distingue c'est que l'une n'est qu'un mode du *Cogito* quand l'autre possède une valeur objective.

> . . . Si la démonstration de l'existence de Dieu comme cause et modèle de mon idée permet d'attribuer à celle-ci une valeur objective pleine et assurée, c'est qu'elle est parvenue à nous révéler que la réalité objective de l'idée est l'empreinte même de l'existence, ou de l'être, ou de la réalité intelligible, ou de l'essence actuelle de la chose hors de moi.[22]

Cette validation objective qui, chez Descartes, fait de l'idée en moi une essence en soi et qui légitime la preuve ontologique, n'équivaut nullement au réalisme exemplariste qui hypostasierait *extra cogitationem meam* les essences hors des existences, comme il arrive à quelque degré chez Malebranche et chez Leibniz.[23] En face de la puissance infinie de Dieu, les existences créées ne se distinguent précisément pas des essences rationnelles[24]. Ainsi le cartésianisme consiste dans cette conjonction remarquable: justifier la valeur objective des idées en les transformant en essences, mais se garder de leur prêter une vie qui leur permettrait autre chose que de sauver les phénomènes. Ce trait remarquable n'est autre que la marque de l'intuitionnisme métaphysique. L'intuitionnisme s'oppose au scepticisme en requérant un critère, c'est-à-dire une méthode. Il s'oppose au dogmatisme et particulièrement au réalisme, par sa règle d'économie, en refusant tout engagement ontologique auquel ne correspondrait pas une existence en acte.

A première vue, on pourrait penser que les preuves du *Proslogion* se rapprochent de celles de Descartes et se distinguent des preuves du *Monologion* précisément parce qu'elles posent comme unique prémisse le *id quo nihil maius cogitari potest*. Car, indépendamment du fait qu'un élément à la fois épistémologique et modal intervient dans la prémisse,[25] la considération de la quantité d'être, sur laquelle repose la preuve, paraît être extrinsèque à l'essence elle-même ; elle ne la désigne ni absolument, ni naturellement, ni simplement, mais seulement relativement.[26] Cette

relation essentielle de la preuve anselmienne aux effets
exclus ne l'établit-elle pas précisément au niveau même de
la première preuve cartésienne par les effets, c'est-à-dire
au niveau des réalités objectives en tant que, privées
encore de valeur objective, elles se distinguent des
essences ou de ce qui, selon Anselme, est "significatif de
la substance ou de l'essence?"[27]

Mais pressons l'analogie et nous en verrons s'évanouir
le fondement. La réalité objective de l'idée, chez Descartes, est indubitable parce qu'elle représente une chose
sans qu'elle assure en quoi que ce soit l'existence de cette
chose hors de la pensée. S'il en allait ainsi pour Anselme,
la validité de la première preuve, au chapitre II du *Proslogion*, s'effondrerait. Surtout, l'assimilation des effets
négatifs selon Anselme avec la réalité objective interdit de
comprendre ce qu'a de spécifique la preuve du *Proslogion* et
la confond avec le genre de preuve caractéristique du *Monologion*.

Ce dernier genre de preuve consiste, en effet, à partir
d'une *gradatio* de perfections données dans la création pour
conclure à l'existence d'un terme, situé hors de la série,
indépendant d'elle et fermé sur lui-même, ce qu'Augustin
désignait du nom de *circuitus*, et qui est cette perfection
même. A l'intérieur de la *gradatio* (1) chaque terme a cette
perfection à un degré plus ou moins grand relativement aux
autres termes de la série, (2) sa place est fixée par le
degré plus ou moins grand de similitude qu'il a avec la perfection placée hors de la série. Les termes de la *gradatio*
ont donc cette perfection par participation ou prédication
ou imitation; par exemple, d'un homme on dira qu'il est
vivant. Mais le terme transcendant du *circuitus* est, quant
à lui, identique à cette perfection: la souveraine nature
est substantiellement la Vie.[28]

Lorsque nous disons alors que Dieu a créé ce qui lui est
inférieur en ayant dans son intelligence "comme un exemplaire de la chose à faire ou, pour parler plus précisément
une forme, une ressemblance ou une norme"[29] et quand nous
comparons les différents degrés donnés de dignité de ces
formes, car qui douterait que le cheval soit meilleur que le
lion et l'homme supérieur au cheval ne mériterait pas d'être
appelé un homme,[30] notre discours et notre comparaison
doivent être rapportées à deux instances et à deux critères
différents. D'une part il y a la suite de la gradation ou
chaîne de similitude, au sein de laquelle les individus participent par imitation au degré de perfection qui leur donne
l'être de façon approchée. D'autre part il y a dans le
Verbe divin les essences vraies, simples et absolues.[31] Un
abîme sépare donc d'un coté ma science des choses créées

laquelle porte sur la seule ressemblance, de l'autre la nature des choses et les essences telles qu'elles sont dans le Verbe.

Mais cette distinction a pour conséquence que les preuves du *Monologion* n'atteignent Dieu que relativement, en tant qu'il appartient à la chaîne de similitude des effets. Indépendamment des difficultés logiques qui regardent les conditions rendant valide le passage de la *gradatio* au *circuitus*,[32] une difficulté théologique de premier ordre grève ces preuves, puisque le *summum omnium* n'est précisément considéré que dans sa relation avec ce qui n'est pas lui. Ce sont des preuves par la ressemblance.

On rêve donc d'une preuve qui s'affranchirait de la similitude et qui, sans pour autant prétendre comprendre l'incompréhensible, s'élèverait cependant à l'existence divine en tant que, conformément à l'essence propre de Dieu, elle est entièrement étrangère aux accidents et aux fluctuations des similitudes de la création. Or le *Proslogion* fournit cette preuve. Tandis que le *Summum omnium* rattache le Créateur aux créatures, le *id quo nihil maius cogitari potest* pose Dieu absolument hors de la gradation en le posant par l'impossibilité qu'il y a à penser quoi que ce soit de plus grand que lui. Le *nihil cogitare potest* est la marque qu'on ne sort pas de Dieu ; le *nihil maius* est la marque qu'on raisonne à partir de Dieu et non plus (comme lorsque Dieu était le terme du mouvement) à partir de la ressemblance avec le créé.

Le problème que devait résoudre Descartes était celui de la valeur objective des idées y compris l'idée de *summum omnium*. Il le résolvait en montrant que l'idée du parfait en moi est telle que la lumière naturelle me contraint, par le moyen des principes de correspondance et de causalité, à poser Dieu comme existant et vérace. Dès lors, l'idée de Dieu devient essence véritable et la preuve ontologique est validée.

Anselme ignore le problème cartésien. Quoi qu'on ait dit, les preuves du *Monologion* sont conformes au schéma réaliste tel qu'Augustin l'avait développé à partir de Platon.[33] Le parfait existe, sans quoi la chaîne des degrés de perfection que révèle la création resterait sans fondement.[34] Mais ce genre de preuve a quelque chose d'insatisfaisant. Non parce qu'il utilise le réalisme des idées et le passage qui fonde l'imitation de l'archétype sur son existence, mais parce qu'il ne peut l'utiliser à plein étant donné qu'il part non d'une multiplicité sensible participant d'un même intelligible, mais d'une multiplicité de sensibles hétérogènes participant à des intelligibles différents tous rangés dans une échelle de perfection croissante. La diffi-

culté que rencontre Anselme n'est pas la difficulté du
réalisme. C'est une difficulté concernant l'application du
réalisme à la considération d'une chaîne de ressemblance,
difficulté que la tradition platonicienne rencontrait quand
elle se demandait s'il y a idée de ce qui est susceptible du
plus ou du moins. C'est cette difficulté particulière que
résout le *Proslogion*. Les preuves du *Proslogion* comme
celles du *Monologion* dépendent rigoureusement de la thèse
métaphysique du réalisme, et cette thèse consiste à postuler
la valeur objective des idées et leur transformation en
essences dont l'intuitionnisme cartésien devait faire un
problème.[35] Mais, le postulat reçu, il fallait encore
l'appliquer à la théologie et échapper à cette objection que
la gradation des essences, sur laquelle repose la preuve
réaliste, reste extérieure et relative par rapport aux
essences intrinsèquement considérées. En recourant à la foi
(*Deo donante*), Anselme a su répondre à l'objection. Car
c'est à l'essence de Dieu et non à la similitude des créatures que la foi rapporte la similitude même par laquelle il
nous est donné de le saisir. Et c'est cette essence, vue
par une similitude qui lui est intrinsèquement rapportée,
qui pour notre intelligence (*Deo illuminante*) représente le
point culminant du réalisme métaphysique, d'un réalisme tel
que son objet même est plus grand que tout ce qui peut être
pensé.[36]

Notes

[1] B. Geyer, éd., *Die patristische und scholastische
Philosophie*, Vol. II de *F. Überwegs Grundriss der Geschichte
der Philosophie*, 15ᵉ éd. (Darmstadt: Wissenschaftliche
Buchgesellschaft, 1958), p. 201.

[2] La dépendance est par exemple affirmée par F. R. Hasse,
Anselm von Canterbury (Leipzig: 1843-52; réimp. Frankfurt
a. M.: Minerva, 1966), II, 262-72, et niée par Geyer, *Die
patristische*, p. 201.

[3] Je ne m'arrêterai pas ici aux questions historiques
d'influence.

[4] La différence entre Descartes et Anselme tient à ce
que, selon Descartes, le principe de causalité a une validité universelle, tandis que pour Anselme il ne porte que
sur tout ce qui devient (*fit*), non sur tout ce qui est
(*Monologion* VIII: Schmitt I,22,25-27). Encore ne fau-
drait-il pas exagérer cette différence comme on le remar-

quera pour Descartes quand il dit qu'en Dieu la cause for-
melle est "quasi efficiente" (*Réponses aux IV*[es] *Objections*,
Vol. VII de *Oeuvres*, éd. C. Adam et P. Tannery [Paris: L.
Cerf, 1897-1910], p. 243,23-26).

[5] J. Vuillemin, *Le Dieu d'Anselme et les apparences de la
raison* (Paris: Aubier Montaigne, 1971), pp. 11-14.

[6] Concernant Anselme, Vuillemin, *Le Dieu*, p. 19; concernant Descartes, M. Gueroult, *L'Ame et Dieu*, Vol. I de
Descartes selon l'ordre des raisons, (Paris: Aubier Montaigne, 1968), pp. 357-60.

[7] Gueroult, *L'Ame et Dieu*, pp. 159-168.

[8] Ainsi: *Meditatio III*: . . . illa [idea] per quam
summum aliquem Deum, aeternum, infinitum, omniscium, omnipo-
tentem, rerumque omnium, quae praeter ipsum est, creatorem
intelligo . . . (*Réponses*, p. 41), ou: Dei nomine intelligo
substantiam . . . (p. 48).

[9] *Proslogion* II: Schmitt I,101,14-15.

[10] *Réponses*, pp. 42 et 44.

[11] Gueroult, *L'Ame et Dieu*, pp. 210-213, 369, 373.

[12] *Méditation III*: *Réponses*, p. 43: En sorte que la
lumière naturelle me fait connaître évidemment, que les
idées sont en moi comme des tableaux ou des images, qui peuvent à la vérité facilement déchoir de la perfection des
choses dont elles ont été tirées, mais qui ne peuvent jamais
rien contenir de plus grand ou de plus parfait. . .

[13] Si l'on se réfère à la note précédente, on voit que
l'original qui ne contiendrait pas l'existence serait moins
grand ou moins parfait que le tableau ou l'image qui contient l'idée ou la représentation de l'existence.

[14] Le texte latin, *Réponses*, p. 50, dit: Sed forte maius
aliquid sum quam ipse intelligam.

[15] Ibid., p. 51.

[16] *Réponses*, pp. 40-41: . . . Si ces idées sont prises en
tant seulement que ce sont de certaines façons de penser, je
ne reconnais entre elles aucune différence ou inégalité, et
toutes semblent procéder de moi d'une même sorte; mais, les

considérant comme des images, dont les unes représentent une
chose et les autres une autre, il est évident qu'elles sont
fort différentes les unes des autres. Car, en effet, celles
qui me représentent des substances, sont sans doute quelque
chose de plus, et contiennent en soi (pour ainsi parler)
plus de réalité objective, c'est-à-dire participent par
représentation à plus de degrés d'être ou de perfection, que
celles qui me représentent seulement des modes ou accidents.
De plus, celle par laquelle je conçois un Dieu souverain,
éternel, infini, immuable, tout connaissant, tout puissant,
et Créateur universel de toutes les choses qui sont hors de
lui; celle-la, dis-je, a certainement en soi plus de réalité
objective, que celles par qui les substances finies me sont
représentées. Pour Anselme, Vuillemin, *Le Dieu*, pp. 32 et
seq., 62.

[17] *Réponses*, p. 75; Gueroult, *L'Ame et Dieu*, pp. 338,
356.

[18] Gueroult, *L'Ame et Dieu*, p. 353.

[19] *Proslogion* III: Schmitt I,104,4-7.

[20] Ibid.: Schmitt I,104,1-2.

[21] *De veritate* IV: Schmitt I,180,21-22.

[22] Gueroult, *L'Ame et Dieu*, p. 371.

[23] Ibid., p. 373.

[24] Ibid., pp. 382-384.

[25] *Ad Proslogion* V: Schmitt I,134,27-28: Non enim idem
valet quod dicitur "maius omnibus" et "quo maius cogitari
nequit" . . .; Vuillemin, *Le Dieu*, p. 21 et seq.

[26] *Monologion* XVI: Schmitt I,30,5 et seq.: Cum natura
summa dicitur justa vel magna vel aliquid similium, non
ostenditur quid sit, sed potius qualis vel quanta sit; ou
ibid. XV: Schmitt I,28,11-13: Hoc ipsum quod summa natura
summa omnium sive maior omnibus, quae ab illa facta sunt,
seu aliud aliquid similiter relative dici potest: manifestum
est, quoniam non eius naturalem essentiam designat; ou ibid.
XV: Schmitt I,28,20-22: Summum non simpliciter significat
illam essentiam, quae omnimodo melior et maior est quam
quidquid non est quod ipsa.

[27] Ibid. XV: Schmitt I,28,9-10.

[28] Ibid. XV-XVI et XXVIII: Schmitt I,28-31 et 56. C'est sur le juste et la justice qu'Anselme raisonne.

[29] Ibid. IX: Schmitt I,24; *Anselm of Canterbury*, éd. et trans. J. Hopkins and H. Richardson (Toronto et New York: Edwin Mellen Press, 1974), I,148,n. 20.

[30] *Monologion* IV: Schmitt I,16-18.

[31] Ibid. XXXI: Schmitt I,50,7-13: Satis itaque manifestum est in verbo, per quod facta sunt omnia, non esse ipsorum similitudinem, sed veram simplicemque essentiam; in factis vero non esse simplicem absolutamque essentiam, sed verae illius essentiae vix aliquam imitationem. Unde necesse est non idem verbum secundum rerum creatarum similitudinem magis vel minus esse verum, sed omnem creatam naturam eo altiori gradu essentiae dignitatisque consistere, quo magis illi propinquare videtur. Le *itaque* du début s'entend aisément; voir Augustin, *Sermo CCXIII: In traditione symboli*, Opera omnia . . . studio . . . s. Mauri (Paris: Muguet, 1688-1700), V,939B: Deus ita magnus est in operibus magnis, ut minor non sit in minimis.

[32] *Monologion* XXXVI: Schmitt I,54,18-55,2: Nam nihil dubium creatas substantias multo aliter esse in seipsis quam in nostra scientia. In seipsis namque sunt per ipsam suam essentiam; in nostra vero scientia non sunt earum essentiae, sed earum similitudines; voir Augustin, *De Genesi ad litteram* VIII: *Opera omnia* III,I,242G: Deus loquitur aut per suam substantiam, aut per sibi subditam creaturam.

[33] Vuillemin, *Le Dieu*, pp. 91-93.

[34] Sur cette preuve, Vuillemin, *Le Dieu*, pp. 87-131.

[35] Sur l'intuitionnisme cartésien: J. Vuillemin, *Nécessité ou contingence: L'aporie de Diodore et les systèmes philosophiques* (Paris: Editions de Minuit, 1984), pp. 208-29, 390-99.

[36] *Proslogion* XV: Schmitt I,112; Vuillemin, *Le Dieu*, pp. 16 et 58 et seq.

"Nul n'a plus grand amour
que de donner sa vie pour ses amis" (Jn 15:13).

La Signification de l'*unum argumentum* du *Proslogion*

Michel Corbin, SJ

1. Question

Pourquoi, après la redécouverte barthienne de la signification négative du *Quo majus cogitari nequit*, continuer à traiter *Proslogion* II et IV de S. Anselme comme une argumentation "ontologique"? Pourquoi continuer, presque unanimement, à projeter anachroniquement sur ce texte, déjà difficile, une expression kantienne qui vise et critique la preuve cartésienne de l'existence de Dieu à partir de l'idée de Parfait, présente en l'esprit de l'homme? Malgré toutes les précisions, nuances, et restrictions qui se peuvent ajouter, nul ne parvient, semble-t-il, à proposer, sous cette précompréhension, autre chose que le pseudo-syllogisme suivant: (1) Dieu est la totalité des perfections concevables (*omnitudo perfectionum*); (2) Or l'existence réelle (*esse in re*) est une telle perfection; (3) Dieu possède donc l'existence réelle. Ou, pour reprendre les paroles mêmes de Descartes:

> Je trouve manifestement que l'existence ne peut non plus être séparée de l'essence de Dieu, que de l'essence d'un triangle rectiligne, la grandeur de ces trois angles égaux à deux droits: ou bien de l'idée d'une montagne, l'idée d'une vallée; en sorte qu'il n'y a pas moins de répugnance à concevoir un Dieu (c'est-à-dire *un être souverainement parfait*) auquel manque l'existence (c'est-à-dire auquel manque quelque perfection) que de concevoir une montagne qui n'ait point de vallée.[1]

Une telle déduction analytique de l'existence de Dieu à partir de son essence -- *essentia involvit existentiam* -- ne diffère pas fondamentalement de la parabole de l'île perdue sous laquelle Gaunilon croit pouvoir résumer la démonstration d'Anselme, mais dont celui-ci récuse l'identification à sa propre démarche, parce qu'elle confond deux termes -- ou deux Noms de Dieu -- que lui-même a pris grand soin de distinguer: *majus omnibus (sive summum omnium)* et *quo nihil majus cogitari possit*, l'excellence superlative du Parfait et la fonction négative qui permet de reconnaître, dans l'intelligence de la foi, "tout ce que nous croyons de la substance divine."[2] Au III comme au § V de sa *Réponse*, l'abbé du Bec dit à son objectant:

> Si quelqu'un me trouvait quelque chose qui existât dans la réalité ou dans la seule pensée, hormis "Tel que plus grand ne se puisse penser," à quoi pût s'adapter l'enchaînement de cette mienne argumentation, je trouverais et lui donnerais l'île perdue pour qu'elle ne fût plus jamais perdue. Dire "Plus grand que tout" et dire "Tel que plus grand ne se puisse penser" n'ont pas la même valeur pour prouver que ce qui est dit est aussi dans la réalité.[3]

Et Karl Barth commente ces affirmations en écrivant:

> La formule que Gaunilon introduit dans la discussion par négligence: *quod est majus omnibus*, et qui correspond au premier état de l'opinion d'Anselme . . . n'est que la *retraduction ontologique* de la version noétique choisie délibérément et soigneusement affinée par Anselme.[4]

Si cette lecture est indiscutable, pourquoi semblable "retraduction ontologique" se poursuit-elle, même chez les auteur qui repèrent avec exactitude les sophismes de Gaunilon? Cette permanence étonnante mérite réflexion.

Un premier éclaircissement est apporté par l'examen des sources augustiniennes du *quo majus cogitari nequit*. Dans une longue note de son étude sur la doctrine trinitaire de S. Augustin, Olivier de Roy a rassemblé de nombreux fragments qui ont pu inspirer S. Anselme dans le choix définitif de son argument.[5] Certains ne contiennent guère qu'une simple équivalence:

> Quo nullus est superior (*De libero arbitrio* II,vi,14).

> Ita cogitatur ut aliquid quo nihil melius sit atque sublimius illa cogitatio conetur attingere (*De doctrina christiana* I,vii,7).

> Nihil est majus voluntate Dei (*De LXXXIII
> quaestionibus* XVIII).

> Unum certe quaerimus quo simplicius nihil
> est (*De vera religione* XXXV,65).

D'autres, en revanche, identifient ces équivalents aux divers superlatifs de *super, bonus* et *altus*, c'est-à-dire à: *summum, optimus* et *altissimus*:

> Ad tale bonum pervenisse quo amplius non
> potest, id autem quod dicimus *optimum*.

> Solus enim Deus *altissimus* quo nihil est
> altius.

> Illud *summum* bonum quo non est quiddam
> melius aut superius.

> *Summum* bonum omnino et quo esse aut cogitari
> melius nihil possit.

> (*De moribus ecclesiae catholicae et de mori-
> bus manichaeorum* I,iii,5; xvi,29; II,i,1;
> xi,24)

Pareilles identifications conduisent d'autant plus l'auteur à rapprocher les deux docteurs de l'eglise que sa note est intervenue à propos de la démonstration de Dieu tentée dans le *De libero arbitrio*. En voici la conclusion:

> Chez l'un comme chez l'autre, la grandeur de
> Dieu est une hauteur au-dessus de laquelle
> l'homme ne peut s'élever pour juger celui
> qui le juge. Mais, si Augustin est un tour-
> nant tellement important dans l'histoire de
> la pensée platonicienne sur Dieu, la faisant
> passer de l'*epekeina tès ousias* à l'*id quo
> majus cogitari nequit*, c'est qu'il conjugue
> une philosophie du Bien et de l'Un avec une
> ontologie créationniste. Dans l'une on
> remonte par l'intérieur à une unité au-delà
> de la pensée, dans l'autre on pose un être
> *maximal* au principe de tous les êtres.
> Mais, en conjuguant cet Un au-delà de l'être
> et cet Etre *suprême*, Augustin insère le
> dynamisme d'un dépassement de toute limite

> au sein de la positivité ontologique, en
> même temps qu'il problématise Dieu au sein
> d'une philosophie mystique.[6]

Cette lecture des sources augustiniennes de l'argument
procède, en fait, à deux *identifications* qui, toutes deux,
se trouvent attestées dans le *Monologion*: (1) "Est
suréminent cela qui surémine sur les autres choses de telle
sorte qu'il n'ait ni égal ni plus excellent";[7] (2) "Le
secret d'une chose si *sublime* transcende toute fine pointe
de l'esprit humain et ainsi, je pense, tout effort pour
expliquer comment il doit être maintenu."[8] La première
identification réunit *summum*, qu'Olivier du Roy nomme "être
maximal" et "être suprême," avec une ébauche de l'argument.
Elle est réitérée au début du *Proslogion* XIV quand Anselme
s'interroge sur ce qu'il a trouvé: "Tu cherchais Dieu et tu
as trouvé qu'il est quelque chose de suréminent à toutes
choses, dont rien de meilleur ne peut être pensé."[9] La
seconde rassemble le même superlatif et cette "unité au-delà
de la pensée" qui n'est sans doute pas autre chose que "l'un
au-delà de l'être." Elle est reprise, à son tour, à la fin
du même chapitre du *Proslogion*: "Certainement plus que la
créature ne pourrait reconnaître."[10]
    De telles identifications s'opposeraient-elles à ce que
Karl Barth souligne sous la différence entre "version
noétique" et "retraduction ontologique?" Imposeraient-
elles, contre tant d'affirmations d'Anselme, la lecture traditionnelle qui, sous le *quo majus cogitari nequit*, entend
toujours le *Perfectissime*?

> Par le nom de Dieu, disait Descartes, j'en-
> tends une substance infinie, éternelle,
> immuable, indépendante, toute connaissante,
> et par laquelle moi-même, et toutes les
> autres chose qui sont (s'il est vrai qu'il y
> en ait qui existent) ont été créés et pro-
> duites.[11]

Il semble toutefois qu'à défaut d'imposer l'interprétation
"ontologique," les identifications en soient une cause
majeure, car une *identification* non reconnue comme telle,
c'est-à-dire comme le résultat d'une séquence logique commençant par une *différenciation*, devient nécessairement une
confusion. Peut-être la lecture traditionnelle est-elle
incapable de sortir de la confusion et de retenir les leçons
de Karl Barth parce que celui-ci, comme inversement, a
dégagé la différence, mais n'en a pas fait une différen-

ciation ordonnée, dans le processus d'intelligence, à une identification ultérieure. En ce cas, l'analyse des sources renverrait à une difficulté fondamentale du texte, celle même qu'Anselme indique dès les premières lignes de son Préambule quand il rappelle la requête d'unité *noétique* qui l'a saisi devant le constat de l'insuffisance du *Monologion*.

Le docteur magnifique s'est demandé, tous le savent, s'il se pouvait trouver un argument unique qui n'ait besoin que de lui seul pour se prouver (*quod nullo alio ad se probandum quam se solo indigeret*) et pour prouver, dans cette auto-probation: (1) que Dieu est vraiment; (2) qu'Il est le Bien suréminent (*summum*) n'ayant besoin de nul autre pour être; (3) "tout ce que nous croyons de la substance divine."[12] Si l'argument, qui doit trancher toutes alternatives possibles entre foi et incroyance, est bien le Nom de Dieu dont nous cherchons la signification exacte: *quo nihil majus cogitari possit*, si le projet du livre conjoint l'autoprobation de ce Nom et la double preuve de l'existence et de l'essence de Dieu comme *bonum summum*, il ne peut y avoir passage logique d'un Nom à l'autre, passage intérieur au *Credo* dont les articles forment totalité (*concatenatio veritatum*), passage dialectique sous mode de reconnaissance par l'absurde de ce qui est déjà connu par la foi, que sous la présupposition d'une différence préalable entre le Nom-argument et les autres noms relatifs à l'existence comme à l'essence de Dieu. Cette différenciation est double. Elle joue d'abord entre le Nom-argument et *summum* qui n'est reconnu comme tel, grâce à l'argument, qu'à la première argumentation de *Proslogion* V. Elle distingue ensuite *quo majus cogitari nequit* de *quiddam majus quam cogitari possit*, qui se trouve reconnu de la même manière en *Proslogion* XV et ne désigne pas autre chose que "l'au-delà de la pensée." Les deux différenciations étant ordonnées, dans le processus d'*intellectus fidei*, aux identifications qui ont été relevées, le progrès du *Proslogion* par rapport au *Monologion* devient manifeste. Au lieu de n'avoir qu'un seul nom -- *summum* -- pour désigner la transcendance de Dieu, de devoir toujours répéter les mêmes expressions: *summa essentia, summa natura* . . ., le *Proslogion* dispose de trois Noms pour signifier le Toi seigneurial auquel il s'adresse. Ces trois Noms de l'unique transcendance de Dieu ne signifient pas de la même manière et se peuvent numéroter selon l'ordre de leur apparition:

I.   *Quo nihil majus cogitari possit*
(*Proslogion* I)

II.   *Summum   omnium   (sive   majus omnibus)*
(*Proslogion* V)

III.   *Quiddam   majus   quam   cogitari   possit*
(*Proslogion* XV)

Que,   dans   leur   différenciation   même,   ils doivent s'identifier au terme du processus de reconnaissance de la foi,
cette coexistence d'une différenciation et d'une identification   est   un   problème   qu'aucune   lecture   jusqu'ici,   ni
l'ontologique   ni   celle   de   Karl   Barth,   n'a pris en considération. Les sources augustiniennes ou l'unilatéralité
de la polémique expliquent, pour une part, cet oubli, mais
il est possible que la difficulté textuelle ait   encore   une
autre   dimension, plus profonde et plus cachée, en sorte que
le premier éclaircissement en exige un second.
Pour respecter en même temps différenciation et   identification,   une   grande   attention   est   requise aux formulations
mêmes du texte, aux manières différentes dont les trois Noms
signifient   l'une   et   identique   transcendance de Dieu. Ne
contenant qu'un superlatif et ne   faisant   référence   qu'aux
étants,   le Nom II (*summum omnium*) signifie de manière POSI-
TIVE et ONTIQUE. Ne contenant pas de   négation,   mais   rem-
plaçant le superlatif par un comparatif et la référence aux
étants par le rapport au pouvoir de la pensée,   le   Nom   III
(*quidam   majus   quam   cogitari   possit*)   signifie de manière
POSITIVE et NOETIQUE. Ajoutant au comparatif   et   à   la
référence au pensable une négation, le Nom I ou Nom-argument
(*aliquid quo nihil majus cogitari possit*) ne peut que signifier   de manière NEGATIVE et NOETIQUE. Mais comment distinguer ONTIQUE et POSITIF de NEGATIF   et   NOETIQUE?   Comment
procéder pour les autres combinaisons possibles?
Karl   Barth   a   très   rigoureusement   opéré la première de
ces distinctions -- la seule qui nous intéresse ici -- en se
reportant à la phrase de *Proslogion* III qui revient, après
les deux preuves imbriquées de l'existence de Dieu,   sur   le
sens   du   Nom   I: "Si quelque esprit pouvait penser quelque
chose de meilleur que Toi, la créature s'élèverait au-dessus
du   créateur,   jugerait   du   créateur,   ce   qui est très absurde."[13]   Négative   est   ici   la   signification car   elle
énonce, à propos du Dieu de la foi, l'impossibilité de
saisir son essence à l'intérieur de l'horizon de   la   représentation   sous lequel l'homme peut penser plus grand. Elle
interdit de se placer au-dessus de Dieu pour   juger   de   son
essence   ou de son oeuvre à partir de plus grand. Et, parce
qu'elle concerne le pouvoir de recul de la pensée, elle   est
encore   noétique.   Elle consonne avec les mots fameux de S.
Augustin: "*Si comprehendisti, non est Deus; si comprehen-*

dere potuisti, aliud pro Deo comprehendisti.[14] NEGATIF et NOETIQUE: les deux dimensions de la significations sont rassemblées dans ces quelques lignes du théologien réformé:

> Pour comprendre plus profondément la signification de ce nom, il faut avant tout faire bien attention *à ce qu'il ne dit pas*. Il ne dit pas que Dieu soit la chose la plus élévée que l'homme conçoive véritablement, et au-dessus de laquelle il ne pourrait rien concevoir de plus élévé. Il ne dit pas non plus que Dieu soit la chose la plus élévée que l'homme puisse concevoir . . . Ce que la formule dit de (son) objet, *c'est seulement une chose négative*: on ne peut concevoir quelque chose de plus grand; on ne peut rien concevoir qui la surpasse ou puisse le surpasser, sous quelque rapport que ce soit; aussitôt qu'on a conçu quelque chose qui soit plus grand que lui sous un rapport quelconque, on n'a pas encore commencé à le concevoir (dans la mesure où l'on peut le concevoir), ou bien on a cessé de le concevoir.[15]

Impossible de douter de la justesse de cette lecture, que tous du reste accordent. Mais comment se fait-il que tous, ou presque, après cette concession, oublient la distinction ainsi opérée d'avec l'idée de Parfait et réitèrent la confusion qu'Anselme reproche à Gaunilon? Quelques lignes du célèbre article de Jacques Palliard sur "Prière et dialectique"[16] offrent, semble-t-il, une réponse très sûre. Adoptant une perspective "réflexive," ce philosophe voit dans la preuve anselmienne une remontée vers la condition *a priori* de tout exercice de la pensée humaine:

> La signification essentielle de l'argument ne consiste nullement à passer du logique au réel, mais à saisir au sein même d'une expérience spécifiquement intellectuelle la réalité qui la conditionne et qu'elle réfléchit en objet. Tu ne m'affirmerais pas, pourrait-on dire, si déjà tu ne me possédais.[17]

Quelle est cette réalité qui conditionne l'expérience intellectuelle, cette "aspiration qui s'éprouve comme un progrès indéfini?" Elle est nommée *l'infini* car, est-il dit, "seule

l'expérience de la réflexion peut livrer un infini
actuel,"[18] l'infini ou l'indépassable, toutes expressions
qui peuvent transcrire, en langue française, l'argument
anselmien:

> L'idée originaire n'est nullement un concept
> logique comme le croit Gaunilon, l'adver-
> saire d'Anselme. Dieu, en effet, ne re-
> semble à rien, n'appartient à aucun classe-
> ment conceptuel. C'est tout autrement qu'il
> faut entendre l'idée de Dieu: non l'essence
> s'offrant au regard de l'homme, mais la
> désignation de l'essence: *aliquid quo nihil
> majus cogitari potest*, quelque chose de tel
> que rien de plus grand ne peut être conçu.
> Pour éviter la paraphrase dans un texte où
> les substantifs abstraits sont rares, on
> peut traduire d'un mot: *l'infini*, et mieux
> encore *l'indépassable* qui exprime l'impos-
> sibilité de concevoir quelque chose de plus
> grand.[19]

De fait, *indépassable* veut dire: tel qu'on ne puisse le
dépasser, et *infini*: tel qu'on ne puisse lui assigner de
fin, ce qui renvoie à *Proslogion* XIII sur l'impossibilité de
circonscrire l'essence de Dieu. Mais Jacques Palliard n'use
pas de l'adjectif. Le faisant précéder de l'article défini,
il le substantifie de sorte que *l'indépassable* signifie: *ce*
qui ne peut être dépassé, et *l'infini*: *ce* qui n'a pas de
fin. Avec cette introduction de l'article, compréhensible
pour des raisons d'abbréviation, se produit alors -- pour
parler comme S. Thomas -- le virage dangereux de l'infini
négatif vers l'infini *privatif*. Dans le passage de l'adjectif au substantif, la proposition relative qui suit *aliquid* et dont la signification est proprement négative
puisqu'elle conjoint négation, comparatif et référence au
pensable, devient la désignation d'une *excellence superlative*. Après le rappel des négations -- impossibilité de
tout "classement conceptuel" -- vient donc la nécessaire
suppression de la négation et l'auteur peut parler d'"idée
originaire," de "désignation de l'essence," d'"idée de Dieu"
puis, quelques lignes plus loin, de "l'infini en tout genre
comme pourraient dire Spinoza ou Malebranche."[20]

Etrange dérapage. Peut-être manifeste-t-il que la formulation du Nom I est moins simple qu'il n'y paraît. La
phrase [21] comprend, en effet, une principale: *credimus* et
une subordonnée: *te esse aliquid quo nihil majus cogitari
possit*, qui attribue au Toi seigneurial de Dieu un Nom

lui-même composé de deux éléments: (1) un neutre de désignation *positive*: "quelque chose"; (2) une relative à fonction noétique et *négative*: "dont plus grand ne se puisse penser." Or cette dualité n'a pas été relevée par Karl Barth dont l'argumentation s'est principalement appuyée sur la *Réponse* à Gaunilon où la position du "quelque chose" est très souvent omise. L'argument s'y trouvant réduit à la seule relative: *quo nihil majus cogitari possit*, le théologien suisse peut parler de *fonction négative*, se borner à rappeler comment le Nom se distingue de l'idée cartésienne de Parfait, sans se demander comment *aliquid* peut bien *porter* cette signification purement négative. Son interprétation est en quelque sorte l'inverse du philosophe français qui, lui, met sous le boisseau la fonction négative en maintenant le "quelque chose" *porteur* de la fonction. Alors s'éclaire d'un jour nouveau l'opposition des interprétations. Dans un premier temps, Karl Barth pose la différence entre idée de Parfait (Nom II) et argument (Nom I), mais sans ajouter que cette différenciation est ordonnée à une identification; ses adversaires, inversement, font de l'identification un résultat. Dans un second temps, Karl Barth souligne la fonction et la signification négatives de l'argument, mais sans s'interroger sur l'*aliquid* qui la porte et soutient; ses adversaires, inversement, Jacques Palliard en tête, insistent sur cet *aliquid*, mais sans s'inquiéter de l'inexorable logique qui joue entre l'adjectif et l'adjectif substantivé. Pareil conflit déploie la question posée au commencement de cet essai, lui apportant une réponse plus profonde qu'auparavant. Il renvoie, nul n'en peut douter, à la difficulté de penser ensemble ce que l'abbé du Bec a juxtaposé dans un même nom: *une position et une négation*, un "quelque chose" et l'impossibilité de penser "plus grand." La dualité explique le conflit, mais cette réponse est aussitôt question: *comment approcher et penser une coexistence qui ressemble à une contradiction?*

2. Eclaircissement

Pour que soit juste la lecture du conflit, et vrai que continuer la lecteur "ontologique," après les analyses de Karl Barth, procède d'une incapacité à penser jusqu'au bout le caractère d'*exception* de l'*unum argumentum*, il faut que le paradoxe de sa formulation soit pensable, que la coexistence d'une position et d'une négation ne soit pas une contradiction, bref que se puisse désigner le "quelque chose" qui, en Dieu, porte et soutient l'impossibilité des idoles dont l'homme peut toujours penser plus grand. Pour y parve-

nir, il suffit, semble-t-il, d'examiner comment fonctionne
la fonction négative et de chercher comment ce fonctionne-
ment présuppose la position d'un "quelque chose." Un exemple privilégié paraît tout désigné: les cc. IX à XI sur
justice et miséricorde qui préparent la christologie du *Cur
deus homo* et qu'ignorent d'ordinaire les commentaires du
Proslogion. Il s'agit, pour Anselme, d'y lever une contradiction notoire:

> Mais en vérité comment épargnes-Tu les mé-
> chants si Tu es tout entier et suréminem-
> ment juste? Comment le tout entier et
> suréminemment juste fait-il quelque chose
> qui n'est point juste? Ou quelle est cette
> justice de donner la vie éternelle à qui
> mérite la mort éternelle? D'où vient donc,
> Dieu bon, bon envers les bons et les mé-
> chants, d'où vient que Tu sauves les mé-
> chants, si ce n'est point juste et si Tu ne
> fais rien qui ne soit juste?[21]

Si justice et miséricorde, apparemment, se contredisent
et si cette *repugnantia* constitue l'aporie à résoudre, la
difficulté ne concerne pas la justice et la miséricorde
prises isolément, mais uniquement leur *conjonction*. L'énoncé
de l'aporie suppose alors que, dans un premier temps, soit
montrée la nécessité d'attribuer à Dieu la justice *isolément*, puis la miséricorde *isolément*. Ce fut l'objet de
Proslogion V, essentiel à notre propos car il contient la
reconnaissance du Nom II (idée de Parfait) à partir de la
fonction négative contenue dans le Nom I (argument):

> Qu'es-Tu, Seigneur Dieu, dont rien de plus
> grand ne puisse être pensé? Mais qu'es-Tu
> sinon cela qui surémine à toutes choses et,
> seul existant par soi, fit toutes les autres
> choses de rien? Tout ce qui n'est pas tel
> est moindre, en effet, que ce qui peut être
> pensé. Mais on ne peut le penser de Toi.
> Quel bien manque donc au Bien suréminent
> (*summum*) par qui est tout bien? Ainsi es-Tu
> juste, véridique, heureux et tout ce qu'il
> est meilleur d'étre que de n'être pas. Car
> il est meilleur d'être juste que non-juste,
> heureux que non-heureux.[22]

Développons: puisque justice et miséricorde appartiennent
aux x tels que x > non-x, refuser ce qu'atteste la Bible, à

savoir que Dieu est juste et miséricordieux, serait contredire au Nom I. S'il disait: Dieu n'est pas juste, ou: Dieu
est non-juste, l'homme penserait quelque chose de plus grand
que Dieu: ce "juste" qui est meilleur que le "non-juste,"
et un bien manquerait au Bien suréminent et parfait. L'argumentation est simple, en tout semblable à celles de *Proslogion* II et III sur l'existence, mais exige aussi quelques
précisions pour n'être point confondue avec le syllogisme
"ontologique" qui semble voisin: (1) Dieu est la somme de
toutes les perfections (*omnitudo perfectionum*); (2) Or
justice et miséricorde sont de telles perfections; (3) Dieu
possède donc la justice et la miséricorde. La preuve anselmienne, à l'encontre de ce raisonnement pourtant valide,
suppose qu'il soit déjà connu par la foi que Dieu est juste
et miséricordieux. Ce présupposé biblique apparaît en
Proslogion XI avec la citation explicite de deux versets de
psaumes: "Toutes les voies du Seigneur sont miséricorde et
vérité" (Ps 24:10); "Le Seigneur est juste en toutes ses
voies" (Ps 144:17). Ainsi la foi sait-elle ce qu'il s'agit
de démontrer, et la démonstration n'a sens qu'à reconnaître
(*intelligere*) cette connaissance préalable en *excluant* toute
proposition incroyante qui la contredit.

Pour découvrir cette modalité négative de la démonstration, Anselme a sans nul doute pris modèle sur un texte
des *Confessions* qu'Olivier du Roy a curieusement omis de
ranger parmi les sources augustiniennes de l'argument:

> C'est ainsi que je faisais effort pour
> trouver le reste, comme j'avais déjà trouvé
> que l'incorruptible est meilleur que le cor-
> ruptible, ce qui me faisait confesser que
> Toi, quoi que Tu sois, Tu es incorruptible.
> Car *jamais aucune âme n'a pu ou ne pourra
> penser quelque chose qui soit meilleur que
> Toi*, qui es le Bien suréminent, et le meil-
> leur. Or, puisque c'est en toute vérité et
> certitude qu'on place l'incorruptible avant
> le corruptible, comme déjà moi-même je l'y
> plaçais, j'aurais pu déjà par la pensée
> atteindre quelque chose qui eût été meilleur
> que mon Dieu, si Toi, Tu n'avais pas été
> incorruptible.[23]

Dans son identification même au *bonum summum*, l'impossibilité de penser meilleur que Dieu se différencie des superlatifs et de la dénomination d'incorruptibilité qui leur est
attachée parce qu'elle intervient comme la fonction d'exclusion rendant possible la reconnaissance de la dénomination.

La fonction *exclut* que soit attribuée au vrai Dieu la cor-
ruptibilité des idoles faites de main d'homme, parce que
l'incorruptible est pensable, qui est plus grand et meilleur
que le corruptible.

Impossible de refuser à Dieu le comparatif "plus grand"
du moment qu'il est pensable, au moins à titre d'hypothése;
impossible de ne pas faire le saut vers la foi qui confesse
"plus grand!" Bien qu'inséparable du comparatif "plus
grand," l'impossibilité de penser "plus grand" que le Dieu
de la foi en diffère par la manière de signifier. Déjà
cette différence était présente en *Monologion* XV qui sert de
chaînon intermédiaire entre la source augustinienne et le
Proslogion. Au terme d'une réflexion assez embrouillée sur
le transfert à Dieu des biens et dénominations venus des
créatures, et sur le statut herméneutique de *summum* qui doit
servir de *correctif* et précéder toutes dénominations ainsi
transférées -- *summa vita, summa justitia* . . . --, Anselme
concluait:

> (L'essence suréminente) est la seule en
> regard de laquelle absolument rien n'est
> meilleur; elle est meilleure que toutes les
> choses qui ne sont pas ce qu'elle est . . .
> Bref, il faut TAIRE qu'elle soit de ces
> chose auxquelles est *supérieur* ce qui n'est
> pas ce qu'elles sont; et DIRE, comme la
> raison l'enseigne, qu'elle est de ces chose
> auxquelles est *inférieur* tout ce qui n'est
> pas ce qu'elles sont.[24]

Deux règles herméneutiques ordonnent ici le transfert: une
règle *négative*, taire de Dieu tout x tel que x < non-x (ce
qui est le cas de "corruptible" ou de "corporel") et une
règle *positive*, dire de Dieu tout x tel que x > non-x (ce
qui est le cas de justice et miséricorde). Elles sont
situées sur le même plan dans le *Monologion* mais se trouvent
en déséquilibre dans le *Proslogion*. Le règle négative
devient, en effet, le Nom I, fonction de reconnaissance par
l'absurde de toutes les dénominations divines, tandis que la
règle positive est intégrée au Nom II comme le quantifica-
teur logique qui en définit la richesse. Dans cette
différenciation, tout se passe comme si la positivité de
"plus grand" -- des biens et dénominations qui s'ensuivent
-- exigeait, pour être une véritable positivité, que se produise la négation d'une négation: d'abord l'idolâtrie comme
NON injuste au juste rapport de créature à Créateur, puis le
Nom-argument comme NON au NON de l'idolâtrie. Comme si
l'opération d'exclusion de l'incroyance idolâtre, essen-

tielle à la fonction de reconnaissance, était devenue essentielle au véritable contenu de la perfection divine!

Confirmation de cette lecture diachronique, depuis la
source augustinienne jusqu'au *Proslogion* reprenant et corri-
geant le *Monologion*, apparaît dans la confrontation de
justice et miséricorde qui fait l'objet et la difficulté
propres de *Proslogion* IX à XI. Les deux dénominations
bibliques ayant été accordées *isolément* en *Proslogion* V, par
l'exclusion de leurs contraires, la nouveauté de ces trois
chapitres consiste à creuser le contenu de ces deux "biens"
à partir de l'apparente contradiction qui suit immédiatement
leur confrontation. Le procédé, classique depuis Boèce,
constitue la *quaestio disputata* au sens strict. Dans le
corpus anselmien, il prend toute son ampleur dans la
dernière oeuvre: le *De concordia*. Si le dire biblique, en
effet, se diffracte en deux registres de langage, qui font
question parce qu'ils semblent se contredire, mais si la
Bible consigne de manière normative une Parole de Dieu qui
n'est "pas à mesure humaine" (Ga 1:11), l'immédiate contradiction peut être résolue dès qu'elle est accueillie comme
la trace, dans le discours étroit de l'homme, d'un *surplus*
d'intelligibilité, ou d'une *concors veritas* plus logique que
toute logique. Dans cette perspective, il devient impossible, comme l'eût fait le *Monologion*, de se contenter
d'ajouter le correctif *summe* aux deux dénominations en
cause, pour conclure: *Deus est summe justus et summe miseri-
cors*. Dieu l'est, certes, mais le correctif, du fait qu'il
ne contient aucune négation dans son expression linguis-
tique, s'entend nécessairement selon la positivité de l'excellence superlative: Dieu est *infiniment, parfaitement et
suprêmement* juste et miséricordieux. Pour que soit réelle-
ment prise en compte — et surmontée — la contradiction
initiale, il faut qu'une négation soit dûment explicitée.
Or, puisqu'une telle explicitation au coeur de *summum* ne
peut s'accomplir autrement que par l'intervention de
l'argument, fonction *négative* interdisant de penser plus
grand que Dieu, c'est la différenciation de *quo nihil majus
cogitari possit* d'avec *summum* qui permet de reconnaître la
vérité de ce superlatif. Cet approfondissement du contenu
de *summum* peut se nommer: *redoublement* de transcendance en
sur-transcendance. Il est attesté dans l'argumentation par
l'absurde que *Proslogion* IX propose en complet parallélisme
avec *Proslogion* V.

Analysons les grandes lignes de ce *mouvement* de pensée.
S'il apparaît une contradiction entre justice et miséricorde, en sorte qu'apparemment la miséricorde est non-
justice et la justice non-miséricorde, si ces deux appela-
tions, d'autre part, s'identifient dans la simplicité

divine, en sorte que la miséricorde est la justice, et toute autre dénomination semblable, il est possible de prendre une troisième appelation qui serve d'intermédiare pour la solution de l'aporie. Cette tierce perfection est la *bonté* et autorise le raisonnement suivant:

> Ta miséricorde ne naît-elle pas de ta justice? N'épargnes-tu pas les méchants par justice? S'il en est ainsi, Seigneur, s'il en est ainsi, enseigne-moi comment. Est-ce parce qu'*il est juste que Tu sois si bon qu'on ne puisse Te reconnaître meilleur*, et que Tu oeuvres si puissamment qu'on ne puisse Te penser plus puissant? Qu'est-il de plus juste? De toute façon, cela ne se ferait pas si Tu étais bon en rétribuiant seulement et en n'épargnant pas, si Tu faisais les bons à partir des seuls non-bons et non à partir des méchants. Il est juste de la sorte que Tu épargnes les méchants et fasses les bons à partir des méchants.[25]

En se rappelant la variante qui a précédé ce passage: "Tu serais moins bon si Tu n'étais bienveillant envers *aucun* méchant,"[26] il est permis de formaliser et de distinguer trois étapes:

(1) *La reprise de Proslogion V*: "Il est juste que Tu sois si bon qu'on ne puisse Te reconnaître meilleur." La justice désignant ici une relation de Dieu à Dieu ou, plutôt, du Nom II ["si bon"] au Nom I ["qu'on ne puisse Te reconnaître meilleur"], la proposition qui identifie les deux Noms est à la fois commencement et terme de l'argumentation. Elle présuppose et pose que l'impossibilité de penser "meilleur" que Dieu, en excluant toute limitation de la bonté de Dieu, fasse reconnaître *le surcroît de bonté* qu'atteste la Bible en racontant la miséricorde qui pardonne et épargne les pécheurs. Se déroulant par l'absurde, l'argumentation présuppose ce qu'elle pose, à savoir que soit déjà connu par la foi ce qui doit être reconnu par le Nom I.

(2) *L'établissement du surcroît de bonté*: "Cela ne se ferait pas si Tu étais bon en rétribuant seulement." Si l'homme peut penser, au moins à titre d'hypothèse, certaine inégalité quantitative à propos de la bonté, si le fait d'être bon "pour les bons et les méchants" (Mt 5:45) est plus grand et meilleur qu'être bon pour les bons *seulement*, si la bonté a *plus d'extension* en s'exerçant par rétribution

ET pardon qu'en rétribuant SEULEMENT, en se limitant à la
seule rétribution des bons et de leurs mérites, refuser
d'attribuer à Dieu ce "plus grand" -- qui est pensable --
serait contredire au Nom interdisant de penser plus grand.

(3) *La conclusion*: "Il est juste que Tu épargnes les
méchants." Si la deuxième étape démontre -- par l'absurde
-- que la miséricorde naît de la justice, il est juste que
Dieu soit miséricordieux et, puisque la miséricorde déborde
la *simple* justice, *juste que Dieu soit plus que juste*. Dieu
est juste en étant plus que juste: quoique paradoxale,
cette conclusion est conforme au témoignage biblique, notamment à ce que l'apôtre prononce au sujet de la divine surabondance (*hyperperisseuein*): "Là où le péché s'est multi-
plié, la grâce a surabondé" (Rm 5:20). Qu'elle soit aussi
une des pensées décisives de S. Anselme, bien d'autres
expressions interdisent d'en douter, à commencer par celle
qui termine le *Proslogion* en rassemblant toute promesse
faite par Dieu: "J'ai trouvé certaine joie, pleine et plus
que pleine (*plenum et plus quam plenum*)."[27]

Comment ne pas remarquer maintenant que le mouvement de
pensée induit par le Nom I pour prouver l'accord entre justice et miséricorde qu'atteste la Bible se superpose exactement au mouvement selon lequel le premier chapitre de la
Première aux Corinthiens témoigne de la sagesse de la croix.
Là où Paul proclame : "*Ce qui* est folie de Dieu est plus
sage que les hommes, et *ce qui* est faiblesse de Dieu est
plus fort que les hommes" (I Co 1:25), Anselme montre que *la
miséricorde de Dieu*, laquelle apparaît *non-justice, est plus
juste que toute justice d'homme*; soit en formalisant: non-x
est plus x que x. S'il existe une telle homologie avec le
dire paulinien, c'est parce que la fonction négative et
noétique contenue dans le Nom -- argument a creusé le sens
de *summum*, qui n'équivaut plus, comme précédemment, au
simple: "infiniment, parfaitement et suprêmement," mais
signifie désormais: *plus qu'*infiniment, *plus que* parfaitement, *plus qu'*éminemment ou *sur-*éminemment. La transcendance, ouparavant superlative, s'est clairement redoublée
et, dans la nécessité de penser une justice qui n'est justice qu'à se faire plus que justice, miséricorde, l'union
des contraires s'est manifestée plus logique que toute
logique. *La conjonction de justice et miséricorde est plus
juste que la justice seule.* Mais le redoublement suppose,
rappelons-le, que soit exclu le refus incroyant de ce surplus, et que ce même surplus soit pensable, pour autant que
l'homme est capable d'appliquer à lui-même, à sa pensée, le
comparatif "plus grand" dont il use pour penser et repré-

senter le monde des étants. L'homme peut se décentrer, penser [sans pouvoir le représenter] l'au-delà de tout au-delà spatialisé dont il use en ce monde, redoubler le "plus" dont il est capable. Du moment que ce double "plus" est pensable [non pas représentable], il est nécessaire en vertu du Nom qui exclut toute circonscription de Dieu. C'est par cette exclusion, précisément, qu'est reconnue la surabondance gracieuse de Dieu, c'est-à-dire le contenu de la foi chrétienne auquel appartient le Nom. Par une opération intérieure à la foi, le simple "plus grand" est devenu un "plus grand" *redoublé*: plus que grand, *plus que perfection*, ce qui ne dit pas autre chose que le Nom III: *plus quam a creatura valeat intelligi*.[28] Dès lors, puisque ce devenir présuppose ce qu'il pose: l'identification des Noms I et II, de la fonction négative et de l'idée de Parfait, puisqu'il est reconnaissance de ce qui est déjà connu par la foi, la démarche laisse supposer que le "quelque chose" porteur de la fonction, et encore caché, est lié à ce redoublement. En donnant de reconnaître -- négativement -- que la perfection divine est plus que perfection, la fonction exprimée par *quo majus cogitari nequit* rejoint sans doute le "quelque chose" qui la porte et lui donne d'appartenir à la foi.

Avec *Proslogion* X et XI qui suivent, allons-nous assister au dépassement inverse de la miséricorde par la justice, en sorte que l'hypothèse précédente se vérifie? Allons-nous trouver la proposition qui semble nécessaire pour que la *concors veritas* de justice et miséricorde soit complète, découvrir que la justice, laquelle apparaît non-miséricorde, est plus miséricordieuse que toute miséricorde d'homme, ou, équivalemment, que la conjonction inouie de justice et de miséricorde est plus miséricordieuse que la *simple et seule* miséricorde? Le *Proslogion* ne le dit pas tout à fait, mais s'engage sur une dialectique assez embrouillée, ce qui est signe, chez un auteur aussi logicien qu'Anselme, d'un inachèvement de la recherche. Le raisonnement peut, semble-t-il, être articulé un quatre étapes:

(1) *La réitération de la difficulté*: s'il est juste, depuis la démonstration précédente, que Dieu épargne *certains* méchants, il demeure juste, la miséricorde n'étant confessée que pour ceux-là, que Dieu punisse les autres. Il est alors juste ET que Dieu pardonne ET que Dieu punisse, ce qui subsume la contradiction initiale de justice et miséricorde sous un seul chef: la justice comme rapport de Dieu à Dieu.

(2) *Une première solution*: une première possibilité s'ouvre: poser une distinction que reprenne et élargisse celle que *Proslogion* VIII a élaborée à propos de la seule miséricorde. Quand il pardonne, Dieu serait juste non pas *selon nous* mais *selon soi*; quand il punit, il serait juste non pas *selon soi* mais *selon nous*:

> Quand Tu punis les méchants, ceci est juste parce que convenant à leurs mérites; quand, par contre, Tu les épargnes, ceci est juste non parce que digne de leurs mérites mais de ta bonté.[29]

(3) *Une seconde solution*: la distinction précédente ne suffit pas à résoudre l'aporie parce qu'une seconde argumentation par l'absurde, en tout semblable à celle de *Proslogion* IX, exclut que Dieu ne soit pas juste *selon soi* quand il punit:

> Mais n'est-il pas juste aussi selon Toi, Seigneur, que Tu punisses les méchants? Il est juste assurément que Tu sois si juste qu'on ne puisse Te penser plus juste. Et Tu ne le serais jamais si tu rendais seulement les biens aux bons, et non les maux aux méchants. Qui rétribue les mérites des bons et des méchants est en effet plus juste que celui qui rétribue seulement les mérites des bons. Il est donc juste selon Toi, Dieu juste et bienveillant, ET que Tu punisses ET que Tu épargnes.[30]

Comme plus haut, l'argumentation présuppose et pose l'identification des deux Noms I et II. Entre présupposition et position, prend place une inégalité quantitative aussi simple que précédemment: la domaine où s'exerce la justice quand elle rétribue les bons ET les méchants est plus grand que lorsqu'elle rétribue SEULEMENT les bons. Si donc la justice que AUSSI punit est plus grande que la justice qui ne punit pas [et SEULEMENT pardonne], nier cette justice de Dieu serait contredire au Nom I, ce qu'il fallait démontrer.

(4) *La confession de l'élection gratuite*: justice et miséricorde devant désormais s'entendre de Dieu selon Dieu, leur coexistence n'est compéhensible qu'à distinguer leurs domaines d'application. Certains méchants sont pardonnés, les autres sont punis. Suit alors une conclusion, entière-

ment dépendante de la théorie augustinienne de la prédestination et quelque peu décalée par rapport à l'argumentation de *Proslogion* IX sur la miséricorde: si la raison de
la foi reconnaît que Dieu est juste *selon soi* et quand il
pardonne "certains" et quand il punit "certains," et quand
il est SEULEMENT juste et quand il est PLUS QUE juste, nulle
raison ne peut pénétrer l'élection gracieuse:

> S'il est possible de saisir, en quelque
> manière, pourquoi Tu peux vouloir sauver
> les méchants, il n'est certainement nulle
> raison qui puisse faire comprendre pourquoi,
> entre semblables méchants, Tu sauves par ta
> bonté suréminente ceux-ci plutôt que
> ceux-là, ni pourquoi Tu condamnes par ta
> justice suréminente ceux-là plutôt que
> ceux-ci.[31]

Incompréhensible grâce de l'élection! Excluant que la
miséricorde par laquelle Dieu est juste en étant plus que
juste puisse être une donnée à disposition de l'homme, la
seconde argumentation par le Nom I rappelle la prédication
des prophètes et, plus particulièrement, la diatribe de
Jérémie dans le Temple de Jérusalem: "Ne vous fiez pas aux
paroles mensongères: 'c'est le sanctuaire de YHWH, le sanctuaire de YHWH, le sanctuaire de YHWH'" (Jr 7:4). Car c'est
la pire des perversités, aux yeux de Dieu, qu s'appuyer sur
le pardon de Dieu, sur l'Alliance dont le Temple est le
signe, pour pécher de plus belle, "voler, tuer, commetre
l'adultère, se parjurer, encenser Baal, suivre des dieux
étrangers" (Jr 7:9). Le pardon de Dieu, *don par-delà tout
don*, est un acte libre qui échappe à la saisie de l'homme et
demeure l'acte de Dieu, son *libre* amour. Impossible, en
conséquence, que l'homme puisse le situer ou comprendre par
rapport à lui-même. Comme le dit Paul dans un passage que
citera le *De concordia*: "Qui a prévenu [le Seigneur] de ses
dons pour devoir être payé de retour?" (Rm 11:35). Bref,
comprendre la libre et gracieuse miséricorde de Dieu serait
détruire sa liberté, enfermer Dieu sous la nécessité et contredire au Nom qui interdit de penser plus grand.

3. L'événement de la croix

Rappelons la difficulté que nous espérons, sinon
résoudre, du moins éclairer: comment peuvent coexister,
dans la formulation du Nom de Dieu (I) qui sert d'argument,
la position d'un "quelque chose" et la négation de toute

idolâtrie qui prétende penser plus grand que ce "quelque chose?" Comment S. Anselme peut-il faire suivre *aliquid* d'une fonction purement négative, user de cet *aliquid* comme d'un intermédiaire entre Dieu et la fonction, placer le tout sous une principale: *credimus?* Devant ce paradoxe, nous avons émis l'hypothèse qu'en voyant fonctionner la fonction, nous trouverions le "quelque chose." De fait, nous avons découvert que le Nom I conduit au redoublement de la transcendance divine [qu'il présuppose]. Parce qu'il porte le Nom I, parce qu'il est identifiable au "quelque chose" dont on ne peut penser plus grand, Dieu n'est pas seulement juste et parfait, mais *plus que juste et parfait*. Il est juste que Dieu soit plus que juste en étant miséricordieux pour certains. Mais la proposition inverse, nécessaire pour une totale concorde de la justice et de la miséricorde, pour un complet débordement de la pensée humaine dans sa possibilité même de penser "plus grand" que son "plus grand," n'a pas trouvé sa formulation dans le *Proslogion*. Elle est restée prisonnière des thèses fort discutables de S. Augustin sur la prédestination et sur la limitation à "certaines" du libre pardon de Dieu.

Où trouver, sous la plume d'Anselme, ce que Thomas d'Aquin apprit de lui et qui semble correspondre à notre attente?

> Hoc fuit abundantioris misericordiae (quando Deus satisfactorem dedit Filium suum) quam si peccata absque satisfactione dimisisset.[32]

> Quand Dieu donna son propre Fils pour satisfaire, ce fut miséricorde plus abondante que s'Il avait remis les péchés sans satisfaction.

Où lire l'inversion rigoureuse de la proposition sur la miséricorde comme non-justice plus juste que toute justice? Pour reconnaître que la justice exigeant satisfaction, et comme telle non-miséricorde, est plus miséricordieuse que toute miséricorde, il faut attendre le *Cur deus homo*, d'une quinzaine d'années postérieur au *Proslogion*. Car la question qu'entend résoudre ce livre énigmatique est bien celle que suppose l'inversion attendue: devant l'attestation biblique du salut par la croix du Fils, Anselme veut exclure, par raisons nécessaires, que Dieu puisse vraiment sauver par la seule miséricorde (*sola misericordia sine omni debiti solutione*).[33] Un tel salut serait moins grand que le salut qui se peut penser à la lecture de la Bible et contre-dirait au Nom qui rend impossible toute pensée de "plus grand." Une telle miséricorde [sans justice] serait moins miséricordieuse que le salut accompli par la passion et la mort de l'Unique, et comportant la *satisfactio justitiae debitae*. Les raisons nécessaires supposant ainsi l'usage répété du Nom, c'est l'exclusion d'une éventualité contraire au Nom I -- la grâce à bon marché comme dirait Dietrich Bonhoeffer -- qui démontre la nécessité de la satisfaction christique, satisfaction signifiant non pas *expiation* comme on le croit trop souvent, mais *libre réponse d'amour* qui procure à Dieu agrément, joie de voir son oeuvre menée à bonne fin. Où trouver la proposition qui contrebalance, dans la *concors veritas*, le débordement de la justice par la miséricorde? Il suffit de se reporter à *Cur deus homo* II,20 et d'en relever la première phrase:

> Misericordiam vero Dei quae tibi perire
> videbatur, cum justitiam Dei et peccatum Dei
> et peccatum hominis considerabamus, tam mag-
> nam tamque concordem justitiae invenimus, ut
> nec major nec justior cogitari possit.[34]

> Quant à la miséricorde de Dieu, qui te sem-
> blait périr quand nous considérions la jus-
> tice de Dieu et le péché de l'homme, nous
> l'avons trouvée si grande et si accordé à la
> justice que ni plus grande ni plus juste ne
> se peut penser.

Comme en *Proslogion* IX à XI, une identification est posée entre les Noms I et II, entre l'interdiction de penser plus grand et la perfection divine reconnue plus que perfection dans la coïncidence de justice et de miséricorde. Coïncedence et identification s'entr'appartenant, cet ajointement marque la superposition possible du mouvement de la pensée anselmienne avec la parole paulinienne sur la croix. De même que la non-sagesse de la croix est plus sage que toute sagesse d'homme, et la non-force plus forte que toute force d'homme, de même la miséricorde -- ou non-justice -- est plus juste que toute justice d'homme, et la justice exigeant satisfaction -- c'est-à-dire non-miséricorde -- plus miséricordieuse que toute miséricorde d'homme. C'est dans cette superposition à la "parole de la croix" (1 Co 1:18) que la fonction négative signifiée par le Nom I: *quo majus cogitari nequit*, trouve enfin le "quelque chose" qui la porte et soutient. Entre Dieu et la fonction négative, entre la plus que perfection et l'impossibilité de penser "plus grand," au coeur de l'identification des deux

Noms I et II, il y a *l'événement de la croix glorieuse* que
S. Paul appelle justement: *"ce qui* est folie de Dieu . . .
ce qui est faiblesse de Dieu" (1 Co 1:25). Car, recevant
son sens de la *concors veritas* où perfection et transcendance se redoublent, présupposant ce redoublement que Paul
nomme encore surabondance, le posant dans l'exclusion de
toutes possibilités moins grandes, la fonction négative ne
peut être *portée* que par *cela* qu'elle présuppose et qui
déborde toute pensée du "plus grand": l'acte dans lequel
Dieu s'est librement déterminé pour le salut de sa créature
perdue, l'événement historique de son libre amour pour les
hommes, le lieu de sa révélation ultime. Tout cela est
affirmé par Anselme en un texte magistral que tous connais-
sent:

> Nihil autem asperius aut difficilius potest
> homo ad honorem Dei sponte et non ex debito
> pati quam mortem, et nullatenus seipsum po-
> test homo dare Deo quam cum se morti tradit
> ad honorem illius.[35]

> Pour l'honneur de Dieu, l'homme ne peut, de
> son plein gré et non par dette, souffrir
> rien de plus âpre ni de plus difficile que
> la mort; il ne peut jamais se donner davan-
> tage à Dieu que lorsqu'il se livre à la mort
> pour son honneur.

L'identification précédente des Noms I et II laisse ici
la place à l'identification mutuelle de la fonction négative
[*nihil asperius aut difficilius*] et d'un événement de notre
histoire. Mais c'est la seconde identification qui rend possible la première, et le redoublement de transcendance et
perfection qui l'accompagne. Le "quelque chose" sur quoi
repose la fonction négative est identique à Dieu puisqu'il y
passage d'une identification à l'autre. Mais, "quelque
chose" n'est divin, identifiable à Dieu dont il redouble la
hauteur en hauteur d'au-delà toute hauteur, qu'à être
d'abord CET acte déterminé d'amour et de don de soi où se
concentre le chemin du Fils unique vers son Père qui est
"plus grand" (Jn 14:28), CETTE livraison spontanée de soi
pour les hommes (cf Jn 10:17-18), CETTE libre détermination
de Dieu devenu CET homme crucifié "pour l'honneur de Dieu."
Car Dieu s'est librement déterminé à se faire plus que juste
et plus que miséricordieux, juste et miséricordieux *à la
fois*, librement déterminé à être encore plus Dieu, Dieu
encore plus grand, en ne voulant pas être Dieu sans l'homme.
En conséquence de quoi, le "quelque chose" qui *porte* la

fonction négative pour former le Nom I que *porte* la divine
transcendance, n'est autre que cette petite chose dans
l'immensité de l'histoire du monde que sont "les jours de la
chair" (He 5:7) du Fils unique, ce "peu" ou ce *mikron* comme
il est dit en S. Jean (16:16) dont l'homme s'efforce toujours de penser plus grand en le situant dans une vision
générale du monde, mais qui vient dénoncer et briser toutes
ces tentatives en manifestant leur caractère idolâtre. Sur
la face du Fils mis en croix, se livrant librement aux
méchants, se lit, en effet, la vanité mortifère des idoles
sous lesquelles l'homme justifie sa volonté de saisir et sa
violence. Sur la figure défigurée de l'Unique, est démasqué
ce que l'homme fait de l'homme en se faisant un dieu dont il
puisse penser "plus grand." Voulant disposer du dieu,
l'homme donne à l'homme la mort, forme dernière de la contradiction. Mais, de cette chair décharnée, de ce visage
"qui n'a plus figure humaine" (Is 52:14), quand s'ouvre le
coeur sous le coup de lance, s'écoule la surabondance de
Dieu: *gaudium plus quam plenum* dans le *Proslogion*,[36] *plus
in infinitum* dans le *Cur deus homo*.[37] En somme, la coexistence d'une position et d'une négation dans l'*unum argumentum*, d'un "quelque chose" et d'une interdiction de penser
plus grand, trouve sa réalité et sa possibilité à la croix
de Jésus. Si l'argument, nom révélé de Dieu, se distingue
de l'idée cartésienne du Parfait, c'est parce qu'il désigne
l'événement déterminé où Dieu est Dieu en étant encore plus
Dieu. Si ce Nom exceptionnel peut, au terme des argumentations par l'absurde qu'il permet, s'identifier à la perfection, c'est parce qu'il la redouble, Dieu étant "plus que
lui-même"[38] en donnant à l'homme son Fils. Dieu est juste
en étant plus que juste, miséricordieux en étant plus que
miséricordieux: ce n'est plus hasard si *Cur deus homo*
II,20 fait suivre la *concors veritas* de justice et
miséricorde par une extraordinaire confession:

> Nempe quid misericordius intelligi valet,
> quam cum peccatori tormentis aeternis dam-
> nato et unde se redimat non habenti Deus
> Pater dicit: accipe Unigenitum meum et da
> pro te; et ipse Filius: tolle me et redime
> te.

> Que peut-on reconnaître de plus miséri-
> cordieux? Au pécheur condamné aux tourments
> éternels, n'ayant rien d'où se racheter,
> Dieu le Père dit: Reçois mon Fils unique et
> donne-le pour toi; et le Fils lui-même:
> emporte-moi et rachète-toi.[39]

Espace et temps manquent, dans le cadre limité de cet essai, pour évaluer les conséquences de cette lecture du *quo majus cogitari nequit*. Elle confirme pleinement ce que Karl Barth avait perçu de la preuve de l'existence de Dieu: "qu'il existe une relation étroite et démontrable entre le nom de Dieu et la révélation de son existence et de son essence."[40] Elle fait de ladite démonstration, par l'absurde redisons-le, le déploiement du lien qui conjoint, dans le décalogue, la deuxième parole et le court prologue: "Je suis YHWH ton Dieu . . . Tu ne te feras aucune image sculptée, rien qui ressemble à ce qui est dans les cieux, là-haut, ou sur la terre, ici-bas, ou dans les eaux, au-dessous de la terre" (Ex 20:2,4). Disant ainsi la *concatenatio* qui interdit de dissocier l'être de Dieu et sa révélation dans l'exclusion des idoles sculptées ou écrites, la preuve anselmienne s'accomplit dans une entière superposition -- ou *homologie* -- avec le verset qui clôt le prologue de l'Evangile selon S. Jean: "Dieu, nul ne l'a jamais vu; le Fils unique qui est, tourné vers le sein du Père, lui, l'a fait connaître" (Jn 1:18). La justification plus complète de cette interprétation qui *prolonge* Karl Barth paraîtra bientôt, *Deo adjuvante*, dans le deuxième tome de *L'inouï de Dieu*.[41]   Qu'il suffise, pour conclure, d'ajouter trois remarques:

(1) Il n'y a plus lieu de s'étonner que le premier titre donné par Anselme à son livret ait été: *Fides quaerens intellectum*.   L'intelligence de la foi, comme reconnaisance de ce qui est déjà connu par la foi, admet comme présupposé l'impossibilité de se situer au-dessus de la Bible pour la juger à partir de 'plus grand." Lecture du sens intérieur déployé par le texte extérieur, elle s'accomplit dans le respect scrupuleux du Nom I ou, équivalemment, dans l'écoute fidèle de la parole de Jésus: Le serviteur n'est pas plus grand que son maître, ni l'envoyé plus grand que celui qui l'envoie: (Jn 13:16). Il en va donc des Ecritures saintes, *verbum Dei scriptum*, comme de l'événement de Jésus, *Verbum Dei incarnatum*:   impossible de penser plus grand que ces "quelque chose" d'où nous advient la surabondance de Dieu.

(2) Il est permis, en pensant à *Proslogion* IX à XI, qui forment la première ébauche du *Cur deus homo*, de mettre un lien entre les deux contresens qui défigurent la pensée d'Anselme: la preuve ontologique et la satisfaction vicaire [entendue comme expiation des péchés]. Ce lien fait apparaître, avec grande clarté, la raison profonde du premier contresens par-delà les raisons *techniques* que nous venons

d'exposer. A en croire le Père Hans Urs von Balthasar, dans
sa brève monographie sur l'esthétique théologique de S.
Anselme:

> Une déduction de l'existence de Dieu à par-
> tir d'un concept, et même déjà la represen-
> tation que nous pourrions penser Dieu comme
> un concept, une telle opération n'aurait pu
> apparaître à Anselme que comme la caricature
> d'un acte philosophique. Au contraire,
> *l'achèvement du véritable acte philosophique
> est cette expérience théologique* en présence
> de la révélation de la miséricorde du Père
> dans le Fils souffrant. Miséricorde par
> laquelle toute justice reçoit satisfaction
> d'une manière inconcevable: *ut nec major
> [misericordia] nec justior cogitari pos-
> sit.*[42]

Si quelqu'un se prend à désirer, comme Descartes, une preuve
purement philosophique de l'existence de Dieu, une démarche
purement rationnelle qui fasse abstraction de la foi chrétienne et de son libre risque, il ne pourra, comme Descartes, que penser son projet à l'intérieur de la distinction classique entre philosophie et théologie qui fut élaborée, pour la première fois, dans la *Summa contra gentiles*
de S. Thomas. Il ne pourra que situer ladite preuve parmi
les *praeambula fidei* qui doivent servir, sous cette précompréhension, de préalable et de fondement pour la foi. Mais,
ce faisant, il ne pourra aussi que contredire au projet anselmien, le lire anachroniquement. Car l'abbé du Bec a non
seulement énoncé son argument comme un Nom que la foi donne
à Dieu -- *credimus enim te esse aliquid quo nihil majus
cogitari possit* -- mais encore posé ce Nom comme l'unique
fonction pour reconnaître "*tout* ce que *nous croyons* de la
substance divine." Les anachronismes s'accordent: à la
précompréhension de l'argumentation comme "preuve ontologique" correspond la précompréhension de l'intelligence de
la foi sous le couple philosophie/théologie [ou: raison/foi]
qui lui est postérieur d'environ deux siècles. A cette critique de toute interprétation visant à supprimer le *credimus*
dans l'intelligence de l'*argumentum*, objectera-t-on que la
perspective inaugurée par Descartes s'impose comme une des
colonnes de notre monde intellectuel, que la distinction
entre une philosophie sans présuppositions et une théologie
reposant sur la Bible demeure une vérité intouchable? L'objectant ferait sans doute bien de se souvenir que l'holo-
causte de six millions de Juifs sous le coup des totalita-

rismes et de leurs idoles violentes a replacé sous les regards de tous la prophétie du Serviteur souffrant (Is 52:13-53:12), déjà accomplie à la croix de Jésus, et probablement sonné le glas de toute théodicée à la manière de Leibniz.

(3) S'il est question de perfection dans l'idée cartésienne de Dieu, il convient de rappeler que, jouant sur cette présupposition -- commune à tous les hommes -- d'un *Perfectissime* épuisant, dans son excellence superlative, toute réalité et toute possibilité, l'argument d'Anselme en renverse et déborde l'*ideatum*, vers un redoublement de transcendance et de perfection qu'Emmanuel Levinas a sans doute en vue lorsqu'il dit de "la relation appelée 'idée de l'infini' et décrite par Descartes": "Elle a ceci d'exceptionnel que son *ideatum* dépasse son idée."[43] Que peut être *concrètement* ce débordement de l'idée de perfection? En commençant sa *quaestio* sur justice et miséricorde, S. Anselme a nommé Dieu: "Dieu bon, bon envers les bons et les méchants."[44] Une telle appelation renvoie manifestement au passage du sermon sur la montagne qui s'achève sur le commandement d'être parfait: "Vous donc, vous serez parfaits comme votre Père céleste est parfait" (Mt 5:47). De quelle perfection s'agit-il sinon d'être "bon envers les bons et les méchants," ou encore: plus que juste en aimant les ennemis, en pardonnant les offenses, en exerçant la miséricorde? L'Evangile le dit en toutes lettres: "Aimez vos ennemis et priez pour vos persécuteurs, afin de devenir fils de votre Père qui est aux cieux, car il fait lever son soleil *sur les bons et sur les méchants*, et tomber la pluie sur les justes et sur les injustes" (Mt 5:44-45). Cette perfection au-delà de toute perfection s'est manifestée en plénitude à la croix quand le Fils unique de Dieu s'est librement déterminé à ce "quelque chose" qui brise toute tentative de penser plus grand amour. La plus que perfection de Dieu s'identifiant ici à l'amour des ennemis, apparaît en filigrane, sous la lettre de l'*argumentum*, le verset johannique que nous avons donné pour titre à cet essai: "Nul n'a plus grand amour que de donner sa vie pour ses amis" (Jn 15:13).

Notes

[1] René   Descartes,   *Meditationes   de   prima   philosophia* (Paris: Vrin, 1978), p. 65.

[2] *Proslogion*, Proemium: Schmitt I,93.

[3] *Quid ad haec respondeat editor ipsius libelli* IV: Schmitt I,133-34.

[4] Karl   Barth,   *La Preuve de l'existence de Dieu* (Neuchatel: Delachaux & Niestlé, 1958), p. 76.

[5] Olivier du Roy, *L'Intelligence de la foi en la Trinité selon S. Augustin* (Paris: Etudes Augustiniennes 1966), p. 245, n. 5.

[6] Ibid., p. 246.

[7] *Monologion* I: Schmitt I,15.

[8] Ibid. LXIV: Schmitt I,74.

[9] *Proslogion* XIV: Schmitt I,111.

[10] Ibid. XIV: Schmitt I,112.

[11] *Méditation* III, p. 45.

[12] *Proslogion*, Proemium: Schmitt I,93.

[13] Ibid. III: Schmitt I,103.

[14] *Sermo LII*, XVI.

[15] Barth, *La Preuve*, p. 66.

[16] Jacques Palliard, "Prière et dialectique: Méditation sur le *Proslogion* de saint Anselme, *Dieu vivant* 6 (1946), 51-70.

[17] Ibid., p. 57.

[18] Ibid., p. 55.

[19] Ibid., p. 55.

[20] Ibid., p. 57.

[21] *Proslogion* IX: Schmitt I,106-07.

[22] Ibid. V: Schmitt I,104.

[23] *Confessions* VII,iv,6.

[24] *Monologion* XV: Schmitt I,29.

[25] *Proslogion* IX: Schmitt I,108.

[26] Ibid. IX: Schmitt I,107.

[27] Ibid. XXVI: Schmitt I,121.

[28] Ibid. XIV: Schmitt I,112.

[29] Ibid. X: Schmitt I,108-09.

[30] Ibid. XI: Schmitt I,109.

[31] Ibid.

[32] Thomas d'Aquin, *Summa theologica* IIIa, q. 46, a. 2, 3m.

[33] *Cur deus homo* I,12: Schmitt II,69.

[34] Ibid. II,20: Schmitt II,131.

[35] Ibid. II,11: Schmitt II,111.

[36] *Proslogion* XXVI: Schmitt I,121.

[37] *Cur deus homo* II,18: Schmitt II,127.

[38] Hans Urs von Balthasar, *La gloire et la croix* (Paris: Aubier, 1975), III, 367.

[39] *Cur deus homo* II,20: Schmitt II,131-32.

[40] Barth, *La Preuve*, p. 67.

[41] Cet ouvrage paraîtra aux mêmes éditions: Le Cerf, Paris, que l'édition bilingue [latin-français] de *L'oeuvre de S. Anselme* à laquelle son empruntées toutes les traductions ici utilisées.

[42] von Balthasar, *Las gloire*, II, 212. Dans son petit ouvrage sur *La foi du Christ* (Paris: Aubier, 1968), p. 106, le Père Urs von Balthasar a encore écrit ces lignes pour lesquelles cet essai lui est dédié: "On peut situer l'évidence unique qui brille à travers cet événement [de la croix et de la résurrection de Jésus] entre les deux formules de saint Anselme de Cantorbery, sur Dieu qui est: *id quo majus cogitari nequit*, et sur l'homme qui: *rationabiliter comprehendit incomprehensibile esse* [*Monologion* LXIX]. Si les deux formule valent de la connaissance de Dieu . . ., elles ne sont plus valables *a priori* . . . mais vérifiées *a posteriori* par l'expérience de la Révélation de Dieu. L'homme qui, dans la foi, saisit pour ce qu'elle est l'oeuvre révélatrice de Dieu dans le Christ, doit être ainsi capable de voir paraître ici quelque chose *quo majus cogitari nequit*, la manifestion d'un amour divin absolu, laissant évidemment en arrière tout ce que l'homme peut inventer de plus sublime comme révélation."

[43] Emmanuel Levinas, *Totalité et infini* (La Haye: Martinus Nijhoff, 1971), p. 19.

[44] *Proslogion* IX: Schmitt I,108.

Parmenides: Anselm *eminenter*[1]

Michael P. Slattery

The claim being made in this paper is that Anselm was
not in fact the first proponent of the ontological argument
for the existence of God but that Parmenides was. In fact
by the time that Anselm came to put it forward, the ontological argument had had a long and varied career, starting
with Parmenides, and continuing with Plato and his followers. A case can even be made that, with Anselm, the ontological argument was for the first time called into question, a point that will come up later. Parmenides, on the
other hand, not only originated the ontological argument:[2]
he also gave it its most extreme form, by expounding a second negative ontological argument which disproved the
existence of everything else apart from God.

No special interpretation of the texts will be involved
in making this claim. The standard traditional interpretation of Parmenides' thought is taken for granted. Furthermore no claim is made that Parmenides had achieved some
early insight into the nature of the God of Christianity.
On the contrary the claim of Parmenides' priority over
Anselm is quite consistent with the view that Parmenides was
a materialist, and even an atheist, that is, if a materialist must be thought of as an atheist. So even the interpretation of Parmenides as a materialist or an atheist is quite
compatible with his being the true originator of the ontological argument for the existence of God.

Parmenides provided the basic logical structure of the
ontological argument. This basic structure that he gave to
the argument never changed throughout all the later formulations that the argument took. The only thing that substantially changed was the name or description that was given to
the entity that was asserted to have the characteristics of
true being.

The central part of the argument lies in the claim that
it is in principle possible to argue from the concept of
something to an assertion of that thing's existence. A crucial step in the argument involves the notion of perfection
and the claim that existence is a perfection. And this we
find already stated in Parmenides' *Way of Truth*.

Three possible positions can be taken with respect to
the ontological argument. The first position is the claim
that one can validly argue to the existence of anything at
all from the concept of that thing. Plato's doctrine of
forms illustrates this position. According to Plato, when

one thinks of Justice, or Goodness, or the Ideal Bed, providing one is thinking correctly, one sees that such things
must have real being. Such things cannot fail to exist.
Admittedly only one of each exists, but that is another
matter. The second position has it, not that one can argue
to the existence of anything of which one can form a concept, but that one can argue to the existence of at least
one thing of which one can form a concept, namely an absolutely perfect being. Anselm exemplifies this position, as
do all those who accept the ontological argument. The third
position is a completely negative one. It simply denies
that there is even one being whose existence can be inferred
to from its concept. All those who deny the validity of the
ontological argument hold this position.

There are numerous passages in which Parmenides affirms
that correct thinking necessitates affirming existence, the
existence of absolute being. For example the statement that
"To think is the same as the thought that it is; for you
will not find thinking without being, in regard to which
there is an expression,"[3] clearly makes the inference from
thought to existence. Take also the passage, "It is the
same thing to think and to be."[4]

Parmenides specifically denies that ordinary experience
can ever give us knowledge of true existence. Ordinary
experience, for him, simply fails to put us in touch with
what truly is. He describes everyday experience as the "way
along which wander mortals knowing nothing two-headed, for
perplexity in their bosoms steers their intelligence astray,
and they are carried along as deaf as they are blind."[5] The
same point is made when he says, "You must debar your
thought from this way of search, nor let ordinary experience
in its variety force you along this way, (namely of allowing) the eye, sightless as it is, and the ear, full of
sound, and the tongue, to rule; but (you must) judge by
means of the Reason (*Logos*) the much-contested proof which
is expounded by me."[6]

The principle basic to the ontological argument is that,
for at least one object of thought, its existence does not
consist simply in being part of a thinker's consciousness.
The perfect being, the being that is in question in the
argument, is such that it exists whether or not one thinks
of it. If you think correctly you will discover that you
have to admit that it exists. If you think incorrectly
about it, it will still exist. In other words, the absolutely perfect being, so the argument goes, is not some
aspect of consciousness. It is independent of one's thought
processes. The Fool can say and even think, in his unthink-

ing way, that there is no God. The absolutely perfect being
still exists anyway.

Whether or not one calls such a being "God" or not is a
matter of indifference from the point of view of the logic
of the argument. In the same way, whether or not one says
that such a being exists, or is real, or is, or even has
being, is a matter of indifference from the point of view of
the logic of the argument. The real issue is whether there
is any being whose existence, or independent reality, is
demanded just simply because of the very concept of that
being.

What is important here is to note that the word "exists"
in the argument does not have negative overtones. Existence, with respect to this argument, cannot be something
negative. Gilson claims that, according to the existential-
ists, existence is a disease in being.[7] If existence is a
disease in being, then the ontological argument cannot conclude that God exists, for then it would conclude that a
perfect being was imperfect. Again existence here cannot be
the etiolated existence of characters of fiction, since fictional existence is not perfection in existence -- whatever
existence one might wish to grant it. Nor is the existence
of correct ideas or true propositions the kind of existence
that the ontological argument aims at asserting for God;
nor, for that matter, is existence when interpreted as a
Kantian category of the understanding.

Furthermore the word "God," or the phrase "divine
being," cannot be understood in the argument to indicate a
being which is less than absolutely perfect. We do, however, find in early Greek thought the view that divine being
is less than absolutely perfect being.[8] In that context,
divine being, even though of a very high order, is still not
complete in perfection. Accordingly the ontological argument could not conclude with the assertion that God exists,
or that a divine being exists, since it would then be concluded that a less than absolutely perfect being exists,
which is not what the argument aims at.

Furthermore, in the Neo-platonic tradition, faithful in
this to Plato, even being itself is a mark of inferiority.[9]
The form of the Good, for Plato, is beyond being; and the
One of Plotinus is also beyond being. On this premise, the
absolutely perfect "being," to use a word we can hardly
avoid, cannot be said to be, or to exist, since that would
stigmatize it with inferiority. Since in this context,
being is a falling away from perfection, we would be forced
to say that the perfect "being" is not, that it does not
exist. It enjoys the higher state of nothingness or non-
being.[10]

Once again, the normal terminology of the ontological argument is not that of Neo-platonism. In the normal terminology terms like "exists" and "is" do not indicate limitations or imperfections in being. Whether rightly or wrongly, proponents of the ontological argument treat terms like "exists" and "is" as being positive in themselves, as indicating perfection without any necessary limitation on perfection. Because of this, when proponents of the ontological argument assert that the absolutely perfect being exists, they do not contradict themselves. They do not affirm a predicate which is in contradiction to the subject of the proposition. On the same premise the proponents of the ontological argument are not limited to meaning by the term "exists" that something is an object of immediate sense perception. In fact, proponents of the argument never mean this, since they accept that what is an object of immediate sense perception has limitations to its being, and is therefore not absolutely perfect in being.

What the ontological argument does need is the distinction between something being real, objective, and something being unreal, only subjective. Greek philosophy did have this distinction in various forms. Parmenides was able to dismiss the world of everyday experience as lacking true being. In Plato's allegory of the cave, most people live their lives in a world that is not really there. It is merely a fantasy world. Aristotle denies that, for physical objects, there are such things as separate forms in Plato's sense of the term. Such separate forms, thinks Aristotle, just do not exist. For Aristotle, forms only exist in the physical world, unseparated from physical objects.

The other basic thing that the ontological argument does need is the notion of an absolutely perfect being, a being which lacks no perfection. What is defined as a perfection, provided reality or existence is included as a perfection, is irrelevant to the logic of the argument. Descartes includes total freedom and power of creation as part of perfection of being. Such notions cannot be found in Parmenides. Melissus, generally taken to be a follower of Parmenides, gives psychological characteristics to his perfect being. Thus Melissus says, ". . . nor does it feel pain or grief. For if it suffered any of these things, it would no longer be One."[11], and again, "Nor does it feel pain; for it could not be complete if it were in pain; for a thing which is in pain could not always be. Nor has it equal power with what is healthy. Nor would it be the same if it were in pain; for it would feel pain through the subtraction or addition of something, and could no longer be the same."[12] These psychological characteristics that Melissus finds in being or the One are not stated by Parmenides to be there. Nevertheless the logic of the argument whereby Parmenides finds quantitative characteristics in such a being is no different from the logic whereby Melissus finds qualitative characteristics. One might say that they both have the same variable, but they put different values in its place. They have different, though not necessarily conflicting, notions of what constitutes perfection of being. One can find the same kind of differences between proponents of the ontological argument in modern times, just by comparing Descartes and Spinoza, for example.

Parmenides argues that when you think properly you can only think what is. You cannot think non-being. Furthermore when you think properly you can only think total being. You cannot properly think of something that lacks being, since you cannot properly think non-being. Nothingness is not, properly speaking, an object of thinking. The upshot of all this is that the being of Parmenides is, as he says, "not lacking,"[13] and again, ". . . it is complete on every side, like the mass of a well-rounded sphere, equally balanced from its centre in every direction. . . . For, in all directions equal to itself, it reaches its limits uniformly."[14] And of course there cannot be two such beings since they could only be separated from one another by non-being, and non-being cannot be thought, and *a fortiori* cannot be. We have here all the basic materials for producing the ontological argument. The first step is to affirm that true thought cannot be about what is not. Correct thinking cannot end up with anything else than what is. Furthermore correct thinking cannot end up with anything except total, or absolute, or perfect being, for correct thinking can only think being, and is therefore forced to think total being, "complete on every side", "equally balanced from its centre in every direction" to use Parmenides' own phraseology.

Admittedly the argument from the time of Anselm has been put forward in the context of a multiplicity of beings. Anselm did not deny the possibility of there being other entities besides the absolutely perfect entity, "a being than which no greater can be thought" to use a time-honored formula. So the argument in its best known formulation envisages many other beings besides God. Nevertheless it is not of the essence of the argument to include the possibility of other beings besides God. Nobody has ever, to my knowledge, denied the validity of the argument on the grounds that there either could be or alternatively that there could not be other beings besides God. What other beings there could be or could not be is a matter of irrelevance to the argument. The core of argument lies with the validity of the inference from conception to the affirmation of existence, and with the meaningfulness of the notion of an absolutely perfect being. So the implied multiplicity of being in the phrase "than which no greater can be thought" is not essential to the argument. For Parmenides there is no greater being that can be thought other than the being about which he is thinking, namely the being that is "complete on every side." But for Parmenides it is equally true that that no other being can be thought other than such a being. There is only one, and no more than one object of true thought, and that is absolutely perfect being. Parmenides' monism, while stricter than that of Spinoza or Hegel, nevertheless does belong to the general family of monism, and when Spinoza and Hegel with their ontological monism can be included among proponents of the ontological argument, there is no justification for excluding Parmenides from such a company simply on the grounds of his monism. Furthermore, if the ontological argument really depended on bringing in the existence of other beings, it would cease to be ontological and become "cosmological," to use Kant's other term.

Gilson notes a family resemblance between the various proponents of the ontological argument, one that we have already mentioned. Gilson says about the ontological argument:

> There have always been philosophers to take it up and refashion it in their own way, and its implications are so manifold that the sole fact of having rejected or admitted it almost suffices to determine the doctrinal group to which a philosophy belongs. Saint Bonaventure, Descartes, Leibniz and Hegel took it up again, each in his own way . . . What all those who accepted it have in common is the *identification of real existence with intelligible being conceived by thought*.[15] (my italics)

This "identification of real existence with intelligible being conceived by thought" is not a principle limited by time. While Gilson applies it to thinkers that come after Anselm, there is no reason to prevent us from applying it to thinkers that come before Anselm. In fact Bertrand Russell, in his *History of Western Philosophy*, does precisely this. He maintains that Plato puts forward a kind of ontological argument; Russell says:

> The real question is: Is there anything we
> can think of which, by the mere fact that we
> can think of it, is shown to exist outside
> our thought? . . . If yes is the right
> answer, there is a bridge from pure thought
> to things; if not, not. In this generalized
> form, Plato uses a kind of ontological argu-
> ment to prove the objective reality of
> ideas. But no one before Anselm had stated
> the argument in its naked logical purity.
> In gaining purity, it loses plausibility,
> but this is also to Anselm's credit.[16]

So, according to Russell, Anselm was not the first to
use the ontological argument. He was the first to *clarify*
it; and in so doing unwittingly put his finger on its controversial point. In fact when Russell describes Parmenides' *Way of Truth* as "the first example in philosophy of
an argument from thought and language to the world at
large,"[17] Russell is himself getting close to making Parmenides the father of the ontological argument.

There is a further aspect to the ontological argument
that Russell points out. Admittedly its most specific form
consists in an argument for the existence of an absolutely
perfect being. But in a more generalized form it was used
by Plato to prove the existence of beings perfect in their
own nature, while not containing all possible perfections.
Thus Plato's forms, for example the form of dog, and the
form of horse, each contained all the perfections in its own
area of being, including the perfection of existence or true
reality. In a similar way we find a generalized version of
the ontological argument hidden within the folds of Aristotelian logic. Controversy connected with it is usually
called the problem of existential import. The question is:
Do universal propositions have existential import? To use
an example from medieval thought, does the proposition that
all men are animals involve the existence of men, so that if
men did not exist it would be false? Around the time when
Anselm was clarifying the existential aspects of the ontological argument, we find logicians raising the question of
existential import of universal propositions. Thus they
raised the question whether the proposition that all men are
men is true if there are no men,[18] and likewise whether it
is true that all chimeras are chimeras when there are no
chimeras.[19] There is a certain appropriateness in the fact
that the question of existential import was raised in the
eleventh and twelfth centuries during the same period when
questions were raised about the ontological argument. The

same kind of issue is at stake in each case, namely whether
the correctness of an idea or the truth of a certain kind of
proposition demands the existence of the being or beings
mentioned in the given idea or proposition, so that, just as
the ontological argument maintains that the perfect being is
not perfect if it does not exist, so Aristotelian logic
maintains that men are not men unless men exist.

In the thirteenth century we get the question of the
exis-tential import of universal propositions connected with
the controversy over the necessity or the contingency of the
existence of the world. The Averroists, or radical Aristotelians, af-firmed the necessary existence of the world,
while the Christian thinkers affirmed its contingent
existence.[20] Siger of Brabant, the leader of the Averroists, and the specific opponent of St. Thomas on this point,
posed the question whether the proposition that man is an
animal is true if no men exist. As a good Aristotelian he
said it was not. Van Steenberghen notes that, ". . . the
question is answered in accordance with radical Aristotelianism, by the affirmation of the eternity of the human species."[21]   St. Thomas, on the other hand, had a philosophy
that denied the necessary existence of the world, this position being in line with his Christian viewpoint. In accordance with this viewpoint St. Thomas maintained that if no
men existed, it would still be true that rationality
belonged to humanity.[22] Albert the Great, his teacher,
maintained the same position, replying specifically to the
question asked by Siger of Brabant. Mandonnet notes Albert
the Great's answer, namely that, ". . ., if no individual
human beings existed, it is still true that man is an animal, along with suchlike other statements."[23]. The fourteenth century logician, Vincent Ferrer, as Ivo Thomas tells
us, maintains that universal propositions are still true
when there are no individuals of the subject class existing.[24] This goes to show that by the fourteenth century the
ontological argument implicit in Aristotelian logic, with
its implicit affirmation of the necessary existence of the
world, had become subject to serious criticism.

Summing up we can say that Parmenides originated the
ontological argument, which, in its various forms, flourished in the Greek philosophy of essence,[25] while the Fool
of Gaunilo signals the beginning of an attack on the ontological argument in its various forms, an attack that is in
keeping with the medieval philosophy of existence.

Notes

[1] See Michael P. Slattery, "The Negative Ontological Argument", *The New Scholasticism* 43, 4 (1969), 614-17; and Vincent J. Ferrara, "Some Reflections on the Being-Thought Relationship in Parmenides, Anselm and Hegel", *AA* III, 95-111. Perhaps see also Bertrand Russell, "Parmenides," *A History of Western Philosophy*, (London: Clarion-Simon and Schuster, 1945), Ch. v (p. 49). The first time that this thesis came to the attention of the present writer was from a philosophy undergraduate, Mr. Anthony Banet, of Bellarmine Colleqe, Louisville, Ky.

[2] A. H. Armstrong, *An Introduction to Ancient Philosophy* (3rd ed. London; Methuen, 1957; rpt. Totowa, N.J.: Rowman and Allenheld, 1983), p. 12, notes that "Parmenides is the first Greek philosopher who reasons."

[3] Parmenides, *Ancilla to the Pre-Socratic Philosophers*, trans. K. Freeman (Oxford: Blackwell, 1956), p. 44.

[4] Ibid., p. 42.

[5] Ibid., p. 43.

[6] Ibid.

[7] E. Gilson, *Being and Some Philosophers* (Toronto: Pontifical Institute of Medieval Studies, 1952), pp. 10, 152, 208.

[8] Armstrong, *An Introduction*, p. 4.

[9] Gilson, *Being*, p. 24.

[10] Ibid., p. 22.

[11] Parmenides, *Ancilla*, p. 48.

[12] Ibid., p. 49.

[13] Ibid., p. 44.

[14] Ibid., p. 44.

[15] E. Gilson, *History of Christian Philosophy in the Middle Ages* (New York: Random House, 1955), p. 134.

[16] Russell, *A History*, pp. 417-18.

[17] Ibid., p. 49.

[18] W. and M. Kneale, *The Development of Logic*, (Oxford: Clarendon Press, 1964), pp. 210-11.

[19] Ibid., p. 264.

[20] T. Gierymski and M. P. Slattery, "Existential Import and Latin Averroism", *Franciscan Studies* NS 18 (1958), 127-32; and "*A* Propositions", *The Modern Schoolman* 36 (1959), 91-106.

[21] F. van Steenberghen, *Aristotle in the West: The Origins of Latin Aristotelianism*, trans. Leonard Johnson (Louvain: E. Nauwelaerts, 1955), p. 214.

[22] Thomas Aquinas, *Quaestiones disputatae et quaestiones duodecim quodlibetales ad fidem optimarum diligenter reclusae* VIII,i,ad 1: Marietti 1931: Remotis omnibus singularibus hominibus adhuc remaneret rationalitas attribuibilis humanae naturae. Again, *ibid.* ad 3: Si omnes creaturae ab esse deficerent natura humana maneret talis quod ei competeret rationalitas.

[23] P. Mandonnet, *Siger de Brabant et l'averroisme latin au XIIIᵐᵉ Siecle: Etude critique et documents inédits*, (Fribourg en Suisse: Librairie de l'Université, 1899), p. cxxxviii; Albert the Great, *Liber de intellectu et intelligibili* II,iii: ed. Vives, Paris 1890, IX,494b: . . .patet quod nullo existente homine particulari, adhuc est vera, homo est animal, et hujusmodi aliae locutiones.

[24] See I. Thomas, "St. Vincent Ferrer's *De suppositionibus*", *Dominican Studies* 5 (1952), 82-102. The text from Vincent Ferrer is as follows: Non sequitur pluvia est aqua guttatim cadens, igitur hec pluvia et illa, etc., quoniam antecedens est verum etiam si nulla pluvia sit, ut statim dicetur, et tamen consequens non est verum nec etiam satis intelligibile, quoniam nulla pluvia existente non potest dici: nec pluvia, vel illa, qui iam implicaretur contradictio.

[25] In his paper, "Why Existence Does Not Emerge As A Distinct Concept In Greek Philosophy", in *Philosophies of Existence: Ancient and Medieval*, ed. P. Morewedge (New York: Fordham Univ. Press, 1982), pp. 1-17, Charles Kahn

denies that Parmenides could have produced the ontological argument. But his thesis concerning existence, as embodied in the above title of his paper and exemplified in his many writings on the subject, is quite compatible with the ontological argument being *implicit* in Eleatic and Platonic thought. In fact the criticism levelled by contemporary logicians at the existential import involved in Aristotle's logic is an indication of the widespread implicit ontological inferences made in classical Greek thought.

Some Remarks on the Prehistory of the Logical Form of St. Anselm's Argument in *Proslogion* II

Wolfgang Röd

The background to Anselm's proof for the existence of God in *Proslogion* II has been thoroughly investigated. However, it seems that the presuppositions of the argument with respect to its logical form have not received as much attention in those researches as Anselm's metaphysical and substantive claims. In what follows some of those less known aspects of the context in which Anselm developed his argument will be discussed, and its origins in the notion of indirect proof in metaphysics will be emphasized with a view towards showing that the formal side of Anselm's argument had a long period of incubation (to adopt the metaphor used by M. Heidegger with regard to the principle of sufficient reason).

It can be shown that the form of indirect proof is as old as metaphysics itself, but also that it can only be employed in a proof for the existence of God on the basis of certain presuppositions: first, that God must be characterized with superlatives such as *quo maius cogitari non potest*; second, that existence independent of thought represents an ontological perfection; and third, that God has a place within the hierarchy of being. By way of conclusion will be considered what might have made indirect proof so attractive to Anselm.

The History of Indirect Proof before Anselm

Indirect proof not only has a long history, but we can go so far as to say that it was the original mode of justifying metaphysical claims. It functioned as such already for the Eleatics, with whom metaphysical argumentation originates. However, fifteen hundred years lay between the Eleatics and Anselm, and it is almost certain that Anselm did not know Parmenides or Zeno. Thus, the connection between Anselm's mode of argumentation and theirs can only be indirect. We must, therefore, keep an eye out for possible mediators between them.

On account of the huge influence that Augustine exerted upon Anselm, he is the first who comes to mind. Yet, seemingly Augustine did not make use of the indirect argument when he tried to prove the existence of God. Close examination, nevertheless, shows that his argument in *De libero arbitrio* can be presented as an indirect proof without difficulty. In order to prove that God exists, it is necessary to show that there is something which cannot be surpassed by some thing more perfect (*superius*). It cannot be denied that there is something more perfect than the human mind, because the mind claims to be able to pass true judgements and, thus, assumes truth as an objective standard. Evidently, truth, being immutable, is more perfect that the human mind, which is the most perfect part of human nature:

> Ratio caeteris in homine praestat.

And with regard to truth:

> Aeterna (incommutabilia) temporalibus (commutabilibus) potiora sunt.[2]

Now, either truth is something objective, which cannot be surpassed by anything else, in which case it is divine; or there is something which is more perfect than it is, which is nothing other than the deity:

> Si enim aliquid est excellentius, ille potius Deus est; si autem non est, iam ipsa veritas Deus est. Sive ergo illud sit, sive non sit, Deum tamen esse negare non poteris.[3]

This mode of arguing can also be expressed in the following way: Let us assume that the human mind, capable of knowledge, is the most perfect being. In that case there would be no standard upon which it depended; for that standard would clearly be superior to it. However, knowledge depends upon truth as a standard. Thus, the initial assumption is untenable and, consequently, its opposite is true. The human mind is not the most perfect being; rather, there is a more perfect being, God.

Heinrich Scholz has observed with respect to this argument that its formal elegance assumes acquaintance with truth functional logic and, in all probability, can be traced back to Stoic models.[4] Indeed, we do find related argumentation in the Stoa. For example, Chrysippus argues as follows:

> If there is something, which man cannot cause, then whoever can cause this is superior to man. Man cannot cause what is in the world. Whoever can do that is superior

to man. Who can excel man except God?
Therefore, God exists.

Aother example of indirect proof is to be found in Zeno the
Stoic (although it is in fact close to being a sophism):
The gods are justifiably (*eulogos*) honored. If they did not
exist, they would not be justifiably honored; so gods
exist.[6]

If we go a step farther back into the history of indirect proof, we find an example in Aristotle which is more
serious than the previously mentioned argumentation. Aristotle assumes that no positive predicate can be denied to
nous as the most perfect entity:

> . . . if he (the *nous*) thinks, but this
> depends on something else, then (since that
> which is its substance is not the act of
> thinking, but a potency) it cannot be the
> best substance . . . Further . . . what does
> it think of? Either of itself or of some-
> thing else . . . Evidently, then, it thinks
> of that which is most divine and precious,
> and it does not change; for change would be
> change for the worse, and this would be
> already a movement . . .[7]

An entity is clearly the most perfect (*ariste ousia*) if all
positive predicates appertain to it. If we conceive thinking in act or the thought of the perfect as positive predicates, then it would be a contradiction to ascribe to *nous*
only a potency for thinking or a thought of something imperfect. So, we have an incontestable case of an indirect
proof here, even if it is with respect to particular properties of the divine mind, rather than to God's existence.

Finally, the search for the historical roots of this
form of philosophical proof leads us to the Eleatics. Thus,
Melissus proved the thesis that being is without beginning
indirectly. We need merely mention Zeno's arguments against
motion in passing. It is not so clear that this form of
reasoning is present at the crucial point in Parmenides
where he tries to establish the thesis that being is limited. There he argues: Because being has no defects, it
lacks nothing; thus, it cannot lack a limit. Now, assuming
that unlimitedness is a defect, the claim that being-
without-defects is unlimited proves to be contradictory.
Therefore, its negation has to be true, which means that
being cannot lack limit.[8]

An indirect argument in which it should be established
that being is without origin is merely implicit in Parmenides. However, that argument is explicitly formulated by
Xenophanes, if the account in *De Melisso Xenophane Gorgia* of
Pseudo-Aristotle is reliable: In order to show that God is
without origin Xenophanes analyzes the negation of that
proposition and indicates that its consequences are contradictory. If we assume that God has been generated, he must
be generated by something more perfect or by something less
perfect. But both sides of the alternative are impossible.
God cannot be generated by something greater than he is, for
he is insuperable; and he cannot be generated by something
less perfect, for then being would generate from nothing,
which is impossible. Therefore, God must be eternal.[9]

It seems as if Xenophanes was the first to have employed
indirect arguments in metaphysics. It is worthy of note
that in the time of Xenophanes we find the first traces of
indirect proof in mathematics, namely in connection with
demonstrations of the incommensurability of certain propor-
tions in geometry. Thus, the proof of the irrationality of
the square root of 2, reported in Euclid's *Elementa*, Book X,
Appendix 27, which is Pythagorean in origin, is a clear
example of an indirect argument: In order to demonstrate
that the diagonal of a square is not commensurable with its
side, it is assumed that they are commensurable. By means
of a purely arithmetical demonstration it can be shown that
this assumption is contradictory, and therefore its negation
necessarily true.[10]

Certainly, in the period between Xenophanes and Anselm
it is not difficult to find further examples of this mode of
arguing in philosophy. The examples set forth here ought to
make it sufficiently clear that Anselm was indebted to a
logical tradition when he developed his proof in the *Proslogion*.

The Definition of "God"

Wherever philosophers have tried to justify assertions
about the divine by means of indirect proofs, this has been
done on the basis of characterizations in terms of superlatives of the sort we find in Anselm's formula, *quo maius
cogitari non potest*. Characterizing the divine by means of
superlatives which indicate absolute insuperability has its
roots deep in early antiquity, as they gradually came to be
distinguished from characterizations in terms of superlatives which define a maximum relative to a set of entities.
It is necessary to elaborate upon this distinction; we

employ superlatives of the latter kind when we say with
respect to some specific thing that it is the best, highest
or most perfect of its kind. *Maximum omnium*, used by Anselm
in *Monologion* I, is an example of this sort of superlative.
We employ superlatives of the first kind, on the other hand,
when we characterize something as insuperable pure and
simple, as for example by means of the formula *quo maius
cogitari nequit*. In the following these two kind of superlatives will be distinguished as *maximum* concepts and *supremum* concepts. These terms function only as abbreviations
here; no connection with the mathematical concepts of *maximum* and *supremum* is involved.

We first encounter *maximum* concepts. Thus, Hesiod
called Zeus "the most excellent of gods and the greatest
with respect to power."[11] With Xenophanes we find the first
glimmering of a transition to *supremum* concepts in the view
that divinity and divine power consist in the ability to
surpass and not to be surpassed.[12] This is noteworthy,
because with Xenophanes the indirect proof is first employed
as a means of justification with respect to metaphysical
claims. The contemporaneous appearance of *supremum* concepts
and the indirect proof in metaphysics is not an accident;
for it can be argued, with the aid of "non surpassable,"
that the assumption that any positive predicate is lacking
in the deity is a contradiction. In the end, however,
Xenophanes does not manage to establish fully the distinction between the two kinds of superlatives mentioned above;
for, on his view, God means "the greatest among the gods and
men"[13] or "the most excellent of all,"[14] which shows that
his formulation boils down to a *maximum* concept.

It is only with Parmenides that we find a turn of phrase
which implies a *supremum* concept, namely when he calls being
ouk epideues or "lacking no positive determination."[15] The
previously cited Aristotelian usage, *ariste ousia*,[16] that
is, most excellent entity is meant as a *supremum* concept,
although it seems to be a *maximum* concept at first glance.
This is clear from the context, that is, from the function
of the designation in the indirect proof. There is a similar case in Cleanthes, who characterizes God, not only as
the most perfect and the best, but also as the fullness of
all positive determinations (*aretai*), and, then, deduces
that the nature of such a being could not include anything
negative.[17] Here we have arrived at a point from which an
indirect proof for the existence of God can be reached in a
single step, the step that Anselm was the first to take.
This consists in conceiving existence as an *arete*, that is,
as a positive determination.

We find *supremum* concepts in various Stoics, who should
be recognized as anticipating Anselm's characterization.
Thus, Chrysippus characterized God as that being above whom
nothing more excellent can exist,[18] and Seneca, extending
the formula to conceivability, ascribed to God a greatness
beyond which nothing greater can be thought.[19] This is the
clearest anticipation of Anselm's characterization of God.
But Seneca justified his definition on the basis of the
assumption that God is everything that exists, and this
view, of course, could not be adopted by Anselm, regardless
of the extent that his formulation agrees with Seneca's. In
Seneca's argument, there is no longer any trace of a characterization of God on the basis of a *maximum* concept. Similar characterizations appeared frequently in the Stoa.

Augustine's concept of God is developed entirely along
the lines of absolute insuperability. "God" means something
than which nothing higher exists: *quo nullus est superior*.[20] Thus, on Augustine's view, we call that being "God"
for whom it can be established that it is surpassed by nothing. The more complete formulation, *quo esse aut cogitari
melius nihil possit*,[21] is the next logical step in this
direction: here God is not only determined as something
which cannot be surpassed by another; but, beyond that, as
something of which it cannot be conceived that it should be
surpassed by anything else. This formula, being an adequate
expression of a *supremum* concept, anticipates Anselm's *quo
nihil maius cogitari potest*, which can be conceived as the
continuation of Augustine's efforts toward an adequate characterization of God.

The Concept of Existence

The definition of "God" with the help of *supremum* concepts is necessary, but not sufficient for an indirect proof
of God's existence. The assumption that existence is a
property whose absence signified a defect and whose presence
is, consequently, a perfection has to be added. This is no
longer a logical assumption, but an ontological one, which
only needs to be discussed here to the extent that it has a
logical aspect to it.

It is crucial to note that "existence" can only be conceived as a positive attribute, if "being" can be treated as
an adjective. This can appear possible on the condition
that "being" admits of gradation, that is, that we can speak
of "being more" and "being most," or of "existent," "more
existent" and "most existent." This possibility is tied to
the notion of a hierarchy of being, which originates with

the Eleatics and Plato, and which all later Platonists
developed. If "being" can be compared like any other adjective, then existence seems to be a property, and it is but a
short step to the view that "existence" cannot be denied
without contradiction to an entity which lacks no positive
property because it is insuperable.

Although the assumption of a hierarchy of being was made
by Plato, the Neo-platonists and later by Pseudo-Dionysius,
we do not find indirect proofs for the existence of God in
their works. This would seem astonishing, if the reason
were not clearly because God was conceived as transcending
being in the Platonic tradition such that "existence" even
in the highest degree, could not be attributed to Him. Only
where the notion of a hierarchy of being was tied to the
assumption that God has a place in the hierarchy of being,
was an indirect proof for the existence of God possible.

This was the case in Augustine, who explained how it is,
on the basis of a hierarchical ontology, that finite things
do not exist in the same way as the Creator, that they do
not even exist relatively to God:

> Nec ita pulchra sunt nec ita bona sunt nec
> ita sunt, sicut tu conditor eorum, cui com-
> parata nec pulchra sunt nec bona nec sunt.[22]

At the same time, he ascribed existence of the highest order
to God: *summe est.*[23] If this account is correct, Augustine
was also in a position where he could have produced a proof
of the sort that Anselm later did. The fact that he did not
do so is not something that lends itself to philosophical
explanation.

To sum up: An indirect proof of God's existence is
based upon (at least) the following presuppositions: (a)
"God" must be defined as absolutely insuperable; (b) "being"
must be defined as an attribute capable of gradation; and
(c) God has to be conceived as belonging to the realm of
being.

Condition (a) is met by the Eleatics, Aristotle, several
Stoics, Augustine, Anselm; condition (b) by Plato and all
representatives of a Platonic ontology; it is implied by
Parmenides' distinction between phenomenal and "true" being;
condition (c) is met by Aristotle, Augustine, Anselm. If
only some of these conditions are met (or none of them), an
indirect proof of God's existence is impossible. This is
the case with those philosophers who characterized God by
means of *maximum* concepts, instead by means of *supremum*
concepts; it is the case with those who -- like the Stoics
-- did not accept the idea of the gradation of being; and

finally it is the case with those who -- like the Neo-
platonists and the Gnostics -- conceived God (or the One,
the Good, and so forth) as transcending the realm of being.
Only where all these conditions are met, an indirect proof
of God's existence is possible, as was the case with Anselm.

Philosophers who did not meet the conditions mentioned
above had to choose other kinds of reasoning, if they wished
to prove God's existence, as for example the Stoics who preferred teleological arguments; or they had to assume the
possibility of direct intuition of the divine, as Neo-
platonists or Gnostics did.

The conditions under discussion belong to a metaphysical
framework which would have to be taken into consideration if
one were to make a complete analysis of this topic. To do
that was not the aim of the present paper. We can, however,
ask why Anselm found an indirect proof for God's existence
attractive.

The Attractiveness
of the Indirect Proof for God's Existence

It is not accidental that indirect proof is most typically found in mathematics and metaphysics and that it
appears in these disciplines almost at the same time. In
both spheres it opens the door to the possibility of justification without deduction from substantively established
premises, but merely on the basis of definitions and logical
principles. Thus, in mathematics for example, proceeding
from the definition of "prime number" and propositions about
divisibility, it can be shown that there is no greatest
prime number. The reason is that the assumption that a definite prime number is the absolutely greatest prime number
can be proved to be contradictory. Similarly, a proof for
God's existence such as Anselm's should rest upon the definition of God and the rules of logic alone, even if critical
analysis shows that it cannot dispense with certain substantive assumptions.

If we ask, what might have made indirect proof of God's
existence so attractive in Anselm's eyes, we can identify a
number of reasons. These are worth sketching.

(1) The indirect proof is self-sufficient inasmuch as it
does not presuppose any other arguments, as Anselm himself
emphasized in the *Prooemium* of the *Proslogion*. It seems to
be a disadvantage of all types of direct proof for God's

existence that there appears among their premises at least
one matter of fact. But this seems to make the knowledge of
God's existence dependent upon knowledge of finite things.
This could be construed as a restriction upon the knowledge
of God, and, thus, as a restriction upon the infinite perfection of God Himself.

(2) Because indirect proof proceeds from characterizations of the form *id quo maius cogitari non potest*, God does
not have to be defined on the basis of specific characteristics. This allows us to skirt the difficulties which appear
without fail with characterizations such as "uncaused cause"
or "necessary being."

(3) The indirect proof is appealing from the point of
view of apophatic theology inasmuch as the basic characterization it employs is negative. It excludes from the divinity everything than which a greater can be thought. Anselm's definition of "God" as *quiddam maius quam cogitari
possit* is in the tradition of apophatic theology.[24]

(4) Indirect proof assumes on our part, nevertheless, a
certain capacity to conceive the divine nature, and, thus,
seems compatible with kataphatic theology, too. The characterization, *quo maius cogitari non potest*, is intelligible,
which is shown by the fact that it is in the intellect of
the person who understands and even of the *insipiens*:

> Intelligit quod audit, et quod intelligit in
> intellectu eius est.[25]

If God is unfathomable, he is, nevertheless, conceivable.
This corresponds to the restricted nature of our knowledge
of God, which Anselm explains as the consequence of sin.

(5) The indirect proof is, therefore, from the point of
view of Anselm's assumptions the more fitting because it is
proper to our state; inasmuch as we are only capable of
knowing God on the basis of analogy, which is to say, indirectly. That does not mean that the proof in the *Proslogion*
rests upon the principle of analogy. Yet, as Anselm was
generally convinced of the analogical character of our
knowledge of God, a proof of God's existence which took this
into account would be preferable in his eyes. The shortest
expression of the assumption of analogy seems to be the following sentence in *Proslogion* I:

> Fateor Domine, et gratias ago, quia creasti
> in me hanc imaginem tuam, ut Tui memor Te
> cogitem, Te amem.[26]

And in *Proslogion* XVII the idea of analogy is expressed with respect to the attributes of beauty, harmony, and so forth:

> Habes enim haec, Domine Deus, in Te Tuo
> ineffabili modo, qui ea dedisti rebus a Te
> creatis suo sensibili modo. . .[27].

This should in no way be taken to imply that an "ontological" proof for God's existence could not arise from other motives than those discussed here. A glance at the history of this argument shows how its later champions were moved to accept it by quite different considerations. The factors I have cited as attracting Anselm to this mode of proof are, then, historically contingent. For that reason, these reflections do not aim at anything more than clarifying the historical origins of Anselm's argument from a particular perspective.

Notes

[1] *De libero arbitrio* II,vi: *PL* XXXII,1248.

[2] Ibid. II,xiii,34:   *PL* XXXII,1259.

[3] Ibid. II,xv,39:   *PL* XXXII,1262.

[4] H. Scholz, "Der Gottesgedanke in der Mathematik," *Mathesis Universalis: Abhandlungen zur Philosophie als strenger Wissenschaft*, ed. H. Hermes et al. (Basel: Schwabe, 1961), p. 303, n.

[5] H. v. Arnim, *Stoicorum veterum fragmenta* (Leipzig: Teubner, 1903-1905), II, 1011.

[6] Ibid. I, 152.

[7] *Metaphysica* XII,ix,1074b20.

[8] H. Diels and W. Kranz, eds., *Die Fragmente der Vorsokratiker: The Older Sophists; a Complete Translation by Several Hands* ed. Rosamund Kent Sprague (Columbia: Univ. of South Carolina Press, 1972) I,[16]; 28 B 8,30-33. The deci-

sive passage is the following one: ". . . ouk ateleuteton to eon themis einai, esti gar ouk epideues, [me] eon d'an pantos edeito." The fact that, according to Parmenides and contrary to the modern conception, limitation is supposed to be a positive attribute, whereas absence of limitation is conceived as a defect, shows the historical relativity of the meaning of "perfection." Modern metaphysicians considered limitation as a defect and consequently rejected the assumption of God's finitude as contradictory. Thus, Spinoza argued in *Ethica* I, prop. VIII, schol. 1: "Cum finitum esse revera sit ex parte negatio, et infinitum absoluta affirmatio existentiae alicuius naturae, sequitur . . . omnem substantiam debere esse infinitam."

[9] Pseudo-Aristotle, *De Melisso Xenophane Gorgia*, c.3; 977a14ff.

[10] Cf. K. v. Fritz, "The Discovery of Incommensurability by Hippasus of Metapontium," *Annals of Mathematics* 46, No. 2 (1945), 242 ff.

[11] Hesiod, *Theogonia* v. 49: "phertatos esti theon kratei te megistos."

[12] Pseudo-Aristotle, *De Melisso Xenophane Gorgia* 977a28: "kratein, alla me krateisthai."

[13] Diels and Kranz, *Die Fragmente* ,21 B 8,23.

[14] Pseudo-Aristotle, *De Melisso Xenophane Gorgia* 977a28: "panton kratiston."

[15] Diels and Kranz, *Die Fragmente*, 28 B 8,33.

[16] *Metaphysica* XII,ix,1074b20.

[17] Arnim, *Stoicorum*, I,529.

[18] Ibid., II,1012: "quo nihil potest esse praestantius."

[19] *Naturalium questionum liber I*, praefatio, 5.

[20] *De libero arbitrio* II,vi,14: *PL* XXXII,1248: "Hunc plane fatebor Deum, quo nihil superius esse constiterit."

[21] *De moribus Manichaeorum* II,xi,24: *PL* XXXII,1355: "quo esse aut cogitari mrlius nihil possit."

[22] *Confessiones* XI,iv: PL XXXII,811; cf. *De civitate dei* VIII,11:   PL XLI,236.

[23] Ibid. XII,2:   PL XLI,350.

[24] .Cf. *Proslogion* XV: Schmitt I,112.   Cf. Augustine, *Sermo CXVII* III,5:   PL XXXVIII,663:   "Si enim comprehendis non est Deus." The negative character of Anselm's reasoning is underlined by J. Vuillemin, *Le Dieu d'Anselme et les apparences de la raison*, (Paris: Aubier Montaigne, 1971), p. 16: "La force analytique de la preuve repose sur son caractère négatif." Cf. p. 19: "Seule la forme négative et épistémologique est caractèristique de la preuve ontologique d'Anselme et la distingue essentiellement de toutes les formes positives et dogmatiques soit des preuves ontologiques classiques, soit des formes auxquelles on a souvent réduit la preuve d'Anselme lui-même."

[25] *Proslogion* II: Schmitt I,101. T. A. Losoncy, "Language and Saint Anselm's Proslogion Argument," in *Acta conventus neo-latini bononensis: Proceedings of the Fourth International Congress of Neo-Latin Studies: Bologna, 26 August to 1 September 1979*, ed. R. J. Schoeck, Medieval and Renaissance Texts and Studies, No. 37 (Binghamton, N.Y.: Center for Medieval and Early Renaissance Studies, 1985), p. 286, points out to the fact that according to Anselm it is possible to know God "in some measure" (aliquatenus), notwithstanding the limitedness of our knowledge. Cf. on p. 287: "This limited knowledge of God is likened to the kind of knowing one experiences when endeavoring to grasp something not completely comprehensible or understandable."

[26] *Proslogion* I: Schmitt I,97.

[27] Ibid. XVII: Schmitt I,113.

Augustine's Concept of Purification
and the Fool of the *Proslogion*

Robert A. Herrera

In an article in the *Revue Internationale de Philosophie*'s celebration of a Plotinian centenary in 1970, John J. O'Meara stressed what he called the "conversion syndrome" in Augustine's thought, pointing to its inspiration in Plotinus, principally in *Ennead* I,6, itself indebted to Plato's *Symposium*. He indicates that the practical aspect of Augustine's spiritual elevations is represented by purification, one that was propounded by both Plotinus and Porphyry.[1] It should be added that the purification of the soul, which plays such a pivotal role in Augustine's thought, is, at least in his early works, a relatively simple affair, an external training, an educational process buttressed by authority and directed to preparing the path for rigorous thought. Later, purification takes on a deeper dimension and a more austere character, due perhaps to Augustine's realization that the depredations caused by original sin were more serious than he had previously believed. It begins to include deeper regions of the soul. No longer a sort of training, it becomes an effort to increase the capacity of the soul, to "deepen" the soul. But even this view was modified once Augustine came to the realization that even thinking of the highest level is grounded on sources which escape the level of consciousness and the human will. Thinking of this caliber is rooted on the capacity to love and this is a gift of God and not a natural attainment. Wisdom is no longer seen as close at hand but is now an aspiration whose fulfillment remains in question. Mankind is viewed as surrounded by dark, subterranean forces which conspire to shut out the light of God.

As noted, these notions of purification preserve a considerable pagan sediment. It was a common notion of later antiquity that those higher powers who populated the realm of the daemonic prompted, inspired, and revealed thoughts to men. This notion is included within Augustine's thoughts on the torturous complexity of the human soul and the multiplicity of forces that are there at work. His ongoing meditation on the fall -- not unmixed with intimations of Plotinus' fall -- may well have led to the realization that man was involved in both fall and redemption on levels both below and above that of consciousness and will. As Peter Brown indicates, for Augustine evil is not a surface phenomena, a matter of mere choice, but a profound a permanent dislocation, a *discordia*, that strives, however perversely, to seek resolution in harmony and balance, in *concordia*.[2]

It is a matter of grave consequence that the very depths out of which reason issues can be corrupted by the fall. This is reflected by Augustine's belief -- commonplace with many later rationalists -- that reason can be corrupted by the imagination, a belief which reaches down to Anselm and finds voice in his remarks concerning the "heretics of dialectics" in *De incarnatione verbi*,[3] a passage which also invokes purification. The modern, secular analogue to the work of the imagination, thinking in pictures, is the Freudian notion of mentation, common to primitives, psychotics, and children, which comprises the language of dreams. Both Augustine and Anselm approach the position that speech is a disengagement of the soul from itself, from its inner dialogue with the source of truth.

In Augustine as well as Anselm there is a definite link between reasoning and prayer. The fact that the *Confessiones* were presented in the form of a prayer, Peter Brown indicates, actually increased its value as a philosophical work.[4] This is a tacit recognition that the complex of forces which prepare the way for thought and surround thought include elements that transcend the natural order. It is a safe generalization to state that this is also true of a later example of praying in thought: Anselm's *Proslogion*. Prayer elicits thought which, in turn, generates a quest for the experiencing of God, the *gaudium in spe* of *Proslogion* XXVI.

Augustine is unambiguous on the need for purification. In *De doctrina christiana*, he indicates that the soul must be purified in order that it be able to contemplate and adhere to the Divine Light.[5] He compares the procedure to "travelling" and "navigating" to the celestial fatherland.[6] This journey to the fatherland has its pagan counterparts in Plotinus, who considered that Ulysses' escape from Circe and Calypso represented the attempt to ascend to the fatherland on high, and Proclus, who interpreted Ithaca as the mystic port to which the hero is destined to return.[7] What separates Augustine from his "Platonist" predecessors is his insistence that purification is impossible without the incarnation. In his elegant phrase, "being himself the fatherland, he made himself the path to take us to the fatherland."[8]

The perennial aspiration of the philosophers, the possession of complete happiness, now hinges on the acceptance of Christ. All must pass through the mediator who is both bridge and door. To enjoy the vision of the splendor of God the human heart must be purified by means of faith.[9] Augustine admonishes those autodidacts who would attempt to purify themselves that the enterprise is engendered by pride, and pride closes the path to spiritual elevation. He admits that some of these "proud men" were able to attain "a tenuous ray of immutable truth" because of the acuity of their intelligence, but insists that this is merely a temptingly fleeting vision. The humble and speculatively unchurched Christian may well have a lengthy wait in the offing but is nevertheless certain that passage has been taken on a ship which will unfailingly arrive at the fatherland.[10]

The principal obstacle to reaching immutable truth is sin. Because of this, the love of temporal things, characteristic of sinful man, must be purified by these very temporal things. The remedy must be proportionate to the sickness. Faith is presupposed. Once it is purified, the rational mind can apply itself to the contemplation of the eternal. In his gloss on the Gospel of St. John, Augustine indicates that the truth of the *Verbum* itself -- that it is the life which is the light of men -- is hidden to the foolish because of the weight of their sins:

> He is blind in his heart as are all fools,
> evil men, and impious men ("*omnis stultus,*
> *omnis iniquus, omnis impius*").[11]

If the fool wishes to correct the unfortunate situation in which he finds himself, Augustine suggests that he purify that part of himself which has the power to contemplate God.[12] He indicates that it is fundamentally a question of a sickness of the "eyes of the heart" which dovetails, on a more popular level, with his many admonitions to his congregation to purify their hearts by rectifying their lives.

It is noteworthy that purification plays a major role in his late, encyclopaedic, *De civitate dei*. Porphyry somewhat hesitantly mentioned a purification by means of theurgy which, whatever its effectiveness in other domains, does not purify the intellectual soul. Augustine remarks that such an endeavour is contemptible as well as useless since the purification of the intellectual soul is the only path to the vision of God and the contemplation of those things "that really are."[13] Moreover, to a mankind distanced from God through sin, purification is a result of divine mercy and not of human industry.[14] Christianity offers mankind the "universal way of salvation" which Porphyry had searched for in vain. Jesus Christ, "the purifier and saviour", had taken on all of man including his intellect. This purification leads to the vision of God.[15]

Anselm echoes Augustine's principal themes in a less complex, perhaps less profound, but clearer way. The rational mind is the privileged point of departure for the knowledge of God as by considering itself it is able to rise to this knowledge.[16] The soul was created to be eternal, for the purpose of loving God endlessly, with only the proviso that it always wills to fulfill the purpose for which it was created.[17] Because he is distanced from God by sin, mankind requires a purification which can come only from God: "no man has from himself either the truth which he teaches or a just will. . . he has these from God."[18] Original sin causes a loss of rectitude in the will, a loss of justice, and its effect is to limit albeit not subvert the intellect. The rectitude of the will is, according to Anselm, the "debt which both men and angels owe to God and which only God is able to restore."[19]

Another way of addressing the question of purification is by again considering the notion of "heart," but now with many of Augustine's psychological nuances excluded. Anselm indicates that the man who believes rightly and understands rightly, but fails to will rightly, does not have an upright heart.[20] Purification becomes the necessary propedeutic to an upright heart, and is in fact presupposed by the "*credo ut intelligam.*" The heart must be cleansed by faith before examining the "deep things of faith" and also, in the words of the *Cur deus homo*, "confounding the foolishness of unbelievers and breaking through their hardheartedness."[21] In the *Responsio*, the fool is contrasted with the *catholicus*. He is a man who refuses to accept the authority of Scripture.[22]

A nostalgia for wholeness and the necessity of purification surfaces in the very first chapter of the *Proslogion*: "I was made for seeing you, but I have not done that for which I was made . . ."[23] ". . . straighten me so that I can look towards your light."[24] This plea takes on special importance in a treatise characterized by Anselm as dealing with the plenitude of human happiness,[25] and which, in addition, fuses into one *persona* the search for understanding and the quest for contemplation.

It is fairly well established that the fool's denial of God's existence is really a statement concerning his own deficient mode of thought. He exits from the *Proslogion* at a crucial point, precisely at the hiatus between *intellege ut credas* and *crede ut intelligas*. The fool is open to the exigencies of reason, though, from Anselm's point of view, hardly making good use of it. In any case, he is outside of the ambit of Christian faith and waits upon God. If Anselm is correct, the fool has made a mistake, and a mistake can be rectified. His acceptance of faith is problematic, and, at this point he does not possess that "therapeutic" knowledge which issues from faith which purifies the soul and leads it to God.

Anselm encounters the fool on the common ground of reason, the only point of mutual agreement. It would appear that the fool is deaf to both its inner exigencies, which prod him towards faith, and its outer formulation, as developed by Anselm. There appears to be nothing except his own "foolishness" which prevents him from following Anselm's argument and in this way attaining a correct, though truncated, knowledge of the existence of God. It may be necessary to postulate a prior, intellectual purification of the intellect, one which would restore discipline to the fool's use of reason and be in line with Augustine's early speculations on the theme.

It is clear that spiritual (supernatural) purification takes place only after the acceptance of faith. It is a gratuitous *modus* and, to some extent, resembles the purification of the later Augustine. Anselm is rather more sanguine than Augustine concerning the powers of reason, even reason laboring under the disadvantage of being detached from the faith which provides it with spiritual wings. The fool should be able to become aware of his sloppy ways and revise his thinking without any appeal to, or acceptance of, the Christian faith.

In this interpretation, the fool is defective in the intellectual as well as the spiritual domain. The "eyes" of his "heart" are impaired on the levels of both faith and reason. It follows that his "foolishness" requires both an intellectual and a spiritual purification. While the intellectual purification would be necessary for the fool to think rigorously and attend to the argument of *Proslogion* II-III, the spiritual purification is illustrated in the soul's vertical ascent to the light in the later books of the treatise. This intellectual purification would entail an asceticism of thought which would act as a defense against the image-glutting propensities of the imagination and the errors to which reason gone wild ineluctably leads.

This suggestion follows from the fool's ability, albeit unrealized in the *Proslogion*, to recognize his error. In addition, the acceptance of a pre-faith purification coincides in many ways with Anselm's own thematic presuppositions, and is bolstered by passages in his extensive correspondence, especially those letters with a pedagogical turn. In any case, there is no doubt that Anselm believed that all traces of foolishness must be excised from the human soul before man can reach the ultimate goal of living the life of angels, delighting in God and in each other.[26] The fool ends up with the worst of both worlds.

Notes

[1] Cf. J. J. O'Meara, "The Neoplatonism of St. Augustine." *Neoplatonism and Christian Thought*, ed. D. J. O'Meara (Norfolk: International Society for Neoplatonic Studies, 1982), p. 37ff.

[2] Peter Brown, *Augustine of Hippo* (Berkeley: Univ. of California Press, 1969), p. 366.

[3] *De incarnatione verbi* I: Schmitt II,9,20-10,13; *Anselm of Canterbury*, ed. and trans. J. Hopkins and H. Richardson, (Toronto; New York: Edwin Mellen Press, 1974-76), III, 13-14.

[4] Brown, *Augustine*, p. 155ff.

[5] *De doctrina christiana* I,x,10: *CC* XXXII,12 (author's translation).

[6] Ibid.

[7] *Enneads* I,6,8; *In Platonis Parmenides* V; cf. J. Pepin, "The Platonic and Christian Ulysses," in *Neoplatonism and Christian Thought*, pp. 3-23.

[8] *De doctrina christiana* I,xi,11: *CC* XXXII,12.

[9] *De trinitate* I,xiii,30: *CC* L,73.

[10] Ibid. IV,xv,20: *CC* L,187.

[11] *In Ioannis evangelium* I,19: *CC* XXXVI,11.

[12] Ibid. XIV,12: *CC* XXXVI,149-50.

[13] *De civitate dei* X,9: *CC* XLVII,281-83.

[14] Ibid. X,22: *CC* XLVII,296.

[15] Ibid. X,32: *CC* XLVII,309-14.

[16] *Monologion* LXVI: Schmitt I,77,7-24.

[17] Ibid. LXIX: Schmitt I,79,12-80,6.

[18] *Cur deus homo* I,9: Schmitt II,63,20-21.

[19] Ibid. I,11: Schmitt II,68,3-12.

[20] *De concordia* III,2: Schmitt II,264,5-9.

[21] *Cur deus homo*, commendatio: Schmitt II,39,2-40,2.

[22] *Responsio*, introductio: Schmitt I,130,3-5; *Responsio* VIII: Schmitt I,137,28-30.

[23] *Proslogion* I: Schmitt I,98,13-15.

[24] Ibid.: Schmitt,100,4-6ff.

[25] *Epistola 112*: Schmitt III, 246, 73-77.

[26] *Epistola 230*: Schmitt IV, 135,20-25.

"Existence in the Understanding" in *Proslogion* II

Brian Leftow

The core of *Proslogion* II's argument runs this way:

> when the fool hears the this thing which I
> say, "something than which nothing greater
> can be thought," he understands what he
> hears. And what he understands is in his
> understanding . . . (as) when an artist
> envisions what he is about to paint, he has
> it in his understanding . . . because when
> he hears this, he understands this, and
> whatever is understood is in the understand-
> ing. But . . . if it exists only in the
> understanding, it can be thought to exist
> also in reality -- which is greater. There-
> fore . . . this same thing than which a
> greater cannot be thought is a thing than
> which a greater can be thought. But surely
> this cannot be. Hence something than which
> a greater cannot be thought exists both in
> the understanding and in reality.[1]

It is not altogether clear just what Anselm meant by the
claim that "something than which no greater can be conceived" (henceforward G) is "in the understanding." Contemporary interpreters sometimes take this phrase to mean no
more than that a G is "conceivable" or "logically possible,"
i. e. that the description "a G" is comprehensible.[2] But
Anselm's text resists this reading. *Proslogion* II and
Response II argue that if a G exists in the understanding
alone, then *it* would be less great than a G existing both in
the mind and beyond the mind, and so it would not be a G.
That is, Anselm appears to think that if one understands "a
G," there exists *in intellectu* a G: to represent the argument Anselm actually gave, it seems, one must refer to or
quantify over individuals *in intellectu*. Thus any analysis
which is reasonably faithful to *Proslogion* II's text will
have to include some principle rather like one of the following:

> (1) For all x, if a person P understands the phrase "an
> x," an x exists in P's understanding;

(2) If a person P understands the phrase "a G," a G exists in P's understanding.

Gaunilo took *Proslogion* II to involve (1) and so attacked (1) vigorously.[3] Anselm plainly believed (1) and believed that its truth matters to *Proslogion* II, for he defends (1) explicitly in *Response* II.[4]   Let us therefore ask how we should understand (1).

The argument of *Proslogion* II is a *reductio ad absurdam*. The absurd entailment Anselm ascribes to the claim that there is no actual G seems to be that the very *in intellectu* individual which is a G is not a G. So Anselm is committed to the claim that a G *in intellectu* is a G. (1) is Anselm's backing for the claim that what exists *in intellectu* is a G. If (1) is a general principle entailing that a G *in intellectu* is actually a G, then (1) must assert that if one understands "an x," there exists *in intellectu* an individual with the essential attributes of an extramentally actual x.[5] So taken, (1) is clearly false. If I think of a dog, I do not increase the world's canine population; a mental dog is not a dog or animal.   So if (1)'s consequent assets the existence of mental individuals, Anselm's claim that a G exists *in intellectu* rests on a falsehood.

Suppose on the other hand that we take (1) as claiming only that if one understands "an x," some mental representation of an x exists. Anselm claims that if *what exists in one's mind* existed extramentally, *it* would be greater.   But a mental representation is not the sort of thing that can exist outside the mind. If so, "what exists in one's mind exists extramentally" may be mere nonsense, a category mistake. If it is, the conditional whose antecedent it is is nonsense as well. Further, according to Anselm, *Proslogion* II's conclusion, that a G exists extramentally, entails that what existed in the fool's mind exists extramentally. Thus if (1) is nonsense, Anselm must grant that his conclusion entails a piece of nonsense -- an uncomfortable admission. It might also be, however, that "a mental representation exists extramentally" is not a category mistake but a necessary falsehood. If so and if for Anselm what exists in one's mind is a mental representation, "if what exists in one's mind existed extramentally, it would be greater" is a counterfactual conditional with a necessarily false antecedent. On standard theories of counterfactuals, then, this claim would be true. But if Anselm purchased the truth of this conditional in this way, he would be paying too high a price.   For again, according to Anselm, *Proslogion* II's conclusion, that a G exists extramentally, entails that what existed in the fool's mind exists extramentally. So if this

latter is necessarily false, then *Proslogion* II's conclusion
is false. If (1)'s consequent asserts the existence of mental representations, then Anselm cannot accept (1).

We cannot save (1) by saying that what exists within or
without the mind is the attribute of being of G. For it is
not the attribute which is supposed to be greater if it
exists extramentally, but rather what *has* that attribute.
Suppose then that we take (1) to claim that if we understand
"an x," there exists a possible individual which possibly
but not actually is a an x. This would strain Anselm's
text, for taking being *in intellectu* as being metaphysically
possible would ignore the evident connection between the
phrase *in intellectu* and *Proslogion* II-IV's talk about what
the fool can and does think and say to himself: talk of
being *in intllectu*, being thinkable and being sayable seems
to deal with what is conceivable, and being metaphysically
possible neither entails nor is entailed by being conceivable. But let us see if thus straining the text will help.
Anselm's *reductio* seems to turn on the claim that if the G
in intellectu is not also in reality, it is not actually a
G. But if the G *in intellectu* is merely a possible G to
begin with, the unpleasant consequence of denying the actu-
ality of a G cannot be that this possible G is not an actual
G. So on this reading, the unpleasant consequence must be
something like "the possible G is not the/a (possible) G."
Taking both occurrences of "the possible G" as rigid designators, this statement asserts that an individual is not
identical with itself. While this is impossible, it is
unclear why it would follow from anything in *Proslogion* II.
Taking only the first occurrence of "the possible G"
rigidly, we get the claim that a possible individual picked
out as possibly G is not in fact possibly G. But there is
nothing problematic about making successful reference to
something via an attribute it does not possess, so long as
the person to whom one points this thing out understands
what one means to say or shares one's delusion. So this
consequence would not be unacceptable, and thus would not
force the Fool to grant that there is an extramental G.

If being *in intellectu* is being metaphysically possible,
Anselm's *reductio* might instead turn on the claim that if
there is no actual G, the possible G is such that were it
actualized the result would not be a G. If this is so, of
course, the putative possible G is not truly a possible G.
Anselm could argue for this claim in a variety of ways --
for instance, by arguing that no G can be caused to exist by
something other than itself, but a non-actual possible G
would have be actualized by something other than itself.
However, no such argument occurs here. Instead, on this

reading, we are told that "the possible G is not a possible G" follows directly from the claim that no G is actual. But this follows directly, given the present reading of existence *in intellectu*, only if necessarily whatever is a G is actual. Thus the claim that this follows directly would presuppose *Proslogion* II's conclusion.

Let us note one more possibility. We will suggest below that "exists in the understanding" may mean "is or has been directly encountered in experience." On this reading, (1) claims that to understand a phrase denoting an individual or an attribute one must have encountered or have had acquaintance with that individual or attribute. This amounts to extending to definite descriptions a Russellian view of proper names. This theory of proper names now has few backers. This extension would find fewer still.

The approaches we have tried all read (1) as committing us to the existence of objects of acts of conceiving or of experience, be they *possibilia*, *intentionalia*, or whatever. The failure of these approaches may suggest that we take Anselm as ontologically committed only to acts of conceiving. That is, we might ascribe to him an "adverbial" analysis of the objects of conceivings, and read *Proslogion* II's *reductio* as involving not a contradiction about an object of conception but one about an act of conceiving. If we do this, the *reductio* of "a G is *in solo intellectu*" will look something like this:

(1) We can conceive G* to be a G and to be *in solo intellectu*.

(2) We can conceive some G** to be a G and to be *in intellectu et in re*.

(3) Therefore we can conceive some G** to be greater than G*.

(4) Therefore we do not conceive G* to be a G.

(5) Therefore (by *reductio*) if we conceive G* to be a G and to be *in intellectu*, we must conceive G* to be *in re*.

This construction of Anselm's argument has promise. It seems valid intuitively, thought doubtless it would require a high-powered logic able to deal with intentional contexts to show this formally. It also suggests a closer connection with *Proslogion* IV than would otherwise be the case. The latter chapter seems to have as its conclusion that the fool just cannot meaningfully assert his atheism. *Proslogion* II taken as just suggested would conclude not that a G exists but that the fool must conceive that a G exists.

Again, this reading of the chapter would conform to the concern to avoid the use of "necessary" and "necessarily" in statements about God which Anselm manifests in *Cur deus homo* II,17-18. There Anselm argues that since the basic meaning of "necessity" is "constraint" or "coercion," talk of God as necessitated is inappropriate, since nothing can constrain or coerce an omnipotent being. Anselm concludes that statements of the form "necessarily God . . ." or "God necessarily . . ." have misleading surface forms and so should be eliminated from logically perspicuous God-talk. Anselm also suggests that where such surface-forms occur, the states of affairs they are trying to express are not constraints upon God but constraints or inabilities in other things: for instance, the claim that God is necessarily truthful, says Anselm, asserts only that God's will is so firmly set toward truthfulness that nothing is able to make Him lie. If these are genuine concerns of Anselm's, he would not be happy stating the conclusions of *Proslogion* II or III in the form, "necessarily, God exists." He would however find it wholly suitable to state them in such forms as "necessarily, if we think of God at all, we must think that he exists."

Despite these advantages, the proposed interpretation has two serious problems. First, if read this way, *Proslogion* II involves neither (1) nor (2). But we have already seen that Anselm thinks this argument does involve (1) (or perhaps [2], as we will suggest shortly). Second, in criticizing the artist-picture analogy of *Proslogion* II, Gaunilo suggests that before it is painted, a picture is just "a part of (the artist's) understanding" rather than some sort of distinct intentional or possible existent.[6] This seems to adumbrate the claim that we need be ontologically committed only to conceivings, not to objects of conceiving. Thus Gaunilo gave Anselm a fairly clear chance to say that this was what he "really meant." Anselm did not do so.

(1), in any event, is hard to interpret and seems on any construction to be more liability than asset to Anselm. Now given the *Response*'s defense, it might seem plausible that Anselm holds (2) because he holds (1), and that (2) is a mere instantiation of (1). However, there is some reason to suspect that in fact Anselm holds (1) because he holds (2). In her *Anselm and Talking about God*, Gillian Evans builds a persuasive case that Anselm's philosophy of language begins from what holds true of God and the divine Word, then interprets human words and language as images of this primal Word.[7] If Anselm had special reason to believe that understanding terms and phrases referring to God requires God's

presence *in intellectu*, then this could have led him to
adopt (1) as a generalization of this. Again, the claim
that Anselm works from (2) to (1) rather than vice-versa
accords well with Barth's stress on the genuinely theological or God-centered character and method of the *Proslogion*
and of Anselm's work generally. It may be, then, that to
find why Anselm thought (1) plausible, we ought to investigate (2).

If we do, I submit, we will find that (2) follows from a
thesis Anselm plainly held and that this thesis does not at
all support (1). We will thus be able to call (1) merely an
illicit generalization from (2) We will also see that (2)
lacks (1)'s ontological inflation and other difficulties and
that, if suitably understood and given one assumption, (2)
is true. If all these things are so, using (2) in place of
(1) certainly can strengthen *Proslogion* II's argument.

Let us therefore see what we can say on (2)'s behalf.
Given (1)'s difficulties, we should seek so to justify (2)
that (2) will not commit Anselm to (1). One way to succeed
at this would be to base (2) on some attribute of a G which
is such that no other entity can share it. We may find such
an attribute in Anselm's claim that any G must be metaphysically simple:

> whatever is a union of parts . . . can be
> dissolved either actually or in a mind. But
> these consequences are foreign to you, than
> whom nothing better can be thought. There-
> fore there are no parts in you . . . but
> rather, you are . . . unity itself, divi-
> sible in no mind.[8]

When we sketch what Anselm thinks metaphysical simplicity to
involve, we will see that in fact, if a G is simple, nothing
other than that G can be simple.

In this and parallel passages, Anselm's examples of
"parts" are distinct attributes such as life, wisdom, and
goodness. Attributes are in no ordinary sense parts. While
the part-whole relation is transitive, the attribute-subject
relation is not, for that my finger is part of my hand and
my hand is part of my body entail that my finger is part of
my body, but if grass is green and green is a color, it does
not follow that grass is a color. Still, something has distinct attributes as "parts" iff its being actual entails
that the distinction between subject and attribute is exemplified. So we can preserve the point of Anselm's metaphor
by saying that if something is simple, it is not identical
with anything the existence of which entails that the dis-

tinction between subject and attribute is exemplified. Given the earlier and later history of the doctrine of divine simplicity, it would be reasonable to generalize and strengthen this claim and say that something is simple iff it is not identical with anything the existence of which entails that any metaphysical distinction is exemplified.

Speaking of *metaphysical* distinctions allows Anselm a *caveat* on which he insists. Anselm wants to say that the G which he shows to exist is the God of orthodox Christianity. He believes that orthodoxy demands that the Trinity's Persons be distinct in God and not merely in our thinking about God. So he grants that though a G is simple relative to all distinctions metaphysics can make, a G may yet be complex in a further way of which theology tells.[9] (Whether one really can thus divorce Trinitarian and metaphysical distinctions is a question we cannot raise here.)

If a G is simple in Anselm's sense, then, for all non-Trinitarian attributes F, if a G is F, it is false that it is the subject of a distinct attribute, F-ness. Rather, the real condition which makes it true that the G is F is in no way really distinct from makes it true that the G is itself. Anselm took this lack of distinction seriously enough to infer from it that if a G "has" the attribute of goodness, it is identical to goodness.[10] This lack of distinction also seems to entail that if a G is just and merciful, justice and mercy are identical. Thus Anselm conceives a G to be relevantly like a single being which has the ontological roles and status of a fusion of apparently distinct Platonic forms.

To show that these conclusions are not the scandal they seem to be would take us far afield. Let us rather note that it is not possible that there be more than one being which is actually or possibly simple in Anselm's sense. For suppose that there are two actual simple beings, A and B. A must have the attribute of identity with A, or else whatever set of attributes is necessary and sufficient for being A. This attribute (or set) either is or is not identical with the attribute of being simple. If it is not, A has at least two distinct attributes, and so is not simple. If it is, B, by being simple, is identical with A. So either way we have at most one actual simple being. Further, for any simple A, the attribute of simplicity = the attribute of being identical with A, or = whatever set of attributes is necessary and sufficient for identity with A. Hence any being which is possibly simple is possibly A. But only A is possibly A. So for any simple A, nothing other than A is possibly simple.

It seems, then, that the attribute of simplicity can have at most one possible bearer. And of course, it is impossible that any non-simple thing share in the attribute of simplicity. For since all of a simple thing's attributes are identical with its attribute of simplicity, for any A, the attribute of being simple is identical with the attribute of being A. Therefore any non-simple B which is not identical with A is possibly simple only if it is possibly A -- that is, possibly not B. Since nothing is possibly not identical with itself, then nothing non-simple is possibly simple. Further, since real identities are one and all necessary, nothing possibly non-simple is possibly simple. It appears, then, that simplicity is an absolutely unshareable attribute: it cannot have more than one actual or possible bearer. Hence if we can justify (2) on the basis of a G's simplicity, we will lend (1) neither aid nor comfort. Let us now attempt to justify (2) in this way by examining a constraint on our understanding of propositions about a being which is simple in Anselm's sense.

Because every attribute of a simple being is identical with the attribute of simplicity, a simple being can share attributes with other things only if there can be two instances of the attribute of simplicity. As this last is not possible, a simple being cannot have an attribute literally in common with anything distinct from itself. Now if we assumed that "A is good" and "B is good" are both true only if there is a single real attribute, goodness, which both possess, the claim that a simple being cannot share attributes would render false every affirmative proposition using the language we use for talking about other things to ascribe an attribute to a simple being. That is, we would be forced into a purely negative theology.

So a defender of divine simplicity not content with negative theology must seek some basis other than literally common attributes for the ascription of common predicates. We will not be able to discuss here the questions this raises. Let us rather note that Anselm's Platonistic language throughout the *Monologion* and *Proslogion* certainly suggests that he considers common attributes the basis for the ascription common predicates, and that *Monologion* LXV-LXVI and *Proslogion* XV certainly suggest an uneasy awareness of teetering on the edge of purely negative theology. In the latter chapters, Anselm ascribes the change of meaning predicates undergo *in divinis* to God's being a G. But this does not really count against the claim that Anselm may have connected the possible equivocity of talk about God with God's simplicity. For Anselm considers God's simplicity a direct consequence of His being a G.[11]

Let us see how far we can possibly move from negative theology, given a common-attribute theory of predication, if we do not have direct experience of a simple being. Lacking experience of a simple being is not like lacking experience of a particular individual of a known kind, or of a particular kind of a known super-kind, or of any ontologically complex thing. In each of these other cases we have experienced or can experience something with some attribute in common with the thing we have not experienced. With a simple being, such experience is impossible. If likeness entails the possession of common attributes, further, there cannot be anything in any way naturally suited by likeness to stand proxy for a simple being. Given these assumptions, a simple being is the sole literally and absolutely unique thing. If this is so, only direct experience of such a being can bring it within our cognizance or give us a clue as to what it is really like in and of itself.

Without such experience of a simple being, we know only the following about it. We know that the real truth-conditions of statements about such a being must be facts about or involving the simple being. We know some formal properties of these truth-conditions (e. g., their obedience to the laws of logic) and the meanings of any transcendental terms statements of them may involve. We know some attributes which they cannot involve. We also know some logical forms they cannot have. For as a simple being is necessarily unique, nothing else can satisfy any description or predicate which a simple being satisfies. It follows that all terms or descriptions referring to or satisfied by a simple being designate it alone, and so rigidly. Thus they have the logical force of rigid designators. If so, all apparent predications linking terms referring to and/or descriptions satisfied by such a being have the logic of identity-statements: no true statement about a simple being alone has the logic of a predication. But without experiencing the simple being, we know nothing beyond all this. Let us sum up this situation by saying that without such experience, we have and can have only formal knowledge of a simple being. In the absence of direct experience of a simple thing, we cannot understand any proposition about one non-formally. Thus without this experience, sentences which appear to express non-formally informative propositions about a simple being either convey only formal knowledge to us, or convey to us propositions which are not about the simple thing but rather about other things, or are to be interpreted in accord with the canons of negative theology.

Experience of a simple thing in itself need not be experience of nothing but that thing. But an experience's

simple component must be independent of whatever else the
experience contains, i. e., a new primitive quality added to
our experience, irreducible to any other. For if no attribute of a simple being is even possibly identical with any
attribute of a non-simple thing, no experience of any
attribute of something non-simple can be experience of an
attribute of something simple, and so no experience of a
simple thing can be or reduce to experience of any non-
simple thing. But any attribute of a simple being is identical with that being itself. So it is a necessary condition of having experience-based non-formal understanding of
talk about a simple being that it be present to our minds
propria persona. If this being is simple, further, it must
be present in its entirety if it is present at all. (This
is not to say that we will or can wholly comprehend what is
thus present.)

We can understand talk of a simple perfect being non-
formally, then, if and only if this perfect being actually
(if perhaps only inchoately) is or has been present in some
way in our experience, or "*in intellectu*." Thus if we take
"presence *in intellectu*" to mean present or past presence in
experience and take (2) to be talking about a G which is
simple in the context of a common-attribute theory of predication, it appears that (2) is a conceptual truth about a
constraint imposed on our non-formal knowledge of a perfect
being by the logic of metaphysical simplicity. The claim
that it is the Christian God who is a G appears to be non-
formal. Hence if the fool has understood and granted this
claim -- the more fool he -- he must grant that a G is or
has been present *in intellectu*.

In sum, if a perfect being is simple in the way Anselm
thinks, then given a common-attribute theory of predication,
we face a dilemma: either our talk of a perfect being at
best conveys only formal knowledge, or this talk conveys
more to us only because it expresses and articulates a
direct experience of the simple perfect being. (2) is true
given the common-attribute assumption, I submit, because it
expresses a consequence of this dilemma. Now nothing in
Anselm's writings suggests explicitly that he saw this
dilemma. But we do not know that Anselm did not see this
problem, and we do not know that he did not have some ink-
ling of it when he considered (1) and (2). If reading *Proslogion* II in light of the above reasoning strengthens its
argument, the principle of charity may dictate a cautious
suggestion that we take this chapter to involve (2), not
(1). And if doing this does not seem warranted, at least
those who find Anselm's argument appealing may take heart in
the thought that it may admit of a more powerful presenta-

tion than Anselm himself gave it. I believe that in fact Anselm's doctrine of divine simplicity not only warrants (2) but will also warrant the claim that if that than which no greater can be conceived exists *in intellectu*, it exists *in re*. But that is a tale for another day.

Notes

All citations will be from the Schmitt text as reprinted in M. J. Charlesworth, ed. and trans., *St. Anselm's Proslogion* (London: Oxford Univ. Press, 1965).

[1] *Proslogion* II: Charlesworth, p. 116. My translation.

[2] Cf., e. g., Charlesworth's "Commentary," in his *St. Anselm's Proslogion*, pp. 58, 62.

[3] *Quid ad haec respondeat quidam pro insipiente*: Charlesworth, pp. 156-58, 162.

[4] *Quid ad haec respondeat editor ipsius libelli* II: Charlesworth, pp. 172-74.

[5] I take it as obvious that to Anselm, being a G is essential to a G. Anselm would surely think that a G is more perfectly G if it is essentially rather than accidentally G., and so an argument paralleling that of *Proslogion* III would lead him to this conclusion.

[6] *Quid ad haec respondeat quidam pro insipiente*: Charlesworth, p. 158.

[7] Evans, G. R., *Anselm and Talking about God* (London: Oxford University Press, 1978), pp. 20 ff.

[8] *Proslogion* XVIII: Charlesworth, p. 140. My translation.

[9] Ibid. XXIII: Charlesworth, pp. 144-46.

[10] Ibid. XII: Charlesworth, p. 132.

[11] Ibid. III: Charlesworth. p. 118; ibid. XVIII: Charlesworth, p. 140.

III

Truth: Anselm and Augustine

Anselm

. . . veritas est rectitudo mente sola perceptibilis.

(*De veritate* XI)

Augustine

Noli foras ire, in te ipsum redi; in interiore homine habitat veritas, et si tuam naturam
mutablilem inveneris, transcende et te ipsum.
Sed memento cum te transcendis, ratiocinantem
animam te transcendere.

(*De vera religione* XXXIX,72)

Truth: Augustine and Anselm

Edward A. Synan

Three Names

Augustine of Hippo and Anselm of Bec are two names which honor our race. In a special way they have honored the guild of Christian scholars. "Truth," these two saints strongly believed, refers to more than epistemic success: truth is a divine Name (Jn 14:6). Each name -- Augustine, Anselm, and Truth -- evokes an indeterminately enormous wealth of material. Hence, the title assigned presents a daunting challenge.

Still, the three names interact to bring that wealth of material within manageable limits. If they seem to threaten words-without-end (to which you would hardly be willing to say "Amen!"), juxtaposed, they provide a defense against infinite regress.

First, a focus on the theme of truth will preserve us from an aimless wandering through the disheartening mass of the two Saints' *Opera omnia*. Our inheritance from Augustine is of literally proverbial magnitude. An aunt of Giovanni Papini was repeating a local proverb when, seeing her small nephew scribbling away at his exercises in elementary Latin, she cried out: "He writes as much as Saint Augustine!", *Scrive quanto Sant'Agostino!*[1] If Saint Anselm did not match the bulk of Augustine's production, the critical edition of Anselm's writings has required five large volumes and those volumes are doctrinally so densely packed that a sixth volume of comparable size has been required for their indexing. Faced by these two formidable collections, we shall welcome the focus on truth; there is a *sensus plenior* in which "Truth will set us free" (Jn 8:32).

Second, because Saint Anselm is the primary figure in this conference, we are authorized to prescind from aspects of Saint Augustine's doctrine on truth that may not be conspicuous in the work of the great Benedictine.

A further economy is based on the fact that Augustine seems to have made what might well be taken as a kind of *ratio seminalis* of his perceptions on truth in his first extant work. That work is the Cassiciacum dialogue *Contra academicos* of November, 386. In a negative sense this interpretation is guaranteed by the estimate Augustine made of the dialogue in his *Retractationes* of 426. Here, as everywhere, Augustine had his reservations, to be sure, but

they do not bear upon his presentation of truth. Augustine
regretted that he had so often written *fortuna* where he
ought to have written *providentia*[2] and he was not altogether
happy with the mild parading of what Greek he possessed on
the terms *philocalia* and *philosophia*.[3] It may be noted here
that we shall advert to another snippet of classical learning that one might have expected the exigent old bishop to
have withdrawn but which he passed over without a word.   In
a positive sense, a number of Augustine's most characteristic contributions to the epistemic, if not to the noetic,
aspects of truth are already visible in this first of his
works as a convinced believer in Jesus Christ.[4] This reading could be pressed too far: the epistemology of the *Contra acadmicos* is "seminal" only. The mature doctrine of the
De magistro (389) and especially that of the second book of
the *De libero arbitrio* (394-395) was not fully developed at
Cassiciacum. Those later works would hardly have been written had Augustine thought the theme of truth exhausted in
his first effort to deal with it.

What, you may wonder, is intended by the phrase "most
characteristic contributions" of Augustinian epistemology?
First, his insistence, never to be abandoned, that happiness
requires the possession of wisdom and that the possession of
wisdom entails a secure grasp of truth; second, an emphasis
on the immutable, the necessary, quality of truth and wisdom, even in human knowledge of creatures where both what is
known and the one who knows are mutable and contingent;
third, an unwavering conviction that the presence of God to
the human mind is an illuminating factor, indispensable if
such a mind is to transcend its creaturely limitations.

Here it will be contended that all three of these characteristics are conspicuous in Anselm's perspectives on
truth. Furthermore, Anselm's preoccupation with these characteristics illumines the exegesis of Anselmian materials
that otherwise pose insuperable difficulties, notably, his
probatio of divine Being in the *Proslogion* and his search
for "necessary reasons" throughout his examination of the
data of faith in the mighty deeds of the sovereignly free
Creator.

It will be argued too that Anselm, within his assumptions, has given satisfying solutions to every enigma he has
touched; where those assumptions bear on truth, they are
Augustinian. Somewhat as the mature Augustine advanced
beyond his Cassiciacum positions without abandoning them, so
Anselm has advanced beyond Augustine without unsaying what
the mature Augustine had bequeathed to the Christian centuries.

To conclude these introductory remarks: my limitations, of which limited available time is the least significant, dictate that what follows will focus upon Augustine's perceptions of truth, mainly as found in the *Contra academicos*, and this only to the point that those Augustinian insights can be shown to have been used creatively by Saint Anselm.

Truth and the *Contra academicos*

When Augustine arrived at his philosophical retreat he brought with him both a firm faith in Christian truth[5] and a disturbing memory of his own recent brush with scepticism.[6] He was also anxious to provide his instinctively anti-sceptical, but philosophically innocent, patron Romanianus with a set of simple, convincing arguments to the effect that a grasp of truth, even a grasp of wisdom, is not necessarily beyond us.[7] Cicero's *Hortensius* had acquainted Augustine with the joy of philosophy; by his *Academica* the same author had acquainted him with the scepticisms engendered among the successive heirs of Plato.

A stanza from a poem by Godfrey of Saint Victor in praise of Saint Augustine, although written two long generations after the life-time of Saint Anselm, has peculiar value as an introduction to the *Contra academicos*. Godfrey, a Canon of Saint Augustine from the great Parisian house of his Order, had the knack of writing catchy verses in accented, rhyming Latin. Having devoted ten stanzas to Augustine in his *Fons philosophiae* (against only one or two for each of the other major Latin Fathers of the Church -- Ambrose, Jerome, and Gregory the Great)[8], Godfrey composed one hundred and twenty-seven more on Augustine under the title: *Preconium Augustini*.[9] One stanza, lines 101 to 104, echoes an exchange between Alypius and Augustine[10] in the *Contra academicos*:

> Hic est enim Protheus ille latens divus,
> Vultu variabili, semper fugitivus,
> Quem non capit animus quantumcumque vivus,
> Sed prodente numine ducitur captivus.

Lest twelfth century Latin, pronounced by a pre-Vatican II ex-seminarian, needlessly obscure ideas, in themselves less than crystal-clear, an English version may be ventured:

> Proteus, that hidden god, camouflage well-tended,
> Always changing shape lest one make the catch intended,

By no mind, however deft, is he comprehended,
But should God betray his game -- then he's apprehended.

These lines refer to a number of points about truth that
were made by Alypius under the figure of Proteus. According
to the myths, this minor divinity, a son of Neptune and
charged with herding the sea-god's seals, was notable for
his ability to evade capture by changing his shape at will.
Despite this, so the legends have it, Proteus could be taken
by guile, provided there was help from some divinity. The
fourth book of *The Odyssey* might have served, but more
likely the fourth *Georgic* of Virgil[11] provided all relevant
data on Proteus for Alypius and Augustine.

Alypius likened truth, as seen by sceptical philosophers, to the elusive godling. The sceptics had put their
tenets in two statements: "Nothing can be comprehended" and
"Assent must not be given to anything," not even to these
pronouncements.[12] If truth is so evasive that these aphor-
isms are sound, then truth is Protean indeed. Within the
terms of the myth, however, Proteus can be captured provided, in the words ascribed to Alypius, "some sort of divinity point the way," *indice alicuiusmodi numine*.[13] It was
noted above that, although in his *Retractationes* Augustine
would express some scruples on his references to *fortuna* and
on his *quasi fabula* concerning *philocalia* and *philosophia*,
he had no second thoughts on what might have been counted a
more serious impropriety. This is the praise he had handed
out so lavishly to Alypius for his application of the Proteus myth, a remarkable departure from Augustine's habitual
severity against his youthful references to pagan conceptions, as here in the case of *fortuna*. In any event, Augustine's presentation of his own response to Alypius is worth
citation at some length:

> Now you have said with both brevity and
> piety that only some divinity, *numen ali-*
> *quod*, can show a human what the true might
> be. Nothing have I heard in this conversa-
> tion of ours with more pleasure, nothing
> more weighty, nothing more plausible, *proba-*
> *bilius*, and, if that divinity be at hand (as
> I am confident is the case!), *si id numen,*
> *ut confido, assit*, nothing more true, *uer-*
> *ius*. For that Proteus, *Proteus ille* --
> noted by you with so much profundity of mind
> and with so great a thrust toward the best
> sort of philosophy -- that Proteus is intro-
> duced as an image of truth, *in imaginem*

> ueritatis, in order that you young men might
> see that poets ought not to be condemned
> totally by philosophy. In poems Proteus
> exhibits and plays the role of truth, the
> role, I say, of what no one can seize if,
> deceived by false images, one loosen or let
> slip the bonds of comprehension, *comprehen-*
> *sionis nodos*. For these are images which,
> in the usual way of corporeal things, work
> to deceive and delude us through the very
> senses we employ for the necessities of life
> -- and they do this even when truth is
> grasped, held, as it were, in our hands.[14]

There can be no doubt but that Godfrey had this passage in
mind when he wrote the lines we have cited from his *Preco-*
nium. His grasp of Augustinian epistemology apart, Godfrey's very terms are those of Augustine: *ille Protheus* and
prodente numine, the object and condition of a successful
effort to know, are too close to Augustine's *numen aliquod,*
id numen . . . assit, Proteus enim ille, for the thing to be
accidental.

More to the purpose than the fact of Godfrey's having
read (and understood) the *Contra academicos* is the fact that
this brief text adumbrates Augustine's illumination theory
of human knowing. In its developed form this theory holds
that a human mind grasps truths in the light of Truth itself
and Truth itself, for this Christian Platonist, is God.[15]
Here divinity, Augustine was confident, will be at hand to
assist in the capture of truth, however "Protean," that is,
truth whose shifting guises are on the plane of corporeal,
mutable, things, imperfectly grasped through the formation
of equally mutable sense images. Only in the light of present divinity can truth be comprehended and this only if the
"bonds of comprehension," that is, only if an intellectual,
and not a merely corporeal, grasp of what is real be maintained. Hence Augustine's praise for Alypius on the appeal
he had made to the Proteus myth. As a *rhetor* of profes-
sional standing, whose set-books included at least some
philosophical dialogues by Cicero, Augustine could grant the
accolade that the Proteus analogy was "more true" than anything yet articulated. The same Cicero who drew Augustine's
fire for having given scepticism a platform in the *Acade-*
mica[16] was also the author of the *Hortensius*, a dialogue
that had made a life-long "lover of wisdom" of Augustine and
had reconciled his two pupils, Trygetius and Licentius, who
were with him at Cassiciacum, to philosophy.[17] On all
counts he was glad to have his students see that *belles-*

lettres can and ought to have a role in more substantive
studies; this is one more indication of future work for in
his *De doctrina christiana*, begun in 397, but finished only
in 426, he would justify the liberal arts for the millennium
to come as equipment necessary for a knowledgeable reading
of Sacred Scripture.

Augustine was particularly exercised by the notion he
ascribed, and not without reason, to Cicero according to
which the happy life might be achieved apart from the possession of truth: The search alone suffices.[18] More than
sixty years ago Charles Boyer suggested this may well have
been the position of the *Hortensius* which had first drawn
the young Augustine to the philosophical life and he was
able to cite a line from the *Confessiones* to that effect:

> . . . having read Cicero's *Hortensius* I was
> spurred on to the study of wisdom, and I was
> putting off rejecting all earthly felicity
> in order to be free for the tracking down of
> that whose mere seeking, *not the finding*,
> must now be preferred . . .[19]

This attitude Augustine and his companions had left
behind them when they made their way to Cassiciacum: happiness can be assured only by the possession of truth, not by
its pursuit.[20] This conviction was the philosophical dynamic
that moved him to undertake the refutation of sceptical
claims. Those claims, he realized, were formidable, weap-
ons, *arma*, forged "as it were, by Vulcan," and Augustine
thought it right to invoke "the power and wisdom of the most
high God" against them.[21]

Sceptical philosophers did not confine themselves to
objecting against the validity of sensation, but they did
invoke a number of instances in which our senses can be
impugned and we have heard Augustine himself refer to illu-
sory sense images.[22] Philosophers of the Academy were
unwilling to grant that sensations are reliable indices of
truth and Augustine was not insensitive to their reasons; in
one mood he might seem to have joined them:

> . . . chest pains forced me to abandon the
> windy profession (rhetoric both taught and
> practiced, see *Confessiones* V,xiii,23;
> VI,vi,10; IX,ii,4) and to fly to the bosom
> of Philosophy. For she teaches -- and
> teaches truly! -- that whatever is seen by
> mortal eyes, whatever any sense attains,

> must in no way be cultivated, no, the whole
> business ought to be contemned . . .[23]

We may be excused for turning to the *Retractationes* in the
hope that second thoughts might have been more benign, but
the old Bishop's single adjustment was to concede that he
ought to have added the phrase "of a mortal body" to qualify
the sense and what sense can attain; in 426 he wanted to
make room for "senses of the mind."[24] Thus Augustine's
strongly Platonic bias in favor of the intelligible as
against the sensible, visible in this passage, invited his
somewhat nonchalant dismissal of sceptical arguments. That
sort of objection "is not valid against all philosophers,"
for some do not grant knowledge in any strict meaning,
scientia, to the senses; the abode of knowledge is in the
intelligence, in the mind. It was among such philosophers,
he more that hinted, that the "wise, whom we seek" will be
found.[25]

What of the distortion of reality by sight -- the "bent"
oar, the moving tower, the shifting color of a bird's plu-
mage? What of sleep, insanity, and their illusions? "The
whole mass and machine of bodies within which we are," he
responded, "whether we sleep or rave or are awake and sane
either is one, or is not one" -- this he challenged sceptics
to deny. Besides, if an oar in water appeared to be
straight this would be a "false report" and so for all other
instances. Finally, Augustine could not see how an Academic
scepticism could refute one who confined himself to saying:
"I know that this seems white to me, I know I am delighted
by this hearing, I know this odor is pleasant to me" and so
for the rest.[26]

All but buried in this jaunty rebuttal of scepticism is
Augustine's final resource in the emergency: This is the
incontrovertible truth of the disjunctive proposition. No
matter what the disturbances of sense in our world, the
world is necessarily one world or it is not one world. What
may go wrong on the plane of sensation is ultimately irrelevant; one may well be deceived concerning what pertains to
the senses of the body, but:

> . . . that three times three is nine and the
> square of intelligible numbers is necessary
> must be true even though the human race lie
> prostrate.[27]

Not only must the sceptic contend with the necessary
truth of disjunctives, even though no one knows which dis-

junct is true, the sceptics' most objectionable   statements,
that "nothing can be perceived" and "assent must be given to
nothing" are self-refuting.   If they are   false,   scepticism
goes   down   with them; if they are true, then at least something true is known and to this assent must   be   given.   So
too, the device of taking refuge in the "truth-like" entails
the concession that truth is   knowable;   to   deny   truth   as
known   is   to close off the possibility that any position be
"like" that unknown.[28]   No more can one be "wise," yet   not
know wisdom.[29]

All   of this wears a dialectical guise and Augustine was
the first to note the fact; he admitted that   "I   know   more
(of   dia-lectics)   than of any part of philosophy."   Indeed,
through dialectics he had come to know "many other   truths,"
truths beyond numbering.[30]

Finally,   parallel   to   his   dialectical   fencing was an
unabashed appeal to his   new-found   Christian   faith.   The
presence   of divinity, necessary for the capture of Proteus-
like truth, is the incarnate Wisdom of the   biblical   God.[31]
Did   Augustine waver in his zeal for the philosophical life?
"Thus wavering I hurried to seize upon   the   Apostle   Paul."
What   is   more,   Philosophy then revealed her face to him.[32]
There is also the celebrated pledge   of   allegiance   to   the
authority   of   faith   and   to rationality, to Plato as to one
who will not weaken his attachment to Messiah.   Thus did the
late Anton C. Pegis render Augustine's Latin:

> .   .   .   everyone agrees that we are impelled
> to   learning   by   a   double   urge,   that   of
> authority   and   that   of   reason.   From this
> moment forward it is   my   resolve   never   to
> depart   from   the authority of Christ.   For I
> find none that is stronger.   However, I must
> follow after this with the greatest subtlety
> of reason.   For I am so disposed now that   I
> have   an unbounded desire to apprehend truth
> not only by believing it, but also by under-
> standing   it.   In the meantime, I am confi-
> dent that among the Platonists I shall   find
> what   is not opposed to the teachings of our
> religion.[33]

By a paradox the   very   last   criticism   of   the   *Contra
academicos* by Augustine in the *Retractationes* enhances the
value of its arguments.   Augustine had used the term   *nugae*,
"trifles,"   of those arguments and his mild, class-room joke
had raised a laugh on which the   dialogue   ended.   "Joking"
and "irony," yes, the septuagenarian bishop would allow, but

the arguments of Cicero he had refuted "with supremely certain rationality," *certissima ratione refutaui,* and the term was inappropriate: *non debuit tamen dici.*[34]

Nothing remains but to balance the books on this earliest of Augustinian essays on truth. He saw the subject as one which philosophers had done both well and badly: on one hand, the authentic *platonici,* on the other, those fallen angels of Plato's Academy. Philosophy has every right to speak out on truth and she does so because she participates in the light of Truth itself, in the light of Truth which is the incarnate Wisdom of God among us. Our world is corporeal and by nature deceptive, but our minds operate above the corporeal relations within a mutable and contingent cosmos. Philosophy and reason have a precious role, but that role is exercised within authority and faith; Christ is the measure of Plato's value, not the reverse.

Saint Anselm: The Necessity of Truth

As everyone knows, Anselm of Bec and Canterbury has provoked nine centuries of controversy thanks to a pair of his positions. One arose in his own day on whether the "single argument" he contrived for the monks of his house as a "proof," a *probatio,* of divine Being is logically and philosophically valid. The second controversy concerns his persistent search for what he termed "necessary reasons" for articles of faith. Is not the discovery of such reasons impossible in principle? Between Augustine and Anselm, Pope Gregory the Great delivered himself of a *sententia,* a "view," to this effect which made its way into the collection of "sentences" assembled by Peter Lombard and thus into the systematized teaching of divinity in mediaeval schools: "Faith has no merit in one to whom human reason proffers experience,"[35] that is, should the exercise of reason produce necessary arguments, this experiential "seeing" would inevitably dissipate the darkness of faith; with that darkness would go the merit attached to committing oneself to the Lord in faith. Since Bible and Church extol faith and its merit, "necessary reason" for Christian beliefs cannot be found nor ought we to seek for them. Anselm himself had invited just such criticism; after succeeding in formulating the *Proslogion* "proof," he prayed:

> I give You thanks, good Lord, because by Your gift, what I formerly believed, thanks to Your illumination, I now understand in such a way that, if I should be unwilling to

> believe You to be, I could not fail to
> understand You to be.[36]

Since our interest is in Anselm's conception of truth,
it is impossible to pass over his dialogue on just that
theme, the *De veritate*, which dates between 1080 and 1085,
notably later than the *Monologion* and *Proslogion* which he
had composed between 1076 and 1078.[37] In the *De veritate*
Anselm proposed a theory of truth which demonstrates at once
his own originality and the profoundly Augustinian character
of his world. That world can be called a "world of truth,"
for in it "truth" characterizes not only statements, but
things and actions as well. Truth was conceived to be a
relationship between signs and the beings, "essences," of
which signs are similitudes. As for Augustine, God for
Anselm is the highest Truth, thanks to whom there is created
truth. Because we have no direct access to divine Being
this side of the tomb, we reach some knowledge of God
through similitudes and no creature of our direct experience
is a better similitude than is the human being, made as we
are according to Genesis 1:26 "in the image and likeness" of
the Creator. This human similitude includes a trinitarian
seal: memory, intellect, and will; to know oneself is to be
on the road to a knowledge of God. The rational mind is a
kind of "mirror," for in it we gaze upon what, in this life,
we never see directly. No other creature plays the role of
image so well.[38]

If these reflections transcribe Augustinian materials in
the *Monologion*, Anselm broke new ground in the *De veritate*
by applying the notion of truth and of similitude, of rectitude, of the correct, of ought, and of exist, in an unprece-
dented way. Anselm noted that there was no lack of dialec-
ticians to deal with problems raised by the truth of propositions, the truth, as he put it, "of signification." No
doubt Aristotle, in his *Categories* and *Perihermeneias*, and
Boethius as translator and commentator on those two logical
treatises, had made many an eleventh-century reader as
familiar with the truth of propositions as was Anselm, but
few had much to say on the "truth of things":

> Let us return to the truth of signification
> from which I began so that from the better
> known I might guide you to the unknown. For
> everyone talks about the truth of significa-
> tion, whereas few there are who consider the
> truth which is in the essence of things.[39]

To the truth of logic, therefore, Anselm added an ontic truth. Furthermore, the logical truth of signification can introduce an ethical truth as well. Because, from an ethical point of view, some things ought to be done and some things ought not to be done, every morally significant act can be taken as an implicit statement that what one does is what one ought to do, and if a statement, then susceptible of truth or of falsity:

> For not only in those things we are accustomed to call "signs," but also in all the other things we have mentioned there is a "true" or a "false" signification. Since nothing is to be done by anyone except what one "ought" to do, by the very fact that anyone does anything he states and signifies that this he ought to do. If one ought to do what he does, he states a truth; if he ought not, he lies.[40]

Saint Anselm associated, in a dialectic co-terminous with all reality, the terms "true," "ought," "exist," "correct," and "rectitude." This allowed him to transfer the terminology of true sentences to the area of moral choices, to evaluate beings as "signs" of their essential functions as built into them by their Creator or even as intended by a human craftsman. A human artifact "truly" is what it was intended to be only if it fulfills the finality implicit in its design; the knife that does not cut is not "truly" a knife. On the standards of a soldier, the "sword" of an actor on the stage is not "truly" a sword, although, of course, it is "truly" a sword on the standards set by the stage and its requirements. A portrait is a "true likeness," as Renaissance painters were fond of noting, if and only if it achieves "rectitude" in its order by resembling its model. Is it necessary to remark that this ingenious theory was not universally welcomed by Anselm's successors; as Aristotelianism grew, truth was more often relegated to "truth of signification" and beneath that level, to the "truth of judgment." Still, support can be found in Augustine for the notion that the immutable Creator alone "truly is," whereas mutable creatures, in a sense, "are not."[41]

Anselm's threefold truth, that of propositions, that of the will choosing as it ought to choose, and that of things, for which to be false is not to be, are as many correlations of the true, the good, and being. All three are susceptible of signifying and of being signified; all three are exper-

ienced in our world in grades that invite us to rise to
their source in the supreme Truth, the highest Good, Being
itself. On the plane of creatures, he was fond of using the
term *debet*, "one ought," "one is in debt to," when specify-
ing that truth, or rectitude, is or is not present. God is
not only the highest Truth, but is also supremely Rectitude;
a sharp distinction sets off divine from created rectitude:

> Consider that all the rectitudes discussed
> above are such because those in which they
> exist either are what they ought to be or do
> what they ought. The highest Truth is a
> Rectitude, but not because It is indebted to
> anything. For all things are in debt to It,
> whereas it is in debt to nothing; nor is It
> what It is for any reason other than that It
> is.[42]

This dialogue on truth goes well beyond Augustine, but
it is faithful to the Augustinian insight that our human
truths are diminished participations in divine Truth which
is also Truth Itself. If to reap a logical, ontic, and
moral harvest from seed sown by Augustine is to be "Augustinian," then Anselm's *De veritate* presents an Augustinian
doctrine on truth.

Truth and the *Proslogion*

What application, one may ask, does this doctrine of
truth have to the *Proslogion*? First, it puts us on notice
that Anselm in his effort to "understand a little" concerning divine Being, was working within an Augustinian
ambiance. The very formula, "That than which a greater cannot be thought," had been used by Augustine[43] (as it had
been used before Augustine by Cicero[44] and by Seneca[45] and
before Anselm, but after Augustine, by Boethius).[46] Furthermore, Augustine had taken as his starting point the
Psalmist's fool who had "said in his heart: 'God is not!'"[47]
when he composed the second book of the *De libero arbitrio*
to which reference has been made as an advance on the *Contra
academicos*. Despite its brilliant originality, the *Proslogion* argument moves within the world of Augustine, a world
of truth, a world of hierarchic order, and a world of participation.

A second "Augustinian" characteristic of the *Proslogion*
is that, like the later *De veritate*, it is an effort to
penetrate rationally truths already held strongly on faith.

Gilson was right to have preferred its original title:
Fides quaerens intellectum,[48] for the argument moves within
faith for all its renunciation of biblical authority. It
is, in short, the opposite of a prelude to faith, suitable
for an intelligent atheist; Anselm intended it for monks and
when Gaunilon ironically wrote against it his *Pro insipiente*, Anselm refused to take the bait:

> The author of these objections is by no
> means a fool, but a Catholic speaking "in
> behalf of the fool"; enough, I think, that I
> respond to the Catholic.[49]

For Gaunilon too was a monk and no atheist; within Gaunilon's faith the *Proslogion* argument might be hoped to
operate by helping him "to understand a little" what he
already held on faith.

The God who is "that than which a greater cannot be
thought" is Truth Itself and Anselm was compelled by the
principles he would set out in his *De veritate* to proceed in
"rectitude," to speak as "he ought," if the *Proslogion* were
to be marked by truth. Its affirmations would be true only
if their author's will were what it ought to be in his probing the faith handed down to him, thanks to a free decision
of the Holy One. That "probing" was a reverent search for
the inner necessities, embedded within what Anselm believed,
and which would leave his faith as faith untouched. Superficial readers of the *Proslogion* have often thought the
formula "that than which a greater cannot be thought" an
effort to "define" God and from that definition to deduce
his Being, "superficial" because they have failed to notice
that Anselm knows this thought is not a definition of the
divine nature:

> Therefore, Lord, not only are You that than
> which a greater cannot be thought, but You
> are something greater than can be thought.[50]

Necessary Reasons

A question broader than the validity or invalidity of
the *Proslogion* argument is Anselm's general intention to
identify necessary reasons within the data of faith. The
Proslogion argument may be taken as a dramatic application
of Anselm's habitual approach to issues in divinity. His
Cur deus homo will persuade us that Anselm thought he had
found necessities verified in the very work of our rede-

mption and that those necessities in no sense contravene the
sovereign freedom and grace with which the Holy One has
willed and carried out that saving work. Neither did Anselm
spurn what help might be provided by the pagan Aristotle who
knew nothing of redemption, but had provided useful reflections on the purely logical plane. Hence Anselm cited the
Perihermeneias on the necessity that marks logical relations, including those between facts and sentences, even
when the facts might be contingent: "What is must needs be
when it is; what is not cannot be when it is not."[51] Let a
state of affairs be as contingent as you like; when the cat
is on the mat, the sentence that says so is true and necessarily true. The connection between that contingent, singular, state of affairs and the singular, contingent sentence
is a necessary one for as long as the cat stays on the mat.
This necessity in no way contaminates the contingency of the
fact and of the consequent expression of that fact in words.
Anselm's long chapter in the *Cur deus homo*[52] on his claim
that neither necessity nor impossibility can be ascribed to
God and that there is a compelling and a non-compelling
necessity, is evidence that he thought his readers needed
(perhaps had demanded) explanations of his incarnational
discourse in the language of "necessary reasons."
      From this perspective the *Proslogion* proof is a proof
indeed, but not a "proof" in the usual sense. It is an
application of dialectic to show that the reference-fixing
formula, "that than which a greater cannot be thought," commands the identification of the reality to which alone the
name "God" refers. For as long as the state of affairs
expressed in a sentence is the case, that sentence is necessarily true. Thanks to his "single argument," Anselm was
convinced that he, and his readers, will perceive within
their freely-revealed faith in the Holy One an authentic
necessity, a non-compelling necessity from the side of God,
but a necessity that no logician is free to reject. Until
the clear vision of the world to come, it is necessarily
true for Anselm that the God of faith and the Bible is, not
quite "seen," but "understood," to be and to be necessarily.
Saint Anselm has put this with all the clarity that could be
demanded and the sentence in which he did so was chosen by
Gilson as one of the two epigraphs (the other is 2 Co 5:7)
for his landmark article on "the sense and the nature" of
the *Proslogion* argument:

          Finally, since it is my understanding that,
          between faith and vision, *speciem*, there is
          a median understanding which we grasp in
          this life, I think that, by as much as any-

one advances toward that understanding, by just so much does one draw near to the vision to which we all aspire.[53]

It does not seem possible to square this estimate with an intention to provide a "proof" of divine Being in the sense of a demonstration such as might move an atheist from his atheism to an acceptance of God. Yet Saint Anselm has used the terms *probatio* and *probare* in his dialectical *tour de force*; in what sense ought those terms to be taken? My suggestion is that they be taken in the sense so common in the Vulgate version of the Scriptures as "a probing" and "to probe." As gold is "proved" in a furnace and as a believer is "proved" in tribulation, so Anselm proposed that our words, signs of thoughts, and our thoughts, signs of things, those things in their turn signs of the Creator and best of all the human mind, all be "proved." Might it not be the case that our centuries-long dissent over Anselm's desire to establish "necessary reasons" for the data of faith and over the most striking instance of that desire, the *unum argumentum*, has been dissent over something the saint never intended? What is left unresolved if we take his *Opera omnia* as so many responses to the challenge of Augustine's world of truth, so full of truths that must be the case? Thus the work of Anselm can be seen to be a penetrating examination of the data of faith for those necessary intelligibilities consequent upon God's merciful freedom and his blinding Being.

Notes

[1] G. Papini, *Sant'Agostino* (Florence: Vallechi Editore, 1929), p. 5; *Saint Augustine*, trans. M. Pritchard Agnetti (New York: Book League of America, 1930), p. 9.

[2] *Retractationes* I,i,2: ed. P. Knöll, *CSEL* XXXVI(1,2), 12,1-13,4.

[3] Ibid., I,i,7: *CSEL* XXXVI(1,2)14,14-15,5.

[4] C. Boyer, SJ, *L'Idée de vérité dans la philosophie de saint Augustin* (Paris: G. Beauchesne, 1920), p. 7, n. 13, has listed a number of references indicating Augustine's permanent adherence to his *Contra academicos* stance.

[5] In times past this was controverted, v. g., P. Alfaric, *L'Evolution intellectuelle de saint Augustin* (Paris: E.

Nourry, 1918), but the weight of contemporary scholarship accepts the categoric evidence of, among other sources, *Contra academicos* III,xx,43; see below, note 33.

⁶ See *Confessiones* V,x,19:   *CC*   XVII,68,24-27,   and V,xiv,25:   *CC* XVII,72,29-38;   *Contra academicos* III,xx,43: *CC* XXIX,60,1-3.

⁷ On Romanianus,   see   *Contra   academicos*   II,iii,8:   *CC* XXIX,22,   36-38:   Saepius   enim   suscensuisti Academicis eo quidem grauius, quo minus eruditus esses, eo libentius, quod ueritatis amore inliciebaris . . .

⁸ Godfroy   de   Saint   Victor,   *Fons   philosophiae*,   ed. P. Michaud-Quantin,   Analecta   medievalia   Namurcensia,   No.   8 (Louvain: Éditions   Nauwelaerts,   1956)   ;   *The Fountain of Philosophy*,   trans. E. A. Synan (Toronto: Pontifical   Institute   of   Mediaeval   Studies,   1972); Gregory: lines 681-688; Ambrose: lines 689-92; Jerome: lines   693-700; Augustine: lines 701-740.

⁹ "The *Preconium Augustini* of Godfrey of St. Victor," ed. Phillip Damon, *Mediaeval Studies* 22 (1960), 92-107.

¹⁰ That the exchange was between Alypius and Augustine is a   convention   of the dialogue, see *Contra academicos* I,i,3: *CC* XXIX,5,100-101, where Augustine explained   to   Romanianus that   "Sane in hoc libro res et sententias illorum: that is of Trygetius and Licentius, "mea uero et Alypii etiam   uerba lecturus es . . ."

¹¹ Homer,   *Odyssey*   IV,364-570;   Vergil,   *Georgics* IV,422-529.

¹² *Contra   academicos*   III,x,22:   *CC* XXIX,47,2-4:   Duo sunt,   quae ab Academicis dicuntur, contra quae, ut ualemus, uenire instituimus: nihil posse percipi et nulli rei debere assentiri . . .

¹³ Ibid. III,v,11:   *CC* XXIX,41,19-20.

¹⁴ Ibid.   III,vi,13:   *CC* XXIX,42,3-17:   Etenim   numen aliquod aisti solum posse ostendere homini, quid sit   uerum, cum   breuiter   tum   etiam   pie.   Nihil itaque in hoc sermone nostro libentius audiui, nihil   grauius,   nihil   probabilius et,   si   id   numen, ut confido, assit, nihil uerius.   Nam et Proteus ille -- quanta ab te mentis altitudine commemoratus, quanta   intentione   in optimum philosophiae genus -- Proteus

enim ille, ut uos adulescentes non penitus poetas a philosophia contemnendos esse uideatis, in imaginem ueritatis inducitur; ueritatis, inquam, Proteus in carminibus ostendat sustinetque personam, quam obtinere nemo potest, si falsis imaginibus deceptus comprehensionis nodos uel laxauerit uel dimiserit. Sunt enim istae imagines, quae consuetudine rerum corporalium per istos, quibus ad necessaria huius uitae utimur, sensus nos, etiam cum ueritas tenetur et quasi habetur in manibus, decipere atque inludere moliuntur. This is the response of Augustine to the words ascribed to Alypius, Ibid. III,v,11: *CC* XXIX,41,7-22.

[15] *De libero arbitrio* II,xiii,36: *PL* XXXII,1260: Imo vero quoniam in veritate cognoscitur et tenetur summum bonum, eaque veritas sapientia est, cernamus in ea, teneamusque summum bonum, eoque perfruamur. Beatus est quippe qui fruitur summo bono. Haec enim veritas ostendit omnia bona, quae vera sunt, quae sibi pro suo captu intelligentes homines, vel singula, vel plura eligunt, quibus fruantur . . . sic fortis acies mentis et vegeta cum multa vera et incommutabilia certa ratione conspexerit, dirigit se in ipsam veritatem . . .

[16] *Contra academicos* III, xviii,41: *CC* XXIX,59,19-22: De-inde in nostrum Tullium conflictio ista durauit iam plane sancia et ultimo spiritu Latinas litteras inflatura. Nam nihil mihi uidetur inflatius quam tam multa copiosissime atque ornatissime dicere non ita sentientem.

[17] Ibid. I,i,3: *CC* XXIX,5,97-98: Hortensius liber Ciceronis iam eos ex magna parte conciliasse philosophiae uideretur . . .

[18] Ibid. I,ii,5: *CC* XXIX,6,16-18: . . . existimatisne beatos nos esse posse etiam non inuenta ueritate? -- Tunc Licentius: Possumus, inquit, si uerum quaeramus . . .; ibid. I,iii, 7: *CC* XXIX,7,16-18: Placuit enim Ciceroni nostro beatum esse, qui ueritatem inuestigat, etiamsi ad eius inuentionem non ualet peruenire . . .

[19] C. Boyer, *Idée*, p. 16, n. 4: "Très probablement l'*Hor*tensius de couleur néo-académique . . . cujus (sapientiae) non inventio, sed vel sola inquisitio jam praeponenda erat etiam inventis thesauris" (*Confessiones* VIII,vii,17: *PL* XXXII,757).

[20] *Contra academicos* I,ix,25: *CC* XXIX, 17,46-49: Nam cum beati esse cupiamus, siue id fieri non potest nisi

inuenta siue non nisi diligenter quaesita ueritate, postpo-
sitis ceteris omnibus rebus nobis, si beati esse uolumus,
perquirenda est . . .

[21] Ibid. I,ii,1:   *CC* XXIX,18, 14-27:   . . . eoque fit, ut
Academicorum arma, quando cum eis ad manus uenitur, nec
mediocribus uiris sed acutis et bene eruditis inuicta et
quasi Vulcana uideantur . . . oro autem ipsam summi dei uir-
tutem atque sapientiam. Quid est enim aliud, quam mysteria
nobis tradunt dei filium?

[22] See text cited above, n. 14.

[23] Ibid. I,i,3:   *CC* XXIX,4,71-5,80:   . . . . me pectoris
dolor uentosam professionem abicere et in philosophiae gre-
mium confugere coegisset . . . Ipsa enim docet et uere docet
nihil omnino colendum esse totumque contemni oportet, quicquid mortalibus oculis cernitur, quicquid ullus sensus
attingit.

[24] *Retractationes* I,1:   *CC* XXIX,13,4-11.

[25] *Contra   academicos* III, xi,26:   *CC* XXIX,50,80-85:
Quidquid enim contra sensus ab eis disputatur, non contra
omnes philosophos ualet.   Sunt enim qui omnia ista, quae
corporis sensu accipit animus, opinionem posse gignere con-
fitentur, scientiam uero negant, quam tamen uolunt intelle-
gentia contineri remotamque a sensibus in mente uiuere.   Et
forte in eorum numero est sapiens ille, quem quaerimus.

[26] Ibid. III,xi,24-26:   *CC* XXIX,48,71-50,61.

[27] Ibid. III,xi,25:   *CC* XXIX,49,37-39:   . . . nam ter
terna nouem esse et quadratum intelligibilium numerorum
necesse est uel genere humano stertente sit uerum.

[28] Ibid. III,xviii,40:   *CC* XXIX,59,9-11: Quomodo enim
approbat sapiens aut quomodo simile sequitur ueri, cum ipsum
uerum quid sit ignoret?

[29] Ibid. III,ix,19:   *CC* XXIX,45,18-25: Hoc si ita est,
dicendum potius erat non posse in hominem cadere sapientiam
quam sapientem nescire, cur uiuat, nescire, quem ad modum
uiuat, nescire, utrum uiuat, postremo, quo peruersius
magisque delirum et insanum dici nihil potest, simul et
sapientem esse et ignorare sapientiam.   Quid enim est
durius, hominem non posse esse sapientem and sapientem nescire sapientiam?

[30] Ibid. III,xiii,29:   *CC* XXIX,51,6-10:   . . . ego uero
plura quam de quauis parte philosophiae. Nam primo illas
omnes propositiones, quibus supra usus sum, ueras esse ista
<dialectica> me docuit. Deinde per istam noui alia multa
uera. Sed quam multa sint, numerate, si potestis. . .

[31] Ibid. III, xix,42:   *CC* XXIX,60,10-19: Non enim est
ista huius mundi philosophia, quam sacra nostra meritissime
detestantur, sed alterius intelligibilis, cui animas multi-
formibus erroris tenebris caecatas et altissimis a corpore
sordibus oblitas numquam ista ratio subtilissima reuocaret,
nisi summus deus populari quadam clementia diuini intellectus auctoritatem usque ad ipsum corpus humanum declinaret
atque summitteret, cuius non solum praeceptis sed etiam factis excitatae animae redire in semet ipsas et resipiscere
patriam etiam sine disputationum concertatione potuissent.

[32] Ibid. II,ii,5:   *CC* XXIX,21,63-64:   Itaque titubans
properans haesitans arripio apostolum Paulum . . .

[33] A. C. Pegis, "The Mind of St. Augustine," *Medieval
Studies* 6 (1944), 3, translated, for consistency's sake,
from *Contra academicos* III,xx,43:   PL XXXII,957 (= *CC*
XXIX,60,16-61, 24): Nulli autem dubium est gemino pondere
nos impelli ad discendum auctoritatis atque rationis. Mihi
ergo certum est nusquam prorsus a Christi auctoritate discedere; non enim reperio ualentiorem. Quod autem subtilissima ratione persequendum est -- ita enim iam sum affectus,
ut quid sit uerum non credendum solum sed etiam intellegendo
apprehendere impatienter desiderem -- apud Platonicos me
interim, quod sacris nostris non repugnet, reperturum esse
confido.

[34] Ibid. III,xx,45:   *CC* XXIX,61,50-56: Academicos et,
cum ibi uictorem -- quid enim facilius? -- istarum nugarum
Ciceronem inueneritis, cogatur ista a uobis hunc nostrum
sermonem contra illa inuicta defendere. Hanc tibi, Alypi,
duram mercedem pro mea falsa laude restituo. -- Hic cum
arrisissent, finem tantae conflictionis -- utrum firmissimum
nescio -- modestius tamen et citius, quam speraueram, feci-
mus; Augustine's strictures, *Retractationes* I,1:   CSEL
XXXVI(1,2),17,10-14: . . . illud etiam, quod in conpara-
tione argumentorum Ciceronis, quibus in libris suis Academicis usus est, meas nugas esse dixi, quibus illa argumenta
certissima ratione refutaui, quamuis iocando dictum sit et
magis ironia dicebatur, non debuit tamen dici.

[35] *Liber duarum homiliarum in evangelium*, Homilia 26, n. 1: *PL* LXXVI,1197 C: Nec fides habet meritum, cui humana ratio praebet experimentum. This text is cited by Peter Lombard, *IV Sententiarum*, dist. 11, cap. 3.

[36] *Proslogion* IV: Schmitt I,104,5-7: Gratias tibi, bone domine, gratias tibi, quia quod prius credidi te donante, iam sic intelligo te illuminante, ut si te esse nolim credere, non possim non intelligere.

[37] F. S. Schmitt, "Zur Chronologie der Werke des Hl. Anselm von Canterbury," *Revue Bénédictine* 44 (1932), 350.

[38] *Monologion* LXVI-LXVII: Schmitt I,77-78

[39] *De veritate* IX: Schmitt I,188: Sed redeamus ad veritatem significationis, a qua ideo incepi, ut te a notioribus ad ignotiora perducerem. Omnes enim de veritate significationis loquuntur; veritatem vero quae est in rerum essentia, pauci considerant.

[40] Ibid: Schmitt I,189: Namque non solum in iis quae signis solemus dicere, sed et in aliis omnibus quae diximus est significatio vera vel falsa. Quoniam namque non est ab aliquo faciendum nisi quod quis debet facere, eo ipso quod aliquis aliquid facit, dicit et significat hoc se debere facere. Quod si debet facere quod facit, verum dicit. Si autem non debet, mentitur.

[41] *In Joannis evangelium* XXXVIII,viii,10: *PL* XXXV,1680: O veritas qui vere es . . . in omni prorsus agitatione creaturae duo tempora invenio, praeteritum et futurum . . . in veritate quae manet, praeteritum et futurum non invenio, sed solum praesens, et hoc incorruptibiliter, quod in creatura non est; *Confessiones* XI,iv,6: *PL* XXXII,811: Nec ita pulchra sunt, nec ita bona sunt, nec ita sunt, sicut tu conditor eorum cui comparata nec pulchra sunt, nec bona sunt, nec sunt.

[42] *De veritate* X: Schmitt I,190: Considera quia, cum omnes supradictae rectitudines ideo sunt rectitudines, quia illa in quibus sunt aut sunt aut faciunt quod debent: summa veritas non ideo est rectitudo quia debet aliquid. Omnia enim illi debent, ipsa vero nulli quicquam debet; nec ulla ratione est quod est, nisi quia est.

[43] See *Confessiones* VII,iv,6: *CC* XVII,95,1-21; *De libero arbitrio* II,vi,14: *CC* XXIX,246,27-33; *Epistola CLV* IV,13:

CSEL XLIV,ii,iii,443,11-14;   *Enarratio III in psalmum XXXII* II,15:   *CC* XXXVIII,265,33-35.

[44] See *De natura deorum* II,vii,18.

[45] See *Ad Lucillium naturalium quaestionum liber* VII I, prologus

[46] See *Consolatio* III,pr.10.

[47] Opening verse of two Psalms: 13 (14) and 52 (53).

[48] E. Gilson, "Sens et nature de l'argument de saint Anselm," *Archives d'histoire doctrinale et littéraire du moyen âge*, 9 (1934), 5-51; see p. 19, "Le titre primitif de l'ouvrage était *Fides quaerens intellectum*, et l'on fait bien de le lui restituer . . ."

[49] *Responsio*: Schmitt I,130: Quoniam non me reprehendit in his dictis ille "insipiens," contra quem sum locutus in meo opusculo, sed quidam non insipiens et catholicus pro insipiente: sufficere mihi potest respondere catholico.

[50] *Proslogion* XV: Schmitt I,112: Ergo domine, non solum es quo maius cogitari nequit, sed es quidam maius quam cogitari possit."

[51] *Cur deus homo* II,17: Schmitt II,125: Haec est illa necessitas quae, ubi tractat ARISTOTELES de propositionibus singularibus et futuris, videtur utrumlibet destruere et omnia ex necessitate astruere . . . in which Anselm refers to the puzzle illustrated by Aristotle with a future sea-fight, *Perihermeneias* IX, 18b 7-19a 7; see especially Aristotle's dictum, Ibid., 19a 24, 25.

[52] *Cur deus homo* II,17: Schmitt I,122-6

[53] Denique quoniam inter fidem et speciem intellectum, quem in hac vita capimus, esse medium intelligo, quanto aliquis ad illum proficit, tanto eum propinquare speciei, ad quam omnes anhelamus, existimo. Gilson cited this pericope according to the *PL* edition as from the *De fide trinitatis*, praef., *PL* CLVIII,261 A; in the Schmitt edition which appeared four years later the passage occurs in a letter Anselm addressed to the Pope: *Commendatio operis ad Urbanum Papam II* where the work commended to Urban's attention is the *Cur deus homo*: Schmitt II,40.

Freedom as Keeping the Truth: The Anselmian Tradition

Richard Campbell

In the modern era freedom has emerged as an ultimate value, both in the thought of many philosophers and in the rhetoric of many political activists. It has acquired the power to win assent to a wide variety of causes. Especially in our own cultural tradition freedom has come to be enshrined in the personal and political *credos* which inform people's actions at a quite fundamental level.

Yet to invoke freedom as an ultimate value is rather odd. One can reasonably ask what is one free *for.* The question here is not *why* is one free, in the sense of by what reason or cause, but rather: in order to do what is one free? The point here is a logical one; if it be admitted that one is free *for* some particular end, then freedom cannot be an ultimate value. But appearances can be deceiving, even when we are presented with an apparently straightforward logical point. In this case, behind the appearance of a reasonable question is an assumption that talk of freedom is to be understood in terms of "being free to act in some particular way." Such an understanding must be rejected by those who take freedom as an ultimate value. These people indeed are committed to rejecting the apparently reasonable question. For them, freedom is not *for* anything. On the contrary, *not* having some preset end or ends is intrinsic to freedom itself. Those who take this view are operating with a conception of freedom formulated in terms of one's being able to choose amongst an array of possibilities which one to actualize, where one could have actualized any particular one.

Such a conception of freedom might well seem unremarkable. After all, it or something like it seems to be the popular conception invoked in much of the philosophical literature and political rhetoric mentioned above. For our purposes a useful and quite typical example taken from a recent analytical article is worth quoting:

> . . . an agent is truly free with respect to
> an action only if the situation in which he
> is placed is logically and causally compa-
> tible with both his performing and his not
> performing the action.[1]

This conception of freedom runs deeply through the Western intellectual tradition, from at least as early as Augustine

to the present. Thus, for example, Augustine wrote in his
polemic against Felix the Manichee:

> I prove not only in divine Scripture (which
> you fail to understand) but even in the
> words of your own Manichaeus himself that
> there is free determination and that as a
> result of it someone sins if he wants to and
> does not sin if he does not want to.[2]

And Augustine summarizes the outcome of Book I of his *De
libero arbitrio* with his respondent saying:

> unless I am mistaken, we do evil from the
> free determination of the will. . . . But
> now I am asking whether he who created us
> should have given us that very freedom of
> determination by which it has been shown
> that we have the power to sin.[3]

As we will see, it seems to be that Augustinian way of pos-
ing the question of freedom which Anselm takes as his own
point of departure.

Before we begin our examination of that, however, let me
cite one more witness to the apparent obviousness of this
conception of freedom. David Hume writes in his *An Enquiry
Concerning Human Understanding*:

> it will not require many words to prove that
> all mankind has ever agreed in the doctrine
> of liberty as well as in that of necessity.
> . . . By liberty . . . we can only mean *a
> power of acting or not acting, according to
> the determinations of the will*; that is, if
> we choose to remain at rest, we may; if we
> choose to move, we also may.[4]

Significantly, it is precisely this conception of freedom
which Anselm rejects. He begins his dialogue *De libertate
arbitrii* by immediately citing this traditional conception
-- formulated as "being able to sin and not to sin" -- and
dismissing it. Although this dismissal is quick and summary, how it is to be interpreted has proved to be not as
simple and straightforward as might appear at first sight;
it needs dwelling upon. The contention of this paper will
be that Anselm is engaged in drawing a quite radical distinction between two fundamentally different conceptions of
freedom and, in departing from the traditional conception

formulated in terms of a range of alternatives, is initiating a different tradition which can also be traced through later thought.

Two grounds are offered by Anselm for rejecting this definition in terms of ability to sin and not to sin. The first is that if freedom were to be so defined neither God nor the angels would have free *arbitrium*, since they are not able to sin, but to say that they have no free *arbitrium* is blasphemous.

There is a problem of translation here, which must be discussed before we can begin to evaluate the arguments. *Arbitrium* has been translated by Hopkins and Richardson as "choice"[5] but that translation renders Anselm's argument very curious indeed. For he then would be arguing that God and the good angels have free choice although they are not able to sin. The notion of *choice* involves a range of alternatives, any one of which could be chosen. But on Anselm's argument here, God and these angels are not able to choose to sin and it is doubtful that he is operating with the notion that their free choice consists in their choosing from amongst an array of equally good alternatives. The word *arbitrium* has its paradigm use in relation to a judge in a court case, an *arbiter*, who makes a determination in order to settle a legal dispute. The word is used classically to refer to the legal process, the action or process of deciding generally, the task of doing so, the power to do so and the findings of an arbiter.[6] In Anselm's own usage, as Stanley Kane has pointed out, it is linked closely with volition and is used to refer either to the will-as-instrument or to the will-as-use, an act of will.[7]

Given then, that the word *arbitrium* is used generally to mean a judgment or determination of what to do in some circumstance and that meaning suits this argument so much better than "choice," it would better be translated as "determination." God and the good angels can be said to make certain determinations even if they are not able to choose to sin.

We need next to clarify the logical structure of the ability under discussion. Anselm formulates it as the ability to sin *and* not to sin. But since he obviously is not discussing an ability to do the impossible, we must understand this as the ability to sin on some occasion, not to sin on another and to do either on any occasion. It therefore would be better to consider it as a *disjunctive* ability. In this sense, one can only have a disjunctive ability, an ability to do A or to do B, if one has *both* abilities: the ability to do A and the ability to do B. That is why, in this argument, he can take it that the ability in

question entails the ability to sin. Accordingly, he uses
the argument to conclude:

> Now, since the free determination of God and
> the good angels is unable to sin, being able
> to sin does not belong to the definition of
> freedom of determination.[8]

This argument, however, relies upon the prohibition, on pain
of blasphemy, on saying that God has no free determination.
Anselm characteristically seeks a second ground which is not
so strictly theological. He clearly acknowledges the persu-
asiveness of that conception of freedom which takes it to
consist in being able to choose from amongst an array of
alternatives, such that the wider the range the more free
the determination. This is unveiled by the Teacher's asking
his Student:

> Which seems the more free to you: the will
> which so wills and is so able not to sin is
> such that it can in no way be turned away
> from the rightness (*rectitudo*) of not sin-
> ning, or the will which can in some way be
> turned to sinning?[9]

To this the Student replies that it seems to him the second
will, which is able either to sin or not to sin, is the more
free. Manifestly, it is that conception which Anselm is
concerned to refute. His reason for doing so is given in
the following passage:

> But do you not see that someone who pos-
> sesses what is seemly and fitting in such a
> way that he cannot lose it is more free than
> someone else who possesses the same thing in
> such a way that he can lose it and be drawn
> towards what is unseemly and not fitting.[10]

Given his agreement that sinning is always unseemly and
harmful, the Student comes to agree that the will which is
not able to be turned away from the rightness of not sinning
is more free than the will which can desert its rectitude.
Thus he is driven to agree that the ability to sin, when
added to the will, decreases its freedom and so neither is
freedom nor a part of freedom.

Lying behind this second argument is the view already
laid out in the earlier dialogue *De veritate* that creatures
each have proper functions, built into their natures by "him

from whom they have their being," that is, the Creator. These functions are, in fact, the proper exercise of their natures, and when they so act they do as they ought. In the case of non-voluntary things, they cannot but so act; but voluntary things have the ability to misuse their native abilities, and when they do so, they fail to act as they ought, that is, to do what is proper to their being.[11] In that dialogue Anselm had already sketched a metaphysics of immanent teleology by which he establishes a series of equations: of truth with rightness (*rectitudo*), with something's doing what it ought (*facit quod debet*) and with its being what it is in the Supreme Truth. From this investigation it emerges that the rightness of a thing consists in its doing what it ought, that is, acting in accordance with the proper function of its nature, as it was created to be. It is this conception of things which is powerfully at work in all Anselm's thinking.

In the light of this metaphysics of immanent teleology we can see why he should maintain that the will which is not able to be turned away from the rightness of not sinning is more free than the will which can desert its rightness. For the sinful will is one which initiates action which is not in conformity with what is the proper function of its own nature. It is being used in a way contrary to how such a nature was made to be. It is involved, in short, in a denial of its own true being. While people have the ability to do this, any determination to do so cannot be called free; instead of enhancing one's abilities to do what is fitting and advantageous and thus to express one's own being in a proper way, it involves turning one's back on one's essential being. To do that is not an exercise of, but a derogation from, the freedom of the will.

Anselm's argument here is very sparse and compressed; it only makes sense when read in conjunction with the analyses of *De veritate*. His expressed wish that the three dialogues — *De veritate*, *De libertate arbitrii*, and *De casu diaboli* — be always bound together indicates his consciousness of how closely the arguments of each are interwoven. And just as in *De veritate* he sees that his conclusion that whatever is rightly is precipitates him into the problem of evil,[12] so here he sees that this conception of freedom immediately raises the problem that it would seem to follow that the only way that people can act freely is by doing what is right. If the ability to sin does not belong to free determination, how can we say that angels and people sinned by free determination? If they did not sin by a free determination, the Student objects, it seems that they sinned of necessity.

One interesting feature of this objection is that it shows Anselm investigating the opposition in meaning between freedom and necessity. We will return to this general opposition later. For the moment we should note that the Teacher, in his reply, glosses "sinning of necessity" as "being compelled by something to sin" and contrasts it, not with "freely" but with "of its own accord (*sponte*)."

The reply the Teacher gives to the objection is that it was through the ability to sin, and of their own accord and by a free determination, and not of necessity that our and angelic nature first sinned and was able to serve sin. But the Student does not find that that helps, so the Teacher has to elaborate. The apostate angel and the first man sinned by their own determination, which was so free that it could not be compelled to sin by anything else. They sinned of their own accord, with nothing else compelling them nor any other necessity. He then draws a puzzling distinction:

> They sinned by their own determination, which was free, but not by that in virtue of which (*unde*) it was free, that is, by the ability they had not to sin and not to serve sin. Rather [each sinned] by the ability he had for sinning, which neither helped him towards the freedom of not sinning nor compelled him into the service of sin.[13]

The point Anselm is seeking to make here appears to be that since Satan and Adam were not forced to sin, but did so of their own accord, their sinful acts were effected by their own determination. That power to determine their own actions is, however, not what the *freedom* of their determination consists in. That power is free, in Anselm's view, but not for the reason that a choice was made. Rather that power is free because it *can* be exercised in ways which refrain from sin; the ability to determine one's own actions in ways that are not sinful -- that is, the ability not to sin -- is what makes that power to determine one's own actions free. The other ability which they also had, namely, the ability to sin, is not a compulsion, but it forms no part of freedom, which has to do with not sinning.

If that is a fair articulation of Anselm's distinction, it is remarkable that it has been seriously misunderstood. The crucial question is: what is the conception of freedom which Anselm is opposing? It is the contention of this paper that Anselm is not engaged in merely proposing some subtle refinement to the Augustinian conception of freedom.

Rather, he is mounting a radical opposition to any way of thinking of freedom which takes it to consist in the ability to actualize any one of an array of alternatives. The rational deliberation which is an essential aspect of determination (*arbitrium*) might well *contemplate* an array of alternatives -- in the cases of Satan and Adam it did, since Anselm allows that they each had the ability to sin and the ability not to sin although both chose to exercise the former and thus committed their original sins. But the *freedom* of determination, he is arguing, does not consist in being able to choose from amongst such alternatives. That is what he explicitly says.

Anselm's investigations into the nature of freedom have not attracted much attention from modern commentators, but the few who have discussed it have found difficulties with this argument. For example, Jasper Hopkins remarks:

> There seems to be something suspect about supposing that the ability to sin and the ability not to sin are two different abilities. A man who is able to kill another may do so in self-defence or in murder. In the one case he acts admissibly, in the other inadmissibly. But he exercises the same ability in both cases. That is, the description of the act changes, but the ability to act remains unchanged.[14]

More recently, Stanley Kane has interpreted the argument in such a way as to draw the opposite conclusion to that being advanced here. Being concerned lest the connection between Satan and Adam's possession of freedom and their performance of an unjust act might be merely accidental, like the connection between someone's possession of freedom and his stomach growling, Kane suggests that these sins occurred "as a direct result of the exercise of free choice on their part, whereas the growling of the stomach does not come about as a result of an exercise of free choice."[15]   In this suggestion we can see the seduction of the English term "free choice."   With *arbitrium* translated as "choice" and operating with a pre-understanding of freedom in terms of the conventional conception of it as consisting in the ability to choose amongst alternatives, it is all too easy to slide into ascribing to Anselm the very conception which he rejects. In this way Kane tries to explain the position he has ascribed to Anselm:

> . . . even though in his view freedom is not
> to be *defined* as the power either to sin or
> not to sin, nevertheless the form that free-
> dom takes under the conditions of human
> existence is the ability either to sin or
> not to sin. Hence anything, even sin, which
> occurs as a result of the ability to sin or
> not to sin occurs as a result of freedom.[16]

There are serious confusions in all this. Taking Kane's
first, and trying to reconstruct how such a sensitive interpreter of Anselm could have come to ascribe to him a view he
disavows, we can speculate as follows:

Satan and Adam had the ability to sin (since they did)
and they had the ability not to sin;

but sinning and not sinning are alternatives;

so they had the ability either to sin or not to sin;

if freedom is a form of the power of determination, for
a creature who has the ability to sin or not to sin, that
determination must involve a choice between the alternatives;

therefore, for such a creature freedom takes the form of
that disjunctive ability.

On the face of it, this looks like a plausible argument, but
since Anselm quite explicitly says that the ability to sin
neither is freedom nor a part of freedom,[17] we should look
more closely at this talk of abilities. We have already
seen that Anselm accepts that the ability to do A or to do B
implies the ability to do A. But the converse does not
hold. If I have the ability to drive home it does not follow that I have the ability to drive home or fly home.
Still, one might say that if I do have the ability to do A
and also have the ability to do B, I then have the ability
to do A or to do B and that is the form of the case we are
considering. Even if we concede that point, it does not
follow that freedom "takes the form of" that disjunctive
ability in the case of creatures.
     Consider an analogy. If musical talent is the ability
to play a musical instrument well and someone has the ability not only to play an instrument well but also to play it
badly, it would be utterly fallacious to conclude that that
person's musical talent consists in the ability to play an

instrument well or badly. On that basis, we all would be talented musicians! For Anselm freedom is a form of a voluntary creature's ability to act in accordance with the proper function of its nature. The fact that certain creatures have as well the ability not so to act, and can determine not so to act, does not imply that freedom consists for such creatures in the ability to choose between these alternatives.

Turning now to Hopkins' difficulty, we have come to see how important it is for Anselm that the ability to sin and the ability not to sin are two different abilities. Yet Hopkins uses the difference between killing in self-defence and murder to suggest that there is something suspect in this distinction. But the alleged counter-example cannot withstand examination. While the ability to kill may find expression in either of those two ways, the ability to keep the law is not thereby shown to be the same as the ability to commit a crime. Of course, killing someone in certain circumstances is to commit murder, which is a crime; in other circumstances killing might not be against the law. But all that goes to show is that the ability to kill is not the same as the ability to keep the law, nor the same as the ability to commit a crime. Thus, on closer investigation this example readily generates an instructive analogy for just the distinction which Anselm is relying upon.

With those difficulties now sorted out, we can see more clearly how Anselm deals with the Student's objection that if the ability to sin does not belong to free determination, how can we say that Satan and Adam sinned by free determination. As Kane has pointed out, it follows from Anselm's answer that strictly speaking it would be incorrect to say that they sinned freely (*libere*). Their sin was committed "of their own accord" (*sponte*) and therefore was not coerced. Accordingly, they are blameworthy. And their sinful acts were a result of their own determination, which he does call free, since it is *able* to be used rightly. But the freedom of determination is *not* a matter of being possessed of what we today conventionally call "free choice."

The obstacles which this modern conventional notion places in the way of a clear understanding of Anselm are exceedingly difficult to remove. In order not to underestimate the magnitude of these conceptual obstacles, let us come at the question of the link between freedom and choice via a different route. For Anselm, someone's being responsible for their action is a matter of being self-determined: that is developed in painstaking detail in *De casu diaboli*. Later, in the *Cur deus homo* Anselm returned to this topic in order to argue that angels are not to be praised for their

justice because they were able to sin and did not, but
because as a result of this they possess their present
inability to sin from themselves (*a se*) in some respects.
He elaborates:

> when an angel could have deprived himself of
> justice and did not, and could have made
> himself unjust and did not, it is correct to
> say that he gave himself justice and made
> himself just. In this way, then, he pos-
> sesses justice from himself -- since a crea-
> ture cannot possess it from himself in any
> other way -- and for that reason he is to be
> praised for his justice.[18]

Here then is a case of someone (the angel) who has both the
ability to do what is just and the ability to do what is
unjust. It seems reasonable to describe the situation envisaged as one involving a *choice* between two moral alternatives. Given that, and in the light of the above quotation,
it seems only a redescription of the situation to say that
self-determination in a creature is possible only if there
are alternatives from which one can choose, thus making
one's choice the decisive factor in bringing about the act
which is elected. And, given the conventional link between
freedom and self-determination, that seems to lead to the
conclusion that human freedom requires that we have the
ability to sin, since otherwise human action could not be
self-determined and thus free.[19] So, once again -- this
time by thinking about freedom in terms of self-determination -- we are led to the conclusion that for creatures
like us freedom is essentially a matter of having choices
and choice involves the ability to sin or not to sin.

  For all its plausibility, this argument cannot be sound
-- at any rate, not as a purported analysis of Anselm's conceptual scheme. For it leads to a conclusion which he
explicitly denies. If the argument were a sound analysis of
Anselm's thought, we would have to say that his position is
self-contradictory. Given the hermeneutical rule that one
should make such an accusation only as a last resort, we
should re-examine the argument.

  What the passage from the *Cur deus homo* quoted above
commits Anselm to is that, if a creature is to be just from
himself (*a se*), he must have the ability to do what is
unjust, that is, the ability to sin. Let us allow that that
implies there being for him a choice between moral alternatives. But while this can be summarized as self-deter-

mination in a creature only if choice, it does not follow that freedom *consists* in having choices, even in a creature. Anselm is quite firm and explicit that the same definition of freedom should apply to both God and creatures. In creatures self-determination involves the possibility of sinning, whereas in the case of God it does not. So if the term "freedom" means the same in both kinds of cases it must be wrong to conclude that freedom consists in having choices and thus the possibility of sinning. The right conclusion is only that in creatures choice and thus the possibility of sinning provides the *condition* for self-determination and thus the *condition* in which creatures can exercise their freedom: it does not follow that human freedom is essentially a matter of having choices.

Not surprisingly, the logic of this analysis has driven Stanley Kane into a tight corner. Kane himself argues that Anselm's treatment of these topics leads to the "startling consequence" (Kane's own admission)[20] that human freedom takes the form of having the ability either to do or not to do what is unjust. Consequently he is driven to saying that strictly speaking the definition of freedom which Anselm eventually gives, in a strict and literal sense, applies only to God. Kane tries to explain away this "difficulty" which has been generated by his own interpretation, since he acknowledges that Anselm is seeking a single defining formula for freedom which will apply to all beings who are said to be free: God, angels, and humans.

But the difficulty need not have arisen in the first place. What our analysis has revealed is that interpreters of Anselm must wrestle with an inconsistent triad:

(1) The term "free" means the same when applied to God, angels, and humans;

(2) Self-determination is a necessary condition of freedom;

(3) Freedom in creatures consists in having choices.

Since Kane argues himself into accepting propositions 2 and 3, he is then consistent in denying 1. But since Anselm himself endorses 1 and 2 an interpreter of Anselm is required to challenge 3. For a modern that seems hardly possible; the conventional notion of freedom has drawn so close a conceptual link between freedom and choice that to deny it hardly makes sense. But if our analysis is anywhere near right, what Anselm is intending is precisely to chal-

lenge this conception of freedom. If we are to understand
him we are called upon to *think* differently from our
habitual custom.

The conventional conception of freedom, involving as it
does what we have called a disjunctive ability, is in an
important sense contentless. That is, on that conception of
freedom no particular action, no kind of action, no way of
acting, no objective in acting is taken to be free, or more
free, when compared with any other. Freedom simply consists
in the state of being able to choose amongst an array of
alternatives. That Anselm is operating with a quite different conception is evident from his developing his own definition by way of asking for what purpose (*ad quid*) Satan and
Adam had freedom of determination before they sinned.[21] For
Anselm the very character of freedom essentially involves
what one is free *for*. Accordingly, for him it is not contentless.

In developing his answer to this question -- as if to
emphasize how important it is for him that freedom have positive content -- Anselm considers and has the Student reject
the suggestion that what freedom is for is simply to attain
what one wills. The purpose for which Satan and Adam had
freedom of determination was to will what they ought to will
and what it is fitting (*expediret*) for them to will, which
he glosses as rightness (*rectitudo*) of will. Some further
discussion leads to his preferred definition: freedom of
determination is the ability to keep rightness of will for
its own sake.

Precisely because Anselm is rejecting a contentless conception of freedom, he has turned to a normative definition.
The plausibility of his proposal is, however, obscured for
us by the standard translation of *arbitrium* as "choice." The
term "choice" does not, of course, exclude the thought that
choices might be made in order to accord with some objective
or norm. But the conventional idea of a free choice tends
to treat such objectives or norms as extrinsic to freedom.
If, however, we go back to the root meaning of *arbitrium*, we
note that in determining, for example, the appropriate sentence to be passed upon a convicted criminal, the deliberation by a judge is not, in our modern sense, arbitrary; it
is guided by standards and norms. The sentence must be *fitting*. Hence, when Anselm says that Satan and Adam had freedom of *arbitrium* for willing what they ought and what it is
fitting (*expediret*) to will, he is doing no more than to
draw out the meaning of *arbitrium*. By contrast, this statement of what freedom is for must seem capricious and
unargued if it is taken to assert the purpose or point of
freedom of *choice*. It is only when we rigorously eschew

this misleading notion of choice that we are in a position to appreciate the train of thought leading Anselm to his own definition of a free *arbitrium*.

The definition he proposes for freedom -- namely, *rectitudo* of will kept for the sake of *rectitudo* itself -- stitches freedom into that interlocking network of concepts he had already explored in *De veritate*. There truth had been defined as *rectitudo* perceived by the mind, the qualifying clause serving to distinguish that sense of *rectitudo* which equates with truth from the sense in which a Latin-speaker would use it to speak of the "straightness" of a stick. Also there justice had been defined as rectitude of will kept for its own sake. From this latter definition it follows that, for Anselm, freedom can be glossed simply as the ability to be just.

The linkage with truth is, however, the more intriguing. In *De veritate* Anselm had discussed truth of the will and had concluded that it can only be understood as rectitude. His reasoning is that:

> As long as Satan willed what he ought to have willed -- namely, the end for which he received a will -- he was in the truth and in rectitude: and when he willed what he ought not to have willed, he deserted this truth and rectitude.[22]

So, he concludes, the truth or rectitude in Satan's will consisted only in his willing what he ought. From this it is apparent that in Anselm's thinking truth and rectitude are inseparably connected. It was thus with only a little licence that this paper was entitled "Freedom as Keeping the Truth." Rectitude of will is willing to remain in the truth, which is equivalent to willing to do what one ought (*facere quod debet*), which is willing to be what one is in the Supreme Truth. So the ability to keep rectitude of will for the sake of *rectitudo* itself, in Anselm's tight conceptual network, consists in the ability voluntarily to keep one's actions in conformity with the proper function of one's nature, as it was created to be and as it truly is, for no extrinsic reason.

The understanding of truth at work in all this is much richer than that bare conception of it which has seduced the majority of modern philosophers, namely that "true" is a predicate of sentences applicable if and only if the sentence states what is. Of course, anyone operating with such a formalized conception of truth will not be able to see the connections between it and freedom which Anselm sought to

explicate. But even though that be so, the Western philosophical tradition is not bereft of those who have seen such
a linkage.

Accordingly, in the final section of this paper I will
draw attention to a tradition of thinking about freedom
which has kept alive the Anselmian insight that there is
indeed a linkage. Dwelling on this tradition will serve, in
an indirect fashion, to show that the Anselmian insight
deserves more serious consideration than it has to date
received. It therefore cannot be dismissed as a medieval
peculiarity.

Although Anselm's treatment of freedom received little
attention from later medieval writers, with the resurgence
of Christianized Neo-platonism at the end of that era a conception of freedom re-emerged which links it directly with
the normative power of truth. In particular, the Anselmian
insight renders intelligible a passage in Descartes' *Meditations* which has often appeared obscure to commentators.

The passage in question is in the fourth *Meditation*,
where Descartes is pondering how could he ever go wrong,
since God exists as the source of all reality and truth and
is not a deceiver. It has emerged that his deepest problem
is not concerning the attainment of truth, as a fixation on
the first two meditations has led many a student to believe.
Rather, like all Platonists and Plato himself, his fundamental problem is how to explain the occurrence of error. His
answer turns on his will outstripping his understanding; we
will typically decide many issues when we do not *know* the
truth of the matter. He gives an initial account of will,
which he glosses as freedom of determination (*libertas arbitrii*), which is remarkably close to what we have here called
the conventional conception of freedom:

> Will consists simply in the fact that we are
> able alike to do and not to do a given thing
> (that is, can either assert or deny, either
> seek or shun);

But he then immediately qualifies that:

> or rather, [will consists] simply in the
> fact that our impulse towards what the
> intellect presents to us as worthy of asser-
> tion or denial, as a thing to be sought or
> shunned, is such that we feel ourselves not
> to be determined by any external force.[23]

This is a familiar formation of freedom which had come down from Aristotle via Aquinas and which puts in negative terms the conventional notion. But it soon becomes clear that Descartes' objection to his initial formulation of free will was quite fundamental. He seems to have in mind Buridan's ass, the unfortunate animal placed equidistantly between two bales of hay for want of a reason to choose between that on his left and that on his right. Anyone in such a position, faced with alternatives any of which might indifferently be done, is barely free at all. What is lacking are standards or norms by which the will can determine how to act. Descartes puts it thus:

> Indeed, the indifference that I am aware of when there is no reason urging me one way rather than the other, is the lowest grade of liberty; it argues no perfection of free will, but only some defect or absence of knowledge.[24]

That is why Descartes rejects what we have called the contentless conception of freedom. Like Anselm, he considers that one is more free to the extent that one cleaves to truth and goodness -- what Anselm called *rectitudo*.

> There is no need for me to be impelled both ways in order to be free; on the contrary, the more I am inclined one way -- either because I clearly understand it under the aspect of truth and goodness, or because God has so disposed my inmost consciousness -- the more freely do I choose that way.[25]

Descartes is not here writing a treatise on freedom, so it is not remarkable that he did not elaborate on this account. It is, however, clear that he regards truth as the proper end, or *telos*, of the intellect such that when it is perceived clearly and distinctly it naturally is drawn to assent and in doing so be entirely free.

Elements of this conception are carried forward from Descartes by Spinoza, for whom the notion that we are free in the sense that we have the ability to choose from amongst an array of alternative actions is at bottom absurd. Yet Spinoza does not deny human freedom altogether; on the contrary, Part V of the *Ethics* is entitled "Of Human Freedom." For him, freedom consists in a mental condition which knows thoroughly the springs of action; freedom is thus intimately

connected with truth.   Not that a person is free when one
has a list of true propositions.   Rather, the free man   is
one   who understands nature,   and in understanding nature,
understands himself.[26]

That the basic link   in Spinoza's thought   is between
freedom and truth is obscured for us by the fact that in his
metaphysical system truth is linked to necessity.   Spinoza's
Deus sive natura is expressed necessarily in all finite
modes and the order and connection between things is the
same   as   the order and connection of ideas; both are necessary.   Accordingly, Spinoza maintains that our   belief   that
things   in   the   world are as they are quite contingently is
merely the result of our ignorance.   But while he thus has a
different   conception   of   the   truth   of things than either
Anselm or Descartes, Spinoza is carrying forward   the   basic
point   about   freedom: that it consists in adhering to the
truth while error and ignorance are the root of   human   bondage.   He does, of course, reject the kind of teleology in
God and created things by which Anselm explicated his understanding   of   truth.   But with that substantial modification
in how Spinoza understands truth, he likewise sees it as the
ground of freedom:

> I call free him who is led solely by reason;
> he, therefore, who is born free and who
> remains free, has only adequate ideas.[27]

Since   he   defines an adequate idea as one which has all the
intrinsic marks of a true idea, this conception of freedom
comes remarkably close to Anselm's own formulation.

In   this way of thinking of freedom Spinoza was followed
closely by Hegel, for whom the essence of Spirit (*Geist*)   is
freedom,   that   is,   self-contained   being (*Bei-sich-selbst-
sein*).[28] Hegel acknowledges that his conception   of   freedom
is   at   one with Spinoza's conception of *Amor intellectualis
dei*. As the note to paragraph 158 of the *Lesser Logic* puts
it:[29]   man   is most independent when he knows himself to be
determined by the absolute idea throughout.

Freedom thus presupposes necessity: it is the truth   of
necessity,   as   the revelation of its inner nature raised to
consciousness and accepted concretely and positively.   This
notion Hegel contrasts with the "merely abstract" freedom
which takes it to lie only in "the form   of   choosing."   As
the note to paragraph 145 says:

> Freedom of choice, or the capacity of deter-
> mining ourselves towards one   thing   or
> another, is undoubtedly a vital element in

> the will (which in its very notion is free);
> but instead of being freedom itself, it is
> only in the first instance a freedom in
> form.[30]

In fact, there is a contradiction between this form, which
appears to be contentless, and the content of the decision
made, which is dependent on circumstances beyond the will
itself. For Hegel, the genuinely free will is "conscious to
itself that its content is intrinsically firm and fast." It
is that content alone which can account for the will giving
its decision to the one and not the other of the two alternatives. These connections between freedom, reasons, and
inner necessity which Hegel draws are what lead him to maintain that to think is *ipso facto* to be free. Here is how
freedom is tied back to truth, for he also maintains, and in
the same place,[31] that to think is "to bring out the truth
of our object, be it what it may."

The strain of necessity which runs through the metaphysics of Spinoza and Hegel is, of course, quite foreign to
Anselm's thinking and it would be a crude mistake to assimilate the three. That is not the point being made here. But
all three do reject the conventional notion of freedom as a
disjunctive ability and all three do stoutly maintain that
genuine freedom is a matter of holding fast to the truth,
not just as an external constraint, but as the determining
principle by which a person determines himself in his decisive actions. The way Hegel puts it could be endorsed by
all in this tradition of thinking about freedom:

> A good man is aware that the tenor of his
> conduct is essentially obligatory . . . But
> this consciousness is so far from making any
> abatement of his freedom, that without it
> real and reasonable freedom could not be
> distinguished from arbitrary choice -- a
> freedom which has no reality and is merely
> potential.[32]

Turning to our own century we find that while most philosophers in the logical empiricist tradition have confined
truth to items of a linguistic structure -- propositions,
statements, or sentences -- one major thinker has been
striving to re-establish the essential tie between truth and
freedom without the complication of necessity. That thinker
is Martin Heidegger. He challenges the traditional assignment of truth to statements as the basic locus of truth --
not that he is denying that statements are properly said to

be true. The correctness of statements is not, however, the
primary occurrence of truth.   Rather, that correctness
becomes possible only through our having a way of being, a
"comportment," towards entities in the world such that they
are opened up as to reveal themselves, to be manifest.   So
the very possibility of correctness comes about through our
comporting ourselves towards entities in the world in an
open fashion, that is, in an open stance which directs that
our thinking and speaking about them be subordinated to what
they are and how they are.

It is this binding directedness of thought and speech to
adhere to the way something shows itself in its openness
which leads Heidegger to posit a two-way tie of an essential
kind between truth and freedom.   This pre-given directedness, he suggests, comes about because our binding ourselves
to be open to how entities are is to let something which has
itself been opened up in an open region be accepted as binding upon us. He continues:

> To free oneself for a binding directedness
> is possible   only by *being free* for what is
> opened up in an open region.   Such being
> free points to the heretofore uncomprehended
> essence of freedom. The openness of com-
> portment as the inner condition of the pos-
> sibility of correctness is grounded in free-
> dom. *The essence of truth is freedom.*[33]

This talk of a binding directedness, for all the difference
of its manner of expression, is strongly reminiscent of
Anselm's account of the truth of statements in his *De veritate*. The proper function of a statement, he there maintains, is to signify as being that which is. When a proposition is uttered in such circumstances that it does that,
it does what it ought and is accordingly said to be true.
Thus, for Anselm, a statement has a "binding directness" to
conform to what entities are and how they are. That subordination of statements to what-is simply expresses the point
(the *ad quod*) of statements. What Heidegger is adding is
that this *telos* of statements can be achieved only if one
holds oneself freely open to how what-is shows itself. So
the possibility of the correctness of statements is grounded
in freedom.

We should note that in presenting this account Heidegger
characteristically speaks of being free *for* what is opened
up in a confrontation with what-is, in what he calls "an
open region." That already signals that he is not operating

with the conventional conception of freedom. And so it is no surprise to read later in his essay:

> Freedom is not merely what common sense is content to let pass under this name: the caprice, turning up occasionally in our choosing, of inclining in this or that direction. Freedom is not mere absence of constraint with respect to what we can or cannot do. Nor is it on the other hand mere readiness for what is required and necessary (and so somehow a being). Prior to all this ("negative" and "positive" freedom), freedom is engagement in the disclosure of beings as such.[34]

That is, what philosophers have standardly called negative and positive freedom, including that rational acceptance of necessity which Spinoza and Hegel made of it, has to be seen as grounded in "engagement in the disclosure of beings as such." Being open to that disclosure is the ground of the inner possibility of that state generally called freedom. So engaging oneself with what-is in such a way that beings are allowed to show themselves as they are proves to be the essence of freedom. As Heidegger puts it, "Freedom now reveals itself as letting beings be."[35] The disclosure which then occurs, the unconcealment, is truth in its "primordial" sense.

If, now, Anselm's *rectitudo* of the will can legitimately be interpreted as willing to remain in the truth, as was suggested earlier, then Heidegger's explication of freedom as engagement in the disclosure of beings as such has to be seen as a powerful and original modern articulation of that conception of freedom first articulated by Anselm. For his "ability to keep *rectitudo* of will for its own sake" is precisely the ability required to "adhere to something opened up as such," to engage with beings in such a way as to let them be.

Admittedly, Anselm's definition could be taken in a narrower sense, through a strictly moralistic reading which interpreted *rectitudo*, correctly understood in terms of *facere quod debet*, as confined strictly to moral duties. But such a narrow reading would be a mistake. From *De veritate* it is clear that *facere quod debet* is intended to summarize a thoroughgoing teleological metaphysics in which the natures of all things are determined by their immanent *telei* and find expression in their proper ways of behaving, their proper functions. Thus a wider reading of *De liber-tate arbitrii* is also required which, while it will compre-hend the moral, is of broader scope. On this wider reading, the reading which has informed this paper, freedom for Anselm is the ability to comport oneself in such a way that the springs of one's actions (one's will) are congruent with the proper functioning of other beings in the world. These teleological natures of things result, for Anselm, from their being created thus by God such that, if sin had not been committed to disrupt it, the whole system would have been a properly functioning, that is, just order. Because of sin, the conditions for our comporting ourselves so as to maintain that order have been lost -- and can only be restored by divine grace. But he points out that losing the conditions for exercising a capacity is not the same as los-ing the capacity. So long as we have the *reason* by which to recognize what just order would be and the *will* by which to hold it fast, we can properly be said to have the capacity to keep rectitude of the will. That, of course, once again makes no sense if freedom in created beings requires the capacity for choice between alternatives, since we cannot choose something for which the conditions are lost.[36]   But on Anselm's own conception of freedom his point is valid. Because of sin we try to impose our own wills in the world and thus remain closed off from that order which God created. Its truth, the disclosure of its proper function-ing, eludes us. But the original capacity is not thereby denied.

The account given here, in which freedom has been glossed as the ability to keep the truth, has not reduced it to the maintenance of correct opinions. That Anselm sets to one side in chapter 13. The gloss is only illuminating if truth itself is understood in a Heideggarian way as the unconcealment of beings. But read in the light of this remarkable modern restatement of the essential tie between truth and freedom, the Anselmian definition warrants much deeper consideration than it has been granted hitherto.

Notes

[1] T. P. Flint, "The Problem of Divine Freedom," *American Philosophical Quarterly* 20, No. 3 (1983), 255.

[2] *De actis cum Felice Manichaeo* I,ii,3: Latin quotation in Schmitt I,207.

³ *De libero arbitrio* I,i,16, n. 35. The translation given is an adaptation of that by R. P. Russell, OSA, in Vol. LIX of *The Fathers of the Church* (Washington, DC: Catholic Univ. of America Press, 1968), pp. 106-07.

⁴ David Hume, *An Enquiry concerning Human Understanding*, s. VIII, part I, par. 73: L. A. Selby-Bigge, ed., 2nd ed. (1902; rpt. Oxford: Clarendon Press, 1963), p. 95.

⁵ J. Hopkins and H. Richardson, *Anselm of Canterbury* -- Truth, Freedom, and Evil (New York: Harper Torchbooks, 1967). See also their *Anselm of Canterbury* (London: SCM Press, 1976), Vol. II.

⁶ *Oxford Latin Dictionary*, ed. P. G. W. Glare (Oxford: Clarendon Press, 1982).

⁷ G. Stanley Kane, *Anselm's Doctrine of Freedom and the Will* (New York and Toronto: Edwin Mellen Press, 1981), p. 120.

⁸ *De libertate arbitrii* I: Schmitt I,208, 9-10.

⁹ Ibid.: Schmitt I,208 14-16.

¹⁰ *De libertate arbitrii* I: Schmitt I,208,18-21.

¹¹ For a fuller account, see my "Anselm's Background Metaphysics," *Scottish Journal of Theology*, 33, 317-43, esp. 330.

¹² *De veritate* VIII: Schmitt I,186-88. I have discussed his solution to the problem in "Anselm's Background Metaphysics," pp. 329-30.

¹³ *De libertate arbitrii* II: Schmitt I,210,6-10.

¹⁴ J. Hopkins, *A Companion to the Study of St. Anselm*, (Minneapolis: Univ. of Minnesota Press, 1972), p. 144.

¹⁵ Kane, *Anselm's Doctrine*, p. 126.

¹⁶ Ibid., pp. 126-27

¹⁷ *De libertate arbitrii* I: Schmitt I,209,5.

¹⁸ *Cur deus homo* II,10: Schmitt II,107,31-108,4.

[19] The   passage   is analyzed in terms of this argument by Kane, *Anselm's Doctrine*, pp. 128-29.

[20] Ibid., p. 170.

[21] *De libertate arbitrii* III: Schmitt I,211,5.

[22] *De veritate* IV: Schmitt I,181,4-6.

[23] Descartes, *Philosophical Writings*, trans. and   ed.   E. Anscombe and P. T. Geach (London: Nelson, 1964), p. 96.

[24] Ibid.

[25] Ibid.

[26] See   G. H. R. Parkinson,   "'Truth is its Own Standard': Aspects of Spinoza's Theory of Truth," in R. W.   Shanan   and J. I. Biro, eds., *Spinoza: New Perspectives* (Norman: Univ. of Oklahoma, 1978), p. 50.

[27] *Ethics* IV, Prop. LXVIII.

[28] G. W. F. Hegel, *The Philosophy of History*,   trans.   J. Sibree (New York: Dover, 1956), p. 17.

[29] *The   Logic   of   Hegel*,   trans.   W.   Wallace   (London: Oxford, 1904), p. 283.

[30] Ibid., p. 264.

[31] Ibid., p. 44.

[32] Ibid., p. 283.

[33] M.   Heidegger, "The Essence of Truth," in D. F. Krell, ed.,   *Basic   Writings from Being and Time (1927) to The Task of Thinking (1964)* (London: Routledge & K. Paul, 1978),   p. 126.

[34] Ibid., p. 128.

[35] Ibid., p. 127.

[36] Kane,   *Anselm's   Doctrine*,   p.   131,   argues   in   this fashion.

St. Anselm and the Linguistic Disciplines

Desmond Paul Henry

It is a truism that many themes on language, meaning, and understanding are enunciated by St. Augustine of Hippo. Of these, several are taken up by St. Anselm (of Aosta and Canterbury) but few become so consistently prominent in his works as does that of *proprietas loquendi*, propriety of speech. Just one of Augustine's declarations on this subject may serve as an adequate preface to Anselm's corresponding expansions. Thus in *Confessiones* XI,xx,26, Augustine stresses the exclusive presentness of time as such, but is willing to let pass our customary abuse of language (*sicut abutitur consuetudo*) which occurs when we say that there exist three times, i.e. not only the present, but also the past and the future. He is willing to let this false assertion pass because we nevertheless manage to understand what is said. Then comes his generalization on propriety of speech: *Pauca sunt enim, quae proprie loquimur, plura non proprie, sed agnoscitur quid velimus.*[1] This Pusey renders as "But few things are there, which we speak properly, most things improperly; still the things intended are understood."[2]

The quantitative extent of Anselm's exploitation of this theme is now visible almost at a glance, given the information made available in the weighty Anselmian concordance prepared by G. Evans.[3] Therein we see that of the sixty-one occurrences of *proprie* in his works, along with those of the *proprietas*, *proprietate*, *proprietatem*, and *proprietates* entries (twenty-one more cases in all) there is scarcely one which is not concerned with speech, understanding, or meaning. Even the apparent exceptions, which come mostly from the "Philosophical Fragments" revolve around the very general proverb *facere*. This successor to Priscian's corresponding *agere* has an important role to play in Anselm's canonical or categorial language[5] which he uses for linguistic analytic purposes. Throughout, therefore, the concern is still with propriety of speech.

However, already in Augustine's declarations a certain conundrum is embodied. One would have thought that the rules for propriety of speech were available in traditional grammar. Yet here we have Augustine, in his remarks on time, accusing of impropriety forms of speech which violate none of the canons of usual grammar. Does this mean that traditional grammar is somehow lacking as regards the standards of propriety now in question? Indeed, need tradi-

tional grammar be adhered to at all when philosophical or
theological   truth   has to be expressed? Anselm's *Monologion*
is permeated throughout with   reminders   of   the   linguistic
difficulties of expression which arise when speech concerning God is attempted.   Thus   when   *Monologion* XVI overtly
authorizes the   predication of abstract nouns of God, while
still tolerating also predication of the corresponding concrete and participial forms, we are on the brink of an obvious collapse of what normally   makes   sense.   For   example,
Iustus (or *iusta*) *est iustitia* and, in general a whole host
of odd interpretations of abstract and concrete, would
appear to be consequences authorized by that chapter.

Anselm must have had his confidence in the licitness of
such threatened violations of traditional   canons   considerably reinforced   when   he   turned   from   theology to logic.
Authority for just such violations comes directly from Aristotle,   to whom Anselm makes no less than eleven overt allusions by name.   Most of these are in *De grammatico*, and
concern a problem which arises in connection with Aristotle's modes of expression in his *Categoriae*, a work which
is also overtly alluded to twice by name.[6] Anyone having
the minutest familiarity with the *Categoriae* in its medieval
Latin version will recognize immediately the textual sources
in question, and the problems which they embody or raise.
In the fourth chapter of that work Aristotle gives examples
of the various categories.   For the category of quality we
have,   in   the   Latin version, *Qualitas, ut album, grammaticum.*" From this forthwith follow, *Album est qualitas,*" and
Grammaticum est qualitas," which already sound awry, since
one would normally expect the abstract, rather than the concrete, form of the adjective in this context.   Still,
granted the initial Aristotelian thesis, there should be no
objection to particularizing so as to make manifest which
quality is in question in each case, thus yielding *Album est
albedo* and *Grammaticum est grammatica* respectively.   Since,
for logical purposes, the gender of the subject-term is
immaterial, the latter example becomes *Grammaticus est grammatica,*" and its already-quoted general version may also be
correspondingly amended, yielding *Grammaticus est qualitas.*"
Here we have an Aristotelian mode of expression which, on
the face of it, propounds odd locutions concerning grammarians, while at the same time authorizing not only that interpredication of abstract and concrete which we have already
noted in theological contexts, but also, at least one point,
a blatantly ungrammatical confusion of genders.   This mode
of expression certainly continued to exercise the ingenuity
of medieval commentators long after Anselm had given his
solution to the problem as to why the Philosopher had

expressed himself in these strange fashions, leaving the way
open to such outlandish inferential commitments.[7] Anselm's
own fascination with it may be judged from the fact that the
Aristotelian *grammaticus* example (in its various Latin
cases) occurs no less that two hundred and sixty-one times
in his works, sometimes associated with the original's other
paronym (*album*) and sometimes with the one used as a further
example in Boethius' commentary (*iustus*).

Anselm makes it clear that he believes that a special
technical Aristotelian mode of speech is in question here,[8]
and that he believes it to be used by philosophers[9] and by
writers on logic.[10] This mode of speech, he opines, differs
from *usus loquendi* in a most interesting way, semantically
speaking.   Thus *usus* takes up, or at least presupposes, the
common and unsophisticated view of signification, according
to which words have meaning by standing for concrete things.
In Anselm's terms, the paronyms or denominative names with
which *De grammatico* is concerned are said to be *appellative*
of concrete objects. Signification, on the other hand, in
its proper, precise, and logical sense is to be contrasted
with appellation. This significatory side of the contrast
embodies the already-observed Aristotelian logical, philosophical, and linguistic oddities.[11]   It is in Anselm's
actual words at this point that the connection with that
Augustinian concern for propriety of speech with which we
began becomes visible:

> Et   hoc   nomen   [grammaticus]   quamvis   sit
> appellativum hominis, non tamen *proprie*
> dicitur eius significativum; et licet sit
> significativum grammaticae, non tamen est
> eius appellativum.[12]

> And   although this name [literate] is appel-
> lative of man, it is nevertheless not prop-
> erly said to be significative of man; and
> although it is significative of literacy, it
> is, nevertheless, not appellative of it.

As we are to see in due course, this Augustinian concern
with what is properly said is connected in a most interesting way with both the Augustinian and Anselmian condemnation
of the rational incapacity of those who are entrapped by the
senses and who hence are unable to have a true understanding
of higher things.

Thus Anselm himself does not remain within the bounds of
mere assertions around these points.   He spells out the
nature and consequences of his semantic doctrines in great

and perfectly intelligible detail. He makes it clear that the oddities associated with these proper, logical (and, coincidentally, theological) ways of talking, oddities which separate them out from the normal conventions of *usus loquendi*, carry with them at least three consequences. First we have a contrast with traditional grammar, which is, by Priscian's own avowal, based on the *usus loquendi* of the best authors.[13] Further, the logician is committed to giving a more than merely negative account of what is going on when *significatio* (in the logical sense) is being distinguished from standing-for, in the appellative and usage-gathered sense outlined above. Finally, the already noted remarkable convergence of the logical and theological ways of talking and the attitudes which go with them must be further enlarged on and explained. The three points may now be followed up in the order indicated.

First, then, we have the constant contrast with *usus loquendi*, a contrast which is going to confirm the separation out of logical grammar from traditional grammar, based as it is on usage. This contrast has been surveyed elsewhere,[14] and is further enhanced by an overt *riposte* to any grammarian who might object to the logician's technical locutions and their consequences: the grammarians also have peculiar technical assertions, the apparent consequence of which do not intrude into ordinary speech any more than do the logician's theses. For example, one does not consider oneself licensed in current speech to refer to literacy by means of the name "literate," even though logicians assert that "literate" signifies (or that *literate* is) literacy.[15] Similarly, when the grammarian says that *lapis* is masculine, *petra* feminine, and *mancipium* neuter, no one inferentially carries forward into ordinary language the *prima facie* apparent consequences that a stone is masculine, a rock feminine, and slave neither masculine nor feminine.[16]

Again, the Aristotelian contention (which Anselm supports by means of his arguments in terms of a proper, *per se*, strict sense of signification) that paronyms such as the "literate" with which we are concerned signify *just* a quality, runs directly contrary to the grammatical thesis that *all* names (in the broad, classical, sense of "name") signify both substance and quality.[17] Abelard has an account of a continuation of this clearly widespread discussion,[18] and John of Salisbury records as equally well-known the distinction which affords a solution to it, namely that between signification and nomination.[19] This is clearly akin to the Anselmian solution, with *nominatio* now the counterpart of *appellatio*, and both of them representing a concession to the substance-claim in the grammarian's the-

sis. In their turn these two notions represent the beginnings of the later doctrine of *suppositio* as contrasted with
significatio.

Thus far, the removal of technical linguistic propriety
from the control of traditional grammar and usage has been
merely recounted. Our discourse has, as Boethius of Dacia
would express the matter, been in the *narrative* mode (*modus
narrativus*). Now, however, the task is to appreciate further, and in depths, the details and theoretical location of
Anselm's version of the accompanying crucial and persistent
distinction mentioned in the last paragraph. (The *modus
demonstrativus* thus comes into play, in terms of the same
Boethius' methodological distinction.[21]) Until this appreciation is effected, it is impossible to advance towards our
third point, namely recognition and appreciation of the full
extent of the remarkable convergence of the logical and the
theological which appears to have so impressed itself upon
Anselm. It is, after all, easy enough to merely assert that
standing-for (or *appellatio*, or *suppositio*, or *nominatio*) is
to be distinguished from *significatio* (in the strict,
proper, *per se* sense). The former are, after all, technical
adaptations of a fairly familiar pre-theoretical vision as
to how language has meaning, i.e. by standing for or referring to reality, with the relation between the proper name
and its bearer as the central paradigm. The question now
is, however, to determine the nature of the contrast between
this simple paradigm and its offshoots, on the one hand, and
the logical sophistication represented by *significatio* in
the strict or proper sense, on the other.

It has already been intimated that Anselm himself presents us with a means of understanding this contrast, but he
does so against the background of a context which can easily
lead twentieth-century readers into a misapprehension of his
point. Taking the reader back to the original Aristotelian
statements in the *Categoriae*, he construes them as having a
bearing on *significatio* in the strict, proper, *per se* sense,
as opposed to the improper, *per aliud* referential or appellative sense. The student of the dialogue *De grammatico*
generalizes beyond the names which are its particular concern, and in respect of all parts of speech says that their
significatio, as indicated in their definition, is *de illa
qua per se significant ipsae voces et quae illis est sub-
stantialis*, as opposed to the other *quae per aliud est et
accidentalis*.[22] In other words, the contrast between
significatio in the strict or proper sense and meaning in
some sort of referential or allusive sense is being extended
beyond the field of names alone. Up to this point one is
able to follow, at least superficially, the point of his

declarations.   But what exactly *is* this *significatio* in the
per se sense, if it is not some sort of   referential   standing-for?   How can the detail of it made concretely intelligible to the twentieth-century researcher?   Does the   answer
lie in Anselm's saying that the whole question can be looked
at either in the *de re* (thing-centered) mode or   in   the   *de
voce* (word-centered) mode?   Thus, he says, *de voce*, "literate" is a word signifying a quality; *de re*, "literate" is   a
quality.[23]   Here   the   temptation   is to construe the whole
discussion as turning on the first alternative.   The   apparent   *de   re* assertions, such as *Literate* is a quality" which
(as we have seen) derive directly from   Aristotle's   *Categoriae*,   are   thus disarmed and made intelligible as disguised
de voce propositions, perhaps induced into existence by   the
antique   lack   of   the modern linguistic device of quotation
marks.   Thus Anselm would *really* be talking about   names   or
utterances   after   all.   However, any such facile reduction
would in fact eliminate a whole   dimension   of   the   discussion.[24]   This dimension is one which is shared with much of
the rest of medieval thought, but which has tended to remain
unappreciated   until   the recent present, simply because modern logical languages are only now re-acquiring the capacity
for handling it efficiently and unmysteriously.   We may draw
attention to this dimension of utterance by calling   it   the
quidditative,   from   the   medieval Latin *quidditas*, which in
turn derives from the *Quid sit?* question, preliminary   to   a
definition explaining the *esse* of a thing.[25]
     Briefly   (since   this lost dimension is explained at the
appropriate points in Henry 1974:   *Commentary* (pp.   118-22)
and in   § 3 and   § 4 of Henry 1984a: *That Most Subtle Question*)   quidditative   discourse of the sort with which Anselm
and his successors are concerned is pitched at a level which
is   certainly not disguised *de voce*; rather it is definitely
de re. It concerns the essence, nature, or quiddity   of   the
type of thing in question, and although it may indeed in the
end found a *de voce* meaning statement, it certainly need not
do   so,   and even more certainly must not be identified with
such a *de   voce* statement.   The   earlier   chapters   of   *De
grammatico* are replete with expressions which are either in
this quidditative *de re* mode, or in its companion *intelligi-*
mode.[26]   On Anselm's own principles the *res* here in question
cannot be concretely-sensed substances such as human   beings
or   physical   objects,   since it has already been noted that
these, as in the case of the referents of his paronyms, have
been   relegated   by   him to the accidental, appellative, *per
aliud* field.   Does this mean that the things in question   in
this   technical *de re* discourse must hence be quasi-Platonic

abstract universals, viewed by the eye of the mind alone? If not, where are such *res* to be located?

In fact Anselm ingeniously explains his point, with reference to paronyms at least, in such a way as to extract himself from the necessity of any such Platonic threat.[27] Indeed, the logical grammar of his position at this point is not only eminently clear, but also most usefully serves to explain at least one aspect of our contemporary query as to how it comes about that we are forever able to use old words in entirely new contexts, and yet make ourselves understood without any difficulty. First, however, a reminder of a present-day notion with which Anselm was evidently familiar, must be injected into the discussion.

Indeed, this reminder may in fact be gathered from one of Anselm's contemporaries, Garland the Computist, who lists precisely the range of certain possible sentence structures thus: one can, he says, predicate a name of a name, as in "(the) man is (an) animal," or a verb of a name, as in "Socrates reads," or even a verb of a verb, as in "Reading is acting."[28] Like the English of this last-quoted proposition, the Latin version also has participles as its terms (*Legens est faciens*) but, as Garland reminds us, the reason why this counts as an instance of a verb being predicated of a verb is that participles are classified as verbs by logicians. It is in this Latin version that the option here presupposed as open to the medievals now becomes evident. Participles ending in *-ens* (or *-ans*) can be taken in Latin either as names (in which case, *-er*, an English name-generating termination, duly preceded by stylistically and contextually apt articles, constitutes the appropriate translational correlate) or as verbs (in which case, the *-ing* used in the foregoing translation is a more appropriate English correlate). It is on the verb-termed construal that attention must now be concentrated, since this is one way of representing the form of that quidditative level of discourse which endows Anselm and other medievals with a sense of *res* other than that which involves concrete and sometimes kickable referents of which the concrete form of the name is, in Anselm's scheme, appellative. (Use of infinitives as terms is another way of expressing truths at the quidditative level: see Henry 1984a, *That Most Subtle Question*, § 3.11).

Now a verb is clearly an incomplete expression (or "functor," to use a present-day term) which, when appropriately completed by a name, forms a proposition (in the medieval and hence non-Platonic sense). Thus ". . . reads," completed by "Socrates" forms "Socrates reads." Anselm

expressed this functoriality by eliminating the initial sub-
stance-names (*homo, corpus*) from the second terms of
equations such as that of *grammaticus* with *homo habens* (or
sciens) *grammaticam*, or that of *albus* with *corpus habens
albedinem*, and so on.[29] It is the resultant participial (and
hence functorially verb-like) ". . . *sciens grammaticam*
which is offered as the sense in which *grammatica* is in this
context the strict significate of *grammaticus*. This is
offered by Anselm as his elucidation of, and *de voce* correlate of, the scandalous Aristotelian *de re Grammaticus est
grammatica* from which most of the discussion originally
stemmed, in the fashion described initially. Thus Anselm's
definitional *de re* sentences may be seen as being structured
like cases such as:

> (Being) literate is . . . having literacy;

> (Being) white is . . . having whiteness;

> (To be) literate is (to have) literacy;

> (To be) white is (to have) whiteness.

Such indications of the logical grammar of Anselm's
quidditative and hence *de re* discourse not only justify the
departures from traditional grammar which Anselm believes he
has inherited from Aristotle, but also facilitate the second
task envisaged above, namely his explanation of the way in
which new tokens of established word-types (in this case
paronyms) perform their miraculous sense-conveying function
in perpetually novel concrete situations. In such situations the open form of the functor is completed by the
appropriate substance-name which makes it nominal and concrete, as when ". . . having whiteness" (the functorially-
structured signification of "white") is completed by the
sense-indicated *horse* on the occasion of someone's receiving
the command "Strike the white!" in the presence of a *black*
bull and a *white* horse. It is to the sensed horse-having-
whiteness, as opposed to the bull (to which ". . . having
whiteness" is inapplicable) that the word "white" refers in
this context. At this particular point and in this particular place, the functorial verb (sometimes represented in
comparatively natural language by the abstract noun) is completed, saturated, made concrete, in terms of a locally
appropriate concrete noun. This whole process is described
in great detail in *De grammatico* XIV.

And now we are in a position to turn to the third task
envisaged above, namely Anselm's exploitation of the

astounding coincidence between the Aristotelian departures
from ordinary grammatical propriety and the similar departures found in theology. It is an exploitation which serves
to underpin Augustinian attitudes to sense and intellect in
theological contexts, and the coincidence mentioned must
have seemed to Anselm to be a most striking fulfillment of
the points so acutely made, centuries before, by Augustine.
Some of the coincidental departures have already been
recorded, as in the case of the interpredication of
abstract and concrete. However, the details of Anselm's
interpretation of the Aristotelian doctrine of paronyms, and
in particular some further as yet unnoted details of the
example of the white horse, align themselves beautifully
with the theological and philosophical requirements of both
Augustine and Anselm. Thus we have seen how, properly
speaking, "white" signifies whiteness, or, in *de re* style,
white is whiteness. Here "whiteness" has the full import of
". . . having whiteness" and this quidditative functorial
incompleteness is completed by allusions to sense-experi-
enced objects on particular concrete occasions. This suggests that the quidditative assertions (such as the four
suggested in detail above) must, by way of contrast, concern
subjects somehow independent of the senses, and surely
enough, spatio-temporal predicates, as well as predicates
associated with generation and corruption, are here quite
inappropriate in a logical-typological sort of way.[30] Now in
fact we have here exactly the ingredients for a theoretical
basis, purporting to be supported by purely rational pre-
Christian sources, for the rectification of mistakes concerning Trinitarian discourse. Augustine had already
observed, towards the beginning of his *De trinitate*, how
immersion in things of sense brings about incapacity for
dealing with the incorporeal, spiritual, non-temporal. It
is precisely at this point that Anselm's findings on paro-
nymy, and indeed his very example of the white horse, are
not only capable of being brought to bear in order to sus-
tain Augustine's thesis, but are in fact actually and
overtly produced by Anselm himself in this supporting
office. In a very well-known and often-quoted passage from
his own *Epistola de incarnatione verbi* Anselm inveighs
against the "heretics of the dialectic" who are unable to
understand rightly the doctrine of the Trinity. They are so
involved in sense-generated imaginations that they identify
color with body, and hence are incapable of distinguishing
between a given individual horse and its color. All this
is, of course, a direct reference back to the findings of *De
grammatico*,[31] with which a detailed correlation can be made.
Thus in the preliminaries to the above-described resolution

of the white horse case, inclusion of *body* in the meaning of
"white" was said to arise from experientially-based custom:
white, says the tutor interlocutor, no more includes *body*
than *literate* comprises *man*. Even as *literate* is just the
equivalent of the functorial ". . . having literacy," so
also *white* is just the similarly functorial ". . . having
whiteness." In both cases it is custom-grounded imagination, arising from immersion in the senses, as opposed to
intellectually-contemplated quiddity, which gives rise to
the confusion.[32]

Anselm has, in fact, now offered a detailed and intelligibl
analysis of the sense/intellect contrast. Lack of intellectual
appreciation of the functorially-termed, unsaturated, and even
nonsensical discourse at the quidditative level, as opposed to
the nominally-termed and often referential (appellative)
discourse concerning sensed concretes, is what is lacking in
both the student interlocutor of *De grammatico* and in the
dialecticae heretici. The student's identification of
literate and *man having literacy* would commit him also to
the identification of *white* and *body having whiteness*, or
even, in a particular context, of *white* and *this horse
having whiteness*, with all these equations purporting to
represent an adequate basis for signification-statements
embodying *significatio per se*. However, such identifications hold true at the appellative, nominally-termed level
only. Ordinary grammar can cope with such situations without any strain. No novel or non-grammatical way of speaking
need be imported to express them, since the semantic categories involved are perfectly standard. The dialectical heretics to whom Anselm alludes as lacking the capacity to distinguish between a horse and its color owe this incapacity
to their persistence in just this trite sort of merely contingent, sense-grounded, appellative level of identification. It was against such triteness that Anselm had considered it worthwhile to devote the two final chapters of *De
grammatico*. There the student defended a generalization of
his previous position, which would replace the *man*, *body*, or
horse and similar components of the equations with the
colorless pronoun "something" (*aliquid*). According to
Anselm inclusion of the *aliquid* (or its grammatically appropriate variants) gives rise to infinite regress.[33] Since
aliquid, like the *man*, *body*, *horse*, or suchlike components,
represents substance, this makes the resultant compound
expressions nominal in nature, and the whole *de re* background to meaning statements is thus still left to be carried out in nominally-termed appellative-equational discourse, as opposed to the participially-termed quidditative

discourse of the sort explained, exemplified, and championed
by the tutor of *De grammatico* (and hence by Anselm himself).

The contrast thus stressed between the two possible
positions is in itself a reminder of what must have appeared
to Anselm as a most remarkable coincidence between the ver-
dicts of theology and logic on the limits (or lack of limits) of the sayable. In both disciplines the authorities
(Augustine and Aristotle respectively) either by word or
linguistic practice suggest that the canons betokened by
ordinary usage and the grammar based thereon are in some way
lacking as guarantors of propriety of speech in technical
contexts. These suggestions are conveyed in theology at
points where discourse concerning the divine is concerned,
and in logic where intellectually-viewed quiddities are in
question. In *both* cases we go beyond the level of the
senses, thanks to our having transcended the level and limits imposed by a correspondingly limited usage-based
grammar.

The same Anselmian contrast is quite prophetic in
respect of the future history of the medieval linguistic
disciplines in general, and in respect of logic in particular. Nominalism of the Ockhamist type does indeed tend to
restrict or reduce such technically-approved discourse to
exactly the nominally-termed level, with a tendency to
assimilate *significatio* to *suppositio* (in a "standing-for"
sense).[34] Non-Platonic realists such as Aquinas and Scotus
require and presuppose precisely the hitherto unappreciated
functorially-termed type of discourse when speaking at the
quidditative or formal level.[35]

Finally it may be noted that perhaps in view of the
point made by Augustine in his *Confessiones* and quoted
above, namely that in spite of impropriety of speech, we
somehow often manage to communicate successfully, Anselm
does not go in for wholesale condemnations of the actual use
of ordinary language, nor does he abandon customary literary
modes of expression for his thought, save on appropriate
occasions. He describes the situation as follows: "Lots of
things are improperly expressed in ordinary speech, but when
it is necessary to get to the heart of the truth, one has no
alternative but to remove that worrying impropriety as far
as is desirable and possible, given the subject-matter."[36]
Appropriate occasions of the sort here envisaged reach their
peak in *De grammatico* and the "Philosophical Fragments,"
with more occasional exercises scattered about the rest of
the saint's works. The rectifications sometimes involve
elucidations of vocabulary, but more often than not are
matters of logical syntax, with propriety of speech in the
fullest and deepest sense as the ultimate target.[37]

Notes

[1] *The Confessions of St. Augustine*, trans. E. B. Pusey, ed. Ernest Rhys, Everyman's Library (1907; rpt. London: Dent; New York: Dutton, 1913), p. 435.

[2] *Confessions of St. Augustine*, trans. E. B. Pusey (Oxford: Parker, 1853), p. 239.

[3] G. R. Evans, ed., *A Concordance to the Works of St. Anselm* (Millwood, N.Y.: Kraus International Publications, 1984).

[4] R. W. Southern and F. S. Schmitt, eds., *Memorials of St. Anselm* (London: Oxford Univ. Press for the British Academy, 1969), pp. 334–51.

[5] Desmond Paul Henry, *That Most Subtle Question: Quaestio subtilissima: The Metaphysical Bearing of Medieval and Contemporary Linguistic Disciplines* (Manchester: Manchester Univ. Press, 1984), pp. 543–44; hereafter cited as Henry 1984a: *That Most Subtle Question* or Henry 1984b: *The Metaphysical Bearing*.

[6] *De grammatico* XVI–XVII: Schmitt I,161–63.

[7] Desmond Paul Henry, *The Logic of Saint Anselm* (Oxford: Clarendon Press, 1967), § 3.121 contains detailed references; hereafter cited as Henry 1967: *The Logic*.

[8] *De grammatico* XVI: Schmitt I, 161–62.

[9] Ibid. I: Schmitt I,145–46.

[10] Ibid. XI: Schmitt I,155–56.

[11] Ibid. XII: Schmitt I,156–57.

[12] Ibid.

[13] Henry 1967: *The Logic*, pp. 16–17.

[14] Ibid., § 2, § 3.124.

[15] *De grammatico* XVIII: Schmitt I,163–64; XI: Schmitt I,155–56.

[16] Ibid. XVIII: Schmitt I,163–64.

[17]Henry 1967:   *The Logic*, pp. 64-65.

[18]Ibid., pp.   65-66.   See also John Marenbon, *Early Medieval Philosophy (480-1150): An Introduction* (London; Boston: Routledge and Paul, 1983), pp. 106-08.

[19]*Metalogicon* II,20:   *PL* CXCIX,877-88.   See also Desmond Paul Henry, *Commentary of De Grammatico: The Historical-logical Dimensions of a Dialogue of St. Anselm's* (Dordrecht; Boston: Reidel,   1974),   p.   209; hereafter cited as Henry 1974:   *Commentary*.

[20]Henry 1984a: *That Most Subtle Question*, pp. 91-95.

[21]Ibid., § 1.

[22]*De grammatico* XVII: Schmitt I,162-63.   See also *Monologion* XVI: Schmitt   I,30-31   for the same *per se/per aliud* contrast.

[23]*De grammatico* XVIII: Schmitt I, 163-64.

[24]Henry 1974:   *Commentary*, pp. 294-96.

[25]*De grammatico* VIII: Schmitt   I,152-53;   Henry   1984a: *That Most Subtle Question*, § 4.1.

[26]Henry 1984a: *That Most Subtle Question*, § 4.4.

[27]Henry 1967:   *The Logic*, § 3.3.

[28]Garlandus Compotista, *Dialectica*, introd. L. M. de Rijk (Assen: Van Gorcum, 1959), p.   48,   lines   8-13.   See also Henry 1984a: *That Most Subtle Question*, § 3.1.

[29]*De grammatico* XIII, XIV: Schmitt I,157-61.

[30]Henry 1984a: *That Most Subtle Question*, pp. 180-81.

[31]Henry 1967:   *The Logic*, § 3.35

[32]*De grammatico* XIV: Schmitt I,159-60.

[33]The   validity of this claim is examined in Henry 1974: *Commentary*, pp. 320-34 and Henry 1984a: *That Most Subtle Question*, § 3.43.

[34]Henry 1984a: *That Most Subtle Question*, § 2.6.

[35] Ibid., § 4.6, § 5.

[36] *De casu diaboli* XII: Schmitt I,251-55.

[37] For   general   appreciations see Henry 1967:   *The Logic* and Henry 1984b: *The Metaphysical Bearing.*

Some Problems with Anselm's View of Human Will

Robert F. Brown

Introduction

Anselm refined Augustine's innovative but inconsistent
doctrine of human will into one of the most careful treatments of this topic by a theologically orthodox Christian
philosopher.[1] This brief paper examines several remaining
difficulties with Anselm's view of human will, to the best
of my knowledge from a different angle than that taken by
other commentators. My focus is mainly on philosophical
aspects of the topic -- what human will is, and its condition apart from considerations of fallenness -- rather than
on theological views of the unjust will or the will restored
by grace. I assume an audience familiar with the texts and
with Anselm's general theory,[2] and so, without sketching the
broader background, I will address directly three topics:
(1) will depicted as an ability; (2) degrees of wanting and
willing; (3) the constraint upon will by desire and the
beneficial (*commoditas*). But first a quick comment about
Anselm's definition of freedom (*De libertate arbitrii* XIII:
Hopkins and Richardson II,124-25) as "the ability to keep
uprightness [rectitude] of will for the sake of this
uprigntness itself."

Anselm intends this definition of freedom to be neutral
with respect to the special circumstances of humans, angels,
and God, and to require further specification as applied to
each.[3] Freedom so defined entails an ability to maintain
sinless perfection but not an ability to sin (*De libertate
arbitrii* I: Hopkins and Richardson II,105-06). Therefore
human freedom as such is not the ability to choose between
good and evil alternatives, although the humans who may or
may not have such freedom also have this power of choice.[4]
Thus Anselm has his own version of the Augustinian distinction between *libertas* and *liberum arbitrium*. This paper is
not about the special Anselmian notion of freedom, but
rather about some problems with his view of the natural
human will with respect to the power of choice among alternatives. My own conviction, which will emerge at the end,
is that only a more truly indeterminist conception of human
will than Anselm's is compatible with Christian beliefs
about divine goodness and justice, and about responsible
fallenness. I would also be critical of Anselm's (and
Augustine's) conception of the freedom of God, of the good

angels, and of the blessed in heaven, as an inability to
sin, but limit my remarks in this paper to the theme of
human will with respect to its power of choice.

Will as Ability

In *De concordia* Anselm distinguishes three senses in
which we speak of will: (1) as *instrumentum* or faculty of
the soul; (2) as *aptitudo* or *affectio*, a disposition or
inclination to choose in a certain way; (3) *usus* or actual
choosing.[5] Our first concern will be with the first and the
third senses, will as faculty and as actual choosing.
Anselm's simpler characterization of will as an ability
(*potestas*), in the much-discussed example of the bull and
the ram (*De libertate arbitrii* VII: Hopkins and Richardson
II,116-18), bridges and blurs the distinction between the
two. (We will come to will as disposition later on.) A man
who has previously demonstrated the strength and skill to
hold a wild bull now allows a ram, a smaller and weaker animal, to break free from his grasp. The teacher invites the
student's comment on this, in a discussion of the will's
ability to resist temptation. The student's straightforward
reply (p. 118), "I would judge him to be equally strong in
each task, but would maintain that he did not use his
strength equally . . . ," sets up the teacher's conclusion
that the will has a strength to will X that it may not fully
use, because it is instead willing Y more strongly. There
is a problem with language about willing strongly to which
we will return later; but first let us look at another feature of the example.

Jasper Hopkins argues that Anselm should discard the
example of the bull and the ram. He analyzes various meanings of "having an ability," and reminds us that special
circumstances may make an ordinarily sufficient ability
insufficient on a particular occasion: perhaps the strong
man slips in the mud, is ill due to something he ate, etc.
Similarly, for a person overcome by temptation, we ought to
search outside the will itself for the causes of its suc-
cumbing, rather than saying with Anselm that the person just
did not will strongly enough.[6]

Hopkins is correct that Anselm's example is a poor one,
but not for the reason he gives. *Willing* to hold the
animal and *physically succeeding* in holding the animal are
not the same. In physical performance one can only will *to
try* to do X; other factors apart from the willing itself
affect whether or not the effort is successful. The weak
man may want to hold the bull as much or more than does the

strong man, and try to do so; when he tries, his failure is not due to insufficient will but to insufficient physical strength and skill. Even Sartre, that most radical advocate for free will, affirms that willing a project consists in "trying to do X," not in "succeeding in doing X." Hopkins criticizes Anselm for overlooking this distinction, since the passage ignores extraordinary circumstances that might on occasion prevent the strong man from holding the ram. But Anselm's point is a different one, namely that the would-be ram holder chooses instead to release it, just as a person who wants to give in to one temptation sometimes does not do so because of wanting more strongly to do something else instead. The example may not be the best one for Anselm's purposes, but he should not be faulted for making a different point with it than the one Hopkins wants him to make.

The serious difficulty with the bull and the ram example is rather that will is not analogous to physical strength, and so ought not to be reified in this way. Will is not a thing with a specific nature, such as a muscle capable of handling weights up to a certain limit. We speak only figuratively of will as an instrument or faculty, ". . . an instrument that moves itself" (*De concordia* III,11: Hopkins and Richardson II,218); why does the *potestas* of willing in reality have to be embodied in a particular faculty or an aspect of the soul's nature?[7] "Willing" (as a verbal, not a nominative, element) is a term for the act of the person, soul, or self, in "choosing to try to do X." It is misleading to compare this possibility of choice to the ability of a strong man, whose "ability" can refer either to his muscles and nervous system as bodily structures, or to his prowess demonstrated in the act of gripping the animal; that is, either to a seat of latent strength or to an instance of displayed strength. A strong man cannot lift without muscles (indeed would not be a strong man without them), but a free person can will without having to be or possess a will construed as a structure of his human nature. Necessary conditions for the activity of willing, allegedly corresponding to latent muscular strength, comprise such ephemeral factors as being consciously awake, being aware of one's physical and mental capacities, being aware of X as a possibility for oneself, and the like. Of course Anselm operates within a theological tradition that hypostatizes will; therefore I am really attacking a high water mark in this long tradition more so than singling him out for individual criticism. Since I have ready to hand no general argument to discredit all hypostatization of will as a faculty or instrument of the soul (rather than its activity),

my circumscribed contention is only that hypostatization of
will that treats it analogously to muscular strength or a
similar physical property is misleading. Points introduced
in the next part will provide additional backing for this
contention.

Degrees of Wanting and Willing

The pertinent issue in the moral domain is the goodness
or evilness of will as disposition and act. Anselm discusses the case where one either does or does not withstand
a temptation to which it would on that occasion be wrong to
yield. Here analysis in terms of the *degree of effort* seems
appropriately applied to will, analogously to the case of
the strong man, but actually it is not. The reason the ram
escapes from the strong man is not because he is using those
muscles more vigorously for some other task; rather, he is
not using them at all, or at least not up to their full
capacity. The proper comparison involving degrees of effort
does not concern will as such, but is rather a comparison
between two different desires, in this instance a desire to
use one's full strength, and a desire to relax one's grip.
Not only is will not like a physical structure with latent
power, but also its exercise is not something to which we
should attribute a relative strength or weakness.

The ambiguity of *velle*, which can refer to both "willing" and "wanting" ("desiring") in English, causes the confusion. What I call "wanting" or "desiring" falls under the
second of Anselm's meanings for "will": *affectio* as inclination or disposition. He writes (*De concordia* III,11:
Hopkins and Richardson II,215):

> The inclination (*affectio*) of the instru-
> ment-for-willing is that by which the in-
> strument is so inclined to will some given
> thing (even when a man is not thinking of
> that which he wills) that if this thing come
> to mind, then the will wills [to have] it
> either immediately or at the appropriate
> time.

Wanting or desiring is feeling a need and also perhaps the
tug of an attractive object or course of action that prom-
ises to satisfy that need. Anselm's example in this context
is that of wanting good health; this desire is a natural
consequence of our animal and rational natures and so is a
given in us. He might, however, also grant that some spe-

cific desires can be learned, such as a desire to behave properly in school. My point here is simply that there can be degrees of wanting or desiring. Jane can want X more strongly than she wants Y. Willing, on the contrary, is the actual choosing or deciding to try to do something or to obtain something. Faced with mutually exclusive alternatives, Jane can only will one of them, even though she may want both. Anselm himself says, in introducing the "lying-or-dying" example (*De libertate arbitrii* V: Hopkins and Richardson II,112): "But a man cannot will against his will, because he cannot will if he is unwilling to will." Even though in a case purged of all complicating factors we would expect Jane to choose X (to try to do or obtain X), we can see clearly the difference between her wanting X and her willing X.

The following example further illumines the difference. Jill, a world-class distance runner, is competing today in one of the lesser meets on the European tour. She *wants* to win her event (as does nearly every runner in every race ever contested), but she *also wants* to save her strength for more important meets in the weeks to come. So she is *actually willing* to try to run at only ninety percent of her capacity, and then *concomitantly willing* to try to win if that degree of exertion should prove sufficient, but not if it be insufficient. On the final lap she glimpses her parents in the stands. They have never seen her run in international competition, and have kept their transatlantic flight to today's meet a secret in order to surprise her. Seeing them, she discards her race plan and runs all out in an effort to overtake the runners ahead of her before they reach the finish line. How should we properly describe this situation? Both before and after glimpsing her parents Jill wants to win. But after spotting them, she wants to make her parents proud of her today more than she wants to conserve her strength; therefore she turns on her maximum effort and speed. So much for her desire and her effort. What should be said about her willing? Is it correct to say that she is now willing more strongly to win than she was previously? No, for she has in fact changed not the strength of her willing but its very content; she changed it from "trying to run at ninety percent capacity, and also to win only if that degree of effort permits it," to "trying to win at all (physical) costs." Wanting and effort expended admit of degrees; willing does not.

How then do we ascertain what a person wills? Absent coercion, and without reliance on self-reporting (which we would need in Jill's case), the relevant analysis for ordinary instances is made after the decision is taken. In

retrospect one judges, for example, either that Jack willed
to withstand the temptation or that Jack willed to succumb,
depending on which alternative he in fact chose.   To say
that "Jack struggled mightily against the temptation but
finally succumbed" may tell us a good deal about Jack's conflicting desires, but it tells us no more about his willing
that does the simple declaration that "Jack decided to succumb."   Observing what someone does is not an infallible
guide to what that person wills, for the manifest outcome
might result from his failure to succeed at some other
attempted act (for example, if a seriously ill strong man
loses his grip on the ram, appearing to let it go intentionally when he is actually trying to hold onto it).   But it is
incorrect to describe wanting something not actually chosen
as if that desire were a willing that was overridden by
another and conflicting willing on the part of the same person.   What one wills is none other than what one actually
tries to do.   Whether the confusion of wanting with willing
is a real one in Anselm's own mind or just an apparent confusion due to the limitations of the language he is using,
it causes serious misunderstanding of the issue.

The Constraint of Desire and the Beneficial

The final topic before us is whether, or to what extent,
the soul or self is free to choose the *kinds* of things that
it shall will.   Here the issue of determinism vs.   indeterminism arises.   Anselm writes (*De concordia* III,11: Hopkins
and Richardson II,217):

> So the instrument-for-willing has two apti-
> tudes, which I am calling inclinations.
> One of these is the inclination to will what
> is beneficial; the other is the inclination
> to will what is right.   To be sure, the will
> which is the instrument wills nothing except
> either a benefit or uptightness.   For what-
> ever else it wills, it wills either for the
> sake of a benefit or for the sake of
> uprightness. . . .

He subsequently adds (*De concordia* III,11: Hopkins and
Richardson II,217): "Indeed, because of the inclination to
will what is beneficial, a man always wills happiness and to
be happy."   Also in discussing the possibility of willing
uprightness or rectitude, he remarks (*De concordia* I,6:
Hopkins and Richardson II,193):

> It is the prerogative of the will to reject
> and to elect in accordance with what ratio-
> nal discernment teaches . . . and where only
> the will's choosing is operative, there the
> force of necessity accomplishes nothing.

A disagreement between Kane and Hopkins centers on passages such as these.

In an extended analysis of Kane's book, *Anselm's Doctrine of Freedom and the Will*,[8] Hopkins criticizes him for equating determinism with compulsion and for treating the human will's power of choice (which Kane calls "freedom of self-determination") as a species of indeterminism. Hopkins concludes (p. 481):

> There is no textual basis for supposing that
> Anselm would not regard a man's choices as
> "determined" by his inclinations, motives,
> goals, and rational assessments. And there
> is no legitimate philosophical justification
> for labeling this kind of determinism *compulsion*.

He attributes to Anselm a determinist account of human will, though the sort that views it not as outwardly coerced but as determined from within by one's affections or desires. This is where Anselm does end up, but I do not agree that it is a satisfactory conclusion about human will as the power of choice. Let us look again briefly at wanting in relation to willing.

Two things incline one to will something: the strength of one's natural desire for it (for example, ice cream); the attractiveness of its presentation in a form eliciting or matching the desire (the ice cream cone in the advertisement). Anselm supposes that in this case one wills to get some ice cream unless a competing desire is concurrently stronger, so that one wills to satisfy it instead. Such desires can of course pull us toward rational objects as well as to physical ones, toward noble ends as well as to ignoble ones. Therefore reason gives us leverage by which to resist crudely physical desires, though the rational objects or goals it presents to us are also species of the beneficial for which we have desires naturally implanted in us (cf. *De virginali conceptu* X: Hopkins and Richardson III,156-57). One must will what one desires most strongly. Anselm says (*De libertate arbitrii* VII: Hopkins and Richardson II,118): "Hence, when presented with that which it wills less strongly, the will does not at all desert what

it wills more strongly . . ." This is what he intends by
"willing X more strongly than Y" (the correct statement
actually is: "willing X because one wants X more than Y").
In speaking this way he is, for a theologian, dangerously
close to Plato and Aristotle, neither of whom has a conception of will sufficiently developed to countenance a notion
of sin responsibly (that is, freely and knowingly) committed.

Anselm's ingenious treatment of rectitude as an alternative possible object of will avoids some problems engendered
by the Augustinian notion of the fallen will as utterly in
bondage to the objects of its love. For Anselm the fallen
will never loses the ability to keep rectitude, though that
ability cannot actually be exercised until God restores rectitude to the will (*De libertate arbitrii* VIII-X: Hopkins
and Richardson II,118-21). The fallen will thus has the
capacity (unactualizable by itself alone) to will something
other than the beneficial as satisfaction of its own strongest natural desires. This conception is more than a merely
cosmetic improvement of Augustine, so far as analysis of the
fall is concerned, but it does not go far enough. Adam
before falling was able to resist whatever beneficial object
he most strongly desired, and able instead to will to uphold
rectitude for its own sake. So Adam's possession of justice, as "uprightness of will kept for its own sake," evidently enabled him to be freed from determinism of his willing by his natural desires for physical and rational goods.
But evidently Adam as fallen and all his heirs are in actu-
ality unable to will other than in accord with their strongest desires. Anselm says (*De conceptu virginali* V: Hopkins and Richardson III,151):

> The will . . . lacking justice, driven on by
> various appetites, being inconstant, unres-
> trained, and uncontrolled, plunges itself
> and everything under its control into mani-
> fold evils -- all of which justice, had it
> been present, would have prevented from
> happening.

If Anselm intends this to be a *theological* account of the
will as fallen (and I think he does), then he ought to
segregate such notions more clearly from the *philosophical*
account of human will as such. As a philosophical factor,
determinism (not just influence) of the will as such, by
natural desires for physical and rational goods, would have
to be a property of Adam before the fall as well; yet Anselm
quite correctly will not have it this way when it comes to

speaking about Adam's original ability and responsibility. By not more clearly restricting this determinism by desires to the doctrine of sin, by not keeping it more clearly out of the doctrine of human will as such, Anselm appears to be wanting to have his cake and eat it too, namely, to suggest the contradiction that a responsibly self-determining will can be determined by desires it did not choose to have.

A truly indeterministic view of human will would sit better with Christian notions of responsible fallenness, and therefore of divine justice in punishing sin than does an inheritance from ancient philosophy that confuses wanting with willing, that makes willing a tool of desire as a natural property of the self. Anselm polished up this ancient paradigm about as well as can be done, and placed it within a setting of other conceptions that try to limit the philosophical and theological damage it does. This is his great achievement in the history of classical Christian reflection on the will. In my view, however, a willing that is truly free (in the ordinary, not the special Anselmian sense) is one that can, in significant ways though not of course in all respects, choose and rank order its own dispositions and desires, and not a willing that is merely free to act, without external compulsion, as the tool of internal desires it finds itself already having. The history of Western thought had to wait until Kant, and some of his successors, for the appearance of a truly uncompromising articulation of the human will as free in its self-determining power of choice.

Notes

[1] My own account of some of Augustine's inconsistencies appears in "The First Evil Will Must be Incomprehensible: A Critique of Augustine," *Journal of the American Academy of Religion* 46 (1978), 315-29.

[2] The principal texts for this topic are: *De libertate arbitrii*; *De casu diaboli*; *De veritate* IV and XII; *De concordia*; *De conceptu virginali*. Citations and quotations are from the English translations by J. Hopkins and H. Richardson, *Anselm of Canterbury*, 4 vols. (Toronto and New York: Edwin Mellen Press, 1974-76).

[3] G. S. Kane therefore argues that *De libertate arbitrii* is not *primarily* concerned with *human* freedom, and so has a different aim from modern philosophical treatments of the will. See his "Anselm's Definition of Freedom," in *Religious Studies* 9 (1973), 297-306, especially p. 298.

[4] In   the foregoing article Kane, using M. Adler's terms, designates these two notions as "freedom of self-perfection" and "freedom of self-determination." He says that ability to sin is antithetical to the former (though   the two co-existed   in Adam and Satan before each fell!), and determinism is antithetical to the latter (p. 305). Cf. *De liber-tate arbitrii* I: Hopkins and Richardson II,105-06.

[5] *De   concordia* III,11:   Hopkins   and   Richardson   II, 214-18. *De libertate arbitrii* VII: Hopkins and Richardson II,116-18, draws a two-fold distinction: instrument and use.

[6] J. Hopkins, *A Companion to the Study of St. Anselm* (Minneapolis: Univ. of Minnesota Press, 1972), pp. 145ff. Cf. *De casu diaboli* XII: Hopkins and Richardson II,150-54, for Anselm's general discussion of ability (*posse*).

[7] Anselm might reply that he is not relying simply on an argument from ordinary language, but also on the conviction that will is something good created by God. Cf. *De casu diaboli* VIII: Hopkins and Richardson II,144:   "We cannot deny, it seems to me, either that the will or that the turning of the will is something. For although the will and its turning are not substances, nevertheless it cannot be proven that they are not beings. . . ."

[8] G. S. Kane, *Anselm's Doctrine of Freedom and the Will* (Lewiston, NY: Edwin Mellen Press, 1981); J. Hopkins, "Anselm on Freedom and the Will: A Discussion of G. Stanley Kane's Interpretation of Anselm," *Philosophy Research Archives* 9 (1983), 471-94.

Anselm and the Problem of Evil

Hiroko Yamazaki

Anselm defined evil as "not-good, or the absence of good where good either ought to be or is advantageous to be" (*non-bonum, aut absentia boni ubi debet aut expedit esse bonum*).[1] Anselm's understanding of evil as "aversion from good" derives from Augustine. Nevertheless, the two figures differ in the ways they think about evil and in the points they emphasize.

Freedom as *non posse peccare* and the Origin of Evil

Anselm as well as Augustine considers "to be able not to sin" (*posse non peccare*) as man's first freedom and "not to be able to sin" (*non posse peccare*) as the highest kind of freedom.[2] Two reasons support this distinction. First, if "to be able to sin and not to sin" (*posse peccare et non peccare*) is freedom of choice, God and angels, who cannot sin, cannot have this freedom of choice.[3] Second, although God, angels, and men share the same definition of freedom, nonetheless "to be able to sin" (*posse peccare*) is not in the character of God or angels.[4] Sin is caused not by absence of will, but by misuse of will. Then what is the human misuse of will? Why does man misuse his will?

In *De concordia* Anselm distinguishes three meanings of the word will: (1) "the instrument-for-willing" (*instrumentum volendi*),(2) "the inclination of this instrument" (*affectio instrumenti*), and (3) "the use of this instrument" (*usus eiusdem instrumenti*).[5] When man sins by the misuse of will, the cause of his fault is found in any of these three kinds of will. The instrument-for-willing is created good insofar as it exists, because will itself is a work of, and a gift from, God. Similarly, the will is good as long as it is not misused. The cause of moral evil, therefore, is in the inclination of will. About this inclination of will Anselm states:

> . . . so the instrument-for-willing has two
> aptitudes, which I am calling inclinations.
> One of these is the inclination to will what
> is beneficial; the other is the inclination
> to will what is right. To be sure, the will
> which is the instrument wills nothing except
> either a benefit or uprightness.[6]

This statement makes the nature of these two inclinations
readily apparent.

The highest state of Augustinian freedom, "not to be
able to sin" (*non posse peccare*), emerges in Anselm's
expression, "to be able to keep uprightness-of-will for the
sake of uprightness itself."   When man does not have the
inclination to will what is right, he cannot maintain his
uprightness, and thereby relinquishes it. Therefore, if one
lacks the inclination to will what is right, he falls immediately into evil.   Inclination to will what is right is
indispensable in order to attain true freedom and avoid a
"depraved turning of the will" (*prava voluntatis conversio*).

On the other hand, the inclination to will what is beneficial is possessed by every man from his birth: the happiness which every rational nature wills consists of benefits;[7] and a will to avoid disadvantage or to possess what
is beneficial is natural.[8]   Therefore, sin is caused by
man's inclination to will what is beneficial, because he
only wills for benefit or uprightness. When man deserts
uprightness, this inclination moves him towards what he
wills more ardently.

The relation between inclinations of will and sin can be
explained by means of this line of reasoning. But when he
wills benefit, he does not always maintain uprightness-of-
will. When man wills uprightness and benefit simultaneously, or when he wills only uprightness, he maintains
uprightness-of-will. For the will's object is not always
its final purpose: if its ultimate purpose has no relationship to the good, to will something not for its own sake but
for the sake of something else allows man to fall into sin,
even though certain benefits might ensue. To will a benefit, therefore, does not always ensure that man can retain
uprightness-of-will; in fact, a strong probability that he
will desert uprightness exists.   Consequently, these two
inclinations must coexist. Only "a just will-for-happiness"
(*justa beatitudinis voluntas*) makes it possible for man to
attain the state of constancy in justice and happiness,
which enables him to enjoy God.

Aversio as *Conversio ad quod non debet*

Augustine defined evil as *aversio voluntatis ab incommu-*
tabili bono et conversio ad mutabilia bona (*De libero arbi-*
trio II,xix,53).   If the idea of moral evil needs to be
paraphrased, we may define it as "turning away," and so
Anselm believes.   Yet Anselm does not use the word *aversio*
as much as the word *conversio*. Evil is, however, consti-

tuted by both *conversio* and *aversio*. Why does not Anselm use the term *aversio* in the case of evil? Of course, *conversio* and *aversio* are not totally different, and in order for evil to proceed they must work together. On this point, Anselm agrees with Augustine. But the cause of moral evil in the strict sense is understood as *aversio* rather than *conversio*. So the origin of evil is found not in *conversio* but in *aversio*. In other words, it is a question whether *conversio* is the final cause which constitutes moral evil.

The solution to this problem is connected with the essence of Anselm's theory of evil, because Anselm shows us the contents of "aversion" without using the word *aversio*. For instance, he says "this uprightness is separated from the will" (*separatur haec rectitudo a voluntate*).[9] In another place, he states "he [the evil angel] departed solely by an evil will" ([*diabolus*] *sola mala voluntate abiit*).[10] Among others, the following statements can also be seen: "to desert uprightness-of-will" (*deserere voluntatis rectitudinem*);[11] "he [the devil] deserted the truth" ([*diabolus*] *veritatem deseruit*).[12] The expression in *De casu diaboli* VII and XX especially interests us: *convertere voluntatem suam ad id quod non debuit* ("[to] turn its will . . . towards what it was not supposed to will," and in Chapter XX, "turned his will to what he ought not to have [willed]").[13] This last expression deserves our particular attention because it does use the word *conversio*, but it represents precisely the meaning of both *conversio* and *aversio*, which Augustine defines as evil.

Anselm's Understanding of Moral Evil: Comparison with Augustine

Before Anselm uses the word *convertere* in *De casu diaboli* VII, he explains his understanding of the problem of evil more clearly. There he says that " . . . when it [the will] is turned to what it ought to will, it becomes a good will, but when it is turned to what it ought not to will, it is called an evil will."[14] The following diagram illustrates Anselm's meaning (in comparison with Augustine's).[15] In the case of good will both Augustine and Anselm use *convertere*: the object of will is according to Augustine, "God," while according to Anselm, it is "what it ought to will." In the case of evil will, Anselm again uses *convertere* (instead of Augustine's *avertere*): here, according to Augustine, the will turns away from "God," while in Anselm's view, it turns to "what it ought not to will." In other words, they comprehend similarly the idea of good will,

though they differ in their view of evil will. Augustine
expresses the object which the will turns to and turns away
from in one word, "God" and gives two expressions to show
the state of will: *convertere* for good will and *avertere*
for evil will. On the other hand, Anselm needs to use the
two phrases for the object of will, "what it ought to will"
and "what it ought not to will" respectively.

VOLUNTAS

            ad hoc quod debet velle conversa[16] = voluntas bona
           /
Anselmus   (*De casu diaboli* VII)
           \
            ad id quod non debet conversa   = voluntas mala

            quod ad deum nos convertimus   = voluntas bona
           /
Augustinus (*De peccatorum meritis et remissione* II,xviii,31)
           \
            quod a deo nos avertimus   = voluntas mala

He adds the word *non* because he wishes to demonstrate the
content of "turning" by one word *convertere*. The phrases,
"to turn the will to what it ought not to will," "to turn to
what it ought not to will," "the will's turning to what it
ought not to" (*voluntatis conversio ad quod non debet*) and
"to will what it ought not to," are in Anselm equivalent
phrases.
    With this analysis in mind, we may now compare the
phrase, "will's turning to what it ought not," with Augustine's *aversio* and *conversio*. When the will becomes evil by
free choice, it deserts freely what it ought to will, as it
wills what it ought not. Therefore, this will is evil,
insofar as it abandons what it ought to have willed, and
becomes unjust. What it ought to will is justice, which is
the good, or a benefit. Since a benefit does not always
assure uprightness (as indicated above), what it ought to
will in this case must be justice. Hence, to desert freely
what it ought to will, i.e., to sin and to fall into evil,
means relinquishing justice, and this notion of relinquishing justice applies to Augustine's *aversio voluntatis ab
incommutabili bono*, since Anselm understands justice as
immutable good.

On the other hand, other objects besides justice are, strictly speaking, what it ought not to will. So the "will's turning to what it ought not" applies to Augustine's *conversio ad mutabilia bona*. Consequently, Anselm's expression *conversio ad quod non debet* includes the contents of Augustine's definition of evil, *aversio voluntatis ab incommutabili bono et conversio ad mutabilia bona*, which may explain why Anselm does not emphasize *aversio* particularly. Anselm also regards the cause of evil as an *aversio* even though he does not use the word itself. Therefore, *conversio* which Anselm does use in the phrase *conversio ad quod non debet*, expresses evil to its fullest extent.[17] *Aversio* is implicit in this use of *conversio*.

Conversio ad quod non debet and Justice

How, then, does Anselm consider uprightness in terms of what the will ought to will? Man cannot enjoy God and be happy until he becomes just, so he must not only will a benefit but also uprightness. If one wills only a benefit and not uprightness, he cannot attain happiness. Even if he seems to attain happiness, it is misdirected happiness, since it is not attained justly. Here, "uprightly" and "justly" have the same meaning, and from this we understand that "inclination to will what is right" means "inclination to will what is just" (*affectio ad volendum iustitiam*). As far as freedom is concerned, *rectitudo* is synonymous with *iustitia*.

Although Anselm considers every nature good, he nonetheless speaks of two virtues, justice (*iustitia*) and benefit (*commodum*) and two vices, injustice (*iniustitia*) and disadvantage (*incommodum*).[18] Anselm's idea of *rectitudo* ultimately centers on justice, with strong ethical overtones, since his concept of justice underlies thinking of evil as a privation of good. Injustice is *ipsum malum*, because the privation of justice is also the privation of good.[19] The will becomes evil by being unjust.

Anselm's concept of *debere* and *iustitia* explains why *conversio ad quod non debet* includes both *conversio* and *aversio*. *Debere* does not connote inevitability but suggests a norm for free action. The human will turns toward God. God, on the other hand, attracts the human will, which nevertheless remains free. "I must do something" means "someone wants me to do something." What one ought to will in this case, therefore, is understood as "to will what God wills him to will" (*velle quod deus vult illum velle*).[20]

Therefore, if *debere*'s connotation as a norm for free action
is denied, the whole system is undermined. Thus, evil,
which is to desert the uprightness, means not to achieve
quod debet.

   Debere, applied to the situation of evil, has the following two meanings: (1) *facere quod non debet* or   (2) *non
facere quod debet.*[21]   Even if one achieves his goal, *quod
non debet* implies that the act has been done unjustly.   So
facere quod non debet means to desert uprightness.   On the
other hand, if one does not achieve his goal, *quod debet*
still suggests the act of turning away, thus losing the
uprightness. Consequently, from the viewpoint of *debere*,
"doing evil" and "not doing good" are the same thing as
deserting uprightness.

   Justice, on the other hand, is "uprightness-of-will kept
for its own sake" (*rectitudo voluntatis propter se ser-
vata*),[22] requiring not to will for the sake of something
else but for its own sake. Moreover, the expression "for
its own sake" suggests another perspective: its focus is
not whether or not to will justice, but whether to will justice or things other than justice.   To will things other
than justice means to will what one is inclined to consider
a benefit; when the will abandons uprightness and becomes a
servant of this inclination, it simultaneously becomes "servant of injustice" (*ancilla iniustitiae*).[23] Concerning the
problem of evil Anselm characteristically emphasizes *debere*
and justice, while accepting Augustine's thought.   And his
use of the expression *conversio ad quod non debet*, which
explains evil without *aversio*, indicates this accommodation.

Notes

   [1] *De casu diaboli* XI: Schmitt I,251,6-7; *Anselm of
Canterbury*, ed. and trans. J. Hopkins and H. Richardson (New
York: Edwin Mellen Press, 1976), II, 150. All quotations
from Anselm's works, hereafter, are from these texts.

   [2] Cf. Augustine's view of freedom: *Enchiridion de fide,
spe, et caritate* XXVIII,105; *De correptione et gratia*
XII,33; *De civitate dei* XXII,xxx,3.   Analogous expressions
are employed in various works, for example, *libertas voluntatis* in *De correptione et gratia*, and *liberum arbitrium* in
the *Enchiridion* and *De civitate dei*.

   [3] *De libertate arbitrii* I: Schmitt I,207,11-13.

⁴ Ibid. I: Schmitt I,208,3-12.

⁵ *De concordia praescientiae et praedestinationis et gra*
tia Dei cum libero arbitrio III,11:   Schmitt II,279,13-14;
Hopkins and Richardson, p. 215.

⁶ Ibid.:   Schmitt II,281,5-8; Hopkins and Richardson,
p. 217.

⁷ *De casu diaboli* IV: Schmitt I,241,13-14.

⁸ Ibid. XII: Schmitt I,254,23-26.

⁹ *De concordia* III,4:   Schmitt II,268,3-4; Hopkins and
Richardson, p. 203.

¹⁰ *De casu diaboli* XXV: Schmitt I,272,28; Hopkins and
Richardson, p. 173.

¹¹ *De libertate arbitrii* III: Schmitt I,212,3; Hopkins
and Richardson, p. 109.

¹² *De veritate* IV: Schmitt I,181,2; Hopkins and Richardson, p. 81.

¹³ *De casu diaboli* VII: Schmitt I,245,12; Hopkins and
Richardson, p. 144; Ibid. XX: Schmitt I,265,21; Hopkins and
Richardson, p. 165.   In *De casu diaboli* XX, *suam* and *id* are
omitted, and the past tense is employed.

¹⁴ Ibid.:   Schmitt I,245,4-7:   Quod si dicitur quia
voluntas aliqua essentia et ideo bonum est aliquid, sed conversa ad hoc quod debet velle fit bona voluntas, ad id vero
quod non debet conversa dicitur voluntas mala: quidquid
dixi de voluntate, video posse dici de ipsa conversione
voluntatis.   Hopkins and Richardson, p. 143.

¹⁵ *De peccatorum meritis et remissione* II,xviii,31:   *CSEL*
LX,102: Quocirca quoniam quod a deo nos auertimus, nostrum
est -- et haec est uoluntas mala -- quod uero ad deum nos
conuertimus, nisi ipso excitante atque adiuuante non possumus -- et haec est uoluntas bona -- quid habemus quod non
accepimus? (Here the good will and the evil will are compared, so Augustine does not mention *conversio* of the evil
will, but only *aversio* which is final cause of evil.)

[16]A minor change of the word order has been made by the author to show the contrast more clearly.

[17]Passages in which Anselm considers evil under the aspects of both *conversio* and *aversio*, or in which he stresses *aversio* are in evidence. But expressions without *aversio* are more evident. For example, *De casu diaboli* IX: Schmitt I,246,30-247,1: Cum vero [voluntas] avertit se ab eo quod debuit et convertit ad id quod non debuit: non stetit in originali ut ita dicam rectitudine in qua facta est. *De libertate arbitrii* V: Schmitt I,216,24-26: . . . si nulla tentatio potest illam [voluntatem] nisi volentem avertere a rectitudine ad peccatum, id est ad volendum quod non debet?

[18]*De casu diaboli* XII: Schmitt I,255,4-8.

[19]Ibid. IX: Schmitt I,246,22-26.

[20]*De libertate arbitrii* VIII: Schmitt I,220,22; Hopkins and Richardson, p. 119.

[21]F. S. Schmitt, "Ein neues unvollendetes Werk des hl. Anselm von Canterbury," *Beiträge zur Geschichte der Philosophie und Theologie des Mittelalters*, 33, No. 3 (1936), 28.

[22]*De veritate* XII: Schmitt I,194,26; Hopkins and Richardson p. 96; *De libertate arbitrii* III: Schmitt I,212,15; Hopkins and Richardson, p. 110.

[23]*De concordia* III,13: Schmitt II,287,3-5; Hopkins and Richardson, p. 221.

Theological Method: Augustine to Anselm

Anselm

Non tento, domine, penetrare altitudinem
tuam, quia nullatenus comparo illi intellectum
meum; sed desidero aliquatenus intelligere veritatem tuam, quam credit et amat cor meum. Neque
enim quaero intelligere ut credam, sed credo ut
intelligam. Nam et hoc credo: quia "nisi credidero, non intelligam."
(*Proslogion* I)

Augustine

Nisi enim aliud esset credere, et aliud
intelligere, et primo credendum esset, quod magnum et divinum intelligere cuperemus, frustra
propheta dixisset, "Nisi credideritis, non
intelligetis."
(*De libero arbitrio* II,ii,6)

Zur philosophisch-theologischen Denkform
bei Augustinus und bei Anselm von Canterbury

Klaus Kienzler

Michael Schmaus hat einer Abhandlung über Augustinus den
Titel gegeben: *Die Denkform Augustins in seinem Werk De
trinitate*.[1] Er hat damit die Denkform des Augustinus als
eigenes Problem erkannt und sie als Grundlage des grossen
Werkes über die Trinität herauszuarbeiten versucht. Mit
Denkform wird im allgemeinen Sinn die wissenschaftliche
Methode eines Philosophen oder Theologen verstanden.[2] In
dieser Hinsicht ist schon einiges zur Methode Anselms von
Canterbury gesagt worden.[3] Aber die Frage nach der Denkform
führt weiter. Es ist zum Beispiel zu vermuten, dass Philosophie und Theologie des Augustinus nicht von seiner
Denkform zu trennen sind. Dies könnte gerade an *De trinitate* aufgezeigt werden. Es wäre zu erläutern, wie sehr
Augustinus von der trinitarischen (bzw. triadischen) Struktur des menschlichen Geistes und damit seines Denkens über-
zeugt war und es deshalb wohl nicht von ungefähr kommt, dass
er sich beständig um trinitarische Gehalte bemühte und
schliesslich in einer Theologie der Trinität sein höchstes
Ziel menschlichen Denkens erkannte.[4] Denkform und Denkin-
halt haben bei Augustinus in *De trinitate* eine Entsprechung
gefunden. Sie sind nicht voneinander zu trennen. Etwas
Ähnliches will ich bei Anselm zu erheben versuchen.
Wenn ich im folgenden vor allem von einer weithin
gemeinsamen Denkform bei Augustinus und Anselm ausgehe --
Unterschiede sollen nicht eingeebnet werden, aber es sind
zuerst einmal Gemeinsamkeiten sichtbar zu machen --, so gibt
es dazu bekanntlich viele Einzelindizien.[5] Damit ist aber
noch nicht ausgemacht, worin denn eigentlich diese gemeinsame Denkform bestehe; gerade dieser will ich Schritt für
Schritt näherzukommen versuchen. Ich will mich dafür vor
allem auf den augustinischen Umkreis um Anselms *Proslogion*
beschränken. Denn in dieser Schrift dürfte Anselms Denkform
auf besonders charakteristische Weise zur Anschauung kommen.
Einzelindizien für den Zusammenhang des *Proslogions* mit
einigen augustinischen Schriften gibt es ebenso eine Reihe:
Zuerst die Aussage Anselms, in seinen Schriften nichts
anderes als Augustinus darlegen zu wollen.[6] Dann der Name
des *Proslogions*, der nicht nur von Ferne an die *Soliloquia*
erinnert. Auch werden immer wieder Einzelbelege aus Augustinus' *De libero arbitrio* vor allem für Anselms "Argument"
angeführt. Ich würde dazu auch einen Grossteil von *De vera
religione* nennen. Schliesslich hat etwa F. S. Schmitt dar-

auf hingewiesen, dass das *Proslogion* über alle einzelnen
Hinweise hinaus besonders die Atmosphäre der *Confessiones*
atme.[7] Damit sind im wesentlichen auch die Schriften Augustinus' genannt, die ich im folgenden des näheren und im
Blick auf das *Proslogion* betrachten will. Dabei geht es mir
allerdings weniger um einzelne Parallelen, sondern um die in
ihnen zum Vorschein kommende Denkform. Denn sollte gerade
der Hinweis von F. S. Schmitt auf die *Confessiones* stichhal-
tig sein, so läge es auf der Hand, dass mögliche Entsprechungen zum *Proslogion* nicht mehr durch unmittelbare
Verweise erhoben werden könnten, da es sich ja eher um eine
atmosphärische Ähnlichkeit handelte, sondern der Zusammenhang von *Confessiones* und *Proslogion* wäre dann am ehesten
durch strukturale und literarische Gemeinsamkeiten zu
erheben -- oder sie liesse sich durch eine gemeinsame
Denkform aufschliessen, wenn eine solche bestehen sollte.
Dafür wäre allerdings zuerst die charakteristische Denkform
der *Confessiones* zu beschreiben, um dann zu zeigen, dass im
Proslogion eine ähnliche und doch verschiedene Denkform
zugrunde liegt.

Nun wird man ebenfalls davon ausgehen können, dass eine
augustinische Denkform nirgends fertig vorliegt. Wenn ich
aber einmal annehme, dass, wenn von einer augustinischen
Denkform mit Recht gesprochen werden kann, diese in den
Confessiones einen grossartigen Ausdruck gefunden hat, dann
wird man im Blick auf die anderen genannten früheren Schriften Augustinus' sagen müssen: In ihnen ist die Denkform
der *Confessiones* höchstens in Ansätzen zu erkennen -- in
den *Soliloquia* etwa im grossen Eingangsgebet, in *De libero
arbitrio* vor allem in ihrer radikalen philosophischen Kompo-
nente und in *De vera religione* bereits in einer grösseren
Ausgewogenheit ihrer philosophischen und theologischen Merkmale. In diesen in Frage kommenden Schriften wären also
bestimmte Akzente der zu besprechenden Denkform wahrzuneh-
men. Ich werde diese Aspekte im Blick auf Struktur und Gestalt des *Proslogions* anzudeuten versuchen.

Die entscheidende Frage ist aber durchaus noch
ungeklärt: Wie wäre vom Stand der *Confessiones* her dann
diese charakteristische Denkform des Augustinus zu bestimmen. Ich möchte sie einmal im Anschluss an R. Berlinger als
"philosophische Dialogik" und -- über diesen Autor hinaus --
als "christliche Dialogik" bezeichnen. Dies scheint mir
eine Formel zu sein, die vor allem zur Beschreibung der
Confessiones geeignet ist. Ich möchte an dieser Stelle nur
unterstreichen, dass ich die Bedeutung dessen, was ich mit
"christlicher Dialogik" bezeichnen will, nicht von irgend-
welchen neueren philosophischen oder theologischen Richtung-
en hernehmen, sondern zuerst allein von Augustinus und

Anselm her gewinnen will. Was "christliche Dialogik" für
Augustinus bedeuten könnte und welche Konsequenzen   --
zunächst für die Philosophie -- damit verbunden sind, sei in
einer Aussage R. Berlingers angedeutet:

> Um dem gestaltenden Prinzip augustinischen
> Denkens (d.i. der Denkform) auf den Grund zu
> kommen, ist zu fragen: Was hat sich im Den-
> ken Augustins beispielhaft zugetragen. . . .
> Es setzt in seinem Denken, um ein Wort aus
> den *Ennarationes in Psalmos* aufzunehmen,
> eine *innovatio*, und zwar eine *innovatio
> metaphysica* ein. Diese meint aber nicht nur
> eine Neubesinnung auf das, was Metaphysik
> heisst. Augustinus entdeckt in der Tat ein
> *novum*, das die Frage nach der Wahrheit in
> ihm entzündet. Deshalb wird durch diese
> philosophische Initiation nicht Altes neu
> gedacht, sondern er denkt Neues schlechthin:
> die triadische Struktur des Menschen als
> Person und seine Geschichtlichkeit als ein
> Moment der Gewordenheit. Erst diese *innova-
> tio metaphysica* lässt begreifen, warum Pro-
> bleme wie Zeit, Geschichte und Person durch
> ihn sozusagen in die akmé gebracht wurden.
> Die Problematik der Zeitlichkeit, der
> Geschichtlichkeit und der Personalität wur-
> den seit Augustinus zu einem Moment der
> abendländischen Philosophie.[8]

R. Berlinger hat diese neue Art der Philosophie des Augustinus als "dialogische Metaphysik" bezeichnet -- und der Name
scheint mir sehr treffend gewählt zu sein. Aber es wäre
über R. Berlinger hinaus nach der Herkunft und nach der
Möglichkeit einer solchen Philosophie zu fragen. Und so
scheint es mir, dass eine solche philosophische Dialogik bei
Augustinus nicht zu verstehen sein dürfte ohne "christliche
Dialogik," die ihr vorausgeht und von der sie herkommt.
Diese "christliche Dialogik" -- die Grunderfahrung des
christlichen bei Augustinus -- wäre der Auslöser auch jener
folgenreichen "dialogischen Metaphysik." Diese Zusam-
menhänge scheinen mir exemplarisch in den *Confessiones* zur
Sprache zu kommen. Die *Confessiones* werden mir deshalb vor
allem als Dokument dienen, wenn ich im folgenden einige
Merkmale dieser augustinischen Denkform erheben will.
    Wenn ich im folgenden "christliche Dialogik" als charak-
teristische Denkform des Augustinus -- und dann auch des
Anselm -- einführen will, dann habe ich deshalb vor allem

etwa diesen komplexen Sachverhalt im Blick: Augustinus ist
von seinen christlichen Wurzeln schwer zu trennen (obwohl
ich mir bewusst bin, damit eine kontroverse Diskussion einfach übergehen zu müssen). Die christliche Bekehrung prägte
zusehends seine philosophisch-theologische Denkform. Diese
muss deshalb in ihrem Ansatz als christliche Denkform
festgehalten werden. Mit dieser christlichen Denkform verbinden sich für Augustinus aber sofort und fast immer ge-
wichtige originäre philosophische Fragestellungen. Denn
wenn es für Augustinus zwar selbstverständlich ist, dass das
entscheidende christliche Grundverhältnis ein dialogisches
Verhältnis zu Gott ist, so erhebt sich für ihn meist sofort
die charakteristisch philosophische Anfrage, wie dies denn
möglich sein könne, wie also überhaupt ein Verhältnis zwischen Gott und Mensch bestehen und gedacht werden könne.
Dabei zeigt es sich, dass sich mit den Jahren bei Augustinus
das Verständnis christlicher Dialogik zunehmend vertiefte,
und dass sich in einem gleichen Ausmass bei ihm auch die
philosophische Problematik radikalisierte.

Ich will dieser Entwicklung ein Stück weit nachgehen und
zeigen, dass Augustinus etwa in den *Soliloquia*, nachdem er
eben Christ geworden ist, selbstverständlich mit der Grund-
form christlicher Dialogik, dort mit dem grossen Eingangs-
"Gebet", beginnt, dass er dann aber recht unvermittelt seine
eigenen philosophischen Überlegungen verfolgt. Die *Confessiones* dagegen zeigen eine ganz andere Gestalt: Für sie
bleibt die Gebetsform von Anfang bis Schluss prägend; in
ihnen kommt christliche Dialogik exemplarisch zur Sprache.
Aber gerade diese Hochform christlicher Dialogik löst in den
Confessiones die wichtigsten philosophischen Reflexionen
aus. Mit anderen Worten treibt die Grunderfahrung christlicher Dialogik Augustinus zur Erörterung ihrer philosophisch-theologischen Grundproblematik, die nun für seine
Theologie und Philosophie charakteristisch wird. Augustinus
hätte dann in den *Confessiones* diese seine Grunderfahrung
christlicher Dialogik philosophisch-theologisch zu verantworten gesucht. In dieser Bahn sehe ich sodann auch die
Entwicklung, die bis zu Anselm hinüberreicht.

"Gebet" bei Augustinus und Anselm

Anselm hat seiner Schrift *De trinitate* nachträglich den
Namen *Monologion* gegeben und ihr damit einen Hinweis auf
Augustinus' *Soliloquia* mitgegeben. Dann wollte er das
Proslogion vom *Monologion* unterscheiden und zugleich wohl in
einem wichtigen Merkmal charakterisieren. Während das eine
ein philosophisch-theologischer Monolog "über" Gott ist,

erwächst der philosophisch-theologische Inhalt des *Proslogions* aus dem Dialog "mit" Gott. "Christliche Dialogik" als Tiefendimension des *Proslogions* scheint mir für dessen Verständnis unverzichtbar zu sein. Ich will dem Zusammenhang von *Proslogion* und *Soliloquia* nun einmal nachgehen.

Das einleitende "Gebet" *Proslogion* C. 1 (= P 1) hat aus diesem Grund seine eigene Bedeutung. Es charakterisiert Anselm nicht weniger als das folgende rationale "Argument." Im Gegenteil ist auf den Zusammenhang von Gebet und philosophischer Argumentation hinzuweisen. Das ist nun aber auch ein Kennzeichen des sehr frühen Augustinus. Ein wertvolles Zeugnis dafür sind gerade die *Soliloquia*. Dort steht am Anfang des I. Buches ein sehr langes und schönes, am Anfang des II. Buches ein kurzes Gebet[9]. Danach folgen jeweils lange philosphische Erörterungen. Anders wird es in den *Confessiones* sein. Dort prägt die Gebetsform das Ganze; dort erheben sich aber aus dem Gebet auch immer wieder lange philosophische und theologische Erörterungen. Was in den *Soliloquia* noch schiedlich getrennt wird, ergibt sich in den *Confessiones* aus einem Entwurf. Es ist aber auch immer wieder erkannt worden, dass das grosse Gebet am Anfang der *Soliloquia* bereits in einer grossen Nähe zu den *Confessiones* steht. Dies wäre an seiner Struktur zu erheben. Für uns ist nicht weniger wichtig, dass bei diesem Gebet der *Soliloquia* ebenfalls manches an Gestalt und Gehalt des *Proslogions* erinnert. Alle drei Schriften verbindet diese gemeinsame Form des Gebetes als Anleitung zur philosophischen Reflexion.

Eine genauere Analyse des grossen Gebetes am Anfang der *Soliloquia* würde dort schon eine kunstvoll und genuine Sprach- und Denkform entdecken, die für Augustinus charakteristisch geworden ist: das Gebet ist durch und durch -- von der Gesamtgestalt bis in einzelne Satzsequenzen hinein -- triadisch komponiert. Was zunächst noch wie eine Zusammenfassung seines neuplatonischen Weltbildes erscheint, entpuppt sich dann in einem ersten Teil als ein grosser Entwurf trinitarischer Anrufungen. Der triadische Sprachgestus antwortet dem trinitarischen Anruf.[10] In einem zweiten grossen Teil jedoch, der uns hinsichtlich der *Proslogion* besonders interessieren dürfte, antwortet eine nicht weniger triadisch verfasste Seele (der Beter Augustinus) dem angerufenen trinitarischen Gott.[11] Wenn der Ternar von *memoria* -- *intelligentia* -- und *amor* dort auch noch nicht zur späteren Höhe entwickelt ist, so ist er doch schon als Ausdruck des menschschlichen Geistes, der sich zum Gebet erhebt, deutlich sichtbar. In diesem dichten Gebetsteil fallen allerdings bereits eine Reihe von Aussagen auf, die eine unverkennbare Nähe zur Sprach- und Denkform des *Proslogions* zeigen: Auch

Augustinus will sich in der gläubigen *memoria* zuerst seines Standes[13] vor Gott vergewissern;[12] dann will er "erkennen" (*intelligere*), was er glaubend wahrnimmt, um schliesslich ein "vollkommener Liebhaber" Gottes zu werden (*amor*).[14] Die Grossstruktur des *Proslogions* zeichnet sich bereits ab: Auch Anselm gewinnt seinen Stand durch die Vergewisserung des "Glaubens" im Gebet (P 1); dann will er im philosophischen Argument von P 2-4 "erkennen," was er glaubt; und schliesslich sucht er im restlichen *Proslogion* immer mehr einzustimmen und einzuwilligen in die grössere "Liebe" Gottes (P 14 et seq.).

Nach dem grossen Gebet zu Anfang der *Soliloquia* spricht Augustinus in kurzen Sätzen ein Programm aus, das für ihn später weithin gültig geblieben ist, und das auch für Anselm immer wieder als gültig anerkannt worden ist:

> Siehe nun habe ich zu Gott gebetet. Was also willst du wissen? All das, worum ich betete. Fass es kurz. Gott und die Seele erkennen: das ist mein Wunsch (*Deum et animam scire cupio*). Nichts weiter? Nein, sonst nichts.[15]

Zwar ist hier die Augustinus' prägende Absicht deutlich ausgesprochen, dass er nur auf philosophische Weise erkennen wolle, was er zuvor im Gebet gesprochen hat, aber was dann in den *Soliloquia* folgt erscheint doch gleichsam wie ein Bruch, wie ein neuer Einsatz, der mit dem vorausgehenden Gebet unverbunden bleibt. Gebet und philosophische Reflexion stehen noch getrennt nebeneinander. Das grosse Gebet weist wohl auf die künftige Denkform des Augustinus voraus. Es weist vielleicht aber noch mehr auf seine neuplatonische Herkunft zurück. Denn es war Plotin gewesen, der etwa in seiner Schrift "Über die drei ursprünglichen Wesenheiten", die Augustinus zu dem Zeitpunkt schon gekannt haben dürfte, vorschlägt, sich im Gebet zu sammeln, bevor der Philosoph daran geht, über Gott zu sprechen.[16] Es mutet noch wie eine solche Sammlung vor der philosophischen Rede über Gott an, wenn Augustinus am Anfang der *Soliloquia* sein Gebet spricht.

Christliche Dialogik

Bereits die *Soliloquia* kennen das christliche Gebet als Beginn der philosophischen Betrachtung. Beten ist aber ohne Zweifel der höchste Ausdruck christlicher Dialogik zwischen Gott und Mensch. Für Augustinus ist Beten in den *Soliloquia* noch unproblematisch. Wenn ich die Denkform des Augustinus als "christliche Dialogik" charakterisiert habe, dann meine ich vor allem jene wichtige Entwicklung, wo diese Selbstverständlichkeit christlicher Dialogik für Augustinus höchst problematisch wird. Christliche Dialogik liegt also im philosophisch präziseren Sinne dort vor, wo sich Augustinus dessen bewusst wird, was es bedeutet zu beten und Gott anzurufen, dort, wo ihm das christliche Beten zur genuinen Form christlichen Lebens und zugleich zur höchst problematischen Form wird. Dann nämlich wird ihm das Gebet zum Ansatz und Impuls einer philosophisch-theologischen weitreichenden Reflexion, wird es für ihn zum Einsatz aller weiteren Betrachtungen, wird ihm die christliche Dialogik selbst zum Grundproblem aller weiteren philosophischen wie theologischen Fragen. Das aber geschieht in den *Confessiones*. An den Anfangskapiteln der *Confessiones* können wir etwa ablesen, was gemeint ist, wenn wir von der Zuspitzung "christlicher Dialogik" bei Augustinus sprechen, und wir können dort in dichten Aussagenreihen erkennen, wie christliche Dialogik nun zum grundlegenden Ausgang aller Philosophie und Theologie werden kann. Es sei nur thetisch vorweggenommen, dass nicht nur Augustinus' Denkform aus der Reflexion auf die christliche Dialogik erwächst, sondern dass auch Anselms Denken aus ihr zu leben scheint.

Einige grobe Andeutungen zur Struktur der ersten fünf Kapitel des *Confessiones* I müssen genügen, um ihre Nähe zum Anfang des *Proslogions* und zur Gestalt der ganzen Schrift festzustellen. Augustinus beginnt die *Confessiones* bekanntlich sehr programmatisch. Den kunstvoll gegliederten Auftakt kann ich nur andeuten. Vor allem wäre auch hier auf die triadische bzw. trinitarische Sprechform hinzuweisen:

A (1)   "Gross bist Du, Herr, -- und hoch zu preisen" (Ps 144:3)

(2)   "und gross ist Deine Macht

(3)   und Deine Weisheit unermesslich" (Ps 146:5).

B (R)   Und preisen will Dich der Mensch, ein kümmerlicher Abriss Deiner Schöpfung,

(1)   ja der Mensch, der herumschleppt sein Sterbewesen,

(2)   herumschleppt das Zeugnis seiner Sünde

(3)   herumschleppt das Zeugnis, dass Du "den Hochfährigen widerstehst."

C (R)   Und dennoch will Dich preisen der Mensch, ein
           kümmerlicher Abriss Deiner Schöpfung.

(1)   Du selber reizest an, dass Dich zu preisen
           Freude ist;

(2)   denn geschaffen hast Du uns zu Dir,

(3)   und ruhelos ist unser Herz, bis dass es
           seine Ruhe hat in Dir.[17]

Augustinus beginnt also mit der Hochform christlichen
Selbstverständnisses: mit dem Lobpreis Gottes oder mit dem
rühmenden Gebet (A). Aber dieses christliche Selbstverständnis wird sogleich problematisiert (B): Wie vermag
der Mensch Gott zu loben, da er doch nur ein kümmerlicher
Abriss von Gottes Schöpfung ist. Die innerste christliche
Problematik ist von allem Anfang an offengelegt. Es ist die
Problematik christlicher Dialogik schlechthin. D.i. die
Frage nach der innern Möglichkeit des Gebetes zu Gott und
damit eines jeden Sprechens zu ihm. Es ist zugleich eine
intrikate Dialektik damit verbunden. Zwar erscheint die
erste Selbstverständlichkeit des Betens durch den Hinweis
auf den Stand des Menschen verunmöglicht, doch weist ein
"dennoch" sogleich darauf hin, dass der Mensch Gott trotzdem
preisen soll, wenn er auch nur ein kümmerlicher Abriss der
Schöpfung ist (C). Diese Dialektik ist durch die stanzenar-
tige Wiederholung der Aussage, der Mensch solle Gott
preisen, obwohl er nur eine gebrochene Natur ist, deutlich
herausgehoben (R). Mit kurzen Sätzen hat also Augustinus
programmatisch das Wesen der christlichen Dialogik und ihre
innere Dialektik gleich zu Anfang unüberhörbar angekündigt.
Aus ihr erfolgt nicht nur der Einsatz für die nächsten
Aussagreihen, sondern sie sind im Grund auch der Ausgang für
die *Confessiones* insgesamt.
     Im Hinblick auf Anselm ist aber über die allgemeine
Charakteristik christlicher Dialogik hinaus ein Blick in
ihre innere Dialektik bedeutsam. Augustinus hat sie in
einer dreifachen Stufung formuliert und ihre Auflösung in
einer ebenfalls dreifachen Stufung angedeutet: Der Mensch
ist nicht nur eine gebrochene Schöpfung oder ein Sterbewesen, sondern er hat seinen Zustand noch durch seine eigene
Sünde und seinen Fall verschlimmert und er verharrt darüber
hinaus seither in seinem sündigen Hochmut vor Gott (B, 1-3).
Deshalb muss Gott selbst den Anfang machen, damit der Mensch
Gott wieder loben kann; Gott hat den Anfang dadurch schon
gemacht, dass er den Menschen zu sich hin geschaffen hat,
und dass er den Menschen nicht los lässt, bis sein ruheloses

Herz in Gott Ruhe findet (C, 1-3). Es könnte ausgeführt werden, dass Anselm in P 1 diese programmatische Zustandsbeschreibung des Augustinus breit extemporiert, indem er auf ähnliche Weise die innere Dialektik christlicher Dialogik entfaltet: Der Mensch ist noch nicht einmal dem nachgekommen, wozu er von Gott geschaffen worden ist; schlimmer, er ist durch den Sündenfall zu einem erbarmungswürdigen Wesen herabgesunken; sein Wesen ist nun so pervertiert, dass nur durch Gott eine Erneuerung erhofft werden kann. Gott ist es also, der den Menschen wiederschaffen, erlösen und von Grund auf erneuern muss. Ohne auf einzelne textliche Entsprechungen eingehen zu können, mag festgehalten werden, dass die Aporie christlicher Dialogik sowohl den Ausgang der *Confessiones* als auch des *Proslogions* ausmacht.[18]

Ich würde diesen ersten Anfang der *Confessiones* als eine Vergewisserung der "Seins"-ordnung des Menschen durch Augustinus charakterisieren. Sie hat ihre Entsprechung am Anfang des *Proslogions*. Beidemal handelt es sich um eine Zustandsbeschreibung, wie es um den Menschen steht. Der nächste Abschnitt ist aber auch für Anselm nicht weniger bedeutsam: "Lass mich, Herr, wissen und erkennen . . ."[19] Es ist dieses "Erkenntnis"-Interesse, das für Augustinus wie für Anselm so charakteristisch ist, wissen und erkennen zu wollen, was der Glaube am Anfang sagt. Ich muss es mir wiederum versagen, den Übergang vom "Glauben" zum "Erkennen" präzise mit Augustinus nachzuvollziehen; es kann nur darauf hingewiesen werden, dass er bei Augustinus wie in der entsprechenden Passage von P 1 durch das Einführen der Grundworte von "suchen" (*quaerere*) und "finden" (*invenire*) und durch ihr wiederum dialektisches Verhältnis geschieht. Auf die Bedeutung dieser Grundworte bei Augustinus wie bei Anselm ist immer wieder genügend hingewiesen worden. In ihnen spielt sich der Vorgang christlicher Dialogik vor allem ab.

Dagegen mag auf den weiteren Fortgang der Anfangskapitel der *Confessiones* (I,ii,2-v,5) aufmerksam gemacht werden. Mit ihm beginnt eine erste philosophische Reflexion auf das Wesen christlicher Dialogik. Augustinus beginnt offensichtlich mit einem neuen Aufschwung der Betrachtung und zugleich mit den fast gleichen Fragen wie zuvor: die neue Reflexionsstufe ist damit gekennzeichnet. Die Aporie solcher Dialogik wird aber nun als Frage nach dem "Ort" formuliert, wo denn ein Gespräch mit Gott stattfinden könnte: "Wie aber soll ich meinen Gott anrufen, meinen Gott und meinen Herrn, da ich doch, wenn ich ihn rufe, in mich herein rufe? Und welches ist der Ort in mir, wohin er kommen soll, mein Gott? Wohin soll Gott in mir denn kommen, Gott, der 'den Himmel gemacht hat und die Erde.'" (Gn 1:1)[20] Es sei auf die

Entsprechung wiederum in P 1 hingewiesen, wo Anselm dieselbe
Aporie in derselben Weise formuliert, da auch er nicht
weiss, an welchen Ort er sich wenden soll, um Gott zu finden. Es ist geradezu ein durchgehendes Motiv von P 1, immer
wieder die Ortlosigkeit feststellen zu müssen, deren der
Mensch gewahr wird, sobald er sich Gott zuwenden will.[21] Die
philosophisch-theologischen Überlegungen, welche Augustinus
nun aber der Frage nach dem Ort anschliesst, sind dann so
weitreichend, dass sie geradezu einen ersten Vorblick auf
die Grossstruktur des *Proslogions* im ganzen zu geben
vermögen.

Vergewissern wir uns aber zunächst noch einmal der Frage
nach dem "Ort," die für Augustinus wie für Anselm offensichtlich zur Grundfrage christlicher Dialogik geworden ist.
In der Tat meint die Frage nach dem Ort die aporetische
Grundfrage, wo denn der Mensch vor Gott einen Stand und
Anhalt haben könne, damit Gott in ihn komme. Ist der Mensch
überhaupt ein fester Ort, der sich vor Gott behaupten
könnte, so kann die weitere Überlegung von Augustinus wie-
dergegeben werden. Ist der Mensch vielleicht nicht eher ein
Un-Ort vor Gott, da alle Wege vom Menschen aus nur zu erneuten Aporien führen? Vom Menschen aus kann nur ein Bruch,
ein Grund-Riss, eine wesenhafte Diachronie festgestellt
werden, die nie zu Gott selbst hinüberführen werden. Dieser
Bruch und diese Diachronie kennzeichnen die christliche
Dialogik zutiefst. Sie zeichnen sich folgenschwer in die
Grundstruktur der *Confessiones* wie des *Proslogions* ein. Sie
dürften der Grund der inneren Dramatik in beiden Werken
sein, die schliesslich keine Auflösung findet.

Auf welche Weise nun bringt Augustinus im weiteren Verlauf der Anfangskapitel diese Diachronie christlicher Dialogik zur Sprache und mit welcher Dramatik trägt er sie aus?
Zusammengefasst können etwa drei Schritte unterschieden werden. Sie gipfeln jeweils in neuen Anrufungen an Gott, die
sich aussprechen liessen: "Wer bist Du dann Gott, Du
selbst, wenn ich Dich soweit erkannt habe?"[22] Ein erster
Schritt beginnt beim Menschen und führt über ihn hinaus; ein
zweiter vergegenwärtigt sich die Grösse Gottes; ein dritter
kehrt von der Grösse Gottes zum Menschen zurück. Ich sehe
in Anselms *Proslogion* ein ähnliches Vorgehen.

Eine erste Stufe beginnt beim Menschen: Gott soll in
ihn kommen. Aber sie führt über den Menschen hinaus: Gott
muss in den Menschen kommen. Besser: Gott muss schon im
Menschen sein, damit der Mensch Ort der Ankunft Gottes werden kann: "Nicht also wäre ich, mein Gott, ja gar nicht
wäre ich, wenn Du nicht wärest in mir. Oder vielmehr, wäre
ich nicht, wenn ich nicht wäre in Dir." (I,ii,2)[23] Ich
vermute, dass im Argument von P 2-4 auf philosophische Weise

eine ähnliche Vergewisserung statthat und eine ähnliche
Umwendung vom Aufstieg des Menschen zu Gott, zur Erkenntnis
göttlichen Seins im Menschen hin geschieht.
In einem zweiten Schritt muss dann notwendigerweise die
Besinnung auf die Grösse dieses Gottes erfolgen. Die Frage
nach Gott bricht auf: "Was also bist Du, mein Gott? Ja,
was anders denn als Gott der Herr?" (I,iv,4) [24] Wird man
hier nicht an die erneut aufbrechenden Fragen nach Gott in P
5 erinnert? Und die Attribute Gottes, die Augustinus
anschliesst, erinnern nicht weniger an die weitertreibenden
Reflexionen über Gottes Eigenschaften, die Anselm in P 5-13
entwickelt:

> Du, über alles bist Du der Hohe, der Gute,
> der Mächtige, der Allmächtige, der Erbar-
> mende, der Gerechte, der Geheime und der
> Offenbare, der Schöne und Gewaltige, der
> Feste und der Unergreifliche, der Unwandel-
> bare, der alles wandelt usw. [25]

Hier wäre ein Aufschluss möglich, warum sich Anselm dort vor
allem auf Gottes Eigenschaften des Unwandelbaren, des
Mächtigen und des Gerechten und Barmherzigen einlässt.
Der dritte Schritt steht sodann unter der Leitfrage:
"Was bist Du mir? Erbarme Dich, dass ich reden kann"
(I,v,5). [26] Zu denken wäre an die weitertreibende Suche nach
dem personalen Du, die ab P 15 zu einem Höhepunkt gelangt.
Von da an ringt Anselm nicht weniger darum, wie der Mensch
ob solcher Grösse Gottes von ihm noch reden könne, und mehr
noch, was dieser Gott ihm bedeute. Augustinus Antwort weist
auf die entsprechenden Passagen des *Proslogions* voraus:
"Was sagen wir nun, mein Gott, mein Leben, meine Köstlich-
keit (*dulcedo*)? . . . Sagt meiner Seele: Dein Heil bin Ich.
. . ." [27]
Zusammenfassend kann in den Anfangskapiteln der *Confessiones* und im *Proslogion* eine gleiche Absicht und eine
gleiche Problematik erkannt werden: Beidemal ist "christliche Dialogik" der Ausgangspunkt. Diese wird aber bald
problematisch und wirft schwere philosophische Anfragen auf.
Eine tiefe philosophische Vergewisserung wird nötig. Diese
bezieht sich auf den "Seins"-Status des Menschen vor Gott,
auf Gottes Grösse und auf Gottes Heil für den Menschen. Die
philosophische Reflexion hat offensichtlich beidemal die
Funktion, den Ansatz christlicher Dialogik zu stützen und
ihre Grundproblematik zu klären. Christliche Dialogik zieht
offensichtlich ein ganzes philosophisches Programm nach
sich.

Christliche Dialogik in neuplatonischem Kontext.

Die christliche Dialogik führt in eigentümliche Aporien. Sollte meine Vermutung zutreffen, dass Augustinus immer mehr von dieser Denkform eingenommen wurde, dann wäre damit zugleich gemeint, dass er auch immer mehr auf ihre inneren Aporien aufmerksam wurde. Die Anfangskapitel der *Confessiones* scheinen mir dafür die Bestätigung zu sein. Meine Interpretation sollte darauf hinweisen, vor welche Probleme sich Augustinus angesichts christlicher Dialogik gestellt sieht und welche weitreichenden Folgen sich damit zugleich ankündigen. Um sie noch einmal zu nennen, so sind sie zwar zuerst theologischer Natur, aber Augustinus lässt ebensowenig einen Zweifel daran, dass sie philosophische Grundfragen herausfordern. Es sind dies einmal die Fragen nach dem Menschen vor Gott, der über sich hinaus muss, damit Gott zu ihm komme; dann die Erkenntnis der Grösse Gottes in sich und schliesslich die neue Erkenntnis des Menschen, wenn es wahr ist, dass Gott zum Menschen spricht und der Mensch auf neue Weise mit Gott zu sprechen vermag. Augustinus wird diese Grundfragen durch die ganzen *Confessiones* hindurch verfolgen. Er wird dazu Antworten teils theologischer teils philosophischer Art formulieren. Er wird dazu auf eigene frühere Schriften zurückgreifen. Wir wenden uns diesen früheren Versuchen zu. Sie waren für Anselm offensichtlich von nicht geringerer Bedeutung.

Was die philosophische Seite der anstehenden Grundfragen einer christlichen Dialogik betrifft, so hat sie Augustinus in den *Confessiones* offensichtlich weitgehend mit den Mitteln der "neuplatonischen Philosophie" zu lösen versucht. Das Ineinander von neuplatonischer und christlicher Sicht innerhalb der *Confessiones* ist allerdings ein besonderes Problem, auf das ich bald in seiner Bedeutung für Anselm zu sprechen kommen werde. Deutlicher sind die Konturen von Augustinus' neuplatonischer Philosophie in früheren Werken zu erkennen. Im Hinblick auf Anselms Rezeption kommt für uns dafür vor allem das II. Buch von *De libero arbitrio* in Frage. Denn ohne Zweifel finden wir dort die meisten Einzelbelege, die fast unmittelbar in das *Proslogion* eingegangen sind. Vor allem ist dort der philosophische Gottesbegriff, den Anselm an den Anfang seines "Argumentes" stellt, bereits deutlich eingeführt. Es genügt aber offensichtlich nicht, sich mit dieser Schrift allein zu befassen, um den ganzen Kontext der neuplatonischen Argumentation zu erkennen, wie sie für Augustinus wichtig wird, sondern ich verweise darüber hinaus auf einen grossen Teil der Schrift *De vera religione*, wo Augustinus den ganzen Komplex neuplatonischer Philosophie relativ zusammenhängend diskutiert.

Dort wird erst der Stellenwert neuplatonischer Philosophie in seinem frühen Denken begreifbar. Um zu diesen Hintergründen hinzuführen, wird es unumgänglich sein, auch kurz auf redaktionelle Eigenheiten dieser genannten Schriften einzugehen.

Um die Bedeutung der neuplatonischen Philosophie für Augustinus und dann auch für Anselm im voraus zuerst anzudeuten, so erscheint der anselmische Gottesbegriff "*id quo maius cogitari nequit*" gerade in diesem philosophischen Kontext des Augustinus. Auf mögliche stoische und andere Transformationen dieses Gottesbegriffes (schon bei Augustinus) und auf weitere Umformungen bei Anselm kann ich hier nicht eingehen.[28] Es ist nur der erste systematische Ort aufzuweisen. Es ist aber deutlich, dass Anselm den langen neuplatonischen Argumentationsgang des Augustinus in seinen Schriften *De libero arbitrio* und *De vera religione* nicht nachvollzieht, sondern dessen Ergebnis aufnimmt und das "*id quo maius cogitari nequit*" einfach mit seinem philosophischen Gottesbegriff identifiziert. Aber die Implikationen dieses Gottesbegriffes bleiben nichtsdestoweniger neuplatonischaugustinisch.

Die erste Redaktion von *De libero arbitrio* (388) dürfte vor *De vera religione* (389-391) liegen. Zu dieser ersten Redaktion wird man den ganzen grossen Komplex des II. Buches zählen müssen, in dem Augustinus eine Art Gottesbeweis vorlegen will. In der Tat kündigt Augustinus in II,iii,7 einen solchen Weg an, während die beiden anderen Punkte, die er dort vorschlägt, bereits die zweite Redaktion (nach 391) betreffen dürften. Es dürfte plausibel zu machen sein, dass Augustinus in der früheren Redaktion einen Weg der Gotteserkenntnis vorlegte, der mit dem II. Buch einsetzt und mit dem 15. Kapitel endet. Der Rest gehört der späteren Redaktion an.[29]

Es ist immer schon die Nähe dieses Entwurfs eines Gottesbeweises in *De libero arbitrio* zu P 2 bis 4 aufgefallen. In der Tat sind es die gleichen Ausgangsbedingungen hier, die auch Anselms Einsatz des "Argumentes" in P 2-4 kennzeichnen: Es ist die Einrede des "Toren" aus Ps 52:1 bzw. 13:1 auf der einen Seite, der in seinem Herzen sagt, es gebe keinen Gott, der die argumentative und rationale Form des Gottesbeweises erzwingt.[30] Dann ist es aber die fast gleiche rigide Überzeugung auf der anderen Seite, die Augustinus hier wie sonst selten artikuliert, dass, was der Glaube vorlegt, rational untersucht und durch die Vernunft erkannt werden muss. Wiederholt führt Augustinus dazu Jr 7:9 an, wie es Anselm nicht anders tut.[31] Überhaupt fällt bei diesem Gottesbeweis in *De libero arbitrio* auf, dass er scheinbar einen ähnlichen Rationalismus atmet, wie er oft

bei Anselms "Argument" angenommen wird. Die Ähnlichkeit
beider Texte ist nicht zu verkennen.

Der dann folgende Gottesbeweis ist von Augustinus aber
dann deutlich aus neuplatonischen Motiven gewonnen. Augustinus trägt hier seine Gedanken zur Existenz Gottes lang und
breit vor, wie er sie später bisweilen sehr verkürzt wieder-
gibt. Es ist darin das neuplatonische Aufstiegsschema zu
erkennen, das Augustinus offensichtlich seit Mailand
geläufig ist. Die augustinische Wendung des neuplatonischen
Aufstieges zielt aber in seiner Spitze auf eine "Wesenheit,"
die die menschliche Vernunft noch übersteigt. Nach einer
früheren Übereinkunft zwischen Augustinus und Evodius muss
diese Wesenheit schliesslich Gott sein:

> Wie nun, wenn wir etwas finden können, was
> zweifellos nicht nur ist, sondern auch noch
> unsere Vernunft überragt (*ipsa nostra
> ratione praestantius*), wirst du dann Beden-
> ken tragen, dies, was es auch sein mag, Gott
> zu nennen. (Evodius:) Ich möchte doch nicht
> ohne weiteres Gott heissen, was dem Besten
> meines Wesens noch überlegen ist. Denn mir
> scheint, man sollte Gott nicht das nennen,
> dem meine Vernunft untergeordnet, sondern
> dem nichts übergeordnet ist (*quid melius
> quam id quod in mea natura optimum est -- id
> quo mea ratio est inferior, sed quo est nul-
> lus superior*). . . . Ich kann nur das als
> Gott erkennen, dem unzweifelhaft nichts
> überlegen ist (*plane fatebor deum quo nihil
> superius esse constiterit*).[32]

Offensichtlich sind in diesen Formeln die Elemente enthal-
ten, die zum philosophischen Gottesbegriff Anselms geführt
haben. Es sei nur auf zwei Veränderungen aufmerksam
gemacht, die dann bei Anselm von Bedeutung sein dürften.
Anselm rekurriert nicht mehr auf den neuplatonischen Unter-
bau, der zu diesem Gottesbegriff hinführt, sondern er hält
das "*id quo maius cogitari nequit*" in sich für philosophisch
schlüssig. Zum anderen beschränkt sich Anselm auf die philosophische Analyse allein dieses Begriffes, während Augustinus nur zu einer philosophischen Hypothese kommt. Augustinus bedarf ja so etwas wie eines weiteren Gottesbeweises,
um seine philosophische Hypothese zu bestätigen . Er zeigt
ja in der Folge der Schrift auf, dass diese überlegenen oder
transzendenten Wesenheiten tatsächlich existieren. Erst
dann kann der eigentliche Gottesbeweis in seinem Sinne
erbracht werden: Es müssen jene transzendenten Wesenheiten

anerkannt werden; dann müssen sie Gott zugesprochen werden; sie verweisen auf Gottes Sein. Anselm hat in seiner Antwort auf Gaunilo eine solche Argumentation abgelehnt.[33] Er hat sein Argument allein aus dem "*id quo maius cogitari nequit*" gewonnen. Anselm hat offensichtlich die augustinische Vorlage auf eine bestimmte Weise radikalisiert.

Man wird mit einigem Recht auf *De libero arbitrio* als die nächste Parallele zu Anselms Argument im *Proslogion* hinweisen. Aber diese Parallele allein scheint mir nicht zu genügen. Sie hebt zwar den strengen philosophischen Rationalismus von P 2-4 deutlich hervor; sie verliert aber dadurch auch den ganzen Kontext des *Proslogions*. Die Kapitel P 2-4 erscheinen dann recht funktionslos in der ganzen Schrift. Dies ist im Grunde schon bei Augustinus so. Zwar zeigt der Gottesbeweis in *De libero arbitrio* eine gewisse Eigenständigkeit, aber Augustinus macht in anderen Schriften nicht weniger darauf aufmerksam, dass sein Gottesbeweis in einen bestimmten neuplatonisch-philosophischen Kontext hineingehört, von dem er ohne Verlust nicht herauszutrennen ist. Gerade dieser Kontext wird aber auch für Anselm aufschlussreich sein.

Zu dem grösseren neuplatonisch-augustinischen Kontext führt Augustinus' andere Schrift *De vera religione*. Auch in ihr hat der neuplatonische Weg zu Gott eine bestimmte Position. Aber hier ist er in einen grossen und ganzen philosophisch-theologischen Komplex eingelassen. Es wäre zunächst durch eine redaktionelle Analyse wiederum zu erläutern, dass ein Grossteil dieser Schrift der neuplatonischen Philosophie gewidmet ist. Auch in dieser Schrift sind offensichtlich verschiedene redaktionelle Stufen zu unterscheiden. Ich würde aus Gründen einiger Beobachtungen am Text und zum Inhalt die Auseinandersetzung des Augustinus mit dem Neuplatonismus mit XXIV,45 beginnen lassen und sie bis zum Ende der Schrift sich hinziehen sehen.[34] Könnte diesem Vorschlag zugestimmt werden, so stellte sich diese Auseinandersetzung aber als eine grosse und in sich geschlossene Abhandlung Augustinus' zum Neuplatonismus heraus.

Sodann wären dabei in etwa drei grosse Etappen zu unterscheiden. Die beiden ersten Etappen hat Augustinus selbst gekennzeichnet: Er spricht nämlich am Anfang dieser Abhandlung von den zwei verschiedenen Wegen der christlichen Wahrheit, die er danach auch getrennt behandelt, nämlich einmal von der "Autorität des Glaubens" und dann von der "Erkenntnis der Vernunft."[35] In einem ersten Gang behandelt er deshalb den Weg des "Glaubens," der auf die Heilsgeschichte baut (XXIV-XXVII). Dieser Weg muss in einem zweiten Gang in den Weg der "Vernunft" einmünden; die Glaubenswahrheiten müssen nach Augustinus von der Vernunftwahrheit durchdrungen und vor ihr ausgewiesen werden (XXIX-XXXVI). Denn nur so gelingt nach ihm der Aufschwung vom "Zeitlichen zum Ewigen." Während die erste Etappe deutlich einen genuin christlichen Einstieg im Glauben nimmt, stimmt der zweite Gang durch die Vernunft im wesentlichen mit der neuplatonischen Philosophie überein. Hier greift Augustinus wiederum auf den neuplatonischen Aufstieg zu Gott zurück. Die dritte Etappe dagegen (XXXVII-LV) macht auf die inneren Gefahren aufmerksam, die sich aus einem reinen geistigen Neuplatonismus ergeben. Die Einwände Augustinus' dazu können bündig so zusammengefasst werden, dass der Neuplatonismus zwar eine grosse geistige Höhe erreicht, aber für das Leben und für die christliche Tugend der "Liebe" unfähig bleibt. Es ist nur anzumerken, dass in diesem Dreischritt der Schrift der augustinische Ternar von "Glaube"-"Erkenntnis"-"Liebe" offensichtlich eine führende Rolle einnimmt.

Nach dieser Interpretation läge uns in einem Grossteil von *De vera religione* eine relativ geschlossene Abhandlung der neuplatonischen Philosophie durch Augustinus vor. Sie besteht teils in der Übernahme teils in der Kritik wesentlicher Merkmale dieser Philosophie -- ein Verfahren, das Augustinus' Umgang mit ihr bis zu den *Confessiones* charakterisiert. Es dürfte aber daran kein Zweifel sein, dass bei einem solchen Umgang mit der neuplatonischen Philosophie bei Augustinus etwas Neues entsteht. Es ist seine eigene genuine Komposition, die er in der Schrift vorträgt, und mit der er der neuplatonischen Philosophie einen bestimmten Platz zuweist. Damit verändert er aber auch den Charakter dieser Philosophie. Denn nun ist die gesamte Komposition bedeutsam. Und es scheint mir ohne Zweifel zu sein, dass Augustinus mit ihr den gesamten christlichen Heilsweg beschreiben will. Dieser christliche Heilsweg erinnert bereits an die *Confessiones*, er erinnert an deren Anfangskapitel, die wir vorher interpretiert haben, und er würde uns der Grossstruktur der *Confessiones* näher bringen, wenn wir uns auf eine Betrachtung des Vergleichs beider Schriften einliessen. Denn die Grossstruktur des christlichen Heilsweges hat für Augustinus von nun an eine sehr charakteristische Gestalt: Er beginnt mit der Einstimmung in den "Glauben"; dieser drängt aber zur "Erkenntnis;" so nur findet er seine Vollendung in der "Liebe." Zwar werden wir erst ab den *Confessiones* von der augustinischen Denkform christlicher Dialogik im besonderen Sinne sprechen, aber die entscheidenden Grundzüge dafür sind im christlichen Heilsweg von *De vera religione* schon sichtbar. In den *Confessiones* entspringt alles der christlichen Dialogik des Gebetes, in *De vera*

religione sehe ich den Versuch, vorgegebene und eigene Erkenntnisse in eine ganze christliche Gestalt umzuschmelzen.
Mit dieser Einlagerung der neuplatonischen Philosophie zwischen "Glaube" und "Liebe" in *De vera religione* verändert sich für Augustinus auch der Charakter dieser Philosophie. Darauf will ich besonders aufmerksam machen. Denn diese Veränderung scheint mir erheblich zu sein für den darin gewonnenen Gottesbegriff, bedeutsam auch für den Gottesbegriff des späteren *Proslogion*. Die neuplatonische Philosophie wird dadurch nämlich zu einem Stück des gesamten religiösen Heilsweges. Dieser Charakter wird im Vergleich zwischen *De libero arbitrio* und *De vera religione* deutlich. Zwar greift Augustinus beide Male auf die gleiche neuplatonische Philosophie zurück, vornehmlich auf ihr Aufstiegsschema, um zu Gott zu gelangen. Aber während er dort ein rigides Stück metaphysischer Gotteserkenntnis vorlegt, erscheint die neuplatonische Philosophie hier als ein wichtiger Schritt der philosophischen Reflexion über eben diesen Heilsweg. Sie führt zur Erkenntnis dessen, was der Glaube vorgibt; sie gibt Rechenschaft von dem, was der Gläubige lebt; sie sucht philosophisch zu verantworten, was der Glaube von Gott aussagt. Hier lassen sich die *Confessiones* bereits vorausahnen, wo dem Neuplatonismus im VII. Buch eine ähnliche Rolle zukommen wird.
Dies gilt vor allem auch für den zur Diskussion stehenden Gottesbegriff. Augustinus scheint mir hier nämlich den in der neuplatonischen Philosophie vorgefundenen Gottesbegriff in einer Weise zu entwickeln und zu gebrauchen, der ihn religiös einfärbt und verwenden lässt. Dieser Gebrauch scheint mir ihn dem neuplatonischen Erbe nicht zu entfremden, sondern nur dessen religiöse Anknüpfung zu enthüllen. Aber was Augustinus daraus macht, gehört bereits in den religiösen Umkreis der *Confessiones*, wie schon oft bemerkt worden ist. Er scheint mir für das Verständnis des *Proslogion*-Arguments Anselms nicht weniger wichtig. Denn mir scheint die innere Absicht des *Proslogion*-Argumentes und die Funktion des Gottesbegriffes "*id quo maius cogitari nequit*" bereits ausgezeichnet getroffen, wenn Augustinus in der entsprechenden Passage von *De vera religione* nun diesen Gottesbegriff so formuliert:

> Geh nicht nach draußen, kehr wieder ein bei dir selbst (*Noli foras ire, in te ipsum redi*)! Im inneren Menschen wohnt die Wahrheit. Und wenn du deine Natur noch wandelbar findest, so schreite über dich selbst

hinaus (*transcende et te ipsum*). Doch
bedenke, dass, wenn du über dich hinaus-
schreitest, die vernünftige Seele es ist,
die über dich hinausschreitet (*memento cum
te transcendis, ratiocinantem animam te
transcendere*). Dorthin also trachte, von wo
der Lichtstrahl kommt, der deine Vernunft
erleuchtet. Denn wohin sonst gelangt, wer
seine Vernunft recht gebraucht, wenn nicht
zur Wahrheit? Die Wahrheit kommt ja nicht
durch den Vernunftgebrauch zu sich selber,
sondern sie ist das, wonach alle, die ihre
Vernunft gebrauchen, trachten. So sieh,
hier ist die denkbar höchste Übereinstimmung
(*convenientiam qua superior esse non possit*), und nun stimme auch du mit ihr
überein. Bekenne, dass du nicht bist, was
sie ist (*confitere te non esse quod ipsa
est*). Denn sie selbst sucht sich nicht, du
aber bist suchend zu ihr gelangt (*tu autem
ad eam quaerendo venisti*), nicht einen Raum
durchmessend, sondern von Sehnsucht des
Geistes getrieben.[36]

Der Hintergrund dieser Aussage ist ohne Zweifel neuplatonisch. In ihr ist derselbe Weg zu Gott und derselbe neuplatonische Gottesbegriff am Werk wie in *De libero arbitrio*: die Rückkehr in sich selbst und darin die Bewegung der Transzendenz. Diese Bewegung der Transzendenz wird aber vornehmlich durch die vernünftige Seele vollzogen. Zugleich ist die Aussage ganz augustinisch und weist auf die *Confessiones* voraus. Die Bewegung der Rückkehr in sich selbst und darin der Transzendenz sind dort das Kernstück "christlicher Dialogik." Ich erinnere an die Anfangskapitel der *Confessiones*; wir werden bald die gleiche Grundstruktur in zentralen Teilen der *Confessiones* wiedererkennen. Die Doppelbewegung des "*Noli foras ire, in te ipsum redi*" und des "*transcende et te ipsum*" wurde immer wieder zu Recht als das Programm der *Confessiones* erkannt.

Es ist aber nun von grossem Interesse, dass Augustinus hier in *De vera religione* deutlich und in den *Confessiones* ebenso die gesuchte Transzendenz im Aufschwung der Vernunft (*Nous*) erkennt. Im Aufschwung der Vernunft vollzieht sich zuhöchst die Einsicht in die Transzendenz. Ist dies nicht die Anknüpfung, die Anselm aufgenommen hat, um in seinem *Proslogion*-Argument diesen Charakter der Vernunft auszuleuchten und aufzuzeigen? Das "Denken" (*cogitare*) transzendiert sich in der Spitze seines Vermögens selbst.[37] Was aber im Aufschwung des Denkens sichtbar wird, ist zugleich auch Antwort auf die Grundproblematik "christlicher Dialogik." Denn wenn diese in die Aporie führte, wie es denn möglich sei, dass Gott in den Menschen komme, so ist durch das transzendierende Vermögen der Vernunft bereits erhellt, dass Gott schon immer im Menschen ist, als Bedingung der Möglichkeit des Denkens sozusagen schon in der Vernunft selbst ist. Dies aber ist die "denkbar höchste Übereinstimmung" (*convenientia qua superior esse non possit*) von Vernunft und Gott, die das Denken zu erreichen vermag, eine denkbar höchste Übereinstimmung aber auch, nach der "christliche Dialogik" auf der Suche ist. Augustinus weist durch die Wahl der Worte selbst darauf hin, dass die genuine Dialektik "christlicher Dialogik" nun eine Auflösung erfahren hat, da die Sehnsucht seines Geistes nun "fand," was sie "suchte" (*ad eam quaerendo venisti*). Mit anderen Worten scheint mir hier Augustinus für die Grundproblematik "christlicher Dialogik" eine neuplatonisch-philosophische Aufklärung erreicht zu haben. Wir werden sehen, dass er diese Aufklärung vor allem in den *Confessiones* immer wieder durch die neuplatonische Philosophie versuchte.

Vor diesem ganzen Panorama neuplatonisch-augustinischer Theologie und Philosophie und vor ihrer weitreichenden Bedeutung für die augustinische Denkform, wie wir sie aus *De vera religione* erhoben haben, wird nun aber auch eine ganz andere Sicht auf Anselms *Proslogion* möglich. Der Gesamtzusammenhang des *Proslogion* dürfte deutlich werden. Wie Augustinus in *De vera religione* einen Gesamtzusammenhang des christlichen Heilsweges organisch entwickelt, so ist ein gleicher auch für Anselms *Proslogion* zu vermuten. Es lässt sich für beide Schriften eine gleiche Grossstruktur erheben: Wie für Augustinus zuerst der "Glaubens"-Einstieg nötig ist, so versichert sich Anselm im Gebet von P 1 im Glauben. Zugleich gerät er dabei aber in die Krisis, wie ein solches Gebet zu sprechen möglich oder wie christliche Dialogik zu vollziehen ist. Diese Aporie provoziert aber bei Augustinus wie bei Anselm die "Vernunft." Sie wird zur tieferen Erkenntnis des Glaubens gefordert. Diese Vernunft erscheint dadurch aber nicht mehr isoliert. Sie ist durch die Aporie des Glaubens herausgefordert; sie steht im Dienst des Glaubens. Andererseits muss die Vernunft ihren philosophischen Charakter auch nicht aufgeben: Augustinus kann die neuplatonische Philosophie anerkennen und in seine Dienste stellen; Anselm kann auf Vernunftautonomie bestehen. Denn die Rückkehr des Denkens in sich wird der ihm innewohnenden Transzendenz gewahr. Solche Philosophie bringt dem Glauben erst Gewissheit und der christlichen Dialogik erst ihre Grundlage. Der Glaube kommt zu sich und vermag sich in der

"Liebe" zu vollenden. So muss sich die neuplatonische Philosophie bei Augustinus fragen lassen, ob sie zur "Liebe"
hinführe, und Anselm schliesst seine Schrift mit einer liebenden Kontemplation.

Sollten meine Überlegungen zur Stellung der neuplatonischen Philosophie bei Augustinus aber zutreffen, so hätten
wir auch einen Hinweis zum Ort des "anselmianischen Arguments" im *Proslogion*. Das leitende Paradigma sowohl augustinischen wie anselmianischen Denkens wäre wie angenommen
die "christliche Dialogik." Ihre Grundproblematik würde von
Augustinus mit Hilfe der neuplatonischen Philosophie zu
klären versucht. Darin spielte deren philosophischer Gottesbegriff eine entscheidende Rolle. Anselm hätte diese
Aufgabe fortgeführt und radikalisiert. Denn er hätte das
philosophische Argument in P 2-4 ausgesondert und in seiner
Tragfähigkeit eigens überprüft. Dazu hätte er sich allein
auf den philosophischen Gottesbegriff verlassen. Dies ist
die Funktion des "anselmianischen Arguments" im *Proslogion*.
Es stünde aber nicht anders als bei Augustinus im Dienst der
Vergewisserung "christlicher Dialogik." Der Gesamtzusammenhang des *Proslogions* scheint mir diese Vermutung zu
erhärten.

Christliche Dialogik in den *Confessiones* und im *Proslogion*

Wir haben bisher zwei Traditionen bei Augustinus verfolgt, die für das *Proslogion* Anselms relevant zu sein
scheinen. Augustinus hatte seine *Confessiones* mit dem Programm der "christlichen Dialogik" eingeleitet und es in
seiner Dialektik vorläufig umrissen. Wir haben ein
ähnliches Programm in P 1 wiedergefunden. Das anselmianische "Argument" in P 2-4 dagegen führt uns in neuplatonische Kontexte bei Augustinus zurück, wie sie besonders in
De libero arbitrio und *De vera religione* deutlich sind. Es
ist nun meine weiterführende These, dass uns in den *Confessiones* in einem Grossteil eine Kombination beider Traditionsströme vorliegt. Das heisst aber für das Programm der
Confessiones in einem groben Vorgriff: Für Augustinus ist
dort die Denkform der christlichen Dialogik führend.
Allerdings wirft diese Denkform typische theologische und
philosophische Probleme auf. Augustinus versucht ihre
Lösung in den *Confessiones* vor allem mit den Mitteln der
Philosophie des Neuplatonismus. Augustinus hätte also die
Grundprobleme einer christlichen Dialogik mit bedeutsamen
Teilen der neuplatonischen Philosophie zu bewältigen
versucht.

Was das heisst wird besonders an den herausgehobenen neuplatonischen Stücken der *Confessiones* deutlich. Gemeint ist vor allem der dreifache Versuch des Aufstieges zu Gott im VII. Buch und ihr erfolgreicher Abschluss in der "Vision von Ostia" im IX. Buch.[38] Es dürfte dabei deutlich sein, dass es Augustinus dabei jeweils um die Vollendung des christlichen Weges geht, der Augustinus im ganzen Buch vorschwebt und den er nun mit neuplatonischen Mitteln zu begehen versucht. Andererseits wird an diesen Texten auch deutlich, wie sie unter Augustinus' christlicher Denkform zu einem religiösen und christlichen Weg transformiert und umgeschmolzen werden. Augustinus integriert den neuplatonischen Weg in seine genuine christliche Denkform und versucht dadurch, die christliche Dialogik philosophisch zu rechtfertigen.

Es ist nun überraschend, bei Anselms *Proslogion* deutliche Anklänge gerade an diese zentralen Passagen der *Confessiones* zu finden, auf die meines Wissens noch nicht aufmerksam gemacht worden ist. Zwar wurde immer schon einmal auf die Nähe von *Confessiones* und *Proslogion* hingewiesen, aber sie wurde kaum einmal näher überprüft. Auch im folgenden kann kein detaillierter Nachweis erfolgen. Es sind in einer ersten Vergewisserung nur einige auffallende Parallelen zu erheben. Diese Parallelen sind, wie angedeutet, vor allem den "ekstatischen Texten" im VII. Buch und der "Vision von Ostia" im IX. Buch entnommen. Sie verteilen sich aber auf das gesamte *Proslogion* und scheinen dort in einige wesentliche Aussagen eingegangen zu sein.

Ich möchte mit einer überraschendend Bemerkung beginnen. Es ist bekannt, dass Anselm in seinen Schriften mit Bibelzitaten äusserst sparsam umgegangen ist und sie nur sehr bewusst gebraucht hat. Etwas anders stellt sich der Sachverhalt im *Proslogion* dar, wo am Anfang und im Schlussteil ausgiebig von Bibel- und Psalmzitaten Gebrauch gemacht wird. Es scheint mir nun kein Zufall zu sein, dass der Schlussteil des *Proslogions* geradezu leitmotivisch von zwei Zitaten durchzogen ist, mit denen Augustinus die "Vision von Ostia" eröffnet und beschliesst. Augustinus beschreibt dort die Sehnsucht nach der Schau als Suche nach der Wahrheit, die nach 1 Co 2:9 "kein Auge geschaut und kein Ohr vernommen, und das in keines Menschen Herz gedrungen ist."[39] Anselm führt dasselbe Schriftzitat in den beiden Schlusskapiteln P 25 und P 26 gleich zweimal an, behandelt es ausführlich und zeigt, dass es diese Kapitel weithin beherrscht.[40] Auf die gleiche Schriftaussage zielt aber auch schon P 17 ab und es wird klar, dass der ganze Schlussteil des *Proslogion* unter diesem Leitmotiv steht.[41] Anselm extemporiert immer wieder dieselbe Aussage. Augustinus beendet dann die "Vision von

Ostia" mit Mt 25:21: "Geh ein in die Freude deines Herrn."
Auch dieses Schriftzitat wird von Anselm zweimal ausdrücklich in den beiden Schlusskapiteln P 25 und 26 verwandt.[42]
Es ist aber ähnlich wie das andere von 1 Co 2:9 im ganzen
Schlussteil präsent, da Anselm immer wieder auf die "Freude"
der Gotteserkenntnis und auf die künftige eschatologische
Freude zu sprechen kommt. Anselm ergänzt dabei Mt 25:21 vor
allem mit Jn 16:24, das von der "vollkommenen Freude"
spricht und als Steigerung des augustinischen Schriftzitates
verstanden werden kann.[43] Der gesamte Schlussteil will in
diese "vollkommene Freude" der Schau einführen.

Ich denke, dass diese Entsprechungen nicht auf einem
Zufall beruhen. Ich vermute vielmehr, dass sich Anselm
dieser Nähe zu einigen Teilen der *Confessiones* sehr bewusst
war und aus dieser Nähe wichtige Aussagen des *Proslogions*
formulierte. Ich will nun dieser Vermutung nachgehen und
einige weitere Beobachtungen anfügen, die dem gesamten Text
des *Proslogions* in grossen Etappen folgen. Demnach fällt
auf, dass sich bei Anselm Entsprechungen vor allem zu den
klassischen und zentralen Teilen der *Confessiones* finden und
dabei wiederum besonders zu dem Text der "Vision von Ostia."

Oder ist es nicht so, dass der Einstieg des *Proslogions*
in P 1[44] unüberhörbar an jene berühmte Passage der "Vision
von Ostia" erinnert, die Augustinus wahrscheinlich selbst in
Anlehnung an Plotin so zur Sprache bringt?

> Wir sagten uns also: Brächte es einer
> dahin, dass ihm alles Getöse der Sinnlich-
> keit schwände, dass ihm schwänden alle
> Inbilder von Erde, Wasser, Luft, dass ihm
> schwände auch das Himmelsgewölbe und selbst
> die Seele gegen sich verstummte und selbst-
> vergessen über sich hinausschritte, dass ihm
> verstummten die Träume und die Kundgaben der
> Phantasie, dass jede Art Sprache, jede Art
> Zeichen und alles, was in Flüchtigkeit sich
> ereignet, ihm völlig verstummte -- wenn also
> nach diesem Wort das All in Schweigen
> versänke, weil es sein Lauschen zu dem
> erhoben hat, der es geschaffen, und wenn nun
> Er allein spräche . . .[45]

Sollte es also nur ein Zufall sein, dass die siebenfache
Aufforderungs Anselms zum Schweigen dem siebenfachen
"Schweige" (*sileat*) des Augustinus so genau korrespondiert?
Ich glaube kaum. Wie gesagt, kann ich auf Unterschiede bei
Anselm nicht näher eingehen, da es zuerst einmal wichtig

ist, Entsprechungen zu entdecken. So will ich auch im folgenden verfahren.

Es dürfte nicht zu übersehen sein, dass P 1 einige bedeutsame Leitmotive für die ganze Schrift einführt. Die wichtigsten davon haben auch in den *Confessiones* einen hervorragenden Platz. Dazu gehört das Ps-Zitat 26:8: "Ich suche Dein Antlitz; Dein Antlitz, Herr, suche ich", das in P 18 wiederholt wird und das Anselms personale Gottessuche im ganzen *Proslogion* motiviert.[46] Anselm konnte es bereits am Anfang der *Confessiones* und im wichtigen Buch IX lesen und damit sein Anliegen mit dem des Augustinus verbinden.[47] Offensichtlich ist sodann die Rede vom "unzugänglichen Licht" nach 1 Tm 6:16 ein Stichwort, das Anselm im Verlauf des *Proslogions* immer wieder meditiert, und das jeweils im Zentrum wichtiger Etappen wiedererscheint.[48] Diese Rede vom alles überstrahlenden "Licht" Gottes ist aber ein nicht weniger durchgängiges Motiv in den Berichten der drei "ekstatischen Versuche" der Schau bis hin zur "Vision von Ostia" bei Augustinus.[49] Das "unzugängliche Licht" macht bei Augustinus und Anselm gleicherweise die Dialektik der gesuchten Schau aus.

Ich habe schon früher darauf hingewiesen, dass ich im weiteren Verlauf von P 1 eine Extemporation der programmatischen Aussagen von *Confessiones* I,i,1 sehe.[50] Anselm hat die dortige Zustandsbeschreibung des auf Gott hin geschaffenen Menschen und seiner Sünde ausgeführt und bis zur Krisis des Menschen vor Gott dramatisch gestaltet. Diese Krise kommt aber bei Anselm in den dramatischen Anfragen an Gott zur Sprache: "Du, o Herr, wie lange noch?" Sie wird durch ein dreifaches "Wie lange? (*usquequo*)" und ein dreifaches "Wann? (*quando*)" unterstrichen.[51] Ist hier nicht an Augustinus' Lebens- und Glaubenskrise erinnert, wie sie in seinem letzten Glaubenskampf vor der Bekehrung unübertroffen dargestellt wird: "Und Du, Herr, wie lange noch? Wie lange noch, Herr (*usquequo*)?" -- "Wie lange noch, wie lange dieses 'Morgen, ja morgen' (*quamdiu, quamdiu*)."[52] Anselm hat die Krise des Menschen vor Gott mit der Lebenskrise des Augustinus verbunden und in Worten der *Confessiones* artikuliert. Das *Proslogion* muss wohl deutlich auf dem augustinischen Hintergrund der *Confessiones* gelesen werden.

Auf die augustinischen Quellen im Umkreis des anselmianischen Arguments von P 2-4 habe ich früher schon eingehend hingewiesen. Sie sind in den Schriften *De libero arbitrio* und *De vera religione* auszumachen. Aber sie haben auch in *Confessiones* I,i,1 ihren Anhalt. Anselms Eingangsbitte um die rechte Erkenntnis: "Gib mir, dass ich, soweit Du es nützlich weisst, einsehe . . . (*da mihi, ut, quantum*

scis expedire, intelligam)"[53] hat dort eine fast gleiche
Entsprechung: "Lass mich, Herr, es wissen und erkennen
. . . (*Da mihi, domine scire et intelligere*)"[54] und führt
hier wie dort von der "Glaubens" -- zur "Erkenntnis" -- ordnung hinüber. Neben anderen Entsprechungen will ich nur
darauf aufmerksam machen, dass sich vor diesem Hintergrund
der *Confessiones* der Wunsch nach Erkenntnis organisch aus
dem vorhergehenden Gebet ergibt. Mit anderen Worten führt
die Hochform christlicher Dialogik bei Augustinus und Anselm
nun organisch zur philosophischen Reflexion. Die Denkform
christlicher Dialogik wird sich ihres Tuns bewusst und ruft
die philosophische Vergewisserung darüber heraus. Die philosophische Antwort darauf ist bei Augustinus vor allem in
den neuplatonisch-augustinischen Teilen der "ekstatischen
Versuche" zu sehen; Anselm versucht sie in seinem "*unum
argumentum.*"

Das philosophische "Argument" Anselms führt zu einem
philosophischen Gottesbegriff. Es führt zur Erkenntnis,
"dass Gott 'ist'", zum göttlichen "Sein." Es ist voraus-
schauend zu sagen, dass diese Erkenntnis Anselms nicht
genügen wird, und dass er damit nur eine erste -- philosophische -- Stufe seiner Erkenntnisbemühung gewonnen hat.
Etwas Ähnliches ist in den "ekstatischen Versuchen" des
Augustinus zu beobachten. Was in allen Versuchen angedeutet
wird, formuliert Augustinus in der dritten Ekstase des VII.
Buches so:

> Damals aber, als ich, vom Lesen jener plato-
> nischen Bücher zur Suche nach der unstoff-
> lichen Wirklichkeit aufgefordert (wurde)
> . . . da war ich des einen gewiss, dass Du
> bist (*certus esse te*) und unendlich bist
> (*infinitum esse*), freilich nicht ausge-
> breitet über endlich oder unendlich gedach-
> ten Raum hin, und war mir auch des anderen
> gewiss, dass nur Du wirklich seiend bist
> (*vere te esse*), weil Du immerdar "ein und
> derselbe" bist (*idem ipse*), in keiner Hin-
> sicht Deines Wesens und durch keine Verän-
> derung ein anderer oder einmal anderswie,
> dass aber das übrige jegliches aus Dir her
> ist (*cetera vero ex te esse omnia*), wofür
> allein schon als sicherstes Zeugnis spricht,
> dass es ist (*quia sunt*). In diesen Fragen
> also hatte ich Gewissheit, und war doch viel
> zu schwach, in ganzer Freude Dein zu sein
> (*infirmus ad fruendum te*).[55]

Diese Stufe der Erkenntnis, dass Gott "ist," ist in allen Berichten der Schau der *Confessiones* auf mehr oder weniger deutliche Weise zu erkennen. Ich muss es mir versagen, den zitierten Text und seine Parallelen *in extenso* zu interpretieren. Ich erkenne in ihnen die Stufe wieder, die Anselm mit dem Argument erreicht hat. Auch die zusammenfassende Aussage Anselms dazu: "Und das bist Du, Herr, unser Gott (*Et hoc es tu, Domine Deus noster*)"[56] hat ihren Anhalt an dem Ausklang der ersten Ekstase des Augustinus: "Du bist es, Du mein Gott (*Tu es deus meus*)."[57]

Der zitierte Text des Augustinus und seine Parallelen machen aber auch unüberhörbar darauf aufmerksam, dass Augustinus mit dem Erreichen des "Seins selbst" (*id ipsum*) noch nicht am Ziel seiner Suche ist: Er kann noch nicht in "ganzer Freude" bei Gott sein. Der Aufstieg muss sich fortsetzen. Es ist der gleiche Sachverhalt, den wir bei Anselm in P 5 antreffen: Die philosophische Gotteserkenntnis befriedigt nur teilweise, sie fordert neue Fragen nach Gott heraus: "Was also bist Du, Herr-Gott?"[58] Wohin diese Anfragen Anselms zielen, kann wiederum ein Stück weit aus seiner augustinischen "Vorlage" geklärt werden. Das Ziel ist ohne Zweifel die Suche nach dem personalen Gott, wie sie auch bei Augustinus zu verfolgen ist.

Zuerst ist aber das bisher erreichte Ziel zu vergewissern; es ist die Grösse Gottes in sich zu betrachten. Anselm tut es in P 5-13. Augustinus scheint mir dazu in der "Vision von Ostia" folgende passende Passage zu bieten:

> Da erhoben wir uns mit heisser Inbrunst nach dem "wesenhaften Sein" (*id ipsum*) . . . Und höher stiegen wir auf im Betrachten, Bereden, Bewundern Deiner Werke, und wir gelangten zu unserer Geisteswelt. Und wir schritten hinaus über sie (*transcendimus*), um die Gefilde unerschöpflicher Fülle zu erreichen, auf denen Du Israel weidest mit der Speise der Wahrheit; und dort ist das Leben die Weisheit, die Weisheit, durch die alles Geschöpfliche entsteht, was je gewesen ist und was je sein wird; und sie selbst ist ohne Werden, sie ist, was sie gewesen ist, und also wird sie stetsfort sein; vielmehr, es gibt in ihr kein Gewesensein noch ein Künftigsein, sondern Sein allein, weil es ewig ist; denn Gewesensein und Künftigsein ist nicht ewig. Und während wir so reden von dieser ewigen Weisheit, voll Sehnsucht nach ihr, da streiften wir sie leise in

> einem vollen Schlag des Herzens; da seufzten
> wir auf, liessen dort festgebunden "die
> Erstlinge des Geistes" . . .[59]

Augustinus steigt also zur Betrachtung von Gottes "Wahrheit," "Weisheit" und "Ewigkeit" auf, die für den Menschen
überreiches Leben bedeuten. Zur Eigenschaft der "Ewigkeit"
Gottes haben wir bei Anselm in P 13 und 18-21 fast wörtliche
Parallelen. Warum Anselm in seiner Betrachtung der Eigenschaften Gottes daneben besonders auf die "*Sensibilitas*,"
die "Allmacht" und "Barmherzigkeit" Gottes eingeht, kann
Anhaltspunkte in den Anfangskapiteln der *Confessiones* haben,
wie wir schon andeuteten, oder sie wären aus anderen augustinischen Kontexten zu erheben.[60]

Anselm hat bisher Gott gesucht und etwas von ihm gefunden. P 14 fasst den gefundenen Gott zusammen: Er ist "das
Leben selbst, das Licht, die Weisheit, die Güte, die ewige
Seligkeit und die selige Seligkeit, allerorts und alle-
zeit."[61] Und doch hat er noch nicht gefunden, was er
eigentlich suchte. Er suchte ohne Frage nach dem personalen
Gott "wie Du bist" (*sicuti es*).[62] Auf eine ähnliche Weise
ist Augustinus' Suche in der "Vision von Ostia" auf "Ihn
selbst" (*ipse*) ausgerichtet und kommt nur bei Ihm zur
Erfüllung:

> Wenn also . . . das All in Schweigen ver-
> sänke, weil es sein Lauschen zu dem erhoben
> hat, der es erschaffen, und wenn nur Er
> allein (*ipse solus*) spräche, nicht durch die
> Dinge, nur durch sich selbst (*per se ipsum*),
> so dass wir sein Wort vernähmen nicht durch
> Menschenzungen, auch nicht durch Engelsstim-
> men und nicht im Donner aus Wolken, noch
> auch in Rätsel und Gleichnis, sondern Ihn
> selbst (*ipsum*) vernähmen, den wir in allem
> Geschaffenen lieben, Ihn selbst (*ipsum*) ganz
> ohne dieses, wie wir eben jetzt uns nach ihm
> reckten und in windschnell flüchtigem Gedan-
> ken an die ewige, über allen beharrende
> Weisheit rührten. . . .[63]

Aber diese Schau ist eschatologische Schau, die nur geahnt
zu werden vermag.

Warum dieses letzte Ziel der Schau vom Menschen selbst
nicht erreicht werden kann, wird schon in der ersten Ekstase
durch Augustinus deutlich erkannt. Auch dort will Augustinus wegen seiner Schwäche verzagen, Gott nicht ganz sehen zu
können. Da ruft ihm Gott von ferne seinen Offenbarungsnamen

nach Ex 3:14 zu: "Nein! Ich bin es, der Ich bin. . ."[64]
Gott muss sich ohne Zweifel selbst offenbaren, muss sich und
seinen eigenen Namen selbst kundtun, damit der Mensch seiner
gewiss sein kann. Augustinus sucht zwar nach dem personalen
Gott, dieser wird aber nur durch personale Kundgabe bekannt.
Darauf dürfte auch Anselm hinweisen, wenn er in P 22 wahrscheinlich ebenfalls Ex 3:14 in Erinnerung rufen will: "Du
allein also Herr, bist, was Du bist (*tu es qui es*)."[65] Dies
wäre auch sein Ziel, das ihm aber nur durch Gott selbst
zuteil werden kann.

P 14-16 versichern sich dieser Dialektik des gesuchten
und noch nicht gefundenen personalen Gottes. Sie bleibt für
den Menschen konstitutiv; Gott bleibt der nahe und ferne,
der gegenwärtige und abwesende Gott. Dies zeichnet seine
Person aus, dass er sich in freier und ungeschuldeter Kundgabe dem Menschen zeigt. Und doch kann sich Anselm in P 15
zu der höchst erreichbaren Gewissheit erheben, dass dieser
Gott diese Person ist ("*quiddam maius*"), die nun alles
Denken übersteigt.[66] Diese Gewissheit bleibt ihm unausrott-
bar. Sie löst die eschatologische Vorfreude aus, in die nun
der Schlussteil des *Proslogions* ausmündet. P 17 leitet
diese Freude mit dem Anklang an 1 Co 2:9 ein: "was weder
ein Auge gesehen noch ein Ohr gehört noch in eine Menschen
Herz aufgestiegen ist," das Motiv, das wir am Anfang der
"Vision von Ostia" bei Augustinus gefunden haben und das
leitmotivisch die Schlusskapitel durchzieht.[67]

Die neue Gewissheit und den eschatologischen Vorgeschmack des personalen Gottes versucht Anselm ab P 17 in
Worte zu fassen. Dazu hat F. S. Schmitt für P 17 eine sehr
nahe literarische Parallele in C X gefunden. Dort spricht
sich auch Augustinus darüber aus, was er bisher von Gott
gefunden habe:

> Was aber liebe ich, da ich dich liebe?
> Nicht die Schönheit eines Körpers noch den
> Rhythmus der bewegten Zeit; nicht den Glanz
> des Lichtes, der da so lieb den Augen; nicht
> die süssen Melodien in der Welt des Tönens
> aller Art; nicht Blumen, Salben, Spezereien-
> Wohlgeruch; nicht Manna und nicht Honig;
> nicht Leibesglieder, die köstlich sind der
> fleischlichen Umarmung: nichts von alledem
> liebe ich, wenn ich liebe meinen Gott. Und
> dennoch liebe ich ein Licht und einen Klang
> und einen Duft und eine Speise und eine
> Umarmung, wenn ich liebe meinen Gott: Licht
> und Klang und Duft und Speise und Umarmung
> meinem inneren Menschen. Dort erstrahlt

> meiner Seele, was kein Raum erfasst; dort
> erklingt, was keine Zeit entführt; dort duf-
> tet, was kein Wind verweht; dort mundet, was
> keine Sattheit vergällt; dort schmiegt sich
> an, was kein Überdruss auseinanderlöst. Das
> ist es, was ich liebe, wenn ich liebe meinen
> Gott.[68]

Bei Anselm heisst es in vielen fast gleichen Wendungen:

> Meine Seele schaut umher und sieht nicht
> deine Schönheit. Sie horcht und hört nicht
> deinen Wohlklang. Sie riecht und empfindet
> nicht deinen Wohlgeruch. Sie schmeckt und
> erkennt nicht deinen Wohlgeschmack. Sie
> tastet und fühlt nicht deine Zartheit. Denn
> Du, Herr-Gott, hast dies in Dir auf deine
> unaussprechliche Weise.[69]

Nicht nur in P 17, sondern in den weiteren Schlusskapiteln ist die angeführte Aussage Augustinus' vielfach präsent. In ihnen extemporiert Anselm geradezu diese neue dialektische Erfahrung der *Confessiones*. Anselm gewinnt durch sie eine neue "Sensibilität," den personalen Gott zu erahnen und aus-zusprechen.[70]

Der Schlussteil und vor allem das Schlusskaptiel P 26 sind sodann dominiert von der eschatologischen "Freude" des kommenden personalen Gottes und seiner Schau von "Angesicht zu Angesicht." Das *Proslogion* endet so wie die "Vision von Ostia" mit der Einstimmung in die verheissene "Freude" nach Mt 25:21. Anselm steigert sie noch mit der Bitte von Jn 16:24: "Bittet, und ihr werdet empfangen, dass eure Freude vollkommen sei."[71] Mit diesem Vorgeschmack auf die "voll-kommene Freude" klingt das *Proslogion* aus.

Anmerkungen

[1] M. Schmaus, *Die Denkform Augustins in seinem Werk De trinitate*, Bayerische Akamdemie der Wissenschaften. Philo-sophisch-Historische Klasse. Sitzungberichte; Jahr, 1962, Heft 6 (München: Verlag der Bayerischen Akademie der Wis-senschaften in Kommission bei Beck, 1962).

[2] G. Söhngen, "Denkform", *LTK* III, 230 et seq.

[3] Etwa von F. S. Schmitt, "Die wissenschaftliche Methode in Anselms *Cur deus homo*", *SB* I, 349 et seq., und

Einführungen zu den lat.-dt. Ausgaben des Monologion (Stuttgart: F. Fromman, 1964) und *Proslogion* (Stuttgart: F. Fromman, 1962).

[4] Dazu unerlässlich O. Du Roy, *L'intelligence de la foi en la Trinité selon Saint Augustin: Genèse de sa theologie trinitaire jusqu'en 391* (Paris: Etudes Augustiniennes, 1966).

[5] R. Pouchet, *La rectitudo chez Saint Anselme: Un itinéraire augustinien de l'âme à Dieu* (Paris: Etudes Augustiniennes, 1964); F. J. Thonnard, "Caractères augustiniens de la méthode philosophique de Saint Anselme," *SB* I, pp. 171 et seq. Cf. auch die wichtige Auseinandersetzung zwischen K. Flasch, "Der philosophische Ansatz des Anselm von Canterbury im *Monologion* und sein Verhältnis zum augustinischen Neuplatonismus," *AA* 2 (1970), 1 et seq., und F. S. Schmitt, "Anselm und der (Neu-)Platonismus," *AA* 1 (1969), 39 et seq.

[6] *Monologion*, Prologus: Schmitt I,8,8-14.

[7] F. S. Schmitt, Einführung, Anselm von Canturbury, *Proslogion*, (Stuttgart: F. Fromman, 1962), p. 33.

[8] R. Berlinger, *Augustinus dialogische Metaphysik* (Frankfurt: V. Klostermann, 1962), p. 15 et seq.

[9] *Soliloquia* I,i,2-6: *PL* XXXII,869-872 und *Soliloquia* II, i,1: *PL* XXXII,885.

[10] *Soliloquia* I,i,2-3: *PL* XXXII,869-871; O. du Roy, *L'intelligence*, pp. 196 et seq.

[11] *Soliloquia* I,i,4-6: *PL* XXXII,871-872; O. Du Roy, *L'intelligence*, pp. 203 et seq.

[12] *Soliloquia* I,i,4: *PL* XXXII,871.

[13] *Soliloquia* I,i,5: *PL* XXXII,872.

[14] *Soliloquia* I,i,6: *PL* XXXII,872.

[15] *Soliloquia* II,i,1: *PL* XXXII,885.

[16] *Enneads* V,i,6.

[17] *Confessiones* I,i,1:   PL XXXII,659 et seq.: "Magnus es, domine, et laudabilis valde" (Ps 144:3); "magna virtus tua et sapientiae tuae non est numerus" (Ps 146:5). Et laudare te vult homo, aliqua portio creaturae tuae, et homo circumferens mortalitatem suam circumferens testimonium peccati sui et testimonium, quia "superbis resistis." Et tamen laudare te vult homo, aliqua portio creaturae tuae. Tu excitas, ut laudare te delectet, quia fecisti nos ad te et inquietum est cor nostrum, donec requiescat in te. (Ich hoffe bald eine umfangreiche Studie und Interpretation der *Confessiones* vorlegen zu können.)

[18] Zur Interpretation von *Proslogion* I im einzelnen, cf. K. Kienzler, *Glauben und Denken bei Anselm von Canterbury* (Freiburg: Herder, 1981), pp. 50-59; 310-15.

[19] *Confessiones* I,i,1:   PL XXXII,661: Da mihi, domine, scire et intelligere . . .

[20] *Confessiones* I,ii,2:   PL XXXII,661:   Et quomodo invocabo deum meum, deum et dominum meum, quoniam utique in me ipsum eum vocabo, cum invocabo eum? Et quis locus est in me, quo veniat in me deus meus? Quo deus veniat in me, deus, qui "fecit caelum et terram?"

[21] *Proslogion* I: Schmitt I,98,11; cf. *Proslogion* XIII and XIX.

[22] Cf. *Confessiones* I,ii,2:   PL XXXII,661; I,iv,4:   PL XXXII,662; I,v,5:   PL XXXII,663.

[23] *Confessiones* I,ii,2: PL XXII,661: Non ergo essem, deus meus, non omnino essem, nisi esses in me. An potius non essem, nisi essem in te . . .

[24] *Confessiones* I,iv,4: PL XXXII,662:   Quid es ergo, deus meus? Quid, rogo, nisi dominus meus?

[25] *Confessiones* I,iv,4:   PL XXXII,662: Summe, optime, potentissime, omnipotentissime, misericordissime et iustissime, secretissime et praesentissime, pulcherrime et fortissime, stabilis et incomprehensibilis, inmutabilis, mutans omnia . . .

[26] *Confessiones* I,v,5:   PL XXXII,663: Quid mihi es? Miserere, ut loquar.

[27] *Confessiones* I,iv,4: *PL* XXXII,663: Et quid diximus, deus meus, vita mea, dulcedo mea sancta . . . "Dic animae meae: salus tua ego sum." Siehe auch *Confessiones* I,v,5: *PL* XXXII,663. Cf. *Proslogion* XIV: Schmitt I,111,6-15 und *Proslogion* XVII: Schmitt I,113,6-16.

[28] O. du Roy, *L'intelligence*, pp. 245-46, nn. 2-5; A. Beckaert, "Justification platonicienne de l'argument a priori," *SB* I, 185 et seq.; R. Pouchet, "La rectitudo," pp. 70 et seq.; Th. A. Audet, "Une source augustinienne de l'argument de Saint Anselm," in *Etienne Gilson, Philosophe de la Chrétienté*, ed. J. Maritain et alii, Rencontres, t. 30 (Paris: Editions du Cerf, 1949), pp. 105 et seq.

[29] Cf. O. du Roy, *L'intelligence*, pp. 236 et seq.

[30] *De libero arbitrio* II,v,13: *CSEL* LXXIV,40; II,xlvii, 180: *CSEL* LXXIV,82) und *Proslogion* II: Schmitt I,101,6-7; *Proslogion* III: Schmitt I,103,9-11. Siehe n. 25.

[31] *De libero arbitrio* II,vi,17: *CSEL* LXXIV,41, und *Proslogion* I: Schmitt I,100,19. Siehe n. 25.

[32] *De libero arbitrio* II,xiv,54-56: *CSEL* LXXIV,51-52: A.: Quid si aliquid invenire potuerimus quod non solum esse non dubites, sed etiam ipsa nostra ratione praestantius? Dubitasne illud quidquid est deum dicere. E.: Non continuo, si quid melius quam id quod in mea natura optimum est invenire potuero, deum esse dixerim. Non enim mihi placet deum appellare quo mea ratio est inferior, sed quo est nullus superior. . . . Hunc plane fatebor deum quo nihil superius esse constiterit.

[33] *Responsio Editoris* V: Schmitt I,135,8-23.

[34] Cf. O. du Roy, *L'intelligence*, pp. 309-17.

[35] *De vera religione* XXIV,45: *PL* XXXIV,141.

[36] *De vera religione* XXXIX,72: *PL* XXXIV,154: Noli foras ire, in te ipsum redi; in interiore homine habitat veritas, et si tuam naturam mutabilem inveneris, transcende et te ipsum. Sed memento cum te transcendis, ratiocinantem animam te transcendere. Illuc ergo tende unde ipsum lumen rationis accenditur. Quo enim pervenit omnis bonus ratiocinator nisi ad veritatem? Cum ad se ipsam veritas non utique ratiocinando perveniat, sed quod ratiocinantes appetunt, ipsa sit. Vide ibi convenientiam qua superior esse non possit, et ipse

convenit cum ea. Confitere te non esse quod ipsa est;
siquidem se ipsa non quaerit, tu autem ad eam quaerendo venisti, non locorum spatio sed mentis affectu, ut ipse interior homo. . .

[37] Zum folgenden, siehe K. Kienzler, "Glauben und Denk-
en," pp. 255-95; 303-40.

[38] P. Courcelle, *Recherches sur les Confessions de Saint
Augustin* (Paris: E. de Boccard, 1950), pp. 157-67; 222-26;
P. Henry, *La vision d'Ostie* (Paris: J. Vrin, 1938); A.
Mandouze,"L'exstase d'Ostie: Possibilités et limites de la
méthode des parallèles textuels," *Augustinus Magister*
(Paris: Etudes Augustiniennes, 1954), pp. 67 et seq. -- Ich
hoffe bald in einer langeren Studie und Interpretation der
Confessiones diese Texte ausführlich behandeln zu können.

[39] *Confessiones* IX,x,23:   *PL* XXXII,774: Nec oculus vidit
nec auris audivit nec in cor hominis ascendit.

[40] *Proslogion* XXV: Schmitt I,118,14, und *Proslogion*
XXVI: Schmitt I,121,7-8.

[41] *Proslogion* XVII: Schmitt I,113,8-15.

[42] Intra in gaudium domini tui. Siehe *Confessiones*
IX,x,25:   *PL* XXXII,775, und *Proslogion* XXV: Schmitt
I,119,12-13; *Proslogion* XXVI: Schmitt I,121,6.

[43] *Proslogion* XXVI: Schmitt I,120-22.

[44] Dazu P. Henry, "Die Vision zu Ostia," *Zum Augustin-
Gespräch der Gegenwart*, ed. C. Andresen (Darmstadt: Wissenschaftliche Buchgesellschaft, 1962), pp. 204 et seq. -- Zur
folgenden Interpretation des *Proslogions*, siehe K. Kienzler,
"Glauben und Denken" pp. 303-40.

[45] *Confessiones* IX,x,25: *PL* XXXII,774: Dicebamus ergo:
Si cui sileat tumultus carnis, sileant phantasiae terrae et
aquarum et aeris, sileant et poli et ipsa sibi anima sileat
et transeat se non se cogitando, sileant somnia et imagina-
riae revelationes, omnis lingua et omne signum et quidquid
transeundo fit si cui sileat omnino -- his dictis si iam
taceant, quoniam erexerunt aurem in eum, qui fecit ea, et
loquatur ipse solus . . . Cf. *Proslogion* I: Schmitt
I,97,4-10.

⁴⁶ *Proslogion* I: Schmitt I,97,9-10: Quaero vultum tuum, vultum tuum, domine, requiro. Cf. *Proslogion* XVIII: Schmitt I,114,9-10.

⁴⁷ *Confessiones* I,xviii,28: PL XXXII,673; cf. *Confessiones* IX,iii,6: PL XXXII,766.

⁴⁸ *Proslogion* I: Schmitt I,98,4; *Proslogion* IX: Schmitt I,107,4-5; *Proslogion* XVI: Schmitt I,112,20.

⁴⁹ Cf. *Confessiones* VII,x,16: PL XXXII,742; VII,xvii,23: PL XXXII,744; IX,x,24: PL XXXII,774.

⁵⁰ Siehe p. 351 et seq.

⁵¹ *Proslogion* I: Schmitt I,99,15-18: Et o tu, domine, usquequo? Usquequo, domine oblivisceris nos, usquequo avertis faciem tuam a nobis? Quando respicies et exaudis nos? Quando illuminabis oculos nostros et ostende nobis faciem tuam? Quando restitues te nobis.

⁵² *Confessiones* VIII,xii,28: PL XXXII, 762: Et tu, domine, usquequo, domine, irasceris in finem. . . . Quamdiu, quamdiu . . .

⁵³ *Proslogion* II: Schmitt I,101,3-4.

⁵⁴ *Confessiones* I,i,1: PL XXXII,661.

⁵⁵ *Confessiones* VII, xx,26: PL XXXII,746-47: Sed tunc lectis Platonicorum illis libris posteaquam inde admonitus quaerere incorpoream veritatem . . . certus esse te et infinitum esse nec tamen per locos finitos infinitosve diffundi et vere te esse, qui semper "idem ipse" esses, ex nulla parte nulloque motu alter aut aliter, cetera vero ex te esse omnia, hoc solo firmissimo documento, quia sunt, certus quidem in istis eram, nimis tamen, infirmus ad fruendum te.

⁵⁶ *Proslogion* III: Schmitt I,103,3.

⁵⁷ *Confessiones* VII,x,16: PL XXXII,742.

⁵⁸ *Proslogion* V: Schmitt I,104,11.

⁵⁹ *Confessiones* IX,x,24: PL XXXII,774: . . . erigentes nos ardentiore affectu in "id ipsum" . . . Et adhuc ascendebamus interius cogitando et loquendo et mirando opera tua et venimus in mentes nostras et transcendimus eas, ut attin-

geremus regionem ubertatis indeficientis, ubi pascis Israel
in aeternum veritatis pabulo, et ibi vita sapientia est, per
quam fiunt omnia ista, et quae fuerunt et quae futura sunt,
et ipsa non fit, sed sic est, ut fuit, et sic erit semper.
Quin potius fuisse et futurum esse non est in ea, sed esse
solum, quoniam aeterna est: nam fuisse et futurum esse non
est aeternum. Et dum loquimur et inhiamus illi, attigimus
eam modice toto ictu cordis; et suspiravimus et reliquimus
ibi religatas "primitias spiritus" . . .

[60]Cf. *Proslogion* XIII: Schmitt I,110,12-18; *Proslogion*
XIX: Schmitt I,115,6-15; *Proslogion* XX: Schmitt I,115-16.
Siehe oben p. 355.

[61]*Proslogion* XIV: Schmitt I,111,10-11: Et hoc esse
ipsam vitam, lucem, sapientiam, bonitatem, aeternam beatitu-
dinem et beatam aeternitatem; et hoc esse ubique et semper.

[62]*Proslogion* XIV: Schmitt I,111,21.

[63]*Confessiones* IX,x,25:   *PL* XXXII,774: His dictis si
iam taceant, quoniam erexerunt aurem in eum, qui fecit ea,
et loquator ipse solus non per ea, sed per se ipsum, ut
audiamus verbum eius, non per linguam carnis neque per vocem
angeli nec per sonitum nubis nec per aenigma similitudinis,
sed ipsum, quem in his amamus, ipsum sine his audiamus,
sicut nunc extendimus nos et rapida cogitatione attigimus
aeternam sapientiam super omnia manentem . . .

[64]*Confessiones* VII,x,16: *PL* XXXII,742: Immo vero ego
sum qui sum.

[65]*Proslogion* XXII: Schmitt I,116,14: Quod solus sit,
quod est et qui est.

[66]*Proslogion* XV: Schmitt I,112,14-15: Sed es quiddam
maius quam cogitari possit.

[67]Siehe p. 365.

[68]*Confessiones* X,vi,8:   *PL* XXXII,782 et seq.: Quid
autem amo, cum te amo? Non speciem corporis nec decus temporis, non candorem lucis ecce istum amicum solis, non
dulces melodias cantilenarum omnimodarum, non florum et
unguentorum et aromatum suaviolentiam, non manna et vella,
non membra acceptabilia carnis amplexibus: non haec amo,
cum amo deum meum. Et tamen amo quandam lucem et quandam
vocem et quandam odorem et quendam cibum et   quendam

amplexum, cum amo deum meum, lucem,   vocem,   odorem,   cibum,
amplexum interioris hominis mei, ubi fulget animae meae,
quod non capit locus, et ubi sonat, quod non rapit tempus,
et ubi olet, quod non spargit flatus, et ubi sapit, quod non
minuit edacitas, et ubi haeret, quod non divellit satietas.
Hoc est quod amo, cum deum meum amo.

⁶⁹*Proslogion* XVII: Schmitt   I,113,9-13: Circumspicit
enim, et non videt pulchritudinem tuam. Auscultat, et non
audit harmoniam tuam. Olfacit, et non percipit odorem tuum.
Gustat, et non cognoscit saporem tuum. Palpat, et non sen-
tit lenitatem tuam. Habes enim haec, domine deus, in te tuo
ineffabili modo. . . Cf. *Proslogion* XXV: Schmitt
I,118-19.

⁷⁰Siehe K. Kienzler, "Glauben und Denken," p. 335-41.

⁷¹Siehe p. 365.

Relevanz und Dimension
eines erkenntnis-kritischen Philosophierens
Die Artikulation christlichen Glaubens
im Gegenüber zur Position des Nicht-Glaubens
bei Augustinus und Anselm

Adolf Schurr

Was impliziert die Konzeption eines *erkenntnis-kriti-schen* Philosophierens? Wie ist sie zu bestimmen? In welcher Weise wird sie von Augustinus und Anselm so gefasst, dass auch in der nachfolgenden Geschichte philosophischen Denkens ein erkenntnis-kritisches Philosophieren nicht anders verfahren konnte?

Was wir mit unseren Ausführungen aufzuzeigen versuchen, ist die heute nicht unbestrittene These, dass sich der Begriff der Philosophie unter erkenntnis-kritischen Aspekten wissenschaftstheoretisch eindeutig bestimmen lässt, wobei als wissenschafts-konstitutiv folgende Momente angesprochen sind: Legitimation, Voraussetzungen, methodische Verfahrensweise und Fragedimension einer philosophischen Reflexion.

Glaube und Wissen

Wenn wir zu Anfang unserer Überlegungen das Verhältnis von Glaube und Wissen thematisieren, so könnte es scheinen, dass wir uns auf den Ursprung abendländischer Philosophie beziehen: das, was lediglich geglaubt wurde (was bloss als *doxa* gegeben war), sollte daraufhin überprüft werden, ob und inwieweit es sich vermittelst einer *philosophischen* Reflexion als Wissen (als *episteme*) ausweisen liesse.

Wenn wir die Verhältnisbestimmung von Glaube und Wissen bei Augustinus und Anselm aufgreifen, so sehen wir uns vor eine völlig andere Situation gestellt: Glauben wird nicht verstanden also blosses *Meinen* im Gegenüber zur Möglichkeit von *Wissen*. Der Glaube begreift sich als Position, die als *religiöse Glaubens*position für sich in Anspruch nimmt, den *einzig wahren* menschlichen Existenzvollzug zu verwirklichen.

Wie versteht sich christlicher Glaube unter dem Aspekt von Wissen? Ist christlich-religiöser Glaube ein irrationaler Akt -- oder ist er im Medium von Wissen aufschliessbar? Um die gestellten Fragen zu beantworten, muss erstens das Selbstverständnis christlichen Glaubens präzisiert werden; zweitens muss bestimmt werden, was unter Wissen im

strengen Sinne zu verstehen ist; drittens muss für unsere
gesamte Untersuchung zwischen nicht-empirischem Wissen und
Erfahrungserkenntnis unterschieden werden.

Das Selbstverständnis christlichen Glaubens

Unter systematischen Aspekten gibt es nur zwei Möglichkeiten: *Entweder* ist christlicher Glaube der Vernunft
in keinerlei Weise zugänglich; *oder* der christliche Glaube
ist -- zumindest partiell -- der Vernunft erschliessbar. Im
ersten Fall müsste der religiöse Glaube in der Tat zu einem
völlig irrationalen Akt erklärt werden. Es bestünde keinerlei Möglichkeit, mit Hilfe rationalen Denkens auf ihn zu-
rückzukommen. Im zweiten Fall wäre der religiöse Glaube als
Akt eines menschlichen Vernunftwesens mit der Frage angeh-
bar, wie er seinen *Wahrheitsanspruch* begründen könne.
Im Hinblick auf ein mögliches Selbstverständnis christlichen Glaubens haben wir eine fundamentale Alternative aufgestellt. Wie ist sie zu entscheiden? Der Versuch, den
christlichen Glauben als vernunftlosen irrationalen Akt zu
betrachten, scheitert ganz einfach an dem phänomenalen Tatbestand, dass keinem Glaubenden abgesprochen werden kann,
dass er weiss, *woran* er glaubt und *dass* er glaubt. D. h.:
Der Glaubensakt als *Glaubens*akt kann nicht anders gedacht
werden, als dass er sich seiner selbst bewusst ist.
Zu erörtern ist daher nur die zweite Möglichkeit der
angezeigten Alternative: Christlicher Glaube ist der Vernunft nicht prinzipiell unaufschliessbar. Die Offenheit
christlichen Glaubens gegenüber der Vernunft wird von Anselm
in der Formel festgeschrieben: *credo ut intelligam*[1] -- ich
glaube, um einzusehen. Mit einem solchen Programm wird von
seiten christlichen Glaubens keine Vorentscheidung gegenüber
einer einholenden Möglichkeit von Vernunfterkenntnis getroffen. Das Intendierte hat zwei Aspekte:

(1) Der religiöse Glaube soll als Glaube nicht nur
behauptet, sondern als mögliche Vernunfterkenntnis *ausgewiesen* werden;

(2) die religiöse Glaubensposition soll solcherweise
reflektiert werden, dass sie selbst gegenüber einer Position des Nicht-Glaubens philosophisch-argumentativ vertret-
bar ist.

So sprach Anselm:

> Obschon nämlich [die Ungläubigen] nach
> Gründen fragen, weil sie nicht glauben, wir
> dagegen, weil wir glauben, so ist es doch
> ein und dasselbe, wonach wir forschen.[2]

Lässt sich eine solche Voraussetzung begründen, dass die *Fragestellung* einer philosophischen Reflexion sowohl für den Glaubenden als auch für den Nicht-Glaubenden nur ein und dieselbe sein könne? Was wird unter dem Akt des Glaubens begriffen, der von Anselm als *conditio sine qua non* der Vernunfteinsicht veranschlagt wird?

Unterstellen wir, dass sich Anselm im Hinblick auf die Gesamtkonzeption seines reflexiven Bemühens in keine prinzipielle Widersprüchlichkeit verwickelt, so kann dem Glauben nur die Bedeutung einer *notwendigen* Bedingung für *jede* Vernunfteinsicht zuerkannt werden. Nur in diesem Fall könnte davon abgesehen werden, ob von der religiösen Position des Glaubens oder Unglaubens aus reflektiert wird.

Was begreift Anselm unter dem *credere* als notwendiger Bedingung jeder Vernunft-Einsicht? Die entscheidenden Punkte könnten nicht klarer und deutlicher gefasst werden als sie von Anselm und zuvor schon von Augustinus ausgesprochen werden. Was den Menschen als Menschen auszeichnet, bezeichnet *Augustinus* als Möglichkeit des *Fragen*-könnens. Aufgrund ihrer Vernunft-Begabtheit (*iudex ratio*) "vermögen die Menschen zu fragen"[3] und ihr Fragen zu beantworten. *Anselm* präzisiert diese generellste Voraussetzung jeglicher Vernunfteinsicht: "kein Mensch kann gedacht werden ohne Vernunft,"[4] d. h. "Jeder Mensch ist notwendig vernunftbegabt."[5] -- Dieser Sachverhalt "ist so evident, dass es Unverstand wäre, dafür einen Nachweis zu führen."[6]

Aus diesen allerersten Verweisungen geht klar hervor, worin die Möglichkeit einer Argumentation gesetzt wird, in der Glauben und Nicht-Glauben übereinkommen: in die schlechthin vorauszusetzende Vernunftbegabtheit des Menschen und in einen Impetus des Fragens.

Es ist ohne weiteres einsichtig, dass alles, wonach nicht gefragt wird, einer philosophischen Reflexion notwendigerweise verschlossen bleiben muss. Eine Antwort kann nur erwartet werden, *wenn* und insofern es gefragt wird. Wird eine Problematik nicht angegangen, wie sollte sich in diesem Fall eine Problemlösung einfinden können? Wie könnte darüber entschieden werden, ob die Lösung einer bestimmten Problematik möglich ist oder nicht?

Aufgrund der Vernunftbegabtheit gehen *Augustinus* und *Anselm* gleicherweise von der Voraussetzung aus, dass dem

Menschen ein wesentliches und existentiell-relevantes Fragen
nicht bereits anfänglich verschlossen sein kann.

Worauf erstreckt sich ein Fragen, das den menschlichen
Selbstvollzug ohne Einschränkung thematisiert? Was wird
unter dem *credere* als notwendiger Bedingung jeglicher Vernunft-Einsicht reflexiv angegangen? Es könnte scheinen,
dass es sich lediglich um die Möglichkeit von Einsicht in
theoretische Sachverhalte handeln könnte. Aber eine solche
Annahme wäre weit gefehlt. Beider Äusserungen sind unmissverständlich: *Augustinus* stellt die These auf: nur "wer
die Wahrheit verwirklicht (*facit*), kommt zum Licht"[7] -- zu
einer Vernunfteinsicht, die über ein bloss theoretisches
Untersuchungsfeld hinausreicht.

Mit einer solchen These ist eine Konzeption von Wahr-
heits-Erkenntnis angezeigt, die von *Anselm* (in seiner
Schrift *De veritate*) unter systematischen Aspekten entwickelt wird. Die Überlegungen Anselms thematisieren und
analysieren eine strukturelle Seinsverfasstheit, ohne die
sich kein Selbstvollzug des Bewusstseins artikulieren
könnte: das *Urteil* als elementarste Artikulation menschlicher Geisttätigkeit. In seiner Analyse führt Anselm den
Nachweis, dass kein Urteil gedacht werden kann ohne implikativen *Wahrheitsanspruch* seines Behauptens. Die Wahrheits-
Behauptung kann aus *keinem* Urteil eliminiert werden, ohne es
als Urteil aufzuheben, und zwar nicht nur das *theoretische*
Urteil, das bezeichnet *was ist*, sondern ebenso und vor allem
das *praktische* Urteil, das bezeichnet *was sein soll*.

Auf *die* Dimension der Wahrheitskonzeption, die Anselm
angeht, wird von ihm selbst ausdrücklich verwiesen:

> Alle nämlich sprechen von der Wahrheit der
> Bezeichnung; die Wahrheit aber, welche in
> [jedem vernünftigen Handeln] liegt, bedenken
> nur wenige.[8]

In beiden Fällen, sowohl im theoretischen als auch im prak-
tischen Urteil, wird notwendigerweise behauptet, dass etwas
entweder in Wahrheit *ist* oder in Wahrheit *sein soll* -- *oder*
in Wahrheit *nicht ist* oder in Wahrheit *nicht sein soll*.

Den *konstitutiven* Wahrheits-*Anspruch* sowohl für das
theoretische als auch insbesondere für das praktische Urteil
fasst Anselm in die These: "Dass jede Tat entweder Wahres
oder Falsches behauptet."[9] Der notwendige Wahrheits-
Anspruch des Urteils impliziert aber nicht schon die *Verwirklichung* des Anspruchs -- weder im Denken und Sprechen
noch im Wollen und Handeln. Die Realisation des konstitutiven Wahrheitsanspruchs jeder Urteils-Behauptung ist
durch *Freiheit* vermittelt.

Beide Aspekte der Urteilsbehauptung werden von Anselm klar unterschieden: Der Wahrheits-*Anspruch* des Urteils erfolgt aus Notwendigkeit (*ex necessitate*), da er eine strukturelle Seinsverfasstheit indiziert; die *Verwirklichung* des Wahrheitsanspruchs dagegen kann nicht aus Notwendigkeit (*non ex necessitate*) erfolgen, so gewiss als Grundbestimmung des Menschen als Vernunftwesen nur eine Selbstbestimmbarkeit durch *Freiheit* gedacht werden kann.[10]

Was ergibt sich aus dem angezeigten Resultat einer Analyse des Urteils als elementarster Artikulation des Vernunftwesens? Muss der Wahrheits-Anspruch für den gesamten Selbstvollzug endlichen Bewusstseins als strukturelle Seinsverfasstheit fraglos konzediert werden, so kann sich keine Freiheit aus diesem Anspruch selbst entlassen. Jede endliche Freiheit sieht sich aufgrund des *implikativen* Wahrheitsanspruches seines Urteilens aufgefordert, Wahrheit zu verwirklichen. In Anselms Formulierungen heisst das: an die Wahrheit "allein muss jeder Mensch glauben, weil sie das einzige Ziel ist, daraufhin er sich in all seinem Denken und Tun . . . zu richten hat."[11]

Wird der ganzheitliche Akt des Bewusstseins in seiner implikativen Bezogenheit auf Wahrheit als *Glaube* (als *credere*) gefasst, so kann einem so verstandenen Glaubensbegriff keine andere als eine *konstitutive* Bedeutung zugesprochen werden. Anselm begründet eine solche konstitutive Bedeutung seines Glaubensbegriffes für jeden menschlichen Existenzvollzug mit einer präzis gefassten stringenten Argumentation:

> Wer nicht glaubt, wird nicht einsehen. Denn
> wer nicht glaubt, wird nicht erfahren, und
> wer nicht erfährt, wird nicht erkennen.[12]

Mit Anselms Argumentation wird auf einen Sachverhalt verwiesen, der einer philosophischen Reflexion vorausliegt. Ohne selbsttätige Verwirklichung des Wahrheitsanspruches ist eine Erkenntnis von Wahrem undenkbar. Ein solcher Sachverhalt besitzt eine unbestreitbare Gültigkeit, sowohl führ die Position religiösen Glaubens als auch für die Position des Unglaubens. -- Worin aber besteht das zu verwirklichende Wahre jedes menschlichen Existenzvollzugs?

Der religiöse Glaube erhebt -- in Bezug auf seine Glaubens inhalte -- den Anspruch, auf die gestellte Frage nicht irgendeine Antwort geben zu können, sondern die einzig mögliche Antwort zu geben. Dem religiösen Glauben erwächst die Antwort auf die Frage einer letztwahren Sinngebung menschlichen Daseins aus der *metaphysischen Dimension* seines Glaubens*inhalts*.

Mit dem *Inhalt* religiösen Glaubens sieht sich die Reflexion auf eine Fragedimension verwiesen, die eine *philosophische* Reflexion nicht einfach ausklammern kann, der aber auch nicht mehr als eine *regulative* Bedeutung zuerkannt werden kann. Würde der Inhalt religiösen Glaubens nicht als blosse Vorgabe für die Fragestellung, sondern als Argumentationsbasis veranschlagt, so wäre eine solche Reflexion nicht Philosophie sondern Theologie. Wenn es um das wahre Selbstverständnis menschlichen Daseins geht, so stellt sich die wissenschaftstheoretische Frage nach der Basis und dem Medium einer philosophischen Argumentation.

Der Begriff philsophischer Erkenntnis

Unsere bisherigen Überlegungen versuchten den Nachweis zu führen, dass der religiöse Glaube nicht als vernunftloser oder gar als widervernünftiger Akt gedacht werden kann. Niemand wird bestreiten können, dass religiöser Glaube in seiner konstitutiven Bedeutung ein Streben nach Wahrheit (ein *tendere in veritatem*) impliziert. Um aber die Frage entscheiden zu können, ob die metaphysische Dimension des Glauben*inhalts* Gegenstand einer philsophischen Reflexion sein kann, bedarf es einer Bestimmung des vorausgesetzten Erkenntnisbegriffes. Der *Inhalt* christlichen Glaubens beruht auf *Autorität* -- auf der Autorität der Schriften des Neuen Testaments und deren Interpretation in der abendländischen Tradition.

Erwartung und Erkenntnisweise einer philosophischen Reflexion formuliert Augustinus in einer höchst bemerkenswerten Weise:

> All das, was wir im Anschluss an die Autorität geglaubt haben, wird einerseits so erkannt, dass es uns mit voller Gewissheit einleuchtet, anderseits gewinnen wir die Einsicht von seiner Möglichkeit, ja seinem Soseinmüssen.[13]

Wie ist die Erkenntnis nicht nur der Möglichkeit, sondern der Notwendigkeit eines Sachverhalts zu bestimmen, um dessen apodiktische Gewissheit behaupten zu können?

Eine Erklärung über die Offenheit christlichen Glaubens gegenüber dem menschlichen Erkenntnisvermögen findet sich im ersten Satz des philosophischen Erstlingswerkes von Anselm, in dessen *Monologion*:

Ich meine, dass jemand sich selbst, wenn er
auch nur von mittelmäsiger Begabung ist, von
dem, [was wir glauben] durch blosse Vernunft
überzeugen kann. [Anselm fügt jedoch hinzu]
Vermag man zu verstehen, so danke man Gott;
vermag man es nicht, so setze man sich nicht
Hörner auf um wegzustossen, sondern neige
verehrend sein Haupt.[14]

Die Möglichkeit einer reflexiven Erhellung des Glau-
bensinhalts gilt Anselm nicht als intellektuelle Spielerei.
Im ersten Kapitel seines letzten Hauptwerkes *Cur deus homo*
verweist Anselm auf den Beweggrund, aus dem sein Frage ent-
sprungen ist: "es scheint mir eine Nachlässigkeit, wenn wir
. . . uns nicht zu verstehen bemühen, was wir glauben."[15]
Die Legitimation des Postulats einer philosophischen Reflexion auf die Glaubensposition resultiert aus Anselms Wahr-
heitsbegriff: "Keine Sache wird geliebt ohne Bewusstsein
oder Erkenntnis von ihr."[16]

Von Anselm wird ein Sachverhalt angesprochen, der als
phänomenaler Tatbestand verifizierbar ist: Wirkliche Liebe
setzt das Bewusstsein und die Erkenntnis dessen voraus, was
geliebt wird. Anselm reflektiert auf den Tatbestand eines
positiven Verhaltens zur Wahrheit und generalisiert ihn mit
einfachen Worten:

Es hat jemand die Absicht im Herzen, die
Wahrheit festzuhalten, weil er erkannt hat,
dass die Wahrheit lieben das Richtige ist.[17]

Kann keinem menschlichen Selbstvollzug die Möglichkeit
von Erkenntnis abgesprochen werden, auch nict die Erkenntnis, welche Bedeutung der Erkenntnis überhaupt für den
Selbstvollzug eines Vernunftwesens zuerkannt werden muss, so
stellen sich zwei Fragen:

(1) Weshalb bedarf es eines zusätzlichen philosophischen
Erkenntnisbemühens, um den religiösen Glauben reflexiv ein-
zuholen?

(2) Wie ist der Begriff von Erkenntnis zu bestimmen, der
einer erkenntnis-kritischen Konzeption von Philosophie zu-
grundegelegt werden muss?

Ist dem Menschen als Vernunftwesen Erkenntnis möglich,
so impliziert ein solches Vermögen nicht schon dessen Verwirklichung in dem Sinne, dass bereits erkannt wäre, was den

wahren Selbstvollzug endlichen Bewusstseins ausmacht und
worin er gründet. Die Beantwortung einer solch fundamen-
talen Fragestellung ist zwar dem religiösen Glauben vorge-
geben; sie im Medium von Erkenntnis auszuweisen, bedarf aber
in jedem Fall -- sowohl für den Glaubenden als auch für den
Nicht-Glaubenden -- einer sich auf den *gesamten* Selbstvollzug erstreckenden Reflexion.

Nur dann, wenn angenommen werden muss, das Erkenntnisvermögen den unmittelbaren Selbstvollzug nicht in der angezeigten Weise reflektiert bzw. ihn auszuweisen vermag, kann
das Faktum einer zusätzlichen philosophischen Reflexion
überhaupt erklärt werden. Ihre Aufgabe kann daher nur darin
bestehen, fundamentale Fragestellungen aufzugreifen und sie
einer möglichen Antwort zuzuführen oder erklären zu müssen,
dass sie im Medium von Erkenntnis nicht beantwortbar sind.

Das Faktum des Unzureichens einer dem unmittelbaren
Lebensvollzug inhärenten Reflexion benennt Anselm ausdrücklich als Anlass seines philosophischen Erkenntnisbemühens; er versteht es als Erörterung dessen, "was er
zuvor nicht beachtet hatte."[18] Mit einem solchen Hinweis
ist eine *radikale* Fragestellung angezeigt. Die Möglichkeit
von Erkenntnis soll nicht bloss angehoben bleiben, sondern
vermittelst reinen Denkens (*sola cogitatione*) durchvollzogen
werden. Wie konzipiert Anselm von seiner christlichen
Glaubensposition aus den Begriff einer philosophischen
Erkenntnis?

Die wissenschaftstheoretische Konzeption einer philosophischen Argumentation wird von Anselm im Prolog seines
Erstlingswerkes unmissverständlich ausgesprochen: Die Argumentation soll sich *erstens* nicht auf die "Autorität der
Heiligen Schrift" (auf die *auctoritas scripturae*) stützen;
sie soll *zweitens* ausschliesslich auf der "Notwendigkeit der
Vernunftüberlegung" (der *rationis necessitas*) beruhen, um
einzig und allein dadurch die "Einsichtigkeit der Wahrheit"
(eine *veritatis claritas*) offenkundig zu machen.

Auf die Intention seiner beiden Frühschriften des *Mono-
logions* und des *Proslogions* kommt Anselm später selbst
zurück und bezeichnet sie als Antwortversuch auf die Frage,

> ob das, was wir im Glauben festhalten . . .
> durch notwendige Vernunftgründe ohne Auto-
> rität der Heiligen Schrift erwiesen werden
> könne.[19]

Die angezeigte Konzeption seines Erkenntnisbemühens hat
Anselm bis zu seinem späten Hauptwerk *Cur deus homo* durch-
halten. In dessen Vorrede wird erklärt, in der Fragebeantwortung "mit Beiseitesetzung Christi, so, als ob niemals

etwas von ihm gewesen wäre, mit zwingenden Vernunft-
gründen"[20] zu argumentieren.

Aus den Quellenverweisungen lässt sich deutlich ablesen,
wie ein philosophisches Erkenntnisbemühen verstanden wird.
Nicht nur, dass Anselm die Autorität der Schrift und mit ihr
die christliche Offenbarung ausklammert; ist das reine
Denken mit dem Kriterium der Denknotwendigkeit einziges
Kriterium einer philosophischen Argumentation, so wird
zwangsläufig jegliche Berufung auf Erfahrung ausgeklammert.
Als philosophische Erkenntnis wird nur reine Vernunfter-
kenntnis zugelassen.

Damit stellt Anselm sein Erkenntnisbemühen auf eine
prinzipiell jedem zugänglich Basis, sei er nun religiös
gläubig oder nicht. Bei einem so klar und eindeutig artiku-
lierten Begriff eines *philosophischen* Erkenntnisbemühens
muss es völlig unverständlich bleiben, wenn die Frage gestellt wird:

> Gibt [Anselm] sich nicht einer Illusion hin,
> wenn er meint, seine 'Beweise' könnten von
> denen, die *quaerunt, quia non credunt*, über-
> haupt verstanden werden. . . . An was für
> Ungläubige mag [Anselm] gedacht haben, die
> es sich gefallen liessen, in dieser Weise
> *nolens volens* auch nur in den Raum der
> Theologie versetzt zu werden?[21]

Entgegen eines solchen Vorbehalts zu der von Anselm kon-
zipierten Argumentationsweise kann nur gesagt werden: Wo
immer der Wille zur Wahrheit vorliegt, ist die Voraussetzung
gegeben, dass jemand -- wie es Anselm versucht -- "mit sich
durch blosses Nachdenken das erörtert und erforscht, was er
zuvor nicht beachtet hatte."[22]

Die Legitimation
eines philosophischen Erkenntnisbemühens

Wird in einer philosophischen Reflexion von einer radikalen Fragestellung ausgegangen, so kann sie sich selbst in
ihrem Fragen nicht auslassen. Warum wird der Versuch unter-
nommen, grundlegende Sachverhalte im Medium von Erkenntnis
auszuweisen? Liegt in einer blossen Möglichkeit auch schon
die Legitimation deren Realisation?

Wird die Frage nach der Legitimation der Verwirklichung
einer dem Menschen offenstehenden Möglichkeit in dieser
abstrakten Allgemeinheit gestellt, so ist sie nicht beantwortbar; denn warum sollte etwas allein schon deshalb, weil

es möglich ist, verwirklicht werden? Eine *legitimierbare*
Realisation eines Vermögens muss auf eine Begründung verweisen können, aus der ersichtlich wird, *dass* und *warum* sie
sein soll. Nur ein *wertendes* Urteil vermag darüber zu entscheiden, ob eine offenstehende Möglichkeit ergriffen oder
verworfen, ob ein Vermögen verwirklicht oder nicht verwir-
licht werden soll.

Wenn *Freiheit* als Grundbestimmung menschlichen Selbstvollzugs veranschlagt wird, so kann ein solches Vermögen
erstens nur so gedacht werden, dass es über ihm offenstehende Möglichkeiten entscheiden kann und durch den wirk-
lichen Selbstvollzug schon immer entschieden hat. Die Realisation eines Vermögens zu *freier* Selbstbestimmung kann
zweitens nur so gedacht werden, dass es sich nicht blind
vollzieht, sondern um sein Sich-Entscheiden weiss; denn ein
freier Wille kann sich nur dadurch artikulieren, dass er
weiss, *dass* er will, *was* er will und *warum* er will -- ein
Sachverhalt, der von Anselm klar erkannt wird:

> jeder Wille hat sein Was und Warum. Wir
> wollen nämlich überhaupt nur etwas aufgrund
> eines Warum. . . . So wie der Wille irgen-
> detwas will, will er es so wegen etwas.[23]

Kann kein Freiheitsvollzug gedacht werden, ohne dass er
in der angezeigten Weise in die Dimension des Wissen gehoben
ist, so kann Wissen und Erkenntnis umgekehrt nur als Richt-
mass für den gesamten menschlichen Existenzvollzug gedacht
werden.

Damit ist die Legitimation jeder Reflexion angezeigt,
auch die einer *philosophischen* Reflexion; letztere dann,
wenn die *rationale Ausweisbarkeit* einer dem Lebensvollzug
inhärenten Reflexion gefordert ist, sei es für sich selbst
oder im Gegenüber zu einer der eigenen Lebensposition wider-
streitenden Konzeption menschliches Daseins.

Die Legitimation einer philosphischen Reflexion kann nur
in die ursprüngliche Bezogenheit jeder Reflexion auf die
Freiheit menschlichen Selbstvollzugs gesetzt werden. In
Anselms Generalisierung eines prinzipiellen Sachverhalts
heisst das:

> Dem Vernunftwesen bedeutet vernünftig sein
> nichts anderes, als das Gerechte vom Nicht-
> Gerechten, das Wahre vom Nicht-Wahren, das
> Gute vom Nicht-Guten, das Bessere vom weni-
> ger Guten unterscheiden zu können. Dieses
> Vermögen aber ist völlig unnütz und über-
> flüssig, wenn [die Vernunft] das, was sie

unterscheidet, nicht liebte oder verwürfe,
je nach dem Urteil wahrer Unterscheidung.[24]

Einer philosphischen Reflexion kann demnach keine andere
Aufgabe zugesprochen werden als die einer Ausweisbarket
einer Gesamtkonzeption menschlichen Selbstvollzugs im Medium
von Erkenntnis.

Die Transzendenzbezogenheit endlichen Bewusstseins als transzendental-philosophische Fragestellung

Worin liegt dem Menschen die Notwendigkeit eines Fra-
genmüssens überhaupt begründet? Bewusstsein ist -- in
seiner Reinheit gedacht -- unmittelbares Wissen um sich
selbst, da Wissendes und Gewusstes identisch sind. Verbindet sich dem unmittelbaren Wissen um sich dennoch Problema-
tizität, so kann sie dem Bewusstsein nur aus einer Verwiesenheit auf anderes erwachsen. -- Aus diesem Sachverhalt
ergeben sich zwei Fragen:

(1) Was bedeutet eine konstitutive Relationalität für
das Verstehen eigenen Seins?

(2) Wie ist das zu bestimmen, was Bewusstsein in seinem
Sein ermöglicht und daher nur als absolute Ermöglichungsbedingung gedacht werden kann?

Die Nicht-Absolutheit von Bewusstsein

Die fundamentalste Problematik, die in einer philosophischen Reflexion angegangen werden kann, hat Augustinus so
formuliert: "Gott und die Seele begehre ich zu erkennen.
Nichts weiter? Nichts darüber hinaus."[25] Worin liegt die
Artikulation dieser grundlegendsten philosophischen Frage
begründet? -- Man könnte auf die religiöse Glaubensposition
verweisen, aus der sie entspringt, und hinzufügen, dass aus
ihr die Frage nach Gott erwachsen muss. Die Intention, eine
Glaubensposition im Medium von Erkenntnis auszuweisen, bedarf unter philsophischen Aspekten jedoch einer anderen
Legitimation als die einer Verweisung auf eine religiöse
Glaubensposition.

Muss ein Nachdenken über sich selbst nicht jeden
Menschen zur Frage nach einer absoluten Wirklichkeit führen?
-- Würde sich aufgrund einer Reflexion auf sich selbst jeder
Mensch vor die Frage nach einer absoluten Wirklichkeit ge-
stellt sehen, so wäre die Frage nach dem Absoluten nicht auf

eine vorgegebene religiöse Glaubensposition einzuschränken.
Die Frage einer Transzendenzbezogenheit erwiese sich dann in
der Tat als grundlegendste philosophische Frage, ohne deren
Beantwortung ein adäquates Wesensverständnis des Menschen
gar nicht gedacht werden könnte.

Dass sich Bewusstsein in der Weltvorstellung schon immer
über sich hinausverwiesen sieht, ist ein konstatierbares
Faktum. Vermag Bewusstsein aber darum sein intentionales
Korrelat *Welt* auch schon als absolute Wirklichkeit zu begreifen? Um diese Frage beantworten zu können, bedarf es
einer Differenzierung.

Unter der Vorstellung von "Welt" als eines Transzendie-
rens seiner selbst auf anderes kann zweierlei subsumiert
werden:

(1) eine Verwiesenheit auf eine *apersonale* Wirklichkeit
qua Natur;

(2) eine Verwiesenheit auf eine andere *innerweltlich-
personale* Wirklichkeit.

Im *ersten* Fall würde etwas verabsolutiert, das nicht mit der
Dimension *menschlichen Bewusstseins* mit all seinen Implikationen ausgezeichnet wäre und kein Vermögen besässe, jemals
in diese Dimension gehoben werden zu können. Im *zweiten*
Fall verabsolutierte menschliches Bewusstsein sich selbst
und müsste damit zwangsläufig den Wahrheitsanspruch einer
Transzendenzbezogenheit *religiösen* Glaubens auf eine nicht
innerweltliche göttliche Wirklichkeit ausschliessen.

Wie kann und muss die Frage einer Tranzendez-Bezogenheit
menschlichen Bewusstseins überhaupt unter dem Aspekt der
Bezogenheit auf eine absolute Wirklichkeit *argumentativ*
entschieden werden? Dass dem Menschen der Begriff einer
absoluten Wirklichkeit möglich ist, liegt in seiner Vernunftbegabtheit begründet. Wäre ihm ein solcher Begriff
nicht möglich, so wäre dem Menschen in seiner Geschichte
weder eine *Natur*-Religion noch eine *Offenbarungs*-Religion
möglich gewesen.

Im Begriff einer absoluten Wirklichkeit liegt das Kriterium, um darüber entscheiden zu können, was *nicht* als solche
gedacht werden kann. Dass diese weder in eine apersonale
Natur noch in ein endliches Bewusstsein gesetzt werden kann,
resultiert Anselm aus einer ohne Schwierigkeit nachvollzieh-
baren Argumentation:

Zweifellos kann das, was irgendwo oder irgendwann nicht ist, auch wenn es irgendwo
und irgendwann ist, dennoch als nirgendwo

und nirgendwann seiend gedacht werden, so
wie es irgendwo und irgendwann nicht ist.
Denn was gestern nicht war und heute ist:
kann als niemals seiend begriffen werden,
wie begriffen wird, dass es gestern nicht
gewesen ist. Und was hier nicht ist und
anderswo ist, kann, wie es hier nicht ist,
als nirgends seiend gedacht werden. Wessen
einzelne Teile nicht sind, wo oder wann
andere Teile sind, dessen Insgesamt an
Teilen und daher es selbst als Ganzes kann
in ähnlicher Weise als nirgendwo und niemals
seiend gedacht werden.[26]

Alles, worauf das Kriterium der "Denkbarkeit des Nicht-
seins" anwendbar ist, kann nicht als absolute Wirklichkeit
begriffen werden. Anselm konzipiert die Denkbarkeit eines
Nichtsein-könnens unter den Aspekten der Zeitlichkeit und
Einheit. Es versteht sich von selbst, dass eine *Werdens*-
Einheit nicht als absolut gedacht werden kann, da der
Begriff des Werdens weder einen möglichen *Anfang* noch ein
mögliches *Ende* des Werdens-prozesses auszuschliessen vermag.
Von allem, was einem zeitlichen Werden unterworfen ist,
"wird nicht mit Unrecht verneint, dass es schlechthin und
vollkommen und unbedingt ist, und erklärt, dass es fast
nicht ist und kaum ist.[27]

Mit solchen Überlegungen bestimmt Anselm -- aufgrund des
Kriteriums der Denkbarkeit des Nichtseins -- die notwendig
zu denkende Seinsweise einer zeitlichen Werdens-Einheit. Im
eigentlichen Sinne kann ihr Sein gar nicht zugesprochen werden -- nämlich dann, wenn der Begriff absoluten Seins ein
schlechthin unbedingtes Durchsichsein impliziert.

Wie muss in der von Anselm angesprochenen "ontologischen
Differenz" absoluten und nicht-absoluten Seins das Sein von
Bewusstsein gedacht werden? -- Anselm fasst seine These in
folgende Frage:

Da alles, was [vom höchsten Geist selbst]
verschieden ist, nicht durch sich, sondern
durch ein anderes vom Nichtsein zum Sein
gelangt ist, und da es, soweit es an ihm
liegt, vom Sein zum Nichtsein zurückkehrt,
wenn es nicht durch ein anderes erhalten
wird: wie soll diesem zukommen, schlechthin
vollkommen und unbedingt zu sein und nicht
vielmehr kaum zu sein oder fast nicht zu
sein? . . . jedoch ist es nicht gänzlich
nicht.[28]

Die Notwendigkeit einer "*creatio continua*" verweist auf
die Bedingung der Möglichkeit des Sein- und Bestehen-Könnens
alles nichtabsoluten Seins. Damit ist die entscheidende
Dimension angezeigt, um ein Sein begreifen zu können, von
dem aufgrund der "ontologischen Differenz" gesagt werden
muss, dass es im *eigentlichen* Sinne nicht ist und doch nicht
gänzlich nicht ist.

Die konstitutive Verwiesenheit
von Bewusstsein auf das Absolute

Wie wird von Anselm das Problem einer konstitutiven
Transzendenzbezogenheit endlichen Bewusstseins unter wissen-
schafts-theoretischen Aspekten angegangen? -- Die gestellte
Frage führt auf den zentralen Punkt unserer Überlegungen:
Worauf kann sich eine erkenntnis-kritische Reflexion als
Argumentationsbasis beziehen? Wie ist sie methodisch zu
entfalten?
Dass und wie Anselm um die wissenschaftstheoretische
Konzeption einer Beantwortung der Frage nach dem Absoluten
gerungen hat, geht aus dem einleitenden Passus seines *Pros-
logions* hervor, in dem er seinen sogenannten "ontologischen
Gottesbeweis" artikuliert:

> Nachdem ich . . . eine kleine Schrift als
> Beispiel dafür, wie man über den Grund des
> Glaubens nachdenkt, . . . herausgegeben
> hatte, bedachte ich, wie dieses durch Ver-
> kettung vieler Beweise verflochten sei, und
> begann bei mir zu fragen, ob sich nict *ein*
> Argument finden liesse, das keines anderen
> bedürfte, um sich zu beweisen, als seiner
> allein, und das allein hinreichte, um aufzu-
> weisen, dass Gott in Wahrheit existiert.
> . . . Als ich oft und eifrig darauf das
> Denken hinwandte und es mir einmal schien,
> es liesse sich fassen, was ich suchte, das
> andere Mal der Schärfe des Geistes gänzlich
> entglitt, wollte ich endlich verzweifelnd
> davon ablassen wie von der Erforschung einer
> Sache, die zu finden unmöglich wäre. Aber
> als ich jenen Gedanken von mir vollständig
> fernhalten wollte, damit er meinen Geist
> nicht fruchtlos beschäftige und von anderem,
> worin ich voranschreiten könnte, abhalte, da
> begann er immer mehr und mehr sich mir, der
> es nicht wollte und sich dagegen wehrte, mit

einer gewissen Zudringlichkeit aufzunötigen.
Als ich also eines Tages in der Abwehr
seiner Zudringlichkeit ermüdete, da bot sich
in diesem Streit der Gedanken das, was ich
aufgegeben hatte, so dar, dass ich eifrig
den Gedenken umfasste, den ich ängstlich
zurückwies.[29]

Worin besteht das gesuchte einzige Argumentationsfunda-
ment, das Anselm kurz nach derselben Problemerörterung im
Monologion seinem *Proslogion* zugrundelegt? Das erste
Kapitel seines *Monologion*s trägt den Titel: "Dass es ein
Bestes und Grösstes und Höchstes von allem gibt, was ist."[30]
-- Das gesuchte "*unum argumentum*" des *Proslogions* dagegen
lautet: "wir glauben, dass Du etwas bist, worüber hinaus
nichts Grösseres gedacht werden kann."[31] Beiden Werken
liegt -- wie Anselm im Rückblick erklärt -- ein und dieselbe
Intention zugrunde: nämlich den Nachweis zu führen, dass
das, was wir im Glauben festhalten . . . durch notwendige
Vernunftgründe ohne Autorität der Heiligen Schrift erwiesen
werden könne.[32]

Wenn beide Problemerörterungen dieselbe Thematik angehen
und zudem von derselben Intention getragen sind, so stellt
sich die Frage nach deren methodologischer Differenz. --
Nach Anselms Worten ist an die Stelle einer "Verkettung
vieler Beweise" "ein einziges Argument" getreten. -- Ist
damit eine bloss *quantitive* Differenz angezeigt oder liegt
ein wirklich *wissenschaftstheoretischer Neuansatz* vor?

Achtet man auf die Verschiedenheit der beiden Formulierungen der Frage nach dem Absoluten, so lässt sich ohne
Schwierigkeit ablesen, dass Anselm in dem gesuchten Neuansatz methodisch *die* Bedingung der Möglichkeit *expressis
verbis* veranschlagt, ohne die keinerlei Problemerörterung
mögliche wäre: nämlich das *Denken* als *conditio sine qua
non*.

Welche Konsequenzen ergeben sich aus diesem methodischen
Neuansatz für die Konzeption eines Absoluten? -- Im Denken
und durch das Denken kann ohne Zweifel alle *vorfindbare*
Wirklichkeit, auch die eines "Besten und Grösten und
Höchsten von allem, was ist," überschritten werden. Aufgrund von Anselms *unum argumentum* kann vermittelst des
Denkens nicht nur alle vorfindbare Wirklichkeit überschritten werden; sie muss vielmehr überschritten werden, wenn es
um die Konzeption des Begriffes einer absoluten Wirklichkeit
geht: sie kann und muss gedacht werden als etwas, "worüber
hinaus nichts Grösseres *gedacht werden kann.*"

In Anselms *unum argumentum* wird das *Denken* in dessen
transzendentalkonstitutiver Bedeutung veranschlagt: als

Medium, ohne das keine Wirklichkeit erschlossen sein kann
und das einzig und allein eine Argumentation "durch notwendige Vernunftgründe" zu ermöglichen vermag. Allein im
Medium des Denkens lässt sich darüber entscheiden, wie der
wahre Begriff einer absoluten Wirklichkeit gedacht werden
muss und was aufgrund dieses Begriffes nicht als Absolutes
gedacht werden kann.

Worauf Anselm in seinem *unum argumentum* rekurriert,
erweist sich als unhintergehbare *conditio sine qua non*
jeder Argumentation. Dabei ist ganz entscheidend, dass in
Bezug auf Anselms Argumentation in dessen "ontologischem
Gottesbeweis" gerade nicht der meist erhobene Vorwurf einer
"metabasis eis allo genos" gemacht werden kann; denn das
Denken wird nicht als blosses *Denken* gegenüber einem ihm
transzendenten *Sein* veranschlagt.

Die Argumentationsbasis einer erkenntniskritischen Verfahrensweise wird von Anselm ausdrücklich in das *Sein des
Denkens* und mit ihm in das Sein von Bewusstsein gesetzt. --
In seiner Entgegnung auf Einwendungen gegenüber seiner Argumentation zur Gottesfrage präzisiert Anselm seinen Neuansatz, indem auf den fraglos gewissen fundmentalen Sachverhalt verwiesen wird,

> dass das Sein im Erkennen daraus folgt, dass
> erkannt wird. Wie nämlich, was gedacht
> wird, im Denken gedacht wird, und was im
> Denken gedacht wird, ist, so wie es gedacht
> wird, insofern im Denken -- ebenso wird, was
> erkannt wird, im Erkennen erkannt, und was
> im Erkennen erkannt wird, ist, so wie es
> erkannt wird, insofern im Erkennen.[33]

Aufgrund einer solch unmissverständlichen Präzisierung
seines Argumentationsfundaments muss es völlig unverständlich bleiben, warum Anselms Reduktionsverfahren nicht-
absoluten Seins auf ein absolutes Sein auf die meist rezi-
pierte Kritik stossen konnte, seine Argumentation beruhe auf
einer "metabasis eis allo genos," d. h. auf einem unerlaub-
ten Überschritt des Denkens zum Sein.

Wenn Anselm die Gottesfrage angeht und dabei das Sein
des Denkens *qua* Bewusstsein veranschlagt, dann muss es
völlig uneinsichtig bleiben, warum gegen ein Reduktionsverfahren, das in ein und derselben *Seins*dimension verbleibt,
der Einwand einer *metabasis eis allo genos* erhoben werden
kann. Das angestrengte Reduktionsverfahren bewegt sich
anfänglich und erklärtermassen in der Dimension des *Seins*
von Bewusstsein als *geistigem* Sein und intendiert nichts

anderes als auf reflexivem Wege das zu ermitteln, was als
dessen Ermöglichungsbedingung gedacht werden muss.

Der Einwand einer Metabasis müsste umgekehrt dann
erhoben werden, wenn in der Frage nach dem Absoluten als
einer *geistigen* Wirklichkeit auf eine nicht-geistige
Wirklichkeit als Argumentationsbasis zurückgegriffen würde.
Anselms Argumentation dagegen verbleibt und bewegt sich im
demselben Genus eines in die Dimension der Bewusstheit geho-
benen *geistigen* Seins. Reflektiert wird auf die Ermöglichungsbedingung endlichen Bewusstseins, die als Ermöglichungsbedingung eines *geistigen* Seins nur als *geistiges*
Sein gedacht werden kann.

Das Kriterium, mit dem Anselm ein Argumentationsfunda-
ment eruiert, das jenseits einer Willkürfestsetzung zu
stehen kommt, wird ebenso für die Explikation seines *unum*
argumentum als einziges Kriterium zugelassen. Die Bestimmung der Argumentationsbasis wird auf das reduziert, ohne
das keine Argumentation gedacht werden könnte, da sich unter
dem Kriterium der *Denknotwendigkeit* das *Sein* von Bewusstsein
als apodiktisch gewisse Implikation *jeder* Reflexion erweist
-- auch einer Reflexion, die sich als radikale Skepsis
artikuliert.

Reflektiert man auf das Kriterium, das Anselm seiner
Argumentation zugrundelegt, so könnte es scheinen, dass
Denk-*Notwendigkeit* die Erreichbarkeit von Sein überhaupt
ausschliesst. Man könnte die These aufstellen, dass die
Notwendigkeit eines nicht anders Denken-Könnens gerade
darum, weil sie in einer strukturellen Seinsverfasstheit
endlichen Bewusstseins begründet liegt, nicht mehr sein
könne als die Explikation einer notwendigen Denkstruktur.

Dass *prinzipiell* nicht ausgeschlossen werden kann, dass
das Denken vermittelst des Kriteriums der Denknotwendigkeit
ein Sein erreichen kann, erweist die Bestimmung des Argumentationsfundaments einer erkenntniskritischen Reflexion: der
Selbstvollzug des Denkens impliziert *denknotwendig* dessen
Sein. Wenn darum das Kriterium der Denknotwendigkeit in der
Bestimmung des Argumentationsfundaments zu apodiktischer
Gewissheit zu führen vermag, so kann dasselbe in der Beantwortung der Frage nach dem Absoluten ebensowenig prinzipiell
ausgeschlossen werden.

Die Möglichkeit einer Reflexion *nicht*-absoluten Seins
auf ein absolutes Sein liegt Anselm darin beschlossen, dass
eine sinnvolle Negation einer Position nur gedacht werden
kann unter der Voraussetzung eines Verstehenkönnens der
negierten Position:

> Wer . . . verneint, dass etwas sei, worüber
> hinaus Grösseres nicht gedacht werden kann,
> versteht und denkt gewiss die Negation, die
> er vollzieht.[34]

Anselms Explikation der konstitutiven Transzendenzbezogenheit endlichen Bewusstseins auf das Absolute   erfolgt in
drei Explikationsschritten, wobei auf der Basis seines *unum
argumentum* jeweils zwei alternative Möglichkeiten   des
Denkens in Betracht gezogen werden und argumentativ aufgrund
des Kriteriums der Denknotwendigkeit entschieden wird:

   (1) Das Absolute kann nicht als   nur im Denken seiend
gedacht werden; es kann   nur als in Wirklichkeit seiend
gedacht werden.

   (2) Das Absolute kann nicht so gedacht werden, dass sein
Nichtsein denkbar is; es kann nur so gedacht werden, dass
sein Nichtsein undenkbar ist;

   (3) Das Absolute kann nicht so gedacht werden, dass es
dem endlichen Bewusstsein begreifbar wäre; es kann nur als
unbegreifbare Wirklichkeit gedacht werden.[35]

   Unter methodologischen Aspekten muss festgehalten werden, dass Anselm nicht mehr voraussetzt als das Sein von
Bewusstsein und dass er   seine Argumentationsschritte ausschliesslich durch das Kriterium der Denknotwendigkeit legi-
timiert. Die Argumentation erfolgt nicht unter *Berufung auf
Erfahrung* -- weder unter Berufung auf eine *religiöse* Glau-
benserfahrung noch unter Berufung auf *sinnliche* Erfahrung.
(Im ersteren Fall läge kein *philosophisches* Argumentations-
verfahren vor; im zweiten Fall wäre der *Überschritt* von
einer sinnlichen zu einer nichtsinnlichen Wirklichkeit
uneinsehbar.)
   Anselms Reduktionsverfahren vom Sein endlichen Bewusstseins auf das Sein des Absolutens vollzieht sich in der
Dimension geistigen Seins; seine Argumentation wird dabei
ausschliesslich von dem Kriterium getragen, das ihn in der
reflexiven Ermittlung seines Argumentationsfundaments zu
apodiktischer Gewissheit geführt hatte.
   Unter wissenschaftstheoretischen Aspekten kann daher das
Postulat der "analytischen Philosophie" der Gegenwart nach
einer "Elimination der Metaphysik" aus jeder philosophischen
Untersuchung nur als willkürliche Beschränkung der philosophischen Fragedimension angesehen werden.

Mit welcher Begründung können folgende Thesen aufgestellt werden:

(1) that all metaphysical assertions are nonsensical;[36] und

(2) that a sentence says nothing unless it is empirically verifiable?[37]

Mit welcher Begründung wird anfänglich ausgeschlossen:

(1) that philosophy affords us knowledge of a reality transcending the world of science and common sense;[38] und

(2) that thought is an independent source of knowledge, and is moreover a more trustworthy source of knowledge than experience[39]

Solche Vorbehalte gegenüber einer metaphysischen Problemerörterung ergeben sich dann, wenn der Ausgangspunkt einer philosophischen Argumentation in die Frage gefasst wird: Must [a metaphysician] not begin, as other men do, with the evidence of his senses?[40] Wird die Evidenz von Sinneswahrnehmung als einziger Ausgangspunkt einer philosophischen Reflexion zugelassen, so stellt sich die Frage, ob mit einer solchen These eine legitimierbare Einschränkung der Möglichkeit von Evidenz menschlichen Bewusstseins vorgenommen wird. So gewiss ein Bewusstsein seiner selbst ohne nicht-sinnliche Evidenz undenkbar ist, so gewiss verfehlt die These einer Einschränkung aller Anschauung auf sinnliche Wahrnehmung einen denknotwendigen Sachverhalt.

Die Kritik an einer metaphysischen Problemerörterung überhaupt stösst auch dann ins Leere, wenn unterstellt wird, ihre Argumentation gründe in einer intellektuellen Anschauung von Metaphysischem, indem gesagt wird: that [the metaphysician] was endowed with a faculty of intellectual intuition which enabled him to know facts that could not be known through sense-experience.[41]

Eine philosophische Untersuchung lässt sich ihren Gegenstand weder durch eine sinnliche noch durch eine nicht-sinnliche intellektuelle Anschauung einfach fraglos gegeben sein; sie setzt ihre Aufgabe vielmehr in den Aufweis der Bedingungen der Möglichkeit von Erfahrung überhaupt, was nur durch eine rationale Argumentation vermittelst reinen Denkens geschehen kann. In Anselms Worten: eine metaphysische Problemerörterung erfolgt erklärtermassen allein im Denken (*sola cogitatione*) durch notwendige Vernunftgründe (*rationes necessariae*).

Angesichts einer solchen wissenschaftstheoretischen Konzeption von Philosophie, wie sie sich nicht nur bei Anselm findet, bleibt es völlig unerfindlich, wie *jede* metaphysische Problemerörterung völlig unbesehen mit der Behauptung zu deklassieren versucht wird:

> that those philosophers who fill their books
> with assertions that they intuitively 'know'
> this or that moral or religious 'truth' are
> merely providing material for the psycho-
> analyst.[42]

Der Sinn von Menschsein und Geschichte

Wird mit Anselms Reduktionsverfahren in dessen "ontologischem Gottesbeweis" vorausgesetzt, das *Dass* einer Transzendenzbezogenheit endlichen Bewusstseins auf ein wahres und wirkliches absolutes Sein aufweisen zu können, so stellt sich die weiterführende Problematik einer Bestimmung des *Wie* einer Transzendenzbezogenheit.

Am Ende seines Reduktionsverfahrens formuliert Anselm im Hinblick auf die gewonnene Einsicht in der Beantwortung der Gottesfrage eine höchst bemerkenswerte Bestimmung des Verhältnisses von Glaube und Wissen:

> ich sehe jetzt . . . solcherweise ein, dass
> ich, wollte ich es nicht glauben, dass Du
> existierst, es nicht nicht einsehen
> könnte.[43]

Was bedeutet und impliziert die Formulierung eines solchen Sachverhalts -- Anselm spricht von einer Vernunfteinsicht, die als Vernunfteinsicht nur als unaufhebbare Einsicht gedacht werden kann. Entgegen einer apodiktischen Gewissheit von Eingesehenem soll es aber dennoch möglich sein, *nicht zu glauben*. Was in diesem Kontext unter "glauben" bzw. "nicht glauben wollen" verstanden werden kann ist nichts anderes als die Verwirklichung von Eingesehenem; denn es ist immer möglich, wider besseres Wissen zu handeln. Ist aber sowohl die Realisation von Einsicht überhaupt als auch die hier angesprochene Realisation von Eingesehenem im Wollen and Handeln allererst durch Freiheit möglich, so erweist sich Freiheit als grundlegendste Bestimmung des Menschseins.

Wie konzipiert Anselm die dem Erkenntnisbemühen vorgeordnete und Erkanntes realisieren könnende Freiheit als Prinzip des Menschseins in dessen Geschichte?

Die Undenkbarkeit einer autonomen Sinnstiftung
durch ein endliches Bewusstsein

Anselm veranschlagt Freiheit als Grundbestimmung endlichen Bewusstseins; er expliziert deren Formalstruktur und
begreift sie in ihrer Tranzendenzbezogenheit. Die Konzeption der Freiheit resultiert aus der Konzeption von Wahrheit, die von Anselm als "allein dem Geiste erfassbare Richtigkeit" definiert wird.[44]

Welch notwendig-implikative Momente werden im Begriff
von Freiheit schon immer mitgedacht, um sie in ihrer Formalstruktur aufgrund einer "allein dem Geiste erfassbaren Richtigkeit" zu konzipieren? Freiheit ist die Artikulation
eines Willens, der ohne zwei Momente undenkbar ist: "jeder
Wille hat ein Was und Warum."[45] Kein Wille is denkbar ohne
ein selbstgewolltes Material-Inhaltliches und ebensowenig
ohne einen Beweggrund, dessetwegen er etwas will.

Freiheit kann nur als Grundsein gedacht werden, das aus
sich und durch sich das zu verwirklichen vermag, wozu es
sich selbst als Grundseinkönnen bestimmt. Das Vermögen
freier Selbstbestimmung mit der These infrage zu stellen,
dass das Menschsein schlechthin determiniert wäre, scheitert
allein schon an der Möglichkeit des Begriffes von Freiheit.
Wäre das Menschsein einer durchgängigen Determination ausgesetzt, dann wäre jegliche freie Selbstbestimmung und mit ihr
der Begriff freier Selbsttätigkeit ausgeschlosen. Die
Möglichkeit des Begriffes von Freiheit erweist daher die
Möglichkeit freier Selbstbestimmung als wirkliches Vermögen
menschlichen Daseins.

Wie aber muss das, woraufhin sich Freiheit im Ganzen
entwirft, aufgrund einer konstitutiven und daher unaufhe-
baren Tranzendenzbezogenheit gedacht werden? Dass sich der
reale Selbstvollzug menschlicher Freiheit nur in einem
Nacheinander von Freiheitsakten zu entwerfen vermag, liegt
in dessen Endlichkeit begründet. Dennoch aber kann und muss
eine Mehrheit von Setzungen nur als Ausformung einer Freiheit gedacht werden, da sie in der Einheit des Bewusstseins
synthetisiert sind.

Die entscheidende Frage lautet: Vermag das Durch-sich-
sein endlicher Freiheit allein aus sich heraus das zu entwerfen, was den Sinn seines gesamten Daseins ausmacht?
(Unter "Sinn" wird hier das Worumwillen endlicher Freiheit
überhaupt verstanden.) — Impliziert das absolute Durch-
sich-sein von Freiheit die Möglichkeit einer autonomen Sinnstiftung durch ein endliches Bewusstsein?

Wird in der Fragebeantwortung von einer *konstitutiven*
Tranzendenzbezogenheit ausgegangen, so muss die Annahme
ausgeschlossen werden, dass endliches Bewusstsein das

Vermögen einer absoluten Sinnstiftung besitzen könne. Kann endliches Bewusstsein in seinem Sein und Seinkönnen aufgrund seiner konstitutiven Transzendenzbezogenheit nur als ermöglichtes Sein gedact werden, so kann auch sein absolutes Durch-sich-sein *qua* Freiheit nur als ermöglichtes Durch-sich-sein gedacht werden, das auf seine konstitutiv-unaufhebbare Ermöglichungsbedingung zurückgebunden bleibt.

Die Frage nach einer Autonomie endlichen Bewusstseins kann daher nur so beantwortet werden: Eine autonome Sinnstiftung ist undenkbar, so gewiss Bewusstsein in seinem Sein ermöglicht ist. Kann eine solche Argumentation lediglich für eine in sich schlüssige Gedankenoperation gehalten werden -- oder lässt sich der Nachweis führen, dass sich der Selbstvollzug endlichen Bewusstseins in der Tat in einer unaufhebbaren Weise auf eine andere Wirklichkeit bezogen sieht, die einzig und allein als sinnstiftend gedacht werden kann?

Das Seinsollen von Wahrheit als Sinn-stiftende Normativität

Wir sind der Frage nachgegangen, wie das gedacht werden muss, woraufhin sich die Freiheit endlichen Bewusstseins im Ganzen zu entwerfen vermag, um den Sinn seines Daseins zu verwirk-lichen. Wir haben gesehen, dass die Endlichkeit des Bewusstseins die Möglichkeit eines autonomen Sinnentwurfes ausschliesst und dass ihm eine solche Möglichkeit nur aus seiner konstitutiven Tranzendenzbezogenheit erwachsen kann. Sind diese Überlegungen stringend, so muss sich zeigen lassen, dass sich Bewusstsein in seinem Selbstvollzug schon immer über sichselbst hinausverwiesen sieht.

Eine konstitutive Verwiesenheit auf eine sinnstiftende absolute Wirklichkeit erweist Anselm durch eine Analyse des Selbstvollzugs von Bewusstsein: Keine Tätigkeit des Bewusstseins kann gedacht werden ohne einen ihr notwendig-implikativen Wahrheits-anspruch. Vermag Bewusstsein als ermöglichte Freiheit das, worumwillen sie überhaupt ist, evidentermassen nicht in autonomer Weise aus sich selbst zu begründen, so indiziert der jedem Willen implikative Anspruch eines Seinsollens in Wahrheit die Dimension möglicher Sinnhaftigkeit menschlichen Daseins.

Das Material-Inhaltliche dessen, was die Sinnhaftigkeit menschlichen Daseins in Wahrheit zu begründen vermag, wird von Anselm in die Möglichkeit unmittelbaren Einsehens gesetzt: "Was nämlich zu wollen ist, liegt offen zutage."[46]

Wie kann Anselm von der Voraussetzung ausgehen, der Sinn menschlichen Daseins wäre nicht nur bestimmbar, sondern darüber hinaus in unmittelbarer Evidenz einsehbar? Die *Be-stimmbarkeit* der Sinnhaftigkeit liegt Anselm in der Realisa-tion des implikativen Wahrheitsanspruches *jeder* Tätigkeit des Bewusstseins beschlossen, sowohl des Denkens als auch des Wollens und Handelns; deren *unmittlebare Einsichtigkeit* liegt darin begründet, dass die Artikulation des Wahrheits-anspruches und das In-Anspruch-Genommensein durch Wahrheit in ein und derselben Dimension aufeinandertreffen: in der Wirklichkeit geistigen Seins, das nur als unmittelbare Selbsterschlossenheit gedacht werden kann.

Dass sich ein solch unmittelbares Aufeinandertreffen nicht als blosse Willkürkonstruktion deklassieren lässt, dafür steht Anselms Argumenation seines "ontologischen Got-tesbeweises," die den Nachweis führt, dass als Ermögli-chungsbedingung des Seins von Bewusstsein nur eine abolute Wirklichkeit gedacht werden kann. Der Wahrheitsanspruch endlichen Bewusstseins kann daher nur so gedacht werden, dass er auf ein wirkliches In-Anspruch-Genommensein durch die Wahrheit bezogen ist.

Die Frage, wie ein In-Anspruch-Genommensein endlichen Bewusstseins durch eine absolute Wirklichkeit gedacht werden muss, trifft genau das, worum es in Anselms Überlegungen zur Konzeption von Wahrheit eigentlich geht. Wenn Freiheit als Grundbestimmung der Wesensverfasstheit endlichen Bewusst-seins veranschlagt werden muss, denn kann die unmittelbare Präsenz eines In-Anspruch-Genommenseins durch eine absolute Wirklichkeit nur in der Weise eines absoluten *Sollens* ge-dacht werden, da *Determination* die Möglichkeit einer freien Selbstbestimmung notwendigerweise ausschlösse.

Woraufhin die Freiheit endlichen Bewusstseins im Ganzen bezogen ist, um das Worumwillen ihres Seins verwirklichen zu können, liegt in deren konstitutiver Ermöglichungsbedingung als absolutes Sollen begründet. -- Wie muss ein durch ein Absolutes gesetztes Sollen und dessen Erschlossenheit ge-dacht werden? Impliziert der Begriff des Absoluten eine differenzlose Identität jenseits aller Zeitlichkeit und Wan-delbarkeit -- eine "für kein Denken teilbare Einheit,"[47] so kann auch ein im Absoluten begründetes Sollens nicht anders gedacht werden, als dass es keinerlei Wandelbarkeit unter-worfen ist. Kann ferner das Absolute nur als absolutes Durch-sich-Sein gedacht werden -- als ein Sein, "das allein durch sichselbst ist,"[48] so kann auch ein absolutes Sollen nicht anders gedacht werden, als dass es sich in seinem Seinsollen fraglos selbst begründet.

Erweisen sich Unwandelbarkeit und Selbstbegründetheit als notwendig-implikative Formalbestimmungen des Material-Inhaltlichen eines absolut Gesollten, so ist damit eine unhinterfragbare, da sich selbst begründende normative

Werthaftigkeit angezeigt -- eine Werthaftigkeit durch das
Seinsollen der Wahrheit, die für ein endliches Bewusstsein
einzig und allein als Sinnstiftend gedacht werden kann.
    Wird über die Formalbestimmung des Material-Inhaltlichen
eines absolut Gesollten hinausgegangen, so stellt sich die
Frage: Wie muss endliches Bewusstsein in seinem Sein
überhaupt gedacht werden und wie muss das gedacht werden,
wozu die Freiheit endlichen Bewusstseins im Ganzen bestimmt
ist? Die gestellte Frage führt Anselm auf die "ontologische
Differenz" absoluten und nicht-absoluten Seins:

> Was . . . so schlechthin und in jeder Hin-
> sicht allein vollkommen, einfach und unbe-
> .dingt ist, von dem kann natürlich in gewis-
> sem Sinne gesagt werden, dass es allein ist.
> Und umgekehrt, von all dem, von dem . . .
> erkannt wird, dass es weder schlechthin noch
> vollkommen noch unbedingt ist, sondern kaum
> ist oder fast nicht ist, von dem wird frei-
> lich in gewisser Weise mit Recht gesagt,
> dass es nicht ist. Infolge dieser Überle-
> gung also ist allein jener Schöpfer-Geist,
> und alles Geschaffene ist nicht; jedoch ist
> es nicht gänzlich nicht.[49]

    Kann dem endlichen Bewusstsein aufgrund der "ontologi-
schen Differenz" kein Sein im eigentlichen Sinne zugesprochen werden, ist es aber dennoch nicht gänzlich Nichts,
so stellt sich die Frage: Wie muss die Seinsweise nicht-
absoluten Seins positiv gefasst werden? In der Frage ist
deren Beantwortung bereits angezeigt. Kann sich endliches
Bewusstsein nur als nicht-absolutes Sein verstehen, so hat
ein solches Sichverstehen den Begriff des Absoluten zur
Voraussetzung. Aufgrund des konstitutiven In-Anspruch-
Genommenseins durch ein absolutes Sollen kann daher das Sein
endlichen Bewusstseins in seiner zu verwirklichenden
Seinsweise nur als Begriff des Absoluten gedacht werden. In
Anselms Worten: als Bildsein-Können des Absoluten -- als
imago Dei:

> sicherlich erweist [der Geist] sich dadurch
> wahrer, Abbild [der höchsten Wesenheit] zu
> sein, als er sich ihrer bewusst werden, sie
> erkennen und lieben kann.[50]

    Lieg in der erkenntnis- und lebensmässigen Ausformung
von Bewusstsein als Begriff- und Bildsein des Absoluten die

eigentliche Seinsweise des Menschseins überhaupt beschlossen, so kann auch das Prinzip, aus dem der Sinn von Geschichte erwachsen kann, nicht anders gedacht werden, als
dass sich das Zusammenwirken endlicher Freiheiten in der
Rückbezogenzeit auf das in Wahrheit Gesollte gestaltet.
Das Ende alles zeitlichen Werdens von Bewusstsein im
Überschritt zu einem vollkommenen Bildsein des Absoluten
fasst Anselm konsequenterweise in die bemerkenswerte These:

> alle werden *einen* Willen haben, denn sie
> werden keinen Willen haben als allein den
> Willen Gottes. . . . denn wie sie nicht
> anders wollen werden als was er, so wird er
> wollen, was immer sie wollen werden, und was
> er wollen wird, wird nicht nicht sein
> können.[51]

Wie aber muss die Erschlossenheit des in Wahrheit
Gesollten im zeitlichen Werden gedacht werden? Worauf ist
dessen Evidenz als *conditio sine qua non* zurückgebunden? --
Diese Frage führt zum grundlegendsten Sachverhalt christlichen Glaubens.

Die Notwendigkeit einer Inkarnation als Wiedereröffnung einer Sinnrealisation von Menschsein und Geschichte

Die Sinnrealisation menschlichen Daseins setzt Anselm
unter *formalen* Aspekten in die Gemeinsamkeit des Wollens
realdistinkter Freiheiten, unter *materialen* Aspekten in die
Verwirklichung eines absoluten Sollens. Unter formalen
Aspekten ist folgender prinzipieller Sachverhalt ohne
Schwierigkeit einsichtig: Kann etwas nur in der Wechsel-
wirksamkeit zweier Freiheiten realisiert werden, so ist das
daraus Resultierende nur dann evidierbar, wenn das Gewollte
einer Freiheit durch eine *zweite* Freiheit selbsttätig
miterstellt wird. Würde der angehobene Wille einer Freiheit
durch eine zweite Freiheit nicht durchvollzogen, so wäre ein
nur im Miteinander zweier Freiheiten zu erstellender Sachverhalt deshalb nicht evidierbar, weil er nicht zur Wirklichkeit geworden wäre und daher weder anschaubar noch
erfahrbar wäre.
Was resultiert aus der unbestreitbaren Stringenz einer
solche reine formalen Überlegung im Hinblick auf die
Möglickeit einer Sinnrealisation endlichen Bewusstseins
unter materialen Aspekten? -- Entspräche die Freiheit end-

lichen Bewusstseins seinem Sinnkonstituierenden absoluten
Sollen nicht, so würde das, was den Sinn menschlichen
Daseins ausmacht, nicht erstellt werden; es wäre darum in
seiner positiv-materialen Einsichtigkeit auch nicht evidierbar. Was bei einer solchen Nicht-Verwirklichung eines konstitutiven absoluten In-Anspruch-Genommenseins verbliebe,
wäre lediglich eine Einsehbarkeit in den notwendigen Aus-
schluss dessen, was in Wahrheit *nicht* sein soll.

Die Möglichkeit einer positive-materialen Einsichtigkeit
dessen, was in Wahrheit sein soll, könnte in dem hypothe-
tisch angenommen Fall einer ursprünglichen Verfehlung von
absolut Gesolltem nur durch ein erneutes Aufgerufen-Werden
endlicher Freiheit durch die Freiheit des Absoluten eröffnet
werden. Es bedürfte einer erneuten Sinn-Eröffnung von
seiten des Absoluten, die Anselm in seinem letzten Hauptwerk
in die Frage fasst: *Cur deus homo* -- Warum ist Gott Mensch
geworden?

Von Anselm werden zwei fundamentale Thesen aufgestellt:

(1) "dass es notwendig sei, dass sich das mit dem
Menschen vollziehe, um dessetwillen er geschaffen wurde;"

(2) dies könne aber nur geschehen "durch einen men-
schgewordenen Gott."[52]

In der ersten These wird von einer Notwendigkeit gesprochen,
die der Sinn des Gesetzseins nicht-absoluten Seins impliziert; in der zweiten These wird das benannt, was den implikativen Sinn des Gesetzseins nicht-absoluten Seins einzig
und allein notwendigerweise erfüllen kann.

Der Sinn des Gesetztseins nicht-absoluten Seins liegt in
der Verwirklichung des Bildseins des Absoluten. Wird die
Freiheit als Grundbestimmung endlichen Bewusstseins veranschlagt, so kann aufgrund der Absolutheit von Freiheit nicht
ausgeschlossen werden, dass es den Sinn seines Seins nicht
verwirklicht. Soll daher -- Anselms Argumentation -- der
Sinn des Gesetztseins nicht-absoluten Seins nicht gänzlich
verfehlt, sondern verwirklicht werden, so bedarf es notwendigerweise der Menschwerdung Gottes.

Anselms Postulat der Notwendigkeit einer Inkarnation
liegt in einer zweifachen Argumentation begründet: in einer
prinzipiellen und einer *hypothetischen* Argumentation. Die
prinzipielle Argumentation fordert die Notwendigkeit einer
Inkarnation aus dem Grunde, dass die Verwirklichung des
Sinnes des Gesetztseins nicht-absoluten Seins nicht als dem
Zufall überlassen gedacht werden kann. Die hypothetische
Argumentation veranschlagt das aus einer ermöglichten Frei-

heit unableitbare Faktum einer ursprünglichen Verfehlung der
Verwirklichung des Sinnes ihres Gesetztseins, das umwillen
einer Sinn*realisation* von Mensch und Geschichte deren Wie-
dereröffnung von seiten des Absolutens erfordert.

Unter wissenschaftstheoretischen Aspekten ist primär
entscheidend, wie Anselm den grundlegendsten Sachverhalt
christlich-religiösen Glaubens angeht. In der *Praefatio* zur
Erörterung der Frage *Cur deus homo* wird das methodische
Vorgehen der Reflexion eindeutig bestimmt. Die Erörterung
soll erfolgen.

(1) "mit Beiseitesetzung Christi, so als ob niemals
etwas von ihm gewesen wäre;"

(2) die Argumentation soll einzig und allein vermittelst
"notwendiger Vernunft-gründe" durchgeführt werden.⁵³

Wie ist eine Argumentation zu fassen, die das historische Faktum des Offenbarungsanspruches einer Inkarnation,
worin christlicher Glaube gründet, als Argumentationsbasis
ausklammert und sich in ihren Argumentationsschritten
erklärtermassen auf "notwendige Vernunftgründe" beschränkt?
Eine sich so verstehende Reflexion ist nicht theologisch,
sondern philosophisch. Es wird nichts anderes vorausgesetzt
als das Sein endlichen Bewusstseins mit allen bisher aufge-
wiesenen Implikationen und dessen Vermögen, über die Wahrheit prinzipieller Sachverhalte vermittelst notwendiger Vernunftgründe entscheiden zu können.

Im Hinblick auf die Formalbestimmung einer Philosophie
als Wissenschaft werden von Anselm nicht nur die beiden wis-
senschafts-konstitutiven Momente der *Voraussetzung* und der
methodischen *Verfahrensweise* in seinem Gesamtwerk unter
erkenntnis-kritischen Aspekten durchgehalten. Das dritte
wissenschafts-konstitutive Moment des *Fragehorizonts* jeder
wissenschaftlichen Untersuchung wird in Anselms Spätwerk in
der metaphysischen Dimension einer philosophischen Reflexion
so tief gefasst, dass sie über die Erörterung der Frage nach
einer absoluten Wirklichkeit im "ontologischen Gottesbeweis"
hinausführt und die Gründe einer notwendigen Inkarnation des
Absoluten thematisiert.

Dass die Artikulation des gesamten Erkenntnisbemühens
Anselms von einer *radikalen* Fragestellung getragen ist,
ergibt sich aus seiner bereits anfänglich gestellten Frage
nach der Bedingung der Möglichkeit von Einsicht überhaupt.
-- Wie sind Denken und Einsicht vermittelt? Kann das Denken
als *zureichende* Bedingung der Möglichkeit von Einsicht
gedacht werden? Dass Denken als *notwendige* Bedingung jeder

Einsicht gedacht werden muss, hat Anselm in der Definition
von Wahrheit festgeschrieben: dass Wahrheit nur als "eine
dem Geiste erfassbare Richtigkeit" gedacht werden kann.[54]

Muss am Denken als notwendiger Bedingung jeder Einsicht
festgehalten werden, so kann es dennoch nicht als zureich-
ender Ermöglichungsgrund von Einsicht überhaupt gedacht werden, weil gezeigt werden müsste, wie das Denken das ihm
implikative Moment von Einsicht überhaupt allein durch sich
und aus sich entlassen könnte. So gewiss Denken als so kon-
zipiertes Grundseinkönnen nicht gedacht werden kann, so
gewiss ist sein Vermögen zur Einsicht auf eine absolute
Ermöglichungsbedingung verwiesen. Anselm fasst diesen aus
einer radikalen Fragestellung resultierenden Sachverhalt in
die bekannten Worte:

> Dank Dir, guter Herr, Dank Dir, dass ich
> das, was ich zuvor durch Dein Geschenk
> geglaubt habe, jetzt durch Deine Erleuchtung
> so einsehe, dass ich, wollte ich es nicht
> glauben . . . es nicht nicht einsehen
> könnte.[55]

Anmerkungen

[1] *Proslogion* I: Schmitt: I,93,1-100,19.

[2] *Cur deus homo* III: Schmitt II,50,18-20: Quamvis enim
[infideles] ideo rationem quaerant, quia non credunt, nos
vero, quia credimus: unum idemque tamen est quod quaerimus.

[3] *Confessiones* X,vi,10: Homines . . . possunt interro-
gare.

[4] *De grammatico* VII: Schmitt I,151,1-2: nullus homo
potest intelligi sine rationalitate.

[5] Ibid., III: Schmitt I,147,25-26: Omnis . . . homo
rationalis est ex necessitate.

[6] Ibid., III: Schmitt I,147,29 durch 148,1: . . . sic
. . . per se [nota est], ut imprudentia sit [eam] probare.

[7] *Confessiones* X,i,1:   . . . qui facit [veritatem],
"venit ad lucem."

[8] *De veritate* IX: Schmitt I,188,28–29: Omnes enim de veritate significationis loquuntur; veritatem vero quae est in [omne actione rationali], pauci considerant.

[9] Ibid. IX, Titel: Schmitt I,188,26: Quod omnis actio significet verum aut falsum.

[10] Cf. Ibid. V und XII: Schmitt I,181,10–183,7; 191,25–196,25.

[11] *Monologion* LXXVII: Schmitt I,84,9–11: In [veritatem] solam omnis homo debet credere, quia est solus finis quem in omni cogitatu actuque suo . . . debet intendere.

[12] *Epistola de incarnatione verbi* I: Schmitt II,9,5–6: qui non crediderit, non intelliget. Nam qui non crediderit, non experietur; et qui expertus non fuerit, non cognoscet.

[13] *De vera religione* VIII,14: *PL* XXXIV,129: ex quo illa omnia, quae primo credidimus, nihil nisi auctoritatem secuti, partim sic intelliguntur, ut videamus esse certissima; partim sic, ut videamus fieri posse, atque ita fieri oportuisse.

[14] *Monologion* I: Schmitt I,13,10–11: puto quia ea [quae credimus] . . ., si vel mediocris ingenii est, potest ipse sibi saltem sola ratione persuadere. *Epistola de incarnatione verbi* I: Schmitt II,7,2–4: Si potest intelligere, deo gratias agat; si non potest, non immittat cornua ad ventilandum, sed submittat caput ad venerandum.

[15] *Cur deus homo* I: Schmitt II,48,17–18: . . . . negligentia mihi videtur, si . . . non studemus quod credimus intelligere.

[16] *Monologion* L: Schmitt I,65,6: Nulla . . . res amatur sine eius memoria aut intelligentia.

[17] *De concordia* I: Schmitt II,257,8–9: Habet aliquis in corde ut veritatem teneat, quia intelligit rectum esse amare veritatem.

[18] *Monologion*, Prologus: Schmitt I,8,19: . . . quae prius non animadvertisset.

[19] *Epistola de incarnatione verbi* VI: Schmitt II,20, 18–19: . . . ut quod fide tenemus . . . necessariis rationibus sine scripturae auctoritate probari possit.

[20] *Cur deus homo*, Praefatio: Schmitt II,42,12-13: . . . remoto Christo, quasi numquam aliquid fuerit de illo, probat rationibus necessariis.

[21] K. Barth, *Fides quaerens intellectum, Anselms Beweis der Existenz Gottes im Zusammenhang seines theologischen Programms* (München: C. Kaiser, 1931), pp. 72-73.

[22] *Monologion*, Prologus: Schmitt I,8,18-19: . . . secum sola cogitatione disputantis et investigantis ea quae prius non animadvertisset.

[23] *De veritate* XII: Schmitt I,194,3-4:   . . . omnis voluntas habet quid et cur. Omnino namque nihil volumus, nisi sit cur velimus.

[24] *Monologion* LXVIII: Schmitt I,78,21-25: . . . rationali naturae non est aliud esse rationalem, quam posse discernere iustum a non iusto, verum a non vero, bonum a non bono, magis bonum a minus bono. Hoc autem posse omnino inutile illi est et supervacuum nisi quod discernit amet aut reprobet secundum verae discretionis iudicium.

[25] *Soliloquia* I,ii,7:   *PL* XXXII,872:   Deum et animam scire cupio. Nihilne plus? Nihil omnino.

[26] *Contra insipientem* I: Schmitt I,131,18-25: Procul dubio quidquid alicubi aut aliquando non est: etiam si est alicubi aut aliquando, potest tamen cogitari numquam et nusquam esse, sicut non est alicubi aut aliquando.   Nam quod heri non fuit et hodie est: sicut heri non fuisse intelligitur, ita numquam esse subintelligi potest.   Et quod hic non est et alibi est: sicut non est hic, ita potest cogitari nusquam esse.   Similiter cuius partes singulae non sunt, ubi aut quando sunt aliae partes, eius omnes partes et ideo ipsum totum possunt cogitari numquam aut nusquam esse.

[27] *Monologion* XXVIII: Schmitt I,46,14-16: non immerito negantur simpliciter et perfecte et absolute esse, et asseruntur fere non esse et vix esse.

[28] Ibid. XXVIII: Schmitt I,46,16-31:   cum omnia quaecumque aliud sunt quam ipse, de non esse venerint ad esse non per se sed per aliud; et cum de esse redeant ad non esse quantum ad se, nisi sustineantur per aliud: quomodo illis convenit simpliciter aut perfecte sive absolute esse et non magis vix esse aut fere non esse? . . . nec tamen omnino non sunt . . .

²⁹ *Proslogion*, Prooemium: Schmitt I,93,2-19: Postquam opusculum quoddam velut exemplum meditandi de ratione fidei . . . in persona alicuius tacite secum ratiocinando . . . edidi: considerans illud esse multorum concatenatione contextum argumentorum, coepi mecum quaerere, si forte posset inveniri unum argumentum, quod nullo alio ad se probandum quam se solo indigeret, et solum ad astruendum quia Deus vere est . . . sufficeret. Ad quod cum saepe studioseque cogitationem converterem, atque aliquando mihi videretur iam posse capi quod quaerebam, aliquando mentis aciem omnino fugeret: tandem desperans volui cessare velut ab inquisitione rei quam inveniri esset impossibile. Sed cum illam cogitationem, ne mentem meam frustra occupando ab aliis in quibus proficere possem impediret, penitus a me vellem excludere: tunc magis ac magis nolenti et defendenti se coepit cum importunitate quadem ingerere. Cum igitur quadam die vehementer eius importunitati resistendo fatigarer, in ipso cogitationum conflictu sic se obtulit quod desperaveram, ut studiose cogitationem amplecterer, quam sollicitus repellebam.

³⁰ *Monologion* I, Titel: Schmitt I: Quod sit quiddam optimum et maximum et summum omnium quae sunt.

³¹ *Proslogion* II: Schmitt I,101,5: . . . credimus te esse aliquid quo nihil maius cogitari possit.

³² Siehe oben n. 19.

³³ *Contra insipientem* II: Schmitt I,132,16-20: Vide quia consequitur esse in intellectu, ex eo quia intelligitur. Sicut enim quod cogitatur, cogitatione cogitatur, et quod cogitatione cogitatur, sicut cogitatur sic est in cogitatione: ita quod intelligitur intellectu intelligitur, et quod intellectu intelligitur, sicut intelligitur ita est in intellectu.

³⁴ Ibid. IX: Schmitt I,138,15-16: Quisquis . . . negat aliquid esse quo maius nequeat cogitari: utique intelligit et cogitat negationem quam facit.

³⁵ Cf. meine Arbeit: *Die Begründung der Philsophie durch Anselm von Canterbury: Eine Erörterung des ontologischen Gottesbeweises* (Stuttgart: Kohlhammer, 1966).

³⁶ A. J. Ayer, *Language, Truth and Logic* (London: V. Gollancz, 1967), p. 41; cf. dazu meine Schrift: *Eine Einführung in die Philosophie, Existentielle und wissen-*

schaftstheoretische Relevanz erkenntnis-kritischen Philosophierens (Stuttgart-Bad Cannstatt: Frommann-Holzboog,
1977.

[37] Ayer, *Language*, p. 73.

[38] Ibid., p. 33.

[39] Ibid., p. 73.

[40] Ibid., p. 33.

[41] Ibid., p. 33-34.

[42] Ibid., p. 120.

[43] *Proslogion* IV: Schmitt I,104,6-7: iam sic intelligo
. . . ut si te esse nolim credere, non possim non intelligere.

[44] *De veritate* XI: Schmitt I,191,19-20: . . . veritas
est rectitudo mente sola perceptibilis.

[45] Ibid. XII: Schmitt I,194,3: . . . omnis voluntas
habet quid et cur.

[46] Ibid. XII: Schmitt I,191,7: quid enim volendum sit,
palam est.

[47] *Proslogion* XVIII: Schmitt I,114,24: . . . unitas,
nullo intellectu divisibilis.

[48] Ibid. III: Schmitt I,16,21: . . . quod solum est per
se.

[49] Ibid. XXVIII: Schmitt I,46,24-31: Quod . . . sic
simpliciter et omnimoda ratione solum est perfectum, simplex
et absolutum: id nimirum quodam modo iure dici potest solum
esse. Et econtra, quidquid . . . nec simpliciter nec perfecte nec absolute esse sed vix esse aut fere non esse cognoscitur: id utique aliquo modo recte non esse cognoscitur:
id utique aliquo modo recte non esse dicitur. Secundum hanc
igitur rationem solus ille creator spiritus est, et omnia
creata non sunt; nec tamen omnino non sunt.

[50] Ibid. LXVII: Schmitt I,78,4-5: . . . [mens] certe
inde verius esse [summae essentiae] se probat imaginem, quia
illius potest esse memor, illam intelligere et amare.

[51] *Proslogion* XXV: Schmitt   I,119,7-12:   . . . omnibus illis erit una voluntas, quia nulla illis erit nisi sola Dei voluntas.   .   . . quia sicut illi non aliud volent quam quod ille, ita ille volet quidquid illi volent; et quod ille volet, non poterit non esse.

[52] *Cur deus homo*, Praefatio: Schmitt II,42,16-43,2:   . . . necesse esse ut hoc fiat de homine propter quod factus est, sed non nisi per hominem-deum.

[53] Siehe oben n. 20.

[54] Siehe oben n. 44.

[55] *Proslogion* IV: Schmitt I,104,5-7:   Gratias tibi, bone Domine, gratias tibi, quia quod prius credidi te donante, iam sic intelligo te illuminante, ut . . . non possim non intelligere.

L'usage de la sainte Ecriture
chez S. Anselme et S. Augustin
ou
Le projet historique, conçu au XI siècle,
d'une science sacrée rationnelle, non positive

André Cantin

La question proposée se lit, pour ainsi dire, dans S. Anselme lui-même. Dès le prologue de sa première "méditation écrite," connue après sa parution en 1076 sous le titre de *Monologion*, il annonce en effet, comme règle essentielle à son projet, une décision radicale concernant l'usage ou plutôt le non-usage de l'Ecriture. Rien, "absolument rien," *penitus nihil*, ne sera "persuadé par l'autorité de l'Ecriture." La démonstration de "l'essence de la divinité" ne devra trouver argument que dans la "nécessité de la raison."[1] Et, comme pour inviter son lecteur à sonder l'originalité de sa démarche, d'un poids historique incontestable, il le renvoie à S. Augustin.[2]

Il veut qu'on s'assure qu'il n'innove en rien pour ce qui est de la doctrine. Mais il en a déjà l'assurance, la vraie question n'est pas là. Elle porte sur la méthode, et plus précisément sur l'usage de la sainte Ecriture quand il s'agit d'énoncer ce qui n'est connu de Dieu que par elle. Anselme innove-t-il en décidant de ne tirer aucun argument de l'autorité de l'Ecriture? Jusqu'à quel point peut-il, pour cette audace de méthode, se réclamer de l'exemple de saint Augustin?

Il ne s'agit pas seulement de savoir si Anselme est original par rapport au maître auquel il veut se référer, mais encore de comprendre ce qu'il a fait en décidant de ne pas citer l'Ecriture au moment d'établir ce qu'il en est de l'essence de Dieu. Que signifie ce choix et de quelle portée historique est l'exigence qu'il exprime? Anselme commence par nous avertir que le choix lui a été dicté. L'exigence est celle de quelques frères. C'est une exigence collective que nous voyons portée par un courant rationnel, nourri par l'étude de la logique ou dialectique et sur le point d'emporter l'étude sacrée dans une direction nouvelle. *Sola ratione:*[3] en assumant, pour la démonstration des vérités révélées, reçues dans la foi, ce principe de méthode, maintenu assez largement dans la suite de ses méditations, même si l'Ecriture y affleure souvent, Anselme prend une décision de portée historique. Par des formules de chef d'école, quand bien même il est entraîné par d'autres et difficilement imitable, il pose en quelque sorte

l'acte de fondation d'un nouveau mode d'intelligence de la
foi.   On pourra lui attribuer l'instauration d'un nouveau
cours de la science sacrée. Bref, l'interrogation se charge
pour nous de tout le poids de la scolastique. Où peut-on la
voir commencer? Qu'en revient-il à Anselme?

Nous ne chercherons ici qu'à mieux assurer les bases de
cette interrogation, au plus près des textes, au moyen de
trois questions.

Premièrement, avant toute confrontation, quelle est la
véritable attitude que définit Anselme concernant l'usage de
l'Ecriture, et qu'il tient surtout dans son *Monologion*, mais
aussi, dans une grande mesure, tout au long de ses méditations écrites jusqu'au *De concordia* exclusivement?[4]

En deuxième lieu, ce point précisé s'il a pu l'être,
existe-t-il entre son maître Augustin et lui, sur le même
usage et sur l'attitude dont il dépend, une différence
essentielle par laquelle Anselme innoverait véritablement?

Enfin, s'il faut reconnaître à Anselme une originalité
certaine, concernant précisément l'usage de l'Ecriture
sainte dans l'étude des questions sacrées, quelles sont sa
signification et sa portée?

La présence-absence de l'Ecriture

La constatation la plus décisive est celle d'un fait sin-
gulier, au sens propre du terme, car il paraît sans exemple.
Voici un auteur nourri de l'Ecriture et qui, tout au long
d'une douzaine d'ouvrages de sa maturité rapportés par
lui-même à "l'étude de la sainte Ecriture,"[5] ne la cite
pratiquement jamais, alors qu'il entend ne rien dire qui
s'en écarte et qui ne doive être référé et soumis, parût-il
évident et nécessaire, à son autorité suprême.[6] Il aura
gardé pendant plus de vingt ans la "forme" qui lui a été
fournie et demandée pour ses "méditations écrites" lorsqu'on
lui a fait écrire la première. Elle est devenue pour lui
comme sa manière propre.

C'est un usage qui tranche tellement sur celui de son
temps, autant que nous pouvons en juger par les textes con-
servés, que nous ne pouvons pas négliger son propre aver-
tissement: cette habitude de méthode lui vient d'une
demande à laquelle il a consenti non sans peine.[7] Il ne
peut ignorer qu'il va ainsi contre l'enseignement formel de
son maître Lanfranc, lequel se faisait lui-même l'écho d'une
injonction du pape Léon IX: dans les "question sacrées,"
qu'on produise des "autorités sacrées" plutôt que des "raisons logiques!"[8] Anselme ne s'engage pas sans risque ni sans
précaution sur une voie contraire à la norme la plus offi-

cielle et, du reste, la plus traditionelle, saint Augustin
ne faisant point exception. Il rappelle encore, dans la
préface de son *Proslogion*, qu'il a été "forcé par la prière
de certains de ses frères" de publier un premier opuscule
"comme exemple de méditation sur la *ratio fidei*."[9] Il est
prêt à le détruire si Lanfranc ne l'approuve pas, mais il ne
cache pas que le succès aussitôt rencontré le convainc de
l'utilité d'avoir répondu par écrit, donc beaucoup plus
largement, à l'intérêt pressant de quelques-uns, intérêt
qu'on peut dire daté et qui exigeait alors, pour l'intelligence de la foi, des méthodes nouvelles.[10] En un mot, il
fait sienne une certain méthode, singulière, qu'une exigence
logique et rationelle lui imposait dans ces années 1070, et
il en voit les fruits.

Il savait pourquoi on lui demandait de ne pas citer
l'Ecriture comme argument. Cette convention passée entre
lui et quelques disciples, au rebours de l'usage normal en
de tels sujets, ne pouvait pas être un but en soi. La
vérité est d'abord reçue dans la foi; il ne s'agit pas
encore -- on en est loin -- de ramener la religion "dans les
limites de la simple raison." Quel résultat visait donc
l'intention d'exclure tout argument scripturaire? Il ne
s'agit pas, comme pour Bérenger de Tours, d'obtenir une
évidence rationnelle supérieure à l'autorité de l'Ecriture
au sujet même de ce qui n'a pu être connu que par cette
autorité. Anselme ajoute à la certitude de la foi une
évidence rationnelle sans enlever à la foi sa prééminence, à
l'inverse de Bérenger qui, quelques années avant lui, essaie
de plier la foi de l'Eglise à une nécessité de la raison,
reconnue par lui instance suprême, *quia in euidenti res
est*.[11]

Anselme laisse voir, en réalité, à la base de son propos
rationnel une pluralité d'intentions, unifiées par les
exigences de la foi. "Confondre la folie des infidèles et
rompre la dureté de leur coeur" en leur rendant raison de la
foi chrétienne, est une chose. Désirer s'approcher de la
vision béatifiante par "l'intelligence que nous saisissons
en cette vie comme moyen entre la foi et la vision,"[12] en
est une autre. Et les deux répondent à ce que demande une
foi sincère dans le coeur du croyant. Mais, dans tous les
cas, le désir ou le besoin d'une intelligence de la foi, la
confirmant par une certitude rationnelle de l'ordre de
l'évidence, implique-t-il que soit mis à l'écart le texte de
la Parole sacrée, source réelle de la foi?

Dans les années où se formait l'esprit d'Anselme, les
intentions qu'il exprime étaient partagées par d'autres
croyants, préparés comme lui à l'exercice du raisonnement
logique. Tout près de lui, son maître Lanfranc et l'éco-

lâtre de Tours, archidiacre d'Angers, Bérenger, cherchaient
à établir l'un contre l'autre le vrai contenu de la foi en
la conversion eucharistique au moyen d'autorités scriptu-
raires en premier lieu et, secondairement, par des arguments
logiques. Pierre Damien cherchait et enseignait à chercher
tout aussi ardemment que l'allait faire Anselme l'intelligence de la foi, mais "en défrichant les forêts de l'Ecriture,"[13] en la citant à chaque ligne, en s'opposant aux
conclusions faussement "nécessaires" de dialecticiens qui
eux-mêmes ne faisaient que s'attaquer à la Parole sacrée
pour dénoncer ses contradictions dans la lettre.

Pour expliquer la mise à l'écart de l'Ecriture, quelle
part faut-il faire au souci de l'incrédule qui ne connaît
pas l'Ecriture ou qui la rejette et qui, de toute façon, ne
reçoit pas l'autorité de l'Ecriture, laquelle est reçue dans
la foi? Quelle cohérence réelle peut-on trouver entre ces
deux but poursuivis en même temps par le même moyen: la
délectation que donne une certaine intelligence rationnelle
de la foi, intelligence de la Parole de Dieu non séparable
de l'expérience,[14] et le devoir de rendre raison de ce qu'on
espère, en raison de la Parole divine reçue dans la foi? On
dirait qu'Anselme trouve le secret d'être lui-même en se
mettant à la place de l'incroyant sans quitter la sienne.
Il entre comme il est, en croyant, dans le rôle d'un homme
"d'intelligence moyenne," "qui ignore ce que nous croyons
nécessairement, soit qu'il ne l'ait pas entendu dire, soit
qu'il ne le croie pas."[15] Cet homme a besoin de l'aide d'un
croyant pour pouvoir se dire ce qu'il peut se dire par le
seul pouvoir du raisonnement. Car ce qu'il peut se dire en
raisonnant, c'est ce qu'il ne sait pas. C'est ce qu'il
pourra néanmoins se prouver à lui-même par le raisonnement
seul, par le pur exercice de sa raison, à partir d'évidences
communes et sans jamais sortir de l'évidence, du moment
qu'il est guidé par la foi d'un autre qui sait ce qui est à
prouver et qui réussit à le faire en raisonnant comme un
incroyant plein de sens, ignorant la foi. Si cet autre
livrait la source de la connaissance qu'il possède dans la
foi, s'il se mettait à citer comme autorité la sainte Ecriture, aussitôt l'incroyant cesserait de le suivre et il le
priverait de se donner à lui-même la délectation de
découvrir la nécessité rationnelle, indépendante de la foi,
de ce qui'il connaît par la foi.

En tout cela, il reste clair à celui qui raisonne sur
Dieu qu'il faut croire pour "savoir" véritablement ce qu'il
en est de Dieu. Tout ce qu'on fera dire à cet homme incroyant, forcé d'assentir à l'évidence d'une chaîne de propositions nécessairement tirées d'une première évidence commune, est dit à partir de la foi, selon la foi et, secrète-

ment, sans sortir de la foi. Le discours rationnel, sans être aucunement déduit de la foi, ne laisse pas d'être conduit par elle. Comme chaîne d'énoncés à considérer en eux-mêmes, il est pleinement autonome. Mais il ne s'énonce pas primitivement hors de la foi. Il peut tout au plus être redit sans la foi, et garder sans elle cohérence et nécessité irrécusable. Il est discours d'un croyant qui, ayant effacé la source réelle de ses affirmations, s'en retire et les laisse offertes à tous, croyants ou incroyants, comme le discours d'une science objective et impersonnelle. Effaçant par méthode la source de ses affirmations, il ne la cache pas pour autant. Il maintient fermement que la foi est la condition de l'intelligence et de la science.[16] Non seulement il ne peut être question pour lui de faire accéder quiconque par la raison à la foi,[17] mais pas davantage d'épuiser dans l'intelligence qu'on en prend en raisonnant le mystère de la foi. Ce que l'on croit reste objet de foi jusqu'à la vision et ce que l'on comprend le mieux est la nécessité de le croire.[18]

Evodius, dialoguant avec Augustin sur le libre-arbitre, l'invitait déjà à ne pas s'en tenir à la foi, mais, en raisonnant, à chercher la science.[19] Il avait déjà à l'esprit le double désir de savoir et comprendre ce qu'il croyait fermement et de pouvoir démontrer de quelque façon ce qu'il croyait à ces "insensés" qui refusent de le croire.[20] Et lui aussi tombe d'accord avec Augustin qu'il faut encore partir de la foi. Mais de la foi prise en sa source, c'est-à-dire du témoignage des saintes Ecritures, à prendre en considération par la raison. Car pourquoi écarter du chemin de la raison ce qu'elle peut apprendre de l'autorité de témoins accrédités par Dieu auprès de l'homme raisonnable?[21] Au demeurant, comment oublierait-elle ce qu'elle en a reçu? Et de quel droit ferait-elle comme si elle l'avait oublié et le retrouvait par elle-même? Que n'a-t-elle pas reçu? Une "raison pure," oublieuse de ce qu'elle a appris, est une pure imagination. Anselme ne s'abondonne pas plus que son maître Augustin à cette supposition.[22] Mais en suivant la distinction accréditée surtout par l'autorité d'Augustin entre ce qui est connu "par raison" et ce qui l'est "par autorité,"[23] et en condescendant à l'exigence de jeunes esprits séduits par l'exercice logique des forces de la raison, à l'écart de l'autorité, même divine, il se laisse entraîner dans le jeu d'une séparation formelle, cachant ce qui informe sa raison en ses raisonnements de la part de l'autorité de l'Ecriture (*sola ratione, auctoritate nihil*), avec un radicalisme tout nouveau, inconnu de Jean Scot Erigène, et dont on cherche en vain le modèle en saint Augustin.[24]

La raison instruite par l'Ecriture en S. Augustin

Alors que l'Ecriture, lue et méditée dans la foi, est pour Anselme lui-même la source essentielle de ce qu'il énonce *sola ratione*, il a voulu prendre le parti radical d'écarter l'Ecriture pour démontrer la nécessité des vérités qu'elle enseigne. Nécessité, c'est-a-dire impossibilité de ne pas les admettre en leur tout et en leurs relations mutuelles, d'admettre l'une sans l'autre et sans le tout. Le projet d'Anselme: dégager la *ratio fidei* dans l'évidence de sa nécessité par le non-usage de l'Ecriture, en ne tirant aucun argument de son autorité, paraît d'une telle singularité qu'il ne trouve ni équivalent ni modèle, ni dans le maître dont il veut être couvert, saint Augustin, ni en aucun des philosophes chrétiens ou docteurs sacrés qui l'ont précédé.

Suivons d'abord au plus près l'indication par laquelle Anselme nous adresse lui-même à saint Augustin.

> Pour moi, réexaminant souvant mon texte, je n'ai rien pu trouver que j'y eusse dit qui ne s'accorde aux écrits des pères catholiques et surtout du bienheureux Augustin. C'est pourquoi, s'il semble à quelqu'un que j'ai avancé, dans cet opuscule, quelque chose qui ou bien soit trop nouveau, ou bien s'écarte de la vérité, je le prie de ne pas s'exclamer aussitôt, me traitant d'introducteur de nouveautés ou d'auteur de fausseté, mais d'examiner d'abord avec soin les livres dudit docteur Augustin *Sur la Trinité*, et de trancher ensuite, selon ces livres, le jugement de mon opuscule.[25]

Cet appel suffirait à nous faire sentir combien nous avons peine à entrer dans l'état d'esprit d'un homme séparé de nous par une distance et des différences que nous ne savons même pas évaluer. Car la nouveauté dont il se défend, sur le plan des affirmations doctrinales, nous paraît bien peu de chose par rapport à la nouveauté, frappante au contraire, concernant la méthode et dont il ne songe même pas à se défendre, ou plutôt qu'il ne juge pas nécessaire de justifier, alors qu'il vient de dire qu'il l'a lui-même longtemps réfusée.[26]

Que pouvait-il trouver dans les livres du bienheureux Augustin *Sur la Trinité* qui l'autorise, sur un tel sujet, à ne rien prouver, à ne tirer "absolument aucun argument de l'autorité de la sainte Ecriture"? Il pouvait d'abord

remarquer que le livre premier porte en titre: *Sur la Trinité selon les Ecritures*,[27] ce qui pourrait impliquer que
l'auteur admet une autre manière d'en traiter. D'autant que
les premiers mots de l'ouvrage attirent l'attention sur la
ratio en l'opposant aux principes de la foi.   Mais c'est
pour rappeler qu'en un tel sujet tout se fonde sur la Parole
qui inspire la foi, et non pas pour encourager ceux qui
chercheraient à prouver la Trinité par la nécessité de la
raison à prendre du champ par rapport au donné de
l'Ecriture.

> Il convient d'abord que celui qui s'apprête
> à lire nos dissertations sur la Trinité
> sache que notre style demeure vigilant
> contre les faussetés répandues par ces gens
> qui, méprisant l'entrée de la foi, se
> laissent tromper par un amour pervers du
> raisonnement.[28]

Lorsqu'il aura achevé de traiter de la Trinité selon les
Ecritures -- en quoi il ne sera pas suivi par Anselme --
Augustine laisera-t-il le champ libre à la raison, fournis-
sant à son disciple un modèle? Il n'en est rien. Le livre
deuxième ne fait que s'enfoncer plus profondément dans une
étude directement scripturaire. Le prologue ne sépare pas
"la découverte de la vérité et l'examen des livres divins et
saints," même si "de pénibles difficultés" résultent du
"langage complexe et multiforme des Lettres sacrées."[29]   En
fait, aucune difficulté scripturaire n'est esquivée, ni dans
les textes trinitaires du Nouveau Testament, cités et autant
qu'il se peut élucidés en premier, ni dans les théophanies
de l'Ancien, où l'auteur ne cache pas la peine qu'il a à
discerner si

> à travers ces formes corporelles: le buis-
> son ardent, la colonne de nuée ou de feu, la
> foudre sur la montagne . . . s'est manifesté
> aux Patriarches le Père, ou le Fils, ou le
> Saint Esprit, ou tantôt le Père, tantôt le
> Fils, tantôt le Saint Esprit, ou, sans
> aucune distinction des personnes, comme Dieu
> est dit unique et un, la Trinité
> elle-même.[30]

Aussi longuement qu'il le faut, avec le scrupule de respecter et de pénétrer toute indication de la lettre qu'il a
constamment sous les yeux et introduit continuellement dans
son texte, Augustin, comme le fera à sa suite, au temps même

d'Anselme, un Pierre Damien ou un Bruno de Segni, enferme l'exposition de la doctrine révélée dans un patient travail d'exégète, pour qu'elle soit puisée à sa source et sans cesse confirmée par le donné scripturaire, si difficile qu'il soit à interpréter quand il s'agit du mystère de la Trinité, car "à la vérité," remarque l'exégète, "la contexture même de l'Ecriture ne fait jamais sentir qu'elle passe d'une Personne divine à une autre."[31]

Ce que fait Augustin, Anselme le voit. Il sait comment il traite du mystère que lui-même prétend exposer rationnellement sur ses traces, sans introduire le texte de l'Ecriture, à la demande instante de certains frères. En cela, il n'ignore pas qu'Augustin lui donne l'exemple le plus opposé. Il ne semble pourtant même pas s'en apercevoir. "Qu'on examine avec soin, dit-il, les livres du docteur Augustin *Sur la Trinité* avant de s'exclamer et de dire que je suis un introducteur de nouveautés"![32] Si l'on examine en effet les sept premiers livres de saint Augustin sur la Trinité et qu'on mette en regard le texte du *Monologion*, on ne pourra certes pas les opposer sur les processions divines, mais l'on n'en sera pas moins, du fait de la méthode, devant deux mondes de pensée très différents, où s'élaborent deux types de sciences de formes tout opposées.

Une comparaison précise devient possible au moment où une réminiscence scripturaire affleure, pour celui qui peut la saisir, car elle n'est nullement signalée, dans le texte du raisonnement d'Anselme. L'opposition devient encore plus claire. Prenons, par exemple, les premières lignes du sixième livre de saint Augustin:

> Certains estiment que l'égalité du Père et du Fils et du Saint Esprit est rendue inintelligible parce qu'il est écrit: "Christ, Puissance de Dieu et Sagesse de Dieu,"[33] de sorte que l'égalité ne s'y voit pas puisque le Père n'est pas lui-même Puissance et Sagesse, mais générateur de la Puissance et de la Sagesse. Et en vérité c'est l'usage de chercher avec une attention tendue comment Dieu peut être dit Père de la Puissance et de la Sagesse. En effet l'Apôtre dit: "Christ, Puissance de Dieu et Sagesse de Dieu."[34]

Anselme, au *Monologion* XLV:

> Qu'il est plus juste de dire que le Fils est l'Essence du Père que le Père du Fils, et

que pareillement le Fils est la Puissance du
Père et sa Sagesse et autres semblables
choses. Bien que cela soit vrai par la
raison que nous venons de voir, il convient
pourtant beaucoup plus de dire le Fils
Essence du Père que le Père Essence du Fils.
En effet, puisque le Père n'a l'essence de
personne sinon de lui-même, cela manque de
justesse de dire qu'il a l'essence de
quelqu'un au lieu de la sienne. . . .[35]

Parler de la Puissance et de la Sagesse du Père, c'est
assurément évoquer "l'Apôtre" en sa première lettre aux
Corinthiens. Le même passage est présent à l'esprit
d'Anselme et à l'esprit d'Augustin. L'Ecriture est écartée
sans être oubliée; mais parce qu'elle est écartée, elle peut
être aussi oubliée. Lorsqu'Anselme en vient à conclure:

. . . Ainsi le Fils peut être dit avec plus
de convenance Essence du Père que le Père du
Fils . . . Donc pareillement le Fils est la
Puissance du Père, sa Sagesse, sa Vérité, sa
Justice et tout ce qui convient à l'essence
de l'Esprit suprême,[36]

il ne résout pas comme Augustin une difficulté de
l'Ecriture; il ne tire de l'Ecriture explicitement aucun
argument.

Cela est d'autant plus frappant qu'Augustin, en
s'enfermant dans l'Ecriture avec autant de détermination
qu'Anselme -- au niveau de son argumentation, il s'entend --
s'en évade, rencontre déjà les questions que son disciple
aborde et résout dans le même sens que lui. L'identité des
question et des réponses, l'identité surtout de la source
des question accusent l'opposition des méthodes. Augustin a
grand soin de marquer, à la différence d'Anselme, que ces
questions ne se posent qu'à partir du donné positif de
l'Ecriture, et s'éclairent au sein de l'étude et par
l'intelligence spirituelle de l'Ecriture:

De même, dit-il que le Père n'est grand que
par la grandeur qu'il a engendrée, ainsi il
n'est que par l'essence qu'il a engendrée,
puisque ce n'est pas autre chose pour lui
d'être et d'être grand. Mais alors est-il
père de sa propre essence, comme il est père
de sa propre grandeur, comme il est père de
sa Puissance et de sa Sagesse? En effet sa

> grandeur est la même chose que sa Puissance,
> et son essence la même chose que sa gran-
> deur. Ce débat est né de l'Ecriture qui
> appelle le Christ "Puissance de Dieu et
> Sagesse de Dieu."[37]

On ne saurait ramener plus clairement de telles questions et
un tel débat à leur fondement scripturaire. Il n'y a rien
dans l'exemple d'Augustin qui puisse servir de modèle ou de
caution à l'entreprise de traiter ces questions en les
détachant de leur source, en faisant abstraction de l'autorité de la sainte Ecriture.

Avec le livre huitième d'Augustin, commence une approche
nouvelle du même mystère.

> Le livre VIII marque une étape dans le *De
> Trinitate*. Tandis que, dans les sept premi-
> ers livres, Augustin s'appuie sur l'Ecriture
> et la Tradition pour établir le dogme (I-IV)
> et le défendre contre les interprétations
> tendancieuses des hérétiques (V-VII), il
> s'efforce, à partir du livre VIII, d'entrer
> dans l'intelligence du mystère et de com-
> prendre ce qu'il croit.[38]

Ce livre VIII a reçu pour titre: *Intellectus fidei*. Il
ouvre là, incontestablement, une certaine entrée à la tentative d'Anselme. Il peut d'une certaine manière le justifier
d'inviter son lecteur à trouver dans le traité d'Augustin
son modèle. Mais jusqu'à quel point son modèle?

Pour ce qui est de la doctrine, il n'y a aucun doute
qu'Anselme dépend particulièrement d'Augustin dans cette
deuxième partie de son ouvrage.[39] S'il imitait en tout
point cette deuxième partie, on pourrait dire qu'il commence, après quelques siècles troublés, là où l'évêque
d'Hippone finit. Ce serait déjà entre eux une différence
considérable. Augustin achève l'étude qui a rempli sa maturité par une méditation plus rationnelle. Le prieur du Bec,
la quarantaine passée, entame une nouvelle étude de l'essence trinitaire de la divinité en radicalisant la méthode
rationnelle, non plus positive et scripturaire, dont il
trouve l'essai à la fin du grand ouvrage de son maître. Mais
est-il vrai qu'il le suive en sa deuxième manière? C'est
toujours et jusqu'au bout l'usage de la sainte Ecriture qui
les différencie et les oppose formellement. Mais la différence va plus loin, l'opposition est plus radicale qu'on
ne le suppose en simplifiant et schématisant la dernière
partie du projet d'Augustin. Il est vrai qu'il annonce un

changement de méthode. Mais observons bien en quels termes et voyons s'il y a là quelque chose qui annonce le prologue du *Monologion*.

> Maintenant donc, dit-il, pour autant que le Créateur, admirablement miséricordieux, nous vient en aide, portons notre attention à ces choses que nous allons traiter d'une façon plus intérieure que les précédentes, bien qu'elles soient les mêmes, en gardant cette règle que ce qui n'aura pas encore brillé à notre intelligence ne soit pas rejeté hors de la solidité de la foi.[40]

Par l'expression *modo interiore*, Augustin ne peut vouloir annoncer qu'il confie à la *ratio* le relais de l'*auctoritas*. Il ne prétend pas que la raison livrée à ses propres ressources pénétrera plus avant dans l'intelligence de la foi que la méditation du donné scripturaire. En termes thomistes, "Augustin ne raisonne pas en philosophe après avoir réfléchi en théologien."[41] Il n'attribue pas au premier une "intériorité" à laquelle le second n'accéderait pas. Il reste l'homme de l'Ecriture. Mais il pénètre en un domaine nouveau, celui de l'âme humaine, image de Dieu, d'une certaine façon une et trine. L'Ecriture a-t-elle moins à dire sur lâme que sur Dieu? Quel parti va-t-il adopter à son égard, alors qu'elle semble moins nécessaire? Décide-t-il qu'il n'empruntera aucun argument à son autorité? Il en est si éloigné que non seulement il continue à la citer, au contraire, mais encore que c'est au moment où il entre dans le coeur de son nouveau sujet qu'il multiplie les citations et s'appuie le plus et jusqu'au bout de son ouvrage, sur le donné scripturaire.[42]

De quelque façon qu'on s'y prenne pour les rapprocher, il apparaît donc que plus Anselme suit Augustin de près pour ce qui est de la doctrine, plus il innove par rapport à lui pour ce qui est de la méthode. La différence essentielle est irréductible. Augustin a beau confier davantage à la *ratio*, il ne manque jamais de l'appliquer d'une façon explicite à la source réelle de sa connaissance, la révélation donnée à la foi à travers le texte de la Parole sacrée. Augustin ne pose nulle part la convention ou la supposition d'une raison qui n'emprunterait aucun argument à l'autorité de l'Ecriture; qui démontrerait la nécessité de l'incarnation *remoto Christo*. Il agit tout au contraire. Il ne semble même pas concevoir la possibilité d'une démonstration rationnelle de ce qui est reçu dans la foi, faisant abstraction du donné positif de l'Ecriture. Même dans la partie finale du *De trinitate*, l'Ecriture n'est nullement écartée; nous restons dans l'ordre traditionnel de la science sacrée, science positive, science de la Parole de Dieu où se trouvent conjointes en une double attention le texte de la Loi et les oeuvres de la Parole créatrice.

Par dessous la référence qu'il indique lui-même dès les premier pas de sa tentative nouvelle, il serait difficile de nier l'originalité de la démarche d'Anselme. Il s'écarte bel et bien de celui qu'il veut suivre. Il introduit une étonnante nouveauté. Il ne cache même pas qu'il a été lui-même étonné de l'exigence nouvelle qui a fini par l'y engager.

La séparation d'avec Augustin porte donc précisément sur l'usage de l'Ecriture sainte. Nous l'avons considérée surtout dans le *Monologion*. En est-il toujours ainsi? Il est clair que dans le *De concordia*, Anselme n'est plus tenu par la règle qu'il a acceptée au début de *Monologion*. Mais cela ne fait que mieux ressortir l'originalité des ouvrages où elle reste suivie. Surtout lorsqu'ils sont rattachés par l'auteur à l'étude de la sainte Ecriture. Ainsi en est-il du *De libertate arbitrii*. Il a l'intérêt particulier de reprendre le thème d'un ouvrage bipartite de saint Augustin où l'on pourrait voir apparaître une amorce de la méthode rationnelle excluant les citations de l'Ecriture et les arguments tirés de son autorité. La confrontation s'impose donc, mais, sur la question de l'usage de l'Ecriture, elle aboutit aussitôt: le parti adopté par saint Anselme n'a aucun équivalent en saint Augustin. Déjà on peut remarquer que ce n'est pas au début de son traité que celui-ci entreprend de démontrer l'existence de Dieu dans l'évidence rationnelle, par un autre chemin que celui de l'autorité de l'Ecriture, mais au début de second livre.[43] Là encore, ce qui peut être un deuxième temps chez le maître devient pour son disciple démarche initiale. Ce décalage, par lui-même, aurait un sens. Le mouvement de l'esprit n'est pas le même et l'exemple nouveau n'est pas sans signification historique. Mais on ne soupçonne pas toujours l'ampleur de la différence. Augustin est fort éloigné de vouloir mettre la *ratio* à part de l'autorité divine. Il n'entend pas lui réserver un second rôle où elle n'aurait plus à consulter l'Ecriture. Il commence par inviter son interlocuteur, Evodius, à "entrer dans le chemin de la raison soutenu par la piété."[44] Et c'est au moment même où Evodius demande que ce qu'il admettent déjà par la foi, ils le cherchent maintenant comme si tout était incertain, afin de le tenir par la connaissance,[45] qu'il introduit plus généreusement l'Ecriture et, multipliant les citations, s'appuie davantage sur elle.[46] Abordant la démonstration pourtant rationnelle de

l'existence de Dieu, il ne prend nullement le parti de
laisser de côté l'autorité de l'Ecriture. Il ne fait qu'y
recourir encore plus, comme de raison, pourrait-on dire. Il
ne croit pas que l'homme puisse parler raisonnablement de la
raison des choses à moins de lui laisser la parole. Il
tient que l'homme "revient à la raison" par l'unique Chemin
qui est la Parole vivante de Dieu.

Signification et portée de l'adhésion d'Anselme
au projet d'une étude sacrée rationnelle et non positive

Anselme adhère non sans réticence à un projet qu'il n'a
pas conçu et qui a mûri avant lui, porté par un courant
d'exigence où s'exalte la passion dialectique, elle-même
nourrie des rudiments de la logique d'Aristote, encore mal
restituée et indéfiniment remâchée par les commentateurs.
Ce projet nouveau le fait rompre avec l'usage de la sainte
Ecriture qui a prévalu jusqu'en son temps. Usage indispensable en l'étude de questions relevant spécialement de l'autorité de l'Ecriture. Il le sent si bien lui-même qu'il
laissera les réminiscences de l'Ecriture affleurer en son
texte, alors qu'il a convenu de ne pas la citer.[47] Il
protestera que ses conclusions en apparence les plus nécessaires sur le plan du raisonnement restent soumises au
jugement d'une autorité plus haute qui est justement celle
de l'Ecriture, interprétée par l'Eglise. Il tremblera
devant le jugement de son maître Lanfranc et croira devoir
justifier son entreprise de fonder en raison nécessaire
l'incarnation du Christ en faisant abstraction du Christ, en
l'expliquant au pape Urbain II et en la soumettant à son
examen.[48] Il ne peut que se sentir aventuré, la hardiesse
de son originalité est certaine. Pour la mesurer, nous
l'avons confronté à saint Augustin, maître incontesté des
penseurs latins. Nous pourrions le comparer aux maîtres qui
l'ont entouré, à ceux qui l'ont formé, et tout particulièrement à son maître Lanfranc. Lanfranc, aussi dépendant
que lui à l'égard de saint Augustin, se refuse véhémentement
à livrer aux *rationes* le champ de l'étude sacrée, débarrassé
des *auctoritates*, c'est-à-dire des témoignages divins des
saintes Ecritures.[49] Mais son adversaire Bérenger lui-même,
champion de la dialectique au milieu du siècle et plaçant la
raison "incomparablement au-dessus" de l'autorité, même
divine, parce qu'elle possède l'évidence logique, ne laisse
pas de chercher l'appui des autorités sacrées et cite conti-
nuellment l'Ecriture.[50] Ne parlons pas des Pierre Damien,
Bruno de Segni, esprits aussi positifs que possible, constamment penchés sur l'Ecriture, enseignant qu'il faut

éviter de rien dire qui ne soit appuyé sur un fait dûment
constaté ou sur un témoignage authentique de la Parole
divine.[51] Quelque différents que soient les auteurs contem-
porains d'Anselme et du même ordre que lui, aussi richement
variés en leurs attitudes et en leurs solutions aux mêmes
problèmes que les bâtisseurs de l'art roman qui sont leurs
frères, tous néanmoins se réunissent sur un point qui est de
refuser dans leur écrits que rien, "absolument rien ne soit
prouvé par l'autorité de l'Ecriture." Cela n'appartient qu'à
Anselme. Et pourtant Anselme nous dit que d'autres que lui,
qui sont ses proches, l'ont poussé à prendre cette option
inédite. Tout semble se passer comme si l'exigence logique,
attestée aussi bien dans les cloîtres que dans les écoles
séculières,[52] et toujours jusque là tournée vers l'Ecriture
pour en soumettre la lettre à ses lois, se trouvant, en
présence d'Anselme, devant une capacité de prouver incompa-
rable, avait franchi un seuil dans l'esprit de jeunes moines
logiciens, d'ailleurs soucieux de convaincre les incrédules,
en leur faisant concevoir le projet d'une exposition de la
foi catholique exempte de tout recours à l'Ecriture et à
l'enseignment traditionnel de l'Eglise et entièrement fondée
sur "la nécessité de la raison." La puissance de la pensée
qui donne à ce projet une réalisation simple et magistrale,
la vigueur provocante des formules qu'Anselme ne craint pas
d'employer (*auctoritate penitus nihil, remoto Christo . . .*)
donnent en quelque sorte ses lettres de noblesse à une
entreprise ample et diffuse qui cherchait sa voie et qui en
trouvera encore bien d'autres en direction d'une intelligence rationnelle de la foi. La solution adoptée est singulière; elle ne réussit pas à canaliser le courant dialectique qui entraîne déjà l'étude sacrée dans une direction
nouvelle; elle signale sa force et lui donne sa première
victoire. Entre la tentative de Bérenger, à partir de 1049,
et le succès d'Anselme en 1076, "l'intelligence," pour citer
le Père de Lubac, "entre dans un nouvel âge." Dès le milieu
du siècle, "une mentalité nouvelle se répand,"[53] préparant
pour la science de la Loi divine, la plus haute et la plus
influente sur les esprits, un nouveau cours dominé par la
déduction logique. Anselme n'en fixe pas les fondements; il
rappelle seulement que la Parole de Dieu elle-même invite le
croyant à chercher à la comprendre;[54] il atteste par son
exemple que le courant rationnel est irrésistible et que le
nouveau cours de l'étude sacrée auquel il aboutit peut être
fécond et catholique.
    Il reste que la signification du parti adopté par An-
selme, au temps même où il le fut, et plus encore sa portée
ultérieure, dans le développement de la pensée "scolastique"

et ses immense répercussions, ne peuvent être comprises qu'au prix de nouvelles et patientes recherches. Une ébauche de problématique historique pourrait à cela être utile.

Il nous faut d'abord nous assurer que ce choix d'Anselme de ne tirer absolument aucmple en mille ans d'intelligence de la foi chétienne.

Nous pouvons retenir cependant que, quand bien même le même projet, porté par les mêmes exigences, aurait déjà été formé, les circonstances historiques changent complètement la portée de l'entreprise. Le moment de la pensée latine chrétienne où éclôt l'oeuvre d'Anselme est celui de l'essor de l'Europe, pour la première fois libre d'invasions et désormais conquérante. C'est à la faveur de cet essor, qui se continuera jusqu'à notre temps, qu'on peut identifier ce moment historique au départ de l'aventure européene de la raison. Mais en une telle vue, autant de questions que de termes, et qui en susciteront beaucoup d'autres.

Pour aller rapidement ici aux masses les plus grandes, dans quelle mesure peut-on dire que la non-positivité, c'est-à-dire le fait de ne pas faire porter la réflexion et l'étude sur un donné positif, tel que l'Ecriture sainte interprétée par l'Eglise, et de ne pas soumettre à ce donné les conclusions obtenues par le raisonnement pour qu'elles soient vérifiées ou infirmées par lui, caractérise un certain type de *sacra doctrina* auquel s'attachera bientôt le nom de scolastique? Et, si l'on peut définir une méthode scolastique, quels rapports peut-on lui trouver avec la méthode assez précisément définie et pratiquée par Anselme?

Dans l'histoire de la science sacrée elle-même, à partir d'Anselme, peut-on suivre les conséquences de l'option non positive si fortement exprimée par la formule: *penitus nihil auctoritate Scripturae*?

Pour concrétiser quelque peu cette dernière question, portons notre attention, cinquante ans plus tard, par delà Roscelin et Abélard, à la situation qui régnait dans les écoles parisiennes lorsque Pierre Lombard, avant 1159, y fut maître de "théologie," selon le nom donné par le dialecticien Abélard à la science sacrée. La description qu'en ont donnée les Mauristes (PL CXCI,13-14) n'en dit certes pas le dernier mot, mais reste fort significative des changements et des troubles durables produits par l'invasion dialectique ou par l'introduction de la déduction logique dans le champ de l'étude sacrée.

Deux méthodes régnaient dans les écoles de
théologie lorsque Pierre Lombard se mit sur
les rangs pour enseigner. La première, qui
était celle de l'Antiquité, consistait à
expliquer par ordre la doctrine enfermée
dans l Ecriture d'après l'Ecriture elle-même
et la tradition, méthode simple, mais sûre,
pacifique, lumineuse, qui maintenait dans sa
pureté le dépôt de la Révélation, édifiait
en instruisant, et fixait à l'esprit humain
le terme où il devait s'arrêter dans la
recherche des vérités du salut. La seconde,
que notre auteur avait presque vu naître,
était de traiter les matières de la religion
comme celles de la philosophie, d'une
manière contentieuse et par la voie du raisonnement, embarrassée, pointilleuse, plus
propre à satisfaire le curiosité qu'à nour-
rir la piété, elle repoussait les barrières
qui séparent la raison de la foi, ouvrait la
porte à des questions sans fin; et moins
occupée du principal que de l'accessoire,
elle jetait des nuages sur le premier de ces
objets par les efforts que ses partisans
faisaient pour répandre des lumières sur le
second.

Pouvons-nous à bon droit attribuer à une positivité
déficiente la cause principale des écarts de la scolastique
et de ses échecs? Pouvons-nous la critiquer en tenant
compte du prisme à travers lequel nous la voyons, celui du
progrès tout différent de sciences "positives" (positif:
qui est donné à titre de fait par l'expérience), fondées
avec Galilée en opposition et antithèse avec elle, non sans
lui devoir beaucoup, et qui se sont largement substituées à
l'intelligence de la foi et à la vie de la foi dans le rôle
de moteur de l'évolution de l'humanité?
Si la seule science qui peut actuellement accorder tous
les esprits, par la soumission à l'intuition sensible donnée
à tous, ne peut aussi que les décevoir, laissant de côté
l'invisible et l'essentiel et exposant à le négliger ou à le
nier, cette situation, née de ce qu'on a appelé "la rationalité moderne," ne renvoie-t-elle pas aux insuffisances de
la conception de la raison qui s'est affirmée, non sans
variations et lacunes, depuis l'époque d'Anselme, l'auteur
par qui a fait ses premières preuves une confiance nouvelle
en la raison?

Il s'agirait en somme de sonder la double insuffisance, révélée successivement, d'une science sacrée d'un genre nouveau à la fin du XIe siècle, élaborée sous l'emprise de la raison au détriment de la positivité de ses fondements, et d'une science positive pacée ensuite sous le signe de la rationalité à l'écart du sacré et de la raison des choses. Constatant cette double insuffisance historique, ne sommes-nous pas replacés collectivement, en humanité, devant le mystère de la raison? Par là, nous pourrions être renvoyés en particulier à saint Augustin, invoqué par Anselme et les penseurs de son temps comme leur maître commun et, de toute façon, l'un des auteurs les plus constamment et profondément attachés à élucider ce mystère. Il nous indique une ligne de crête dans la recherche de ce que peut être la raison en liant le *regressus in rationem* à l'écoute de la *summa ratio*. Dans la recherche du secret de la raison même, il a guidé Anselme.

Il ne saurait être laissé à l'écart d'une interrogation suscitée par l'étrange décision de ce moine du Bec, son disciple du XIe siècle, qui peut-être ne s'aperçut même pas qu'il dépassait son exemple en voulant démontrer les plus hauts mystères de la foi par la seule "nécessité de la raison," en ne prouvant rien, "absolument rien par l'autorité de la sainte Ecriture."

Notes

[1] *Monologion*, prologus: Schmitt I,7: Cuius scilicet scribendae meditationis . . . hanc mihi formam praestituerunt: quatenus auctoritate scripturae penitus nihil in ea persuaderetur, sed quidquid per singulas inuestigationes finis assereret, id ita esse plano stilo et uulgaribus argumentis simplicique disputatione et rationis necessitas breuiter cogeret et ueritatis claritas patenter ostenderet.

[2] *Ibid.*: Schmitt I,8: . . . Si cui uidebitur quod in eodem opusculo aliquid protulerim quod aut nimis nouum sit aut a ueritate dissentiat, rogo ne statim me aut praesumptorem nouitatum aut falsitatis assertorem exclamat, sed prius libros praefati doctoris Augustini *De trinitate* diligenter perspiciat, deinde secundum eos opusculum meum diiudicet. Cf. *Epistola 77*: Schmitt III,199-200.

[3] *Monologion* I: Schmitt I,13: Si quis . . . quae de Deo siue de eius creatura necessarie credimus aut non audiendo aut non credendo ignorat, puto quia ea ipsa ex magna parte,

si uel mediocris ingenii est, potest ipse sibi saltem sola
ratione persuadere.

[4] Notons qu'au début de son *Monologion*, Anselme, qui de
toute façon pose la foi en principe comme condition de
l'intelligence, ne s'interdit pas de citer l'Ecriture ou
d'en évoquer tel ou tel passage, mais accepte la règle de
n'en tirer, pour sa démonstration, aucun argument qui aurait
sa force dans l'autorité de l'Ecriture. Sauf erreur, il
restera fidèle à cette régle de méthode jusqu'au *De con-*
cordia où enfin il reprendra la liberté du croyant de
prendre explicitement dans l'autorité de l'Ecriture (cf.
chap. 5) les principes de son argumentation.

[5] Comme il le dit de trois d'entre eux, au début de la
préface du *De ueritate*, tous les ouvrages d'Anselme appartiennent à l'étude de la sainte Ecriture du moment qu'il
suit et explicite son enseignement.

[6] *Monologion* I: Schmitt I,14: . . . Si quid dixero quod
maior non monstret auctoritas, sic uolo accipi ut, quamuis
ex rationibus quae mihi uidebuntur quasi necessarium conclu-
datur, non ob hoc tamen omnino necessarium, sed tantum sic
interim uideri posse dicatur.

[7] Cf. *Monologion*, prologus: Schmitt I,7-8; *Epistola ad*
Lanfrancum archiepiscopum (de libro qui dicitur Monologion):
Schmitt I,5-6; *Proslogion*, prooemium: Schmitt I,93-94;
Epistola 72: Schmitt III,193,19.

[8] Cf. Lanfrancus, *De corpore et sanguine domini*: *PL* CL,
413B-416D.

[9] *Proslogion*, prooemium: Schmitt I,93-94: Postquam
opusculum quoddam uelut exemplum meditandi de ratione fidei
cogentibus me precibus quorundum fratrum in persona alicuius
tacite secum ratiocinando quae nesciat inuestigantis edidi
. . . On remarquera qu'il s'agit d'un "exemple" illustrant
une manière possible de méditer sur le contenu raisonné de
la foi, construit par le raisonnement en une certaine
science de la foi.

[10] Cf. *Epistola 72*: Schmitt III,193,20-22; *Epistola* 74:
Schmitt III,196, 14-28; *Epistola 77*: Schmitt III,199-200;
Monologion, epistola dedicatoria ad Lanfrancum: Schmitt
I,5-6; *Proslogion*, prooemium: Schmitt I,93-94. L'exigence
de ces méthodes nouvelles, basées sur la dialectique, se
trouve attestée principalement dans la réponse de Bérenger

de Tours à Lanfranc sur l'Eucharistie: *De sacra coena,
aduersus Lanfrancum*, ed. W. H. Beekenkamp (La Haye: M.
Nijhoff, 1941), et dans la réponse de Pierre Damien à des
moines dialecticiens du Mont Cassin qui lui avaient tendu le
piège d'une objection dialectique contre la toute-puissance
divine: voir n. 52 infra.

[11] Bérenger, *De sacra coena*, p. 47: . . . Ratione agere
in perceptione ueritatis incomparabiliter superius esse,
quia in euidenti res est, sine uecordiae cecitate nullus
negauerit.

[12] Cf. *Cur deus homo*, commendatio operis ad Urbanum papam
II: Schmitt II,39-40: Quamuis post apostolos sancti patres
et doctores nostri multi tot et tanta de fidei nostrae ratione dicant ad confutandum insipientiam et frangendum duritiam infidelium, et ad pascendum eos qui iam corde fide mun-
dato eiusdem fidei ratione, quam post eius certitudinem
debemus esurire, delectantur, ut nec nostris nec futuris
temporibus ullum illis parem in ueritatis contemplatione
speremus: nullum tamen reprehendendum arbitror, si fide
stabilitus in rationis eius indagine se uoluerit exercere
. . . Inter fidem et speciem intellectum quem in hac uita
capimus esse medium intelligo.

[13] *Epistola XXXVII*, Alberico: *PL* CXLV,623A: Tu quoque,
frater . . . mittendus es ad siluas Scripturarum, ubi scilicet continuo labore desudans siluescentia saltus arbusta
succidas, nodos et dubietatum truncos euellas, ac noualia
tibi uelut quibusdam propriae indaginis manibus excolas.
Cf. *Epistola XLV*, Ariprando: *PL* CXLV,704 A: Discumbis,
frater, ad mensam Dei, sufficiant tibi dapes caelestis elo-
quii. *Epistola VIII* 14, sororibus Rodelindae atque Suffi-
ciae: *PL* CXLIV,496D: Spirituales epulae mentes uestras
delectabiliter pascant, uidelicet diuinorum uerborum assidua
meditatio. . .

[14] Cf. *Epistola de incarnatione verbi* I: Schmitt
II,3-10.

[15] *Monologion* I: Schmitt I,13-15: Si quis unam naturam,
summam omnium quae sunt . . . aliaque perplura quae de Deo
siue de eius creatura necessarie credimus, aut non audiendo
aut non credendo ignorat, puto quia ea ipsa ex magna parte,
si uel mediocris ingenii est, potest ipse sibi saltem sola
ratione persuadere.

[16] Sur ce point, voir la même position dans le *Monologion*: quae necessarie credimus . . . ratione persuadere; *Proslogion*, prooemium: Schmitt I,93-94: quaerentis intelligere quod credit.

[17] *Cur deus homo* I: Schmitt II,47,8-9: . . . Non ut per rationem ad fidem accedant . . .

[18] *Proslogion* I: Schmitt I,100,19: Nam et hoc credo: quia nisi credidero non intelligam. L'expression: quae necessarie credimus (*Monologion* I: Schmitt I,13,8-9) peut s'entendre de plusieurs façons: parce que Dieu l'a révélé et qu'il est nécessaire de croire ce qu'il nous enseigne; parce qu'il est nécessaire de croire d'abord pour pouvoir comprendre ensuite: parce que ce qu'on croit apparaît nécessaire une fois démontré. Ce dernier sens de *necessarie credimus*: nous croyons nécessairement ce que nous avons démontré par des raisons nécessaires ne peut être retenu dans ce contexte du début du *Monologion*. Il est suggéré par E. Gilson, *La philosophie au moyen-âge*, 2e éd. (Paris: Payot, 1947), p. 242: ". . . tout se passe comme si l'on pouvait toujours arriver à comprendre, sinon ce que l'on croit, du moins la nécessité de le croire."

[19] *De libero arbitrio* II,ii,5: *BA* 6,271: Quanquam haec inconcussa fide teneam, tamen quia cognitione nondum teneo, ita quaeramus quasi omnia incerta sint . . . Hoc non contemplando, sed credendo inconcusse teneo.

[20] Ibid.: Si quis ergo illorum insipientium . . . uellet . . . cognoscere utrum uera credideris . . .

[21] Ibid.: Tum ego demonstrarem, quod cuiuis facillimum puto, quanto esset aequius, cum sibi de occultis animi sui quae ipse nosset, uellet alterum credere qui non nosset, ut etiam ipse tantorum uirorum libris, qui se cum Filio Dei uixisse testatum litteris reliquerunt, esse Deum crederet . . .

[22] Cf. *De ordine* II,xi,30: *BA* 4,416: Ratio est mentis *motio*, ea quae discuntur distinguendi et connectendi potens (*motio* ne suppose aucune catégorie *a priori* pour relier et distinguer "ce qui s'apprend"); *Monologion* I: Schmitt I,14,5-7: . . . cum tam innumerabilia bona sint, quorum tam multam diuersitatem et sensibus corporeis experimur et ratione mentis discernimus . . .

[23] Cf. *De ordine* II,9,26: ad discendum item necessario dupliciter ducimur: auctoritate atque ratione.

[24] Entre Augustin et Anselme, Jean Scot pourrait leur être comparé pour l'ampleur de la pensée spéculative; or "ce prétendu rationaliste fonde entièrement sa philosophie sur une base scripturaire, en quoi il ne fait d'ailleurs que suivre l'exemple de ses deux maîtres préférés, Augustin et Denys" (Gilson, *La philosophie au moyen-âge*, p. 203). Cf. *In Iohannis euangelium* I,29: éd. Ed. Jeauneau, Sources Chrétiennes, No. 180 (Paris: Cerf, 1972), p. 156: Duo pedes uerbi sunt, quorum unus est naturalis ratio uisibilis creaturae, alter spiritualis intellectus diuinae scripturae.

[25] *Monologion*, prologus: Schmitt I,7-8.

[26] Ibid.: Schmitt I,7,13-14: Quod quidem diu tentare recusaui atque me cum re ipsa comparans multis me rationibus excusare tentaui.

[27] *De trinitate secundum Scripturas*. Bien qu'on ne puisse pas faire remonter la tradition manuscrite jusqu'à l'auteur lui-même, on ne peut douter que ce titre du *liber primus*, inscrit ou non par lui en tête de l'ouvrage, corresponde à son intention. Cf. *De trinitate* I,ii,4: *BA* 15,94: Sed primum secundum auctoritatem Scripturarum sanctarum, utrum ita se fides habeat, demonstrandum est.

[28] *De trinitate* I,i,1: *BA* 15,86: . . . fidei contemnentes initium, immaturo et peruerso rationis amore falluntur. Il semble ici préférable de traduire *ratio* par: le raisonnement, plutôt que par: la raison.

[29] L'auteur résiste à deux vices (présomption et obstination): *De trinitate* II, prooemium: *BA* 15,182: A quibus duobus uitiis nimis inimicis inuentioni ueritatis et tractationi diuinorum sanctorumque librorum . . . experti difficultates laboriosas, siue in ipsa acie mentis conantis intueri inaccessibilem lucem, siue in ipsa multiplici et multimoda locutione litterarum.

[30] *De trinitate* II,vii,12-13: *BA* 15,212-16.

[31] Ibid. II,x,17: *BA* 15,224: Contextio quidem ipsa Scripturae nusquam transire sentitur a persona ad personam.

[32] *Monologion*, prologus; voir n. 25.

[33] Cf. 1 Co 1:24.

[34] *De trinitate* VI,i,1:   *BA* 15,468-70; cf. 1 Co 1:24.

[35] *Monologion* XLV: Schmitt I,61-62.

[36] Ibid., in fine.   Entre les deux passages cités, voir la partie la plus subtile de l'argumentation rationnelle.

[37] *De trinitate* VII,i,2:   *BA* 15,506: Haec disputatio nata est ex eo quod scriptum est: "Christum" esse "Dei uir- tutem et Dei sapientiam."   Cf. *De trinitate* VII,i,1:   *BA* 15,502.

[38] P. Agaësse et J. Moingt, Introduction à "cette seconde partie du *De trinitate*," *BA* 16,7.

[39] A partir du *Monologion* XLVIII, Anselme reprend à son compte l'analogie augustinienne de l'âme: mémoire, intelli- gence, amour, à l'image de Dieu, notamment au chapitre 67.

[40] *De trinitate* VIII,i,1:   *BA* 16,26:   . . . seruata illa regula ut quod intellectui nostro nondum eluxerit, a firmi- tate fidei non dimittatur.

[41] Introduction, *BA* 16,8.

[42] Cf. notamment: *De trinitate* VIII,ii,3:   *BA* 16,28; iv,6: *BA* 16,38; vii,10-11:   *BA* 16,58-62; viii,12:   *BA* 16,62.

[43] *De libero arbitrio* II,ii,5:   *BA* 6,271.

[44] Ibid. I,vi,14:   *BA* 6,214:   Rationis uias pietate fretus ingredere.

[45] Ibid. II,ii,5:   *BA* 6,271.

[46] Ibid. et seq.

[47] Pour le seul *Monologion*; Gn 1; Si 6:32; Is 53; Jn 1, 4, 5, 14; Rm 11; 1 Co 1, 8, 13; Col 1; He 1; Je 2. Rémi- niscences beaucoup plus nombreuses dans le *Proslogion*, mais absence d'argumentation scripturaire sur la question traitée jusqu'au *De concordia* exclusivement.

[48] Cf. *Monologion* I: Schmitt I,14; supra, n. 10, et *Epistola ad Lanfrancum* I,6:   Schmitt II,39-40.

[49] Cf. Lanfranc, *De Corpore et Sanguine Domini aduersus Berengarium Turonensem*: *PL* CL,413B, 416D-417A.

[50] Cf. Bérenger, *De sacra coena adversus Lanfrancum*. Voir n. 10 supra.

[51] Sur Pierre Damien, cf. *PL* CXLIV et CXLV; G. Fornasari, *S. Pier Damiani e la storiografia contemporanea: osservazioni in margine a recenti studi damianei* (Rome: 1979); A. Cantin, *Les sciences séculières et la foi: Les deux voies de la science au jugement de S. Pierre Damien* (Spolète: Centro italiano di studi sull'alto Medioevo , 1975). Sur Bruno de Segni: D. R. Grégoire, *Bruno de Segni, exégète médiéval et théologien monastique* (Spolète: Centro italiano di studi sull'alto Medioevo, 1965).

[52] Pierre Damien en reste le principal témoin. Cf. notamment: Pierre Damien, *Lettre sur la toute-puissance divine* (aux dialecticiens du Mont-Cassin, en 1067), Sources Chrétiennes, No. 191 (Paris: Cerf, 1972).

[53] Cf. H. de Lubac, *Corpus mysticum: L'Eucharistie et l'Eglise au Moyen Age* (Paris: Aubier, 1944), p. 262.

[54] En citant, au pape Urbain II par exemple, la formule tirée d'Isaïe 7:9: "nisi credideritis, non intelligetis," il ne met pas l'accent sur la foi première, sans laquelle l'intelligence est impossible, mais sure l'invitation à chercher l'intelligence, que l'Ecriture adresse aux croyants: *Cur deus homo*, commendatio operis: Schmitt II,40,7-10 . . . . Sacra pagina nos ad inuestigandam rationem inuitat . . . aperte nos monet intentionem ad intellectum extendere, cum docet qualiter ad illum debeamus proficere.

Anselm's *Brevitas*

Burcht Pranger

It cannot be denied that Anselm's way of writing shows a tendency towards brevity. A partial explanation of this phenomenon can be found in Anselm's Benedictine background in which brevity of speech directed towards both the most efficient and the most elegant way of putting things plays such an important role. It is, however, more difficult in this regard to assess the meaning of the other main stream of influence: the Augustinian way of thinking and the Augustinian rhetoric. Augustinian in substance and style though Anselm's thought may be, he does not seem to be in need of the continuous verbal and rhetorical flux which keeps Augustines mind going. On the other hand, it cannot be said that Augustine writes at random, without a strong idea of composition. As Henri-Irénée Marrou has shown in his *St. Augustin et la fin de la culture antique*.[1] Augustine's rhetoric is meticulously planned. *Exercitatio mentis*: that means that language can be used as a vehicle to shape the mind in order to make it stronger and more prepared to approach the inaccessible God. Analysing either the state of his mind as in the *Confessiones* or the state of human society as in *De civitate dei* he has travelled a long verbal way in order to create images of a person or images of history emerging from the confrontation between the invisible ends of God and the celestial city on the one hand, and man and the terrestrial city on the other.

The question of the status, the permanence or the consistency of those images can only refer to the underlying stream -- or should one say structure? -- of language and thought. In the midst of this stream there is at least one fixed point, that is the human mind as the image of God. However besieged and troubled by sin, doubt and confusion, it is there that the link between God and man is to be found, it is there in the memory palace with its infinite number of treasures that the human mind is reminded of itself and its origin beyond.

In what is undoubtedly one of the most elaborate Augustinian passages of Anselm's work, the first chapter of the *Proslogion*,[2] the starting point of the discourse is precisely this miserable "condition humaine": the situation in which the divine image has become almost invisible. At the end of the same work Anselm has in one way or another managed to reverse this situation: instead of misery there is mere joy: *Inveni namque gaudium quoddam plenum, et plus*

quam plenum. In the meantime it has been made crystal clear
where this joy has to be found, that is, in the whereabouts
of the inaccessible light itself. However, it is not merely
rhetorical means which are being used in order to establish
this place, but rather, as it seems, dialectical ones. Now,
it lies in the nature of dialectical argumentation to be as
strict and brief as possible, excluding all superfluous and
"rhetorical" elements. To this should be added Anselm's
special intention and concentration in the *Proslogion* to
find one and only one argument which can prove the necessity
of God's existence. Having found this argument in the formula, *id quo nihil maius cogitari potest,* Anselm is able to
move around in concentric circles, proving whatever has to
be proven both with regard to the attributes of God and the
situation and status of man.

     In this paper it is argued that the close-knit argumen-
tation by means of which Anselm has established   the
"existence" of God is reflected at different levels of manifestation both human and divine. Paradoxical though it may
seem, this variety does not lead to amplification. Throughout this process one seems to keep moving around within the
limits of the same space, or, to put it in stylistic terms,
the same brevity seems to be maintained throughout.   As a
consequence this brevity turns out to be a double-edged
knife. On the one hand it connects what ought to be connected by nature: God and the human mind, a process which
is supposed to find its zenith in perfect joy. On the other
hand the very perfection (*plenitudo*) might raise problems
with regard to the identity of different beings, human or
divine, who find themselves enclosed in one and the same
circle of perfection. In that respect the question might be
raised whether or not Anselm has become a victim of his own
success. Does the proof of the existence of God as well as
the achievement of pure joy which follows from it, still
leave room for the human mind to find its way back to the
"condition humaine"?   Of course, in strict consideration,
those questions are beyond the Anselmian "ordre du discours." It seems, nevertheless, not without sense to ask
them and to look for answers in order to elucidate the very
structure of the text. Starting from Anselm's description
of God as one an endeavour will be made to track down the
aspects of this unity which manifest themselves as the
created side of being.

     At the end of the *Epistola de incarnatione verbi,* Anselm
recommends to his adversary Roscellinus, who has much trou-
ble in imagining the Trinity because he is unable to see
such a thing in reality (*in aliis rebus*), to confine himself

to faith only, to stop disputing christian authority and,
most of all, to refrain from trying to compare God who is
beyond the laws of space and time and is not composed of
parts, with that which is to be found within the limits of
space and time.[3] These rather sharp remarks only serve as
an introduction to a comparison between the Trinity and the
laws of space and time: the famous metaphor of the Nile and
its source. In spite of the fact that Anselm in this passage admittedly reasons from imperfection to perfection
there remains a problem: the supreme nature is *sine partibus*, as Anselm has made abundantly clear, especially in his
Response to Gaunilo; in other words, it is perfect, though
at the same time three. Now this metaphor might help to get
a better view of the Trinity in one's imagination, but does
it really help to think the Trinity as one, and to find
one's reason capable of doing so? However it may be, after
having used this metaphor Anselm returns to an exposition of
the unity of God. lt is there that Roscellinus' problems
with regard to the status of the Trinity are to be found.
As far as Anselm is concerned, one might expect from him a
demonstration of the fact that the link between God and the
human mind is not a *flatus vocis perfectionis* in the same
way as, in Roscellinus' view, universals are a kind of
flatus vocis partium.

> However, because these terrestrial things
> are far removed from the supreme nature, let
> us,with her help,raise our eyes to that
> spirit and let us contemplate in her mod-
> estly and briefly what we are saying.[4]

After having used a metaphor, Anselm reminds both himself and his adversary yet another time of the fundamentals
of thinking about God: God himself is the a priori of
thought as well as the criterion of what can be said about
Him. God is identical with himself, he is his own limit.
He is nothing but *ipsa simplex aeternitas*. Outside this
eternity no eternity is to be found. It is a perfect eternity in the same way as it can be said that in God there is
perfect unity: *perfecta unitas*:

> Perfecta namque concordia est, quae in unam
> identitatem et eandem unitatem convenit.[5]

There is no God outside/apart from God. This is all very
well but does it help to understand the Trinity? At this
point Anselm introduces again a metaphor; not one, this
time, which in the end turns out to be subject to *partes*, as

was   the   case with the metaphor of the Nile; but one which,
even under close intellectual consideration,   remains indivisible.   As a consequence, it transcends human reality in a
sense.

> Omnipotence in omnipotence is but one omni-
> potence.   This can be illustrated by means
> of a similar state of affairs in the created
> world which does not possess the divine
> nature. A point in a point is only one
> point. For example, the center/middle point
> of the world and a point in time,   that is,
> the present time.   Such a point displays
> some similarity with eternity, which can be
> helpful when one thinks about eternity. Let
> it suffice here that a simple point, that is
> one without parts, is as indivisible as
> eternity; and that is why a point with a
> point without any space in between them is
> only one point, in the same way as   eternity
> with eternity is only one eternity.[6]

It ·is clear that *punctum* (a point) is used here as an
image of indivisible unity from which,   or, within which,
even the *processio* within the Trinity can be discussed. Now
this metaphor seems to "work" with regard to the divine,
that is, perfect reality.   But what can be said in this
respect about the human side of it? Has the human factor to
be defined in terms which are the exact opposite of *punctum*?
Certainly, it has to be admitted that Anselm considers the
creation to exist of parts as opposed to the perfection of
the divine.   On the other hand, on a more true and realistic
level of language and thought, even human reality does not
escape from the claim of perfection.   A parallel can be
drawn here with the relation between Father and Son in the
Trinity. Of course, the two are different, but it is
equally true that they are one. What then is the precise
nature of this relation, of the similitude between Father
and Son? In a sense this relation has to be called perfect,
as Anselm puts it in the *Monologion*:

> Sed utique verbum quo se dicit summa sapien-
> tia, convenientissime dici potest verbum
> eius secundum superiorem rationem, quia eius
> perfectam tenet similitudinem.[7]

Of   course, this is quite a paradoxical way of putting
things which demands the impossible from human speech. Seen

from a different angle, however, what is at stake here is
not only the presence of God within human reality and language, but also the presence of his image and similitude in
divine reality and language. In other words, however true
it may be that human thought is composed of parts (*partes*),
that does not remove the fundamental fact that human
reality, in a sense, is, or has to be perfect. At least,it
has to be in conformity with true and superior being in a
perfecta similitudo.

   This state of affairs can pehaps best be imagined as a
punctum, analogous to the way in which the Trinity has been
described by Anselm. Surely, that is not common language,
no *usus loquendi*. Within this point, however, what is basic
in human reality can and has to be expressed, and that is
the will, the idea which God has about it. It is God's
propositum and his *ordo* which are the true shape of his own
creation. In the absence of any aspect of prior or post-
erior, in other words, by resembling in one way or another
a *punctum*, this order will appear to be small and "brief"
and therefore function as a shortcut in the multiplicity of
human experience.

   The theme of *ordo* plays an important role in *Cur deus
homo*. In true Anselmian style it is especially the negative
form that is given most attention in the argumentation:
inordinate. It is against God's nature to allow for something *inordinatum*. If, against the will of God, the order
is broken, this negation has to be denied in a double negation which is based on the divine honor (*honor*). God's
honor cannot permit that sin, once committed, goes unpunished. *Honor* is God himself:

>   Idem namque ipse sibi est honor incorrupti-
>   bilis et nullo modo mutabilis.[8]

This divine *honor* has a kind of counterpart in the created
world, where the presence of divine perfection consists of
the *honor* which, on the part of man, is due to God: honor
in the sense of *debitum*. Man fulfils the demands implied in
this *debitum* if he adheres to the beautiful order of God and
as long as he does not want something *inordinate*.
   No disturbance of this order can be tolerated and is in
fact impossible:

>   Nihil minus tolerandum in rerum ordine, quam
>   ut creatura creatori debitum honorem auferat
>   et non solvat quod aufert.[9]

In conclusion it can be said that honor is to be considered
a link between the divine order and human experience. If
man deforms this precious possession of his and takes away
what, in strict consideration, does not belong to him, he
will have to restore the former situation: satisfaction
will be demanded. Now one could raise questions from two
different points of view. Seen from the perspective of
divine reality one might ask in which way the divine honor
which is inaccessible and perfect, can be reflected in the
world of space and time. In principle this question has
been solved in the explanation which has been given with
regard to the *punctum* metaphor. However, even then there
remains another problem unsolved, considered now from the
human view point: is man able to experience or to comply
with the divine honor and order without being eliminated
because of his poor and partial status? Is there an area
where he can move freely or does one have to admit that
under the pressure of God's immutable *honestas* the created
world has come under the reign of necessity and perfection?

In *Cur deus homo* the notion of perfection is strongly
tied up with the (Augustinian) theme of the *civitas caelestis*. This can be seen where the main argument in favor of
the necessary existence of a God-man is presented:

> Si ergo, sicut constat, necesse est ut de
> hominibus perficiatur illa superna civitas,
> nec hoc esse valet, nisi praedicta satisfac-
> tio, cuam nec potest facere nisi deus nec
> debet nisi homo: necesse est ut eam faciat
> deus-homo.[10]

Prior to this final argument it had already been proven that
God, in creating this world, had put himself under the obligation to complete whatever he had undertaken with regard to
humanity; an obligation from which followed, as far as man
was concerned, the demand of full satisfaction.

Can anything be said about the nature of what God, who
is eternal and perfect, has undertaken in the beginning?
This question is raised by Anselm in his lengthy excursus
about the angels (I,18; II,76-84). Starting from the Biblical quotation, *qui vivit in aeternum, creavit omnia simul*
(Si 18:1), which might be used as a counter-argument against
the view upheld by Anselm that angels and man cannot have
been created simultaneously, he tries to differentiate the
simultaneity of God's action. This *simul* which, as a token
of what is *sine partibus*, traditionally belongs to the
definition of eternity, raises quite some questions when

related to the creation. What is the reason of this earthly delay in the execution of divine perfection? In his little treatise on the angels Anselm tries to counter the view according to which angels would have been created in a perfect number. This thesis would lead to absurd consequences: the fall of the angels would have been necessary in order to create room for man and the blessed would be obliged to rejoice in the fall of the angels as the cause of their beatitude. Demonstrating that the number of angels which are elect has to surpass the number of the reprobate, Anselm is able to disprove the second argument. There is a surplus of angels beyond the number of the reprobate. Accordingly perfection is a quality of those *plures*; a surplus that cannot but find its origin in God.

Why then still this delay, this waiting for the state in which the number of elect, decided upon by God himself, will be complete? In Anselm's view this delay is intended to emphasize the radiance of perfection, so as to comprehend even the *insensibilis natura*. And even if Adam had not sinned, this delay would have taken place in order to give real immortality to him who first had just the *potestatem* not to die.

Next, two arguments *ad absurdum* demonstrate the impossibility of the *perfectus numerus in principio*: in that case the celestial city would be perfect only *in numero* but not *in confirmatione*. Since, however, no valid reason for this delay can be found, the necessity of perfection would speed up the restoration of created being; and that would be another absurdity. The only conclusion which can be drawn after those incongruities is that an imperfect number of angels has to be assumed. Consequently, the celestial city has to be completed with a surplus of men.

The pressure of perfection can be felt in this chapter. Some relief might be brought in perhaps by imagining those things as taking place in the future. However, that is seen from a human standpoint where space and time are presupposed: *partes*. The real question is: how does one deal with the divine order, not in the celestial city but here and now, amidst *partes*?

In that respect a unique example can be provided: the atoning death of Christ -- the *perfecta similitudo* of the Trinity -- in whose presence and through whose action divine perfection has "touched" terrestrial reality. It is through the atonement of Christ that God's proposal has been excuted so as to reserve a surplus of men for the celestial city.

Now satisfaction itself is also based on a surplus, originating in the perfect God-man. For it was he who was able

to give back to God more than man had taken away. His *debitum* was, unlike the perverted human version of it, founded
in the honor and justice of God, and as such it could truly
be called free.

If at this stage we raise the question as to the scope
of satisfaction in history, that is in the world of space
and time -- considering satisfaction to be a performing
aspect of perfection -- we actually mean to ask about the
power and the capacity of history in view of the satisfaction and perfection of divine being. In other words, we want
to examine to what extent history can profit from satisfaction and perfection without necessarily evaporating into the
closed circle of perfect being. In *Cur deus homo* II,16,
Anselm deals extensively with this subject matter. Anselm
and his partner in the dialogue, Boso, discuss the seemingly
inevitable assumption that the virgin who has given birth to
Christ is, as far as she herself is concerned, conceived and
born in sin because she also has sinned in Adam in whom all
mankind has sinned.

In order to solve this problem, which, in a wider sense,
is the question after the effect of Christ's action before
and after his Incarnation, Anselm uses a parable.   The
famous story of the king to whom all subjects are in debt,
except one innocent man. Because of the latter the king is
prepared to forgive.   To that purpose he fixes a date of
requital. Since, however, not everybody is able to be present that particular day, the king decides that whoever
wants forgiveness, either before or after that day, will be
free from guilt.   Only one condition remains: nobody is
allowed to enter the palace before atonement and forgiveness, be it in anticipation, have really taken place.

This parable allows for the following conclusion:

> Since not all people who were to be saved
> could be present at the moment of Christ's
> redemption, it can be said that the power
> and effect of his death were such as to
> extend itself to those who in time and place
> were absent at the moment.

This result fits in very well in the original and sus-
tained propositum of God. Consisting as this propositum did
of the perfection of human nature which finds its fulfilment
in the completeness of the celestial city (*civitas perfi-
cienda*), it makes it improbable that the world would ever be
so empty as to prevent man from reaching this state. This
same *propositum* makes ground for the assumption that also

Adam and Eve profit from this reconciliation, even though
this is not expicitly taught by the *divina auctoritas.*
    Adam, Eve, Mary, what does it matter? After all that
has been said about perfection, are not all those names
interchangeable? From the view point of perfection it seems
quite easy to travel around in time! And yet the apparent
mythical circle is broken by a historical event: the atoning death of Christ. A unique, momentary event determines
history, be it in a paradoxical way. This paradox arises
when one, because of the unchangeable will of God which is
manifested in Christ's satisfaction, will no longer be concerned with the celestial paradise but with the very reality
of time, space and history. Here Anselm returns to the
starting point of this chapter: how can Mary's purity be
reconciled with the notion of original sin against the background of Christ's death?

> Virgo autem illa de qua homo ille assumptus
> est, de quo loquimur, fuit de illis qui ante
> nativitatem eius per eum mundati sunt a pec-
> catis, et in eius ipsa munditia de illa
> assumptus est.

> The virgin from whom the man whom we are
> talking about, is received, belongs to those
> who are cleansed from sins by him before his
> birth and in her very purity has he been
> received from her.[11]

When Boso replies that Christ ought to have purity from
within himself -- which is not the case in Anselm's phraseology -- Anselm asks him to consider cause and effect differently.

> Non ita est; sed quoniam matris munditia per
> quam mundus est, non fuit nisi ab illo, ipse
> quoque per se ipsum et a se mundus fuit.

> It is not so; yet, because of the fact that
> the mother's purity through which he is pure
> can only derive from him, he himself has
> been pure through himself and from him-
> self.[12]

    Who is the actual subject of this discussion? Is it
God, or is it man? Is it Christ, or is it Mary? The discussion must deal equally with both of them, for in the

relation between God and man neither of them can be absent.
With regard to Christ, it should be said that, in *Cur deus
homo* II,17, the notion of *necessitas* develops into freedom,
that is, the freedom of the actual occurrence. But this
occurrence does not take place without man playing his part.
The "necessity" of the divine satisfaction will ultimately,
having passed through different layers of distance, strange-
ness and improperness, meet with the human experiehce, which
is concentrated here in Mary's religious experience.   What
is the precise character of Mary's experience? How does she
take her bearings in this reality of *partes*? Can there be
freedom in time and place for her who, just as Adam and Eve
participate in the atonement in retrospect, became pure herself through her belief in the purity and the future death
of her son (*per huius fidem certitudinis*)? Or does she
stand immutable, in an almost mythical manner, under the
same suppressive weight of the true perfection as Christ?
Does that "strange necessity" not apply to her as well? In
Cur deus homo Boso derived from the compelling presence of
the *ordo* of the true being the only possible conclusion:
Christ died out of necessity. Let us consider this same
passage with special attention to Mary's experience:

> Sed tamen hoc mihi semper occurrit quod
> dixi, quia si vellet non mori, non magis hoc
> posset, quam non esse quod erat.   Vere
> namque moriturus erat, quoniam si vere non
> fuisset moriturus, non fuisset vera fides
> futurae mortis eius, per quam et illa virgo
> de qua natus est, et multi alii mundati sunt
> a peccato. Nam si vera non fuisset, nihil
> prodesse potuisset.   Quapropter si potuit
> non mori, potuit facere non esse verum quod
> verum erat.

> And yet, what I have just said still engages
> me, namely that he, if he would not want to
> die, would be no more capable of this than
> of not being what He was. Indeed, he would
> truly die, for, if he would not truly die,
> the belief in his future death would not be
> true; the belief through which the virgin by
> whom he was borne, and many others have been
> cleansed from sin. For if that belief had
> not been true, it would have had no effect
> at all.   Therefore, if he was capable of not
> dying, he could make not true what was
> true.[13]

This quotation induces us to ask whether Mary has now become part of the circle of perfect being. In other words, is her belief hope or delusion? God and Christ are not subject to any compelling necessity. For the necessity of Christ's death coincides with the spontaneous event; that is the necessity which runs through all ages:

> Quidquid fuit, necesse est fuisse. Quidquid est, necesse est esse et necesse est futurum fuisse. Quidquid futurum est, necesse est futurum esse.[14]

Seen against the background of this free event Mary's belief makes sense. One can even say that, because of her true belief, things should necessarily happen just as she believed they would. The story of the atonement -- it is there that the divine plenitude ultimately touches the human experience -- can only be told just as it happened, in the same manner as the highest reason for God's existence consists of the fact that he is and is not capable of not being; a story which is neither construed with *picturae* nor built on a strange necessity. If somebody would still object that the faithful Mary functions as a *pictura* within narrow boundaries, we can point at the effect of the full life which reaches beyond the immutable image:

> Vitam autem huius hominis tam sublimem, tam pretiosam apertissime probasti, ut sufficere possit ad solvendum quod pro peccatis totius mundi debetur, et plus in infinitum.

> Concerning the so exalted and precious life of this man you have proved in a very clear way that it can suffice for the requital of what was due for the sins of the whole world, and infinitely more.[15]

At last, Anselm's circular arguments give way to progression. Perfection remains; it has, however, obtained an additional aspect: infinite plenitude.

Let us return once more to the *Proslogion*, to the labyrinth of the opening passage in which the exile, far from his country, wanders about. At the beginning of this paper attention was paid to the outcome of this quest: the mere joy which is experienced by the very same man whose fate seemed to be hopeless at the beginning. Through what means has this happy result been achieved? Through an appeal to the structure of man's mind, which, in spite of all confu-

sion, remains the *imago* and *similitudo* of God. The secret
of this anthropological treatise, as the *Proslogion* could be
called, lies in the establishment of the nature of divine
reality by means of the *unum argumentum*. As a result of
this operation there is a growing awareness of the *simili-*
tudo as a reflection of this perfect reality.   In other
words, *similitudo* turns out to be *punctum*-like. As such it
brings about short cuts -- *brevitas* -- in the law and order
of human experience. And if the human mind still wanders in
the boundless realm of language, thought or imagination, it
will perceive reality as it is: compact and aloof like a
romanesque Christ or Mary.

Notes

[1] H. I. Marrou, *St. Augustin et la fin de la culture*
antique (Paris: E. de Boccard, 1958).

[2] *Proslogion* I: Schmitt I,97-100. Translations are my
own.

[3] *Epistola de incarnatione verbi* XIII: Schmitt II,31.

[4] Ibid. XV: Schmitt II,33.

[5] Ibid.

[6] Ibid: Schmitt II,33-34.

[7] *Monologion* XXXIII: Schmitt I,52.

[8] *Cur deus homo* I,15: Schmitt II,72.

[9] Ibid. I,13: Schmitt II,71.

[10] Ibid. II,6: Schmitt II,101.

[11] Ibid. II,16: Schmitt II,119.

[12] Ibid.

[13] Ibid.: Schmitt II,122.

[14] Ibid. II,17: Schmitt II,125.

[15] Ibid. II,18: Schmitt II,127.

Can Christianity be Proven?:
St. Anselm of Canterbury on Faith and Reason

Katherin A. Rogers

A perennial issue in the study of St. Anselm of Canterbury is the question of his views on the relationship
between faith and reason. The problem arises because Anselm
has some rather startling, even contradictory, things to say
about his methodology. On the one hand, he says that, if
the theologian's reasons lead away from the conclusions of
faith, man must prefer faith: hence the famous phrase,
"*Credo ut intelligam.*" But, on the other hand, Anselm says
that he will prove *sola ratione* that God exists. He will
show *remoto Christo* that the Incarnation was necessary. At
the end of *Cur deus homo* the interlocutor, Boso, says that
Anselm has proven the necessity for God to become man by
reason alone "not only to the Jews but even to the pagans."[1]
This statement is remarkable.

This apparent ambiguity has given rise to two camps
among Anselm scholars. One camp holds that Anselm's work is
ultimately intrafideistic: Anselm attempts to help the
Christian understand his beliefs, without trying to convert
the unbeliever with the use of reason. The commitment to
the faith must be the first step. Karl Barth is probably
the most famous proponent of this view.[2] The other camp
holds that Anselm, in addition to helping the Christian
understand what he believes, really tries to reach the unbeliever and bring him to faith through reason. This seems to
be Gillian Evans' conclusion. She writes: "An unbeliever
who is prepared to listen without condemning the principles
of belief on which Anselm builds will also find his reason
convinced."[3]

This paper defends the second interpretation -- what may
be called the "rationalist" position -- by looking at three
questions. First, if reasons can bring people to faith, why
does Anselm argue that "authority" is to be preferred if his
reasons should conflict with it? Second, what sort of
intellectus is Anselm talking about when he says, *credo ut
intelligam*? And third, looking at the actual reasons
advanced by Anselm in defense of the faith, especially in
the *Cur deus homo*, could Anselm have thought it plausible
(and could it be plausible) that such reasons would bring
the unbeliever to Christianity?

Often throughout his work Anselm seems to denigrate his
powers of reasoning. In the first chapter of the *Monologion*, just after his statement about proving the faith *sola*

ratione, Anselm adds that, if he should say something which is not demonstrated by a higher authority, even if it seems to be necessary based on his reasons, it should not be taken as absolutely necessary, but only as necessary for the time being.[4] He seems to place authority above his reasons.

In *De incarnatione verbi* Anselm says it would be laughable if he, *contemptibilis humuncio*, were to attempt to write something to strengthen the Christian faith. He concludes that when he discusses the strength of the faith he does not do so in order to confirm it.[5]

Again in the *Cur deus homo*, Anselm says that anything which he says, even if it seems proven by reason, is only to be considered as certain for the time being if it is not confirmed by a higher authority. And if he says anything which opposes Sacred Scripture, that statement is false.[6]

A recent interpreter of St. Anselm, Stanley Kane, cites these passages and others like them in defending his view that, according to Anselm,

> all the factual knowledge that a person needs to have is given in the doctrinal content of the faith, and it is given with certainty. Reason is powerless to function as an instrument to come to the faith; it cannot of its own power generate any of this knowledge or add anything new to it.[7]

However, in the majority of passages where Anselm insists that his reasoning is not to be taken over a higher authority, he seems not to be talking about reasoning in general, but only about his own reasoning. In many of these passages Anselm may well be saying that he does not want his readers to place his reasoning above that of men whom he judges to be better and wiser than himself.

The authority which Anselm says supersedes his reasoning if there should be a conflict includes, as Kane points out,[8] not just the Bible, but also the teaching and practice of the Church. In *De processione spiritus sancti*, for example, Anselm points out that the doctrine of the Trinity does not appear spelled out in the Bible. Nevertheless, he says, the things which we believe about the Trinity follow from what we read in the Bible. "Therefore we ought to receive with certainty not only those things we read in Sacred Scripture, but also what follows from them by rational necessity, providing there is no reason against it."[9] Thus reason may, in fact must, interpret Scripture. Sometimes reason errs, as Anselm believes it has in the case of the Greeks who fail to see that the Holy Spirit proceeds from the Father and the Son. But when reason errs, Anselm adopts reason to prove the mistake.

In the *Monologion* the authority whom Anselm takes as the touchstone of the value of his own thought is Augustine, who brought his learning and intellectual powers to bear in his *De trinitate*. Augustine meditated, he analyzed, and he produced this great work which offers both an image of God and a way to God. When Anselm insists that "authority" is to be considered as more important than his own reasoning, he may well have come to the very reasonable conclusion that the great teachers of the Church, especially Augustine, were wiser than he, and that if his reasoning seems to conflict with Augustine's reasoning, Augustine is probably right. Many of the passages which seemed to Kane to pit reason against faith in fact say nothing about reason *per se*. They show, rather, that Anselm, being both humble and sensible, would not place his own reason over that of those whom he himself considered wiser than he. This notion does not prove that Anselm believed that one could use reason to convert the unbeliever. That question remains to be answered. It does show that Kane's claim that reason can add no knowledge to faith is extreme.

Further evidence exists that, for Anselm, faith must precede reason in his famous phrase, derived from Isaiah and Augustine, "*Credo ut intelligam*." At the beginning of the *Proslogion* he says, "I do not seek to understand in order that I may believe, but I believe in order that I may understand."[10] The alternate title for this work was *Fides quaerens intellectum*. Again in *De incarnatione verbi* Anselm writes, "unless you have believed, you will not understand." It is absurd, he says, to try to ascend to knowledge through the intellect first. Those who try will descend into all kinds of errors through the weakness of the intellect.[11]

Moreover, at the beginning of the *Cur deus homo* when Anselm explains why he chooses to respond to the request that he expound upon the necessity of the Incarnation, he makes a great point of insisting that those who make the request are not trying to come to faith through reason, but rather wish to delight in the understanding and contemplation of the things they believe.[12]

Given that Anselm is adamant about this principle, "unless you have believed you will not understand," one must examine his claims about proving the truths of faith by reason alone, asking, for example, what he means when he says he will prove the necessity of the Incarnation, *remoto Christo*.

One   could, of course, argue that Anselm's method or his
expressed principles (or both) are inconsistent and   contradictory.[13]   One   could   ignore one set of principles or the
other.   It might seem that a more   fruitful   approach   would
involve   steering   some middle course, as John McIntyre does
in his *St. Anselm and His Critics: A   Reinterpretation   of
the Cur deus homo.*[14]

McIntyre begins his discussion of Anselm's method in *Cur
deus homo* by comparing the principles which Anselm   advances
in   the   *Commendatio   operis   ad   Urbanum Papam II* (Anselm's
covering letter to the *Cur deus homo*, according   to   F.   S.
Schmitt)   and   the principles stated at the beginning of the
work itself.   In the *Commendatio* Anselm   once   again   says,
"You   shall   not   understand   unless you have believed."   He
writes that the understanding which people   can   achieve   in
this   life is half-way between faith and vision (*inter fidem
et speciem intellectum quem in hac vita capimus esse   medium
intelligo*).[15]   But   in   the   *Praefatio* of the *Cur deus homo*
where he explains the method he   intends   to   adopt,   Anselm
says   that   he   will   set aside what we know in faith of the
Incarnation and the atonement and then show   by   reason   the
necessity   for   all   that we believe.[16]   McIntyre says, "The
principle involved almost becomes: *intelligo ut credam.*"[17]

McIntyre attempts to resolve the apparent   contradiction
by   meshing   the *credo ut intelligam* and the *remoto Christo*.
He concludes that, although Anselm does   address   the   unbeliever   as well as the believer,[18] he does not use reason to
go from universally acceptable extra-fideistic   premises   to
the   conclusions   of faith.   McIntyre suggests, for example,
that Anselm in the *Monologion* was aware   that   reason   could
lead   from   the   original   premises of that work to entirely
different conclusions from the Christian ones   which   he   in
fact   reaches.   According to McIntyre, when Anselm argues he
consciously   moves   "within   the   limits   which   Scripture
defines."[19]

McIntyre says that Anselm consciously aimed his premises
and arguments at those who shared   his   world-view.   Anselm
could   not have expected a Moslem to accept his premises, so
he must not be trying to convince   the   Moslems.[20]   Nor   do
Anselm's   arguments   speak   to   believers of any period, but
rather to his contemporaries who share his general system of
beliefs.[21]   McIntyre writes:

> What,   therefore,   St.   Anselm places before
> his opponents is not so much   a   conclusion,
> or   set   of conclusions, which are claimed to
> be credible because dependent   upon   certain
> premises,   as   a   whole   pattern   of thought

> which challenges the credence of those who
> follow St. Anselm as he weaves his way
> through it. It is the whole argument, pre-
> mises and conclusion, an argument through
> which revelation is understood, which is up
> for consideration, and not simply the con-
> clusion by itself. . . . Revelation is his
> theme and all else is subordinated to
> that.[22]

McIntyre always carefully defends Anselm against the charge
of rationalism. Yet he argues against those who hold that
the understanding of what one believes does not strengthen
one's faith. McIntyre writes that "The firmness of the
belief is reached only through the lengthy process of the
intellectus . . . failure to complete the proof would have
led to a debilitation of the conclusion."[23] Thus the *credo
ut intelligam* can be viewed as a move from a tentatively
held belief to one strongly held because thoroughly understood. Anselm attempts to achieve this *intellectus* by
adopting the method of *sola ratione* and *remoto Christo*, and
he even hopes to carry the unbeliever with him, but, according to McIntyre, he never really steps outside the faith in
his arguments.

A number of problems arise with McIntyre's middle-course
interpretation. For one thing, it is ultimately very con-
fusing. How can Anselm possibly hope that his work will
have any impact on the unbeliever if all of his arguments
move "within the limits which Scripture defines?" Further,
if it is so obvious that Anselm did not intend his premises
to be accepted by anybody who did not share his world-view,
Moslems for example, why does Anselm not correct Boso at the
end of the *Cur deus homo* when Boso says that Anselm's arguments have shown the necessity of the Incarnation "not only
to the Jews but even to the pagans"?[24] McIntyre does not
seem to give Anselm's arguments as much credit as Anselm
does. On the other hand, McIntyre's point, that the *intellectus* strengthens us in a belief that had been only tentative, is too strong. At the beginning of the *Cur deus homo*
Boso assures Anselm that, even if he should not be able to
comprehend by reason the things which he believes, nevertheless nothing could destroy his constancy (*ut etiam si nullo
possum quod credo ratione comprehendere, nihil tamen sit
quod ab eius firmitate me valeat evellere . . .*).[25] If his
interlocutor is any indication, Anselm does not think we
should base the firmness of our faith on the degree of our
understanding.

The key to resolving the problem of the apparent contradiction in Anselm's method lies in that statement in the *Commendatio*: *intellectus* is half-way between faith and vision. If one takes this phrase seriously, then one must conclude that, by as far as the beatific vision exceeds the understanding which one can achieve of God in this life, that understanding exceeds mere belief to the same extent. Gaining *intellectus* is far more than just learning some facts, seeing some connections. It takes one a long way upon the journey to God. This journey can have four stages for the convert. First comes investigation of the reasons to believe. Next comes commitment to the faith. From faith the believer can move to understanding. The fourth stage, unattainable in this life, except perhaps in a mystical experience, is the beatific vision.

Thus in the phrase *credo ut intelligam, intelligere* is a technical term to describe a sort of understanding which brings the believer closer to God. (For Anselm, as for Augustine and for many thinkers influenced by the Platonic tradition, the will and the intellect are not isolated from one another. Virtue is wisdom and vice versa. So *intellectus* applies to the whole person, not to a compartmentalized reason.) This sort of understanding presupposes the commitment of faith. A person certainly could not travel far on the journey to God if he constantly doubted everything about his destination.[26] This point counts against McIntyre's view that the *credo ut intelligam* moves to understanding from a faith which is tentatively held. The believer seeking *intellectus* could not proceed without first making a firm commitment.

So the understanding which can follow from faith, if the believer is willing and able to make the intellectual exertion, is quite different from the reasons which might convert the unbeliever. McIntyre is wrong to suggest that the *Praefatio* to the *Cur deus homo* is almost an invitation to the unbeliever to understand in order to believe. The understanding of the *credo ut intelligam* could not possibly precede faith.

Jasper Hopkins in *A Companion to the Study of St. Anselm* recognizes that Anselm argues both to convert the unbeliever and to help the believer understand his faith.[27] However he does not recognize the full significance of the *intellectus*, how great an advance it is over mere belief. Like McIntyre, Hopkins says that ". . . in a sense Anselm's charge to unbelievers is indeed something like *intelligite ut credatis . . .*"[28] But Anselm repeatedly and emphatically insists that such a process is impossible.

Hopkins attempts to explain the *credo ut intelligam*, writing that:

> The imperative *crede ut intelligas* does not involve the high-handed and erroneous principle that any time someone believes a proposition he is better able to understand it than someone else who does not believe it. Rather, it embodies the modest but viable conviction that, since the participant does not always share the same perspective as the onlooker, there are some things which he, but not the onlooker, will understand. For insofar as understanding is a product of perspective and not simply of accumulated information, and insofar as the standpoint of the religiously committed individual differs from that of the nonreligiously committed individual -- so far may understandings diverge.[29]

But for Anselm there in nothing "modest" about the conviction that one can move from *credo* to *intelligo*. Hopkins talks of the divergent understandings of the non-believer and the believer. But again, this interpretation does not do justice to Anselm's notion of *intellectus*. Whatever "understanding" of God the unbeliever has is so shallow and rudimentary that it cannot be compared to the believer's *intellectus*, the half-way point on the journey to the beatific vision.

One cannot argue that every time Anselm uses the words *intelligere* or *intellectus* he means to refer to this special understanding which moves from belief to vision. In the *Proslogion*, for example, Anselm says that the fool who hears that God is that than which a greater cannot be conceived, "*intelligit quod audit; et quod intelligit in intellectu eius est . . .*"[30] Here Anselm uses the words to refer to the ordinary sense of understanding and intellect. Whether Anselm means ordinary understanding or the special understanding which must be preceded by faith can be gathered from the context.

The interpretation of the *credo ut intelligam* offered here leaves some problems. For example, it is hard to see how one and the same argument could do two quite different things; convert the unbeliever, and help the Christian attain *intellectus*. Yet this seems to be exactly what Anselm is attempting in the *Monologion*, the *Proslogion*, and the *Cur deus homo*. At the beginning of *Cur deus homo* Boso

insists that his faith is unshakeable. He is not asking to
be converted, but rather to understand what he believes.
But at the end of the work, he not only rejoices in his new
comprehension of his faith, he also claims that the arguments would convince a non-Christian. This double purpose
can be seen where Boso says that the unbelievers seek "such
a reason because they do not believe, and we because we do;
nevertheless we all seek one and the same reason" (*unum
idemque tamen est quod quaerimus*).[31]

Clearly Anselm believes that his writing can achieve the
two goals simultaneously. The arguments in the *Cur deus
homo*, for example, might lead the unbeliever to make the
initial commitment to the faith, while the Christian, reading the same arguments, will come to a deeper understanding,
one which will bring him closer to God, farther along the
road to the beatific vision. One example from *Cur deus homo*
can illustrate the double effect.

In *Cur deus homo* I,xxi, Anselm tries to impress upon
Boso the gravity, the horror, of sin. He shows Boso that if
there is a God who really is the Supreme Being, then it
would be better to permit the destruction of the universe or
even of an infinite number of universes rather than to dare
one glance contrary to the divine will.[32] Consider the
response of an open-minded unbeliever to this argument. (In
the case of the *Cur deus homo* the unbeliever in question
might be a Moslem, or a classical Neo-platonist -- someone
who accepts the notion of a supreme being, but who does not
have the Christian's sense of sin.) He might think it over,
weigh the issues, and conclude that if a God exists, source
of all goodness, all beauty, all being, nothing could be
worse than to disobey Him. Having accepted that point, the
unbeliever can read on, following where the argument leads.

In contrast, consider an appropriate Christian reaction.
The Christian already accepts a Supreme Being who became
incarnate, who suffered, and died to free men from their
sins. He has made a personal commitment to this God. Now
he reads that it would be better to permit the destruction
of the universe rather than to dare one glance contrary to
the divine will. The Christian, if he reads Anselm
seriously at all, will stop and examine his conscience:
perhaps he was unjustly angry this morning or envious yesterday. He will feel convicted by Anselm's words. He may
take a moment to pray and repent. He has grown closer to
God, and will continue the journey in the joy he will feel
when Anselm goes on to discuss the necessity and the method
of salvation.

At each step of each argument the reaction of the Christian must be quite different from that of the unbeliever.

The Christian (at least the one who is sympathetic to Anselm's views and methods) in reading the *Monologion* will delight in reaching towards the triune God through the image of memory, intellect, and will. But when he discovers, in the *Proslogion*, that God is so great that he cannot even be thought not to exist, he will be lost in admiration.

> Gratias tibi, bone domine, gratias tibi,
> quia quod prius credidi te donante, iam sic
> intelligo te illuminante . . .[33]

That a work of theology could have this double effect might have seemed odd, but in fact it is quite natural that, upon seeing the reasons for the things believed set out, the unbeliever and the believer react differently. If the non-Christian should read the *Cur deus homo*, should be convinced by the reasons, and should then commit himself to Christ, he could expect to turn back to the beginning of the work, and, upon a new reading, start to gain a real understanding of what he has come to believe.

A further problem may occur with this reading of *credo ut intelligam*. If the *intellectus* which one can achieve by studying the *Cur deus homo* (for example) provides such an advance over mere *fides*, we may be in danger of saying that the intellectual, the one who understands, is a better person, is closer to God, than the good person of simple faith. Perhaps this good man does not have the time, or the innate intellectual ability, to grasp the reasons which lead to understanding. That the man of simple faith should be unable, at least in this life, to approach as near to God as his more scholarly brother seems at best unfair.

To approach this problem, it seems appropriate to look to Anselm's great teacher, Augustine. There is no doubt that for Augustine (the early Augustine, at least) it is better to know than to believe. It is better to be wise than to be foolish. Wisdom and virtue are inextricably bound together. In *De utilitate credendi* he writes:

> By wise I mean not prudent and clever men
> but those who have, as far as possible,
> clear and strongly established knowledge of
> God and man, and live and conduct themselves
> in a way that answers to that knowledge.
> All others, however skilled or ignorant,
> however excellent or depraved their manner
> of life, I put in the number of the
> foolish.[34]

Given what Anselm says of his sources, and given his conclusions, one can reasonably assume that he agrees with Augustine, unless there is good reason to deny it in a particular
case. Anselm does say that the believer ought to seek
understanding and that understanding is half-way between
faith and vision. He probably does think that the virtuous
intellectual who achieves understanding of those things he
believed is closer to God than the good man of simple faith.
Such a stance may suggest a basic unfairness at the heart of
Anselm's views on God and man.

If "fairness" means a kind of modern, democratic, egali-
tarianism, then Anselm's universe and his God are not
"fair." For Anselm it is better to be a bird than a rock
and better to be a man than a bird. And it is better to be
wise and to know than to be ignorant and believe.   And
surely inequality is a fact about the world which we must
accept, acknowledging, "There have always been people more
beautiful than I, smarter than I, more virtuous than I."
But if God is infinite love, if He fills each vessel to its
capacity, then one cannot worry about whether or not someone
might be ahead of him in the race for the beatific vision.
The *credo ut intelligam* does lead to the conclusion that the
believer who is capable of understanding can come closer to
God than the one capable only of simple faith, but, for
Anselm at least, this is not a problem. It is just what one
would expect.

If this reading of the *credo ut intelligam* is correct,
no textual evidence exists to support the belief that Anselm
held that reason could not bring one to faith. The many
passages where he speaks humbly of his own reasons as
opposed to authority do not apply to reason in general at
all, and so do not show that faith must precede reason for
Anselm.   The *credo ut intelligam* does say that one cannot
gain understanding, *intellectus*, unless one believes, but
intellectus here has a special meaning: it is the sure
knowledge which stands mid-way between belief and vision.
This special *intellectus* cannot precede belief, but that
does not mean that reasons cannot lead one to faith. A number of passages have already been cited where Anselm seems
to be proposing to give the non-Christian reasons to
believe.   It remains now to look at some of those reasons,
especially in the *Cur deus homo*, to determine whether Anselm
really intended them to convert the unbeliever.

At the very outset some will argue that Anselm's premises cannot command general assent, and so he could not
have meant to prove the faith through arguments which even
the non-believer will accept.   One might point out, for
example, that the *Monologion* takes its departure from the

Platonic formula that, if there are many goods, there must be one good through which they are all good.[35] If one does not accept this premise, the argument to the *summum bonum* at the beginning of the *Monologion* cannot proceed. And clearly one can reject the premise. So how could Anselm possibly have thought to prove anything about God here *sola ratione*? Again, in the *Proslogion*, Anselm seems simply to assume the characteristics attributed to the classic "God of the philosophers" when he unpacks his notion of that than which a greater cannot be conceived.

One could solve the problem by saying, as McIntyre does, that Anselm was well aware that his arguments would only appeal to those in his own circle, or with his own worldview. He proceeds *sola ratione* once his basic system is accepted.

> It is no criticism of St. Anselm to suggest that arguments which would convince the native of Canterbury would be rejected by the member of the court at Cordova. St. Anselm never thought otherwise.[36]

A less sympathetic interpreter, David Pailin, argues that Anselm is attempting to move from generally acceptable premises to the conclusions of faith, but that the premises which his argument takes as obvious simply reflect the "prejudices of his day."[37] Perhaps Anselm really intended his arguments in the *Monologion* and the *Proslogion* to appeal to any reasonable person, but he is quite mistaken, according to Pailin, to take his premises for granted. He wrongly believes he is proceeding *sola ratione*. In fact he is carrying with him, from the start, a load of Platonic baggage. His arguments could only convince one who already accepts his basic worldview. Anselm is flatly incorrect to think that the unbeliever could be converted by his reasons.

Several answers may be made here. It is true that Anselm starts from certain Platonic premises. But these premises probably would have been accepted by at least the majority of intellectuals in the Western world for the preceding millennium. (Alfarabi and Avicenna, the greatest Moslem philosophers to pre-date St. Anselm, are both considered Neo-platonists.) Anselm had good reason to assume that anyone his work would reach would be willing to grant his original premises. McIntyre is wrong to think that Anselm's premises must necessarily fare better at Canterbury than at Cordova.

This response does not answer Pailin's point, however. One can argue that a particular idea held for for a thousand

years by the greatest thinkers in the West remains merely   a
prejudice.   And   perhaps one can assign this unsavory label
to Anselm's Platonic assumptions. Arguably, however, if   one
could   confront St. Anselm with a twentieth-century perspective, he might still find Platonism defensible, despite   the
vagaries   of philosophical fashion.   St. Anselm will have no
reason to abandon his arguments, since reasons   continue   to
exist   for   accepting the theory of ideas, of participation,
of recollection, of illumination.   The Western   intellectual
landscape   has never been devoid of Platonists, sometimes in
the majority and   sometimes   not;   all   ages   have   nurtured
thinkers   who   found   the arguments in favor of the Platonic
approach compelling.   We have no reason to think that Anselm
could not explain why he adopts his Platonic premises.

     In fact, Anselm does precisely this in *Monologion* I.   He
wants to show that in all the various good things there must
be   one   good   through   which they are all good -- a typical
Platonic position.   But he asks (perhaps as one of the foolish objections he mentions in the preface) whether different
goods might be good through   different   things.[38]   That   he
even raises this objection leads F. S. Schmitt to argue that
Anselm is actually de-Platonizing Augustine.[39]   (Schmitt's
position   turns out to be untenable because Anselm concludes
by upholding the Platonic view.)   The important point   here,
however,   is   that   this is a case where Anselm deliberately
goes out of his way to defend, by argument, a basic Platonic
thesis.   One   might look at the reasons for adopting a Platonic worldview and reject them, but surely it is   wrong   to
call Anselm's premises prejudices.

     Anselm's   use   of   Platonic   premises obviously need not
count against the thesis that he is trying   to   convert   the
unbeliever *sola ratione*.   Anselm had every reason to suppose
that the literate unbeliever would accept his premises.   For
the   unbeliever   who   rejects   them, we cannot fairly assume
that Anselm could not lead him to see the error of his ways.

     Up to this point, this paper has   dealt   primarily   with
the   *Monologion* and   the   *Proslogion*.   In   terms of scope,
however, neither work addresses rational inquiry as   remarkably   as   the   *Cur deus homo*.   Many philosophers have thought
that one could show by reason that a   Supreme   Being   exists
and that he has certain attributes.   Even the arguments concerning the triune nature of God become less startling   when
we   recall   that   pagan   philosophers, Plotinus for example,
held similar views.   But in the *Cur deus homo* Anselm   claims
to prove that it is necessary that God become man.   One must
ask if his arguments could plausibly convince an unbeliever.

     First, by way of background, in the *Cur deus homo* Anselm
is   not speaking to the atheist or agnostic.   One who denies

the existence of God would have to go to the *Monologion* or
the *Proslogion* first; having accepted the arguments there,
he can then move on to the *Cur deus homo*. Anselm expects
the unbeliever of the *Cur deus homo* -- the Jew, Moslem, or
Neo-platonist -- to share many assumptions with him, especially his concern with the "God of the philosophers." To
illustrate this point, we see that one of Anselm's first
tasks is to defend Christianity against the notion that for
God to humble himself and become man is improper, even
absurd.[40]

In his argument proper, in *Cur deus homo* I, Anselm shows
the necessity of the Incarnation by the process of elimination. He says, "If then it is false that man cannot be
saved at all, or that he can be saved in any other way, his
salvation must necessarily be by Christ."[41] This explanation, however, does not quite satisfy Boso, the interlocutor, who asks that Anselm go even further, to show how this
salvation is achieved, the theme of Book II. The presentation of Anselm's argument here will follow his development
of the argument in Book II, with references back to Book I.

Anselm's first premise is that God made man to be happy
in the enjoyment of God (*Cur deus homo* II,i).[42] The
unbeliever of the *Cur deus homo* could certainly accept this.
Aristotle had made it abundantly clear that people desire
happiness, and surely an all-good God would not create a
being to see it suffer unappeasable frustration.

But man has sinned and cut himself off from God. Perhaps the non-Christian Anselm has in mind could balk at
this. The pagan Neo-platonists, for example, do not seem to
have the same sense of sin as the Christian. On the other
hand, perhaps Anselm could appeal to the empirical evidence
that all men have sinned. He could safely argue that the
notion of an original and all-pervasive sin accords with all
known history, with experience, and with introspection. In
the twentieth-century, if someone asserts that he has been
to the moon, the possibility exists, if remote. Some people
have been to the moon. But if someone asserts he has never
done anything wrong, people must suppose he is lying or mistaken. Nothing he could do will change most people's minds.
It is entirely reasonable to assume that men are sinful.

So God made man to be happy in the divine presence, but
man cut himself off by sinning. Nonetheless, because God's
plans may not be thwarted, a solution must be found. Now in
sin, says Anselm, the creature takes away the honor of God
(*Cur deus homo* I,xiii).[43] Man can only be restored to his
proper state if he makes satisfaction for what be has taken,
and this satisfaction must be proportionate to his guilt
(*Cur deus homo* I,xix-xx).[44] But the burden of sin is

enormous   (*Cur deus homo* I,xxi).[45]   It is so great that none
but God can pay the debt.   But it is man who is the   debtor.
Therefore, the only one who can make restitution and restore
human kind is the God-man (*Cur   deus   homo* II,vi).[46]   Here
Anselm has shown why the Incarnation was necessary.   Next he
will explain how Christ's death achieved our salvation.

The God-man pays mankind's debt by His perfect obedience
which   transcends   that owed by any creature to its creator.
He chooses to suffer death voluntarily when not bound by any
obligation   (*Cur   deus   homo* II,xi).[47]   In dying the God-man
not only sets a perfect example for men to follow (*Cur   deus
homo* II,xviii),[48]   but   he   also   merits a reward, and this
reward he gives to mankind in the form of remission of   our
debt   (*Cur   deus   homo* II,xix).[49]   Anselm has shown that man
must be saved, that salvation can only come through the God-
man, and even how that salvation is achieved.

Many questions arise at this point.   The central concept
of the honor of God, for example, may bother   the   contemporary   reader.   This   paper's   scope   does   not   allow it to
explain or defend the argument of the *Cur   deus   homo*.   For
purposes of the topic here, one must notice only two things.
Anselm's proof of the necessity of the Incarnation does   not
use   any   specifically   Christian   premises.   Moreover, even
admitting that the argument incorporates difficult concepts,
Anselm's   premises   and successive steps are at least defensible.   An example might clarify this last point.

In *Cur deus homo*   I,xii Anselm   and   Boso   discuss   the
question of whether God could have simply forgiven man's sin
and saved him without any payment for   the   debt   man   owed.
Anselm says no, for a number of reasons, none very satisfactory to the modern reader, at least on the   surface.[50]   One
might   even be tempted to abandon the argument here, reasoning that God cannot be very loving if He cannot just   choose
to   forget man's sins without exacting payment.   But looking
further,   and   asking   about   some   underlying   assumptions
(theistic,   but not necessarily Christian) at work here, one
may find that a good case can be made for God's   choice   not
to save mankind by simply overlooking its sins.

Consider   St. Anselm's explanation for why God permitted
sin.   God wanted people to be able to choose uprightness   of
will for its own sake.   If they had done so, they would have
"given themselves" righteousness.   In a way they would   have
helped in their own creation.   Here, Anselm departs from the
teaching of Augustine (at least, the Augustine of *De   civitate   dei*).   Augustine   holds   that   man sinned because God
withheld from him the grace to persevere.   If God had   given
him   the   grace,   then man would not have fallen.   Augustine
denies that man was capable of   freely   remaining   righteous

precisely because he does not want to say that it was up to man himself whether or not he would persevere; he feels to do so would be an affront to God's omnipotence. But for Anselm, God's greatest gift of love grants mankind the ability freely to remain upright or to sin, for in giving us the chance to help create ourselves he renders us children rather than slaves.[51]

If this gift is why God permitted sin, then it really does seem unfitting that God should just pick His children up, almost in spite of themselves, clean them off, and put them back into His presence where they belong. Surely it is better, if people are to be children rather than slaves, that one of their own race[52] should reopen the gate to heaven and, by living among them, set an example which they can choose to follow to return home. At first glance this step in Anselm's argument is at best uncompelling, and at worst makes God seem like a jealous tyrant. But on closer inspection a good case can be made that underlying Anselm's argument is not a failure to appreciate God's mercy, but rather, all-too-good an understanding of the Creator's hard love for his free creatures.

Thus we see that Anselm's premises and arguments are not specifically Christian, and they are defensible. The evidence seems overwhelming that Anselm genuinely believed that the unbeliever could be converted by reason, that he could even be made to see the necessity of the Incarnation. Anselm begins the *Cur deus homo* by explaining that he will prove by necessary reasons, *remoto Christo*, that God had to become man to achieve salvation for the human race. At the end of the dialogue he has his interlocutor exclaim that the work must convince both Jews and pagans of the truth of the Christian faith, *sola ratione*.[53] That Anselm expresses some humility about his own capacity to reason, or that he holds that the true *intellectus* must follow upon belief, does not count against the view that, for Anselm, reason can bring one to believe the tenets of Christianity.

A final problem remains: interpreters of St. Anselm are often loath to admit that he is really trying to give the unbeliever reasons to convert. (Some, of course, accept that he is doing this, but only with regret.[54]) Two possible reasons come to mind.

First, one could argue that the commitment to faith must be seen as a free act of the will. If one is given "necessary reasons" to believe, then one will be forced to assent to the faith, and hence this element of choice will be lost. Accepting Christ will no longer be a virtuous act, the first step towards salvation, but only assent to an hypothesis. The Anselm scholar, shaken by this difficulty, might conclude that Anselm could not have made the mistake of thinking that the faith can be proven by reason, or, if he did, he should not have.

Two responses can be made here. First, a great difference exists between merely accepting the accuracy of the Christian world-view and making the commitment to become a Christian. Anselm discusses this difference at the end of the *Monologion* LXXVIII, "What is living faith and what is dead faith." He begins by saying that however much one believes the things which he has shown (that God exists, that He is three persons with one nature, etc.), "faith will be useless and almost dead, as it were, unless in love it lives and is strong."[55]

Second, one might argue with the view that one is forced to believe what can be shown by reason to be the case. The temptation to down-play or ignore a fact that does not fit one's pet theory certainly exists among academics, and a commitment to Christianity is much more radical than commitment to an academic theory. The compartmentalization of the will and intellect presupposed by this criticism is one alien to Anselm, and the Augustinian tradition, and alien, as well, to our everyday experiences.

A second fundamental problem occurs with Anselm's view that reasons can lead one to see the truths of faith. If mere human reason suffices to come to belief, then it might seem that the philosopher could no doubt "storm the gates of heaven" without the help of God. The view might seem to lead to a sort of Pelagian rationalism. Surely Anselm could not have thought that man could come to faith without God's aid.

A confusion about Anselm's epistemology underlies this criticism. The confusion may arise, at least among medievalists, from a tendency to study the history of medieval philosophy backwards. One studies Thomas Aquinas first, and then, when one comes to earlier thinkers like St. Anselm, one sees their thought through the lens of Thomas' categories.

Thomas Aquinas distinguishes between natural knowledge and supernatural knowledge. Supernatural knowledge occurs, here or in the hereafter, when God himself appears, presenting himself as he is. Such knowledge can be had in this life, but only through a miracle.[56] Natural knowledge, the way we know almost everything we know on earth, occurs because God has created us with the capacity to abstract intelligibility from the sensible universe. We can know something of God through our natural faculties, but only what we can deduce from our study of the sensible universe. The mysteries of the faith -- that God is triune, that he became incarnate -- must come to us through revelation. Natural knowledge cannot tell us much about the Christian God, nor does it require any special divine grace. God made us to learn through abstraction, and we can go about doing it without any special help from Him.[57]

According to Anselm, man in his natural state, without any miracle, can come to belief in the deep truths of faith through reason. But Anselm is not guilty of any foolish rationalism that would place man beyond the need for God's help. With Anselm (as with his teacher Augustine) no distinction exists between natural and supernatural knowledge. All knowledge comes directly from God through divine illumination.[58] Whether one knows that $1 + 1 = 2$, or that trees are green, or that the Incarnation was necessary for man's salvation, it is the immediate presence of God to one's soul which gives knowledge. One might disagree with Anselm's epistemology (Thomas Aquinas would), but one cannot accuse him of implying that man can penetrate to the deep truths of faith without the aid of God. Quite the contrary: we cannot penetrate to anything without God.

Given Anselm's epistemology, one can assert that reason can lead the unbeliever to faith, and the believer to understanding. If God really is "that light from which shines all truth which illumines the rational mind,"[59] then that process is exactly what one would expect.

Notes

[1] *Cur deus homo* II,22: Schmitt II,133,8.

[2] K. Barth, *Anselm: Fides Quaerens Intellectum*, trans. I. W. Robertson (London: S. C. M. Press, 1960).

[3] G. Evans, "The *Cur deus homo*: The Nature of Anselm's Appeal to Reason," *Studia Theologica* 31 (1977), 50.

[4] *Monologion* I: Schmitt I,14,1.

[5] *Epistola de incarnatione verbi* I: Schmitt II,5,7-21.

[6] *Cur deus homo* I,18: Schmitt II,82,6-10.

[7] G. S. Kane, "*Fides Quaerens Intellectum* in Anselm's Thought," *Scottish Journal of Theology* 26 (1973), 56-57.

[8] Kane, "Anselm's Thought," pp. 55-56.

⁹*De processione Spiritu Sancti* II,11:   Schmitt II,209, 12-16.

¹⁰*Proslogion* I: Schmitt I,100,18.

¹¹*Epistola de incarnatione verbi* I: Schmitt II,7,10-8,1.

¹²*Cur deus homo* I,1: Schmitt II,47,8-9.

¹³This suggestion is made by D. A. Pailin in "*Credo ut Intelligam* as the Method of Theology and of its Verification: A Study in Anselm's *Proslogion*," *AA* 4 (1975), 112.

¹⁴J. McIntyre, *St. Anselm and His Critics: A Reinterpretation of the Cur Deus Homo* (Edinburgh: Oliver and Boyd, 1954).

¹⁵*Cur deus homo*, commendatio: Schmitt II,40,10-11.

¹⁶Ibid., praefatio: Schmitt II,42-43,11-13.

¹⁷McIntyre, *St. Anselm*, p. 5.

¹⁸Ibid., pp. 5, 10.

¹⁹Ibid., p. 17.

²⁰Ibid., p. 20.

²¹Ibid., p. 44.

²²Ibid., p. 46.

²³Ibid., p. 23.

²⁴R. Roques has written concerning just who the "*pagani*" are in "Les *pagani* dans le *Cur deus homo* de Saint Anselme" in *Die Metaphysik im Mittelalter. Ihr Ursprung und ihre Bedeutung*, ed. P. Wilpert and P. Eckert (Berlin: de Gruyter, 1963), pp. 192-206. He concludes that Anselm probably had the Moslems in mind. He points out that, according to Eadmer at least, Anselm would have converted many Moslems during his stay in Sicily, if Roger, the Count of Sicily, had not objected. However, there is no reason why Anselm could not also be speaking to the sort of pagans Augustine talks about in *Confessiones* VII,ix,13, when he discusses the books of the Platonists.

[25] *Cur deus homo* I,1:   Schmitt II,48,20-21.

[26] Augustine makes the startling point that the truly wise man could skip the step of belief on his journey to understanding.   He suggests in *De utilitate credendi* X,24: *PL* XLII, 81-82 that Honoratus, to whom he addresses this work, may belong to the small number of wise men who are able to "grasp the reasons by which divine power leads to certain knowledge . . ." (Augustine is probably speaking ironically to Honoratus, but he seems serious in saying that faith is not necessary for the truly wise man.)   Such men might do themselves no harm by by-passing faith.   Nevertheless Augustine feels that even one who could achieve knowledge without first believing ought to make the commitment to faith first, so as not to lead the less wise astray, and also so as to remain on the safe and fool-proof path. Still, it is quite surprising to find that Augustine, in *De utilitate credendi*, believes it epistemologically possible to move from reasons to understanding, bypassing faith. Augustine makes a similar claim later in the work (*De utilitate credendi* XVI,34:   PL XLII,89) where he says that for the wise man the Church's appeal to authority through both miracles and the great number of those who accept that authority is not necessary.

[27] J. Hopkins, *A Companion to the Study of St. Anselm* (Minneapolis: Univ. of Minnesota Press, 1972), pp. 39-42.

[28] Ibid., p. 64.

[29] Ibid., pp. 41-42.

[30] *Proslogion* II: Schmitt I,101,8-9.

[31] *Cur deus homo* I,3:   Schmitt II,50,18-20.

[32] Ibid. I,21:   Schmitt II,89,1-17.

[33] *Proslogion* IV: Schmitt I,104,5-6.

[34] *De utilitate credendi* XII,26-27:   *PL* XLII,84-85. English translation is from *Augustine: Earlier Writings*, selected and trans. J. S. Burleigh (Philadelphia: Westminster Press, 1953), p. 314.

[35] *Monologion* I: Schmitt I,14,15-18.

[36] McIntyre, *St. Anselm*, p. 20.

[37] Pailin, p. 120.

[38] *Monologion* I: Schmitt I,14,5-9.

[39] F. S. Schmitt, "Anselm und der (Neu-)Platonismus," *AA* 1 (1969), 50.

[40] *Cur deus homo* I,3: Schmitt II,50,24-28.

[41] Ibid. I,25: Schmitt II,95,13-14.

[42] Ibid. II,1: Schmitt II,97-98.

[43] Ibid. I,13-14: Schmitt II,71-72.

[44] Ibid. I,19-20: Schmitt II,84-88.

[45] Ibid. I,21: Schmitt II,88-89.

[46] Ibid. II,6: Schmitt II,101.

[47] Ibid. II,11: Schmitt II,109-112.

[48] Ibid. II,18: Schmitt II,127,17-128,2.

[49] Ibid. II,19: Schmitt II,129-131.

[50] Ibid. I,12: Schmitt II,69-71.

[51] Compare Anselm in *De casu diaboli*, VI and XVIII with Augustine in *De civitate dei* XII,9.

[52] This notion of shared race should appeal especially to one with Platonic leanings. Anselm insists upon the importance of the shared race in *Cur deus homo* II,21: Schmitt II,132,14-16.

[53] Of course Anselm has not shown the Incarnation to be logically necessary or entirely beyond any conceivable doubt. Such an undertaking really would be impossible. After all, a stubborn sceptic can doubt the laws of logic or his own existence (at least he says he can). As G. Evans, "The *Cur deus homo*", pp. 49-50, points out, Anselm is writing to convince the reasonably open-minded unbeliever.

[54] For example, F. S. Schmitt, "Die wissenshaftliche Methode in Anselms *Cur Deus Homo*," *SB* I, 349ff.

[55] *Monologion* LXXVII: Schmitt I,84,16-17.

[56] See Thomas Aquinas, *De veritate* X,11.

[57] Thomas Aquinas explains his doctrine of abstraction in *De anima* IV. In *De anima* XVI, he argues that God, the angels, and human souls, though intrinsically intelligible, nonetheless cannot be understood by the soul, for it is united to a body and must learn from images of corporeal things.

[58] I discuss this point at some length in "Divine and Human Ideas in St. Anselm of Canterbury," Diss. Univ. of Notre Dame 1982, pp. 163-72.

[59] *Proslogion* XIV: Schmitt I,112,5-6.

V

The Anselmian Worldview

Anselm

Credimus hanc mundi molem corpoream in
melius renovandam, nec hoc futurum esse, donec
impleatur numerus electorum hominum et illa
beata perficiatur civitas, nec post eius perfec-
tionem differendum.
(*Cur deus homo* I)

Augustine

Gloriosissimam civitatem dei sive in hoc
temporum cursu, cum inter impios peregrinatur ex
fide vivens, sive in illa stabilitate sedis
aeternae, quam nunc expectat per patientiam,
quoadusque iustitia convertatur in iudicium,
deinceps adeptura per excellentiam victoria
ultima et pace perfecta, . . . defendere . . .
suscepi . . .
(*De civitate dei* I, praefatio)

Anselm's *Weltbild* as Conveyed in His Letters

Walter Fröhlich

"It will be admitted without difficulty, I think," wrote Langlois at the beginning of his classic series of articles on medieval formularies, "that the most precious documents of history of the Middle Ages are letters, missive letters, both official and private correspondences." Giles Constable underlines the historical value of letters and collection of letters by adding that Langlois' statement may at first sight appear somewhat exaggerated, but in fact it is hard to think of any other single type of source which sheds so much light on medieval history. He concludes his treatise by stating that fictional letters as well as real letters constitute a vast, and in some respects still unexplored, source for the study of medieval history.[1]

This paper endeavors to unfold Anselm's *Weltbild*[2] as contained in his letters and will progress in four major steps. The first step will assess the art and value of Anselm's letters as well as Anselm's intention as revealed in the collecting of his letters and the compiling and editing of collections of his correspondence. Bearing in mind that the art of letter-writing at its best can provide a carefully-drawn portrait of a man,[3] a second step will draw a sketch of Anselm's personality and outline the growth of his monastic outlook over some thirty years as it emerges from his correspondence. A third step will search for the roots of Anselm's monastic thinking and preaching. Finally, a fourth step will describe Anselm's perception of the world and sketch his *imago mundi* as conveyed in the letters by analyzing a few of the key words of the medieval *Weltbild*.

I

From the evidence available it appears that from about 1085 Anselm began collecting his own letters written after 1070 in response to various inquiries and requests.[4] The earliest letter in Anselm's collection was written in 1070 congratulating Lanfranc, Anselm's teacher, the former Prior of Bec and Abbot of St. Stephen of Caen, on the occasion of his elevation to the archiepiscopal see of Canterbury. Lanfranc was consecrated as Archbishop of Canterbury and Primate of all Britain on 29 August, 1070. This letter to Lanfranc occupies the first place in Anselm's letter collection. This is not a place of honor since at least

Epistolae 4, 5, 7, 8, and *11* to *17* were written later than *Epistola 1*.[5] No letters written by Anselm before 1070 have been preserved although it seems very likely that Anselm had written letters before that year.

After some years of wandering in France, Anselm sought out Prior Lanfranc at Bec, his fellow north Italian country-man and the most renowned teacher of his time. Lanfranc had joined the young community at Bec in 1042. In 1059, at the age of twenty-six, Anselm came to Bec and made his monastic profession the following year at the hands of Herluin, the first Abbot of Bec. When Lanfranc left Bec for Caen in 1063, Abbot Herluin appointed Anselm to the office of prior and *magister scholarum* in the face of some resentment by a number of members of the community at Bec. The school of Bec, under the leadership of Lanfranc and Anselm, was the prime establishment of learning in northern Europe. Students from all parts of Europe flocked there. Some of them won elevated preferments such as the papal see, archiepis-copal and episcopal sees as well as abbacies. It seems very likely that Anselm wrote letters to and received letters from his former fellows while a student under Lanfranc him-self or from his students while he was *magister scholarum Beccensis*. None of these letters, either from or to him, were considered worth preserving by the author.

Anselm's motive for collecting his early letters -- those written while he was Prior (1063-1079) and Abbot of Bec (1079-1093) -- seems to have been based upon their moral content of exhortative and spiritual advice rather than upon their literary form. Business matters and day-to-day infor-mation were almost totally excluded and entrusted to the oral report of the bearer of the letter. Anselm's collec-tion of early letters, with a few exceptions, contains only his out-going correspondence.

The first part of Anselm's collection of letters passed through three stages. The oldest manuscript containing this first part is London, British Library, MS Cotton Nero VII (henceforth referred to as N) since it is the only manu-script that styles Anselm merely as Prior and Abbot of Bec. It contains ninety-nine letters on one hundred and forty-two pages. Some pages are missing at the end but the letters on these lost pages can be reconstructed from London, Lambeth Palace, MS 224 (henceforth M). The latter is an autograph of William of Malmesbury who had copied Anselm's works and letters into this manuscript and had used N for this purpose before 1143.[6] The letters in N do not follow any strict chronological order, their only division being the letters written by the prior and those written by the abbot of Bec.

This division is provided by a rubric after letter N69 (= *Epistola 87*) at the bottom of fol. 94r:

> Hactenus continentur epistole domni Anselmi abbatis, quas fecit donec prior Beccensis. Quae vero iam deinceps sequuntur, egit postquam abbatis nomen et officium suscepit.

As this rubric is written on an erasure it appears to be the work of the original scribe or his immediate corrector and not that of a later copyist. This assessment points to the fact that the scribe or his corrector knew Anselm only as Abbot of Bec and not yet as Archbishop of Canterbury. The rubric at the beginning of the collection of Anselm's letters supports this conclusion. It reads: *Incipit liber epistolarum domni Anselm abbatis*. This rubric separates Anselm's letter collection from the letter collection of Lanfranc which is to be found in the first part of N, from fol. 1r to fol. 40v. Both collections appear to have been written by the same hand and approximately at the same time. This observation is supported by the fact that two letters (*Epistolae 30* and *31*) from Archbishop Lanfranc (one to Prior Anselm and one to his nephew Lanfranc at Bec) are excluded from Anselm's collection since they are already among the collection of Lanfranc's letters.

The date for the compilation of this first stage of the first part of Anselm's letter collection is provided by *Epistola 145* sent to Abbot Ralph of Seez congratulating him on his promotion in 1089. This letter is not to be found in N but it can be assigned to N on the evidence of M. Since the itinerary of Abbot Anselm shows no absence of the Abbot of Bec from his monastery in 1089, it would seem that Anselm's first collection of his letters was assembled and written into N at Bec under Anselm's supervision and assistance. The death of Archbishop Lanfranc on 26 May, 1089 and the compilation and edition of a collection of his letters could have been the incentive for Anselm to do the same with his own letters some time in 1089/1090. Anselm's letter to his former pupil Maurice in 1085 (*Epistola 104*) points to the probability that Anselm had been gathering and collecting his letters and thinking about editing a collection of his letters for some time, for this letter closes: "We are still waiting for our letters which Dom Maurice is supposed to have sent us."

Barely two years later Anselm was intent upon improving the first stage of this first part of his letter collection. In autumn 1092 he informed Prior Baldric and the community

of Bec (*Epistola 147*) that he would be delayed returning
from his third inspection journey of the Bec cells and
estates in England because King William II refused to allow
him to leave. He asked Prior Baldric: "Send me the Prayer
to St. Nicholas which I wrote and the letter which I had
started writing against the propositions of Roscelin; and if
Dom Maurice has any other letters of ours which he has not
sent yet, send them as well." It would appear that Anselm
intended using this period of enforced leisure to improve
the first collection of his letters and therefore required
all the letters which had been collected at Bec since the
compilation of N to be sent to him in England. He improved
the rough chronology of N -- which had only divided the letters into those of the Prior and those of the Abbot -- by
rearranging all the letters in their proper chronological
order. He also inserted in the correct order five of the
letters to Maurice which had meanwhile been returned to him.
Having accomplished the purpose of his journey he spent the
autumn and winter of 1092/93 with his friend and former fellow monk, Abbot Gilbert Crispin at St. Peter's, Westminster,
waiting for the king's leave to return to Bec. Therefore
the second stage of the first part of Anselm's letter collection was most likely executed at Westminster during this
period. The best example of this second stage is to be
found in the first part of his collection in Cambridge, Corpus Christi College, MS 135 (henceforth E_1), an early
twelfth century Bury St. Edmund copy of the lost original of
1093.

Anselm's collection of letters, now to be found in London (Lambeth Palace, MS 59 [henceforth L] written at Canterbury) and in Paris (Bibliothèque Nationale, MS 14762 [hence-
forth V] written at Bec), forming L_1 and V_1 respectively,
developed differently in Canterbury and at Bec, and represent the third stage of the first part of the Anselmian letter collection. L_1 and V_1 differ from N and E_1 and from
each other by additions and further letters and in the chronological sequence of the letters they contain. L_1 contains
one hundred and thirty-five letters while V_1 comprises one
hundred and fifty-six of which twenty-seven are duplicated.

Instead of being granted royal leave to return to his
community at Bec, Abbot Anselm was forcibly invested with
the archbishopric of Canterbury by King William II on 6
March 1093. The highly dramatic procedure is well-known --
King William Rufus on his sick-bed, in fear of imminent
death, pressing the episcopal staff into Anselm's clenched
fist; and the elect being led, dragged, rather carried by
his episcopal colleagues to the nearby chapel chanting the

Te Deum. Despite these irregularities at his investiture and his profuse protestations about his unworthiness, Anselm eventually accepted the office of Archbishop of Canterbury after some not very satisfactory negotiations with the king at Rochester. He was consecrated Archbishop of Canterbury and Primate of all Britain on 4 December 1093. Anselm's pontificate lasted from March, 1093 to 21 April, 1109. These sixteen years are divided into five periods:

(1) March, 1093 to November, 1097 was occupied mainly with the struggle against the royal *usus atque leges Normannorum;*

(2) this fight led to the first exile from November, 1097 to September, 1100;

(3) the period from September, 1100 to December, 1103 was filled by the controversy about lay investiture and the ecclesiastical decrees forbidding homage of clerics to laymen;

(4) the obstinacy of both king and pope on this issue drove Anselm into his second exile from December, 1103 to September, 1106;

(5) the years from September, 1106 to Anselm's death in April, 1109 were spent on the reform of the church and the quarrel with York about the supremacy of Canterbury in the English church (*ecclesia in Anglia*).

Anselm's correspondence covering his archiepiscopal pontificate represents the second part of his correspondence and comprises two hundred and fifty-nine items. It contains not only the out-going letters but also some he received, as well as some letters between third parties. In those letters, written while he was Archbishop of Canterbury, the emphasis of the contents shows a shift from pastoral advice and monastic exhortation to political problems of church reform, Anglo-Norman statecraft and the struggle for supremacy between *regnum* and *sacerdotium* within the *corpus christianorum.* Thus the character of the letter collection changes from a compilation valued for its moral content to that of a compilation dealing with state affairs of the utmost political importance. The final part of this second part of Anselm's letter collection contains all the letters bearing upon the renewed outbreak of the primatial controversy between the metropolitan sees of Canterbury and York

which took place in the autumn and winter, 1108 and spring
and summer, 1109. Thus again the character of the collection changes. It acquires the character of a register of
the archbishop's most recent correspondence.

The earliest collection of Anselm's letters written and
received as archbishop of Canterbury (from 6 March, 1093 to
21 April, 1109) is to be found in the second part of London,
Lambeth Palace, MS 59 (L_2) fol. 64r to 160v, since all other
manuscripts containing letters of the archiepiscopal period
depend on this part of L. They were compiled and edited by
Anselm himself during another period of enforced leisure.
From December, 1103 to September, 1106 he was banished from
the Anglo-Norman realm because of the dispute about investitures between King Henry I and Pope Paschal II. Anselm
spent most of his second exile with his friend, Archbishop
Hugh of Lyon. During this time he directed the production
of a final edition of his works and letters. Following
Anselm's instructions (*Epistolae 334, 379*) this task was
conscientiously and meticulously carried out by the scribe
Thidricus at Christ Church, Canterbury. The fruits of Thidricus' labors are the magnificent and most carefully
executed manuscripts Oxford, Bodleian, MS Bodley 271, containing Anselm's philosophical and theological works, and
London, Lambeth Palace, MS 59, comprising his letters.

Soon after Anselm's death an appendix L_a was added to L_1
and L_2. On thirty-one pages L_a contains a miscellany of
letters, tracts, poems, and other documents. Thirteen letters in L_a are referred back to the collection of L_2 by
symbols and instructions in the margin. Two poems in praise
of Anselm appear also in L_a. The second of these is introduced by the following rubric: *Item versus de eodem praesu-*
lis Anselmi quem nuper obisse dolemus. If *nuper* is understood as "recently" just as Anselm himself had used it, as
in *Epistola 104*, it appears that L_a was written shortly
after Anselm's death on 21 April, 1109, but that L_1 and L_2
were written during his lifetime, most likely from about
1105 to November, 1108.

The Bec tradition of the first part of Anselm's letter
collection of V_1 took over the second part of the collection
of L_2 in order to form V_2 without taking cognizance of
possible duplications of letters or the need for inserting
letters of the Bec tradition into the Canterbury tradition.
At the end of this brief survey of the genesis of the collection of Anselm's letters the following stemma may sum up
the relationship of the main manuscripts containing this
collection.

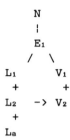

The final edition Anselm made of his letters in L comprises three hundred and eighty-nine items. Dom F. S. Schmitt's edition of *Anselmi opera omnia* contains four hundred and seventy-five letters. The eighty-six letters which Dom Schmitt had found in various other MSS and inserted into his edition seem to have been intentionally omitted by Anselm. In a further one hundred and twenty letters he refers to some written supplication as the cause for his written reply but does not include the writer's letter. All in all, some two hundred and six letters did not find their way into L. This excision would point to the fact that about a third of Anselm's known correspondence or about half of the collection of letters he edited in L were omitted without taking into account any possible Anselmian correspondence before 1070. These considerations demonstrate that Anselm received and wrote a very large number of letters; he also had access to letters exchanged between third persons. They show that Anselm was at the center of a prolific correspondence, with the art of letter-writing a newly-revived feature of the intellectual life of the eleventh and twelfth centuries.

For this reason it seems obvious that Anselm carefully selected from the mass of his correspondence and diligently compiled a collection of those letters he considered worth preserving in L. An examination of the letters included in Schmitt but omitted from L by Anselm provides clues and possible reasons for their omission, and may point to Anselm's method and intention in compiling his collection of letters.

(1) Twelve letters[7] of Anselm's time as Prior and Abbot of Bec were most likely omitted from L because of their relative unimportance, their purely local relevance, their lenient treatment of married priests (which clashed with Anselm's rigorous attitude of later years), or, possibly, their criticism of Archbishop Lanfranc.

(2) Two letters to Pope Urban II were omitted.[8] They dealt with Bishop Fulk of Beauvais, whom Anselm had recommended for that see but who turned out to be a failure in his diocese.

(3) Nineteen letters to the community at Bec or via Bec to various persons in Normandy[9] after Anselm's appointment to the see of Canterbury appear to have been excluded from L because Anselm felt his image might be damaged by their publication; in particular, his too-frequent refutations of his alleged greed for the archbishopric might raise suspicion that he did indeed protest too much.

(4) Eight letters to Bishop Osmund of Salisbury and members of the convent of Wilton[10] in the diocese of Salisbury dealt with the monastic status of some Anglo-Saxon ladies: Eadgyth, daughter of King Malcolm and Queen Margaret of Scotland, Eadgyth's aunt Christina, and Gunilda, daughter of King Harold of England. Having referred to Eadgyth as a *filia perdita* in the early years of his pontificate this letter may have been most embarrassing for Anselm when, with his help, this Eadgyth became King Henry I's bride and queen, then called Mathilda, especially since Anselm enjoyed the queen's close friendship in later years. Moreover, the inclusion of this letter and those connected with it might have stirred the sleep of dormant critics of Anselm's conduct in this affair and blown about the dust of past scandals. Such considerations would explain the omission of these eight letters from L.

(5) Schmitt contains fifty-four letters which name King Henry or Queen Mathilda as sender or recipient. Eight of these, which are correspondence between the king or the queen and Pope Paschal II, are omitted from L.[11] This fact recalls Anselm's letter to Thidricus in 1105 in which he replies to the latter's enquiry:

> Litteras quas quaeris regis ad papam, non
> tibi mitto, quia non intelligo utile esse,
> se serventur (*Epistola 379*).

This letter to Thidricus seems most likely to refer to his work, which had been going on since about 1105, of compiling the collection of the archbishop's letters and copying them into L. While Anselm was forced to suffer his second exile from December, 1103 to September, 1106 he sent these instructions to Thidricus who obediently followed them by omitting from L all but one of the items (*Epistola 323*) of the correspondence between the king, the queen, and Pope Paschal. The pope's cautious negotiations with, and his lenient treatment of, the king while Anselm suffered the hardships of exile for upholding the papal decrees might well have been the reason for Anselm's exclusion of this correspondence from L.

(6) Two letters from Pope Paschal and Cardinal John (*Epistolae 282* and *284*) reminding Anselm of the condemnation of simony, and married priests and deacons, and encouraging Anselm to defend the liberty of the Church were omitted from L. These letters seemed to have irked him because he was suffering exile for the defence of the freedom of the Church and the propagation of its reform.

(7) A group of three short letters representing the correspondence between Bishop Lambert of Arras and Anselm is also omitted from L. Despite the close friendship of the two men, these letters were probably omitted because of their triviality (*Epistolae 437, 438, 439*).

(8) Four letters (*Epistolae 457, 458, 459, 460*) confirming the proposed division of the Diocese of Lincoln and the establishment of the new Diocese of Ely probably never reached Canterbury before Thidricus finished work on L. Therefore they are not in L.

(9) Another group of five letters is missing from L. They are part of the correspondence dealing with the renewed outbreak of the primatial controversy between Canterbury and York, following the promotion of Thomas of Beverly to the See of York after the death of Archbishop Gerard on 27 May, 1108 (*Epistolae 453, 454, 456, 470, 442*). Since the letters from York demonstrate the York opinion in this dispute, and the king did not side wholeheartedly with the claim of Canterbury, it would seem likely that the open and veiled threats to the primatial claim of the archbishop of Canterbury were the ground for the omission of these letters from the final edition of Anselm's letters in L.

(10) Five of the thirteen letters of the correspondence with Archbishop Gerard of York are omitted from L.[12] Anselm appears to have omitted these letters to Gerard, his ecclesiastical opponent in the investiture dispute, even though they might have improved the bad impression conveyed by the other letters of Gerard's correspondence retained in L.

This observation supports the feeling that there was method
in Anselm's omissions. Was the injury inflicted by Gerard's
behavior and actions during the controversy still rankling?

(11) Three more items in the list of omitted letters
level harsh criticism at Anselm for his prolonged absence
from the see of Canterbury and the Church of England due to
his second exile (*Epistolae 310, 365, 366*). Since in
Anselm's eyes this criticism was unjustified, it appears
that he excluded these letters in order not to mar the image
of himself which he wanted to convey and preserve.

Various omissions in the collections suggest that everything was suppressed which might have caused embarrassment
or revived criticism of Anselm's supposed cupidity for the
wealthy archbishopric of Canterbury or of his long absences
from England; furthermore, such letters, which might have
challenged Anselm's claim to be the sole advocate and prota-
gonist for the reform and freedom of the Church and the
mighty defender of the primatial claim of Canterbury, were
(for obvious reasons) not included. The letter collection
displays Anselm as a faithful monk and ardent soldier of
Christ who devoted his life totally to God and his service.
He appears as a zealous laborer in creating a loving and
truly Christian community of monks and as an active reformer
of the Church of God in unity with the pope and in agreement
with papal ordinance. Thus he set an example of the impec-
cable Christian prelate whose faultless public conduct was
to serve as a model and a precedent for others to act in the
same way. The image of his behavior was intended to create
binding customs and, eventually, good laws. Anselm's letter
collection was to be a manual of examples for his own time
and for the future.
Therefore, the letter collection contained in L is a
monument to Anselm's rectitude and firm demeanor as a
churchman vigorously pursuing the demand for *libertas et
reformatio ecclesiae*, and defending the Church of God reso-
lutely in the face of threats and isolation as well as personal suffering and disadvantages. From this survey of the
letters omitted from L it would appear that Anselm took
great care to suppress any correspondence which would have
damaged the picture of himself which he intended for posterity.

II

The examination of how Anselm carefully compiled a selective collection of his letters and edited it three times with the aim of creating a *speculum episcopale* will be followed by a characterization of how Anselm advanced in his monastic profession seeking perfection in order to be counted among the chosen few who are permitted to enter the kingdom of God and share in his glory in the company of the angels adoring him.

In some of his early letters to young men seeking his advice about embarking on the monastic life, Anselm encouraged them with seriousness and fervor to thrust themselves onto the mercy of God, to respond wholeheartedly to his love by leaving the world and its vain glory behind. In counseling those who sought his advice, Anselm draws upon the experience of his own monastic progress and supports his encouragement by the use of examples. In these letters[13] Anselm's growth as a monk as well as the formation of the basis of his *imago mundi* can be perceived. The analysis of *Epistola 2* to the young men Odo and Lanzo, *Epistola 37* to the novice Lanzo at Cluny, and *Epistola 112* to Hugh the hermit, may display evidence supporting this statement.[14]

Circa 1070, Anselm wrote a letter of exhortation to two young men, Odo and Lanzo (*Epistola 2*). Anselm offered this letter as a token of his love for both of them; he encouraged their love of God with advice drawn from Holy Scripture and his own experience. The autobiographical tone of the letter is set by the address:

> Dominis, amicis, fratribus carissimis Odoni
> et Lanzoni: frater Anselmus Beccensis, vita
> peccator, habitu monachus, pro aeternis tem-
> poralia despicere, pro temporalibus aeterna
> percipere.

In these three sets of thesis and antithesis, Anselm summarizes his autobiography of becoming a monk; he threw himself on the love of God and left the sinfulness of the world behind. He offered the example of his own conversion to the monastic life as an invitation for imitation to Odo and Lanzo. In reply to their request about the surest way to salvation, Anselm first of all told them to study Holy Scripture for themselves, but added some pieces of exhortation out of Holy Scripture in his own words. He admonished them to be watchful of what they had gained in daily progress on their pilgrimage towards their celestial home by

pointing to the fact that progress in virtue was hard and
could easily be lessened through idleness and lassitude.
They ought to progress from the many who are called, to
become the few who are chosen. Since nobody knows how many
are chosen, they ought to look ahead and strive to advance
with those who are chosen, and not look behind at those they
think they have overtaken. They should fervently maintain
their fear of God so that it may burn more and more daily
until it becomes the light of eternal security. They should
not abandon their resolution to lead a holy life as monks
but live in such a way that they can progress in their holy
intentions and reach the company of the saints through the
grace of Christ. Since the older they get the shorter they
will have to live, their decision for the monastic life is
very urgent. The further they move away from birth, the
closer they come to death and final judgment; their life
span for living a good life diminishes accordingly. Anselm
closed his letter to Odo and Lanzo by imploring them not to
despise what comes from God but to despise the world, its
snares and rewards, since the friend of the world is the
enemy of God.

As a result of this advice, Lanzo entered the monastery
at Cluny, not at Bec, as Anselm might have hoped for, since
a year or two later he was a novice at Cluny. In about 1072
Anselm, still Prior of Bec, wrote a letter to Lanzo, then
novice (*Epistola 37*). In this letter Anselm assured him
of their lasting mutual love, despite their separation in
obedience to the Lord, and trusted in their eventual union
in the Lord. Lanzo should beware of the snares and tricks
of the devil, resist his temptations and ignore his luring
smile and that of the world. Moreover, *stabilitas loci*,
which helps calm the restless mind of a novice and enables
the young monk to become content with the monastery and its
customs, and to place his trust in divine providence, ought
to be rigorously observed.

Anselm begins his letter praising Lanzo's decision to
leave the world and become a monk because of his love of
God. The young novice should trust that, through divine
clemency, they will be united in the life to come, and that,
although separated, their love will make one of their two
souls. "Our souls present to each in other in love embrace
each other, and being absent from each other in life, long
for one another." As monks not possessing any abode, property, or connections in this world, Anselm encourages Lanzo
to look ahead, and using the metaphor of pilgrims on their
journey to the holy city, he promises him that at the end of
the pilgrimage of their lives they will come together in
that homeland towards which they are striving. "By divine

disposition we shall rejoice in God;" for this reason "we must not resist God's disposition but obey."

Rejoicing that Lanzo had become a soldier of Christ he warns him to beware of the attacks and the violence of the enemy, and to guard against Satan sowing doubt about his decision to join the *militia Christi* by leaving the world. Anselm warns his young friend:

> As long as the malicious one is not able openly to annihilate the young soldier of Christ by inflicting a wound of evil intention, the sly one tries to destroy him by maliciously offering a cup of poisonous reason when he is thirsty.

In this way Satan produces hatred for the monastic life within the novice's mind. Even worse, the devil will make the young novice feel proud of having taken his monastic vow, but lead him to despise life under such superiors and among such fellow monks. Did Anselm experience this at Bec when he was a young monk?[15]

Satan's snares and tricks may persuade the young monk to be ungrateful for the goodness begun by God. Blaming his bad start on others, he will fail to progress and to strive for the goal of perfection but will plan to move to another monastery. Bringing to an end the diagnosis of the young monk's misery due to Satan's whisperings, Anselm writes: "Since the foundation which the young monk has laid displeases him, he will on no account wish to build the frame of a good life upon it." Employing the metaphor of the young tree which, often transplanted or frequently disturbed, will never be able to take root, Anselm compares it to the young monk who will not bring any fruit to perfection.

> If the unhappy monk often moves from place to place following his own whim, [Anselm writes] or remaining in one place is frequently agitated by hatred of his beginning, he never reaches stability with roots of love, and does not grow rich by the fruitfulness of good works. [Moreover] he unjustly assigns the whole cause of his misery not to his own behaviour but to that of others, and hence unhappily works himself up to even greater hatred of those among whom he lives.

Anselm exhorts anybody who takes the monastic vow to strive with total application to take roots with the roots of love and gain *stabilitas loci* in whatever monastery he made his profession. The young monk ought to rejoice about having successfully fled the tempestuous hurricanes of the world and landed in a safe harbor. He should diligently devote himself freely for the rest of his life to the sole pursuit of achieving a holy life. Humility of heart and mind will enable the young monk to progress steadily in his monastery, awaiting the call of divine disposition which never unjustly refuses anything to anybody. Anselm closes his letter of monastic exhortation to Lanzo.

> Let the young monk's mind, continually pro-
> tected by constancy and meekness, be com-
> pletely free to be vigilant in the fear of
> God to delight in his love. For fear guards
> the soul through vigilance whereas love
> leads to perfection through delight.

Anselm's spiritual counsel in this letter and in others[16] is nursed by the experience on his path of becoming a monk; it is an index of his own personal concept of perfection in obedience to God out of fear of Him. These two letters, *Epistola 2* and *Epistola 37*, written about twelve years after he had made his monastic profession, reflect Anselm's progress in the monastic life.

Anselm, and in due course Eadmer, his chaplain and biographer, regarded this letter to the novice Lanzo at Cluny (who later became the first Prior of the Cluniac house of St. Pancras at Lewes [1077-1107), as one of his most important letters dealing with monastic life. Some thirty years later while enduring his second exile in Lyon (1103-1106), Anselm sent a brief piece of spiritual advice to Warner, a novice at Christ Church, Canterbury.[17] For more profound counsel on the monastic life, he advised Warner to look up the letter he had written to Dom Lanzo when the latter was a novice. Eadmer underlined the importance of this letter by inserting much of it into his *Vita Anselmi*.[18]

Fourteen years later, in 1086, Anselm wrote a letter to Hugh, the hermit (*Epistola 112*). At the time of this letter's composition, Anselm was about fifty-three years old, had been a monk for some twenty-six years, Abbot of Bec for seven years, and had reached maturity in the monastic life. With the average life expectancy about thirty-seven years, Anselm must have been fully aware that he was becoming an old man with only a short time to live. The quality of his life was decreasing in a dramatic way. For this reason, the letter displays Anselm's mature and sublime concept of perfection -- a union with God born out of love. A close scrutiny of the letter will support this statement.

Two young men had brought Hugh's petition that Anselm compose a short treatise "with which one could stimulate the minds of secular people towards dispising this world and longing for the eternal kingdom." In his inimitable clarity of mind, Anselm develops his treatise in four main steps: he protests his humility, defines the kingdom of heaven, states the price for gaining it, and demonstrates how anyone can become a citizen of the kingdom of heaven while on earth. Following this protestation of humility, Anselm begins the requested treatise with a resounding metaphor: "Dearest brother, God cries out that he has the kingdom of heaven for sale." However, because the glory of this kingdom of heaven lies beyond the grasp of human senses, even beyond human imagination, Anselm describes the kingdom of God by piecing together four stones of logical reasoning:

(a) The kingdom of heaven is the fulfillment of all the desires of man, all that he has ever hoped for.

(b) Anselm maintains that love is motive for action and attitude as well as the unifying bond in this kingdom of heaven: "So great will the love be between God and those who will be there, and between each other, that all will love each other as they love themselves but all will love God more than themselves."

(c) This all-embracing love creates concord of wills and actions of all the inhabitants of the kingdom of heaven: "Whatever everyone individually wishes, will come about for himself and for all the others, for the whole creation and for God himself."

(d) Anselm concludes that love and will are going to merge to become one: "All of them will be united with God like one man because they will all desire one thing and what they desire will come about."

Thus, through logical deduction, Anselm defines the kingdom of heaven and life therein. This kingdom of heaven is God's merchandise, his offer to man. Anselm progresses in his treatise by inquiring what the price for such an offer by God would be. He points out that there is nothing on earth of adequate value to God's offer, no earthly payment that could buy the kingdom of heaven. Moreover, since God is the creator of the universe, the universe and every-

thing that exists therein is in his possession. For this
reason, "no one can give God anything which he does not
already have since all that is is his." Having dealt with
such negative aspects of the price, Anselm advances his
argument by suggesting that man might conclude that God
grants his gift to man for nothing. This assumption, however, is utterly wrong. On the contrary, "God does not give
his gift for nothing for he does not give it to anyone who
does not love." Love of God and love of neighbor is the
price for the kingdom of heaven. "God asks for nothing but
love without which He is not bound to give." Therefore, man
is exhorted to "love and receive the kingdom: love and possess."

Having set forth man's reward first and then told its
price, Anselm proceeds to relate it to man's present status.
Since the union of will and the love of God, that of angels
and men alike, is the condition for the citizenship of
heaven, it follows: "Love God more than yourself and you
will already begin to hold what you there wish to have in
perfection." Excluding friction as contrary to harmony
since harmony rules the kingdom of heaven, Anselm appeals to
man to seek harmonious identity with God and men. His spiritual advice for men in this world culminates in the following appeal: "Be of one mind with God and men and you will
already begin to reign with God and with all his saints."
This oneness with God and men excludes any other love.
Anselm supports his statement about the exclusive character
of the love of God with the metaphor of the vessel. The
more oil it holds, the less water it contains. Therefore,
"to the extent the heart is occupied by any other love, in
the same measure it excludes the perfect love." If man's
heart is filled to capacity with love of God and neighbor,
it will seek God's will alone.

While on earth, membership of the kingdom of heaven can
be earned by those who dedicate themselves to prayer, meditation, and conversation about heavenly things, by those who
carry out acts of charity according to Christ's command, and
by those who despise riches, power, and pleasure. Therefore, Anselm finishes his exhortation, "Whoever wishes to
possess in full this love with which the kingdom of heaven
is bought, should love scorn, poverty, hard work, and submission as holy men do. For he who humbles himself will be
exalted" (Lk 18:14). By quoting from St. Luke, Anselm puts
the mark of scriptural authority on the fruit of his deliberations.

The analysis of these three letters (*Epistolae 2, 37,*
and *112*) may be summed up as follows:

(a)   Underneath   the   advice   and exhortation offered to others, it is possible to perceive Anselm's own   experiences on   his   pilgrimage towards becoming a perfect monk. By the time the letter to Hugh was written, the personal experience on which he based his advice had been gathered in twenty-six years of monastic life, advancing from fear of God   to   love of God.

(b)   Given   that   Anselm   drew on his own experience, no discrepancy exists between Anselm's conduct as   a   monk   and what he preached to others.

(c)   Anselm urged those who requested his advice to love God completely and thus begin to share the kingdom of heaven in   this   world.   Love for one's neighbor is man's testimony and reflection of this love of God[19] and anything   diminishing or impeding it must be despised and eliminated.

III

Anselm's   reflections   and   meditations on monastic life matured over a period of about thirty years in the monastery of   Bec   --   the greater part of his adult life. This tranquility enhanced and determined his conduct with firm rectitude and righteous firmness, guided by the hierarchy of values of his *imago mundi*. When considering the sources[20]   for Anselm's   thinking as conveyed in his letters Anselm himself must first be listened to. As he wrote in a great number of letters,   he   drew   on   Holy   Scripture   in   his writings.[21] Furthermore, he often referred to the   *Regula   Sancti   Benedicti*,   the   charter   of western monasticism, and to a number of authors of classical antiquity. However, Anselm did   not acknowledge   all   his sources.[22]   He extensively made use of and reinterpreted the ideas and concepts of St. Augustine.[23] This   is   not   surprising   since   St. Augustine was the most influential doctor of the Latin church in the   early   Middle Ages; for this reason the works of St. Augustine constituted a prominent part of the library of the monastery of   Bec   in the early twelfth century.[24]   Anselm's extensive use of them is apparent in his philosophical and   theological   writings. He used them not only as a starting point for his own tracts and dialogues but also as   source   materials.   Despite   the strong   Augustinian   influence, however, differences of substance and emphasis exist between Anselm and Augustine.

In his letters Anselm absorbed   and   then   employed   the fundamental   concepts   of St. Augustine's *De doctrina christiana*[25] and the basic ideas of   *De   civitate   dei*.[26]   These

works shaped his *Weltbild*.   A few citations from both works
will sketch St. Augustine's concepts and will in turn lead
to a better understanding of Anselm's thinking and conduct.
In his advice and exhortation on the monastic life, Anselm
drew heavily on both of these works.   In the *De doctrina
christiana*, for example, St. Augustine subordinates all
earthly good to the supreme good (*summum bonum*).   He differ-
entiates terms.   According to St. Augustine, there are two
kinds of things: those which one may taste and enjoy (*frui*)
and those which one ought to use (*uti*).   St. Augustine
explains:

> Those things which are objects of enjoyment
> make us happy.   Those things which are
> objects of use assist, so that we can attain
> the things that make us happy and rest in
> them. We ourselves, again, who enjoy and
> use these things, being placed between both
> kinds of objects, if we set ourselves to
> enjoy those which we ought to use, are hin-
> dered in our course, and sometimes even led
> away from it; so that, getting entangled in
> the love of lower gratifications, we lag
> behind in, or even altogether turn back
> from, the pursuit of the real and proper
> objects of enjoyment (*De doctrina christiana*
> I,iii,3).

Enjoyment and use, *frui* and *uti*, must be understood in
the meaning which St. Augustine gave them based on his
understanding of Scripture.   These terms represent St.
Augustine's interpretation of the New Testament's command of
love as he analyzed culture and society. They determine how
and to what extent the soul takes possession of the goods
surrounding it.   St. Augustine says:

> For to enjoy a thing is to rest with satis-
> faction in it for its own sake. To use, on
> the other hand, is to employ whatever means
> are at one's disposal to obtain what one
> desires, if it is a proper object of desire;
> for an unlawful use ought rather be called
> an abuse (*De doctrina christiana* I,iv,4)

For this reason, God alone can be the object of our love and
anything that brings us into contact with God may be loved
to the extent it leads us on towards God: the body for the
sake of the soul and the soul for the sake of God.   If love

has learnt to discern in this way, and to order earthly
goods accordingly, it is called *dilectio ordinata*, and will
in turn determine human relationships which up to then were
determined by egoism and greed.

> If God is to be loved more than any man,
> each man ought to love God more than him-
> self. Likewise we ought to love another man
> better than our own body, because all things
> ought to be loved in reference to God, and
> another man can have fellowship with us in
> the enjoyment of God, whereas our body can-
> not; for the body only lives through the
> soul, and it is by the soul that we enjoy
> God (*De doctrina christiana* I,xxviii,27).

This is the reasons that in St. Augustine's thinking love of
one's neighbor is valuable only insofar as it leads the
neighbor to God, the origin and goal of our enjoyment.
Therefore, *frui Deo* is the cardinal point of life in
society.

If, however, the love of one's neighbor is only valuable
if it leads towards *fruitio dei*, it is even more important
in the case of material goods and values which are only
worth anything when they are used to obtain this *fruitio
dei*. That is to say that the intrinsic value of the goods
of this world is abolished. This fact is made quite clear
in *De doctrina christiana* II when St. Augustine critically
scrutinizes the whole breadth of classical education and
eliminates everything which is not conducive to Christian
thinking and in particular to the study of Holy Scripture.
At the end he proposes a selective encyclopedia of pagan
knowledge as far as it is useful for biblical studies and
exegeses. This proposition by St. Augustine is the ultimate
consequence of the radical subjection of earthly goods to
the supreme good (*De doctrina christiana* II,xxxviii,59).
The historical context in which these thoughts were conceived and developed must be remembered. The *De doctrina
christiana* deals with Christian knowledge, or more precisely, with the education and training of Christian scholars. St. Augustine devised a model for the training of
clerics in four stages: training in theology, in other
sciences, in the interpretation of Holy Scripture, and in
the art of preaching. None of these individual stages can
be taught without the assistance of pagan science. Consequently, St. Augustine holds that "the wealth of truths has
to be taken away from the pagans who are unlawful owners and
put to our use" (*De doctrina christiana* II,xl,60). Just as

the Jews when leaving Egypt appropriated the Egyptians' gold
and silver to themselves, in the same way the Christian
scholars have to seize the treasures from the pagans and
lawfully use them for the preaching of the gospel. Thus St.
Augustine closes by saying: "Whatever man may have learned
from sources apart from Holy Scripture, if it is hurtful, it
is there condemned; if it is useful, it is therein contained" (*De doctrina christiana* II,xlii,63). This relationship between the goal and the way of achieving it is
expressed by St. Augustine's distinction between *uti* and
frui. It not merely applies to education and the use of
pagan authors, but also determines the hierarchy of all the
goods, values and institutions of human life and actions.
Going on from *De doctrina christiana*, St. Augustine devel-
opes a code of human behavior and an order of the hierarchy
of values in his *De civitate dei*. In order to establish the
right order of values for human actions, St. Augustine
devotes much thought to man's longing for happiness. He
states that "man's real happiness (*vera felicitas*) is to
spend a good life on earth in order to merit the eternal
life hereafter" (*De civitate dei* IV,3), and elsewhere,
"felicity is the complete enjoyment of all that is to be
desired" (*De civitate dei* V, praefatio). Felicity, however,
is neither made nor conceived by man. Whatever makes man
happy is above him.

> For just as it is not something derived from
> the physical body itself that gives life to
> that body, but something above it, so it is
> not something that comes from man, but some-
> thing above man, that makes his life happy
> (*De civitate dei* XIX,25).

The origin of all happiness, therefore, lies beyond man
and creation. St. Augustine teaches: "God himself is the
happiness of man's life" (*De civitate dei* XIX,26). He is
the creator of all things, and, as absolute being, the final
aim of all human longing for happiness. He is the ultimate
good, *summum bonum*. Having arrived at this conclusion, St.
Augustine then deduces that all human happiness and bliss
are gifts of God, *dona dei*, and this is reiterated throughout *De civitate dei*. Complete happiness, yearned for by
human nature, is a gift of God, is participation in God, and
ultimately God Himself. On the one hand it is obtained by
enjoying God as the absolute, unchangeable good (*bonum
incommutabile*), and on the other hand by permanently remaining in God, not disturbed by any doubts or deceived by any
errors (*De civitate dei* IX,13). Man's quest for complete

happiness will be hindered by desire for earthly goods   such
as wealth, fame, power, and honor. Many people desire these
goods for their own sake. They do not use them in order   to
attain   a   higher   aim or good. They enjoy them to the full
and in so doing they become slaves of the love of themselves
(*amor   sui*) ignoring or even despising the love of God (*amor
dei*). True love of God, and the   total   commitment   to   it,
reduces   all   worldly goods to mere tools. Their only value
is derived from the amount of motivation   they   provide   for
man on his progress towards the love of God.

     According to St. Augustine, the choice between these two
kinds of love, which oppose and exclude each   other,   is   an
option of fundamental character. Every human being is faced
with this choice which divides   mankind   into   two   separate
mystical   and   invisible   societies. If the individual opts
for *amor sui usque ad contemptum dei*,   he   belongs   to   the
civitas   terrena.   His conduct is governed by the desire to
dominate others (*libido dominandi*), and to reap human praise
and   fame   (*cupiditas   humanae gloriae*). The positive moral
decision would be to choose *amor   dei   usque   ad   contemptum
sui*. This option makes man a member of the mystical body of
civitas dei (*De civitate dei* XIV,28). For the   citizens   of
this *civitas dei*, the unimpaired vision and enjoyment of God
in eternal life is the supreme good and final goal of   their
lives.[27]   The   conduct   of   these members of *civitas dei* is
governed by obedience to the will of God, subjection to   his
commandments   and   to those of his representatives on earth,
promulgation of justice, love of truth, and the practice   of
humility.   Their   love   of   God is demonstrated in the love
they show for their neighbors.

     The moral option of man either for *amor sui* or *amor   dei*
creates membership in either *civitas terrena* or *civitas dei*.
These are not visible but   mystical   bodies,   and   therefore
cannot   be identified with the visible institutions of state
or church. These mystical bodies are mixed at   the   present
time.   They become visible on the day of the Last Judgment.
Men living in this age live in *civitas permixta*.

IV

     This brief sketch of the basic ideas and concepts of St.
Augustine's *De   doctrina   christiana* and *De   civitate dei*
points out that Anselm regarded St. Augustine's thinking not
only as the incentive and source material, however modified,
for his own philosophical and theological tracts and   treatises   but   also   as the catechism and normbook for his moral
conduct and his political action. St. Augustine's *De   doc-*

trina christiana and *De civitate dei* formed Anselm's *imago mundi*. Having considered various possibilities, Anselm chose to become a monk.[28] Leaving all worldly goods and honors behind and seeking the love of God alone before any-thing else, he joined the *militia Christi*, adopting and fully bringing to bear St. Augustine's concepts of *frui* instead of *uti*, and *amor dei usque ad contemptum sui* instead of *amor sui usque ad contemptum dei* as the axioms for his moral conduct as a monk living a good life. Thus he con-sciously chose to join the mystical body of the *civitas dei* and positively rejected that of the *civitas terrena*. In his letters, drawing on his experience of striving towards the goal of becoming a perfect monk, he invited others to join him by following his example and encouraged fellow monks to persevere staunchly in their decision of leaving the world for the sake of the love of God. Anselm's love of God becomes apparent in his friendship, his love for his fellow monks and fellow men who also sought the love of God alone. His letters of friendship are a testimony of his love of one's neighbor reflecting his love of God.

In Anselm's view, monks are the most important group in society, advancing the spread and growth of the mystical body of *civitas dei*. They are the vanguard on the pilgri-mage towards the celestial home in search of the beatific vision of God. This evaluation explains why, in Anselm's opinion, all earthly goods and institutions are reduced to the quality of mere tools in order to bring about the cre-ation and growth of this mystical *civitas dei*. Any impedi-ment or obstacle slowing down or even preventing the advance towards the ultimate good, *summum bonum*, would be relegated by him to belonging to *civitas terrena*, and classified as governed by the moral concept of *uti* and *amor sui usque ad contemptum dei*.

A review of the Anselmian use of some of the key terms of the medieval *ordo*, when pieced together like a mosaic, will demonstrate Anselm's perception of the world, his *imago mundi*, and will display the profound influence of St. Augus-tine on his thinking. The Anselmian usage of *ecclesia*, *lex dei*, *pontifex Romanus*, *episcopus*, *rex et regnum*, and *imperator* will be defined.

Anselm's concept of *ecclesia* has been described before, most recently by Yves Congar in 1959.[29] When describing *ecclesia*, Anselm frequently used the image of *sponsa Christi*.[30] This image conveys the mystery of the church in God's plan for man's salvation, and displays its intimate connection with God. Following St. Augustine, Anselm holds that in the beginning God created the angels in order to populate his celestial kingdom.[31] They were to share his glory in adoration. When a number of these angels were expelled from the *civitas superna* because of their pride and vain claim to be like their creator, God decided to create man in order to fill the ranks of his kingdom. Man, therefore, was created to take the place of the fallen angels, and perform their task of adoring God and sharing his glory. Anselm maintains that God made man to be witness and companion, and to populate the celestial kingdom in order to share the vision of God in the company of the obedient and adoring angels. In order to become the fellow citizens and companions of the angels, man would have to organize his life according to the *vita angelica*. The number of those men and women who are chosen to replace the fallen angels is limited by God.

On the basis of this spiritual origin, Anselm's theology of *ecclesia* is characterized as follows:

(a) The basic reality of the church is not on the level of an earthly institution. It is the work of God carried out on earth but on the level of a celestial world.

(b) This characterization of *ecclesia* puts the church in the perspective of St. Augustine's *civitas dei*. The angels are its prime and most authentic citizens; men are called in later and therefore have only the quality of co-citizens to the angels. Anselm expresses his ecclesiology in terms of *civitas dei*, *superna civitas*, *superna Jerusalem*.[32] For Anselm the church (*ecclesia peregrinans*)[33] is the *civitas dei* on its pilgrimage through the world. The situation of the people on this pilgrimage inspired the terms of *ecclesia electorum*, *ecclesia sanctorum*, and *numerus electorum*.

(c) These terms have acquired classical quality since they were derived from St. Augustine and employed by many medieval writers. Yet with Anselm they gain a particular shade because of Anselm's concept of man's loss of the beatific vision and expulsion from paradise because of his fall, and his atonement through Christ's suffering, death, and resurrection. Man was called to complete the angelical society. He had been created for this purpose *sine peccato*.[34] He, however, fell into sin and therefore lost the heritage offered to him. Having a profound sense of the gravity of sin, Anselm defined this sin as that which caused man to lose the vision of God. Man must be punished and is in need of reparation. For Anselm, this need is best answered by the monastic life. Since man had lost paradise, he would find it again in the cloister.[35]

(d) Hence it is quite natural that Anselm has a monastic concept of *ecclesia* in accordance with his idea of Christian life itself. Again and again Anselm fervently encourages young men to abandon the world and embrace the monastic life.[36] He exhorts novices and fellow monks to persevere in the fight in the *militia Christi* in order to win back the lost celestial heritage and share in the company of the angels. According to Anselm, it is very difficult to find salvation in the world, and those who love the world prove themselves to be enemies of God.[37] Such distinctions call to mind St. Augustine's distinction between *amor sui* and *amor dei*.

When we apply these Anselmian qualifications of *ecclesia* to the individual, they mean that a person who makes a moral decision in favor of the former is one who insists on following his own will, asserts his own authority, commands and opposes others, causes discord, and is full of *superbia*, *obedientia*, and *propria voluntas*. A person embracing the latter can be characterized as one who obeys, effaces himself, submits to and serves other in concord and harmony, and practices *humilitas* and *obedientia* in order to gain the *civitas dei*.[38] Anselm's theology of obedience and service for others underlies all of his thought. He frequently quotes St. Paul: "None of you lives for himself, just as nobody dies for himself. Living, we live in the Lord and dying, we die in the Lord" (Rm 14:7-8).

Heaven and the kingdom of God were no distant and strange reality for Anselm. Heaven will be perfect union and complete concordance of the wills of all the citizens with the will of God. In the world, nevertheless, there are certain signs of this union to be found: wherever souls live in obedience, not owning themselves but being at the disposition of others, they are anticipating the spirit of the heavenly union.[39] In his letter to Gunter,[40] canon of St. Quentin of Beauvais, circa 1104 Anselm described this union and transcendental nearness at great length. Although it might lend itself to an easy comparison Anselm in his theology of *ecclesia* never identified *civitas dei* with *ecclesia* nor *civitas terrena* with *regnum*. Consequently, Anselm's *ecclesia* is the body of those souls on earth who took up God's invitation to join Him and the company of angels having chosen *amor dei*. Founded by God and destined to become part of the *civitas superna* Anselm's *ecclesia* is the supreme good on earth: *reginam illam de hoc mundo sponsam sibi Christo placuit eligere* (*Epistola 243*). This idea determined his *imago mundi*. In Anselm's view it is impossible for any man-made institution to be placed above this

gift of God and for anybody or any institution to legitimately throw the divinely founded church into the bondage of
slavery. Following St. Paul, Anselm demanded *liberam esse
ecclesiam.*[41] The church must be free from any secular
influence and tutelage.[42] In order to maintain the freedom
and the reign of the *ecclesia dei*, Anselm not only suffered
exile and loss of his *res omnes*, but he also demanded and
set an example.[43] The Christian should not desert his
position; even the fear of death should not cause him to do
so.[44] Therefore, Anselm praises and encourages everybody
who acts according to the maxim: *qui ecclesiam honorant,
cum illa honorabuntur, qui eam deprimunt cum daemonibus
deprimentur* (*Epistola 243*).

In Anselm's view, *lex dei* and *ecclesia* are closely
related; they become one since *ecclesia* is the institution
which *lex dei* organizes and regulates. Anselm instructs
Queen Mathilda that in baptism and ordination nobody prom-
ises to observe the law of the king or that of Archbishop
Lanfranc, but to obey the law and will of God.[45] Whoever
disregards *lex dei et voluntas dei* is an enemy of God.
Nobody must oppose the law of God which represents the will
of God, for everybody who does not subject himself to both
is an enemy of God according to Holy Scripture.[46]

> Ne credat consilium contra consilium dei;
> consilium autem domini et sacra scriptura et
> earum quibus dixit: qui vos audit, me audit
> et ad Christianam religionem instituta
> (*Epistola 249*).

When in conflict with King William II over his demand that
Anselm should observe and honor the royal *usus atque leges
Normannorum*, Anselm confronted their origin and claim with
lex dei and conclusively argued that they were of human
origin. Consequently, they were arbitrary since they did
not in any way agree with the *lex dei* nor with the *voluntas
dei*.[47] Anselm only accepted one source for righteous
action, as he only accepted one source of truth: the spirit
does not form a true statement unless it is influenced by
the truth of what it is talking about, guaranteed by divine
truth; in the same way a man does not lay claim to a just
deed without having received a measure of justice from the
essential source of justice, the will of God as revealed in
his word which has been transformed into the *instituta apostolica sive ecclesiastica* governed by *lex dei*. In his
letter to Pope Urban II from Lyon in January, 1098, Anselm
complained that, while he was in England, he saw the law of
God, the canons, and the apostolic authorities being overrun

by the arbitrary usages of the king (*Epistola 206*). To
Paschal II, Urban's successor, he went into detail about the
conflict between *lex dei* and the king's *usus atque leges*.
He wrote: "The King demanded of me that under the name of
righteousness I should give my consent to his plans which
were against the law and will of God."[48] The king's duty is
not to work against *lex dei* but to ensure everybody's strict
observance of *lex dei* in *ecclesia* and his realm. In the
course of this important letter Anselm enumerated the various royal laws which he considered to be in conflict with
the law of God. The conflicting demands imposed on Anselm
by the royal *usus atque leges*, as opposed to *lex dei sive
pontifici Romani*, drove him into exile in autumn, 1097, and
in winter, 1103.

On the *pontifex Romanus* Anselm wrote to Robert, Count of
Flanders:

> It is true that whoever does not obey the
> commands of the Roman pontiff, created for
> the protection of the Christian religion, is
> being disobedient towards the Apostle Peter
> whose vicar he is, nor does he belong to the
> flock which was entrusted to him by God.
> Let him seek other gates for the kingdom of
> heaven because he will not enter through
> those for which the Apostle Peter carries
> the keys (*Epistola 248*).

Anselm draws an almost identical picture of the Roman pontiff's position within his *imago mundi* in a letter to Humbert, Count of Aosta (*Epistola 262*). The Roman pontiff is
vicarius Petri, the deputy of the prince of Apostles to whom
Christ entrusted the flock of God.[49] The deputy and successor of St. Peter has the power to bind and loosen and he
grants admission to the kingdom of heaven. The image of St.
Peter being the doorkeeper of heaven, ever-present and ever-
vigilant shepherd of the flock of Christ, was extremely
widespread and fervently adhered to in the beliefs of the
Anglo-Saxons and the Normans.[50] Anselm expressed these
feelings and mystical ideas concerning the prince of
Apostles in his *Oratio ad sanctum Petrum*.[51] For these
peoples, St. Peter governed the Church, being represented in
the world through those who actually had the mission of
representing him sacramentally, namely the *vices eius ager*
-- his vicars (*Epistola 192*). The successor and vicar of
St. Peter had to prove himself as *apostolicus* by bearing
witness to the apostle's authority, his teaching, and way of

life. He is not inferior to the apostle; in fact his
authority is equal to that of St. Peter. Hence, in Anselm's
view, the Roman pontiff was endowed with authority and
responsibility for the whole church just as St. Peter had
been entrusted with the flock by Christ.[52] The pope holds
full authority of leadership for the whole church, not only
legal power, but also authority in teaching, spiritual guidance, and pastoral care.

The pope who rightfully occupies the see of Rome is
vicarius Petri,[53] *summus sanctae ecclesiae pastor*,[54]
universalis pontifex,[55]; but the title which Anselm usually
gave him was that of *ecclesiae catholicae summus pontifex*.[56]
After 1098 -- the first time he went to Rome, in his first
exile -- he only used the title of *summus pontifex*, sometimes affectionately varied by *pater*.[57] The role of the
sovereign pontiff is to conserve and defend Christianity by
carrying out the duties of doorkeeper and shepherd of the
flock.[58] It is worth noting that Anselm rarely made use of
Mt 16:18-19 to uphold the prerogatives of the Roman pontiff.
For him, the absolute value of pontifical decrees and of
communion with the Holy See -- a value so important that to
scorn it means to place oneself outside Christianity -- is
grounded in the fact that the Apostle Peter was invested by
God with the office of doorkeeper of heaven. His keys are
the keys of the doorkeeper. To escape from the shepherd's
crook means to leave the fold of the Lord and to prevent
oneself from entering the kingdom of heaven by the one door
which permits access to it.[59]

As he defines the position of the Roman pontiff within
the Church, Anselm carefully appears to avoid any Gregorian
associations and seems to follow pre-Gregorian and Augustinian doctrine. After 1098, having been to Rome and Lyon
during the course of his first exile (1097-1100), he constantly refers to the pope as *summus pontifex*. It has been
suggested that during this period Anselm learned much about
Gregorian ideas in France and in Italy. However, the title
summus pontifex is not characteristic of the texts of the
Gregorian reform and does not support the theory that Anselm
had accepted Gregorian ideas. His concept of the office of
the Roman pontiff is in keeping with his *imago mundi* as
influenced by St. Augustine.

The rank of *episcopus* and its place in Anselm's *Weltbild*
is defined by pastoral duty. "Every bishop preaching Christ
is Christ" (*Epistola 162*). In Anselm's view bishops are
first and foremost pastors and shepherds of the flock
entrusted to them. The bishop's most important task is preaching the word of God and instructing his flock so that he

may assist them in leading a divine life.[60]   The   more   his
own   conduct   agrees   with Christ, the more his teaching and
sermon will be accepted, his word   believed   in.   *Episcopus
debet   esse   forma et exemplum aliis canonicae religionis.*[61]
Within the hierarchy of *ecclesia* Anselm   placed   the   bishop
under the pope, the primate and the metropolitan archbishop.
His judicial authority is subordinated to that of the   pope.
*Non   pertinet   ad episcopum absolvere quod papa ligat, neque
ligare quod iste absolvit.*[62]   On the other hand, his authority does not go beyond the boundaries of his diocese.   Activities in neighboring dioceses not only require the   consent
of the respective bishops, but also that of the metropolitan
archbishop and the other bishops of the province.[63]   Anselm
condemned   royal   intervention   into episcopal jurisdiction.
He harshly attacked King Henry's disgraceful financial dealings   which   undermined   the canons of the reforming synod of
1102:

> It   has   up   to   now   been   unheard   of   and
> unprecedented   in   the   Church   of God on the
> part   of   any king or prince.   By the   law   of
> God it is not for anyone except the bishops,
> each   in   his   own   diocese,   to   punish   an
> offence   of   this   kind   or,   if the bishops
> themselves are negligent in this,   then   for
> the archbishop and primate (*Epistola 391*).

In the case of a bishop's death, the canons require that the
bishopric not be left vacant for more than   three   months.[64]
The   choice   of   the   new bishop must take place without the
influence of secular rulers.[65]   After canonical election the
bishop-elect   is   to   be   consecrated   by   three   bishops.[66]
Henceforth he can discharge his duties   legally.   *Episcopus
est custos ecclesiae suae (Epistola 281).*   Whoever illegally
seizes a bishop's estates will never be able to   obtain   the
peace   of God unless he restores everything and does penance
for his frivolous deed.[67]   In Anselm's view a bishop has   no
secular duties; on the contrary, such expectations appear as
a threat to his spiritual obligations.   This belief is   why,
towards the end of his pontificate, Anselm remained at variance with the king's expectations of his duties   and   failed
to   gain the support of most of his fellow bishops.   He fervently encouraged the bishops to disregard their   lives   and
honor,   but   rather,   to carry out their pastoral duties most
conscientiously.   Anselm summed up his   advice   by   writing:
*Gloria et laus est episcopo apud deum et bonos homines, quia
spoliatur et expellitur pro iustitia (Epistola 276).*

After this survey of Anselm's concepts of *ecclesia*, *lex dei*, *pontifex Romanus*, and *episcopus*, the essentially secular terms of *rex*, *regnum*, and *imperator* need to be examined. What quality and rank do they occupy in Anselm's *imago mundi*? The quantity of source material dealing with the Anselmian concept of *rex* is very meager in comparison with the wealth of information about *ecclesia*. Although he had been in conflict with two kings of the Anglo-Norman kingdom,[68] he never wrote any tract or treatise about *rex* or *regnum*. In Anselm's letters the word *rex* appears some two hundred and sixty times. The abundance of occurrences, however, is deceptive, because the vast majority of these references are attached to the title of a particular person. Only a minute number refer to king or kingship in general. Anselm does not mention any tracts on kingship by authors of the past or by any of his contemporaries. Nor does he make use of any of the classical images characterizing the relationship between *rex* and *sacerdos* such as sun-moon, gold-lead, Father/Son-king/bishop, or the simile of the two swords. Such omission points out that Anselm did not take part in the literary dispute which accompanied the fierce fighting between empire and papacy for supremacy and leadership of Christianity commonly called the investiture controversy.[69] Whenever Anselm referred to *rex* or *regnum* in his letters, it was to give pastoral advice or some exhortation to royal or noble persons.[70] These exhortations are *speculum regale* in a nutshell.

In 1093, Anselm wrote to Gunhilda, daughter of King Harold II,[71] who had broken her monastic vow, thrown off her veil and left the convent of Wilton near Salisbury:

> What is the value of glory of the world? What is it that you love? You were the daughter of the king and queen. Where are they? They are worms and dust (*Epistola 169*).

He writes in his pastoral exhortation that she should return to her convent, lest she incur eternal damnation. He makes no mention of the divine origin of *rex* and *regnum*. Anselm divested *rex* and *regnum* of all divine and sacramental qualities with which Anglo-Saxon and Norman kings had enhanced themselves. Since Charlemagne's times the kings of Europe had considered themselves to be divinely instituted and sacramentally consecrated by the union at their accession. They were *alteri Christi* and therefore co-leaders, or even sole leaders, of the Christian people. This caesero-

papistic idea of kingship strongly influenced the relationship between *rex* and *sacerdos* in the Ottonian, Salian period
and in the times of William I of England. Despite the prevailing opinion surrounding him, Anselm maintained that
kings were merely mortal beings; like any other man they
would turn to dust. Nonetheless, the paths of kings and
princes into the kingdom of heaven were thornier and more
difficult than those of other men, because the king's
exalted position in this world brought dangers to his soul.

In about 1094 Anselm sent Robert II, Count of Flanders,
a letter congratulating him on his accession to the throne
and advising him about his conduct in his new office. He
invited him to advance from good to better, to consider
seriously what holy authority commands, namely, that as a
prince, he should love justice. He warned him to wield the
power entrusted to him with justice and not to let it dominate him, because "the sharpest pains await the more powerful" (Ws 6:9). He continued: "May you in your prudence
always observe justice in your doings and sweeten it by your
mercy in any offences inflicted on you." Anselm concluded
his brief exhortation by wishing that he might always rule
his earthly realm in such a way that he would merit the
heavenly kingdom in the life to come.[72]   Anselm believes
that the main task of secular rulers is to perform justice
in accordance with the law of God and by so doing guide and
assist the people entrusted to them. Kings are bound to
render this service and are in this sense tools of divine
will and agents for the church towards her final, celestial
destination.[73]

Circa 1101, in the wake of the first crusade, Anselm
sent a letter to Baldwin, the second Christian ruler of Jerusalem, on his ascent to the throne in that city.[74] Having
displayed his close relationship with the family of Eustace
II of Boulogne and Ida of Lorraine and their sons Eustace
III, Geoffrey, and Baldwin,[75] he offered the new ruler a
brief exhortation about the office to which he had succeeded. Anselm wrote:

> Indeed, my dearest lord, even though you
> have no need of my exhortation, yet out of
> the abundance of my heart and as your faith-
> ful friend I beg, admonish, and beseech you,
> and pray to God that by living under God's
> law you may submit your will to the will of
> God in all things. For only if you reign
> according to the will of God will you truly
> reign for your own benefit. Do not think,
> as many bad kings do, that the Church of God

has been given to you as if to a master it
should serve, but that it has been entrusted
to you as its advocate and protector
(*Epistola 235*).

This admonition in the form of a *speculum regale* seems to
reprimand Baldwin for taking on the title of King of Jerusalem which his brother and predecessor Geoffrey had avoided
doing. Geoffrey had chosen and used the title *advocatus
sancti sepulchri*. Anselm's close relationship with the family may have enabled him to influence Geoffrey's decision
not to take the title King of Jerusalem.

Holding up a mirror to Baldwin, Anselm describes the
office and duties of a ruler by using the words *advocatus,
defensor*, and the verbs *commendari, prodesse non dominari*,
and *tractare*. The most significant phrase is doubtless
advocatus et protector ecclesiae. In Anselm's opinion the
king, by the will of God, is not lord of the Church. He is
the advocate of the Church; he is her guard and protector.
The Church, God's gift to man for his salvation, is
entrusted to the care and protection of secular rulers. If
they act according to the will of God they will preserve the
liberty of the church which God loves more than anything
else in this world. Royal domination of the church, on the
other hand, goes against the will of God. Therefore, kings
and princes ought to honor the church like sons their
mother. As *advocati et defensores ecclesiae* kings and
princes had the duty to protect the church and ensure her
unharmed and unmolested progress on her pilgrimage towards
the celestial kingdom.[76] Indeed, an advocate was more than
just a title. It was an institution which bore legal standing. The advocate was a layman wielding military force and
disposing the attributes of justice. He was charged to
defend the temporal goods and the exterior peace of the
abbeys and churches. Consequently, Anselm rejoiced when he
found a ruler who supported without objection the growing
authority of ecclesiastical laws for the advancement of the
Christian religion, because in doing so the ruler obeyed
God, not man.

Anselm believed that, when secular rulers acted in
obedience to the will of God, the commands of the Apostle
Peter, his vicar the Roman pontiff and the bishops, they
proved themselves to be *reges justi*. They ensured the
welfare of the church, defended her temporal goods, and pro-
tected her on her journey towards the celestial destination.
Whoever attempted to dominate the church, to take away her
freedom, and to oppose the will of God became *rex malus*,
that man was *tyrannus*.[77] These *reges mali* were excluded

from the heritage and the gifts promised to the church;
barred from entering the celestial kingdom, they were therefore lost salvation and the vision of the glory of God.
Anselm reiterated his opinion of the fate of those *reges
mali* in his letter to Humbert, Count of Savoy, when he wrote
to him in circa 1102. He grieved that

> the Church of God, whom God calls his beau-
> tiful friend and beloved spouse, is trampled
> upon by evil princes, is oppressed by those
> to whom she has been entrusted by God as
> advocates for protection, to their own eter-
> nal damnation.

Moreover, he complained about the cruelty, unscrupulousness
and disobedience these rulers displayed trying to gain domination over the Church (*Epistola 262*).

These *reges mali sive tyranni* act according to their own
will and arbitrary human laws, and contrary to the will of
God and the canons of the Church. The archetypes of these
tyranni are represented in the eyes of Anselm by Julius
Caesar, Nero, and Julian the Apostate,[78] with Nero prompting
the worst associations. In the minds of medieval people he
was identified with the antichrist whose satanic rule would
precede the Day of the Last Judgment. In Anselm's opinion
these evil Roman rulers were reincarnate in the German kings
and Roman Emperors Henry IV (1056-1106) and Henry V
(1106-1126): these men wickedly opposed the vicar of the
Apostle Peter by stubbornly defending the ancient sacramental concept of divinely-instituted Salian kingship and viol-
ently opposing the papacy's claim of *auctoritas universalis*[79] under Gregory VII (1073-1085), Urban II (1088-1099),
and Paschal II (1099-1118) during the investiture controversy. Anselm's very critical comparison throws an illuminating light on his *imago mundi*.

The title of *imperator* appears only once in the entire
correspondence. Only in his letter of August, 1103 to Gundulf, Bishop of Rochester, does Anselm refer to some legates
to the emperor.[80] Anselm's *imago mundi* held no place for
the emperor; it admitted no dualism between pope and
emperor. The idea of *translatio imperii Romanorum* and the
Salian concept of kingship and empire placing the emperor
above the Roman pontiff into the responsible leadership of
the church was alien to Anselm. His *imago mundi* was determined by his monolithic concept of *ecclesia*. This total
disregard for the idea of the Roman empire and its translation to the German kingdom seems surprising, considering:

(1) that Anselm was born in Aosta, which had become part
of the empire in 1032,

(2) that Anselm was most likely related to the Salian
emperors through his aunt's marriage to Count Conrad of
Egisheim,[81] and

(3) that he was involved in the negotiations which led
to the marriage of Mathilda, daughter of King Henry I of
England, to the Roman Emperor Henry V.[82]

The notions for secular rulers proposed by Anselm are,
above all, moral notions. His idea of royal duty and function within the church, as he proposed it in 1107 to King
Alexander of Scotland, is a wholly religious and moral idea
of service in obedience to the will of God in order to
advance the church on her pilgrimage to the celestial home.
This concept is basically a monastic one. He told Alexander
that

> kings reign well when they live according to
> the will of God and serve Him in fear, and
> when they reign over themselves and do not
> succumb to vices, but overcome their persis-
> tence by constant fortitude.

He exhorted him to follow the example of King David and to

> show himself in such a way that the wicked
> fear you and the good love you. In order
> that your life may always be pleasing to
> God, your mind should always remember the
> punishment of the wicked and the reward of
> the good after this life (*Epistola 413*).

Scrutiny of these letters demonstrates that, in Anselm's
opinion, secular rulers had only an ancillary task and
instrumental function as regards the Church. This opinion
is based on Augustine's ideas of *frui* and *uti*: whoever acts
in such a way as to progress farther towards the vision of
God is doing good; whoever acts in the opposite way is doing
evil.

V

Having noted the genesis and intention of the collections of Anselm's letters, portrayed his progress towards monastic perfection, displayed the roots of Anselm's thinking, and described his *imago mundi* as conveyed in his letters, it is possible to sum up as follows:

(1) Anselm collected letters he had written, some he received, and even some important letters exchanged between third persons. From this vast quantity of epistolary material, he carefully selected those items which he thought worth preserving. They were to convey his pastoral advice and ecclesiastical ideas and demonstrate his courage as bishop and his readiness to defend *libertas ecclesiae*. They are a monument to Anselm's total obedience to the will of God and a *speculum episcopale* to serve as precedent for his contemporaries and for the future. Anselm edited his letter collection three times during his lifetime; a few letters were added shortly after his death on 21 April, 1109.

(2) Anselm's growth as a monk was endangered by many doubts and conflicts. Once he made his profession as a monk, however, he remained faithful to his promise. What he once conceived to be right, he pursued with staunch perseverance. Having perceived the monastic life to be the surest and straightest way to salvation and to the lost heritage of the beatific vision in the company of the angels, he firmly clung to it, progressing from the fear of God to the love of God.

(3) St. Augustine's influence on Anselm is considerable. This influence is apparent not only in Anselm's philosophical and theological writings but also in his pastoral exhortations and political conduct. Although differences in substance and emphasis occur between St. Augustine and Anselm, Anselm accepted St. Augustine's distinction of *frui* and *uti* as regards the perception and evaluation of the world. He also accepted the profound distinction of the two kinds of love which oppose and exclude each other. Anselm chose *amor dei usque ad contemptum sui*, rejecting the opposite kind of love, in order to be counted among the chosen few, the citizens of *civitas dei*, destined to lead to the joys of the kingdom of heaven. Anselm's *amor dei* is reflected in his love for his neighbors.

(4) The adoption of St. Augustine's *frui* and *amor dei* and consequently of the concept of *civitas dei* formed

Anselm's *Weltbild*. Love of God and obedience to his will determined the *ordo* of his *imago mundi*. No trace of Gregorian ideas exists. Anselm did not contribute to the literary polemics of the investiture controversy. God founded *ecclesia* for man's salvation and in order to enable him to regain the beatific vision. The Church is the body of the baptized who are called to receive God's offer. Only those who have totally given themselves up to love of God at the expense of love of themselves are the chosen few, the citizens of the *civitas dei* who will earn the celestial kingdom after their earthly pilgrimage. *Lex dei* should be the guiding line for every human being striving to reach this heavenly home. *Pontifex Romanus* and *episcopus* are institutions given to man to help him find the right path, whereas *rex* and *regnum*, as well as *imperator*, are subordinate to ecclesiastical office. Those performing the duties of these offices can only reach salvation if they follow *lex dei* by protecting and supporting *ecclesia*. Any law resisting or disregarding God's law is arbitrary. Any person in regal power opposing God's will becomes *tyrannus* or even the antichrist himself.

(5) Thus it can be seen that Anselm's *imago mundi*, formed to a large extent by his adoption of Augustinian concepts, did not change as long as he lived. He preached and labored for the growth of the number of the chosen few, the increase of the citizens of the mystical community of *civitas dei*. Since he believed that only the monastic life would certainly lead to this goal, he furthered vocations to this profession in the many letters written to monks, nuns, and those aspiring to these professions, with all the persuasaion his clear thought and logical writing could muster. Monks and nuns were the spearhead, as well as the largest contingent, of the chosen few who would reach the great goal of *civitas dei*. Anselm's letter collection provides living testimony to his ceaseless striving for the growth of *civitas dei* on earth and imparts the essence of his *Weltbild*.

Notes

[1] G. Constable, *Letters and Letter-Collections*, Typologie des sources du Moyen Age occidental, fasc. 17 (Turnhout: Ed. Brepols, 1976), p. 66. The quotation from C. V. Langlois, *Formulaires de lettres du XIIe, du XIIIe et du XIVe siècle* (Paris: Imprimerie nationale, 1890-97), I, 1, is taken from there too.

²For *Weltbild*, see J. Spörl, *Grundformen hochmittleal-terlicher Geschichtsanschauung, Studien zum Weltbild der Geschichtsschreiber des 12. Jahrhunderts* (München: Max Hueber Verlag, 1935); J . Spörl, "Wandel des Welt- und Geschichtsbildes im 12. Jahrhundert? Zur Kennzeichnung der hochmittelalterlichen Historiographie," in *Geschichtsdenken und Geschichtsbild im Mittelalter*, W. Lammers, ed., (Darm-stadt: Wissenschaftliche Buchgesellschaft, 1965), pp. 278-87; W. Kölmel, "*Imago Mundi*, Das Weltverständnis im Schrifttum des Investiturstreites," *Studi Gregoriani* 9 (1972), 168-98.

³A. MacLeish, "His Mirror Was Danger," *Life* 31, No. 3 (1961), 58.

⁴The following passage on Anselm collecting his letters and editing them is a summary of W. Fröhlich, "The Genesis of the Collections of St. Anselm's Letters," *American Bene-dictine Review* 35 (1984), 249-66; W. Fröhlich, "The Letters Omitted from Anselm's Collection of Letters," *Anglo-Norman Studies* 6 (1984), 58-71.

⁵There is a translation of Anselm's philosophical and theological works by J. Hopkins and H. Richardson, *Anselm of Canterbury*, 3 vols. (Toronto; New York: Edwin Mellen Press, 1974-76); of the *Orationes* and *Meditationes* by B. Ward, *The Prayers and Meditations of St. Anselm* (Harmondsworth: Pen-guin, 1973). The first complete translation of the letters by W. Fröhlich is to be published shortly by Cistercian Pub-lications, Kalamazoo, MI.

⁶William of Malmesbury died in 1143.

⁷*Epistola 18*: Schmitt III,125; *Epistola 26*: Schmitt III,134; *Epistola 27*: Schmitt III,134-35; *Epistola 63*: Schmitt III,178-80; *Epistola 64*: Schmitt III,180-81; *Epis-tola 65*: Schmitt III,181-85; *Epistola 88*: Schmitt III,213-14; *Epistola 123*: Schmitt III,263-64; *Epistola 124*: Schmitt III,264-65; *Epistola 126*: Schmitt III,266-68; *Epistola 127*: Schmitt III,269-70; *Epistola 145*: Schmitt III,291-92.

⁸*Epistola 126*: Schmitt III,266-68; *Epistola 127*: Schmitt III,269-70.

⁹*Epistola 148*: Schmitt IV,3-6; *Epistola 150*: Schmitt IV,11; *Epistola 151*: Schmitt IV,12-13; *Epistola 152*: Schmitt IV,13-14; *Epistola 155*: Schmitt IV,16-17; *Epistola*

163:    Schmitt IV,36; *Epistola 165*:   Schmitt IV,38-40;   *Epistola 166*:   Schmitt   IV,40-41;   *Epistola 173*:   Schmitt IV,54-55; *Epistola 174*:   Schmitt   IV,55-56;   *Epistola 178*: Schmitt   IV,61-62;   *Epistola 179*:   Schmitt IV,63; *Epistola 205*:   Schmitt IV,97-98; *Epistola 209*:   Schmitt IV,104-05.

[10] *Epistola 168*:   Schmitt   IV,43-46;   *Epistola 169*: Schmitt   IV,46-50; *Epistola 177*:   Schmitt IV,60-61; *Epistola 183*:   Schmitt IV,67-68;   *Epistola 184*:   Schmitt   IV,68-69; *Epistola 190*:   Schmitt   IV,76;   *Epistola 195*:   Schmitt IV,85-86; *Epistola 337*:   Schmitt V,274-75.

[11] *Epistola 215*:   Schmitt IV,114; *Epistola 216*:   Schmitt IV,115-18;   *Epistola 221*:   Schmitt   IV,123;   *Epistola 224*: Schmitt IV,129-30; *Epistola 305*:   Schmitt   IV,226-28;   *Epistola 348*:   Schmitt   V,286-87;   *Epistola 351*:   Schmitt V,290-91; *Epistola 352*: Schmitt V,292.

[12] *Epistola 255*:   Schmitt   IV,166-68;   *Epistola 362*: Schmitt   V,303;   *Epistola 363*:   Schmitt V,304-05; *Epistola 373*:   Schmitt V,316-17;   *Epistola 440*:   Schmitt V,387-88;.

[13] *Epistola 2*:   Schmitt III,98-101; *Epistola 37*:   Schmitt III,144-48; *Epistola 112*:   Schmitt III,244-46.

[14] Anselm's art of letter-writing has been analyzed by J. D. Loughlin, *Saint Anselm as Letter Writer* (Ann Arbor: Univ. Microfilms, 1967), especially pp. 154-81.

[15] Anselm's   superiors   were Abbot Herluin and Prior Lanfranc who left for Caen in 1063, when Anselm was   appointed prior   by   the abbot in the face of some ill-feeling by some fellow monks; see *Vita Anselmi*, pp. 15-16.

[16] See, for example,   *Epistola 8*:   Schmitt   III,110-11; *Epistola 35*:   Schmitt   III,142-43;   *Epistola 37*:   Schmitt III,144-48; *Epistola 56*:   Schmitt III,170-71;   *Epistola 62*: Schmitt   III,176-77; *Epistola 66*:   Schmitt III,186-87; *Epistola 67*:   Schmitt   III,187-88;   *Epistola 78*:   Schmitt III,200-01;   *Epistola 79*:   Schmitt   III,202;   *Epistola 80*: Schmitt III,203-04; *Epistola 99*:   Schmitt III,229-30;   *Epistola 101*:   Schmitt   III,232-34;   *Epistola 120*:   Schmitt III,258-60; etc.

[17] *Epistola 335*:   Schmitt V,271-72.

[18] *Vita Anselmi*, pp. 32-346.

[19] See, for example, *Epistola 3*: Schmitt III,102-03; *Epistola 4*: Schmitt III,103-05; *Epistola 5*: Schmitt III,105-07; *Epistola 7*: Schmitt III,108-10; *Epistola 13*: Schmitt III,117-19; *Epistola 16*: Schmitt III,121-22; *Epistola 23*: Schmitt III,130-31; *Epistola 28*: Schmitt III,135-36; *Epistola 34*: Schmitt III,141-42; *Epistola 36*: Schmitt III,143-44; *Epistola 37*: Schmitt III,144-48; *Epistola 41*: Schmitt III,152-53; *Epistola 42*: Schmitt III,153-54; *Epistola 43*: Schmitt III,154-56; *Epistola 45*: Schmitt III,158-59; *Epistola 46*: Schmitt III,159-60; *Epistola 47*: Schmitt III,160; *Epistola 50*: Schmitt III,163-64; *Epistola 51*: Schmitt III,164-65; *Epistola 54*: Schmitt III,168; *Epistola 55*: Schmitt III,169-70; *Epistola 57*: Schmitt III,171-72; *Epistola 58*: Schmitt III,172-73; *Epistola 59*: Schmitt III,173-74; *Epistola 60*: Schmitt III,174-75; *Epistola 65*: Schmitt III,181-85; *Epistola 68*: Schmitt III,188; *Epistola 69*: Schmitt III,189; *Epistola 74*: Schmitt III,195-96; *Epistola 75*: Schmitt III,197; *Epistola 77*: Schmitt III,199-200; *Epistola 85*: Schmitt III,209-11; *Epistola 91*: Schmitt III,218-19; *Epistola 93*: Schmitt III,220; *Epistola 96*: Schmitt III,222-23; *Epistola 115*: Schmitt III,250-51; *Epistola 117*: Schmitt III,252-55; *Epistola 119*: Schmitt III,257; *Epistola 141*: Schmitt III,287-88; *Epistola 142*: Schmitt III,288-89; *Epistola 156*: Schmitt IV,17-23; *Epistola 164*: Schmitt IV,37; and many more. In these letters and many others, Anselm expressed his love for his fellow monks and neighbors. See also A. Fiske, "Saint Anselm and Friendship," *Studia Monastica* 3 (1961), 259-90; R. W. Southern, *Saint Anselm and his Biographer* (Cambridge: Univ. Press, 1963), pp. 67-76.

[20] For the sources of Anselm's thinking, see J. Hopkins, *A Companion to the Study of St. Anselm* (Minneapolis: Univ. of Minnesota Press, 1972), pp. 16-37.

[21] For Anselm's use of Holy Scripture, see Schmitt VI,3-18.

[22] For Anselm's use of the *Regula Sancti Benedicti* and other authors of classical antiquity, see Schmitt VI,21-24.

[23] See Hopkins, *Companion*, pp. 16-28.

[24] *Catalogus librorum abbatiae Beccensis circa saeculum duodecinum*: *PL* CL,769ff.

[25] *De doctrina christiana*: *CSEL* LXXX; English translation by J. F. Shaw, in *The Nicene and Post-Nicene Fathers*,

P. Schaff, ed. (Grand Rapids: W. R. Eerdmans, 1979), II, 519-97.

²⁶ *De civitate dei*: *CC* XLVII-XLVIII; English translation by M. Dods, in *Nicene and Post-Nicene Fathers*, Schaff, ed., pp. 1-511.

²⁷ J. Ratzinger, "Herkunft und Sinn der Civitas-Lehre Augustins", *Geschichtsdenken und Geschichtsbild im Mittelalter* (Darmstadt: Wissenschaftliche Buchgesellschaft, 1965), pp. 55-75, in particular, pp. 71-75.

²⁸ *Vita Anselmi*, pp. 8-11; see also Southern, *St. Anselm*, pp. 11-14, 27-30.

²⁹ Y. M. Congar, "L'Église chez Saint Anselme," SB I, pp. 371-99. It served as basis for the section on *ecclesia*.

³⁰ See *Epistola 168*: Schmitt IV,43-46; *Epistola 169*: Schmitt IV,46-50; *Epistola 185*: Schmitt IV,69-71; *Epistola 235*: Schmitt IV,142-43; *Epistola 243*: Schmitt IV,153-54; *Epistola 249*: Schmitt IV,159-60; *Epistola 262*: Schmitt IV,176-77, for example.

³¹ *Cur deus homo* I,1: Schmitt II,47-49; I,16: Schmitt II,74-75 ; I,18 Schmitt II,76-84; I,19: Schmitt II,84-86; II,10: Schmitt II,106-08.

³² See *Cur deus homo* I,18: Schmitt II,76-84; I,23: Schmitt II,90-91; II,15: Schmitt II,115-16; II,16: Schmitt II,116-22.

³³ *Epistola 243*: Schmitt IV,153-54.

³⁴ *Cur deus homo* I,16: Schmitt II,74-75.

³⁵ See *Epistola 231*: Schmitt IV,136-38; *Epistola 278*: Schmitt IV,192; *Epistola 403*: Schmitt V,347-48; *Epistola 418*: Schmitt V,363-64.

³⁶ See, for example, *Epistola 2*: Schmitt III,98-101; *Epistola 8*: Schmitt III,110-11; *Epistola 35*: Schmitt III,142-43; *Epistola 37*: Schmitt III,144-48; *Epistola 56*: Schmitt III,170-71; *Epistola 62*: Schmitt III,176-77; *Epistola 66*: Schmitt III,186-87; *Epistola 67*: Schmitt III,187-88; *Epistola 78*: Schmitt III,200-01; *Epistola 79*: Schmitt III,202; *Epistola 80*: Schmitt III,203-04; *Epistola 81*: Schmitt III,205-06; *Epistola 95*: Schmitt III,221;

Epistola 99: Schmitt III,229-30; *Epistola 101*: Schmitt III,232-34; *Epistola 112*: Schmitt III,244-46; *Epistola 114*: Schmitt III,249 *Epistola 120*: Schmitt III,258-60; *Epistola 121*: Schmitt III,260-61; *Epistola 131*: Schmitt III,273-74; *Epistola 133*: Schmitt III,275-76 *Epistola 134*: Schmitt III,276-78; *Epistola 143*: Schmitt III,289-90; *Epistola 168*: Schmitt IV,43-46; *Epistola 169*: Schmitt III,46-50; *Epistola 335*: Schmitt V,271-72.

[37] *Oratio II*: Schmitt II,6-9; Also *Epistola 8*: Schmitt III,110-11; *Epistola 81*: Schmitt III,205-06; *Epistola 117*: Schmitt III,252-55; *Epistola 405*: Schmitt V,349-50.

[38] See *Epistola 233*: Schmitt IV,140-41; *Epistola 450*: Schmitt V,397-98 for *amor sui*; *Epistola 62*: Schmitt III,176-77; *Epistola 156*: Schmitt IV,17-23; *Epistola 233*: Schmitt III,140-41; *Epistola 403*: Schmitt V,347-48 for *amor dei*.

[39] See *Epistola 403*: Schmitt V,347-48; *Epistola 450*: Schmitt V,397-98.

[40] *Epistola 345*: Schmitt V,282-83.

[41] *Epistola 223*: Schmitt IV,126-29.

[42] *Epistola 249*: Schmitt IV,159-60; *Epistola 262*: Schmitt IV,176-77; *Epistola 329*: Schmitt V,261-62; *Epistola 224*: Schmitt IV,129-30.

[43] *Epistola 339*: Schmitt V,277.

[44] *Epistola 378*: Schmitt V,321-22.

[45] *Epistola 329*: Schmitt V,261-62.

[46] *Epistola 249*: Schmitt IV,159-60; *Epistola 262*: Schmitt IV,176-77.

[47] Anselm fought the Norman *usus atque leges sive consuetudines*; see *Historia novorum*, p. 10; at Rockingham in February 1095, see *Historia novorum*, pp. 54-67; at Winchester in October 1097, see *Historia novorum*, pp. 80-87.

[48] *Epistola 210*: Schmitt IV,105-07.

⁴⁹See *Epistola 248*: Schmitt IV,158-59; *Epistola 262*: Schmitt IV,176-77; *Epistola 278*: Schmitt IV,192; *Epistola 340*: Schmitt V,278; *Epistola 218*.

⁵⁰H. Böhmer, *Kirche und Staat in England und in der Normandie im 11. und 12. Jahrhundert* (Leipzig, 1899; rpt. Aalen: Scientia Verlag, 1968), p. 27.

⁵¹*Oratio IX*: Schmitt III,30-33.

⁵²See *Epistola 262*: Schmitt IV,176-77.

⁵³See *Epistola 192*: Schmitt IV,78-81; *Historia novorum*, pp. 52, 57.

⁵⁴See *Historia novorum*, p. 52.

⁵⁵See *Epistola 127*: Schmitt III,269,70.

⁵⁶See *Epistola 126*: Schmitt III,266-68; *Epistola 193*: Schmitt IV,82-83.

⁵⁷For example, in *Epistola 206*: Schmitt IV,99-101; *Epistola 210*: Schmitt IV,105-07; *Epistola 214*: Schmitt IV,111-14; *Epistola 217*: Schmitt IV,118-19; *Epistola 218*: Schmitt IV,120; *Epistola 219*: Schmitt IV,121; *Epistola 220*: Schmitt IV,122-23; *Epistola 272*: Schmitt IV,187-88; *Epistola 280*: Schmitt IV,193-95; *Epistola 315*: Schmitt V,242-43; *Epistola 338*: Schmitt V,276; *Epistola 340*: Schmitt V,278; *Epistola 388*: Schmitt V,331-32; *Epistola 430*: Schmitt V,376; *Epistola 441*: Schmitt V,388-89 ; *Epistola 451*: Schmitt V,398-99; *Epistola 463*: Schmitt V,412; *Epistola 192*: Schmitt IV,78-81.

⁵⁸See *Epistola 214*: Schmitt IV,111-14; *Epistola 451*: Schmitt V,398-99; *Epistola de incarnatione verbi I*: Schmitt II, 3-4.

⁵⁹Anselm describes St. Peter's and his vicar's position within the flock of God and as regards the kingdom of God in his *Oratio ad sanctum Petrum*: Schmitt III,30-33.

⁶⁰See *Epistola 457*: Schmitt V,405-06; *Epistola 459*: Schmitt V,408.

⁶¹*Epistola 417*: Schmitt V,363.

⁶²*Epistola 218*: Schmitt IV,120.

[63] See *Epistola 404*:   Schmitt V,348-49.

[64] See *Epistola 443*:   Schmitt V,390.

[65] *Epistola 281*:   Schmitt IV,196-98:   Alienum est enim ab ecclesia et a sacris canonibus est inhibitum, ne principes et saeculares viri investituras non solum non dare, sed nec electioni episcoporum se audeant violenter inserere. . . . In septima quippe synodo scriptum est: Sancta et universalis synodus definivit neminem laicorum principum vel potentem semet inserere electioni vel promotioni episcoporum.

[66] See *Epistola 435*:   Schmitt V,382-83.

[67] See *Epistola 331*:   Schmitt V,264-67;   *Epistola 356*: Schmitt V,297-98 ; *Epistola 358*:   Schmitt V,299-300.

[68] Anselm's quarrels with William II and Henry I were more recently dealt with by N. Cantor, *Church, Kingship, and Lay Investiture in England 1089-1135* (Princeton: Univ. Press, 1958); Southern, *St. Anselm*; W. Fröhlich, *Die bischöflichen Kollegen Erzbischof Anselms von Canterbury* (München: Salzer, 1971); F. Barlow, *The English Church 1066-1154* (London: Longman, 1979); idem, *William Rufus* (London: Methuen, 1983); W. Fröhlich, "Anselm and the Bishops of the Province of Canterbury", SB II, pp. 125-45.

[69] G. Tellenbach, *Church, State, and Christian Society at the Time of the Investiture Contest* (Oxford: Blackwell, 1959); I. S. Robinson, *Authority and Resistance in the Investiture Contest: The Polemical Literature of the Late 11th Century* (Manchester: Univ. Press, 1978).

[70] For example, *Epistola 168*:   Schmitt IV,43-46; *Epistola 169*:   Schmitt IV,46-50; *Epistola 235*:   Schmitt IV,142-43; *Epistola 248*:   Schmitt IV,158-59; *Epistola 249*:   Schmitt IV,159-60; *Epistola 262*:   Schmitt IV,176-77; *Epistola 413*: Schmitt V,358-59.

[71] Harold II was king of the Anglo-Saxon realm from 6 January to 14 October, 1066.

[72] See *Epistola 180*:   Schmitt IV,64-65.

[73] Ibid.

[74] *Epistola 235*:   Schmitt IV,142-43.

[75] For Geoffrey of Bouillon, Duke of Lower Lorraine and *advocatus sancti sepulchri* as well as his family, see S. Runciman, *A History of the Crusades* (Cambridge: Univ. Press, 1951), passim.

[76] See *Epistola 319*: Schmitt V,247-48; *Epistola 413*: Schmitt V,358-59.

[77] See *Epistola 235*: Schmitt IV,142-43; *Epistola 248*: Schmitt IV,158-59; *Epistola 249*: Schmitt IV,159-60; *Epistola 262*: Schmitt IV,176-77.

[78] In reply to an inquiry by Walram, Bishop of Naumberg, Anselm, *Epistola de sacrificio azimi et fermentati*: Schmitt II,223, wrote very curtly: Anselmus, servus ecclesiae Cantuarienis, Waleramo, Nuenburgensi episcopo. Scienti breviter loquor. Si certus essem prudentiam vestram non favere successor Julii Caesaris et Neronis et Juliani Apostatae contra successorem et vicarium Petri apostoli, libentissime vos ut amicissimum et reverendum episocopum salutarem. For the entire correspondence between Anselm and Walram, see W. Fröhlich, "Bischof Walram von Naumburg, der einzige deutsche Korrespondent Anselms von Canterbury," *AA* 5 (1976), 261-82; for medieval identification of Nero with antichrist, see R. Konrad, "Kaiser Nero in der Vorstellung des Mittelalters," in *Festiva Lanx*, K. Schnith, ed., (München: Verlag Salesianische Offizin, 1966), pp. 1-15.

[79] *Dictatus Papae* II: ed. E. Caspar, *Das Register Gregors VII*, *MGH*, Epistolae selectae, No. 2, p. 202: sed solus Romanus pontifex iure dicatur universalis.

[80] *Epistola 299*: Schmitt IV,219-21.

[81] Conrad and his brother Brun (later bishop of Toul 1026-1049, then Pope Leo IX 1049-1054) were cousins of Emperor Henry III.

[82] Mathilda was betrothed to Henry in 1109. The marriage took place on 7 January, 1114 at Mainz, the bride being twelve and the bridegroom thirty-three years of age.

A Millenium of Christian Platonism
Augustine, Anselm and Ficino

Vernon J. Bourke

This is a survey of a whole movement in philosophy extending from the fifth to the fifteenth century in the Christian era.[1] The three thinkers selected as representative of Christian Platonism are very different personalities: Augustine, a bishop from Hippo in North Africa who was never taught either philosophy or theology; Anselm, a bishop of the English diocese of Canterbury, born in northern Italy, educated by the Benedictines in France, who probably never thought of himself as a philosopher; and a third cleric, Marsilio Ficino from Florence, trained as a medical doctor in early life, ordained priest at about the age of forty, who devoted much of his mature life to the translation of Greek philosophical works into Latin.

In spite of the fact that only Marsilio Ficino actually read the original Platonic writings, what is common to the philosophical views of these three men is a set of thought positions originating in Plato's *Dialogues* and the writings of his Neoplatonic followers. Since the impression is now widespread that Christian intellectualism before the modern period was largely a systematization of biblical beliefs in terms of Aristotelian philosophy, one might say quite simply that Augustine, Anselm and Ficino were not followers of Aristotle. All three knew varying amounts of Aristotelian logic but, for various reasons, they considered Platonism to be the best philosophy and the most adaptable to the service of Christian doctrine.

Before examining the views of our three authors we must give some definite meaning to the term "Christian Platonism." This kind of philosophical thinking is not identical with the philosophy to be found in Plato's *Dialogues* but it is more akin to Platonism than to other types of ancient philosophy, such as Aristotelianism, Stoicism or Epicureanism. Of course it is colored by the faith of its Christian expositors. There were other types of religious Platonists before the modern period: nearly all early Moslem philosophers, but especially Avicenna, were Platonists in their metaphysics; and in the Jewish tradition Avicebron (Salomon ibn Gabirol) was basically Neo-platonic. But Christian Platonism continued to be prominent throughout the whole premodern era -- and it did not die with the Renaissance.

In a letter to Martino Uranio, Marsilio Ficino answered a question as to the Platonic writings available in the fif-

teenth century to Latin readers.[2] He listed the works of
Dionysius the Areopagite as entirely Platonic (*omnia sunt
Platonica*), and so are many of Augustine's writings. Then
there are the *Consolationes* by Boethius, *On Demons* by
Apuleius, the *Commentary on Plato's Timaeus* by Chalcidius,
Macrobius on the *Somnium Scipionis*, Avicebron's *Fountain of
Life*, and Al Farabi's book *On Causes*. Ficino added that the
writings of Henry of Ghent, Avicenna and Scotus give many
evidences of Platonism. There are translations of Proclus'
writings on theology, providence, and fate. Ficino himself
has translated Hermias on the *Phaedrus* and Iamblichus on
Pythagoreanism. Recent works from Ficino's time are the
Defense of Plato by Cardinal Bessarion and the "Speculations" of Nicholas of Cusa.

This early Renaissance list of Platonic writings is
interesting in several ways. First of all, it predated the
appearance of formal histories of philosophy, yet obviously
Ficino made an effort to treat his authors chronologically
(in his day the Pseudo-Dionysius was still considered a contemporary of St. Paul). Moreover, Ficino mixed pagan,
Jewish and Moslem works with those of the Christian Platonists. But perhaps the most striking feature of these "Platonic" writings is their doctrinal diversity.

In the seven centuries separating Augustine and Anselm a
long line of thinkers developed philosophies that were in
some sense Platonic. Gregory of Nyssa, a contemporary of
Augustine, is a Greek example at the beginning of this tradition. In the fifth century the pagan Proclus wrote metaphysical treatises that fascinated later religious thinkers.
That puzzling author, Dionysius the Pseudo-Areopagite,
flourished around the year 500 and produced Greek writings
steeped in Neo-platonism. Another Greek in the sixth century, the deacon John Philoponus, showed his adherence to
Platonism even in his commentaries on Aristotle. Maximus
the Confessor shared this interest in the next century. The
Latin Christian philosopher with the greatest devotion to
Plato in the sixth century was the Roman Senator Boethius:
the poetic passages in his *Consolatio philosophiae* are often
but digests of Platonic dialogues. The most striking Neo-
platonist in the ninth century was John Scotus Erigena.
Besides translating some treatises by the Pseudo-Areopagite,
Erigena preserved in his *De divisione naturae* much of the
speculative philosophy of the Greeks from Plotinus to Proclus. Greek Neo-platonists of the eleventh century included
Michael Psellus and John Italus. Finally, the early school
of Chartres (represented by Fulbert early in the eleventh
century) was already exploring the cosmological and ontological tradition of Platonism before Anselm appeared on the

scene. A more thorough examination than is possible here
would consider all these pre-Anselmian thinkers.

To give some definiteness to the present investigation,
early Christian Platonism will be treated in four thought
areas: theory of reality, psychology, theory of knowledge,
and moral philosophy. The following summary propositions
are stated briefly and without documentation. They are simply the things that come to my mind as distinctive of Christian Platonism:

> First, besides the world of bodies
> which is mutable and known through sense
> perception, there is a higher and more
> real world of perfect objects of under-
> standing in the mind of God.
>
> Second, the rational soul is the
> important part of man: it moves and rules
> the body and it endures immortally after
> the death of its body.
>
> Third, understanding and reason are of
> much greater cognitive value to man than
> sense experience.
>
> Fourth, virtue (especially wisdom and
> justice) may not be exactly co-extensive
> with knowledge (as Socrates claimed) but
> reason (*logos, ratio*) is the key to a life
> of natural virtue and happiness.

These four positions were adopted by all three of our representatives of Christian Platonism but their ramifications
are somewhat different in the philosophies of Augustine,
Anselm, and Ficino.

Augustine's Psychological Platonism

With Augustine of Hippo we have the first great Latin
Christian writer who is an overt devotee of the philosophy
of the Platonists. Others such as Marius Victorinus and St.
Ambrose might be called Christian Platonists, but Augustine
was more open in expressing his admiration for this type of
philosophy, even though it is quite unlikely that he ever
even saw a copy of Plato's dialogues. Despite the fact that
Augustine's aim in his early *Contra academicos* is to refute
the skepticism of the later Platonic Academy, this little
work calls Plato a "very wise and learned man" (*Plato vir
sapientissimus et eruditissimus*).[3] Similar encomia are
found throughout the writings of Augustine. No reader of

the *Confessiones* (VII,ix,13-14:   *BA* 13,608-610) can fail to
be struck by Augustine's comparison of the divine Trinity
with the Neo-platonic triad of the One, *Logos* and *Psyche*.
The mature treatise *De Trinitate* has at least thirty-five
passages that echo texts from Plato's *Meno*, *Phaedrus*,
Phaedo, *Republic* and *Timaeus*.[4] These are known to Augustine
through later classical writers, such as Cicero. The *De
civitate dei* repeatedly praised Plato as the most brilliant
pupil of Socrates (VIII,4:   *BA* 34,240) and the Platonists in
general as the noblest of the philosophers (X,1:   *BA* 34,
422).   Again he compares Platonism to Christianity (VIII,
11:   *BA* 34,268-272) saying: "Some of our fellow Christians
are astonished to learn that Plato had such ideas about God
and to realize how close they are to the truths of our
faith."   Of course in reviewing his writings in the *Retractationes* (I,1:   *BA* 12,282) Augustine tempered his Platonic
enthusiasm, as an old man explaining that he was displeased
with his excessive praise of Plato and his followers.   He
now says (*Retractationes* I,3:   *BA* 12,286) that he would not
have so stressed Plato's name in his youthful writings if he
had been better acquainted with the writings of Christianity.

Apart from Plato himself, Augustine's Platonists
included Plotinus, Porphyry, Apuleius of Madaura, and Victorinus.   Although he had some partial acquaintance with Neo-
platonic writings, as studies by Pierre Courcelle, Hilary
Armstrong, John O'Meara and others have shown, it appears
that most of Augustine's knowledge of Platonism came through
secondary writers such as Cicero, Apuleius and possibly
Varro.   At one point in the *De civitate dei* (VIII,9:   *BA*
34,262) he shows how broadly he envisioned Platonic philosophy.   Besides the Ionian Platonists, he speculates, there
may be similar wise men in other parts of the world, "Liby-
ans, Egyptians, Indians, Persians, Chaldeans, Scythians,
Gauls, and Spaniards."   Shortly after this text (VIII,
23-26:   *BA* 34,312-326) we find a long discussion of the
teachings of the Egyptian, Hermes Trismegistus.   There is
little doubt, as we shall see later, that this essay in what
might be called Platonic ecumenism strongly influenced Marsilio Ficino's interest in the Hermetic writings.

Reality

As Augustine saw the whole of reality, God is the highest kind of being, immutable in all respects. On a second
level of existence lie all created spirits (angels and human
souls); these are immutable in regard to place but mutable

in temporal duration. The lowest kind of nature is the world of bodies, subject to changes both in space and time. These three levels of reality are described in many of Augustine's writings.[5] But they are presented with admirable brevity in a letter to Coelestinus (*Epistola XVIII: Obras de San Agustin* 8,78) where he says:

> There is a nature that is susceptible of change with respect to both place and time, namely the corporeal. There is another nature which is in no way susceptible to change with respect to place but only with respect to time, namely the spiritual. And there is a third nature which can be changed neither in place nor in time: that is, God.

Whether such a triadic division of natures is Platonic is debatable but there is no question that Augustine thought he was in accord with Plato himself in this teaching. In the *De vera religione* (III,3: *BA* 8,24) we are asked to suppose that Plato is still alive and could be queried about the main points of his philosophy. Plato is made to reply:

> that truth cannot be perceived by bodily eyes but by the intelligence alone; that every soul which clings to the truth becomes happy and complete; . . . that nothing keeps us farther from the truth than a life given over to the pleasures of the body; . . . that it is given only to rational and intelligent souls . . . to enjoy the contemplation of his [God's] eternal nature.

These lines from the time of Augustine's ordination as a priest (A.D. 391) show how he saw the Platonic philosophy of being through eyes colored by Christian beliefs.

This is most evident in the way that Augustine interpreted Plato's theory of the ideal forms. In a famous passage in his *De diversis quaestionibus LXXXIII* (XLVI,1-2: *BA* 10,122-128) he explains that these principles which Plato called "Ideas" are the eternal reasons (*rationes aeternae*) in the creative mind of God. In accord with them all other beings are made. Going well beyond what Plato said about the ideal forms, Augustine concludes:

> If there can be nothing in the divine mind unless it be eternal and immutable, and if Plato called these primary reasons of things

> Ideas, then not only do Ideas exist but they
> are true because they are eternal and they
> endure immutably in this way; and it is by
> participation in these that whatever exists
> is produced, however its way of existing may
> be.

Augustine was not the first to locate the world of ideas in
the mind of the Creator.   One of Cicero's teachers, the
Middle Platonist Antiochus of Ascalon, seems to have identified the ideal forms with God's thoughts.[6]   With Philo of
Alexandria and early Greek Christian writers in Alexandria,
such as Clement and Origen, this divinization of the ideas
became commonplace.[7]

An important axiom in Augustine's metaphysics is the
proposition that an inferior cannot act upon a superior.
Thus, in the discussion of sensation in the *De musica* VI
(VI,v,8-10: *BA* 7,378-382) we are continually reminded that
man's soul can suffer no direct action coming from his body.
Generalizing this, Augustine says that it would be absurd
"to submit the soul in any manner as matter to the working
of its body." (*Nullo modo igitur anima fabricatori corpori
est subjecta materies. De musica* VI,v,8: *BA* 7,376).
Similarly, on the highest level, God can suffer no change
caused by creatures, bodily or spiritual. This is the basic
meaning of divine immutability, as Augustine sees it.[8]
Possibly he owes some of his emphasis on this axiom to Plotinus' treatise on the impassibility of the higher in relation to its inferior.[9]

Light plays a dynamic role in Augustine's philosophy of
reality. As coming from its source it is called *lux*; and as
received in a medium or reflected it is usually called
lumen. The theory that light is a principle of activity in
all beings, and in the illumination of the human mind so
that it may make true judgments, and as a source of sound
values in the moral life, results from Augustine's many meditations on the "*fiat lux*" passage in Genesis 1:3. Speaking
of light in his treatise *Contra Faustum* (XX,7: *PL*
XLII,327), Augustine calls light the beginning of existing
(*initium existendi*), the principle of knowing (*ratio cognos-
cendi*), and the law of loving (*lex amandi*).[10]

While Augustine considered all things that God has made
good, and also that evil, physical and moral, is but a corruption or lack of due order or specific form in anything
(*De natura boni* III,3: *BA* 1,442), he was much less concerned with the natures of corporeal things than with
immaterial beings. This is why he does not have a metaphysics in the Aristotelian sense of a study of difficulties

(*aporiai*) arising from physics. Augustine was quite Platonic when he stated, "*Deum et animam scire cupio*" (*Soliloquia* I,ii,7: BA 5,36). His metaphysics is focused on God and created spirits. Since his own soul is near at hand and most available for consultation, Augustine is a great introspective psychologist.[11]

Psychology

Of course psychology is taken in its root meaning here: the study of soul in its functions and nature.[12] While Augustine admits that souls exist in all living things, it is the human soul that engrosses his attention. In the early works man is identified as a soul using a body which is mortal and earthly (*De moribus ecclesiae catholicae* XXVII,52: BA 1,212). The more mature writings incline to the view that the soul and body are substantially united in man (*De civitate dei* XXII,24: BA 37,662-670). Unlike those of other animals, man's soul is immaterial and immortal. The treatise *De immortalitate animae* (VIII,13: BA 5,195) develops a modification of Plato's argument in the *Phaedo* (86-87) to the effect that the soul cannot die, because life never becomes its opposite, death. Among his many other arguments for immortality is the reasoning expressed in *De trinitate* (XIII,8: BA 16, 295), that man's natural desire to be happy would be incapable of eventual satisfaction unless the human lives on after the death of its body.

As to the origin of the individual human soul, Augustine was never able to find a wholly satisfactory explanation. He could not admit that man's soul was produced by physical causes, but there remained the problem of whether all souls are propagated from Adam's soul, or are specially created individually. And there was the further question of whether, being created, the individual souls are sent to their bodies by God, or are incorporated as a result of their own spontaneous action. This is fully discussed in Books VI to XI of the *De Genesi ad litteram*. Even after searching the Scriptures for many years, Augustine could not solve this problem. "I do not dare to teach," he wrote near the end of his life, "what I do not know." (*Opus imperfectum contra Julianum* IV,104: M X,1192A). Certainly these speculations stemming from the doctrine of original sin range far beyond the thinking of the classical Platonists.

In his analysis of the functions of man's soul Augustine radically distinguished sense experience from intellectual knowing, and the affective functions from cognitive acts. Book X of *De trinitate* describes a soul which exercises

memory, intellect and will. The role of memory is to contain all things experienced, of intellect (*mens aut ratio*)
to understand, and of will to love and act. However this is
not the tripartite soul of Plato's *Phaedrus* and *Republic* but
a *psyche* which is at once memory, understanding, and will:
the whole soul is each of these three. Augustine's is not a
faculty psychology, with powers that are related to soul as
accidents to subject. Everything that his soul does is a
manifestation of will; all its cognitions are simply the
soul knowing; and all its contents are in the soul as memory. Much of the latter half of *De trinitate* is devoted to
the teaching that just as each of the soul's three functions
is identical with the whole soul, so are each of the three
divine persons identical with God.

What is especially characteristic of Augustine's philosophy is his psychological interiorism. He is a master of
introspective analysis and description. This is evident in
all his writings. Two of his best known teachings illustrate it: his psychological explanation of time and his
active theory of sensation. Reacting to the Aristotelian
physical theory of temporal duration and in keeping with the
Plotinian refusal to see time as simply the measure of
bodily movement, Augustine turned to the soul's awareness of
the present as the progressive extension (*distensio*) of the
past into the future. This psychic measuring of time is
discovered in an introspection on one's inner experience of
the difference between long and short measures in the hearing of a psalm (*Confessiones* XI,14-30: *BA* 14,298-340).

Similarly the active theory of sensation presented in
the sixth book of *De musica* (VI,v,9-10: *BA* 7,378-382)
depends on looking inward to what happens in consciousness
when one notices some change in one's body. Sense perception is not a case of a physical stimulus acting on the soul
but rather of the soul acting more attentively than usual,
when it observes some modification in its bodily organs.[14]

Cognition

Augustine's theory of knowledge gives much more value to
intellectual judgment than to sense experience.[15] While the
study of sensation in *De musica* is based on auditory experience, his imagery in other explanations of knowing is
frequently visual: light plays an important role here. In a
key text in the *De Genesi ad litteram* (XII,vi,15 and xi,22:
BA 49,346-362) he describes three levels of vision. The
lowest is sensing through the observation of the bodily
organs; the second is perceiving through the imagination

(this thinking in terms of images is called *cogitatio*); and the highest vision is through an imageless intuition of the mind, by which one sees items such as love, equality, justice, truth, and so on. Solid truths are reached only on the third level, that is, in intellectual vision. As the mind looks for what is true, this gaze (*aspectus*) is called *ratio superior*. There is a lower searching through sense experience by *ratio inferior*. Its proper disposition is named *scientia*, a kind of knowledge that is practical and probable but not wholly reliable. When the soul gazes upward at eternal truths (*rationes aeternae*), it develops *sapientia*, a true wisdom.[16] (We shall note later how St. Anselm speaks of "cogitating" the meaning of the term "God" -- and then moves to the higher level of intellectual vision, when he sees that existence is necessary to this meaning.)

To explain how one makes absolutely true judgments, Augustine introduces his teaching on divine illumination of the mind. As the "Father of Lights," God provides illumination for both the bodily and the immaterial worlds. The things understood by intellectual intuition (*contemplatio*) are seen in the interior light of truth (*in illa interiore luce veritatis*) by which God enlightens men's souls (*De magistro* XII,40: *BA* 6,106). Just how this illumination works is much disputed among modern interpreters; but at least one can say that the light of the intellect makes evident the truth of objects of human judgment (such as that seven plus three equals ten), just as corporeal light makes ocular vision possible.[17]

Morality

Augustine's views on specific moral questions (such as sexual abuse, the purpose of marriage, the evil of lying) have had a great influence throughout later Christian literature: and they have often been criticized. But these special moral positions derive mostly from the Bible, especially St. Paul, and have little relation to Platonic philosophy. It is rather in his general ethical principles that we may see Augustine's debt to Plato and his followers.[18]

That all men naturally and necessarily desire their own well-being, or happiness (*beatitudo*), is a primary ethical axiom for Augustine. He says in the *De civitate dei* (X,1: *BA* 34,422): "It is the sure judgment (*certa sententia*) of all men who reach the use of reason that all men will to be happy." This echoes the theme of one of his earliest works,

De beata vita. Here Augustine owes something to the eudaim-
onism of classical Greek philosophy and in particular to
Plato's *Euthydemus* (279A) and *Laws* (870A), as digested in
later Latin writers. Also implied in this is the view that
there is one highest good or ultimate end for all men, to
the achievement of which all good human actions are
directed. *De civitate dei* XXII discusses the nature of the
eternal felicity which is the reward of all people who live
well.

Also connected with the foregoing is the ethically
important distinction between free choice (*liberum arbitrium*) and eminent liberty (*libertas*). All men are naturally endowed with free choice: its initial movement is the
desire for felicity. But only some humans are confirmed by
divine grace in willing what is morally good. This disposition called *libertas* is the freedom from the inclination to
sin (*posse peccare*) which is one of the dispositions of the
sons of Adam (*Opus imperfectum contra Julianum* VI,11: M.
X,2,1303-07; and *Enchiridion* IX,32: BA 9, 160). In many of
the more recent debates on "free will" in Augustine, this
distinction between free choice and eminent liberty has been
overlooked. It may have a partially Platonic background,
for Plotinus wrote that "true freedom consists in the
absence of any possibility of change for the worse" (*Enneads*
VI,8,10,25-36).[19]

The eternal law of God is for Augustine the absolute
norm of moral judgment. It is known through divine revelation and to some extent through ordinary human understanding, as natural law. Thus in the dialogue *De libero arbitrio* (I,vi,15: BA 6,162) he describes the eternal law as
the *summa ratio* of moral judgment and then suggests that
some of its principles are impressed on our minds (*impressa
nobis est*) and form the bases of human laws. However Augustine's ethics is not primarily legalistic, for, like any
Platonist, he stresses the ethical importance of love[20] and
the value of character development through the cultivation
of moral virtues.

The foregoing are but a few of the key philosophical
positions from Augustine which show some debt to the philosophy of the Platonists.

Anselm's Theocentric Platonism

If psychological interiorism is characteristic of Augustine's thought, then the main thrust of Anselm's thinking is
toward God. This is not to deny the theocentric features of
Augustinianism but simply to suggest that Anselm did not

spread his intellectual efforts over as broad a field as
Augustine's.   It is remarkable, as R. W. Southern has
observed (*St. Anselm and His Biographer*, p. 122), that in
spite of his experience with the administration of a diocese
at the end of the eleventh century, and his difficulties
with Franco-British rulers, Anselm wrote nothing in the
socio-political area. Apart from his work in logic (which
is designed to provide a methodology for the interpretation
of Scripture) Anselm's treatises are theological and moral
in purpose. Something that distinguishes Anselm as a writer
from our other two thinkers is his reluctance to mention the
authors on whom he depends. A glance at F. S. Schmitt's
Index auctorum (Schmitt VI,21-24) reveals Anselm's disdain
for such references.[21]   Augustine is mentioned only seven
times, although his influence is evident on almost every
page that Anselm wrote. Boethius is named in six places and
Aristotle's writings in logic five times. Plato's name
occurs once, in connection with an example in logic. Porphyry's *Isagoge* is named once; Cicero is never mentioned by
Anselm.   Even references to the Bible are somewhat scarce.
St. Benedict's *Regula* is cited more than fifty times. In a
letter written by Anselm as an answer to a non-extant
epistle from Lanfranc concerning emendations of the *Monologion* (*Epistola LXXVII*: Schmitt III,199-200) Anselm defends
himself against the charge that he failed to acknowledge his
debt to theological sources (*divinis auctoritatibus*).   "It
was my intention," Anselm replies, "to assert absolutely
nothing in that disputation that could not be defended
instantly from the canonical writings or from Blessed Augustine."   And later in this letter Anselm explains that there
is nothing in the brief argument of the *Monologion* that
could not be found in Augustine's *De trinitate*. Even in an
age when recourse to the approved *auctoritates* was becoming
the accepted thing, Anselm saw no need to annotate his own
meditations. This does not make it easy to show what Anselm
owed to Platonism.[22]

It is unlikely that Anselm ever read any of Plato's
dialogues. The partial translation of the *Timaeus*, with
commentary, by Chalcidius may have been available to him[23]
but there is no positive evidence that he used it.   Through
Cicero and Augustine he had some general information about
Plato's philosophy. By way of Boethius he knew Porphyry's
introduction to the *Categories* of Aristotle.[24]   Like
Augustine he shows little awareness of other works of Aristotle.   Of the Latin Church Fathers, Augustine and Ambrose
seem the greatest influences. There is no evidence that he
read either Dionysius the Pseudo-Areopagite or John Scotus
Erigena. He was acquainted with the logical works of Boeth-

ius, and also with the *Consolatio philosophiae*, but nothing suggests that Anselm knew Boethius' theological tractates.[25]

Anselm's methodology is well described in the subtitle of the *Proslogion*: *fides quaerens intellectum*. As he says near the start of *Cur deus homo* (I,2: Schmitt II,48):

> Right procedure (*rectus ordo*) demands that
> we believe the profound truths of Christian
> faith before we presume to discuss them. To
> me it would seem negligent if, after having
> been confirmed in the faith, we did not
> zealously endeavor to understand what we
> believe.

And there is no question that he takes the Bible as the main source of the truths available to the Christian. In *De concordia* (III,6: Schmitt II,252) he bluntly states: "Holy Scripture contains the guarantee (*auctoritatem*) for every truth that reasoning gathers." So, unlike the Aristotelian who starts with the reasoned experience of lower beings and rises to the understanding of higher principles, Anselm begins with the highest and uses discursive reasoning for explanation and to reach the lower truths. In this he was embracing the method of theology which Thomas Aquinas was later to distinguish from philosophical procedure.[26]   While there is definitely a philosophy at work in Anselm's writings (and that philosophy is Christian Platonism), his use of such thinking is theological.

Reality

If metaphysics be understood in the Aristotelian way, as a study endeavoring to offer ultimate explanations of difficulties (*aporiai*) that arise in the philosophy of nature, then Anselm had no such speculation. He did have a general view of reality which resembles that of Augustine. God is the supremely existing being. He is that than which nothing greater can be cogitated (*Monologion* I-III: Schmitt I,13-16).[27]   Created beings are ordered hierarchically according to various degrees of perfection.[28] The higher an existent stands in this ordering, the greater is its reality.   Every order of things has a unitary peak perfection which is its limit. This is obviously the justification for Anselm's use of the famous formula, "*quo majus cogitari non potest*" (*Proslogion* II: Schmitt I,101).   We shall see this Platonic view become Ficino's principle of the *primum in aliquo genere*.[29]   That the One is superior to,

and the source of, the many is evident throughout Anselm's
De veritate (where the degrees are of rightness) and in the
third argument of the *Monologion* II (Schmitt I,15 where the
hierarchy is of goods). Every created substance exists more
truly in the mind of the Creator than in the created universe (*Monologion* XXXVI: Schmitt I,55).

The foregoing is closely related to Anselm's realistic
approach approach to words. Most grammarians up to his time
stressed the idea that every noun is the name of some thing.
Even Anselm's discussion of the meaning of *nihil* tries to
show that, when we think or speak of "nothing," we refer to
some positive object or perfection which is negated.[30] Even
universals are things; although there may be some debate
over whether Anselm espoused a crude realism,[31] his whole
attack on the nominalism of Roscelin (in Anselm's *Epistola
de incarnatione verbi)*[32] indicates his basically realistic
position. Following the tradition of later Platonism,
Anselm locates the archetypal forms of all things in the
mind of the Creator. Thus *Monologion* IX (Schmitt I,24)
asserts that, "before all things were made there was in the
thought of the Supreme Nature what they were going to be."
In the creative Word of God creatures are not plural entities but are identical with the unique essence of God. This
teaching on divine exemplarism is not peculiar to Anselm:
it is found in Christian theologians of every century.

Psychology

Anselm's way of describing man's conscious activities is
generally very close to Augustine's but there are some differences. For instance, where Augustine usually gives *ratio*
a directly intuitive function, Anselm follows Boethius in
stressing the discursive, step-by-step character of ratioci-
nation.[35] Again, Anselm never seems to identify man with
his soul alone (as Augustine did in his early works) but
rather sees the individual human person as a unified compos-
ite of soul and body. As to the origin of the individual
rational soul, Anselm differs from Augustine and argues that
rationality is not present from the moment of conception but
enters the fetus later in its development. The reason for
this Anselmian view lies in his claim (in *De conceptu virginali*) that original sin is not present in a person until the
time at which rationality is present.[34] In this Anselm is
less Platonic than Augustine. However, he does use Plato's
imagery of the soul being related to its body as a pilot to
his ship (*De conceptu virginali* V: Schmitt II,146). Actually it is the will (*voluntas*) that is the "pilot" here.

While Anselm does speak of the Augustinian triad, *mens*, *memoria*, *voluntas*, he puts little stress on memory as a psychic function. Once, in discussing the divine Trinity (*Monologion* XLVIII: Schmitt I,63-64), he compares God the Father to memory. Since Augustine's *De trinitate* is clearly one of the great influences on Anselm's thinking, it would not be wrong to say that Anselm's psychology is quite similar to what we find in that Augustinian treatise.

In one of the few places where Anselm attempts to analyze the functions of the human soul (*De concordia* III,11: Schmitt II,278-84), he speaks of the five external senses and their organs and distinguishes between the sense powers (*potestates*) and their instruments. Then he proceeds to the distinctive powers of the human soul, reason, and will, which the soul uses as instruments. Here Anselm is going beyond Augustine, and of course beyond Plato, in speaking of psychic "powers" that are distinct from the soul itself. These powers of the soul may be viewed in three ways: as instruments, as modified by special inclination (*affectiones*), and finally as uses. Thus the Latin word *voluntas* may mean for Anselm: (1) an inborn power of willing which is always present in a human soul; (2) an added disposition (*affectio*) which inclines the will power toward some general object, such as health or justice; and (3) the actual exercise of willing any good. As in Augustine, will is the dynamic aspect of man's soul which moves all the other psychic instruments to perform their operations. This is so not only of immaterial movements but also of sensation and the kinetic workings of the body.

Elsewhere in the Anselmian writings we find the description of two different *affectiones* which incline man's will toward what is naturally good (the *commodum*), or toward a higher good of spiritual righteousness (the *affectio justitiae*).[35] These dispositions play a role in Anselm's understanding of personal freedom and may anticipate the *habitus* theory of later medieval psychology.

Possibly the most distinctive feature of Anselm's psychology is his emphasis on the central role of *willing*, in all of men's conscious activities. He has much more to say about *voluntas* than about *ratio* as a psychic power. However, he was not a voluntarist in any sense of the term, for few Christians have put more confidence in the operation of reasoning than Anselm. In this emphasis on willing there is little evidence of Platonic influence, since classical Greek philosophy has very little to say about will as a power of man's soul.[36]

Cognition

In theory of knowledge Anselm has made some contributions. His notion "faith seeking understanding" is anticipated in Augustine, but it would appear that Anselm is even more insistent than Augustine on the need to begin the search for understanding in the initial act of belief. This Christian reliance on right belief may owe something to classical Greek discussions of *orthodoxa* and, more particularly, to Plato's teaching on faith (*pistis*) and its relation to rationally grounded knowledge of ideal truths (*Republic* 509 D-511 E).

On the meaning of "necessary argument" (*rationes necessariae, argumentatio necessaria,* and *rationabilis necessitas*), as used throughout the Anselmian corpus, there has been a good deal of debate.[37] Anselm's rational explanations of Christian beliefs, such as the incarnation or the Holy Trinity, are not philosophical demonstrations independent of prior faith. Yet he seems to have thought that they would appeal to any person who could read them with ordinary common sense and good will. It is noteworthy that both Cicero and Marius Victorinus spoke of "necessary reasoning" in their treatises on rhetoric.[38]

Significant in Anselm's relation to Augustine's epistemology are two points. First, the theory of truth in Anselm's *De veritate* is more explicitly related to the notion of rightness (*rectitudo*) than it is in Augustine's writings. As a result, moral truth and cognitive truth are more closely connected in Anselmian thought than in Augustinianism. Since Plato's early dialogues portray the Socratic view that virtue is knowledge, with some approval, it would seem that on this point Anselm is quite Platonic.

And in the second place, this *inquisitio*, this searching for profound knowledge, is conducted first on the level of *cogitatio*, a thinking in terms of sense images. Thus when Anselm speaks of a being "*quo majus cogitari non potest,*" he is not talking about an intellectual conception of the divinity: he means what the ordinary person thinks when he uses the word "God" (*deus*). There is some, perhaps vague, image of something bigger than all else.[39] To reach understanding, for Plato, Augustine, and Anselm, one must rise above cogitation to an imageless intellectual confrontation with the highest objects of knowledge or wisdom.

Light as an epistemological principle is important to Anselm -- but not as much as in Augustine. We cannot see the inaccessible light that is God's, says Anselm, but we may see other verities in the divine light (*Meditatio rede-*

mptionis humanae (Schmitt III,85-90; and *Proslogion* XVI:
Schmitt I,112-13). It is not until the thirteenth century
that Christian Platonism will develop a whole philosophy of
light, as in Witelo, Robert Gresseteste, and Roger Bacon.

Morality

Before one examines Anselm's moral theology it is advisable to look at his teaching on evil. Like the Neo-
platonist Proclus,[40] and also like Augustine, Anselm
regarded evil as privation of some sort of good. There is
no being that is evil in its nature. Moral evil, in particular, consists in a lack of righteousness (*rectitudo*) in a
creature's *act* of willing. It is neither the power of will,
nor its unjust inclinations, that is intrinsically evil (*De
casu diaboli* VIII-X: Schmitt I,245-47). The perverse act
of willing is not nothing: it is a real event but its per-
version is a lack of the right order that should characterize every good human action. Now the ultimate criterion of
right moral order is God's commanding will (*Cur deus homo*
I,12: Schmitt II,70). But this is not an arbitrary divine
will which could make any action to be just or unjust. As
Anselm states it:

> But as for the statement that what God wills
> is just and what He does not will is not
> just: we must not interpret this to mean
> that, if God were to will any kind of unfit-
> tingness, it would be just simply because He
> willed it. For this supposition that "God
> wills to lie" does not warrant the inference
> "lying is just," but instead warrants the
> inference "this being is not really God."[41]

So, while Anselmian moral theology is a divine approbative
type of ethics, it is not at all an uncontrolled
voluntarism.

Also basic in Anselm's moral teaching is his much discussed theory of human freedom.[42] Perhaps the key passage
on this topic is *De concordia* VI (Schmitt II,255-57). There
he recapitulates his teaching from *De veritate* and *De
libertate arbitrii*. As in Augustinianism, man is born with
the natural power of choice to do or not do something.
There is free choice on this level (*liberum arbitrium*) in
regard to the election of what is ordinarily advantageous to
a person in earthly life. But such low-grade freedom does

not enable a person to merit salvation: a higher type of freedom may be added to the basic power of will as a special inclination (*affectio*) to will rightness (*justitia*) for its own sake, and not for the sake of some other end. This eminent liberty (*libertas*) is present in a person who wills what God wishes him to will. As such, it is freedom from the bondage of sin, for by *libertas* an agent rises above the appeal of evil and is firmly established as a lover of what is spiritually good. This is the enviable condition of being able not to sin. Obviously Anselm was impressed by the New Testament dictum: "everyone who commits sin is a slave of sin (Jn 8:35)." While this is very different from anything in classical Platonism, there is some parallel between the lower and the higher morality relationship and the Platonic theory of two worlds, one lower and one higher.

Typical of Anselmian morality is the emphasis on the attitude of the moral agent prior to and concomitant with the willing of his action. He pays very little attention to the consequences of moral activity, either in terms of results to the agent or to others. Anselm is not much of an utilitarian. As is clear at the end of the dialogue *De veritate* XII (Schmitt I,191-96) justice is the great virtue for Anselm but this is not the classical virtue of simply giving to others what is their due. Rather, Anselm's justice consists in being right in relation to God. He knows but does not stress virtues such as prudence, fortitude, and temperance. Anselm's morality is not an ethics of many virtues but a prior-attitude ethics. Some interpreters have even likened his moral stance to Kantianism, for Anselm has much to say about duty and what ought to be done (*quod debet*).[43] Motivation determines the moral quality of human actions: the good person acts out of a desire for righteousness itself. It is not enough to desire and act well for the sake of happiness.

Although Anselm's moral teaching owes much to Augustine, and indirectly to Plato, it must be admitted that the Platonic ethics of virtue is not specially favored by Anselm. Yet the key notion of righteousness may be typically Platonic, for we read in the *Theaetetus* (176 B, Jowett version): "Whereas the truth is that God is never in any way unrighteous (*adikos*) -- he is perfect righteousness (*dikaiostatos*); and he of us who is most righteous is most like him."

Of the three authors here considered, Anselm is the least obviously Platonic. But to the extent that he has a philosophy, Anselm's thought resembles Platonism more than any other type of ancient philosophy. As R. W. Southern

puts it, "there can be no doubt that his essential philosophical ideas are Platonic."[44]

Ficino's Literary Platonism

With the extensive writings of Marsilio Ficino, in the
second half of the fifteenth century, Christian Platonism
entered the modern era.[45]   He was both a medieval and modern
man.   Ficino's Latin translations of Plato's dialogues,
together with his versions of other Greek "Platonic" writings, were read and quoted throughout Europe during the next
two centuries.   Their influence on English and other vernac-
ular literatures in the early modern period is widely
recognized.[46]

Unlike Augustine and Anselm, Ficino was familiar with
almost the whole corpus of Plato's dialogues and letters in
the original Greek.   As a young man in Florence he became
interested in Platonism, partly from reading Cicero and
Augustine, but also from contacts with Greek scholars in
north Italy.[47]   However, the young Ficino was advised by
Bishop Antoninus of Florence, a prominent Thomist, to study
the *Summa contra Gentiles* of Thomas Aquinas, possibly as an
antidote to Marsilio's fascination with Plato.[48]   In 1462
Cosimo de Medici provided Ficino with a villa outside Florence where a Platonic Academy was established.   This was
not a teaching center but a meeting-place for philosophical
discussion and research.   Over the years, the Medici family
provided the finances and manuscripts needed to support this
group.

The name of "our Plato" (*Plato noster*) appears again and
again in almost every paragraph that Ficino wrote.   His
Theologia platonica is the most important vehicle for his
personal thinking.[50]   It is not a complete treatise on
theology, for its main purpose is to offer many arguments
for the immortality of the human soul.   Nor is it entirely
Platonic, for it includes views and arguments only remotely
related to Plato's thought. Indeed this is one of the characteristic features of Ficino's scholarship: he is quite
ready to accept as Platonists thinkers representing many
different types of philosophy.   Probably the only philosophers that he could not bring under the wings of Plato were
the Averroistic Aristotelians of his day, whose materialism
Marsilio bluntly rejected.   This tendency to be eclectic and
undiscriminating in regard to the Platonic school is what A.
H. Armstrong, describing a similar attitude in Boethius, has
called "naive concordism."[51]   Of course in appraising

Ficino's scholarship it must be remembered that he was a pioneer in the field of Latin studies of the text of Plato, working with a few Greek manuscripts, with practically no dictionaries and reference works, and with no associates who approached his level of interpretation.

Reality

Since Ficino was well acquainted with most of Augustine's major writings, we can assume that he knew the general outline of Augustinian metaphysics. God is the highest being, perfectly good and all-knowing. The rest of reality is created by God. Bodies are on the lowest level of existence; created spirits occupy a middle position, being subject to temporal changes but not mutable in place as bodies are. In his *Epistola Gazolti* (the letters are not numbered) (B 1,2,769) Ficino accepts Augustine's much quoted statement (*De vera religione* IV,7: *BA* 8,34) that "with a few things changed" (*paucis mutatis*) the Platonists could be Christians. In the same place Marsilio sums up Plato's teachings under three points: (1) God takes providential care of all things; (2) human souls are immortal; and (3) rewards will be given to good people, while prayers are needed for the evil.[52]

The second point, immortality, occupies most of Ficino's attention in his *Theologia platonica*. In this emphasis he is indeed a humanist, for he thinks that both theologians and philosophers can know more about man's soul than any other object. Like Augustine and Cicero, Ficino uses *anima* for the vital principle of any living things, and *animus* for man's conscious spirit. In Ficino's hierarchy of beings the lowest kind of thing (*essentia*) is bodily and quantity is its special characteristic. Ascending to the next grade we find quality, a simple and dynamic form capable of initiating action, contrasting with quantity which is divisible, passive, and incapable of causing action (*Theologia Platonica* I,3: B I,1, fol. 81). The third step upward is to soul (both rational and irrational) and the fourth level is that of the angels. At the peak of Ficino's hierarchy of beings is God, One, True and Good, the Author and Ruler of all (*Theologia platonica* III: B 1, 1, 115-21).

In this scheme of five grades of reality, Ficino stresses quality as something essentially different from quantity, its neighbor in the Aristotelian *Categories*.[53] We know that physics, in its most materialistic interpretation, was then prominent in the schools of northern Italy, espe-

cially at Padua. Many of its Averroistic interpreters were
medical doctors. They derided the notion that man's soul is
immaterial and immortal, claiming that the *psyche* is merely
the structural organization of the living body. As such it
disappears with death. Ficino did his best to show that the
scientific study of matter as quantified does not offer an
adequate explanation of man's distinctive psychic functions.

It will be noticed that Ficino's ascent through five
grades of reality brings him to God. However, unlike
Anselm, he does not stress this analysis as a demonstration
of God's existence. He seems never to question the fact
that there is a supreme divinity. His basis for this
unswerving certitude lies in a principle which he takes to
be basic in Platonic philosophy: This is the axiom that
there is a first item in every genus which serves as the
principle of all other items in the genus (*primum enim in
quolibet genere, totis generis est principium*, see *Theologia platonica* I,3: B I,1,82).[54] Frequently he illuminates
this with the example of the sun as the source of all physical lights (*De sole* and *De lumine* B 1,2,965-86). So it is
almost self-evident to Ficino that there must be one highest
being.

The role of final causality in metaphysics is also vigorously supported by Ficino. God, of course, is the highest
end for all things (*Theologia platonica* II,1-3:   B
I,1,92-96). The end-directedness of the human soul is particularly important. In a little treatise *On Mind*[55] he
answers five questions on this subject: (1) The human mind
(*mens*) strives for an end, as do all parts of man; (2) the
end of its motion is not more motion but rest; (3) the good
that is so desired is not a particular one but universal;
(4) the human mind is strong enough to attain its desired
end which the *summum bonum*; and (5) after it has reached its
perfect good, it never loses it. In answering the last
question (B I,2,682) Ficino says that it is only in eternal
life that the rational soul (*animus*) reaches its final
felicity (*beatitudo*). This, he adds, "is the teaching of
the Prophets and theologians, and it is confirmed by the
Magi and mercurial philosophers."[56] On this point, too,
Ficino was reacting against the growing Renaissance tendency
to exclude final causes from science and philosophy.   In
his *Commentary on Plato's Parmenides* (B II,1187) he argues
that "an innate appetite for the primal cause as the end of
all things is inherent in all things."[57] A generalized
version of the same theme is found in his *Philebus Commentary*: "Natural appetite is the necessary inclination of a
nature striving to go from a want (*indigentia*) to a fulfillment (*plentitudo*)."[58]

In treating the transcendental attributes of being, Ficino says that the good (*bonum*) is superior to being and essence, and that truth (*veritas*) is the shining forth of the good (*veritasque boni lumen*) and is above the ideal forms, beings and minds.[59] On the status of beauty (so often hailed as a Platonic ideal by Renaissance poets) Ficino is not so definite. There is little mention of *pulchrum* in his personal writings but, of course, beauty is often treated in his *Commentaries* on Plato.[60]

Psychology

Like other humanists of the Renaissance, Marsilio Ficino frequently mentions the dignity of man. In this he may be compared with his younger contemporary, Giovanni Pico della Mirandola (who visited with Ficino in Florence in 1484). There is little doubt that Ficino identified man with his soul. In a letter (dated 1473) to Sismundo Stufa (*Epistola I*: B I,2,617), he wrote, "*certe animus homo ipse est, corpus autem est hominis umbra.*" Earlier (probably 1468) a letter to Giovanni Cavalcanti (fol. 616) finds Ficino searching in a very modern way for his own identity. He decides that he is the person who judges that he is doing this questioning. Like René Descartes later, he concludes, "*Solus judicat animus;*"[61] so, he is his conscious soul.

We have already noted that the *Theologia platonica* offers an extended treatise on the immortality of the human soul. Its fifth book (B I,1,235-55) contains fifteen arguments for personal immortality, taken from a variety of authors, including Augustine, Aquinas, and the *Gorgias*, *Phaedo*, *Meno*, *Republic*, and *Phaedrus* of Plato. Sometimes these arguments almost literally parallel their sources. This underscores the point that Ficino is not an original philosopher but rather a well-read literary scholar.

In many places Ficino uses the imagery of the two wings of man's soul (intellect and will) from the *Phaedrus* (246-51). At the beginning of his *De christiana religione* (Proemium: B I,1, fol. 1) he explains that it is by means of these two powers that the soul may fly back to its Father and Fatherland, as it pleased "our Plato" to say. Ficino claims that the philosophers usually stress the intellect, while the priests favor the will. There has been much debate as to whether Ficino was an intellectualist or a voluntarist.[62] It seems to me that this passage fairly represents his judgment that intellect and will are of equal importance, for he adds in the same place that, "the intellect enlightens the will, while the will sparks the intellect" (*intellectus voluntatem illuminat, voluntas intellectum accendat*).

Love, of course, is the basic activity of the will but it is also seen by Marsilio as the bond which holds all things together (the *vinculum universi*, see *Philebus commentarium*: B II,2,1068). With light which is the highest form in the material world, love is a constant companion (*De sole* II: B I,2,966). This theory of universal love has been studied exhaustively by A. M. J. Festugière and Ardis Collins and their interpretations go well beyond the psychological role of love.[63]

One other tenet of Ficino's psychology that is Platonic is the notion that man's soul is stained with evil by its association with the body. In the *Epistola Michaeli Mercato*: B I,2,610 God says to the soul, "*Bonum tibi est esse cum patre, malum tibi est esse cum corpore.*" This dialogue insists that the only good for man's soul is simply *the Good* (*bonum*). Much of Ficino's psychology has this moralizing tone.

Cognition

In theory of knowledge Ficino sharply separates sensory cognition from understanding. Through the senses man is informed about the changing features of the world of bodies. True judgments find no real ground in sense perception (*non est in sensu veritatis judicium constitutum*, see *Theologia platonica* XI,6: B 1,1,261). In producing its true judgments man's intellect gets no solid help from anything below it or on its own level. Only through God's illumination does man reach eternal truths (*Epistola conphilosophis suis* II: B 1,2,682-83). "The highest intelligible object, God, is the cause of understanding, the understanding, I say, that is above cogitative intelligence." Two things are noteworthy in these texts from the *Theologia platonica* and the *Epistola conphilosophis suis*. First, he is not saying, as Kristeller has suggested,[64] that we have here a theory of innate forms in man's understanding. Rather, Ficino is repeating Augustine's theory of divine illumination which he professes to find also in Plato. The little treatises *De sole* and *De lumine* reiterate this view: God impresses truths on man's mind at the time at which judgments are made.

The other point to be observed here is Ficino's use of "cogitation" to designate a level of human thinking in terms of images, beneath imageless intellectual understanding and under the guidance of divine light. When he says *veritas est in ratione* (TP fol. 261), Ficino is not anticipating a Kantian theory of forms innate in man's intellect. Rather, as he explains in reference to our knowledge of moral laws, these truths are divinely impressed (*divinitas impressa*) on our minds (*In epistola d. Pauli commentaria* B 1, 1. 451). Even true judgments about bodily things consist in their conformity to the eternal reasons in the mind of God (TP 11, 6; B 1, 1, 238-58). Such divine guidance is a function of Providence.

Morality

Ficino wrote no special treatise on ethics, possibly because his early mentor, Antoninus of Florence, had written a notable contribution to moral theology in commenting on the second Part of Thomas Aquinas' *Summa of Theology*. However, there are important moral positions to be found in Ficino's writings. The *Commentary on St. Paul* (B1, 1, 425-72) provides a prime example. Explaining Paul's distinction between a natural moral law and a written law, Ficino argues that all peoples have some notions of rightness impressed on their minds by God. He attributes this teaching to Plato (fol. 450) and to Augustine's *City of God* (fol. 451).

But Ficino's main ethical emphasis was on the life of virtue rather than conformity to law. One way to show this is to list the virtues that he attributes to Plato, the greatest of the philosophers: learning, soberness, continence, dignity (*gravitas*), courtesy (*comitas*), eloquence, wisdom, authority, holiness, charity, magnanimity, piety, and gratitude.[65] Some of these attributions might have surprised Plato.

Of course the whole Platonic and Neoplatonic theme of the return of the soul to its origin in God has moral overtones. Man has a natural desire for felicity which can only be satisfied by attaining to the highest good (*Quaestiones de mente*, q. 5; B 1, 2, 682). Man's ultimate well-being does not consist in bodily pleasures but in peace of mind (*De voluptate* 4; B 1, 2, 994). Ficino also shares Augustine's views on the difference between freedom of choice and *libertas*. "Our minds are most free," he writes, "when they are in greatest agreement with the divine will" (*Epist. ad Federicum Urbini*, B 1, 2, 849). Perfect freedom is a divine attribute (TP 4; B 1, 1, 109-14).

Conclusion

In the formative years of Christian intellectualism, from the fifth to the fifteenth century, Platonic philosophy exerted a considerable influence. Augustine, Anselm and Marsilio Ficino illustrate this influence in varying degrees. Anselm is the least obviously Platonic, while Augustine and Ficino are open admirers of Plato and his early followers. Indeed the slogan of medieval Christian intellectualism, "faith seeking understanding," is incorporated in the thinking of all three representatives that have been examined here.

Augustine's Platonism is perhaps most evident in his introspective psychology but it extends to his consideration of most of the major problems of philosophy and psychology. In the case of Anselm it is clear that his efforts to show that the belief in the existing God is quite reasonable are made in the context of a Platonic and Augustinian journey upwards to the vision of a necessary truth. Finally we can see in the scholarly work of Marsilio Ficino the continuation of the medieval fascination with the heritage of Plato, plus the new Renaissance dimension of literary familiarity with the actual *Dialogues*.

The understanding that these three Christian clerics achieved, each in his own distinctive way, owes a good deal to the philosophy that started in the Athenian Academy. But perhaps it takes a poet to distill the essence of this philosophy, so let us end with these lines (180-93) from Robert Browning's *Cleon*:

> Nay, thou art worthy of hearing my whole mind.
> Is this apparent, when turn'st to muse
> Upon the scheme of earth and man in chief
> That admiration grows as knowledge grows?
> That imperfection means perfection hid,
> Reserved in part, to grace the after-time?
> If, in the morning of philosophy.
> Ere aught had been recorded, nay perceived,
> Thou, with the light now in thee, couldst have looked
> On all earth's tenantry, from worm to bird,
> Ere man, her last, appeared upon the stage --
> Thou wouldst have seen them perfect, and deduced
> The perfectness of others yet unseen.

Notes

[1] For the setting of medieval Platonism: E. Gilson, *History of Christian Philosophy in the Middle Ages* (New York: Random House, 1955); A. H. Armstrong, *The Cambridge History of Later Greek and Early Medieval Philosophy* (Cambridge Univ. Press, 1967); R. Arnou, "Platonisme des Pères," *DTC* XII, 2258-392; W. Beierwaltes, *Platonismus in der Philosophie des Mittelalters* (Darmstadt: Wissenschaftliche Buchges-Ellschaft, 1969); F. Copleston, *A History of Philosophy* (Garden City, NY: Doubleday, 1962-63), vols. 1, 2 to 3, 1; R. Klibansky, *The Continuity of the Platonic Tradition* (London: Warburg Institute, 1939); A. J. Festugière, *La révélation d'Hermès Trismégiste*, 4 vols. (Paris: Revue Augustinienne, 1944-54); P. Merlan, *From Platonism to Neoplatonism*, 2nd ed. (The Hague: Nijhoff, 1960); R. T. Wallis, *Neo-Platonism* (New York: Scribner, 1972), ch. 6: "The Influence of Neoplatonism," pp. 160-78; D. J. O'Meara, ed., *Neoplatonism and Christian Thought* (Albany, NY: State Univ. of New York Press, 1982).

[2] For Ficino's *Opera Omnia* see note 45 below: the reply to Martino Uranio is in I, 809.

[3] *Contra academicos* III,xvii,37: *BA* IV,188. Except as otherwise noted the Augustine references are to the *BA* edition.

[4] These Platonic texts are listed in the *Index scriptorum* of *De trinitate*, ed. W. J. Mountain, *CC* 50a,751-52.

[5] For these three levels: *De diversis quaestionibus ad Simplicianum* I,ii,18: *BA* X,486; *De musica* VI,v,12-13: *BA* VII, 384-88; *De vera religione* III,3: *BA* VIII,24-26; *De natura boni* I,1-25: *BA* I,440-66; *De civitate dei* VIII,5-6: *BA* XXXIV, 246-56; and V. Bourke, *Augustine's View of Reality* (Villanova, PA: Villanova Univ. Press, 1964).

[6] On Antiochus: W. Theiler, *Die Vorbereitung des Neuplatonismus*, 2 Aufl. (Berlin; Zurich, 1964), p. 18; and C. Fabro, "Platonism, Neo-Platonism, and Thomism," *New Scholasticism*, 44 (1970), 78.

[7] See J. A. Beckaert, "Les idées dans la pensée divine," in "Notes Complémentaires," *BA* X,726-27.

[8] *De trinitate* XV,7-8: *BA* XVI,434-40.

⁹ See Plotinus, *Enneads* III,vi,1-5; and Wallis, *Neo-Platonism*, p. 74.

¹⁰ Bourke, "Moral Illumination," in *Wisdom from St. Augustine* (Houston: Univ. of St. Thomas, 1984), 106-25.

¹¹ On this psychological interiorism: A. C. Pégis, "The Mind of St. Augustine," *Medieval Studies* (Toronto), 6 (1944), 1-61.

¹² See J. Mourant, ed., "The Augustinian Psychology," in *An Introduction to the Philosophy of St. Augustine: Selected Readings and Commentaries* (University Park: Pennsylvania State Univ. Press, 1964), pp. 105-35.

¹³ On the psychological analysis of time, see "Note Complémentaire," *BA* XIV,581-91.

¹⁴ See M. Ann Ida Gannon, "The Active Theory of Sensation in St. Augustine," *New Scholasticism* 30 (1956), 154-80.

¹⁵ Key Latin texts and notes are in: L. W. Keeler, *Sancti Augustini doctrina de cognitione* (Rome: Universitas Gregoriana, 1934).

¹⁶ See my chapter 4, "Wisdom and Knowledge," in *Wisdom from St. Augustine*, pp. 53-62.

¹⁷ Different interpretations of this intellectual illumination are reviewed in R. H. Nash, *The Light of the Mind: St. Anselm's Theory of Knowledge* (Lexington, KY: Univ. Press of Kentucky, 1969), ch. 7.

¹⁸ J. Mausbach, *Die Ethik des hl. Augustinus*, 2 Aufl. (Freiburg: Herder, 1929) is still the most complete study; see also my *Joy in Augustine's Ethics* (Villanova, PA: Villanova Univ. Press, 1979).

¹⁹ For Plotinus on freedom, see Wallis, *Neo-Platonism*, p. 64.

²⁰ As an antidote to a legalistic view of Augustine's ethics: Oliver O'Donovan, *The Problem of Self-Love in St. Augustine* (New Haven and London: Yale Univ. Press, 1980).

²¹ For many of the works in English: *Anselm of Canterbury*, trans. J. Hopkins and H. Richardson, 4 vols. (Toronto and New York: Mellen Press, 1974-76).   Gilliam Evans

observes that Anselm "looked to Scripture for his only quoted authorities" "Augustine on the Soul," in *Miscellanea Agostiniana*, ed. V. Grossi (Rome: Institutum Patristicum Augustinianum, 1985), p. 290.

[22] On Anselm's philosophical sources: R. D. Crouse, "The Augustinian Background of St. Anselm's Concept of *Justitia*," *Canadian Journal of Theology* 4 (1958), 111-19; A. Forest, F. Van Steenberghen, and M. de Gandillac, *Le Mouvement doctrinal du IXe au XIVe siècle* (Paris: Bloud et Gay, 1951); J. Hopkins, *A Companion to the Study of St. Anselm* (Minneapolis: Univ. of Minnesota Press, 1972); P. I. Kaufman, "A Conformation of Augustine's Soteriology: Human Will's Collaboration with Divine Grace According to St. Anselm," *Medievalia* 4 (1978), 147-60; H. Rondet, "Grace et péché: l'Augustinisme de s. Anselm," *SB* I, 155-68; F. S. Schmitt, "Anselm und der Neu-Platonismus," *Analecta Anselmiana* 1 (1969), 39-71; J. F. Sulowski, "Studies on Chalcidius: Anthropology, Influence, and Importance," in *L'Homme et son destin d'après les penseurs du moyen âge* (Louvain and Paris: Nauwelaerts, 1960), 153-61; S. Vanni Rovighi, *S. Anselmo e la filosofia del Secolo XI* (Milano: Vita e Pensiero, 1949).

[23] Sulowski, "Studies on Chalcidius," pp. 153-61.

[24] See Hopkins, *Companion*, pp. 16-36. There is a quotation from Aristotle's *De interpretione* in *Cur deus homo* II,17: Schmitt II,125.

[25] See *Index auctorum*: Schmitt VI,22.

[26] Thomas Aquinas, *Expositio super librum Beothii de trinitate* 6,4 c; for the English: Bourke, *Pocket Aquinas* (New York: Simon & Schuster, 1978), 148-51.

[27] For Augustine's use of similar expressions: *Epistola CLV*, IV,13 and *De moribus Manichaeorum* II,11: *BA* I,290: quo esse aut cogitari melius nihil possit.

[28] On degrees of perfection among goods, see the third argument in *Monologion* II: Schmitt I,15; compare Hopkins, *Companion*, pp. 18-19.

[29] P. O. Kristeller, *The Philosophy of Marsilio Ficino*, trans. Virginia Conant (Gloucester, MA: Peter Smith, 1964), 146-70.

[30] On thinking *nihil*:   *De casu diaboli* XI: Schmitt I,251.

[31] G. Evans, *Anselm and Talking about God* (Oxford: Clarendon Press, 1978), 36-37.

[32] *De incarnatione verbi* II: Schmitt I,281-90; see also *Epistola 129*:   Schmitt III,271-72, and *Epistola* 136: Schmitt III,279-81, regarding Roscelin.

[33] There is practically nothing in Augustine similar to the discussion of syllogistic reasoning in Anselm's *De grammatico* IV ff.: Schmitt I,148ff.

[34] For the time of origin of rationality, see G. Evans, "Augustine on the Soul," p. 292.   On the integral man: *Monologion* XVII: Schmitt I,31, and Hopkins' comparison with Augustine, *Companion*, pp. 123-24.

[35] The *affectio ad commodum* and *justitiae* are most fully treated in *Liber de voluntate*:   PL CLVIII,487-90, now thought to be a compilation by Anselm's students; but see *De concordia* III,12: Schmitt II ,284-85, and with reference to the will of the devil, *De casu diaboli* XII-XIV: Schmitt I,251-58.

[36] E. R. Fairweather, "Truth, Justice and Moral Responsibility in the Thought of St. Anselm," in *L'Homme et son destin*, pp. 385-91; and Bourke, *Will in Western Thought* (New York: Sheed & Ward, 1964).

[37] One of the best studies is A. M. Jacquin, "Les *rationes necessariae* de s. Anselme," in *Mélanges Mandonnet* (Paris: Vrin, 1930), pp. 67-78.

[38] Jacquin, "Les *rationes necessariae*, p. 72, n. 5, refers to Cicero, *De inventione rhetorica* II,29, and Victorinus, *De rhetorica* X, and Cassiodorus, *De artibus et disciplinis liberalium artium* CXI, for early sources of the expression *rationes necessariae*.

[39] For this thinking in terms of images and words, see G. Evans, *Anselm and Talking about God*, ch. 1.   Also R. W. Southern, *St. Anselm and His Biographer* (Cambridge: Univ. Press, 1963), pp. 57-59, for the *quo majus cogitari* formula in Seneca and Augustine.

[40] On Proclus' privative explanation of evil: Wallis, *Neo-Platonism*, p. 157.

[41] The English of *Cur deus homo* I,12:   Schmitt II, 69-70, is from the Hopkins-Richardson version, vol. III, 70. Fuller explanation in: Sofia Vanni Rovighi, "L'Etica di S. Anselmo," *Analecta Anselmiana* 1 (1969), 73-99.

[42] The basic treatise is *De libertate arbitrii*:   Schmitt I, 201-26.   Key secondary studies are: O. Lottin, "Les définitions du libre arbitre au douzième siècle," *Révue Thomiste* 32 (1927), 104-20, 214-30; R. Pouchet, *La rectitudo chez s. Anselme* (Paris: Études Augustiniennes, 1964);   J. Rohmer, *La Finalité morale de s. Augustin à Duns Scot* (Paris: Vrin, 1939), pp. 139-78; and G. S. Kane, *Anselm's Doctrine of Freedom and the Will* (Toronto: Mellen Press, 1981) which is sharply criticized by J. Hopkins, "Anselm on Freedom and the Will," *Philosophical Research Archives* 9 (1983), 471-93.

[43] *De casu diaboli* IV: Schmitt I,241.   See E. R. Fairweather,   "Truth,   Justice,"   criticizes   Rohmer,   *La Finalité morale*, for his Kantian interpretation of Anselm; see also Pouchet, *La Rectitudo*, p. 260.

[44] Southern, *St. Anselm and His Biographer*, p. 62.

[45] Ficino references   (designated as B)   are   to *Opera omnia*, 2 vols. in 4 tomes (Basel, 1576); reprinted   (Torino: Bottega d'Erasmo, 1959).

[46] See   Jayne   Sears,   *John   Colet   and   Marsilio   Ficino* (London: Oxford Univ. Press, 1963).

[47] A *Letter to Gazolti* (B 1, 2, fol. 769-70) acknowledges a debt to Cicero, Augustine and a whole series of "Platonists." Compare A. T. Canavero, "S. Agostino nella *Teologia Platonica* di M. Ficino," *Rivista di Filosofia Neo-scolastica* 70 (1978), 626-46.

[48] For the influence of Thomism: E. Gilson, "Marsile Ficin et le *Contra Gentiles*," *Archives d'Histoire doctrinale et littéraire du Moyen Age* 24 (1957 101-13.

[49] On Ficino's studies: P. O. Kristeller, *The Philosophy of Marsilio Ficino*, trans. V. Conant (Gloucester, MA: Peter Smith, 1964), pp. 16-17, and Kristeller's *Supplementum Ficinianum* (Florence: Olschki, 1937), I, lxxvii-clxvii.

⁵⁰The *Theologia platonica de immortalitate animae*
(1469-1474) is cited from the Basel edition; R. Marcel's
Latin-French edition (3 vols., Paris, 1964) was not available to me.

⁵¹H. Armstrong, "St. Augustine and Christian Platonism,"
in *Augustine: Critical Essays*, ed. R. A. Markus (Garden
City, NY: Doubleday, 1972), p. 26.

⁵²*Epistola Gazolti*, De Platonica philosophiae natura (B
1, 2, fol. 769).

⁵³See Kristeller, *Philosophy of Marsilio Ficino*, ch. 6:
"Hierarchy of Being," pp. 74-91.

⁵⁴Kristeller, *Philosophy of Marsilio Ficino*, pp. 146-70.

⁵⁵*Quaestiones quinque de mente* (B 1, 2, fol. 675-82),
trans. J. L. Burroughs in *The Renaissance Philosophy of Man*,
ed. E. Cassirer, P. O. Kristeller, and J. H. Randall, Jr.
(Chicago: Univ. of Chicago Press, 1948-50), pp. 185-212.

⁵⁶Ficino refers to the Hermetic corpus, Greek writings
produced in Egypt as revelations of the god Toth but under
the name of Hermes Trismegistus; see Wallis, *Neo-Platonism*,
p. 602; and H. Lewy, *Chaldean Oracles and Theurgy: Mysti-
cism, Magic and Platonism in the Later Roman Empire* (Paris:
Études Augustiniennes, 1978).

⁵⁷The English is from Kristeller, *Philosophy of Marsilio
Ficino*, p. 172.

⁵⁸Ficino, *The Philebus Commentary*, ed. and trans. M. J.
B. Allen (Berkeley: Univ. of California Press, 1975),
p. 83.

⁵⁹*Epistola Martino Uranio*, B 1, 2, `fol. 942; and
Quaestiones de mente B 1, 2, fol. 677.

⁶⁰References to *pulchritudo* or *pulchrum* indexed in the
Basel edition are not to the personal writings.

⁶¹Three selections from *Theologia platonica* on the soul
of man (3,2; 13,3; and 14,3-4) are translated by J. L. Burroughs in *Journal of the History Ideas* 5 (1944), 227-39.

⁶²Kristeller, *Philosophy of Marsilio Ficino*, ch. 10,
argues that Ficino always gave priority to will over intel-

lect, but Allen, ed., *The Philebus Commentary*, p. 534, n. 179, cites a passage where Ficino says: voluntatem scilicet crassum esse intellectum: intellectum autem serenam et liquidam voluntatem.

[63]A.   M.   J.   Festugière,   *La   Philosophie de l'amour de Marsile Ficin* (Paris: Vrin, 1941) and A. Collins, "Love and Natural   Desire in Ficino's *Platonica Theologia*," *Journal of the History of Ideas* 9, No. 4 (1971), 435-42.

[64]Kristeller, *Philosophy of Marsilio Ficino*, p. 51.

[65]For references to these virtues see the *Index* B 1,   2, at the words *Platonis educatio*.

Le dernier Anselme:
Essai sur la structure du *De concordia*

Eduardo Briancesco

Entreprendre l'analyse du dernier ouvrage d'Anselme de Cantorbéry est une tâche ardue. Le lecteur participe, et pas seulement après la première lecture, de la même impression que saisit son auteur en le redigeant: il s'agit d'un traité *de tribus difficilibus quaestionibus quae in spe auxilii Dei incepi* (III,14). La suite du même texte, le dernier chapitre du *De concordia*, donne témoignage d'un état d'esprit semblable à celui de l'auteur lorsqu'il rédigeait son celèbre *Proslogion*:

> si quis mihi quaerenti de quaestionibus eisdem, **quando in eis mens mea rationem quaerendo, fluctuabat,** ea quae scripsi respondisset, gratias egissem, quia mihi satisfecisset.[1]

Moins dramatiques que celles du texte du *Proslogion*, ces lignes laissent entrevoir l'effort que ces questions exigèrent du chercheur Anselme. Et il ne serait pas exagéré d'ajouter que, comme le dit Schmitt,[2] cette recherche ait de plus en plus préoccupé son auteur tout au long de sa vie.

Les réflexions ici proposées veulent aider l'eventuel lecteur du *De concordia* à découvrir, en dirait presque à sentir, la complexité du discours anselmien dans cet ouvrage que, à notre avis, constitue l'aboutissement -- *in actu exercito* -- de toute sa méthodologie théologique.

Le présent essai se veut, pour des raisons évidentes, nécessairement schématique. Bien qu'il suppose une analyse serrée du texte, il se propose plutôt comme une guide de lecture qui appelle la réflexion personnelle et, éventuellement, le dialogue. Le développement tournera autour de deux points également importants:

(I) L'examen de la *structure* du texte de *De concordia* par rapport aux ouvrages précédents d'Anselme; ceci jettera une vive lumière sur l'évolution de son itinéraire intellectuel;

(II) La réflexion *herméneutique* sur la méthode appliquée par l'auteur dans la construction de son texte et découverte par la lecture que l'on propose ici.

Mais il faudra d'abord faire deux observations
préliminaires qui conditionnent ou facilitent l'intelligence
de ce qui va suivre. Il faut en effet remarquer en détail:

(A) Le rapport établi entre les *trois questions* (*de
praescientia, de praedestinatione, de gratia et de libero
arbitrio*) et la *question fondamentale* examinée dans le
livre;

(B) La relation du *De concordia* au reste des écrits
anselmiens *sous la base des indications fournies par le
texte lui-même.*

Les *tres quaestiones* et la question de l'Ecriture

On sait qu'Anselme a elaboré sa trilogie morale (*De
veritate, De libertate arbitrii, De casu diaboli*) autour des
questions posées par l'Ecriture sainte. Bien qu'il
s'articule aussi en trois parties, le *De concordia* ne semble
se référer explicitement au *questionnement de l'Ecriture* que
dans la troisième partie lorsqu'on envisage le rapport entre
grâce et liberté. Les textes du *De concordia* I sont trés
nets. C'est le langage du texte biblique, évoqué au début
et à la fin du chapitre (*quaestio ista inde nascitur quia
divina scriptura ita loquitur . . .; . . . quoniam ergo in
sacra scriptura quaedam invenimus . . .*), qui oblige à
Anselme à préciser son projet:

> in hac itaque quaestione **haec erit nostra
> intentio,** ut liberum arbitrium simul esse
> cum gratia et cum ea operari in multis mon-
> stremus, sicut illud cum praescientia et
> praedestinatione concordare reperimus[3]

Ce qu'il fait en tenant compte d'un double aspect:

(1) Les graves *objections* soulevées par le langage de
l'Ecriture aussi bien du point de vue de ceux qui exaltent
la liberté de l'homme que de ceux qui la récuissent à
presque rien;

(2) Le *contexte* propre du sujet en question, à savoir la
réflexion préliminaire sur le rapport entre prescience et
prédestination, d'un côté, et libre arbitre, de l'autre.
Sous cet angle les deux parties préliminaires du *De concordia* I-II semblent bien être les *conditions de possibilité*
pour penser solidement le travail simultané (*simul esse cum*

et operari cum) de la grâce et du libre arbitre dans
l'activité *morale de l'homme adulte*, où celui-ci engage en
toute responsabilité son *salut* (d'où l'idée du *mérite*), et
d'autre part la réalité incontournable de la profonde
impuissance morale mille fois témoignée par l'expérience
humaine.[4]

Rapports du *De concordia*
au reste de l'oeuvre d'Anselme

En rédigeant son dernier livre Anselme semble avoir sous
les yeux l'ensemble de son ouvrage précédent. Les références explicites à ses écrits sur la morale ne manquent pas
ni dans la première ni dans la troisième partie du *De concordia*. Mais surtout cette troisième partie fait souvent
allusion, quoique implicitement, aux ouvrages christologiques (*Cur deus homo, De conceptu virginali*). Etant donné
qu'il s'agit de la dernière oeuvre d'Anselme cette insis-
tance donne à penser. Est-ce qu'il a voulu recapituler la
totalité de son oeuvre dans un horizon nouveau et plus
large? A-t-il peut-être profité de l'occasion pour retoucher (ou corriger) quelques sujets examinés auparavant?
Comme il n'y a pas le moindre indice qu'Anselme ait voulu
faire, à l'instar d'Augustin, ses propres *Retractationes*,
ni, d'autre part, il est possible de considérer le *De concordia* comme un simple "collage" de ses écrits précédents,
il ne reste qu'à explorer le texte avec patience et recueil-
lir ses indication afin d'arriver à quelque conclusion
satisfaisante.[5]

On ne fera ici que remarquer les donnés du texte qui
semblent s'imposer presque à première vue:

(1) En ce qui concerne la *structure generale*, il est
frappant de constater le parallélisme entre la trilogie
morale, vouée à examiner les **tres questiones** *sacrae scripturae*, et les trois parties qui structurent le *De concordia*
autour de *la question* posée par le langage de l'Ecriture.
Parallélisme de nom et de contenu:

(a) *De veritate* -- *de praescientia*;

(b) *De libertate arbitrii* -- *de praedestinatione*;

(b) *De casu diaboli* -- *de gratia* (par opposition).

Ceci devient d'autant plus frappant si l'on se souvient de
l'hypothèse émise jadis par Schmitt d'après laquelle aussi

bien le *De veritate* que le *De libertate arbitrii* furent
originairement conçus comme des parties (*Teile*) de *De
concordia*.[6]

(2) Plus en particulier l'examen de la première partie
de *De concordia* montre une claire analogie avec le sujet et
l'ordre du *De veritate*. La référence explicite au *De
veritate* XII, au coeur du *De concordia* I,6 est peut être
l'occasion pour découvrir peu à peu le parallélisme existant
entre les deux oeuvres. C'est le même mouvement ascendant
de pensée qui semble s'y réfleter. Ne pouvant pas le
développer on se borne ici à l'exposer schématiquement:

De veritate	*De concordia*
VII. *Summa Veritas*	
	V. *de aeternitate (praesc.)*
X. *Summa Causa*	
XII. *Summa Iusitia*	VI. *de voluntate (iusta)*
XIII. *Una (Summa) Veritas (actus)*	VII. *de scientia dei causante esse facere)*[7]

(3) Dans *De concordia* III, au contraire, s'imposent les
allusions au *Cur deus homo*. Même si elles ne sont pas
explicites, leur importance apparaît aussi bien dans les
endroits du texte où elles sont placées que par les éléments
doctrinaux qu'elles comportent. Leur place dans la structure du texte est capitale, si l'on tient compte surtout que
les références ont toujours un rapport à l'aspect *historique*
de la réflexion. En fait, à partir du *De concordia* III,6.
On ne peut ici que donner les détails le plus saillants:

(a) Le dernier paragraphe du *De concordia* III,6 montre
bien la référence christologique:

> Ostendimus, ut puto, quomodo non sit super-
> vacaneum homines **ad fidem Christi et ad ea
> quae fides exigit invitare**, quamvis non
> omnes hanc invitationem suscipiant.[8]

Ces lignes ramassent en peu de mots le contenu essentiel du *Cur deus homo*, plus concrètement l'articulation de ses deux livres: le passage de la nécessité de croire dans le Christ (le *credendum* qui exprime le *debitum* de l'invitation chrétienne au salut par la foi: *Cur deus homo* I,23-24) à l'exploration rationnelle (*sola ratione*) de toutes le vérités relatives au mystère de l'homme-Dieu (objet du *Cur deus homo* II). Tel est le rythme entre la *fides Christi* et le *ea quae fides exigit* parfaitement souligné dans cet important *De concordia* III,6.

(b) *De concordia* III,9 fait aussi allusion à des éléments capitaux du *Cur deus homo*. La deuxième raison (*Alia quoque ratio*), donnée par Anselme sur la persévérance de la peine du péché, même après le pardon de la faute (*culpa*), est une synthèse concise de toute sa sotériologie. En rappelant qu'il est impossible de *réconcilier* l'homme pécheur avec Dieu sans la *satisfaction* parfaite, d'une part, et d'autre part, sans l'*heritage* finale de la cité céleste promise à Adam, le texte formule enfin la référence décisive: *A quo autem reconciliari quaeat, non est nisi Christus*. Quiconque connaît *Cur deus homo* II, sait bien que la réflexion anselmienne s'y développe selon un rythme tripartite entre satisfaction, réconcilation et restauration (ici *haereditas*) qui doit être parcouru de façon ascendente et descendente.[9]

(c) *De concordia* III,13, enfin, évoque l'*intentio* initiale du Dieu Créateur. Il suffit de lire ces ligne pour se rappeler la doctrine essentielle du *Cur deus homo* II,1: *Intentio . . . Dei fuit, ut **iustam** faceret atque **beatam** naturam **rationalem** ad **fruendum** se.*

On pourrait aussi citer sans difficulté d'autres références implicites au *Cur deus homo* dans le cours du *De concordia* III,[10] mais il semble préférable de remarquer que, contrairement à la première partie du livre qui suit l'ordre ascendant du *De veritate*, les allusion au *Cur deus homo* II montrent une *inversion* dans la dynamique de la réflexion anselmienne. En effet, *De concordia* III,9-13 s'occupent respectivement de la matière qui apparaît à la fin et au début de *Cur deus homo*. D'abord la *réconciliation* opérée par le Christ (tout ensemble avec la satisfaction et l'héritage/restauration), et ensuite l'*intention* première de Dieu dans sa création. C'est exactement l'ordre inverse à celui du *Cur deus homo* II (intention au début et réconciliation après). Pourquoi? C'est un des énigme, et pas l'un des moins significatifs, qui pose la lecture du *De concordia* tout en exigeant par la suite une analyse détaillée.

Quoiqu'il en soit, il semble se vérifier l'hypothèse initiale: pendant la rédaction du *De concordia* son auteur avait bien sous les yeux l'ensemble de son oeuvre écrite. Pour préciser le *forme* prise par cette *mémoire* dans la même *structure* du *De concordia* les données jusqu'ici apportées semblent insiffusantes. La recherche ultérieure du texte contribuera à préciser les éléments indispensables pour pratiquer une lecture vraiment satisfaisante.

Ceci dit à titre de préalable on peut envisager le développement des deux points essentiel de notre exposé relatifs à la *structure* du texte et à la *méthode* appliquée dans son élaboration.

Sur la structure du texte du *De concordia*

On marquera trois choses:

(1) La *lecture* du texte: point de vue du *lecteur* qui montre comment progresse dans l'intellection du texte qu'il parcourt en suivant l'agencement de ses différentes parties (l'*ordo textus* et les mouvements qui rythment sa lecture);

(2) La *construction* du texte: point de vue du *texte écrit* par son auteur qui lui a donné une forme determinée en le construisant d'une certaine manière, et qui fait qui concrètement le *De concordia* soit irréductible à toutes les autres ouvrages d'Anselme;

(3) La *quaestio* envisagée dans le texte: c'est-à-dire l'objet qu'Anselme a voulu vraiment penser en écrivant de cette façon ce livre à la fin de sa vie. Non pas le *quomodo* mais le *quid* du texte en question.

Quoique les trois aspects soient en fait irrémediablement mêlés, il importe de les envisager séparément pour mieux pénetrer dans le sens du texte et dans l'esprit du dernier Anselme.

La lecture du texte

La tâche essentielle est ici de saisir le sens de l'agencement des trois questions que le lecteur doit parcourir successivement pour prendre connaissance de la lettre du texte et entrer dans son intellection. Pour ce faire il

y a tout avantage à établir un rapport, d'abord, avec
l'ordre du texte du *Cur deus homo* et, ensuite, avec les
mouvements du texte du "triptyque" morale anselmien. Dans
les deux cas, similitudes et différences permettront de
mettre en relief des aspects propres au *De concordia*.

L'*ordo textus*

On sait que *Cur deus homo* I,4 expose les trois éléments
indispensables pour montrer la *ratio necessitatis* de la
rédemption: le *fait* de la destruction du genre humain par
le péché (*omnino perierat*), la *convenance* divine de ne pas
permettre la pleine destruction de son oeuvre créatrice, et
la nécessité (conditionnée par cette convenance) de que Dieu
lui-même liberât personnellement l'homme pécheur.[11]
Il semble clair que ces trois parties dominent tout le
texte mais Anselme semble les accentuer de telle façon, à
travers les deux livres, que leur ordre devient le suivant:
le *factum* du péché (*Cur deus homo* I,11-24) la *nécessité* de
l'incarnation rédemptrice (*Cur deus homo* II,1-15 subordonnée
à l'intention créatrice de Dieu), la *convenance* suprême de
la rédemption fondée dans le *Pactum* du Père et du Fils.
C'est-à-dire c'est *vers* la convenance que tend le mouvement
du texte comme vers son aboutissement pour recevoir *de* la
plénitude trinitaire sa pleine lumière. Ce qui arrive
seulement dans *Cur deus homo* II,16-20, surtout 20.
Si, à partir de ces données, on trace un parallélisme
avec les trois parties du *De concordia* on peut aisément
constater que la structure des trois question implique un
ordre du texte *inverse* à l'ordre des accents soulignés dans
le *Cur deus homo*. En effet, comme ont l'a déjà suggéré
auparavant, le rapport entre les *tres quaestiones* et la
quaestio essentielle du *De concordia* est tel que cette
dernière s'occupe du *fait* (*facere*) de l'acte libre salvifique posé tout ensemble par la grâce et le libre arbitre
(*De concordia* III 1-5) à la fin du livre. C'est donc le
factum possibilité pour penser ce *factum*, envisagent plutôt
la *convenance* à la lumière de la prescience et la *nécessité*
sous l'angle de la prédestination. L'*ordo textus* est donc
le suivant: convenance (première), nécessité (deuxième),
factum (troisième). Exactement l'opposé de l'ordre du *Cur
deus homo*, ce qui aura son importance pour saisir le sens de
ce qui va être dit par la suite.

Les mouvements du texte

C'est maintenant le "triptyque" morale d'Anselme qui servira de point de départ. On a indiqué auparavant la similitude entre le mouvement ascendant du *De veritate* et du *De concordia* I consacrée à la prescience. On doit maintenant ajouter que les autres deux ouvrages de la trilogie, *De libertate arbitrii* et *De casu diaboli*, maintiennent aussi le rythme ascendant de la réflexion. En effet, si le *De veritate* culmine dans la Somme (*Una*) Vérité et Justice, le *De libertate arbitrii* le fait dans la Souveraine Liberté de Dieu, et le *De casu diaboli*, qui a évidemment un parcours particulier, se développe sous l'ombre de la Suprême Béatitude-Justice divine.

Le *Cur deus homo* II avait déjà modifié cet aspect des choses car, si les chapitres 1-15 suivent évidemment un itinéraire ascendant qui culmine dans le *Aperte invenimus Christum* du chapitre 15, les chapitres suivants (16-20) qui constituent l'aboutissement de la réflexion, réalisent l'*inversion* de ce mouvement ce pensée dans le mesure où ils envisagent le mystère de la rédemption à partir de la Trinité où a lieu le pacte éternel du Père et du Fils. C'est donc un mouvement *descendant* qui donne forme et parachève la réflexion sotériologique anselmienne. Et partant la lecture de *Cur deus homo*.

Ceci bien compris, si l'on passe à la lecture du *De concordia* il est clair que le mouvement ascendant est présent seulement domine la troisième (grâce). Avant de le montrer en détail il reste à dire que la deuxième partie, laquelle malgré sa brièveté est le centre du texte, constitue un problème particulier qui ne peut être envisagé de façon satisfaisante, au-delà du problème de la lecture, que comme problème de la construction même du texte. On le verra plus loin.

Voici quelques éléments, schématiques mais nets, pour éclairer ce qu'on a avancé auparavant sur les mouvements à parcourir dans la lecture du texte du *De concordia*.

Il y a une triple lecture possible de ce texte:

(A) Lecture *verticale*: qui peut être parcourue de manière ascendante et descendante (dont on a déjà dit quelques mots);

(B) Lecture *horizontale*: qui prend son sens après la lecture antérieure;

(C) Lecture *circulaire*: qui suppose les lectures précédentes et ajoute l'inversion de leurs mouvements et leur inclusion dans un centre que donne forme à toute la construction du texte. C'est donc une lecture, propre de la deuxième partie, que, comme on l'a déjà dit, ne peut être envisagée que plus tard.

On s'occupera ici des deux premières types de lecture qui permettent d'apprécier, à travers l'itinéraire du texte, la progression faite par le lecteur dans la captation de sa structure et de son sens.

Lecture verticale

Elle tâche de mettre en relief les éléments essentiels et les mouvements propres de chaque question. En fait, la première et la troisième.

Question première (de praescientia): mouvement *ascendant*

(1) Son itinéraire passe de la réalité de l'*acte libre* de l'homme *simul necessarium et spontaneum* (*De concordia* I,1-3) à l'acte *juste* d'abord (droit: *rectus, De concordia* I,6), et ensuite à l'*action divine* qui en est la *cause* (*a deo factore, De concordia* I,7). Mouvement, ascendant qui, en montrant la non répugnance de la prescience divine et du libre arbitre, peut être rendu explicite de la façon suivante:

(a) L'exclusion d'abord de la *vis necessitatis* (*De concordia* I,1) capable de determiner l'activité libre de la volonté (distinction: *necessitas sequens et antecedens*);[12]

(b) L'affirmation de la *vis aeternitatis divinae* (*De concordia* I,5) qui embrasse sans violence tout l'ordre temporel, partant aussi le *futurum de futuro* et le *de re futura* (*De concordia* I,3);

(c) L'inclusion explicite de l'*activité libre et salvifique* de l'homme dans l'intérieur de l'éternité divine (*De concordia* I,6): **nec** *aliquid* **facit** *vis necessitatis* **ubi operatur sola** *electio voluntatis*).

(2) Le mouvement ascendant des sept chapitres de la première partie peut être divisé en deux moments: *De concordia* I,1-3;4-7.[13] Jusqu'au chapitre 3 on parle de la concorde *entre* prescience divine et liberté humaine; à partir du chapitre 4 on tâche d'articuler *en Dieu* la science et la volonté opérative: *cum vult aut facit Deus . . . negari nequit scire quae vult aut facit, et praescire quae volet et faciet*. Le chapitre 7 montre, enfin, l'*indentité* divine de la science et de la causalité en rapport avec l'acte libre de l'homme (*esse est a Dei scientia, a deo factore*). Il importe aussi d'ajouter un certain nombre d'affirmations qui ont son importance au point de vue de l'épistemologie théologique qui est ici en jeu:

(a) Après avoir souligné le *simul esse* de ce qui est nécessaire (*ex deo*) et spontané-libre (*ex homine*) (*De concordia* I,1-3);

(b) On passe à l'affirmation *idem diversa ratione oppositum* (*De concordia* I,4) qui marque la possibilité et la nécessité de penser l'opposition des raisons attribuables à une même chose, lesquelles néanmoins doivent être pensées, en dernière analyse, de façon complémentaire, c'est-à-dire comme *inséparables*;

(c) Enfin, le *simul esse* qui est pensable par opposition par et *à partir* de la créature est vue par et *à partir de Dieu* comme *omnia simul sine motu* (*De concordia* I,5) dans son éternité, ce qui n'exclut pas le rapport de causalité créatrice. Telle est la conclusion de la première partie: *res habent esse ab eius scientia* (*De concordia* I,7).

(3) Le mouvement ascendant commence par la *volonté spontanée* de l'homme pour conclure avec la *libre élection* du bien salvifique (justice), tout ceci rythmé par l'action de Dieu qui *voit tout* dans son éternité (*De concordia* I,5) et *à partir de soi-même* (*De concordia* I,7: *a se*). La concorde donc entre Dieu et l'homme, questionnée dès le début de la première partie, devient ainsi claire: il n'y en a pas contradiction.

On voit de la sorte que cet itinéraire ascendant elève la pensée de la *temporalité* de la créature (liberté-nécessité: *non ex vi necessitatis*) jusqu'a l'*éternité* de la science divin enfin présentée comme cause (*factor-auctor*) de la même action libre temporelle. Il n'est guère difficile d'en conclure que ce même rythme du texte prépare le passage ce la première partie aux deux parties suivantes. De même,

en effet, que la prescience s'ouvre, d'abord, à la volonté
(*De concordia* I,3-4) et enfin à l'*action* (*De concordia* I,7:
facere), de même la considération de la science divine devra
préceder celle de sa volonté qui prédestine (deuxieme
partie) et ensuite celle de son activité qui est don de la
grâce (troisième partie).[14]

Question troisième (de gratia):
mouvement descendant

On accentue ici le *dynamisme opératif* des voluntés
divine et humaine. On passe d'abord d'une considération
presque *intemporelle* (dont on verra plus bas le sense
théologique profond) de leur communion dans l'être et
l'action (*esse cum* -- *operari cum*) à l'exposé de leur
insertion dans le développement de l'*histoire* salvifique
(*dispositio providentiae: De concordia III,6-9), et ensuite
à l'expérience psychologique* propre à l'homme pécheur où
puissance et impuissance se trouvent ensemble (*De concordia*
III,10-13)

(1) La simultanéité initialement affirmée (*De concordia
III,1) devient plus explicite à travers l'action que la
grâce (adiuvans)* exerce sur la rectitude (droiture) du libre
arbitre: *quoniam illam liberum arbitrium non nisi per gratiam praevenientem et subsequentem* **habet** *et* **servat** (*De
concordia* III,4). Ces jeux formes de la *gratia adiuvans* (*De
concordia* III,3) soulignant l'aspect "causal" du don divin.
Les cinq premières chapitres ne font que mettre en relief,
en des formules différentes, cette dynamique de la grâce et
de la liberté tout ensemble.[15]

L'effort de penser la *concordia* sous cet angle trouve
peut-être sa plus saisissante formule dans le chapitre 5 où
il est dit à ce sujet: *nullo intellectu gratia separanda
est (a libero arbitrio).* Cette étonnante formule[16] est à
notre avis l'aboutissement de la réflexion épistemologique
d'Anselme sur le problème de la *concordia*. Tenant compte de
ce qu'on a dit plus haut sur le contenu de la première
partie, on peut l'interpréter en grandes lignes de la
manière suivante:

(a) La même chose (l'acte libre de l'homme) est simul-
tanément (*simul esse*) nécessaire et libre;

(b) Il est malgré tout possible de la penser séparement
selon l'angle qu'on choisit pour l'envisager: *ex libertate*

(per liberum arbitrium) aut ex necessitate (quia futurum).
En ce sens vaut l'affirmation déjà rencontrée: *idem diversa
ratione oppositum* (*De concordia* I,4);

(c) Mais si l'on considère cette chose, *en elle-même
simul nécessaire et libre*, on ne peut aucunement l'envisager
séparemment de l'action divine (le don): *nullo intellectu
separanda.* Aussi bien l'*esse* que le *bonum esse* de l'acte
juste doivent être *pensés simul* comme l'oeuvre de Dieu qui
donne sa grâce, et de l'homme qui la reçoit et la garde.
Communion des deux libertés -- don et réception -- qu'il est
impossible de penser séparément soit du point de vue de
l'être (*esse*), soit de l'agir (*operari*). C'est donc la
seule façon de *penser l'action libre existante*, dans
n'importe quelle différence de temps. (D'où notre expression précédente relative à cette considération "intemporelle," ce qui ne veut pas dire abstraite car elle se réfère
à l'*esse* de l'acte libre créé). En d'autres termes, on ne
se réfère à l'*esse* de l'acte libre de l'homme juste en
dehors de son rapport "existentiel" à la grâce divine qui
agit en lui; de même on ne peut pas penser le don gratuit
que Dieu fait à sa créature rationnelle sans la répose libre
que celle-ci, à son tour, fait à Dieu.

(2) A partir *De concordia* III,6 commence une nouvelle
section que répond à un nouvel effort d'Anselme pour penser
l'harmonie de la grâce et de la liberté.[17] Annoncée par le
De concordia III,4 qui, en montrant comment la grâce aide
ces manières différents, dit:

> Denique cum omnia subiaceant **dispositioni
> Dei, quidquid contingit homini** quod adiuvat
> liberum arbitrium ad accipiendum aut ad ser-
> vandum hanc de qua loquor rectitudinem,
> **totem gratiae imputandum,**[18]

on ouvre une perspective qu'on peut appeler *historique* par
sa référence au plan salvifique divin, et qui se développe
entre *De concordia* III,6-9. C'est le plan de la providence
de Dieu -- qui se décide au niveau de la prédestination dont
parle la deuxième partie -- qui est ici envisagé à la double
lumière biblique de Rm 10 (*De concordia* III,6) et de Rm 8
(centre de la réflexion dans la deuxième partie et auparavant dans *De concordia* I,5).
    L'oeuvre de la providence apparaît dans ce texte
d'Anselme comme un infatigable travail de *culture* (*agricultura Dei*) qui embrasse tous les aspect intérieurs (*cogitationes, voluntates*) et les moyens extérieurs (*auditus,*

lectio . . .) nécessaires et utiles pour mener l'homme à la rectitude. En s'inspirant carrément du texte de Rm 10 Anselme accentue la *dynamique préparatoire et descendante* de la *gratia adiuvans*. En voici un passage particulièrement significatif:

> Sed quod mittuntur gratia est. Quapropter et praedicatio est gratia, quia **gratia est quod descendit, ex gratia**; et auditus est gratia, et intellectus ex auditu est gratia, et rectitudo volendi gratia est. Verum missio, praedicatio, auditus intellectus nihil sunt, nisi velit voluntas quod mens intelligit. Quod voluntas facere nequit, nisi accepta rectitudine. Recte namque vult, cum vult quod debet.[19]

Ainsi donc il y a une connexion gratuite de tout le *processus* de conversion polarisé dans son centre: la *rectitudo*. Ce texte montre donc comment Anselme, dans *De concordia* II, *intervertit* radicalement la perspective ascendante de la première partie: celle-ci va de l'homme temporel et changeant à l'éternité de Dieu où l'on découvre la causalité de sa science; tandis que la troisième partie commence par la *simultanéité* de la grâce et de la liberté, saisies, si l'on peut dire, dans la même *éternité* divine (ce que Dieu voit, veut et fait tout ensemble), pour se développer ensuite, par la considération des différents modes que cette action divine prend dans et à travers la *temporalité historique*. Ainsi le don apparaît comme oeuvre de la providence. Sous cet angle Dieu déroule son projet (*dispositio*: *De concordia* III,4;6; *propositum/providentia*: *De concordia* III,9 ; *intentio*: *De concordia* III,13) parfaitement adapté aux circonstances historiques (*missio, praedicatio, auditus, intellectus*) et à la complexité psychologique (*cogitationes, voluntates*) de le'homme. C'est pourquoi Anselme fait ici recours aux considérations sur le péché original accentuant, d'une part, son aspect négatif (l'*impotentia indebita* coupable, *De concordia* III,7-8) mais surtout, d'autre part, valorisant positivement la temporalité, en montrant pourquoi *persévère* dans ce monde la peine du péché (*De concordia* III,9). Le *simul* de la *concordia* entre grâce et liberté rejoint ici le *non statim* de l'action providentielle, dont le plan oriente la souffrance des hommes vers un *magnum bonum*, un *melius*, qui est illustré par une triple référence: la possibilité du mérite dans la créature, la propagation de la cité céleste, et la pleine fidelité dans la foi au rédempteur-réconciliateur. De telle façon la réception de

I	II	III
vis necessitatis	*evenire in potestate*	*gratia et lib. arb.* *nullo intel. separ.*
vis aeternitatis	*verum sicut erit* *mutab./immutabile*	*dispositio Provid.*
sola electio	*servare iustitiam*	*experiri impotentiam*

Il faut ajouter un quatrième rapport entre la première et la troisième question:

esse rerum a scientia Dei	*facere: a Deo,* ab homine (bonum/malum)

l'*héritage* post-adamique répond à la *satisfaction* acquise par le second Adam,[20] *réconciliateur* de Dieu et de l'homme.

(3) *De concordia* III,10 ouvre la dernière section, reprenant la référence initiale à l'*expérience* de la humaine faiblaisse et expliquant son rapport à l'aide de la grâce, soit que celle-ci diminue la force de la tentation, soit qu'elle augmente l'amour de la droiture.[21]

Le mouvement descendant est ici prolongé et accentué de façon *négative*, en mettant en relief la présence du *mal* dans la même droite volonté: *Sed hoc ut plenius intelligatur, investigandum est,* **unde tam vitiosa et tam prona sit ad malum ista voluntas** (*De concordia* III,13).[22] Anselme arrive même à reconnaître après le péché une certaine nécessité dans la présence du mal dans la liberté naturelle de l'homme: celle-ci en devient *otiosa*. Voici l'important texte de ce même chapitre:

> **Voluntas ergo instrumentum,** cum sponte facta sit iniusta, **post** desertam iustitiam **manet, quantum in ipsa est, necessitate** iniusta et ancilla iniustitiae: quia per se redire nequit ad iustitiam, **sine qua numquam libera est, quia naturalis libertas sine illa otiosa est** .[23]

Le désordre librement causé par le péché s'oppose ainsi à l'ordre initial (*Deus ordinavit has duas voluntates*: *De concordia* III,13) qui répond au plan du Créateur (*Intentio . . . Dei fuit*). On peut donc affirmer que ce dernier chapitre de la section trace deux portraits de l'homme: le première Adam juste, d'une part, et de l'autre, le pécheur. Et à partir de ces deux portraits, on est en mesure d'ébaucher les traits de l'homme juste dans sa *situation actuelle*: l'homme rédimé par la foi et le baptême. C'est la juste, la non-coupable, qui se trouve néanmoins dans un état de misère hérité du péché originel. La persévérance de la peine permet la persévérance dans le bien et donc la possibilité du mérite pour arriver à la cité céleste. Mais cette situation comporte une tension entre les deux *voluntés-affectiones* qu'Anselme développe longement dans ces chapitres: la présence d'une *voluntas iustitiae* tout ensemble avec une *voluntas commodi* qui éprouve (*experimentum*) le désordre qu'elle ne doit pas accepter (*consentire*).[24]

On perçoit bien, nous croyons, comment le mouvement descendant qui a commencé pour marquer, au niveau de la réflexion, l'indissoluble unité de la grâce et de la liberté dans l'acte de l'homme juste, doit enfin intégrer dans sa situation actuelle un élément négatif hérité du péché originel et permis et reemployé par l'action providentielle en fonction d'un *melius*, d'un *magnum bonum*, qui n'est autre que celui de la rédemption. C'est donc à la lumière du second Adam qu'il faut penser la *concordia* de la grâce et de la liberté.

Lecture horizontale

Dans un première approche elle se borne en mettre en rapport les trois question du *De concordia*, dont chacune peut être divisée, selon les analyses précedentes, en trois parties. La lecture horizontale précisement les relie en montrant leurs connexions et aussi les oppositions. On ajoute, même si le contenu de la deuxième partie n'a pas encore été détaillé, ce qui correspond à cette partie. Ceci aura l'avantage de préparer la suite de notre réflexion relative à la construction du texte qui développe précisement la question deuxième sur la prédestination.

On propose ici simplement le schéma opposé qui, après les pages précédentes, semble suffisement clair. C'est précisement l'analyse de la deuxième partie qui permettra d'éclairer ce passage. Mais cela suppose qu'on aborde le deuxième moment de notre étude sur la structure du *De concordia* qui a affaire à la construction du texte.

La construction du texte

Le point de vue du texte écrit est ici primordial, son auteur lui a donné une forme déterminée en le construisant d'une certaine façon qui fait précisement l'originalité de cet ouvrage. En fait, *De concordia*, fruit du dernier Anselme, semble irréductible à tout le reste de son oeuvre.

On tâchera de montrer ces deux trait saillants:

(a) L'*inversion* tout à fait originale des perspectives des deux autres questions qu'il opère dans le chapitre 3. Plus exactement comment fait-il le passage, grâce à l'étude de la prédestination, du mouvement ascendant de la première partie au mouvement descendant de la troisième. D'est le fruit d'une opération complexe de pensée qui se reflète dans la lecture du texte, c'est pourquoi il nous faudra commencer par là;

(b) La *circularité* du texte, c'est-à-dire la présence de
la deuxième partie au *centre* même du livre, montre l'intention d'Anselme de faire de la prédestination *l'un des
centres* (pas le seul comme l'on verra plus loin) du *De
concordia*. Mieux encour, il est le centre *textuel* dont
l'effet est de rendre *circulaire inversion* des mouvements de
lecture proposés par les autres deux parties. Il s'agit
d'un effort de pensée pour saisir la réalité de l'acte libre
à partir de son centre *théologique*, ce qui ne peut se faire
que, comme on va le montrer, par une sorte d'"irradiation"
et d'"absorption" par rapport au centre dit.

Voici l'ordre à suivre: (1) *lecture* de la question
deuxième: rappel de ses éléments principaux; (2)
l'*inversion* du texte; (3) la *circularité* du texte.

Lecture de la deuxième partie

Cette partie consacrée à la prédestination est brève
mais décisive. Le rapport à la première question est
clairement exposé:

> Ad quod per ea quae **supra** disseruimus, sicut
> in sequentibus patebit, **non parum profeci-
> mus**; . . . omnia illa quibus **supra** monstra-
> vimus liberum arbitrium praescientiae non
> repugnare, **pariter** ostendunt, illius prae-
> destinationi concordare [25]

Tout le contenu de la première partie vaut donc également
pour la deuxième. Certaines particularités méritent
néanmoins d'être rélevées:

(a) *De concordia* II,1 est en rapport avec *De concordia*
I,5 en assumant la perspective théologique de Rm 8, où
l'éternité est envisagée à la lumière du plan salvifique
fique centré dans le Christ: c'est le *propositum dei* (ce
qui, en termes du *Cur deus homo* I,8-9 est le *decretum* ou la
volonté absolue de Dieu), traduit par *praeordinatio* et
praestitutio (voir aussi *Cur deus homo* I,5: *constituere
apud se inmutabiliter*). Rien n'échappe à ce *plan salvifique
christologique*. C'est là le sens profond de la question
deuxième et de tout le problème théologique posé par le *De
concordia*;

(b) *De concordia* II,2 accentue deux aspects: (1) il
articule la *volunté permissive* de Dieu avec sa volonté

absolue afin de penser la relation du mal et du bien à
l'intérieur de plan salvifique divin; (2) il montre que
autant *la possibilité que l'intérêt (specialis)* de ce plan
s'adressent au bien salvifique. A l'égard du mal il n'y a
qu'une attitude *négative*: *permittere* est traduit par *non
emollire, non liberare, non corrigere*;

(c) Une fois la question posée, *De concordia* II,3, sans
conteste le plus important de la deuxième partie, evisage
enfin le problème de la *concordia* entre prédestination et
libre arbitre sous la base de l'absence de *discordia* entre
préscience et prédestination: *Dubitari autem non debet quia
eius praescientia et praedestinatio non discordant; sed
sicut praescit, ita quoque praedestinat.*

Anselme ne se prive pas de reéxposer le contenu de la
premiere partie mais suivant un *ordre* qui ne correspond pas
littéralement à celui qui est suivi dans les pages précedentes. Dans une certaine mesure on doit même dire qu'il en
fait l'inversion. On ne peut pas nier tout au moins qu'il
commence à énumérer les éléments essentiels pour penser la
prédestination à partir du *salut*: Dieu ne prédestine le
juste au salut sans y inclure sa liberté:

Nam neque praescit Deus neque praedestinat
iustum futurum ex necessitate. **Non enim
habet iustitiam,** qui eam non servat **libera
voluntate.**[26]

Anselme expose donc les éléments relatifs à la
prédestination à partir de la connexión *justice-liberté*,
qui répond au *De concordia* I,6. Ce qui, à la lumière du
texte de Rm 8 (cité d'abord dans *De concordia* I,5) veut
dire: Dieu voit le plan et veut un "monde de justes libre-
ments tels." C'est la *détermination* de la société des
saints (Rm 8: *vocati sancti*) *visualisée* par conformité à
l'image du Fils.
    Il s'ensuit que les actions voulues par Dieu (que Dieu
veut qui soient) doivent arriver: *necesse sit fieri.* Il
n'est pas question de coaction, propre à la nécessité
antécédente, mais de nécessité conséquente. La raison:
*Non enim ea Deus, quamvis praedestinat, facit voluntatem
cogendo aut voluntati resistendo, sed in sua illa potestate
dimittendo.*[27] Par conséquent Anselme articule en deuxième
terme *liberté et nécessité*, objet d'analyse du *De concordia*
I,1-3.

En troisième lieu, ce caractère spontané, non nécessaire, de l'action libre constitue le *verum sicut est*, objet
de la prescience divine et donc aussi de la prédestination
inmuable. Le plan divin détermine ce qui est, et en ces
sens *distingue* (n'articule pas mais oppose) ce qui est
spontané de ce qui est nécessaire (aut necessitate aut
spontaneum). Cette doctrine est présente dans *De concordia*
I,1;2;3;5.

On distingue aussi, enfin, entre l'*immutabilité* de la
prédestination éternelle et la *mutabilité* de ce qui est
temporel: *tamen in **tempore** aliquando **antequam** sit mutari
potest.* La réflexion revient ici au *De concordia* I,5 sur
l'éternité.

Ces deux aspects semblent épuiser le contenu de la
deuxième question. Il reste à developper la *"causalité" de
la science divine (esse **ab** eius scientia)*, ce qui ouvre le
chemin de la réflexion vers la troisième question qui
s'occupe de la *concordia* entre grâce et liberté. On l'a
déjà souligné, cette dernière partie met l'accent sur l'*agir*
divin (*operari, facere*), sur l'opération gratuite de Dieu en
toute sa complexité et sur sa simultanéité avec l'agir divin
de l'homme: *liberum arbitrium **simul** esse **cum** gratia et cum
ea operari.*

L'inversion du texte

Ce qui précède permettra de saisir le sens et
l'originalité de l'inversion opérée dan le chapitre 3 de
cette question. Elle fait le point entre le mouvement
ascendant de la première partie et le mouvement descendant
de la troisième, entre la *scientia **a** deo* et la *gratia
adiuvans **ad** habendum et servandum rectitudinem*: ce serait
l'aspect à souligner dans une lecture *horizontale* de cette
deuxième partie. Mais si l'on prend la peine de consulter
le graphique de la page ?, on se rendra compte que la dite
lecture, en mettant en rapport les contenus des trois questions, ne répond pas à l'ordre d'après lequel ce chapitre 3
sur la prédestination expose ces contenus. En effet, tandis
que le *evenire in potestate* occupe la première place du
schéma en correspondance avec la *vis necessitatis* de la
première partie, et d'autre part, avec la *gratia et libero
arbitrio . . . separandum* de la troisième, il apparaît comme
le deuxième moment de l'ordre de la deuxième partie, après
salus et libertas.

Ceci ne semble compréhensible que si, dans son effort
pour saisir la "causalité" de la science divine (à la
lumière christologique de Rm 8) comme *decretum providentiae*,

On peut donc proposer schéma 1 opposé, qui montre la réexposition de la doctrine en fonction de la prédestination:

Cette réordination, fondée dans la même lettre du texte, devient plus convaincante si l'on établit un rapport avec le rythme *De concordia* I.   On y avait remarqué les accents dans schema 2 opposé.

Or, il est difficile de nier le parallélisme entre les deux parties comme dans schema 3 opposé.

Schema 1

§ salus et libertas   >   **servare** iustitiam

§ libertas et necessitas   >   **eveniunt** (in **potestate** dimittendo)

§ spontaneum **aut** necessarium >   verum **sicut erit** (est)

§ mutabile **et** inmutabile   >   **tempus** et aeternitas (**mutari potes**)

Schema 2

§ *simul esse*: necessité et liberté

§ *diversa ratione oppositum*: à partir de Dieu ou de l'homme (*cum/sine motu*)

§ *esse ab eius scientia*: la "causalité" de la science divine

Schema 3

§ *simul esse*   ≈   salus **et** libertas (servare)
                                 libertas **et** necessitas (evenire)

§ *diversa ratione oppositum* ≈   spontaneum **aut** necessarium
                                 mutabile **aut** immutabile (mutari
                                 potest/ non potest)

Anselme attire l'attention d'abord sur ce qui est le noeud de sa réflexion: la liberté, sans laquelle il ne peut pas penser la justice salvifique, concue comme puissance qui échappe à toute nécessité et toute contrainte.

C'est seulement après la lecture descendante de la troisième partie que l'on peut et, nous croyons, que l'on doit retoucher l'ordre textuel du *De concordia* III,3 et donner la priorité à l'acte sur la puissance (le *verum sicut erit/est* occupe le centre du graphique en correspondance avec l'éternité, d'une part, et à la providence, de l'autre). On expose ainsi mieux la liaison entre *De concordia* II et III; on commence par montrer l'acte juste comme l'oeuvre simultanée de la grâce et de la liberté; c'est seulement à la fin que l'on montre la *voluntas* dans toute sa complexité psychologique (*instrumentum-affectiones-usus*), grâce à laquelle elle devient quasi *causa sui* (*instrumentum se ipsum movens*, dit *De concordia* III,11), en s'ouvrant d'ailleurs à la contamination du mal, même dans la situation de celui qui est juste.

Ce texte semble donc à me-chemin entre les deux autres questions:

(1) Il les relie comme un pont qui fait le passage entre les deux mouvements;

(2) Il avance le sens du mouvement descendant de la troisième partie en identifiant le début (le salut) et la fin (la volunté);

(3) Mais il accentue l'importance de thème de la liberté à travers l'expression pleine de sens: *in potestate dimittere*, dont la profondeur demanderait un effort analytique que l'on ne peut pas entreprendre ici.

Voilà donc le sens de la prédestination: Dieu dans son éternité a fixé auprès de soi (*constituit apud se inmutabiliter: De concordia* I,5) cela même qui, chez l'homme, peut être changé avant de se faire. Autrement dit, il a voulu introduire dans son plan salvifique certaines actions qui sont le fruit de la libre puissance octroyée à l'homme (*apud hominem, priusquam fit mutari potest*).

On perçoit mieux maintenant en quel sens on a parlé d'inversion originale du texte. C'est l'*homme libre* qui est ici pensé, *en direction du Christ* second Adam et parfait exemplaire de liberté. C'est un être avec *la possibilité et la puissance* de décider de ses actes bons et mauvais, qui est voulu par Dieu à l'intérieur d'un ordre qu'il voit et veut de toute éternité. Ce qui nous amène au troisième point de cet analyse.

La circularité du texte

Ce qui precède nous permet de mieux prendre conscience du fait que la deuxième partie sur la prédestination est vraiment le *centre* du texte. En quelque sorte on pourrait dire qu'elle lui donne sa *forme*. Anselme l'a voulu ainsi et ce faisant il s'est écarté de la méthode suivie dans *Cur deus homo* pour suivre celle de *De conceptu virginali*.

En effet, si l'on peut soumettre le *Cur deus homo* à une double lecture diachronique et synchronique, on ne peut pas dire pour autant que la construction de sa forme textuelle soit autre chose que diachronique. Il n'y pas de centre textuel qui attire tout vers lui-même à travers le double mouvement ascendant et descendant. Les deux mouvements, qui se trouvent en fait dans le *Cur deus homo*, font partie de la lecture successive, donc diachronique, qui débouche dans le chapitre 20 du deuxième livre. A ce moment précis le lecteur peut avoir une vue d'ensemble simultanée, donc synchronique, de ce qu'Anselme l'a amené à penser (l'icône du Christ). Il y a donc une lecture synchronique mais il n'y a pas une construction synchronique du texte.

Toute différente est la construction du *De conceptu virginali* qui -- c'est son originalité et son apport méthodique -- pose au centre du texte la figure du Christ, l'*homo natus de virgine sancta* (IX-XXI), et fait tourner tout autour la problématique du péché originel, soit en Adam, soit dans ses descendants (I-VIII; XXII-XXIX).[28]

C'est dans ce dernier sens qu'Anselme semble procéder dans le *De concordia*. Son texte a donc une *construction à forme synchronique* dont le centre est occupé par la deuxième question vouée à la prédestination.

L'effet de cette construction se fait sentir sur la lecture du texte. Elle devient *circulaire* à partir due texte lui-même. Son centre est le lieu d'origine et d'attirance dans la mesure où la *prédestination éternelle dans le Christ est le principe théologique* (donc le centre) *à partir* duquel et *vers* lequel il faut penser tout le problème de la *concordia*. C'est aussi dans ce sens qu'on a pu parler plus haut d'"absorption" et d'"irradiation." C'est un aspect des choses qu'il faut bien garder à l'esprit lorsqu'on envisage le problème de la liberté dans le *De concordia*.

Le contenu du texte: la *quaestio*

Dans ce dernier paragraphe sur la structure du texte il faut faire face à un problème délicat. Comment mêttre ensemble deux affirmations apparemment incompatibles: d'une part, le contenu principal, de *De concordia*, sa *quaestio* centrale, se trouve dans les cinq premières chapitres de la troisième partie (grâce et libre arbitre), et d'autre part, le "centre textuel" est la deuxième partie sur la prédestination.

C'est que l'on propose ici c'est de maintenir la validité des deux assertions et, plus encore, de montrer que dans leur union se trouve la clé pour la dernière intelligence du *De concordia*.

On tâchera de saisir, dans la mesure du possible, ce qu'Anselme a voulu penser en écrivant de cette façon le *De concordia* à la fin de sa vie. Après le *quomodo* du texte, c'est son *quid* qui doit nous occuper maintenant, autrement dit, le contenu de pensée qu'il propose en dernière instance.

Deux choses sont à souligner: (a) le sens de l'*Alliance néotestamentaire*, expression qui semble répondre parfaitement à la *concordia* entre grâce et liberté envisagée par l'auteur; (b) le sens *autobiographique* exprimé dans le *De concordia*, ce qui explique la référence constante de ce livre au reste de l'oeuvre du Docteur Magnifique.

En unissant les deux aspects on aura peut-être le portrait d'Anselme de Cantorbéry à la fin de sa vie. Le dernier Anselme se pense lui-même à la fin de sa vie, et aussi la totalité de sa vie à partir de cette fin, dans le moment d'entrer, pour ainsi dire, dans l'éternité (signée par la prédestination éternelle dans le Christ qu'il vit dan l'Esprit), moment qui coincide en fait avec ce livre qu'il est en train d'écrire. Voilà donc une véritable récapitulation théologique de la vie d'Anselme élaborée par son auteur à la fin de ses écrits. C'est, nous croyons, le véritable contenu de pensée du *De concordia*. Comme cela risque de surprendre quelque peu on tâchera de le montrer le plus clairement possible dans les limites de ce travail.

Le sens de l'Alliance

Les remarques précédentes invitent à admettre que:

(1) Les deux premières question du *De concordia* sont les *conditions de possibilité* pour penser solidement le travail

simultané (*simul esse et operari*) de la grâce et du libre arbitre dans l'activité juste (droite) de l'homme adulte, où celui-ce engage en toute responsabilité son salut (idée du mérite). C'est là donc la vraie question soulevée par l'Ecriture qu'Anselme veut explorer à la fin de sa vie dans le *De concordia* (objet de la deuxième partie);

(2) L'analyse du mouvement descendant de la troisième partie a montré l'importance de ses cinq premières chapitres qui exposent, dans une sorte de considération "intemporelle," l'impossibilité de penser l'*action* libre et juste de l'homme *existant* autrement que comme une *concordia* (dans l'*esse* et l'*operari*) entre la grâce, don de l'Esprit, et le libre arbitre humain. On pense donc l'action libre existante, dans n'importe quelle différence de temps, dans son rapport essentiel au don en dehors duquel elle devient intelligible (et vice versa): *nullo intellectu separanda.*

On souligne donc ici tout ensemble:

(1) La *supratemporalité* de l'acte libre et juste, en des termes plus bibliques, son caractère eschatologique. C'est un acte historique ouvert à l'éternité, ou si l'on préfère, un acte historique par lequel l'éternité se fait chemin dans l'histoire;

(2) Son caractère aussi *pneumatologique* car c'est par le don de l'Esprit, souvent cité dans cette troisième partie,[29] que l'homme est rendu capable de réaliser son salut de façon dynamique par la *fides recta* ou *fides viva*, plénitude de la rectitude dont le déroulement historique (l'*agricultura Dei* du chapitre 6) ne fera que souligner son importance;[30]

(3) Son caractère aussi *christologique*, dans la mesure où, comme le montre *De concordia* III,6-9, c'est l'*héritage* du second Adam qui intéresse ici Anselme. Des trois aspects de la rédemption apportée par le Christ: satisfaction, réconciliation, héritage (restauration dans le second Adam) c'est le dernier qui attire ici son attention. Rien de plus normal. Après avoir étudié dans le *Cur deus homo* la restauration comme culmination de l'oeuvre sotériologique, Anselme se tourne dans le *De concordia* vers cette restauration pour la penser, non pas dans la tête (le Christ), mais dans ceux qui en sont les bénéficiaires: les hommes rédimés, ses héritiers, et ses frères.[31]

Ces trois aspects semblent répondre à des éléments essentiels de la alliance biblique telle que l'expose le

Nouveau Testament. C'est donc bien dans ce sens qu'il faut comprendre l'effort d'Anselme pour penser la *concordia* entre grâce et liberté.

Le reste du rythme ascendant de la troisième partie expose le déroulement temporel de cette action pneumatologique dans la mesure où le don de l'Esprit entre précisement dan l'histoire de chaque nomme et de tous les hommes. Mais, contrairement au *De conceptu virginali* qui expose les trois étapes historiques (Adam, le Christ, les descendents d'Adam) dont le centre -- textuel et objectif à la fois -- est le Christ, le dernier Anselme pense surtout le rapport "supra-temporel" (eschatologique) des deux libertés (de l'Esprit et de l'homme) dans le déroulement possible de l'histoire humaine, conçue plutôt comme drame individuel que comme aventure universelle. Ceci explique pourquoi, dans son mouvement descendant, il envisage l'action historique providentielle et l'expérience négative du péché et de l'impuissance qui s'ensuit, à la lumière et à partir du rapport indissoluble entre grâce et libre arbitre. Ceci explique aussi pourquoi il a séparé les deux centres de son libre: son centre objectif, dont le véritable contenu de pensée est l'acte de l'homme juste, héritier du Christ par la présence agissante en lui du don de l'Esprit (cet homme juste étant, avant tout, Anselme lui-même). Mais, ne pouvant pas penser cette relation eschatologique de l'histoire personnelle des hommes (et avant tout, de la sienne) que par rapport à la prédestination dans le Christ qui en est l'origine et la raison d'être, c'est donc cette prédestination qui doit étre le centre textuel du libre et de la réflexion.

On pourrait peut-être exprimer simplement tout ceci en disant que la prédestination est le centre *théologique* du texte tandis que le don de l'Esprit agissant dans l'homme juste est son centre *théologale*: c'est la *fides viva* qui est en fait le vrai objet de pensée du *De concordia*.

Le *De concordia* comme autobiographie théologique

Il faut franchir un dernier pas, le plus difficile à mettre en lumière. Les remarques initiales ont néanmoins montré que, pensant la rédaction de son livre, son auteur avait sous les yeux l'ensemble de son oeuvre écrite. Le problème était alors de préciser la *forme* prise par cette *mémoire* dans la structure même du *De concordia*. En ce qui concerne le sens de l'Alliance, on a d'ailleurs mis en évidence sa forme eschatologique, pneumatologique et christologique (héritage). Il reste à ajouter sa forme autobiographique, ce qui revient à dire que dans la troisième partie de ce livre Anselme pense, *à la fin* de sa vie et *à partir* de cette fin (c'est-à-dire lorsqu'il écrit), la totalité de son aventure personnelle et ceci dans un double sens:

(1) En *descendant* vers ses origines humains (mouvement descendant de la troisième partie à partir de son centre objectif). Autrement dit, Anselme de Cantorbéry se pense à partir de Cantorbéry (quand il écrit *De concordia*) et descend vers le Bec (l'action providentielle ou *agricultura Dei*) et enfin ver Aosta (où il a pu faire en toute intensité l'expérience négative du péché et de l'impuissance qui en a été la conséquence). Ceci se manifeste d'autant mieux qu'on pratique en même temps la lecture horizontale et verticale du texte comme il a été exposé plus haut;

(2) En *ascendant* vers ses origines divines. C'est-à-dire, en passant du centre objectif au centre textuel, Anselme replonge l'expérience personnelle de sa vie dans l'Esprit du Christ, dans la prédestination éternelle qui, pour ainsi dire, fait partie, d'après la foi chrétienne dont témoigne l'Ecriture (Rm 8), de la *vie même de Dieu*. C'est le pacte de la dernière partie du *Cur deus homo* qui se déploie ici en toute son ampleur.

Ce retour de la troisième à la deuxième partie ne doit pas être vu comme une simple retour "en arrière," mais comme un mouvement ascendant, *vers l'avant*, dans la mesure où le dernier Anselme sait d'expérience qu'il est aux portes de l'éternité et qu'il va enfin avoir la pleine révélation et la vocation divine dans le Christ qui a signé la Création et sa création dès toute éternité. Mieux que toute autre chose, ceci montre le sens circulaire de la lecture exigée par la structure même du texte du *De concordia*. Ce point final à partir duquel Anselme est en train de penser fait l'union des deux lectures, ascendante et descendante, en donnant la *primauté au mouvement ascendant* qui, du point de vue de l'expérience de l'homme juste, est la seule façon de vivre le don qui descend de Dieu. A l'opposé, sa façon de vivre le mouvement descendant est celle du péché qui le plonge de plus en plus dans un abîme sans fond[32] qui correspond précisément à l'absence (par rejet) du don de Dieu dans l'Esprit. C'était le problème du *De casu diaboli* envisagé alors dans une autre perspective.

On pourra peut-être rendre plus claire cette circularité du principe et de la fin dans la forme du texte et dans sa lecture, en se souvenant d'un axiome employé plus tard par la scholastique médiévale, et qui a marqué de son sceau toute la réflexion morale: *finis est primum in intentione et ultimum in executione*. Le dernier Anselme fait et pense l'expérience du don de la grâce dans le moment de sa plénitude finale (*ultimum in executione*) qui est précisement le moment de réjoindre son principe auquel il a été destiné par Dieu (*primum in intentione*).

Il resterait à ajouter que, ce faisant, Anselme rejoint la perspective *trinitaire* de sa réflexion théologique inaugurée dans le *Monologion*. L'union de premier et du dernier dans la vision circulaire de l'eschatologie finale semble fort bien indiquée pour nous introduire dans la vie même de Dieu qui se révèle à l'homme comme éternellement sellée par la prédestination de la création dans le Christ. Autant dire que toute la création pointe vers le Christ qui lui donne sa pleine signification (*signum*) -- ce qui correspond à la première partie du *De concordia* -- mais que ceci n'est réalisable que par le don eschatologique de son Esprit lequel, en divinisant l'homme juste, le fait en quelque sorte entrer dans l'éternité divine -- c'est la *res* pensée par Anselme dans *De concordia* II. La prédestination dans le Christ par le *propositum divinum* (du Père) apparaît comme la source où tout le reste s'origine et prend sens. C'est une nouvelle manière de penser le pacte du *Cur deus homo*, source trinitaire du salut des hommes, qui peut être approché, comme le montre le texte même du *De concordia* dans sa structure et dans la lecture qui s'ensuit, comme une circulation de vie (une *vis*, comme dit le *Monologion*) dont le centre est tout ensemble principe et fin, et fin parce que principe. Affirmation énigmatique qui ouvre la possibilité d'explorer la vie divine en elle-même, c'est-à-dire les "processions" et, à sa suite et comme leur prolongement, les rapports de "causalité" que ce Dieu Trinité qui aime les hommes entretient avec toute sa création. En d'autres termes, le dernier Anselme nous renvoit aussi à son début, le *De concordia* . . . rejoint de manière originale la matière du *Monologion*. On pourrait aller plus loin et demander si Anselme n'a, en fait et sans le dire explicitement, rétouché ou corrigé la méthode de théologie trinitaire exposée dans son première ouvrage.

Quoiqu'il en soit il semble clair que, au point de vue de la méthodologie anselmienne telle qu'elle jaillit de son texte, le *De concordia* se trouve au-delà de ce qu'il avait écrit dans sa trilogie morale, dans ses oeuvres christologiques (*Cur deus homo* et *De conceptu virginali*) et peut-être aussi même dans ses oeuvres théologiques (*Monologion* et *Proslogion*). Ce qui apparaître mieux à la lumière du dernier point qui reste à développer.

Réflexion herméneutique

Ce dernier paragraphe tirera les conclusions de ce qui précède. La lecture du texte du *De concordia* nous a peu à peu dévoilé la méthode appliquée par Anselme lui-même dans la construction de son texte. C'est en quelque sorte l'*acte créateur* d'Anselme, penseur et écrivain, qui jaillit de nos analyses. Dans la même mesure c'est un essai sur l'art de l'interprétation (des textes) qui sera le dernier mot de cette étude.

Pour y aboutir on ne fera que synthétiser les grandes lignes de notre démarche qui, dans la recherche de la structure du *De concordia*, a pris successivement en compte les points de vue du lecteur (la lecture), du texte (sa construction ou sa forme), et du contenu (la *quaestio* pensée par l'auteur). Les deux premières aspects ont trait au *quomodo* du livre en question, tandis que le dernier envisage son *quid*, le problème étudié. Une telle recherche semble jeter une pénétrante lumière non seulement sur le *De concordia* mais sur l'ensemble de l'oeuvre écrite d'Anselme, dans la mesure où l'on perçoit beaucoup mieux l'évolution qu'il a subi dans la façon d'écrire ses livres. C'est ce qu'il nous reste à mettre en évidence pour mieux saisir la valeur de nos conclusions.

Voici donc les divers moments de la réflexion herméneutique ici proposée:

Lecture diachronique et synchronique

Il faut bien prendre à la lettre ces deux termes. Les textes d'Anselme se prêtent à cette double lecture, successive ou simultanée, de son contenu. Parcourir peu à peu la démarche de l'oeuvre avec l'auteur lui-même (lecture diachronique) ou s'efforcer de tirer au clair la vue d'ensemble qui ressort du texte (lecture synchronique).

Mais cette double lecture ne signifie pas nécessairement que la double perspective se trouve dans le texte écrit. En fait, Anselme a écrit des textes à forme diachronique jusqu'a *De conceptu virginali*. Mais ces textes se prêtent à la double lecture indiquée. Et ceci est valable, même si ces textes diachroniques sont construits de telle façon qu'ils soient signés par le double rythme ascendant et descendant. Le cas le plus typique semble être le *Cur deus homo* dont *Cur deus homo* II,15-16 montre l'*inversion de la lecture* dans le moment où l'on passe du mouvement ascendant au mouvement descendant. Comme on l'a déjà dit, le *Cur deus*

AETERNITAS (ALLIANCE — PACTUM)

I. *Praescientia*

II. *Praedestinatio*

III. *Gratia*

causa exemplaris
Filus |voluntas/*pia*
vocatio

causa efficiens
Pater |voluntas absoluta/*decretum*
propositum

causa finalis
Spiritus |voluntas operativa/*permisi*
missio

A Dei scientia

Iustitia (*Rom 8: 2us Adam*)

Gratia *adiuvans*: anteced./conseq.

Lib. arb. (electio):
iust.—voluntas

Gratia: iust.—lib. arbit.
(*meritum*)

Aeternitas
(vis aetern.)

iustitiam (ad Xtum)

evenire (esse)

verum sicut erit,
mutabile antequam . . .

in potestate (ex Adamo)

Dispositio Providentiae
(Historia—cultura)

.verbum
.Scriptura] *redemptio*:
.ratio — satisfactio
— reconcil.
— haereditas
(Civ. Cae 1.0)

instrumentum

Voluntas |affectiones
usus

Necessitas: antechapitre/consequens
(vis necessit.)

servare

evenire: in potestate
dimittere

Praeschapitre: res (aliquid) —
lib. arbit.
(*1us Adam*)

Intentio Creatoris et peccatum:
impotentia-servitus-otiosa
(*filii Adae*)

homo est une oeuvre à structure diachronique dont on peut finalement (II,20) faire la lecture synchronique.

Construction diachronique ou synchronique du texte

C'est à partir du *De conceptu virginali* qu'Anselme de Cantorbéry est arrivé à écrire un texte à forme synchronique. On y trouve un *centre du texte* autour duquel tourne l'ensemble de la question ou des question examinées. En ce sens, la conception virginale est centre par rapport à la complexe problématique du péché originel.

La construction synchronique ainsi centralisée permet une lecture *circulaire* qui englobe les deux mouvements ascendant et descendant et qui exige de les pratiquer à partir et en fonction du dit centre. Il est clair que le première approche du texte est soumis aux avatars d'une première lecture diachronique, mais la vraie intellection du texte, et donc le sens circulaire des mouvements, n'apparaît que dans la perspective proprement synchronique.

Le *De concordia* semble sans doute suivre les pas de la découverte acquise dans le *De conceptu virginali*. Sous cet angle, c'est incontestablement sa deuxième partie sur la prédestination qui est le centre du texte.

Dédoublement du centre: le texte et la *quaestio*

La nouveauté du *De concordia* consiste dans le dédoublement du centre. Il maintient, on vient de le dire, le *centre textuel* et dans ce sens il donne à l'ensemble écrit une forme synchronique. Mais cette construction ainsi centralisée est au service d'un objet de pensée qui ne coincide pas entièrement avec le centre textuel. La *concordia* de la grâce et du libre arbitre est ici le véritable *centre objectif* de la pensée anselmienne. Son attention est attirée pas la *Nouvelle Alliance*, oeuvre du don de l'Esprit qui transforme la liberté de l'homme pour en faire un *homme-dieu* (à l'instar et à la suite de l'homme-Dieu étudié dans le *Cur deus homo*). C'est l'*héritage* du second Adam qui est ici en question.

Mais ce centre objectif doit en quelque sorte se subordonner au centre textuel, même au point de vue de la lecture et de la pensée. La lecture circulaire impose d'envisager la dite *concordia* comme allant *vers* le centre qui est la prédestination dans le Christ, et dont le don eschatologique de l'Esprit reçoit son sens et sa plénitude. Il faut donc donner sa primauté au *mouvement ascendant* de la lecture,

autrement dit, il faut penser le centre objectif à la
lumière et en fonction du centre textuel d'où il tire sa
pleine intelligibilité. Passage de l'histoire, divinisée
par la rédemption du Fils et la grâce de l'Esprit, à
l'éternité qui se dévoile ainsi comme principe et origine de
tout don (création et grâce) et comme fin vers lequel tout
tend.

Unité de principe et de fin qui est, plus que jamais, la
situation d'Anselme au moment d'écrire son *De concordia*. Le
dernier Anselme, l'Anselme de Cantorbéry, est celui qui en
écrivant cette ouvrage difficile, nous livre en même temps:

(1) Sa vue d'ensemble sur l'Alliance Nouvelle (la *concordia*), autrement dit, sur l'homme divinisé dans
l'Esprit[33] : vie *théologale*;

(2) Et sa conscience pleinement mûrie de l'acte créateur
du théologien, en donnant à son livre les traces d'un texte
autobiographique écrit à la fin de sa vie: vie *théologique*.

Ce faisant il a peut-être parfaitement unifié les deux
éléments en montrant, *in actu exercito*, que la conscience
noétique n'est guère séparable de la conscience éthique, et
que le théologien ne parvient à la plénitude de son métier
que lorsqu'il pense et se pense comme instrument de
l'Esprit, comme un moment essentiel du travail de la grâce
dans la divinisation des hommes.

Notes

[1] *De concordia* III,14: Schmitt II,288,14-16.

[2] *Proslogion* I,1-2: Schmitt I,100-02.

[3] *De concordia* III,1: Schmitt II,264,10-13. On trouve
la même idée dans *De concordia* III,5: Schmitt II,269,2-7:
Si bene considerentur quae dicta sunt, aperte cognoscitur
quia **cum aliquid dicit sacre scriptura** pro gratia . . .
neque cum loquitur pro libero arbitrio . . . sicut videtur
illis qui **hanc faciunt quaestionem**. Ita quippe **intelligenda
sunt dicta divina**, ut . . . Les chapitres 6 et 7
développent cette perspective en se référant aux invitations
(*invitat*) et reproches (*arguit*) adressés par l'Ecriture aux
hommes libres.

[4] L'idée de l'adulte est présente dans *De concordia*
III,2 (Schmitt II,264,17-18: postquam intelligibilem habet

aetatem) et reprise dans *De concordia* III,3. Mais on peut déjà la retrouver dans *De concordia* I,6: Schmitt II,256, 6-7: Pro illo autem arbitrio tantum et pro illa libertate ista **ventilatur quaestio,** sine quibus homo **salvari nequit, postquam potest illis uti.**

5 Certains auteurs ont fait attention au caractère synthétique du *De concordia*: R. Pouchet, *La rectitudo chez saint Anselme* (Paris: Etudes Augustiniennes, 1964), pp. 172-85, interessé surtout par la deuxième partie (p. 177); K. Kienzler, *Glauben und Denken bei Anselm von Canterbury* (Freiburg im Br.: Herder, 1981), pp. 381-96, d'après lequel le *De concordia* répresente l'effort d'Anselme pour synthétiser l'ensemble de son oeuvre grâce à l'articulation de nécessité et liberté.

6 *Proslogion* I: Schmitt I,100.

7 *De concordia* I,6 renvoie aussi, sans le citer explicitement, à la doctrine *De libertate arbitrii* VIII (et pas seulement au chapitre 3 sur la définition de la liberté). On sait que le *De libertate arbitrii* VIII est le prolongement et le complément du *De veritate* XII. Cf. notre étude *Un triptyque sur la liberté: La doctrine morale de saint Anselme,* L'oeuvre de S. Anselme de Cantorbéry. Etudes No. 2 (Paris: Desclée de Brouwer, Paris, 1982), pp. 71-72.

8 *De concordia* III,6: Schmitt II,273,4-6.

9 Cf. notre étude "Le portrait du Christ dans le **Cur deus homo:** Herméneutique et démythologisation," *SB* II, 631-46. Je me suis occupé plus longuement de la question dans "Sentido y vigencia de la cristología de San Anselmo: Ensayo de lectura estructural del *Cur deus homo,*" *Stromata* 37, No. 1/2 (1981), 3-18, et 38, No. 3/4 (1982), 283-315.

10 Voici les principales allusions du *Cur deus homo* dans *De concordia* III:

(1) *De concordia* III,3: le salut ne peut être que l'oeuvre de l'homme-Dieu. Idée explicitement reprise à la fin du chapitre 7;

(2) *De concordia* III,6: la *fides Christi* et le *ea quae fides exigit*: rapport entre les deux livres du *Cur deus homo;*

(3) *De concordia* III,7: la situation d'impuissance (*etiam intelligendi*: cf. *De conceptu virginali*) qui vient du péché original blesse autant l'honneur de Dieu que la nature humaine laquelle ne peut être sauvée que par la mort de Dieu;

(4) *De concordia* III,9: le rédempteur apporte avec soi la satisfaction, la réconcilation et l'héritage (restauration);

(5) *De concordia* III,13: la référence à l'*intentio Dei* répète presque les termes du *Cur deus homo* II,1.

On peut ajouter certaines références à d'autres ouvrages:

(1) *De concordia* III,8: l'idée que seule l'injustice (dans la volonté) est *per se peccatum* renvoie au *De casu diaboli* et au *De conceptu virginali*;

(2) *De concordia* III,9: il n'y a pas de mérite si l'on voit un exemple concret expérimental. Le *De concordia* applique dans un sens positif ce que le *De casu diaboli* avait appliqué négativement à l'égard du péché du démon;

(3) *De concordia* III,11: la triple distinction de la volonté complète la division bipartite du *De libertate arbitrii* et *De casu diaboli*;

(4) *De concordia* III,12: la separabilité de justice et volonté reprend une idée du chapitre dernier du *De libertate arbitrii*. Il faut ajouter la référence explicite a la *veritas voluntatis* du *De veritate*;

(5) *De concordia* III,13: le rapport entre l'ordre des deux *volontés-affectiones* complète des éléments importants du *De casu diaboli*.

[11] Voir l'analyse de ce texte dans l'article cité n. 7, *Stromata* 38, No. 3/4 (1982), 293 et seq.

[12] Les nuances au sujet de la nécessité: *necessitas antecedens* (négative et determinante) et *consequens* (positive et *ex libertate*) apparaissent dans *De concordia* II,2-3. Là aussi on précise des éléments déjà élaborés dans le *De casu diaboli* et le *Cur deus homo*.

[13] *De concordia* I,4: Schmitt II,252,7: Cognosci potest **etiam** non omnia quae praescit Deus . . .

[14] Sans pouvoir entrer ici dans le plein de ces question, on peut tout de même suggérer que ces divisions ont un rapport avec les divers aspects de la volonté et à la causalité divines. *De concordia* I,3 présente la volunté divine comme l'exemplaire de celle de l'homme; dans *De concordia* I,4 et 5 et 7, on souligne surtout son aspect efficient; *De concordia*, enfin, est plus près de l'aspect final. Si l'on transpose ces aspects aux tres questions du *De concordia*, il est, semble-t-il, possible de conclure que les perspectives des trois parties correspondent respectivement à l'exemplarité (première) à l'éfficience (deuxième) et à la finalité (troisième). On pourrait même y trouver des résonances trinitaires ce qui permettrait d'approfondir encore plus cette triple considération de l'acte libre de l'homme: pour autant qu'il est libre (exemplarité), juste (finalité), gratuit (éfficience).

[15] *De concordia* III,3, après avoir répondu négativement à la possibilité de ce que le juste puisse avoir la rectitude *a se* ou *ab alia creatura*, affirme carrément que seul Dieu peut la donner: *non nisi per Dei gratiam*. Mais pour rappeler à l'instant le caractère d'aide (*adiuvans*) de cette grâce, voir *De concordia* III,3: Schmitt II,266,21-23: et in intelligentibus ipsa [gratia] semper adiuvet liberum arbitrium naturale, quod **sine illa** nihil valeret ad salutem, **dando** voluntati rectitudinem **quae servet per liberum arbitrium.**

[16] Formule que peut être traduite de différentes façons:

(1) *De concordia* III,5: Schmitt II,269,8: **nec sola** gratia, **nec solum** liberum arbitrium salutem hominis operetur;

(2) *Nec sola* signifie donc qu'aucun des deux élément travaille sans l'autre: *sine libero arbitrio (vel sine gratia)* (chapitre 1). Tout ceci est un commentaire au texte de Jn 15:5: *Sine me nihil potestis facere*, cité dans *De concordia* III,1 et 5.

(3) La négation du *solum sine* conduit à l'affirmation *simul esse eum et operari cum* (*De concordia* III,1);

(4) *De concordia* III,5: Schmitt II,270,5-9, précise, grâce à un exemple curieux, le sens de ces expressions:

Sicut ergo quamvis naturalis usus non procreat prolem **sine**
patre nec nisi **per** matrem, **non tamen removet ullus intellec-**
tus aut patrem **aut** matrem a generatione prolis, ita gratia
et liberum arbitrium **non discordant, sed conveniunt** ad
iustificandum et salvandum hominem.

[17] *De concordia* III,4 distingue les trois aspects de
l'aide de la grâce qui seront développés dans la suite de la
troisième partie: après avoir rappelé les aspects *praeve-*
niens vel subsequens envisagés dans les premières cinq chapitres, on parle de son influence pour vaincre les difficultés (*removendo vim tentationis vel augendo affectum rec-*
titudinis: ce qui répond aux *De concordia* III,10 et seq.)
et enfin, de l'aspect historique de son action (*De concordia*
III,6-9). On peut aisément constater que l'ordre dans
lequel Anselm envisage ces sujets dans la troisième partie
ne répond pas à celui du *De concordia* III,4. Il y là une
inversion explicable par le mouvement descendant de cette
partie.

[18] *De concordia* III,4: Schmitt II,268,10-12.

[19] *De concordia* III,6: Schmitt II,271,11-15.

[20] La n. 11 a indiqué la référence de ce chapitre au *Cur*
deus homo. Il faut quand même préciser que le chapitre 9
donne trois raisons de la persévérance de la peine dont les
deux premières (*Magnum itaque bonum providit Deus . . .*) se
rapportent au *De casu diaboli* tandis que la troisième (*Alia*
quoque ratio) se réfère au *Cur deus homo* et aussi à *De*
conceptu virginali.

[21] Cf. ce qui a été dit sur *De concordia* III,4 dans la
n. 15.

[22] Il faut tenir compte du rapport entre *De concordia*
III,13 et ce qu'on a dit auparavant à *De concordia* III, 7-8
sur l'abîme des péchés (*usque in abyssum peccatorum sine*
fundo).

[23] *De concordia* III,13: Schmitt II,287,3-6. Il faudrait
ici montrer les nuances entre les expressions employées par
Anselme à ce sujet en divers chapitres. Par exemple: *De*
concordia III,7 et 10 et 13.

[24] Par cette doctrine Anselme en même temps dépasse
l'abstraction méthodologique du *De libertate arbitrii*, qui
se bornait à la seule considération de la liberté sans la

grâce, et parachève ce qu'il avait commencé à creuser dans le *De casu diaboli* sur les rapports de deux volontés.

[25] *De concordia* II,1: Schmitt II,260,8-9; II,3: Schmitt II,262,14-16.

[26] *De concordia* II,3: Schmitt II,261,20-22.

[27] Il ne faut pas oublier que cette formule tâche d'expliquer (*enim*) la phrase antérieure où l'on affirme que les actions: **eveniunt** ea necessitate . . . quae rem sequitur. Mais l'intérêt de l'expression apparaît mieux en la mettant en rapport avec tous les textes qui parlent de la liberté comme puissance de l'homme.

[28] Cf. notre étude "Aproximaciones a la doctrina del pecado original en Anselmo de Canterbury", *Patristica et Mediaevalia* 4/5 (1983-84), 45-66.

[29] Voici les textes les plus importants:

(1) *De concordia* III,2: Schmitt II,265,6: iudicat Spiritus, référé au *credere in, intelligere in*, i. e. à la justice (*recte volendum*);

(2) *De concordia* III,6: Schmitt II,271,27-28: **faecundat** Spiritus sacram scripturam ut contineat in se omnem veritatem. C'est l'*auctoritas scripturae* (*ad ea quae fides Christi exigit*);

(3) *De concordia* III,7: Schmitt II,273,10-11: iudicat mundum de peccato quia non credunt in me (Jn 16:9);

(4) *De concordia* III,12: Schmitt II,284,24-26: Rectitudo . . . omnis meriti boni mater est. Haec enim **favet spiritui** concupiscenti adversus carnem, et **condelectatur legi Dei** (cf. *De concordia* III,4 où l'on dit: Adiuvat gratia . . . mitigando . . . aut augendo).

Il faudrait enfin ajouter les textes où l'on parle du *bonus odor Christi*: *De concordia* III,7 et 8 et 12. Tout cet ensemble semble correspondre à la *veritas voluntatis* dont parle le *De veritate* et que Anselme rappelle précisément à *De concordia* III,12.

[30] Il faut garder présent à l'esprit que *De processione Spiritu Sancti* précède d'assez près la rédaction de *De concordia*.

[31] C'est un donné constant dans les écrits anselmienes d'envisager les rédimés comme des frères, héritiers et imitateurs du Christ. A part de le *Cur deus homo*, on peut consulter la *Meditatio III* sur la rédemption, et bien avant cela, ses prères mariales, *Orationes V-VII*. Je renvoie à mon étude, "Teología y espiritualidad en Anselmo de Canterbury," *Teología* 21, No. 43 (1984), 5-22.

[32] Voir le texte du *De concordia* III,8, cité dans la n. 18.

[33] C'est à partir de là qu'il faudrait creuser en détail le contenu des nombreux textes qui s'occupent soit de la liberté humaine soit de l'éternité divine. Mais cela dépasse les limites que nous nous sommes fixés dans le présent travail.

St. Augustine
and the *Orationes sive Meditationes* of St. Anselm

Thomas H. Bestul

St. Anselm composed most of his nineteen prayers and
three meditations between the years 1060 and 1078, while he
was a monk at Bec. As scholars have frequently observed,
those *Orationes sive Meditationes* mark a turning point in
the devotional literature of the Western Church. Composed
in an effusive, exclamatory, highly personal style, making
use of lengthy balanced periods and carefully balanced
cadences, his writings are characterized by an intense, emotional intimacy that is quite unlike anything known before
his time. In seeking to identify the sources of Anselm's
devotional writing, most scholars have rightly identified
three contributing influences: the Psalms, the liturgy, and
the earlier, mainly Carolingian, tradition of private
prayer.[1] Yet these influences, important as they are, do
not adequately account for his achievement. I believe that
Anselm's devotional writings can be better understood if
they are examined in the light of the works of St. Augustine, particularly the *Soliloquia*, the *Confessiones*, and the
De trinitate. While it is true that there are no quotations
or direct borrowings from any of these three works in the
Orationes sive Meditationes, I will argue for a general
influence that is nonetheless profound and fundamental.

The *Orationes sive Meditationes* were written in a period
of Anselm's life when he had given himself to an intense
study of St. Augustine, especially the *De trinitate*, as
preparation for the composition of the *Monologion*, as we
know from Anselm's own account in a letter to Lanfranc and
from the Prologue to the *Monologion*.[2] Apart from the
theology, Anselm seems to have been especially interested in
the form Augustine used for this treatise. The *De trinitate* is a theological discussion combined with meditative
passages drawn from personal experience. The work seems the
record of a personal, inward voice speaking in the presence
of God. This form was essentially Augustine's invention.
He had used a variation of it in his early work, the *Soliloquia*, where the narrator conducts an interior dialogue on
the nature of the Deity with Reason, who is identified as an
aspect of his own being. The dialogue, of course, was well
established as an appropriate form for the conduct of philosophical or theological discussion: it is the interior
character of the conversation which makes Augustine's usage
of the form so novel. Augustine himself sensed this in

coining a new word to give title to his *Soliloquia*. He
speaks to Reason as follows:

> It is ridiculous if you are ashamed, as if
> it were not for this very reason that we
> have chosen this mode of discourse, which
> since we are talking with ourselves alone, I
> wish to be called and inscribed *Soliloquies*
> -- a new name, it is true, and perhaps a
> grating one -- but not ill-suited for set-
> ting forth the fact.[3]

Anselm no doubt has Augustine in mind when in the Prologue
to the *Proslogion* he gives the title of his first work as
Monologion, id est Soliloquium.[4] Anselm found in Augustine's works well-developed examples of the interior dialogue dealing with theological or devotional matter, often in
combination. Anselm's prayers are really inner conversations between the speaker and his soul, or the speaker and
his sins, conducted in the presence of God or of the saint
to whom the prayer is addressed. In the *Meditatio redemptionis humanae* and in the *Proslogion* Anselm treats theological issues in a meditative form, much in the formal and
stylistic manner of Augustine in the *De trinitate* and the
Soliloquia.

The soliloquy form as originated by Augustine was one
that greatly interested Anselm and his age. Isidore's *Synonyma* is a devotional and philosophical dialogue following
Augustine's model, and is sometimes called *Soliloquia* in the
many eleventh- and twelfth-century manuscripts of the work.[5]
In a thirteenth-century manuscript of Anselm's *Proslogion*
that work is described in the colophon as an *opusculum Soli-
loquiorum more compositum*.[6] Certain commentaries on the
Psalms describe them as soliloquies, and Augustine in the
Enarrationes in Psalmos distinguishes in Psalm 37 two different speakers -- Christ as Head and Christ as Body -- who
yet are a single entity, in the manner of his own *Soliloquia*.[7] In the twelfth and thirteenth centuries the soliloquy form became widely used and the title was applied to a
range of works, but Anselm, I think, was perhaps the first
after Isidore to imitate the prototype of Augustine and to
adapt its spirit to his own purposes.[8]

Anselm's use of a cadenced, carefully balanced prose
style is certainly a reflection of contemporary literary
tastes, but its use in the *Orationes sive Meditationes* could
well have been inspired by the example of Augustine's *Soliloquia*. An extract of that work, beginning *Deus universita-*

tis conditor, had circulated independently as a prayer since Carolingian times, and could have given Anselm a stylistic pattern to imitate.[9] Augustine's *Soliloquia* indeed were recognized in the later Middle Ages as a particularly fine example of a cadenced prose style. John of Garland, writing in his *Poetria* of the mid-thirteenth century, describes what he calls the Isidorian style as having clauses not balanced by equality of length but by rhyming cadences, as are found in Augustine's *Soliloquia*.[10]

Yet in reading the treatise one is struck by the cold formality of those balanced periods, which contrast so strongly with the personal ardor permeating almost all of Anselm's *Orationes sive Meditationes*. It is, finally, to Augustine's *Confessiones* that one must turn to discover perhaps the genesis of Anselm's style and method. In the first place, Anselm would have found in the *Confessiones* the detailed record of spiritual strife which had similarities to his own, provided we accept, as seems reasonable, that the first two of his meditations contain at least a core of biographical truth. He would have seen in Augustine another great sinner (and fellow fornicator), who had struggled to control his passions, finally attaining inner peace in the duties of pastor and teacher. We may be certain that Anselm was familiar with the *Confessiones*, even though he does not quote from nor allude to the book. The twelfth-century catalogue of the library of Bec lists a copy, and there is precedent for using extracts from it for devotional purposes as early as the Carolingian age.[11] From the *Confessiones* Anselm could have acquired the traits of his fervent personal style, in particular the extensive use of exclamation and of the successions of agitated questions, directed in part to oneself, in part to God, through which an attempt is made to probe the depths of private religious experience. Like Anselm, Augustine describes his own inability even to begin to approach God in prayer because the burden of sin is so deeply felt. As Augustine laments:

> How shall I call upon my God for aid, when the call I make is for my God to come to myself? What place is there in me to which my God can come, what place that can receive the God who made heaven and earth? Does this mean, O Lord my God, that there is something in me fit to contain you? Can even heaven and earth, which you made and in which you made me, contain you?[12]

Anselm's predicament in his *Oratio ad Christum* is similarly expressed:

> What shall I say? What shall I do? Where
> shall I go? Where shall I seek him? Where
> or when shall I find him? Whom shall I ask?
> Who will tell my beloved that I languish for
> love?[13]

Anselm might also have found in the *Confessiones* many
instances of the sinner's fervent address to the soul, usually in the form of a series of questions and answers:

> Barren soul, what do you do? Why do you lie
> still, sinful soul? The day of judgment
> approaches.[14]

Anselm's first and second meditations often use this device
in ways reminiscent of Augustine. The narrative complexities of Anselm's devotional works, with their speeches
addressed to different aspects of one's interior existence
seem to reflect the subtleties of the *Confessiones*.

As well as providing possible stylistic models, the *Confessiones* offers an articulate apologia for literary explo-
rations of the inner spiritual life, showing their utility
for a Christian reading public. Throughout his career
Anselm seems to have had a sense of himself as a teacher and
spiritual guide, combined with a literary self-consciousness
of a kind that is unexpected in his age and that in some
ways resembles Augustine's. One of the most remarkable
characteristics of Anselm's *Orationes sive Meditationes* is
the fact that they circulated in their own time as an integral collection under the name of their author. There are
few precedents for the circulation of devotional work in
this manner between the patristic age and Anselm's own time.
Isidore's *Synonyma* may be an exception; Carolingian prayers
are usually found anonymously in compendious anthologies
attached to psalters, and when they have attributions, they
usually belong to the fathers, especially Augustine and Gregory.[15] We may well ask what Anselm's intention was in
allowing so personal and intimate a collection to be spread
abroad with his authorship clearly inscribed, and with a
preface instructing the reader how it is to be used. In the
Confessiones Augustine justifies the dissemination to the
public of spiritual autobiography in words that apply to
Anselm's own practice in his devotional writing. Augustine
notes:

> But when others read of those past sins of
> mine, or hear about them, their hearts are
> stirred so that they no longer lie listless
> in despair crying "I cannot." Instead their
> hearts are roused by the love of your mercy
> and the joy of your grace by which each one
> of us, weak though he be, is made strong,
> since by it he is made conscious of his own
> weakness.[16]

As is Augustine, Anselm is keenly aware of the emotional
impact his writing would have, and was meant to have, on
others. Indeed in his Prologue he states that the chief
purpose of the prayers and meditations that follow is "to
stir up the mind of the reader to the love, or fear of God,
or to self examination."[17]

A letter to Anselm from Durand, Abbot of La Chaise-Dieu,
describes in almost Augustinian terms the effect that the
reading of Anselm's *Meditatio ad concitandum timorem* had on
his community:

> When we read these words, your pious tears
> were before us, drawing the same from us, so
> that we marvelled in every way, both that
> such a dew of blessing should overflow from
> your heart, and that from thence without a
> murmur such a stream should descend into our
> hearts. For this is in fact what happened.
> The goodness of the prayers you have written
> stirs this up in us, loving this in you, or
> rather you in them, and above them and
> through them loving God and you.[18]

This truly remarkable letter reproduces the rationale developed by Augustine for publishing the record of an individual's most intimate encounters with the deity: it is given
to the world not so much for personal glory or publicity,
nor even for purposes of biography, but so that persons
reading and contemplating such written records may be
stirred to similar emotions of fear, remorse, and love, and
be inspired to seek God.

Finally, I would like to suggest that a profound understanding on the part of Anselm of Augustine's celebrated
discussion of memory in *Confessiones* X could have formed the
theoretical basis for the methodology used in Anselm's fer-
vid personal meditations. In speaking of human memory
Augustine observes:

Out of the same storehouse, with these past
impressions, I can construct now this, now
that image of things that I have experienced
or believed on the basis of experience --
and from these I can further construct
future actions, events, and hopes; and I can
meditate on all these things as if they were
present.[19]

Augustine then offers an application of this technique
of meditation as he probes his memory, seeking to recall the
history of his search for God. Memory is crucial in
Anselm's *Orationes sive Meditationes* -- the prayers derive
much of their efficacy from our vivid awareness of Anselm's
sinful past, as it is marshalled before his memory with
lively horror and regret. The same faculty can construct
images which evoke the past historical events of Christ's
passion or suggest the future terrors of the Last Judgment.
The *Oratio ad Christum* well illustrates the method:

To this, most merciful Lord, tends this my
prayer, this remembrance and meditation of
your kindnesses, that I may enkindle in
myself your love . . . Thus not as I ought
but as I am able, I remember your passion,
remember your buffeting, remember the
scourging, remember the cross, remember the
wounds, remember how you were slain for
me.[20]

The first two meditations of Anselm especially hinge upon
the recollection of past sin and the formation of powerful
images which summon before the mind the dreadful day of
judgment:

What is this, O God, what is this that I
perceive in the land of miseries and darkness? Horror! Horror! What is this that I
see, where they dwell with no order, but
everlasting horror? Alas, the confusion of
wailing, the tumult of those gnashing their
teeth, an inordinate multitude of sighs.
Woe, woe; again and again and again woe,
woe! The sulphurous fire, the hell-like
flame, the gloomy whirlings, how I see you
swirling with terrific roaring![21]

(margin, handwritten): importance of memory as a method of contemplation

Of course the language of this passage surpasses any standards of stylistic decorum that Augustine would have recognized, but the importance of the memory as a well of tangible images of things not seen (*invisibilia*) is surely evident. This is a technique of meditation and contemplation which realized its full potential in the centuries following Anselm's death, but we can find its beginnings in his works.

The structure of Anselm's *Orationes sive Meditationes* may well owe much to the patristic doctrine of compunction as expressed most notably in Gregory's *Moralia*, as has been noted.[22] Compunction is defined as abasement of the mind with tears arising from the remembrance of sin and the terror of judgment, and the sources of emotion associated with it are the remembrance of past sins, the calling to mind of future punishments, and the desire for the heavenly home.[23] Yet, at the same time, Anselm's force of utterance, his emotionalism, and the intimacy of his diction, all find their nearest analogues in Augustine's *Confessiones*

What part Augustine played in the formation and development of Anselm's *Orationes sive Meditationes* can never be identified with complete certainty and assurance. As R. W. Southern has noted, it is not characteristic of Anselm to use quotations or to identify sources.[24] But just as his reading of the *De trinitate* suffused the *Monologion* with an Augustinian spirit and perhaps gave the impetus to the *Proslogion*, so it seems likely to suppose that Anselm found in Augustine examples to follow and models to imitate, a mode of expression eminently congenial to him as he committed to writing his prayers and meditations in a time of his life when the work of Augustine was much with him.

Notes

[1] See R. W. Southern, *Saint Anselm and His Biographer* (Cambridge: Univ. Press, 1963), pp. 34-47; *The Prayers and Meditations of St. Anselm*, trans. B. Ward (Harmondsworth: Penguin, 1973), pp. 27-46.

[2] *Epistola* 77: Schmitt III,199-200; *Monologion*, prologus: Schmitt I,7-8. On the relation of Anselm to Augustine, see Southern, pp. 31-33.

[3] *Soliloquia* II,14: *PL* XXXII,891: Ridiculum est si te pudet, quasi non ob idipsum eligerimus huiusmodi sermocinationes: quae quoniam cum solis nobis loquimur, Soliloquia vocari et inscribi volo: novo quidem et fortasse duro nom-

ine, sed ad rem demonstrandam satis idoneo; trans. C. C. Starbuck, in Philip Schaf, ed., A Select Library of Nicene and Post Nicene Fathers, Vol. VII (New York: Christian Literature Company, 1908), p. 551.

[4] *Proslogion*, Prooemium: Schmitt I,94.

[5] See *Synonyma*: *PL* LXXXIII,825-68; on the manuscripts, see M. Oberleitner, et al., *Die handschriftliche Überlieferung der Werke des Heiligen Augustinus: Sitzungsberichte der Österreichische Akademie der Wissenschaften, philosophisch-historische Klasse*, 263, 267, 276, 281, 289, 292 (Vienna: Böhlau in Komm., 1969-74).

[6] *Proslogion* XXVI: Schmitt I,122, ad notas.

[7] For the Psalm commentaries, see A. J. Minnis, *Medieval Theory of Authorship* (London: Scolar, 1984), p. 44; *Enarrationes in psalmos* XXXVII,6: *PL* XXXVI,400.

[8] See Hugh of St. Victor, *Soliloquium de arrha animae*: *PL* CLXXVI,951-70; William of St. Thierry's *De contemplando deo* was also often given the title *Soliloquium*: see *On Contemplating God*, trans. Sister Penelope, Cistercian Fathers Series, No. 3 (Kalamazoo: Cistercian Publications, 1977), p. 34.

[9] It is found, for example, in the *Officia per ferias* attributed to Alcuin, and in a ninth-century prayerbook from Fleury; see, respectively, *PL* CI,580 and *PL* CI,1397.

[10] See C. S. Baldwin, *Medieval Rhetoric and Poetic* (1928; rpt. Gloucester, MA: Peter Smith, 1959), p. 194.

[11] See R. Constantinescu, "Alcuin et les 'Libelli Precum' de l'époque carolingienne," *Revue d'histoire de la spiritualité* 50 (1974), 17-56. For the influence of the *Confessiones* on the devotional writing of Anselm's fellow Norman and near contemporary, John of Fécamp (d. 1078), see A. Wilmart, *Auteurs spirituels et textes dévots du moyen âge latin* (1932; rpt. Paris: Etudes augustiniennes, 1971), p. 135. For the copy in the Bec library catalogue, see G. Becker, *Catalogi bibliothecarum antiqui* (Bonn: Fr. Cohen, 1885), p. 258.

[12] *Confessiones* I,ii,2: *PL* XXXII,661: Et quomodo invocabo deum meum, deum et dominum meum? Quoniam utique in me ipsum eum vocabo, cum invocabo eum. Et quis locus est in

me quo veniat in me deus meus?   quo deus veniat in me,   deus
qui fecit coelum et terram?   Itane, domine deus meus, est
quidquam in me quod capiat te?   An vero coelum et terra quae
fecisti, et in quibus me fecisti, capiunt te? -- trans. R.
S. Pine-Coffin (Harmondsworth: Penguin, 1961), p. 22.

¹³*Oratio II*: Schmitt III,9: Quid dicam? Quid faciam?
Quo vadam? Ubi eum quaeram? Ubi vel quando inveniam? Quem
rogabo? Quis nuntiabit dilecto quia amore langueo? -- translations of Anselm are my own unless otherwise indicated.

¹⁴*Meditatio I*:   Schmitt III,77: Anima sterilis, quid
agis? Quid torpes, anima peccatrix? Dies iudicii venit.

¹⁵See the prayerbooks edited by A. Wilmart, *Precum
libelli quattuor aevi Karolini* (Rome: Ephemerides Liturgi-
cae, 1940); two Anglo-Irish prayerbooks from the eighth or
ninth centuries contain a few prayers attributed to contemporaries; see *The Prayer Book of Aedeluald the Bishop, Commonly Called the Book of Cerne*, ed. A. B. Kuypers (Cambridge: Univ. Press, 1902), pp. 143-44, 155, 207, 219.

¹⁶*Confessiones* X,iii,4:   *PL*   XXXII,780-81:   Nam
confessiones praeteritorum malorum meorum, quae remisisti et
texisti ut beares me in te, mutans animam meam fide et
sacramento tuo, cum leguntur et audiuntur, excitant cor ne
dormiat in desperatione et dicat, Non possum; sed evigilet
in amore misericordiae tuae et dulcedine gratiae tuae, qua
potens est omnis infirmus, qui sibi per ipsam fit conscius
infirmitatis suae; trans. Pine-Coffin, p. 208.

¹⁷*Orationes sive meditationes*, Prologus: Schmitt III,3;
see also *Epistola 10*: Schmitt III,113, and *Epistola 28*:
Schmitt III,135.

¹⁸*Epistola 70*:   Schmitt III,190: Deinde: 'terret me
vita mea, namque diligenter discussa,' cum eo quod sequitur,
scriptum hoc et praeter hoc alia piissime de contrito spiritu tuo et de pietate contriti tui cordis edita et scripta:
pias praestant nobis lacrimas tuas legere, nostras edere,
ita ut utrumque miremur: et in corde tuo redundare tantae
rorem benedictionis, et sine susurro inde descendere rivum
in cordibus nostris. Nam ita est vere. Pietas scriptae
tuae orationis excitat in nobis pietatem sopitae compunc-
tionis, adeo ut quasi mente prosiliendo congaudeamus, ea
diligendo in te, vel potius in eis te, super ea et per ea
deum et te; trans. Ward, p. 70.

[19] *Confessiones* X,viii,14: *PL* XXXII,785: Ex eadem copia etiam similitudines rerum vel expertarum, vel ex eis quas expertus sum creditarum, alias atque alias et ipse contexo praeteritis, atque ex his etiam futuras actiones et eventa et spes, et haec omnia rursus quasi praesentia meditor; trans. in *Confessions and Enchiridion*, ed. A. C. Oulter, The Library of Christian Classics, No. 7 (London: Westminster Press, 1955), p. 209.

[20] *Oratio 2*: Schmitt III,7: Ad hoc, clementissime, tendit haec oratio mea, haec memoria et meditatio beneficiorum tuorum, ut accendam in me tuum amorem . . . sic et ego non quantum debeo, sed quantum queo, memor passionis tuae, memor alaparum tuarum, memor flagellorum, memor crucis, memor vulnerum tuorum, memor qualiter pro me occisus es.

[21] *Meditatio 2*: Schmitt III,82: Quid est, deus, quid est quod animadverto in terra miseriae et tenebrarum? Horror, horror! Quid est quod intueor, ubi nullus ordo, sed sempiternus horror inhabitans? Heu confusio ululatuum, tumultus dentibus stridentium, inordinata multitudo gemituum. Vae, vae; quot et quot et quot vae, vae! Ignis sulphureus, flamma tartarea, caliginosa volumina, quam terrifico rugitu video vos rotari!

[22] See *The Prayers and Meditations*, trans. Ward, pp. 53-56.

[23] Gregory, *Moralia* XXIII; Gregory's teaching on compunction is summarized in Isidore of Seville, *Sententiae* II,12: *PL* LXXXIII,613.

[24] Southern, *Saint Anselm*, pp. 31-32.

St. Anselm's *Cur deus homo*
and the *Heidelberg Catechism* (1563)

Derk Visser

Modern Church historians and theologians generally agree
that the doctrine of satisfaction in the *Heidelberg Catechism* is Anselmian, but do not give many specifics about the
precise relationship between this work and Anselm's *Cur deus
homo*. As the *Heidelberg Catechism* provides a foundation for
Reformed Theology, examining that precise relation may be
useful in an age that seems to be moving towards greater
ecumenism. To enable comparison between the doctrine of St.
Anselm and the *Heidelberg Catechism*, a table of parallel
topoi in the *Cur deus homo* and the *Heidelberg Catechism*,
arranged in five major *topoi* follows this text. The *Heidelberg Catechism* phrases are taken from the *Explicationes
catechiseos*, (1563-1576) of Zacharias Ursinus, one of the
Heidelberg Catechism's principal authors, its officially
appointed defender, and its first explicator.[1]

These tables do not by themselves prove direct dependence of the *Heidelberg Catechism* on the *Cur deus homo*.
Similarities could result from their use of the same biblical texts and such early Fathers of the Church as St. Irenaeus and St. Augustine. Yet the organization and argumentation in the *Explicationes* parallel so closely the *Cur deus
homo* that one cannot easily reject Ursinus' familiarity with
St. Anselm.

The *Heidelberg Catechism* introduces its Anselmian matter
in Questions 12-18, following the first section of the
Catechism, entitled "On the Misery of Man." These questions
begin the second section, "On Deliverance." The arrangement
of the Common Places of Christian doctrine differs from the
usual presentations, such as those by Ursinus in his *Loci*
lectures of 1562-1568, or in the *Loci communes* by Ursinus'
mentor, Philip Melanchthon.[2] The *Heidelberg Catechism*
begins instead with the Christological and soteriological
message of "Comfort," after which it treats of "Sin," "Free
Will," "Satisfaction" (the Anselmian matter), "the Gospel,"
and only then the "Apostolic Creed," with its definitions of
the three persons of the Trinity. Such an arrangement purposes to highlight the Anselmian doctrine of satisfaction,
which emphasizes the inability of man to render that satisfaction himself. In this way, the necessity of the God-man,
Christ the Redeemer, receives more visibility than it does
in the *Catechism*'s discussion on the second person of the
Trinity, where, moreover, much of the material is repeated.

This inclusion of the Anselmian doctrine of satisfaction in Questions 12-18, has occasioned much critical evaluation, even apprehension and disapproval. Hendrikus Berkhof points out that neither Anselm nor the *Heidelberg Catechism* rests its argument on the rational method alone but, rather, they both begin with the fact of biblical revelation. He nevertheless objects to their rationalism,[3] fearing that they threaten our understanding of God's wisdom and liberty and so "violate the mystery of free grace." Berkhof also rejects the questions raised as "artificial" and is "happy that the method is an exception in the *Catechism*" which in its other Questions relies on the "spirit" of the First Question, that is, the expression of faith in the comfort through Christ.[4] Though they may be exceptions in the *Heidelberg Catechism* itself, these questions certainly are not so in the *Explicationes*. Such questions occupied part of the general method of instruction by means of disputations and the "defense of theses." We can take both St. Anselm and Ursinus at their word that such questions were actually posed.[5]

Karl Barth's positive disposition towards both the *Cur deus homo* and the *Heidelberg Catechism* is, of course, well known. He also stresses their a priori acceptance of the Scriptural revelation of Christ and calls their methodology and argumentation acceptable for their respective times. Criticisms result from developments in intellectual history and theology during the past centuries. Barth sees no theological separation between Questions 12-18 and Question 1.[6]

Here Barth touches on a major cause for the discomfort some critics feel. Guided by the parallels between Questions 12-18 and the *Cur deus homo*, they treat these Questions as a separate dialogue whose insertion is to be regretted for its commercialism and legalism, for its reliance on human reason, for its emphasis on God's harshness.[7]

Theodore Haitjema's 1962 study on the *Heidelberg Catechism* elaborates similar ideas.[8] He too stresses the organizational and doctrinal unity of the *Heidelberg Catechism*, but in spite of Barth's discussion of the relationship between the *Cur deus homo* and the *Heidelberg Catechism*, Haitjema still sees the Anselmian influence as regrettable scholasticism.[9] Thus Haitjema, in common with other critics, seeks to safeguard the *Heidelberg Catechism*'s content against medieval, that is, Roman influences by decrying the methodology of Questions 12-18. Haitjema finds questions about God's motivation dangerous. Moreover, writing from the perspective of the Reformation, he does St. Anselm an implied injustice when he says that the *Heidelberg Catechism* goes beyond the *aut satisfactio aut poena* of the *Cur deus homo* and opposes the message of the Gospel to Rome's doctrine of merits,[10] a doctrine condemned also in the *Explicationes*. But I do not see much difference between the teachings of the *Cur deus homo* and the *Heidelberg Catechism* dealing with the doctrines that satisfaction is rendered by the God-man and that the good works we do are owed by us already. As Ursinus says, we owe them as works of gratitude, or as Melanchthon has it, we owe them under the new obedience of the regenerated man reconciled to God through Christ.[11]

Haitjema's resurrection of sixteenth century conflicts also influences the recent study by Wulf Metz on Questions 12-18 of the *Heidelberg Catechism*.[12] By way of introduction, Metz summarizes in some detail the scholarly opinion of the last few centuries on Questions 12-18, arranging the criticism chronologically in positive and negative categories.[13] This catalogue creates the impression that most who disliked the insertion of Questions 12-18 also criticized the *Cur deus homo* itself; yet few of those who do accept Questions 12-18 approve of their Anselmian character. In his separate discussion of the *Cur deus homo*, Metz also, though less extensively, indicates the major schools of *Cur deus homo* scholarship.[14]

Although Metz recognizes the doctrinal progression of the *Heidelberg Catechism* and thus its theological integrity, including Questions 12-18, he too defends the *Heidelberg Catechism* against Anselmian influence by attacking the methodology of the *Cur deus homo*. Nor does Metz avoid what I see as the major impediment to interpreting correctly the relationship between the *Heidelberg Catechism* and the *Cur deus homo*.

On the one hand, Metz's examination of Questions 12-18 focuses too narrowly on those questions without pursuing their doctrinal components throughout the *Heidelberg Catechism*. On the other hand -- taking the *Cur deus homo* also as a work that stands by itself -- he stresses its ostensibly polemical purpose against the unbelievers.[15] Relying on such evaluations of St. Anselm as Adolf Harnack's -- in spite of MacIntyre's rebuttal --and that of Ludwig Heinrichs, Metz criticizes the *Cur deus homo*.[16] He quotes Heinrichs as saying that St. Anselm's teaching conflicted not only with Catholic doctrine as defined by Vatican I, but also with the Scriptures themselves. Thus, concludes Metz, the differences between the *Cur deus homo* and the *Heidelberg Catechism* on the role and person of Christ are clear.[17] In addition Metz finds fault with the exposition of the justi-

fication and sanctification of man which shows that they are
consequent and thus secondary to satisfaction, while in the
Heidelberg Catechism, as Metz sees it, they are doctrinally
primary to satisfaction.[18] Such criticisms base themselves
on demands for a work that St. Anselm did not set out to
write, that is, a work relying explicitly and only on biblical texts and dealing *in extenso* with all the ramifications
of its main subject, namely, that the need of satisfaction
by the God-man establishes the assumption of human nature by
God. Thus for Metz, the method, rather than the specific
doctrine of satisfaction, condemns the *Cur deus homo*. The
chief difference between the *Cur deus homo* and Questions
12-18 is, according to Metz, that the *Heidelberg Catechism*'s
Questions "confront the believer with the revealed mystery
of the office and person of Jesus Christ which *cannot be
deduced rationally*."[19]

As a minor objection, Metz suggests that those who see
the *Cur deus homo* in Questions 12-18 must show how the *Cur
deus homo* reached the Heidelberg theologians who composed
the *Catechism*.[20] He himself sees Questions 12-18 as "free
from scholastic speculation" and to be understood on the
basis of the Reformation's "rediscovered *sola scriptura*."[21]
This minor point is nevertheless of some significance. It
disregards the Saint's assertion that his treatise is in
fact based on the Scriptures and the Fathers of the
Church.[22] It also gives too much weight to the Reformation's insistence on *sola scriptura* as if neither the
Fathers nor even human *ratio* were used. The insistence on
sola scriptura not only meant to guarantee doctrinal sound-
ness, but served as well to condemn the rationalism of the
"schools." Thus modern critics, following the sixteenth century Reformers in rejecting scholasticism and the medieval
Doctors, can see the inclusion of the Anselmian matter of
Questions 12-18 as a regrettable lapse that is both out of
place and out of character in the *Heidelberg Catechism*.

Zacharias Ursinus, whose *Explicationes* were the accepted
interpretation of the *Heidelberg Catechism*'s doctrines,
explicitly recognizes the value of the Fathers, of -- God-
given -- *ratio*, and of correct philosophy.[23] For Ursinus,
sola scriptura becomes the criterion on which the Fathers
are accepted and philosophy judged correct. He himself --
in that most important debate on the real presence in the
sacrament of communion -- cites both Latin and Greek
Fathers.[24] Philip Melanchthon is yet more liberal and on
the question of free will; he refers not only to Ambrose and
Augustine, but also to Hugo of St. Victor and Bernard of
Clairvaux.[25] In 1553, when Ursinus studied with him,

Melanchthon wrote that he had been reading the *Cur deus homo* and other works. On the question of Christ's assumption of human nature in the womb of the Virgin Mary he writes: "It does not displease me to retain Anselm's words."[26]

In tracing the sources of many doctrines held by Luther, the "father" of German Reformers, such recent studies as those by Heiko Oberman,[27] Berndt Hamm,[28] and James Preuss[29] demonstrate the close connection between the theological developments of the sixteenth and preceding centuries. I believe that the Reformers accepted without demur the heritage of Christianity, especially in matters not then subjected to controversy. To what extent each of the Reformers read the actual writings of the Fathers and Doctors, rather than relying on collections of sentences arranged by common places and teachers' notes is difficult to determine.[30] The absence of exact quotations and references should not be taken as evidence of a Reformer's independent reexamination of the doctrine under consideration.

In the case of the *Heidelberg Catechism* and the *Explicationes*, such absence is intentional. Just as St. Anselm ostensibly attempts to avoid citing the Fathers and biblical texts to meet the unbelievers with strictly rational arguments, so the *Heidelberg Catechism* and Ursinus avoid the Fathers and other authorities to counter all critics on the basis of Scripture alone.[31] Thus in Questions 12-18 it is methodology rather than doctrine which creates the differences between the *Cur deus homo* and the *Heidelberg Catechism*. It may here be pointed out that, while St. Anselm does not identify the unbelievers by name, Ursinus -- like his mentor Melanchthon -- bluntly addresses the objections and errors of Turks or Mohammedans and Jews, as well as those of Arius, Samotesanus, and some of his contemporaries, such as Michel Servetus.[32] In contrast to Metz, I want to emphasize this polemical objective of both the *Heidelberg Catechism* and the *Explicationes*. Particularly in the case of Ursinus who wrote the official Palatinate defense against Jacob Andrea's accusation of Anti-Trinitarianism after the affair of Johann Sylvan, the questions raised by the *Cur deus homo* and the *Heidelberg Catechism* on the relationship of the three persons of the Trinity and the two natures of Christ were of primary concern.[33] Their importance had earlier been brought home in the *Colloquy* of Maulbronn on the "real presence."[34] Considering the fact that these attacks on Heidelberg theology were made by some of the people who had attacked Calvin and Melanchthon in the 1550's -- when Ursinus sat at the feet of Melanchthon[35] -- and who had attacked Elector Frederick III's alleged moving towards "Sacramentarianism" in 1560,[36] one cannot assume that the *Catechism* was meant only to instruct the young.[37] Certainly the *Explicationes* do not demonstrate that. And it is poor methodology to explain the *Catechism* with the aid of Ursinus, while treating the *Explicationes* as separate in any evaluation. Rather one should assume that the *Explicationes* shows the purpose and use of the *Heidelberg Catechism* as much as they teach its doctrines.

It is in the discussion of the two natures of Christ and the relationship of the three persons of the Trinity that the similarities in both content and purpose of the *Cur deus homo* and the *Heidelberg Catechism* are yet more significant than the parallels in their proof of the necessity for satisfaction. These similarities, incidentally, also rebut the criticism that both the *Cur deus homo* and the *Heidelberg Catechism*, 12-18, "remove the revealed Christ."[38] Instead of removing Christ, both the *Cur deus homo* and the *Heidelberg Catechism*, 12-18, demonstrate his necessity. This they do primarily by rebutting the arguments of unbelievers against God's assumption of human nature.

If Christ is absent in the Questions and Responses of the *Heidelberg Catechism*, 12-17, the catechumen has nevertheless been told, in the exposition of Question 11, that the satisfaction which is going to be discussed is *solius Christi obedientia, quae est satisfactio pro peccatis nostris*.[39]

Ursinus, who was appointed to preach a weekly sermon on the *Catechism* every Sunday afternoon, does not hide Christ in his exposition of Questions 12-17 either. A few examples may suffice:

> The deliverance of man is . . . the restoration of righteousness . . . through Christ"
> (Question 12);
>
> We are able to make satisfaction not in ourselves, but in Christ . . . (Question 13);
>
> The man Christ was perfectly righteous . . .
> (Question 16).

Even in Questions 14-15, where Christ is not mentioned in the *Explicationes*, biblical texts take care of the criticism.[40] St. Anselm's referral of his interlocutor to his earlier treatises issues in fact a similar reminder, as, of course, does Boso himself when he says that he believes even if no proof is forthcoming.[41] The "faith seeking understanding" motivation of the *Cur deus homo* thus remains in the foreground in any appreciation of the theology as opposed to the methodology -- of both works.

As I have attempted to show in my Table of Topical Parallels, the *Cur deus homo* and the *Heidelberg Catechism* agree not only in their major theological doctrines, but also in their descriptive terminology, as for example: the beauty of the order of God's creation or the honor/majesty of God; in such *exempla* as the ransoming of slaves and feudal relationships; and in such categories of Aristotelian thought as consequent necessity. In addition, anyone familiar with developments in Calvinism would find in the *Cur deus homo* a foreshadowing of the concepts of the covenants of creation, works, redemption, and grace.[42] While Protestantism cannot claim the covenant of grace as its exclusive property, the covenant of works has commonly been traced to Zacharias Ursinus, whence it entered the theology of the Reformed Churches.[43]

Even in an argument of such importance as Anselm's thesis that the number of those saved must equal the number of fallen angels, a thesis completely lacking in the *Heidelberg Catechism*, the two works agree about the consequence, that while Christ renders satisfaction sufficient for all, not all will be saved. Saved are those who believe, as Boso puts it, all the things required to obtain eternal salvation.[44] As the Table shows, these two works do not disagree about the concept of election.

One can argue that the authors of the *Heidelberg Catechism*, having taught the misery of man as they do, could have omitted Questions 12-17, slightly rephrased Question 18 to introduce Christ the Mediator with the covenant of grace, and presented the Anselmian matter in Question 29 and the following, where much of it is now repeated (as demonstrated by the citations in the appended table). As I pointed out, both Melanchthon and Ursinus have the Anselmian matter in their *Loci* in the exposition of the Trinity. Ursinus has it there even in his *Catechesis maior*, which is generally considered a preparatory work for the *Heidelberg Catechism*.[45] Whether that would have softened its language -- for which we may blame the sixteenth century rather than St. Anselm -- or its legalism, which Anselm inherited from the Fathers and to which he added a medieval dimension,[46] remains to be seen. Although the arrangement in Ursinus' *Loci* and *Catechesis maior* differs from the *Heidelberg Catechism*, language and concepts remain similar.   Barth correctly called the arguments of the *Cur deus homo* and *Heidelberg Catechism* typical of their times. But the language is also biblical. Thus in the exposition of the second commandment in both his *Loci* and *Explicationes*, Ursinus

uses   *Ego sum Dominus deus tuus, fortis, zelotis, vindicans*,
and glosses: *hoc est, accerrimum sui honoris defensorem ac
vindicem, horribiliter irascentem deficientibus ab ipso*
. . .[47]

Such vain speculations may cause us to overlook an
apparently minor component of the discussions in the *Cur
deus homo*, which has been   given   great   importance   in   the
Heidelberg Catechism: the   gratuitous   character   of   God's
action is not diminished by its necessity, but rather
deserves greater recognition. As St. Anselm puts it:

> When one   submits voluntarily to the neces-
> sity of doing good . . . one deserves
> greater   acknowledgement   for   the   good
> actions. For in that case one does not
> speak of necessity, but of grace.[48]

Melanchthon   echoes   a similar precept when he writes in
the explanation of the fourth commandment in his own   German
version of the *Loci communes*:

> Gratitude is a virtue which comprises two
> other important virtues: truth and   justice
> . . . Justice, for in gratitude we behold
> our special obligations   to   the   benefactor
> and feel that we must return as we have
> received . . . With regard to truth we are
> to confess of whom we have received benefit
> . . . Gratitude should point us to God,   for
> in giving thanks we confess that He is our
> Helper and Savior.[49]

Ursinus takes these precepts and places them not only in
his own explanation of the commandment to honor one's parents, but also in the preamble to the *Heidelberg Catechism*'s
third section, "On Gratitude," which precedes the Questions
on "Good Works" and the "Decalogue."[50] He writes:

> Gratitude is necessary   on   account   of   the
> glory of God . . .   which comprehends
> acknowledgement and praise for   the   benefits
> of Christ . . .

Then, combining both the *Cur deus homo* and Melanchthon's
definition, Ursinus states:

> Thankfulness in general is a virtue acknowl-
> edging and professing the person from whom

> we have received benefits, as well as the
> greatness of the benefits themselves . . .
> , It includes truth and justice . . . Truth
> acknowledges and professes the benefits of
> our free redemption, and renders thanks to
> God[51]

for what Melanchthon had called:

> God's inexpressible great love towards his
> only begotten Son, Jesus Christ, and towards
> us, poor creatures, who have refuge in
> Christ.[52]

The *Heidelberg Catechism*'s adoption of an earlier catechism's threefold division permitted Ursinus to make sure the catechumen will know "that all our good works are expressions of thankfulness and have no merit in the sight of God."[53] Thus the *Heidelberg Catechism* and Ursinus once again highlight the magnitude of the merit of Christ's satisfaction for the sin of man, a magnitude also brought out by the *Heidelberg Catechism*'s inclusion of most of the *Cur deus homo* in its Questions 12-18 at the beginning of the section "On Deliverance." Thus I think it not too improbable a conclusion that both the *Catechism* and Ursinus are teaching the Christology and soteriology also propounded -- if not as extensively and systematically -- by St. Anselm in his *Cur deus homo*. And I believe that, as Melanchthon was reading Anslem's works when Ursinus was among his students, when -- in the aftermath of the *Interim* of 1548 -- questions raised by Anselm became relevant once again, Ursinus may have become acquainted with Anselm. When later he found biblical language on God's wrath, the Anselmian matter, received from his own mentor, was readily incorporated in his lectures.

Notes

[1] All references to the *Cur deus homo* are from *Pourquoi Dieu s'est fait homme*, ed. and trans. R. Roques (Paris: Editions du Cerf, 1963); all the works of Z. Ursinus, cited in this study, are to be found in *Zachariae Ursini opera omnia*, ed. Q. Reuter (Heidelberg: Johannis Lancelot, 1612), hereafter cited as Reuter I; I cite the text of the *Heidelberg Catechism*, found in Ursinus' *Explicationes catechiseos*, from the Reuter edition and/or from Z. Ursinus, *Commentary on the Heidelberg Catechism*, ed. and trans. G. W. Williard (Grand Rapids: Eerdmans, 1956).

[2] Ursinus, *Loci theologici*: Reuter I,426-733; P. Melanchthon, *Loci praecipui theologici* [1559], *Melanchthons Werke in Auswahl*, ed. R. Stupperich (Gutersloh: Mohn, 1980), Vol. 2 in 2; also C. L. Manschreck, *Melanchthon on Christian Doctrine, Loci Communes 1555* (Grand Rapids: Baker, 1956).

[3] H. Berkhof, "The Catechism as an Expression of Our Faith," *Essays on the Heidelberg Catechism*, ed. R. V. Moss (Philadelphia: United Church Press, 1963), pp. 93-122.

[4] Ibid.

[5] Concerning St. Anselm, see Roques' Introduction and *Cur deus homo*, praefatio, and I,1: Roques 198-200 and 210-16; also R. W. Southern, *Medieval Humanism and Other Essays* (New York: Harper and Row, 1970), pp. 12-13; concerning Ursinus, see D. Visser, *Zacharias Ursinus: The Reluctant Reformer* (New York: United Church Press, 1983), passim.

[6] K. Barth, *The Heidelberg Catechism for Today*, trans. S. C. Guthrie (Richmond: John Knox Press, 1964), pp. 47-48.

[7] See the extensive survey of negative evaluations in W. Metz, *Necessitas Satisfactionis?* (Zurich: Zwingli Verlag, 1970), pp. 15-33.

[8] T. L. Haitjema, *De Heidelbergse Catechismus als klankbodem en inhoud van het actuele belijden van onze kerk* (Wageningen: Venemans, 1962).

[9] Ibid., p. 43.

[10] Ibid., p. 41.

[11] On the place of the "works of man," see *Cur deus homo* I,20-21:   Roques 316-26; *Heidelberg Catechism*, Question 13,17; on the merits of saints, see *Cur deus homo* II,18: Roques 438 ff.; *Heidelberg Catechism*, Question 18,30.

[12] Metz, *Necessitas*, pp. 15-33.

[13] Ibid., pp. 15-33 (negative); pp. 33-57 (positive).

[14] Ibid., pp. 185-221.

[15] Ibid., p. 201.

[16] Ibid., pp. 219-21; for the criticism of Harnack's censures, see J. McIntyre, *St. Anselm and His Critics* (Edinburgh: Oliver and Boyd, 1954), pp. 186-97.

[17] Metz, *Necessitas*, p. 203.

[18] Ibid., p. 212.

[19] Ibid., p. 217, (italics added).

[20] Ibid., p. 218.

[21] Ibid., p. 219.

[22] *Cur deus homo*, praefatio: Roques 198-200.

[23] For examples, see Z. Ursinus, *Prolegomena*:   Reuter I, 46-51, and *Loci theologici*, De scriptura sacra: Reuter I,426-58; see also *Melanchthons Werke*:   Stupperich II/1,188: Sequor autem et amplector doctrinam Ecclesiae Witebergensis et coniunctarium, quae sine ulla dubitatione consensus est Ecclesiae catholicae Christi, *id est, omnium eruditorum in Ecclesiae Christi* (my italics); and (on the use of philosophy) *Melanchthons Werke*: Stupperich II/1,190-91.

[24] *Loci theologici*:   Reuter I,276-77.

[25] *Loci communes* (1555):   Manschreck 68.

[26] Letter to Georg von Anhalt (1553, February 19): Corpus Reformatorum 8,30; on the incarnation, see *Melanchthons Werke*: Stupperich II/1,284.

[27] H. Oberman, *Forerunners of the Reformation* (New York: Holt, Rinehart, and Winston, 1966); also *Herbst der Mittelalterlichen Theologie* (Zurich: Zwingli Verlag, 1965).

[28] B. Hamm, *Promissio, Pactum, Ordinatio: Freiheit und Selbstbindung Gottes in der scholastischen Gnadenlehre* (Tübingen: Mohr, 1977).

[29] J. Preuss, *From Shadow to Promise: Old Testament Interpretation from Augustine to Young Luther* (Cambridge: Harvard Univ. Press, 1969).

[30] On the role of *loci communes*, see G. P. Hartvelt, "Over de Methode der Dogmatiek in the Eeuw der Reformatie," *Gereformeerd Theologisch Tijdschrift* 62 (1962), 97–149; and more recently, R. Kolb, "Teaching the Text: The Common Place Method in Sixteenth Century Biblical Commentary," *Bibliothèque d'Humanisme et Renaissance* 49 (1987), 571–85.

[31] *Prolegomena*: Reuter I,46ff.

[32] *Melanchthons Werke*, Question 33, passim: Stupperich II/1,194: Ab Ario furores Mahomatici orti sunt.

[33] Visser, *Zacharias Ursinus*, pp. 147–48, 160–62.

[34] Ibid., pp. 137–40.

[35] Ibid., pp. 45–46, 52–53, and works cited there.

[36] Ibid., pp. 107–10, and works cited there.

[37] *Prolegomena*: Reuter I,46ff.

[38] Barth, *The Heidelberg Catechism for Today*, pp. 47–48.

[39] *Heidelberg Catechism*, Question 11: Reuter I,85.

[40] See also F. Winter, **Confessio Augustana und Heidelberger Katechismus** (Berlin: Evangelische Verlag, 1954), p. 46.

[41] *Cur deus homo* I,20: Roques 316–26.

[42] Covenant theology is an important (and controversial) aspect of Calvinist Theology. For a survey see L. Berkhof, *Systematic Theology* (Grand Rapids, MI: Eerdmans, 1953), pp.

211ff., 265ff., 273ff. I have indicated the appearance of such covenant notions in square brackets in the appended Table.

[43] R. Letham, "The **Foedus Operum**: Some Factors Accounting for Its Development," *Sixteenth Century Journal* 16 (1983), 457-68. But see my "The Covenant in Zacharias Ursinus," *The Sixteenth Century Journal* 18 (1987), 531-44.

[44] *Cur deus homo* I,20: Roques 316-28.

[45] Visser, *Zacharias Ursinus*, pp. 116-18. For a more recent treatment of the relationship between the *Heidelberg Catechism* and *Maior*, see F. H. Klooster, "Ursinus' Primacy in the Composition of the Heidelberg Catechism," in *Conflict and Conciliation: The Palatinate and the Reformation*, ed. D. Visser (Pittsburgh: Pickwick Publications, 1986), pp. 73-100. The arguments of F. Winter, *Confessio Augustana*, pp. 47-48, for inclusion of Question 12-18 as required by the purpose and organisation of the *Heidelberg Catechism* appear to me convincing.

[46] R. W. Southern, *St. Anselm and His Biographer* (Cambridge: Univ. Press, 1963), pp. 107-13; but also K. Strijd, *De Struktuur en Inhoud van Anselmus' Cur deus homo* (Assen: Van Gorkum, 1958), p. 145; D. Cremer, "Die Würzeln des Anselmischen Satisfaktionsbegriffes," *Theologische Studien und Kritiken* 53 (1888), 7-24.

[47] *Explicationes Catechiseos*: Reuter I,344.

[48] *Cur deus homo* II,5: Roques 356-58.

[49] *Loci communes* (1555): Manschreck 107-08.

[50] *Heidelberg Catechism*: Reuter I,306.

[51] Ibid.

[52] *Loci communes* (1555): Manschreck 107

[53] *Commentary on the Heidelberg Catechism* : Williard 82 and 88; also *Heidelberg Catechism*: Reuter I,307

Appendix

Table of Topical Parallels
in Anselm's *Cur deus homo*
and Ursinus' *Explicationes catecheseos*.

NOTE: The left column lists *topoi* in the *Cur deus homo*,
with reference to book and chapter(s): I,1-5; the edition
of René Roques is used. The right hand column gives the
parallel *topoi* and concepts in the *Explicationes cateche-*
seos, with reference to the Catechism's Question and the
place in the *Opera* of Zacharias Ursinus: Question 1, I,54
and/or the pages in Williard's English translation (p. 17).
Relevant parallels in Melancthon's *Loci Communes* are added
at the end of the Ursinus locus as follows: *MW* = Melanchthon Werke II/1,number; or *LC*-1555 = Manschreck's German
translation of Melanchthon,number.

Column I	Column II
Topos I:	*Topos* I:

Ordo et dispositio et pul- *chritudo universitatis*: I,15	As a proof of God's existence: *Ordo naturae* *pulcherrimus . . . non pot-* *est existere et conser-* *vari*, if not because of God: Question 25, I,113 (p. 121) [*MW* II/1,248]
	As synonymous with God's providence: *Cum doctrina* *de creatione mundi cohaeret* *locus de providentia dei* *quae nihil alius est, quam* *creationis continuatio:* *quia gubernatio est conser-* *vatio rerum creatarum:* Question 27, I,127 [*deus* *servat sui operis ordinem:* *MW* II/1,242].
	Ordo non potest a causa *bruta. Ubi enim est ordo,* *ibi est causa ordinans et* *disponens. In rerum natura* *est ordo, aptissima nimirum*

dispositio est: Question 27, I,127 [*Bruta res non est causa naturae intelligentis*: *MW* II/1, 248].

The order of God's justice requires punishment: *ordo justitiae divinae*: Question 10, I,83 (p. 68) [*peccatum est horribilis destructio operis et ordinis divini*: *MW* II/1,251].

* * * * * * *

Genus humanum, tam scilicet pretiosum opus ejus: I,4; *Hominem factum esse justum ut beatus esset*: II,1

[creation covenant]

Ad quid homo sit conditus? Ut cum [deo] beatus in aeternum vivaret . . . Agnitione dei subordinatur felicitas et beatitudo hominis: Question 6, I,61 (p. 29) [*MW* II/1,250].

* * * * * * *

Man created in state of justice: I,19

Question 6, I,61 (p. 27) [*MW* II/1,285].

* * * * * * *

Adam would not have died if he had not sinned: II,2

Where there is no sin, there is no death: Question 7, I,66 (p. 37).

* * * * * * *

Adam in Paradise had order not to sin: I,24

Question 7, I,64 (p. 34).

* * * * * * *

The just will submits to God and does works pleasing to God: I,11

The just will before the Fall: Question 8, I,78 (p. 62) [*MW* II/1,264].

The will begins to do so as result of regeneration:

Question 8, I,79 (p. 64)
[*MW* II/1,267; II/2,431,
435].

* * * * * * *

* * * * * * *

Truth and desire for jus-
tice are gifts of God: I,9

Question 8, I,79 (p. 64);
Question 19, I,103 (p. 104)
[*MW* II/2,429].

* * * * * * *

* * * * * * *

Scriptures teach how to use
grace and make it rule of
life: II,19

Question 2, I,77 (p. 22),
passim.

* * * * * * *

* * * * * * *

*Necesse est ergo, ut de
humana natura quod incepit
perficiat. Hoc autem fieri
. . . nisi per integram
satisfactionem peccati:*
II,4

There are five types of
work in the act of crea-
tion: (1) *creatio;*
(2) *conservatio: qua deus
. . . omnes res creatas
sustentat ne corruant;*
(3) *gubernatio;*
(4) *reparatio: qua omnia
quae propter peccatum ho-
minis obnoxia sunt corrup-
tioni, reparat in Christo;*
(5) *perfectio: qua omnia
ad fines destinatos perdu-
cit, praecipue vero ec-
clesiam perfecte liberat
et glorificat:* Question
26, I,123 (p. 142).

* * * * * * *

* * * * * * *

Voluntary decree of cre-
ation and promise of beatitude becomes necessity:
II,5, and 16; with satis-
faction through Christ:
II,4

Reconciliation of man with
God [through Christ] is
called covenant: Question
12, I,90; Question 18, I,98
(p. 96)

* * * * * * *

* * * * * * *

Consequent, not absolute or coerced necessity: II,17, passim

Objections to God's freedom rejected and necessity defined as "consequent on God's decrees": Question 25, I,115 [*MW* II/1,260].

* * * * * * *

* * * * * * *

Topos II

Topos II

Deus-homo Novum condat Testamentum et Vetus approbat: sicut veracem esse necesse est confiteri, ita nihil in illis continetur verum esse potest aliquis diffiteri: II,22

Doctrina ecclesiae est integra et incorrupta doctrina legis et evangelii de vero deo eiusque voluntate, operibus . . . *a deo patefacta et comprehensa libris prophetarum et apostolorum*: *Prolegomena* I,46.

Quis autem est ille mediator, qui simul est verus deus, et verus perfecte justus homo?: Question 18, I,95. The *Explicationes* contains a subdivision entitled *De foedere dei* in which God's covenant is defined as: *pactio inter deum et homines, qua deus confirmat hominibus se futurum eis propitium remissurum peccata, donaturum justitiam novam* . . . *per et propter filium mediatorem*: I,98: *hoc foedus non potuit fieri sine mediatore*: I,99; *foedus dei est unum substantia, duplex circumstantiis* . . . *Duo autem dicunt foedera: vetus et novum* . . . *Vetus testamentum seu foedus saepe in scriptura synedoche sumitur pro lege* . . . *Novum testamentum seu foedus fere sumitur pro evangelio*, I,100-101.

Question 19: *Unde id scis?*
Resp.: *Ex evangelio, quod
deus primum in paradiso
patefecit, ac deinceps per
patriarchas et prophetas
propagavit . . . ad extre-
mum vero per filium suum
unigenitum complevit:*
I,101.

* * * * * * *

Anselm's inquiry is based
on the Scriptures and
Fathers, *Dedication to
Urban II* (Roques 194-97)

The Scriptures as confirmation of the certitude of
Christian doctrine: *Sola
autem ecclesiae doctrina in
evangelio explicat libera-
tionem a miseria, et firmam
consolationem conscientiis
ostendit. Sola igitur vera
est et divina*: *Prolegomena*
I,49, rephrased in *Explicationes*, Question 1 (on
man's comfort), I,55.

Ursinus, though less than
his mentor Melanchthon,
also quotes the pre-600
Fathers, for example,
Augustine: Question 16,
I,92; Irenaeus: Question
37, I,164; Cyril: Question
53, I,202.

* * * * * * *   * * * * * * *

Topos III   *Topos* III

Anselm posits the thesis
that salvation must come
through Christ: I,25

The satisfaction through
Christ is necessary for our
comfort and salvation:
Prolegomena specialis,
I,53.

*Providentia vero est con-
silium dei . . . secundum
quod deus . . . ad electo-*

rum salutem dirigit: Question 27 (On Providence), I,129 (p. 151).

* * * * * * *

* * * * * * *

Faith is a requirement to obtain eternal salvation: I,20; (Anselm reminds Boso that for the sake of their dialogue this condition must be disregarded. Boso had earlier said that he believed even if no explanation for understanding what he believed was forthcoming: I,1).

Why it is necessary to retain the doctrine of the trinity: *propter nostram consolationem et salutem . . . Nemo enim servatur sine fiducia in filium dei mediatorem*: Question 25 (subquestion), I,121 (p. 133).

Sine vera agnitione dei et filii eius Jesu Christi, hoc est, sine fide et poenitentia nemo servatur neque habet firmam consolationem: *Prolegomena specialis*, I,53 (p. 14, Williard omits "without faith and repentance"). Also Question 2, I,77; "faith is the instrument of justification": Question 19, I,103; Question 20, I,78; a definition and discussion of justifying faith: Question 21, I,107-108; the doctrine of justification: Christ's righteousness is imputed to us by our believing it, which is worked in us by God: Question 59, I,230 [*Fides est fiducia misericordia divinae promissae in Christo*: *MW* II/1 (1521 *Loci*), 110; Faith that sins are forgiven *propter Filium a deo gratis*: II/2,396-7; II/2, 589].

Topos IV	*Topos* IV
The requirement of *deus-homo*: II,6-13	*Potestve ulla creaturarum in coelo vel terra, quae tantum creatura sit, pro nobis satisfacere? Resp.: Nulla . . . nec poterat quidem quod mera tantum creatura sit, iram dei adversus peccatum sustinere, et alios ab ea liberare*: Question 14, I,91 (p. 84).
	Qualis ergo est querendus mediator et liberator? Resp.: Qui verus quidem homo sit, ac perfecte justus et tamen omnibus creaturis potentior, hoc est qui simul etiam sit verus deus: Question 15, I,92 (p. 84).
	Cur necesse est eum verum hominem et quidem perfecte justum esse? Resp.: Quia justitia dei postulat ut eadem natura quae peccavit, ipsa pro peccato dependat: qui vero ipse peccator esset, pro aliis dependere non posset: Question 16, I,92 (p. 85).

* * * * * * *   * * * * * * *

Man is always sinning: I,10, and 21	Question 13, (p. 82-83), passim.

* * * * * * *   * * * * * * *

Man's sinful condition makes satisfaction by him impossible: I,10, and 21-22	*Explicatio* to Questions 13-15 [*MW* II/1,267, 299].

* * * * * * *   * * * * * * *

Sin is not giving God what is owed: I,11

Question 7 (p. 38); Question 126 (p. 649).

* * * * * * *

* * * * * * *

Sin is going against God's will: I,21

Question 7; [*LC*-1555,82].

* * * * * * *

* * * * * * *

Man sinned voluntarily by giving in to the devil: I,22

Question 7, (pp. 33, 50, 53), passim.

* * * * * * *

* * * * * * *

Honor of God requires punishment: I,13

Postulat autem dei justitia, ut omnia peccata quod adversus summam dei maiestatem est, id etiam summis, hoc est, sempiternis cum animi tum corporis suppliciis luatur: Question 11, I,13 (p. 69); God is a jealous God, *hoc est acerrimum sui honoris defensorem ac vindicem, horribiliter irascentem deficientibus ab ipso*, etc.: Question 98, I,344.

* * * * * * *

* * * * * * *

Honor of God requires, and is shown in, maintenance of His order: I,15

Ursinus uses "glory of God" in the same sense, for example:

Glory of God is chief goal of creation: Question 6, (p. 28); Church is distinct from the world to manifest God's glory: *Prolegomena* (p. 1); Glory of God is shown in the deliverance of man: Question 11, I,86; glory of God is chief end of redemption: I,306

God is said to be vindic-
tive: 1,10

Question 25, I,116 (p.
157); the great anger
demanding punishment: Question 10; also I,344, Question 98.

* * * * * * *   * * * * * * *

Aut poena aut satisfactio:
(Roques 102)

*Lex enim obligat omnes vel
ad obedientiam vel ad poenam.* The concept *obedientia* becomes *satisfactio* in
the definition of *lutron*:
*est solius Christi obedien-
tia, quae est satisfactio
pro peccatis nostris*:
Question 11, I,85.

* * * * * * *   * * * * * * *

Satisfaction must be pro-
portionate to sin: I,20-21

Question 11, I,84, quoted
above;

*Debuit autem mediatoris
supplicium esse infiniti
valoris et aeterno aequi-
valens: ut inter peccatum
et poenam esse proportio*:
Question 17, I,93
[*LC*-1555,33].

* * * * * * *   * * * * * * *

God punishes by taking away
the eternal life of beatitude: I,14

Question 7 (pp. 39, 44,
55); Question 25 (p. 122).

* * * * * * *   * * * * * * *

God's mercy must not upset
the order of his justice:
I,12

Question 10, I,83; Question
11, I,84-85; . . . *deus
magis propendet ad miseri-
cordiam quam ad iram.* [Pun-
ishment = *iram*] *In servan-
dis piis declarabit miseri-
cordiam*: Question 12,
I,90.

"Forgive us our sins" (may be an unreasonable petition): I,12; I,19

Forgiveness of sin through intercession *but without satisfaction* by Christ would be asking God to diminish his justice: Question 58 (p. 307); *Remissio peccatorum non pugnat cum dei justitia*: Question 56, I,220; and in the discussion of the Lord's Prayer: forgiveness is not contrary to God's justice after Christ's satisfaction: Question 126 (p. 649).

* * * * * * *   * * * * * * *

Such things as repentance, humility and obedience are due and thus not satisfaction: I,20-21

Whatever good we do we owe under the present obligation of the law: Question 13 (p. 82); also Question 17 (p. 88).

[Reformed covenant of works]

[Good works are the new obedience that follows regeneration: *Debitores sumus. Regeneramur igitur in reconciliatione, ut nova obedientia in nobis inchoetur*: *MW* II/2,422ff].

* * * * * * *   * * * * * * *

Gratitude for gratuitous acts of God: II,5

[Necessity of grace]

Christ has fulfilled the law: Question 16 (p. 86), passim; good works are required to show gratitude: Question 86, I,307; gratuity demands gratitude, (p.464); [*LC*-1555,107].

* * * * * * *   * * * * * * *

Man cannot be reconciled but by God-man: II,21, i.e. Christ: I,25

Question 18, I,95ff.; and *Prolegomena* in *Topos* III, above [*MW* II/2,622-623].

Voluntary promise of beatitude as goal of God's creation becomes necessity:
II,5; II,16

[establishes a covenant]

* * * * * * *

Perfect God and perfect
man: II,7

* * * * * * *

From the seed of Adam:
II,8

* * * * * * *

From a virgin woman: II,8

* * * * * * *

Mary purified before
Christ's birth: II,16

* * * * * * *

The assumption of human
nature: II,8-9, 17-18, 33,
(p. 185). [*MW* II/1,206:
*mihi non displicet Anselmi
descriptionem*, p. 284]

* * * * * * *

Suffered in human nature
only: I,8

* * * * * * *

The two natures, one divine
and one human, in Christ:
II,17-18 (Roques suggests

Question 12, I,90; recon-
ciliation with God [through
Christ] is called covenant:
Question 18 (p. 96).

* * * * * * *

Questions 13-15, quoted
above [*LC*-1555,33].

* * * * * * *

Question 16 (p. 85); Question 36 (p. 209)

* * * * * * *

Question 35 (p. 205ff.).

* * * * * * *

Question 35 (p. 206).

* * * * * * *

The son who assumed our
nature: Question 18
(p. 91); the flesh that
he assumed: Question
33 (p. 185).

* * * * * * *

Question 37 (p. 215) [*MW*
II/1,228; *LC*-1555,35]; both
Ursinus and Melanchthon
quote Irenaeus' "the divine
nature acquiescing."

* * * * * * *

Question 18 (p. 95); Question 25 (p. 135); Question
33; subsection "Of the two

Anselm is arguing against monophysites, etc. in II,7.)

natures of Christ": Question 36 (pp. 207ff.) [Melanchthon quotes Irenaeus and other Fathers and (like Ursinus) directs his remarks against Samosatenus, Arius, Servetus: *MW* II/1,216-218].

* * * * * * *

* * * * * * *

In note 3, pp. 366-368, Roques discusses Anselm and the denial by Jewish and Muslim thinkers that God made himself man.

Both Melanchthon and Ursinus direct their arguments on this issue against Jews and Turks (= the 16th century equivalent): Question 33 (p. 186), passim [*MW* II/1,194, praefatio; it is one of the reasons for the *LC*; *Ab Ario furores Mahomatici orti sunt*, p. 198 (*Locus de deo*)].

* * * * * * *

* * * * * * *

The Word becomes man: II,9

Question 18; Question 33, passim [*MW* II/1,206, where Melanchthon quotes Irenaeus at length.]

* * * * * * *

* * * * * * *

Topos V

Topos V

The effects of Christ's redemptive death: II,14-21

[*Mediator*] *offert se* [*deo*] *ad satisfactionem. Reipsa praestat satisfactionem moriendo pro nobis et luendo poenam sufficientem . . . Dato spiritu sancto efficit in nobis fidem . . . Servat nos in reconciliatione, fide et obedientia nova, ac defendit adversos diabolos et omnes hostes*: Question 18, I,97.

*Quare Filius dei appellatur
Jesus, hoc est salvator?
Resp. Quia nos salvat ab
omnibus peccatis nostris:
nec ulla salus vel peti
aliunde debet, vel alibi
reperiri potest*: Question
29, I,138 .

What does it benefit you to
believe the [Apostolic
Creed]? *Resp. Quod in
Christo iustus sum coram
deo et haeres vitae aeternae*: Question 59, I,230.

*Iustitia evangelica fidei
est impletio legis, non a
nobis, sed ab alio pro
nobis praestita, hoc est
lutron filii dei nobis
imputatum*: Question 60,
I,231, in tabula.

* * * * * * *

Ransomed from slavery: I,6

* * * * * * *

Freedom from slavery of
sin; we are all servants of
God: Question 8 (p. 57);
Question 29 (p. 166); Question 31 (p. 175); re-
demption from slavery to
devil: Question 34 (p.
203).

* * * * * * *

Roques provides a lengthy
note to this chapter on the
concepts of slavery and
freedom and on a ruler's
care and tyranny.

* * * * * * *

The relationship between a
feudal lord and vassal:
Question 9, I,82; in the
Explicationes to the Lord's
Prayer, Ursinus discusses
the benefits (care) the
king bestows on his king-
dom: Question 123 (p.
635).

Divine justice rewards those indicated by Christ: II,19

Question 19 (pp. 101-02), passim.

* * * * * * *

The example of the king and the man who satisfied for others: II,16

[covenant of redemption]

Christ gathers the Church and those in it are justified: Question 54 (pp. 293ff.).

* * * * * * *

Death of Christ surpasses the totality of sins: II,14; "Assumed man" places all humanity in condition of salvation, II,16: yet only the elect benefit: I,17-18; for only part of mankind is destined for eternal salvation: I,23

Question 20 (p. 106); for all, but actually only for those who believe: Question 29 (pp. 166-67); Question 37 (p. 217); "Did Christ die for all?": Question 40 (p. 21) [*MW* II/2,629, 635; all, but faith is necessary: II/1,387-388]. See also *Topos* III.

* * * * * * *

No one entered paradise before the death of Christ: II,16; yet there was always the promise and thus Adam and Eve also redeemed: II,16

The Old Testament figures under the Law also saved through Christ like those under the Gospel: Question 18 (p. 99) [*Quare opus est evangelii promissione*: *MW* II/1,382-383: .]

* * * * * * *

Christ's death as example: II,18

Question 11, I,87.

* * * * * * *

Christ died so man may be reconciled with God: I,9

Question 1; Question 17 (p. 87); Question 19 (p. 102); satisfaction as restoration: Question 29, I,138; Question 60, I,230.

                    * * * * * * *   * * * * * * *

Death of John the Baptist   Question 18 (p. 96); Ques-
[and of martyrs and saints]   tion 30 (pp. 168-69).
for the truth gives no mer-
its for salvation of sin-
ners: II,18

DATE DUE